SUBJECT AND STRUCTURE

An Anthology for Writers

ALTERNATE EDITION

SUBJECT AND STRUCTURE

An Anthology for Writers

JOHN M. WASSON

Washington State University

LITTLE, BROWN AND COMPANY
Boston

PREFACE

This alternate edition retains the dual focus of *Subject and Structure:* in each section, every selection is on the same general subject and illustrates the same rhetorical technique. The student is thus provided with several examples of the kind of thing he himself will be asked to write. This arrangement should stimulate comparison of structure and technique—as well as content—during class discussion.

A new section, Description, has been added to this edition as a transition from personal example to the more difficult rhetorical techniques which follow. The other sections have the same structure as previous editions, but the subject matter varies considerably. A higher percentage of the selections are by contemporary writers, but some important prose stylists of the past have been included. This edition also contains more pieces of imaginative literature and more works by women.

The first selection in each of the nine sections is a purposely short essay approximating the length of a student theme and clearly illustrating the rhetorical technique under consideration. In general, the selections are then arranged in increasing order of difficulty, with short stories and poems placed last.

The introductions to the sections discuss the philosophy, importance, and utility of each rhetorical technique. They also offer general principles to guide the student in his theme writing and to warn him against pitfalls common to each writing problem.

The questions for discussion in this edition have been divided into two categories: "Subject" and "Structure." By this means, the student is encouraged to see that organization, sentence construction, perhaps even word choice depend upon both the subject and the author's choice of rhetorical technique. Most of the "Structure" questions are aimed at solutions to specific writing problems and often refer back to the general principles outlined in the introduction to each section. If the book is to be used effectively, these questions should consume at least as much class discussion time as those dealing with subject matter.

The author and the publisher are eager to receive from students and teachers alike suggestions and evaluations of this book's effectiveness. Only through such communication can we hope to arrive at a truly satisfactory text. To this end we have included at the back of the book an evaluation form which users are urged to complete and return to Little, Brown.

John M. Wasson
March, 1972

CONTENTS

Contents

2
LOOKING AT PEOPLE
Description   41

Contents

5
PROBLEMS OF POSTCIVILIZATION
Process

Contents

Contents

7
WHERE THE POWER IS
Argument

Power
John Cogley
"All power to no one" is Cogley's answer to the revolutionary demand for "power to the people."

Of the Ends of Political Society and Government
John Locke
Locke argues that since man voluntarily quits the state of nature to organize a society, that society's government must be responsive to his wishes and protective of his rights.

The Military-Industrial Complex
Dwight D. Eisenhower
In his farewell message, the late president warns of the increasing and self-perpetuating power of the defense industry.

The Limits of Law and Order
Robert M. Hutchins
Hutchins argues that Nixon's get-tough policy does not reduce crime in the streets and that, instead, we need penal and judicial reforms, as well as a great deal of "decriminalization"—particularly in the areas of gambling and drug use.

On Not Becoming Revolutionary
Raymond Gozzi, Jr.
A young liberal argues for working within the system rather than trying to destroy it.

What Is a Social Problem?
Neil H. Jacoby
If a social problem is the gap between public expectations and social reality, then the current series of "wars" on poverty, slums, discrimination, and crime increases the social problems instead of solving them. Jacoby calls for a more honest view of progress in these areas.

Contents

Contents

1

GROWING UP IN AMERICA

Example

Among the first lessons a writer must learn is that personal opinions and generalizations usually need illustrations drawn from firsthand observation if the reader is to understand them clearly and be convinced of their validity. Although one example cannot prove an opinion's worth, it will at least make clear what the writer means and will indicate that supporting evidence is available. Because of its versatility, the personal example is one of the writer's basic tools: it may be, and usually is, employed as secondary support for every other method of developing ideas described in this book.

Almost certainly the earliest attempts at written communication were in the form of pictures, at first single pictures and then a related series of pictures which told a story, perhaps of a warrior's success in battle or of a narrow escape from some wild animal. From such crude beginnings, written languages were developed, based at first on stylized abbreviations of the earlier picture writing. But as early as the Sumerian culture of 3000 B.C., man had discovered that he needed phonetic characters to express concepts which could not be "pictured." The subsequent history of written languages shows a clear trend toward developing simpler, more flexible alphabets capable of expressing relationships between ideas in words which refer to no "pictures" at all — "God is love," "Truth is Beauty," and so on.

Until comparatively recently, however, man was so accustomed to thinking in pictures that he instinctively avoided such totally abstract statements whenever possible. He preferred to express the abstract thought in "pictorial" language. When the author of Ecclesiastes wrote

1

"all is vanity," he added "and chasing after wind." When Shakespeare wanted his character Macbeth to complain that life is meaningless, he avoided the unimpressive abstract statement in favor of the now famous lines:

Life's but a walking shadow, a poor player
That struts and frets his hour upon the stage,
And then is heard no more: it is a tale
Told by an idiot, full of sound and fury,
Signifying nothing.

The ability to express generalizations in abstract language is certainly an important advance: scientific laws, for instance, can only be expressed with difficulty and at great length in pictorial language. But we must recognize that there are certain weaknesses in abstract language and that we are not justified in dismissing the pictorial techniques of the older writers without good reason.

At its best, a generalization in abstract language forces the reader to supply a concrete illustration from his own experience. The writer thus loses an important means of control, for the reader's illustration may vary widely from what the author has in mind. To avoid this, when the writer of a physics textbook, for instance, states in general terms Boyle's law of gases he is careful either to give specific illustrations of the law's application or to give instructions for a controlled experiment whereby the reader can see for himself the operation of Boyle's law.

At its worst, highly abstract language may leave the reader with only the vaguest notion of its meaning and without a ready example to clarify it. Suppose you were to read, instead of Shakespeare's clear statement, "Life's but a walking shadow . . . ," something as atrocious as this:

In the opinion of the author of the present
investigation, it is a not unjustifiable assumption
that the normal experiences of human existence
seem to indicate that it may be without a demonstrable
teleological basis.

There are two related methods of avoiding this sort of vagueness: (1) the use of specific, concrete language, including figures of speech where appropriate (a figure of speech should always be used to *clarify,* not to *decorate* the writing); and (2) the use of examples. You should not, of course, try to fill your writing with imagery of the florid, "limpid pools in the moonlight" variety. And you need not pile up superfluous examples. But you should remember to support and clarify your generalizations with illustrative evidence.

When asked to write opinion papers, college students often feel handicapped by a lack of adequate knowledge. They may even disregard as unimportant their best source of material, personal experience and observation. The best writers in every age have used their per-

2

sonal experiences as examples of general principles, partly because they can relate these experiences vividly and partly because firsthand reports are usually more reliable than borrowed ones. In "My Puritan Conscience," when Mark Twain wants to illustrate the harmful side effects of a strict religious upbringing, he employs several examples from his own childhood in Hannibal. Many fiction writers — nearly all of the best novelists, in fact — have kept notebooks in which they jotted down for future use firsthand observations of places, events, and people. A wealth of such material is available to anyone who will use his eyes and his memory, even to an "inexperienced" college student. If you think back carefully, you may find that your experience includes acquaintance with such apparently remote subjects as communism (a room and toys "communally" owned by you and a brother or sister) and totalitarianism (a father, perhaps, whose "word was law" in the home).

Even though your personal experiences may not seem to be of tremendous significance, there are several good reasons why you should draw on them for illustrative evidence. (1) Accurate personal observation makes writing more *vivid.* When you give a vague hypothetical example or none at all, the reader gets no mental picture from the writing; and what he can "see" clearly he understands better. If you are writing about the need for minimum speed laws on freeways, describe in graphic detail the time you nearly smashed into the back end of a slow-moving vehicle in the midst of sixty-mile-per-hour traffic.

(2) Such writing is not only clearer, but it is more *interesting.* You must know from experience how dull a textbook can be when the writer fails to give concrete examples. You may "read" several pages and suddenly realize you haven't any notion of what you have read. And you probably remember as a child that you avoided checking out library books which contained no pictures. While an adult can usually maintain interest without pictures, he at least wants "word-pictures."

(3) Personal examples make writing more *convincing.* A hypothetical example beginning, "Someone might be driving along the highway sometime when . . ." would hardly carry the authoritative force of "I had pushed my '59 Ford up to seventy on the long straight stretch of Highway 101 just south of San Jose when. . . ." A reader might, at worst, argue that your example isn't typical, but he would still be convinced that it did actually happen. And if the example does not seem too unlikely, the reader will probably be reminded of supporting evidence from his own experience.

(4) Finally, writing containing accounts of firsthand experiences is necessarily more *personal:* that is, it establishes a bond of intimacy between you and your reader. The reader, feeling that you are taking him into your confidence and that you sincerely want to communicate with him, will be much more willing to give you a fair chance to make your point. Nothing will alienate a reader more quickly than the suspicion that you do not really care whether or not he understands and

agrees with you. An impersonal approach is a great producer of that suspicion.

In relating personal examples, be sure to include enough concrete facts to create a clear picture for your reader. Use actual names of people, places and things when possible, and select verbs which convey a sense of action. "The coffee burned my tongue" is much more vivid than "The coffee was hot" and is just as easy to write if you employ verbs which carry part of the meaning of the sentence instead of being mere *links.* Try to re-create your experience in such a way that the reader can relive it vicariously. As you read the selections in this section, notice how the writers have accomplished this sense of vicarious experience through the use of concrete detail and active verbs. Note, for instance, how Brother Malcolm, in "The First Major Turning Point," gives names of actual people, quotes his teacher as nearly as he can remember, and even recalls such apparently unimportant details as the particular jobs his classmates were interested in — details which, precisely because there would be no sense reporting them unless they were true, give the account its impact of immediacy.

One word of caution: be sure to avoid trite expressions in relating a personal experience. In striving for vividness, you may be tempted to use such "tried and true" phrases as those in this passage from a student theme.

> I was so excited I could hardly wait for the trip to start. But the day finally came. We arose bright-eyed and bushy-tailed, ate a hurried breakfast, and were on our way.

Such worn-out phrases destroy the very bond of intimacy you are trying to establish between you and your reader. The reader feels that you are not interested enough in what you are saying to think up your own expressions. Furthermore, he loses interest because he feels that he has "read all this before." Trite language, in short, destroys the sense of uniqueness your writing should convey. The reader is not just concerned with the nature of your experience; he is interested in your personal view of it and your reaction to it. For it is precisely your point of view that makes your experience unique and therefore worth reading: remember that no two people experience events in precisely the same way. Even two people in the same automobile accident will "see" it differently because of differences in past experience, intelligence, and emotional nature. Do not sell yourself short; your experience does count, and it will be worth reading if you write it so that it will be "seen" in the way that you saw it.

THE FIRST MAJOR TURNING POINT

Malcolm X

Malcolm X, born Malcolm Little in Omaha, Nebraska in 1925, was assassinated in Harlem on February 21, 1965. The ultimate influence in this powerful civil rights leader's turbulent career is still difficult to assess, partly because his own views changed from black militancy to black nationalism to a deep sense of the brotherhood of man. It can be said with assurance that more than any other leader he gave the black man a sense of his manhood, and that, as Wyatt Tee Walker says, "Malcolm had the 'book' on white America and he read it loud and clear for all to hear." The Autobiography of Malcolm X (1964), whatever one thinks of its author, is probably the most sensitive book yet written by an Afro-American. The following extract is about his experience in junior high school at Mason, Michigan early in 1941.

I kept close to the top of the class, though. The topmost scholastic standing, I remember, kept shifting between me, a girl named Audrey Slaugh, and a boy named Jimmy Cotton. 1

It went on that way, as I became increasingly restless and disturbed 2 through the first semester. And then one day, just about when those of us who had passed were about to move up to 8-A, from which we would enter high school the next year, something happened which was to become the first major turning point of my life.

Somehow, I happened to be alone in the classroom with Mr. Ostrow- 3 ski, my English teacher. He was a tall, rather reddish white man and he had a thick mustache. I had gotten some of my best marks under him, and he had always made me feel that he liked me. He was, as I have mentioned, a natural-born "advisor," about what you ought to read, to do, or think — about any and everything. We used to make unkind jokes about him: why was he teaching in Mason instead of somewhere else, getting for himself some of the "success in life" that he kept telling us how to get?

I know that he probably meant well in what he happened to advise 4 me that day. I doubt that he meant any harm. It was just in his nature as an American white man. I was one of his top students, one of the school's top students — but all he could see for me was the kind of future "in your place" that all white people see for black people.

He told me, "Malcolm, you ought to be thinking about a career. Have 5 you been giving it thought?"

The truth is, I hadn't. I never have figured out why I told him, "Well, 6 yes, sir, I've been thinking I'd like to be a lawyer." Lansing certainly had no Negro lawyers — or doctors either — in those days, to hold up an image I might have aspired to. All I really knew for certain was that a lawyer didn't wash dishes, as I was doing.

Mr. Ostrowski looked surprised, I remember, and leaned back in his 7 chair and clasped his hands behind his head. He kind of half-smiled and said, "Malcolm, one of life's first needs is for us to be realistic. Don't misunderstand me, now. We all here like you, you know that. But you've got to be realistic about being a nigger. A lawyer — that's no realistic goal for a nigger. You need to think about something you *can* be. You're good with your hands — making things. Everybody admires your carpentry shop work. Why don't you plan on carpentry? People like you as a person — you'd get all kinds of work."

The more I thought afterwards about what he said, the more uneasy 8 it made me. It just kept treading around in my mind.

What made it really begin to disturb me was Mr. Ostrowski's advice 9 to others in my class — all of them white. Most of them had told him they were planning to become farmers, like their parents — to one day take over their family farms. But those who wanted to strike out on their own, to try something new, he had encouraged. Some, mostly girls, wanted to be teachers. A few wanted other professions, such as one boy who wanted to become a county agent; another, a veterinarian; and one girl wanted to be a nurse. They all reported that Mr. Ostrowski had encouraged whatever they had wanted. Yet nearly none of them had earned marks equal to mine.

It was a surprising thing that I had never thought of it that way 10 before, but I realized that whatever I wasn't, I *was* smarter than nearly all of those white kids. But apparently I was still not intelligent enough, in their eyes, to become whatever I wanted to be.

It was then that I began to change — inside. 11

SUBJECT

1. Do you think Mr. Ostrowski's advice to Malcolm arises from (perhaps unrecognized) prejudice, or from an honest desire to be "realistic"? What does Malcolm think?

6

2.   Malcolm relates this incident with calm objectivity. Since it is to be a "major turning point," should he have jazzed it up a bit?

3.   What is Malcolm's attitude toward Mr. Ostrowski after twenty-four years? Does this attitude seem characteristic of a man who had become an impassioned denouncer of white racism? What clues do you have that the attitude is genuine?

4.   Does the account make clear why Malcolm should have been so disturbed by Mr. Ostrowski's advice — considering that Malcolm had no intention of being a lawyer, anyway? (Note that Malcolm was more upset by the advice than by being called "nigger." Clearly he was already aware of his "difference" from the other students in the class.)

STRUCTURE

1.   Since Mr. Ostrowski is referred to a number of times, it is clearly more convenient to call him by his name than to keep repeating "my English teacher." But the same reasoning does not explain Malcolm's inclusion of the names Audrey Slaugh and Jimmy Cotton, who are not referred to again. What effect does Malcolm achieve by naming them, an effect which would be lost if he simply wrote "two other students"?

2.   Point out some of the descriptive details which have nothing to do with the aim of the story but which help reconstruct the scene in the reader's mind. (Note that Malcolm does not clutter the account with such details — just enough for verisimilitude.)

3.   Malcolm might have achieved more marked contrast between the advice he received and that of the whites had he included some with less realistic ambitions than nurse, schoolteacher, or extension agent. Why do you suppose he doesn't? (Even if he had invented a couple of ambitions — brain surgeon, ambassador, president — no reader would be greatly surprised by such responses from eighth graders.)

4.   This account describes, of course, a purely personal experience; does Malcolm give any indication that he thinks of it as an example of a much more widespread problem? Using this essay as an example, consider the problem of making a personal experience seem both unique and something which "speaks" to the readers.

SALVATION

Langston Hughes

Langston Hughes (1902–1967) was a poet, jazz expert, and columnist for The New York Post. *At the age of twenty, he quit college for several years and worked as a common seaman, whence the title of his autobiography,* The Big Sea *(1940), from which the following episode is taken.*

I was saved from sin when I was going on thirteen. But not really saved. It happened like this. There was a big revival at my Auntie Reed's church. Every night for weeks there had been much preaching, singing, praying, and shouting, and some very hardened sinners had been brought to Christ, and the membership of the church had grown by leaps and bounds. Then just before the revival ended, they held a special meeting for children, "to bring the young lambs to the fold." My aunt spoke of it for days ahead. That night I was escorted to the front row and placed on the mourners' bench with all the other young sinners, who had not yet been brought to Jesus.

My aunt told me that when you were saved you saw a light, and something happened to you inside! And Jesus came into your life! And God was with you from then on! She said you could see and hear and feel Jesus in your soul. I believed her. I had heard a great many old people say the same thing and it seemed to me they ought to know. So I sat there calmly in the hot, crowded church, waiting for Jesus to come to me.

The preacher preached a wonderful rhythmical sermon, all moans and shouts and lonely cries and dire pictures of hell, and then he sang a song about the ninety and nine safe in the fold, but one little lamb was left out in the cold. Then he said: "Won't you come? Won't you come to Jesus? Young lambs, won't you come?" And he held out his arms to all us young sinners there on the mourners' bench. And the little girls cried. And some of them jumped up and went to Jesus right away. But most of us just sat there.

A great many old people came and knelt around us and prayed, old women with jet-black faces and braided hair, old men with work-

1

2

3

4

gnarled hands. And the church sang a song about the lower lights are burning, some poor sinners to be saved. And the whole building rocked with prayer and song.

Still I kept waiting to *see* Jesus. 5

Finally all the young people had gone to the altar and were saved, 6 but one boy and me. He was a rounder's son named Westley. Westley and I were surrounded by sisters and deacons praying. It was very hot in the church, and getting late now. Finally Westley said to me in a whisper: "God damn! I'm tired o' sitting here. Let's get up and be saved." So he got up and was saved.

Then I was left all alone on the mourners' bench. My aunt came and 7 knelt at my knees and cried, while prayers and songs swirled all around me in the little church. The whole congregation prayed for me alone, in a mighty wail of moans and voices. And I kept waiting serenely for Jesus, waiting, waiting — but he didn't come. I wanted to see him, but nothing happened to me. Nothing! I wanted something to happen to me, but nothing happened.

I heard the songs and the minister saying: "Why don't you come? My 8 dear child, why don't you come to Jesus? Jesus is waiting for you. He wants you. Why don't you come? Sister Reed, what is this child's name?"

"Langston," my aunt sobbed. 9

"Langston, why don't you come? Why don't you come and be saved? 10 Oh, Lamb of God! Why don't you come?"

Now it was really getting late. I began to be ashamed of myself, 11 holding everything up so long. I began to wonder what God thought about Westley, who certainly hadn't seen Jesus either, but who was now sitting proudly on the platform, swinging his knickerbockered legs and grinning down at me, surrounded by deacons and old women on their knees praying. God had not struck Westley dead for taking his name in vain or for lying in the temple. So I decided that maybe to save further trouble, I'd better lie, too, and say that Jesus had come, and get up and be saved.

So I got up. 12

Suddenly the whole room broke into a sea of shouting, as they saw 13 me rise. Waves of rejoicing swept the place. Women leaped in the air. My aunt threw her arms around me. The minister took me by the hand and led me to the platform.

When things quieted down, in a hushed silence, punctuated by a few 14 ecstatic "Amens," all the new young lambs were blessed in the name of God. Then joyous singing filled the room.

That night, for the last time in my life but one — for I was a big 15 boy twelve years old — I cried. I cried, in bed alone, and couldn't stop. I buried my head under the quilts, but my aunt heard me. She

9

woke up and told my uncle I was crying because the Holy Ghost had come into my life, and because I had seen Jesus. But I was really crying because I couldn't bear to tell her that I had lied, that I had deceived everybody in the church, and I hadn't seen Jesus, and that now I didn't believe there was a Jesus any more, since he didn't come to help me.

SUBJECT

1. Do you think that Hughes is concentrating more on giving an honest self-analysis or on entertaining the reader with the humorous account itself? What saves the story from being funny but pointless?

2. Does Langston's pretense at salvation seem to be a typical trick for a boy that age? Is it at least believable? How would you have reacted at age twelve to pressures like those exerted on Hughes?

3. Hughes implies in his last paragraph that this apparently harmless event had an important and lasting effect on him. Does this seem psychologically valid? Can you recall any small events from your childhood which have had lasting effects?

4. Do you think that, in addition to the analysis of himself, Hughes intends some social criticism? Of religion? Of "saving" children at too early an age?

STRUCTURE

1. Examine Hughes's employment of concrete detail. Point out details which are especially effective in making the essay vivid, authentic, and interesting.

2. What special devices does Hughes employ to achieve realism? Were you able to picture yourself in his place?

3. How does Hughes convey the impression that the story is told from the point of view of a young boy? Analyze the sentence structure in the second and third paragraphs, for instance.

MY PURITAN
CONSCIENCE

Mark Twain

Samuel Langhorne Clemens (1835–1910), better known by his pen name, Mark Twain, preferred to be thought of as a philosopher and social critic rather than as a humorist. His philosophic bent can be seen in such works as The Mysterious Stranger and The Man That Corrupted Hadleyburg, as well as in the selection from The Autobiography (pub. 1924) reprinted here. Nevertheless, his real genius lay in his ability to make use of the everyday materials from his own experience, to re-create them vividly and concretely.

In 1849, when I was fourteen years old, we were still living in Hannibal, on the banks of the Mississippi, in the new "frame" house built by my father five years before. That is, some of us lived in the new part, the rest in the old part back of it and attached to it. In the autumn my sister gave a party and invited all the marriageable young people of the village. I was too young for this society and was too bashful to mingle with young ladies, anyway, therefore I was not invited — at least not for the whole evening. Ten minutes of it was to be my whole share. I was to do the part of a bear in a small fairy play. I was to be disguised all over in a close-fitting brown hairy stuff proper for a bear. About half past ten I was told to go to my room and put on this disguise and be ready in half an hour. I started but changed my mind, for I wanted to practice a little and that room was very small. I crossed over to the large unoccupied house on the corner of Main Street, unaware that a dozen of the young people were also going there to dress for their parts. I took the little black boy, Sandy, with me and we selected a roomy and empty chamber on the second floor. We entered it talking and this gave a couple of half-dressed young ladies an opportunity to take refuge behind a screen undiscovered. Their gowns and things were hanging on hooks behind the door but I did not see them; it was Sandy that shut the door but all his heart was in the theatricals and he was as unlikely to notice them as I was myself.

11

That was a rickety screen with many holes in it but as I did not know   2
there were girls behind it I was not disturbed by that detail. If I had
known, I could not have undressed in the flood of cruel moonlight that
was pouring in at the curtainless windows; I should have died of shame.
Untroubled by apprehensions, I stripped to the skin and began my
practice. I was full of ambition, I was determined to make a hit. I was
burning to establish a reputation as a bear and get further engagements;
so I threw myself into my work with an abandon that promised great
things. I capered back and forth from one end of the room to the other
on all fours, Sandy applauding with enthusiasm; I walked upright and
growled and snapped and snarled, I stood on my head, I flung hand-
springs, I danced a lubberly dance with my paws bent and my imaginary snout sniffing from side to side, I did everything a bear could do
and many things which no bear could ever do and no bear with any
dignity would want to do, anyway; and of course I never suspected that
I was making a spectacle of myself to anyone but Sandy. At last, standing
on my head, I paused in that attitude to take a minute's rest. There was
a moment's silence, then Sandy spoke up with excited interest and said:
"Mars Sam, has you ever seed a dried herring?"   3
"No. What is that?"   4
"It's a fish."   5
"Well, what of it? Anything peculiar about it?"   6
"Yes, suh, you bet you dey is. *Dey* eats 'em innards and all!"   7
There was a smothered burst of feminine snickers from behind the   8
screen! All the strength went out of me and I toppled forward like an
undermined tower and brought the screen down with my weight, burying the young ladies under it. In their fright they discharged a couple
of piercing screams — and possibly others — but I did not wait to
count. I snatched my clothes and fled to the dark hall below, Sandy
following. I was dressed in half a minute and out the back way. I swore
Sandy to eternal silence, then we went away and hid until the party was
over. The ambition was all out of me. I could not have faced that giddy
company after my adventure, for there would be two performers there
who knew my secret and would be privately laughing at me all the time.
I was searched for but not found, and the bear had to be played by a
young gentleman in his civilized clothes. The house was still and everybody asleep when I finally ventured home. I was very heavy-hearted
and full of a bitter sense of disgrace. Pinned to my pillow I found a slip
of paper which bore a line which did not lighten my heart but only
made my face burn. It was written in a laboriously disguised hand and
these were its mocking terms:

> You probably couldn't have played bear but you played bare very well
> — oh, very *very* well!

12

We think boys are rude, unsensitive animals but it is not so in all cases. 9
Each boy has one or two sensitive spots and if you can find out where
they are located you have only to touch them and you can scorch him
as with fire. I suffered miserably over that episode. I expected that the
facts would be all over the village in the morning but it was not so. The
secret remained confined to the two girls and Sandy and me. That was
some appeasement of my pain, but it was far from sufficient — the
main trouble remained: I was under four mocking eyes and it might as
well have been a thousand, for I suspected all girls' eyes of being the
ones I so dreaded. During several weeks I could not look any young lady
in the face; I dropped my eyes in confusion when any one of them
smiled upon me and gave me greeting; I said to myself, "That is one of
them," and got quickly away. Of course I was meeting the right girls
everywhere but if they ever let slip any betraying sign I was not bright
enough to catch it. When I left Hannibal four years later the secret was
still a secret; I had never guessed those girls out and was no longer
hoping or expecting to do it.

One of the dearest and prettiest girls in the village at the time of my 10
mishap was one whom I will call Mary Wilson, because that was not her
name. She was twenty years old; she was dainty and sweet, peach-
blooming and exquisite, gracious and lovely in character. I stood in awe
of her, for she seemed to me to be made out of angel clay and rightfully
unapproachable by just any unholy ordinary kind of boy like me. I
probably never suspected *her.* But —

The scene changes to Calcutta — forty-seven years later. It was in 11
1896. I arrived there on a lecturing trip. As I entered the hotel a vision
passed out of it, clothed in the glory of the Indian sunshine — the
Mary Wilson of my long-vanished boyhood! It was a startling thing.
Before I could recover from the pleasant shock and speak to her she was
gone. I thought maybe I had seen an apparition but it was not so, she
was flesh. She was the granddaughter of the other Mary. The other
Mary, now a widow, was upstairs and presently sent for me. She was old
and gray-haired but she looked young and was very handsome. We sat
down and talked. We steeped our thirsty souls in the reviving wine of
the past, the pathetic past, the beautiful past, the dear and lamented
past; we uttered the names that had been silent upon our lips for fifty
years and it was as if they were made of music; with reverent hands we
unburied our dead, the mates of our youth, and caressed them with our
speech; we searched the dusty chambers of our memories and dragged
forth incident after incident, episode after episode, folly after folly, and
laughed such good laughs over them, with the tears running down; and
finally Mary said, suddenly, and without any leading up:

"Tell me! What is the special peculiarity of dried herrings?" 12

13

It seemed a strange question at such a hallowed time as this. And so   13
inconsequential, too. I was a little shocked. And yet I was aware of a stir
of some kind away back in the deeps of my memory somewhere. It set
me to musing — thinking — searching. Dried herrings? Dried herrings? The peculiarity of dri . . . I glanced up. Her face was grave, but
there was a dim and shadowy twinkle in her eye which — All of a
sudden I knew and far away down in the hoary past I heard a remembered voice murmur, "Dey eats 'em innards and all!"

"At — last! I've found one of you, anyway! Who was the other girl?"   14
But she drew the line there. She wouldn't tell me.   15
But a boy's life is not all comedy; much of the tragic enters into it. The   16
drunken tramp who was burned up in the village jail lay upon my
conscience a hundred nights afterward and filled them with hideous
dreams — dreams in which I saw his appealing face as I had seen it in
the pathetic reality, pressed against the window bars, with the red hell
glowing behind him — a face which seemed to say to me, "If you had
not given me the matches this would not have happened; you are
responsible for my death." I was *not* responsible for it, for I had meant
him no harm but only good, when I let him have the matches; but no
matter, mine was a trained Presbyterian conscience and knew but the
one duty — to hunt and harry its slave upon all pretexts and on all
occasions, particularly when there was no sense nor reason in it. The
tramp — who was to blame — suffered ten minutes; I, who was not to
blame, suffered three months.

The shooting down of poor old Smarr in the main street at noonday   17
supplied me with some more dreams; and in them I always saw again
the grotesque closing picture — the great family Bible spread open
on the profane old man's breast by some thoughtful idiot and rising and
sinking to the labored breathings and adding the torture of its leaden
weight to the dying struggles. We are curiously made. In all the throng
of gaping and sympathetic onlookers there was not one with common
sense enough to perceive that an anvil would have been in better taste
there than the Bible, less open to sarcastic criticism and swifter in its
atrocious work. In my nightmares I grasped and struggled for breath
under the crush of that vast book for many a night.

All within the space of a couple of years we had two or three other   18
tragedies and I had the ill luck to be too near by on each occasion. There
was the slave man who was struck down with a chunk of slag for some
small offense; I saw him die. And the young Californian emigrant who
was stabbed with a bowie knife by a drunken comrade; I saw the red
life gush from his breast. And the case of the rowdy young brothers and
their harmless old uncle; one of them held the old man down with his
knees on his breast while the other one tried repeatedly to kill him with

an Allen revolver which wouldn't go off. I happened along just then, of course.

Then there was the case of the young Californian emigrant who got 19 drunk and proposed to raid the "Welshman's house" all alone one dark and threatening night. This house stood halfway up Holliday's Hill and its sole occupants were a poor but quite respectable widow and her blameless daughter. The invading ruffian woke the whole village with his ribald yells and coarse challenges and obscenities. I went up there with a comrade — John Briggs, I think — to look and listen. The figure of the man was dimly visible; the women were on their porch, not visible in the deep shadow of its roof, but we heard the elder woman's voice. She had loaded an old musket with slugs and she warned the man that if he stayed where he was while she counted ten it would cost him his life. She began to count, slowly; he began to laugh. He stopped laughing at "six"; then through the deep stillness, in a steady voice, followed the rest of the tale: "Seven ... eight ... nine" — a long pause, we holding our breaths — "ten!" A red spout of flame gushed out into the night and the man dropped with his breast riddled to rags. Then the rain and the thunder burst loose and the waiting town swarmed up the hill in the glare of the lightning like an invasion of ants. Those people saw the rest; I had had my share and was satisfied. I went home to dream and was not disappointed.

My teaching and training enabled me to see deeper into these trage- 20 dies than an ignorant person could have done. I knew what they were for. I tried to disguise it from myself but down in the secret deeps of my troubled heart I knew — and I *knew* I knew. They were inventions of Providence to beguile me to a better life. It sounds curiously innocent and conceited now, but to me there was nothing strange about it; it was quite in accordance with the thoughtful and judicious ways of Providence as I understood them. It would not have surprised me nor even overflattered me if Providence had killed off that whole community in trying to save an asset like me. Educated as I had been, it would have seemed just the thing and well worth the expense. *Why* Providence should take such an anxious interest in such a property, that idea never entered my head, and there was no one in that simple hamlet who would have dreamed of putting it there. For one thing, no one was equipped with it.

It is quite true, I took all the tragedies to myself and tallied them off 21 in turn as they happened, saying to myself in each case, with a sigh, "Another one gone — and on my account; this ought to bring me to repentance; the patience of God will not always endure." And yet privately I believed it would. That is, I believed it in the daytime; but not in the night. With the going down of the sun my faith failed and the clammy fears gathered about my heart. It was then that I repented. Those were awful nights, nights of despair, nights charged with the bitterness of death. After each tragedy I recognized the warning and repented; repented and begged; begged like a coward, begged like a dog; and not in the interest of those poor people who had been extinguished for my sake but only in my *own* interest. It seems selfish when I look back on it now.

My repentances were very real, very earnest; and after each tragedy 22 they happened every night for a long time. But as a rule they could not stand the daylight. They faded out and shredded away and disappeared in the glad splendor of the sun. They were the creatures of fear and darkness and they could not live out of their own place. The day gave me cheer and peace and at night I repented again. In all my boyhood life I am not sure that I ever tried to lead a better life in the daytime — or wanted to. In my age I should never think of wishing to do such a thing. But in my age, as in my youth, night brings me many a deep remorse. I realize that from the cradle up I have been like the rest of the race — never quite sane in the night. When "Injun Joe" died . . . But never mind. Somewhere I have already described what a raging hell of repentance I passed through then. I believe that for months I was as pure as the driven snow. After dark.

SUBJECT

1.   Are the incidents in this chapter told honestly and objectively? Does Twain seem to avoid rationalization in his judgments of himself?

2.   In what way did Twain's puritan background color his interpretation of the tragedies he witnessed? Does it seem to you unlikely that anyone would make such an interpretation?

3.   Is such a personal religious view "selfish," as Twain implies? What sort of God would strike down one person in order to warn another to repent?

4.   What was the psychological effect of Twain's intense religious training? What was the practical effect? Why do you suppose there was such a discrepancy between his resolutions and his actions? Twain links this contrast with the contrast between day and night. Why should his conscience bother him at night but not during the day? Does Twain intend the day-night contrast to be symbolic? If so, of what?

5.   Do Twain's examples seem to be sufficiently convincing to serve as valid evidence about the nature of man? Or would you say that they only help you to understand Twain better, not man in general? If so, is there any value in reading the selection?

STRUCTURE

1. Examine the language: Is it primarily concrete or abstract? Could Twain have achieved the same success in character portrayal without the elaborate background descriptions? Consider the rehearsal, for instance.

2. This account was written some fifty years after the events occurred. How does Twain manage to give the impression that it was written from a fourteen-year-old boy's point of view?

3. This chapter seems to break in half: The first part deals with the "undress rehearsal" and the remainder with various local tragedies. Why does Twain run the two parts together? Should he have made two chapters of this material?

4. Twain's boyhood experiences with violence are far more extreme and frequent than are those of most boys. How does Twain make them believable?

5. What does Twain do to maintain the reader's interest when his subject becomes so personal and unpleasant in the "remorse-and-repentance" part of the chapter?

MARTA

Oscar Lewis

Anthropologist Oscar Lewis (born in 1914) has devoted a considerable part of his distinguished career to studying the culture of poverty, particularly in Mexico. While doing research on poor families in Mexico City to compare with his earlier studies of rural families, Lewis met the almost incredible family of Jesus Sanchez (pseudonym). Jesus had had four common law wives and a total of twelve children by them; although poor, he supported three separate households simultaneously. The Children of Sanchez represents the autobiographies of the four surviving children of Jesus's first marriage. At the time the following passage was written, Marta, the youngest, had had two children by her first common law husband, Crispín, and was again pregnant; as frequently happened, Marta was not currently living with Crispín, an irresolute husband and a poor provider. As the account implies the pilgrimage to the shrine at Chalma was a popular excursion for the poor of Mexico.

That year, I went to Chalma for the first time. All my life, I had wanted to go with my aunt and would cry when my father wouldn't allow me. He would say, "Go? What for? It's pure foolishness! They don't know anything about God and just go to get drunk. And they'd probably leave you there." When I married, it was Crispín who wouldn't let me go. 1

So when my aunt told me she was going with Mati, my uncle's niece, I decided to take my two daughters and go along. We had twenty-five *pesos* among us, two blankets, two quilts, extra clothing for the children, a clay jar, powdered coffee, sugar, and other food. We had to carry the children and two large packs. 2

It began to rain as we were standing in line for the Chalma bus and I bought Concepción a plastic raincape for two *pesos*. She and Violeta both had the measles and were completely covered with red spots . . . that was why I didn't want them to get wet. It was still raining when we got off the bus at Santiago that night, and my aunt took us to the courtyard of the municipal building where a lot of people were stretched out for the night. We spread our bedding and saved a place 3 for my aunt's goddaughter and *comadre,* who were coming on a late bus.

The courtyard looked like a sheep pen with valises, packs and people 4 everywhere. Soldiers were on guard to see that the pilgrims were not robbed, but even then some bundles disappeared. All night, gangs of boys and girls made noise and people kept arriving or leaving, getting up or lying down. Before we went to sleep, we women had hot coffee spiked with alcohol.

At three in the morning, my aunt woke us to leave for the pilgrimage. 5 "Let's go," she said, and we all got up and packed. My aunt's *comadre* Luz had come with her husband and daughter, so there were eight of us when we started out. It was still dark and the only light we could see were the kerosene lamps of little food stands here and there on the road. We stopped at one for coffee, and learned that we had lost our way in the dark and had to go back to find the right road. As we walked up and down the hills, through the woods and over large rocks, I felt happy. I loved being on the move and seeing the little Indian women selling coffee, *tortillas,* chickpeas, cheese and butter to the stream of pilgrims passing by.

We walked all night and the next morning, until we arrived at Ocuila. 6 I couldn't walk any more so we rented a little shed for twenty-five *centavos* per person and rested until the next day. I had to hire a *burro* for three *pesos* to carry our packs, because by that time both children wanted to be carried all the time. I was so tired, I wanted to go back, but all the women said, "You must not turn back, because the road will become very difficult and you will never arrive." I don't know whether that was the truth or just a belief, right? but I kept on until we arrived at the *ahuehuete* tree.

Because it was our first time there, my children and I had to look for 7 a godmother to give us each a crown of flowers so that we might dance before the tree. We gave a *peso* to two old Indians to play for us on their violin and guitar. As we danced, I felt all my fatigue drop away . . . then we placed our flower crowns on the cross.

My aunt told me to bathe the children in the spring because the water 8 was miraculous and cured many illnesses. The girls were burning with fever . . . even their eyes had measle spots. I was afraid to put them in the cold water. I said, "*Ay!* these girls are going to die on me here." They were hot and sweating from the road, but my aunt dipped them in the water. I thought we would be burying them in *petates* right there, but no, the spring didn't hurt them at all.

From there to Chalma was a short walk, only about two hours. We 9 passed the enchanted rocks and arrived at Chalmita, where my aunt's godmother lived. She received us well and let us cook there without charge, before we went to the shrine. All along the decline to the Church, the road is lined with stalls and shops, so that wherever we looked we saw roofs of tin or wood. There were dancers who blew on the *chirimía* as they went along, making a sad kind of music. The penitents on their knees, blindfolded and wearing crowns of thorns, others with cactus leaves on their chests and backs to fulfill vows, bands of musicians playing . . . seeing so many of the faithful who had come to venerate the Lord, I was filled with feeling and began to cry. Pilgrimages and churches have always made me cry and there, at Chalma, almost all those who reached the Church door were crying.

The Lord of Chalma was very miraculous and very punishing. I 10 prayed for my father and all of us to be saved. I asked Him to send me a good job, but He never did, and I prayed that if Crispín was not for me, then for my sake and for my daughters' to take him away from me forever.

The trip back was boring. The children cried and I was tired and 11 desperate to get home. We sold the clay jar on the way because by then we didn't have enough *centavos* for food. I think I had only five *pesos* left. I couldn't walk any more, so I spent two *pesos* for seats for my aunt and myself on a truck from Ocuila to Santiago, where we waited in line for a bus. Mati and the others had remained in Chalma to drink *pulque,* and were no longer with us. The bus fare was three *pesos* each and I didn't have enough money to pay, so I sold an extra pair of shoes I had taken with me. Just think, they gave me only four *pesos* for them and the shoes were almost new! But what else was there for me to do? I couldn't leave my aunt there, could I? So I bought two tickets and we arrived in Mexico City without a single *centavo.*

I would like to go to Chalma at least once a year, because it is a good 12 thing to see the *Señor* and to pray, no? Especially since I hardly go near a church any more. I cannot go to Sunday Mass and confess the way I did when I was a girl because I am living in sin. I pray an Our Father or an Ave Maria to myself at home, or when I get very desperate I go to the Villa to ask the Virgin for help. After I give birth, I go to thank the Virgin.

I may not be very Catholic, but neither am I a Mason or a free- 13 thinker. I send my daughters to Catechism in the Casa Grande every Tuesday to prepare them for their first communion. After that, if they want to stick close to the Church it will be because of themselves, not because of me. I am satisfied to have my pictures of the Virgin of Guadalupe and the Virgin of the Sacred Heart and to pray at home. Besides, I never did like to confess my sins to a priest, who is a sinner like myself. Many say that the priests bother women at confession and deceive them just like other men. When I was eleven years old, I confessed that I took money from the house and had a *novio,* and the priest gave me a whole rosary of penances. After my first communion, I never again confessed.

My prayers were always the same: I asked the Lord that if Crispín 14 were not the one for me, it would be better to take him away once and for all, or if he *was* meant for me, then to please improve him so that we might live a normal life without so many ups and downs, for the sake of the children. But the Lord heard my first prayer better than the second.

My other prayer was always that my father should never be taken 15 from us. When his end comes, I don't want to be alive. When the wall falls, all the bricks fall with it. Then, none of us will be able to get up. If we cannot rise now that my father is alive, it will be impossible later. Like my brother, Roberto. If he cannot marry and lift his head now, how will he later?

When I think of how close death is to us, and that only God knows 16 which of us will wake up the next morning, I say why don't we do everything possible to make life happy for others? For example, my aunt is not going to last much longer on this earth and I would like to do something for her, but all my good intentions turn out bad because the very thought that I too may cease to exist from one moment to the other, prevents me from doing anything.

SUBJECT

1. Can you tell from the context why Marta decided to go on the pilgrimage to Chalma?

2. After her wretched experience, particularly on the return trip, why would Marta "like to go to Chalma at least once a year"?

3. What is Marta's attitude toward organized religion (see paragraph 13)? How does this view square with her attitude toward the pilgrimage?

4. What incidents on the pilgrimage indicate Marta's willingness to sacrifice her commonsense impulses when they conflict with matters of faith?

5. Marta's father had shown a strong sense of economic responsibility but very little love toward his children; he had kicked Marta out of the apartment when she lost her virginity at fourteen. What is Marta's attitude toward him? Do you find "Biblical" overtones in this attitude?

STRUCTURE

1. As Lewis points out in his Introduction to *The Children of Sanchez,* much of the colloquial vividness is lost in the translation of these

accounts into English. What expressions do seem to preserve something of that original flavor?

2. Examine Marta's use of concrete details; do they give the account vividness and a sense of authenticity?

3. What indications are there in the writing that Lewis is justified in using Marta's personal experience as an example of the culture of poverty?

4. Compare the account of the pilgrimage itself to Marta's summary of her religious views at the end (paragraphs 12-16); is the shift from specific to general accompanied by a stylistic change?

5. Is it possible from the details given to characterize Marta's habit of mind as, say, poetical, commonsense, mystical, speculative, etc.?

WE'RE POOR

Floyd Dell

Floyd Dell was born in Barry, Illinois in 1887. Although he was a prolific writer, his radical politics and pacifism fifty years before such beliefs were fashionable have caused him to be virtually obliterated from biographies and histories of politics and literature. During World War I, he was editor of a radical journal, The Masses *(1914–17). When the paper, with Dell as defendant, was accused of violating the Espionage Act, Dell promptly started another radical journal,* The Liberator *(1918–24). During the twenties and early thirties, Dell published ten novels, six books of non-fiction, numerous plays, and his autobiography,* Homecoming *(1933) — from which the following passage is taken. None of Dell's books is now in print.*

That fall, before it was discovered that the soles of both my shoes were 1
worn clear through, I still went to Sunday school. And one time the Sunday-school superintendent made a speech to all the classes. He said that these were hard times, and that many poor children weren't getting enough to eat. It was the first that I had heard about it. He asked everybody to bring some food for the poor children next Sunday. I felt very sorry for the poor children.

Also, little envelopes were distributed to all the classes. Each little 2
boy and girl was to bring money for the poor, next Sunday. The pretty Sunday-school teacher explained that we were to write our names, or have our parents write them, up in the left-hand corner of the little envelopes. . . . I told my mother all about it when I came home. And my mother gave me, the next Sunday, a small bag of potatoes to carry to Sunday school. I supposed the poor children's mothers would make potato soup out of them. . . . Potato soup was good. My father, who was quite a joker, would always say, as if he were surprised, "Ah! I see we have some nourishing potato soup today!" It was so good that we had it every day. My father was at home all day long and every day, now; and I liked that, even if he was grumpy as he sat reading Grant's

"Memoirs." I had my parents all to myself, too; the others were away. My oldest brother was in Quincy, and memory does not reveal where the others were: perhaps with relatives in the country.

Taking my small bag of potatoes to Sunday school, I looked around for the poor children; I was disappointed not to see them. I had heard about poor children in stories. But I was told just to put my contribution with the others on the big table in the side room. 3

I had brought with me the little yellow envelope, with some money in it for the poor children. My mother had put the money in it and sealed it up. She wouldn't tell me how much money she had put in it, but it felt like several dimes. Only she wouldn't let me write my name on the envelope. I had learned to write my name, and I was proud of being able to do it. But my mother said firmly, no, I must not write my name on the envelope; she didn't tell me why. On the way to Sunday school I had pressed the envelope against the coins until I could tell what they were; they weren't dimes but pennies. 4

When I handed in my envelope, my Sunday-school teacher noticed that my name wasn't on it, and she gave me a pencil; I could write my own name, she said. So I did. But I was confused because my mother had said not to; and when I came home, I confessed what I had done. She looked distressed. "I told you not to!" she said. But she didn't explain why. . . . 5

I didn't go back to school that fall. My mother said it was because I was sick. I did have a cold the week that school opened; I had been playing in the gutters and had got my feet wet, because there were holes in my shoes. My father cut insoles out of cardboard, and I wore those in my shoes. As long as I had to stay in the house anyway, they were all right. 6

I stayed cooped up in the house, without any companionship. We didn't take a Sunday paper any more, but the Barry *Adage* came every week in the mails; and though I did not read small print, I could see the Santa Clauses and holly wreaths in the advertisements. 7

There was a calendar in the kitchen. The red days were Sundays and holidays; and that red 25 was Christmas. (It was on a Monday, and the two red figures would come right together in 1893; but this represents research in the World Almanac, not memory.) I knew when Sunday was, because I could look out of the window and see the neighbor's children, all dressed up, going to Sunday school. I knew just when Christmas was going to be. 8

But there was something queer! My father and mother didn't say a word about Christmas. And once, when I spoke of it, there was a strange, embarrassed silence; so I didn't say anything more about it. But 9

I wondered, and was troubled. Why didn't they say anything about it? Was what I had said I wanted (memory refuses to supply that detail) too expensive?

I wasn't arrogant and talkative now. I was silent and frightened. What   10
was the matter? Why didn't my father and mother say anything about Christmas? As the day approached, my chest grew tighter with anxiety.

Now it was the day before Chirstmas. I couldn't be mistaken. But not   11
a word about it from my father and mother. I waited in painful bewilderment all day. I had supper with them, and was allowed to sit up for an hour. I was waiting for them to say something. "It's time for you to go to bed," my mother said gently. I had to say something.

"This is Christmas Eve, isn't it?" I asked, as if I didn't know.   12

My father and mother looked at one another. Then my mother   13
looked away. Her face was pale and stony. My father cleared his throat, and his face took on a joking look. He pretended he hadn't known it was Christmas Eve, because he hadn't been reading the papers. He said he would go downtown and find out.

My mother got up and walked out of the room. I didn't want my   14
father to have to keep on being funny about it, so I got up and went to bed. I went by myself without having a light. I undressed in the dark and crawled into bed.

I was numb. As if I had been hit by something. It was hard to breathe.   15
I ached all through. I was stunned — with finding out the truth

My body knew before my mind quite did. In a minute, when I could   16
think, my mind would know. And as the pain in my body ebbed, the pain in my mind began. I knew. I couldn't put it into words yet. But I knew why I had taken only a little bag of potatoes to Sunday school that fall. I knew why there had been only pennies in my little yellow envelope. I knew why I hadn't gone to school that fall — why I hadn't any new shoes — why we had been living on potato soup all winter. All these things, and others, many others, fitted themselves together in my mind, and meant something.

Then the words came into my mind and I whispered them into the   17
darkness:

"We're poor!"   18

That was it. I was one of those poor children I had been sorry for,   19
when I heard about them in Sunday school. My mother hadn't told me. My father was out of work, and we hadn't any money. That was why there wasn't going to be any Christmas at our house.

Then I remembered something that made me squirm with shame—   20
a boast. (Memory will not yield this up. Had I said to some Nice little boy, "I'm going to be President of the United States?" Or to a Nice little

girl: "I'll marry you when I grow up.""? It was some boast as horribly shameful to remember.)

"We're poor." There in bed in the dark, I whispered it over and over 21 to myself. I was making myself get used to it. (Or — just torturing myself, as one presses the tongue against a sore tooth? No, memory says not like that — but to keep myself from ever being such a fool again: suffering now, to keep this awful thing from ever happening again. Memory is clear on that; it was more like pulling the tooth, to get it over with — never mind the pain, this will be the end!)

It wasn't so bad, now that I knew. I just hadn't known! I had thought 22 all sorts of foolish things: that I was going to Ann Arbor — going to be a lawyer — going to make speeches in the Square, going to be President. Now I knew better.

I had wanted (something) for Christmas. I didn't want it, now. I didn't 23 want anything.

I lay there in the dark, feeling the cold emotion of renunciation. (The 24 tendrils of desire unfold their clasp on the outer world of objects, withdraw, shrivel up. Wishes shrivel up, turn black, die. It is like that.)

It hurt. But nothing would ever hurt again. I would never let myself 25 want anything again.

I lay there stretched out straight and stiff in the dark, my fists 26 clenched hard upon Nothing. . . .

In the morning it had been like a nightmare that is not clearly 27 remembered — that one wishes to forget. Though I hadn't hung up any stocking, there was one hanging at the foot of my bed. A bag of popcorn, and a lead pencil, for me. They had done the best they could, now they realized that I knew about Christmas. But they needn't have thought they had to. I didn't want anything.

SUBJECT

1. At what point in the story does the reader become aware that the Dell family is poor? Why does it take the child so much longer to make this discovery?

2. Given Floyd's new attitude at the end, how might he have felt had his family received some of the Sunday school's gifts for poor children? How does his mother feel about letting people know the family is poor? Why?

3. In some ways Christmas Eve was the worst possible time for Floyd to make his discovery; in what respects might it be the right time?

4. The worst part of the discovery for the boy is the shame over his boast; shouldn't the prospect of hunger and hardship be more of a worry? Which is normally more important to a person, the preservation of his life or of his self-respect?

STRUCTURE

1. Which details in this passage mark it as uniquely Dell's experience? Which details make it a typical example of the experiences of almost all poor children in America?

2. How does Dell separate the immediate experience of the child from his mature comments on that experience? The device is somewhat mechanical; does it work all right? Would there have been a better way to achieve the same separation? What do the "grown-up's" comments add to the story?

3. Contrast the way feelings are communicated in paragraphs 4 and 10; which way is more effective? How could Dell have improved the weaker paragraph?

4. Since the reader finds out almost at once the point of Floyd's much later discovery, how does the author maintain interest (or suspense) until he can come to the boy's crucial reaction to this discovery?

ALBUM OF OLDER WOMEN

Stanley Kauffmann

Stanley Kauffmann was born in 1916. He is best known as the film critic for the New Republic; *but his college training was in drama, and he also writes dramatic criticism for the same journal. His film critiques have been published separately in* Kauffmann on Film *(1969).* "Album of Older Women" *is one of a series of "albums" Kauffmann is currently writing.*

She was twenty-five and I was fourteen. She was a virgin and I was not. 1
She was my high-school teacher of chemistry, the one teacher in any school who ever gave me a failing grade.

Her name was Eleanor Brophy, and she had a touch of Irish accent 2
and a lot of Irish softness. The only time I saw her angry was when one of the boys in class mocked something I said at the blackboard, where I was fumbling an answer, and she turned on him. My work got worse and worse through the year. I had taken chemistry because I was still obeying a willed ambition to be a doctor. The worse my work got, the more often she kept me after school for conferences. "Kauffmann," she would say, "I don't understand it. You write all those poems, but you can't remember valences."

I was writing poems and stories, some of which were published in the 3
school magazine, and whenever she kept me to go over a wretched test paper, or even if she did not, I asked her whether she wanted to read something of mine. I did this partly as tactics, which she saw. But part of it was her gray eyes with the fierce brows so unlike her manner. She saw that, too.

She had long brown hair that she wore in a bun, and a broad brow 4
and serene smile. Her features and her round strong neck I saw again later in the singer Flagstad. Miss Brophy was flat-chested, and she moved with a somewhat graceless pigeon-toed walk. But I couldn't imagine anything about her being different from what it was, which is one definition of perfection.

The school was at the top of the Bronx on the edge of a park. I lived 5
in Manhattan. She had a new Model A Ford, and one day after she had

kept me to go over a paper, she said she was driving downtown a bit and would give me a lift. On the way, she accidentally went through a red light. I gloated. She laughed and blushed. "Ah, now you've got something on me, I suppose."

I failed the state regents' exam at the end of the year, she failed me   6 in the course, and I had to take it again in order to graduate the next June. The second time round I did superbly in chemistry, as I got a sudden vision of how it was supposed to go, basically, and everything followed easily from that. One clean autumn day she and I walked out of school together, and she said she felt like driving up into Westchester to see the leaves. I said impulsively, "Take me," and she said, "All right, Kauffmann."

Perhaps twice a month through the year we drove up there and   7 drove roundabout Kensico Dam and parked for a while and talked. And laughed. In the car the world dropped away, everything of our ages and of school. For her birthday I gave her a poem — not of love but of praise. For my birthday she gave me a novel.

And on my birthday I asked another present. We were sitting in her   8 car on a wooded road, talking and laughing, which was all we ever did. I asked her to take down her hair. She laughed and said, "Don't be foolish, Stanley. What for?" "So I can see it," I said. "It's foolish," she laughed again, and took it down. "There. What's that now?" she asked. But she knew what it was — in the look of it and the meaning of the act — or she wouldn't have done it.

Her hair was long and full, and, cloaking her shoulders, it changed   9 her. I thought it was the most intimate thing a girl had yet done for me, though I had slept with two before that.

We laughed and teased some more, and again on other days. One day   10 we were in the car and her hair was down and we were teasing and her face was close. Swiftly she turned her head away. I didn't kiss her, then or ever. But all at once I knew something I had never known before. I had power. Over a woman. Not just a girl — this was a woman — and I had power. I had never known that. With the two in bed in the country, I had only been the receiver of favors.

I got an almost perfect mark on the next regents' exam, and I gradu-   11 ated. That summer she came, with her sister, to visit me at the farm where I worked, the last summer I ever worked on a farm. In the fall I went to college and saw her a couple of times. Then I called her one day at home and her sister said she was out. I few days later I got a note from her inviting me to the Alumni Assembly, saying that she was always glad to see her former students, and she wished me well in my studies. It was the perfect friendly teacher's note in her perfect teacher's hand.

It was a testament of fear. I was clever enough to be touched, and 12
young enough to be proud. But I liked her so much, I was so grateful,
that I never called her again.

II

In those days it was common for lower-middle-class families to have 13
maids who "slept in." New York apartments often had maids' rooms and
bathrooms; and immigrant girls, called greenhorns, were plentiful.
Irish, German, Polish, mostly. Some families had Negro maids, but it
took another ten years before the supply of white girls dwindled and
most of the maids were black.

So it was quite usual for an apartment to have in it an adolescent boy, 14
son of the family, and a young woman who spent her nights on the
premises. Stories buzzed among the boys, most of them lies or exaggerations.

I exaggerated too. I told my fellow thirteen-year-olds about my wild 15
lovemaking with Anna, our German girl. She was a pleasant, slow farm
girl, near thirty, childlike and prudish. I explained to her in mixed
German and English that I was going to be a doctor, which I thought
was true, and that as part of my education she ought to let me examine
her, which I thought was sly. Occasionally, when she was sure no one
would come home to interrupt, and when I had flattered her sufficiently, she allowed me various gropes and peeks.

By the time we got Polish Anna, I was fifteen and a college freshman. 16
She was in her mid-twenties, chunky and small-breasted and sullen and
strong. The first day she was there, I was home alone for lunch. She put
a dish before me on the table, bumping me slightly; then in the kitchen
doorway, she paused and looked back. "Hey, you know, you look like
one of those movie stars," she said.

It was some sort of invitation, I supposed. What kind? How far? "Yes? 17
Which one?"

"That cute one. Robert Montgomery." 18

In the thickest fumes of adolescent fantasy, I could not think this 19
likely. Nobody could possibly think that. Clearly there was something
else involved. I felt uneasy, incompetent.

The next afternoon, when she was fixing dinner, I went into the 20
kitchen for a piece of fruit. When I took it out of the icebox, I looked
at the pan below that caught the water from the melted ice. I was
supposed to keep an eye on it, and it was nearly full. I carried it past
Anna at the stove to the sink, and while I was tipping it, she grabbed
my ribs hard from behind, in her ten tight fingers. "You're strong,
right?" she whispered.

My mother was in the living room, not far off. I turned around to 21
Anna, excited and scared. I didn't know what to do.

She grabbed my chin in her hand, so tightly that it hurt. "You know 22
Bobby Berger?" she whispered.

I had never heard the name. 23

"He was in the place I worked six years. Fellow like you. He liked to 24
have fun. I bet you like to have fun."

I tried to laugh carelessly, my chin still tightly in her grip. 25

She let me go and jabbed my chest with her fist. Close to her, I could 26
see how beautiful her skin was, how deep and crazy her slitted eyes. "I
don't like the way you got your hair cut," she whispered. "A good-
looking fellow, you should cut it different. I fix it for you some time."

I got away, out of the kitchen, and I kept away from her as much as 27
possible the next few days. Anna said nothing to me in front of others.
But when there was a chance, she gave me sullen looks, as if there were
something between us. I had recently seen a movie in which a girl
found out she was pregnant, and she had given looks like that to her
seducer.

A few nights later I was in bed reading. From the living room I could 28
hear my parents' voices and the radio — that eternal radio with its
comedy hours and variety hours while I was trying to read or sleep. My
door opened, and Anna came in.

"What's the matter?" I said. 29

She whispered sullenly and close, "I'm just checking up. I'm supposed 30
to take care here, right? Make sure everything's all right?" She was next
to the bed. She grabbed my chin again as I lay there. "Everything
okay?"

I heard the radio and the living-room laughter. I wriggled. 31

"You remember Bobby Berger?" she whispered. She slid her hand 32
under the covers. "You should talk to him, he could tell you I take care."
She found what she was groping for.

The radio announcer was selling some kind of automobile. A round 33
and cheery voice.

"Hey, come on," I whispered, "you can't — we can't — " I felt pow- 34
erless, thrilled, caught. I knew this was important, but I didn't know
what to do. I heard that radio.

"You call him up, I give you the number." Her hand was still fixed 35
under the covers. She leaned over me. I didn't know what was going
to happen — to me, to my whole future. Would everything be
wrecked?

Then suddenly she withdrew her hand, twisted my chin again, and 36
went out.

I didn't sleep much that night. Prospects of orgies, true stories to tell   37
my friends. But also sheer fright at having this girl in the house. The
idea of my new, secret world of sex being discovered, impinging on the
other world of my family.

I knew I couldn't handle the situation. I saw that sex always involves   38
safety, in some degree, if one is concerned with status. One has to be
able to rely on the other person, somehow. Anna promised wildness,
and disgrace.

The next morning I asked my mother how she felt about the new   39
maid, and she said that Anna was only fair but that she was willing to
give her another week's trial. "Well," I said "also she's — not so nice."
My mother blushed. When I came home that night, Anna was gone.

I felt relieved and elated. What a narrow escape, what a retrospective   40
triumph. I could store this episode away, I *had* it, complete, it could not
change for the worse. Not for the better, either, of course, but it was
good enough as it was. I told all my friends that Anna had sneaked into
my room every night for the five days she had been in the house, then
sneaked out early in the morning. One morning my mother had discovered her leaving and had fired her on the spot. They almost believed
it, I thought — they believed something, because two of them had got
a glimpse of Anna one day when they called for me.

My conscience used to bother me sometimes about getting her fired,   41
but it had all occurred too early for me. I wonder what happened to her.
Something squalid or terrible, probably. Is she dead? Is she alive? —
the beautiful skin gone, the crazy eyes crazier.

III

Dolly was my girlfriend's mother. They lived in a small house on a   42
street of identical houses in a Long Island suburb, but they were very
different from the neighbors. The father was English, a salesman who
would have been quite successful except for the alcoholism that he had
acquired in the British Army, off in the colonies somewhere. Dolly had
been born in Germany and brought here when she was ten. In her
youth she had been on the operetta stage in a small way. She got her
first job, as understudy, because she resembled the star of the show, a
woman famous in the theater, and later in films, for her exquisite profile
and dainty manner. The producer who hired Dolly said to the star,
"This is what you looked like when I first met you." It tells almost all
about Dolly to say that the star did not hate her after that introduction.

Her daughter Enid was in college, in the drama department, with   43
me. She was fine and also slightly affected; and the fact that this quite
consciously fine girl was devoted to me was more than my ego could

bear. I bullied her a good deal of the time, and although she fought back, she never really bullied me in return. But we often had good times, and we saw each other from our sophomore year until about a year after graduation. Her eyes were her best feature, gray and superior. She had not inherited her mother's profile or figure, or the funny, delicate pathos.

I was in their home often, and often spent the night there, on the sofa. 44 I liked it best when the father was out; and when he disappeared on a week's binge, which he did every couple of months or so, I stayed there as much as I could. Dolly was wretched but somewhat liberated during those episodes. Money was especially tight during the binge weeks, but she was glad to have him out of the house. He was always very courteous to her, but she was his prisoner. She had no way of making a living, his behavior cut them off from having friends because she didn't want the neighborhood to know about the binges, and she had no relatives in this country. She stayed with him for Enid's sake, to see her somehow through college, but she slept in Enid's room. A condition he accepted in his deferential sober weeks.

Often during the binge weeks she and Enid and I had cozy little 45 meals at the bridge table we set up in the living room.

One summer Enid got a job as a counselor at a children's camp. I was 46 going to stay in the city to do some work, and when I saw her off at the railroad station, she said, "Try to get out and see Dolly once in a while. She's so fond of you, and you know how things are likely to be with the pa."

I telephoned Dolly about a week later, then went out for Sunday 47 dinner with her and Gordon. In the cooling afternoon I took her for a walk in the nearly rural streets nearby. She told me stories about her childhood in a German town, including one about the deaf old sexton named Pachs who used to fall asleep in the last row of their church during services. One Sunday near the end of the Mass, the priest intoned loudly, *"Pax vobiscum,"* and the old sexton started awake, sprang to his feet, and called out, *"Hier bin ich, Herr Vater."* As I leaned backward with laughter, Dolly looked at me sideways like a pleased child.

She asked me to come out again in two weeks. When I got there, 48 about noon, I knocked on the door. No answer. I turned the knob. The door was open, and I went in. As I entered the tiny hall, the bedroom door at the top of the stairs opened, and Dolly looked out, her face tired and damp. She had evidently forgotten about me, because she made a cry of surprise. Then she burst into tears and came running down the stairs into my arms. Gordon had been off drinking for about ten days, no word from him, but the checks he wrote when drunk had begun to come in and they had no money in the bank. She was practically penniless, alone — she hadn't wanted to write and upset Enid — she had mostly just been lying there crying. Frightened.

She was wearing something thin. She was a full-bodied, very beautiful woman, clinging to me. 49

In the years since then, I have often had fantasies in which we slipped to the floor of that little hall and, out of a huddle of emotions, made love. I know that we did not; but I still feel as if it had happened. 50

By and by we had sandwiches of something, and iced tea. She held my hand and apologized for being so foolish, and I held her hand and told her not to say such things. She was in her early forties, I was a college boy of eighteen, but the day was ours, as friends, as woman and man, as lovers in spirit. I thought that she knew how close we had come to making love, although there had been no overt sign. The fact that she was Enid's mother only made it more mystical and sad to me. When we went for a walk in the late afternoon, I felt as if we had returned, graver, to reality. 51

Gordon's binge ended; the summer ended. Eventually, after a couple of years, the affair with Enid ended — an overdue ending, considering how I treated her. When she told me she had begun to see someone else, the first thing I thought of was my pride, which was proof enough that she was right to break it off. The second thing I thought of was that day with Dolly; that there would never be another. 52

IV

I was the best senior student in the directing class, so I got the annual plum. Each year an exclusive girls' finishing school in Connecticut did a play, and each year they asked the head of my college drama department to recommend a student of his to direct their show. In my senior year he recommended me, and I felt imperial. The fee was a hundred dollars and expenses — in 1935. Up at that school I met Mireille. 53

They were very careful of their girls. Boys were rarely allowed on the school grounds. All the male parts in their plays were performed by girls, and besides there was a faculty member present every time I rehearsed. Just because I was there, nineteen and appreciative. Like so many of the rich, this school was stingy. Instead of buying copies of the published play for the cast, they typed up copies. The play they had chosen was Barrie's *Quality Street;* and at the casting tryout, we read through the typescripts in the presence of a caricature schoolmistress, black throatband and all. We came to the stage direction, "She runs to the window to peep between the curtains." The typist had left the final "p" off "Peep." There were strangulated giggles in the presence of the 54 granite teacher, and I concentrated as hard as I could on my hundred dollars.

At the first rehearsal, the faculty proctor was the French teacher, Mademoiselle Parlier. She was in her early thirties, long-nosed, full-bosomed, long-waisted, and small. She wore a shirtwaist with flowing sleeves and a dark velvet tam. I thought she looked like the heroine of a French film, very real. After we were introduced, I turned to work and worked hard for about three hours. 55

I had to be taken to the railroad station after every session — I went up there twice a week from the city — and this day Mademoiselle Parlier offered me a lift. As we drove, I could tell from her manner that she had been impressed with my work. I was flattered, but I had no kind of intention toward her, I had no thought of it. She seemed unattainable, French, perhaps thirty-five. Besides, I didn't want to risk that money. 56

We chatted, and in the course of the chat, I presumed to ask her first name. She said, "One that you have never heard, Mireille." I had been given a present, a golden chance. I said, "Isn't that the name of an opera by Gounod?" She was as impressed as I had hoped, and said, "You are the first one in this country who has ever heard of it." 57

In a moment we turned into another road, and she said, "I live just there, a little cottage. Do you have time for a cup of tea? My English habit. I acquired it there. Shall we have some?" I was happy, nothing more; and as there was another train in about an hour, I said yes. 58

It was a pretty house with flowers, and a low-ceilinged living room with a piano and a violin and art books and French paperbound volumes all over. She made tea, and we smoked and talked for a while, very cozily. Then she took me to the station. 59

At the next rehearsal she was the proctor again, again in the velvet tam. "I have told the headmistress that I do not mind attending the repetitions, I am interested in the progress of the play," she said. I forgot her again during the rehearsal, then again she offered me a lift. Again, as we turned into her road, she asked me whether I had time for tea and I accepted. And again I had no slightest intention toward her. But I knew later — anyway I know now — that she had made up her mind about me on the first day, that the first invitation had been to give her the chance to see whether she could rely on my discretion and the second invitation was because she had decided. 60

Again we had tea, and I loved my new state. I was almost finished with college, conversing easily about books and life with a French-woman in her art-filled cottage. 61

It was time to go, and I asked whether I might use the bathroom. She said it was through the bedroom. I went through and closed the bath- 62

35

room door. When I came out, the bedroom shades were drawn, the bedroom door was closed. She was inside, leaning against the door, naked.

What I remember more strongly than my surprise or excitement is   63 the look on her face as she came toward me. Something like hatred. I tried to think it was hunger only, but there was hatred in it. It was wonderful to me. New.

I took a much later train, and every rehearsal day after that, I took   64 that later train. I had never felt anything like this, so immersed. I had slept with girls, I had used the word "love," but it was the first time I had felt drowned, grateful for the drowning.

After five weeks, the play was performed one afternoon. The head-   65 mistress and the parents were very pleased, and there were compliments over the punch. Then Mireille drove me to the station again, and again I took the later train. At the station, in her car, as the train arrived, I said I would telephone her the following week. I wanted it never to end, and anyway I assumed she would be wounded if I did not make some sort of promise. I had no clear idea how it could continue, but that didn't matter at the moment. She said, "Yes, do. Do telephone."

That was Friday. I called her on Monday afternoon, ready to spend   66 some of my hundred dollars on a hotel room if she could come to New York, or on train fare to go up there. She said, "Oh, dear, there are some friends here now. Could we speak tomorrow?" I called the next day, and she said that she wasn't planning to visit New York that week; she was busy with end-of-year affairs, so I couldn't come up there either. I was baffled but tried to write it off as mood. I called again the following week and she very nearly hung up on me. She was much more remote than on the day we had first met. I tried frantically to close the distance over the telephone, but it was ice all the way. She cut off the talk.

I didn't call again. It wasn't my pride, I was ready to be humbled, but   67 I felt that she wasn't even sufficiently interested to humble me. She had cut it.

I couldn't understand. The woman with whom — until two weeks   68 before — the bed had been a universe. Then I remembered the first bedroom day and the look on her face. I supposed that the finish had been in the beginning.

What love might be, I did not yet really know, but I saw now that   69 romance was a male invention, licensed by women and sometimes pitied by them.

SUBJECT

1. Many men like to think back over old affairs, perhaps even keep a scorecard. But in three of these episodes the author did not "score";

what does he see in them that is worth remembering? What do the four experiences exemplify for the author?

2. The notion of pride is brought in toward the end of each episode. Is the whole "album" a story about pride? Is it pride which keeps these relationships from being loves?

3. What does Kauffmann seem to have learned from these experiences with women during his teens?

4. Would you agree with the concluding remark that romance is "a male invention, licensed by women and sometimes pitied by them"?

5. Is there a relationship expressed between romance and sex? (Note that in none of these cases is Kauffmann the aggressor.)

6. Does the context make clear why the French teacher has a look of hate on her face? or why this would be exciting to the young man?

STRUCTURE

1. The only "order" of these accounts is roughly chronological; what, if anything, unifies them?

2. Several times Kauffmann brings in anecdotes which do not seem directly related to the story being told — the lies exchanged by the boys in II, the joke about Pachs in III, and the mistyped stage direction at the rehearsal in IV, for instance. What function do such asides serve?

3. Does Kauffmann relate these episodes from the point of view of the teenager involved or from that of the older man looking back on his youth? What difference does point of view make in a case like this?

4. Discuss Kauffmann's use of vivid detail. How often does he "interpret" the story instead of letting the reader draw his own conclusions? Should he have offered *more* interpretation?

PRETENSE

Howard McCord

Howard McCord was born in 1932 in El Paso, Texas and attended college at Texas Western and the University of Utah. He is one of America's fastest rising poets, having published some seven or eight volumes of poems, as well as numerous pieces in literary magazines from England to Argentina. In the summer of 1971 he was awarded the use of the D. H. Lawrence ranch near Taos, New Mexico to continue his writing. He is currently professor of creative writing at Bowling Green, Ohio. Among his major interests are the culture and social problems of Mexico and of the Southwest Indians. "Pretense" is taken from a volume of poems primarily about those subjects, The Spanish Dark *(1965).*

Writing of the dark,   1
the quinsy, throttling black
back of umber pitch
tucked under the scree
rearward of my tongue,

I am shards of syllables   2
as pot-broken and lost
to history
as a virgin.

'Than which the more of'   3
madmen say and whittle images
into my jaw, mourn dying gods
and daylight's morning,
fabricating (mind you)
vowels
      cretins
          retreats.

A prayer obviously   4
and a lie.

One only increases 5
the danger
by believing.

And what remains 6
is to sell one's parts,
lust on rocks,

and defy 7
the perfect accuracy of the imagination.

SUBJECT

1. To what kind of pretense is the poet admitting?

2. What particular difficulty does he experience in making poems?

3. Does he think it is better to admit the shortcomings or to believe they don't exist? Or does he lose either way?

4. He says that his recourse is "to sell one's parts, lust on rocks"; what does he mean by this?

5. Would it be fair to say that the third stanza is an example of the problem discussed in the first two stanzas?

STRUCTURE

1. In the second half of the poem, McCord turns his very personal experience into an example of the difficulties inherent in the creative process for any artist. How does he do this?

2. Each sentence in the poem has a rational and paraphrasable content except the "sentence" of the third stanza. Does the difference here indicate a flaw in the poem, or does it mark that stanza as especially important? What would happen to the poem if the meaning of the third stanza were expressed in a coherent, grammatically correct sentence?

3. This poem does not have a rhyme scheme, regular stanza form, or lines of patterned metrical length. Would you say that this irregular (or free) form is appropriate to the content? Examine the stanzaic divisions; does the poem seem to be put together "carefully"?

4. Stanza two contains a metaphor of broken Indian pottery and a simile about a virgin; how do these two images relate to one another?

5. What effect is achieved by the unusual word combinations in the opening stanza? The main clause of the sentence comes in stanza two; does it clarify the point McCord is making in the first stanza?

6. If the poem sustains a dominant mood, what is it? Resignation? Frustration?

2

LOOKING
AT PEOPLE

Description

In some ways description is an extension of the use of personal example discussed in the preceding section. It is an extension from the writer's self to the places and people he has observed. If written properly, description conveys the same sense of immediacy, vividness, and interest. And it makes the same demand that the writer keep his eyes and ears open to the world around him. There are differences too, of course. For one thing, the personal experience is usually presented in a narrative framework rather than a purely descriptive one. For another, description has numerous uses other than to provide a concrete illustration of a general principle.

Except in very short pieces, description is seldom found isolated from some other method of developing ideas. Yet it is an essential tool for virtually every kind of writer; a botanist can get along without it no better than a novelist can. For description is normally a means to an end rather than an end in itself — and the possible uses to which it can be put are infinite. The writer of a Boy Scout manual may carefully describe poison ivy so that his readers will be able to avoid it. A public relations man may want to describe a tract of New Mexico scabland in such a way that his readers will want to purchase an acre of it. A playwright describes his protagonist so that an actor will have a better idea of how to play that role. A novelist may describe the setting for action to give a sense of realism to his fiction — or he may use the description to create a mood of cheerfulness or desolation or foreboding. Compare Juliet's description of night as she awaits her new husband —

41

Gallop apace, you fiery-footed steeds,
Towards Phoebus' lodging: such a waggoner
As Phaethon would whip you to the west,
And bring in cloudy night immediately.
Spread thy close curtain, love-performing night,
That runaways' eyes may wink, and Romeo
Leap to these arms, untalk'd of and unseen.
Lovers can see to do their amorous rites
By their own beauties; or, if love be blind,
It best agrees with night. Come, civil night,
Thou sober-suited matron, all in black,
And learn me how to lose a winning match,
Play'd for a pair of stainless maidenhoods:
Hood my unmann'd blood, bating in my cheeks,
With thy black mantle; till strange love, grown bold,
Think true love acted simple modesty.
Come, night; come, Romeo; come, thou day in night;
For thou wilt lie upon the wings of night
Whiter than new snow on a raven's back.
Come, gentle night, come, loving, lack-brow'd night,
Give me my Romeo; and, when he shall die,
Take him and cut him out in little stars,
And he will make the face of heaven so fine
That all the world will be in love with night
And pay no worship to the garish sun.

with Macbeth's description as he prepares to murder Duncan:

Now o'er the one half-world
Nature seems dead, and wicked dreams abuse
The curtain'd sleep; witchcraft celebrates
Pale Hecate's offerings, and wither'd murder,
Alarum'd by his sentinel, the wolf,
Whose howl's his watch, thus with his stealthy pace,
With Tarquin's ravishing strides, towards his design
Moves like a ghost.

Regardless of the writer's purpose, what he is after in description is the "essential nature" of the thing described — the special characteristics of poison ivy which will allow one to distinguish it from other forest plants. The problem is that a thing may have many "essences," and the writer must decide which one best fits his purposes. What is the "essential nature" of a harmless drop of water, for instance? Much depends on the context in which it occurs. Obviously there is a considerable difference between a glistening drop of dew on a rose petal at sunrise and the first drop of rain spattering in the dust at second base during a World Series game. And the writer's attitude toward what he describes is also important: the baseball fan may be dismayed by that drop of rain and see it as an agent of evil; but if the pitcher is in a jam, that lovely mud-producing raindrop may to him seem sent from heaven.

The writer of description, then, must keep in mind both the occasion for which he is writing and the attitude toward his subject which he wants to recreate in the reader. In college writing, the nature of an assignment will frequently suggest the proper approach. (If the biology professor wants you to describe a drop of water as seen under a microscope, it is best to describe as accurately and objectively as possible, leaving your feelings out of it.) But when you are on your own, remember that, important as *accuracy of detail* is, just as crucial is proper *selection of detail*. You cannot describe everything about your subject, nor should you wish to. For many details, perhaps even obvious ones, may be irrelevant to the dominant impression you wish to convey. If you were describing Albert Einstein, his height and weight would probably not be mentioned. On the other hand, a description of Abraham Lincoln might very well employ vivid physical details — the long loose frame, the huge floppy hands, the intense eyes — as outward manifestations of his inner personality. Surely the fact that Lincoln wore formal clothing uncomfortably is revealing of the man. Or what was the significance of Einstein's wild long hair? Was he setting a fashion trend for hippies, was he so modest that careful grooming seemed affectatious, was he so busy that haircuts were a waste of time? The details you select and the way in which you describe them should imply answers to such questions and thus convey a coherent impression of the subject.

The suggestions made in the introduction to the preceding section on proper word choice for personal example apply as well to description; you should review those pages before attempting to write a description. But a few other suggestions need to be added here. Be sure to evaluate the relevance of descriptive details before you include them. Abraham Lincoln may have had a prominent mole on his cheek, but how does that information contribute to the impression you wish to convey? Will a description of poison ivy's root system be useful in avoiding the itch? If not, leave it out.

One danger in writing description is the temptation to control the reader's attitude by using strings of interpretive adjectives — adjectives which really tell how you feel rather than what the subject looked like. "He was quite impressive" or "It was a really beautiful day" tell us little. Was it warm and sunny, or was there a fresh snowfall? Was it still snowing, or had the sun come out? Such details are what the reader needs to know. Not only are readers quite capable of inferring the effect you want — provided you supply the right details — but their impression will be much deeper if you let them draw the conclusion themselves. Cantankerous creatures that they are, readers have a natural resistance to being *told* how to feel, but a pliant willingness to feel anything you want them to if you simply provide the relevant details:

> For all the history of grief,
> An empty doorway and a maple leaf.

Let us go back to that harmless drop of water one more time. Suppose you had written for the biology professor an objective account of what you had seen under the microscope; but then you wanted to convey to a friend your repulsion at the sight of so many "animals" in your drinking water. If you wrote something like this:

> It was just ghastly; I can't tell you how ill the sight of that horrible water drop made me,

you would neither be telling him what you saw nor making him feel what you felt. He would only understand that *you* felt revulsion. But if you left out the "ghastly" and the "horrible," you could describe with vivid details which would recreate your feeling. A beginning of this sort might do:

> Although it was a drop of ordinary tap water — drinking water — under the microscope it came alive. Great green eels squirmed and slithered through it. Purple creatures like tadpoles, all head and tail, thrashed and churned blindly, colliding with other more sluggish monsters. A few blobs without tails for propulsion bobbed in the wake, expanding and contracting like lungs. . . .

Finally, you should remember that to describe what you have experienced, all the senses should be appealed to which were involved in your original experience, not just the sense of sight which inexperienced writers rely on almost exclusively. For the qualities which sight perceives, such as color, shape, size, and movement, are probably not the only "essential" characteristics of a person or a landscape. It might be possible, in fact, to write a vivid description — say of a wharf on a pitch black night — without once appealing to the sense of sight. Sounds would be important: the water lapping, unseen gulls screeching, the rubbing of a boat against the dock. And the sense of touch: the night breeze, the chill moisture in the air, the spongy give of old boards underfoot. Perhaps even taste and smell: the odor of fish, the slight salt taste on the lips. For most descriptions, probably you will rely mainly on the sense of sight, but do not neglect the others; they can bring to life a "photographic" description.

The best way to organize materials for description depends both on what is being described and the impression of it you wish to convey. In describing a person, you might want to go from a photographic

impression — physical features, clothing — to characterizing movements, to deeds and statements which reveal the inner person. In
describing a scene, you might move like a movie camera from left to
right, or from a long range view to a close up, or from the outside (of
a building, for instance) to the inside. Or your purpose might better be
served by proceeding from a broad view — snow-capped mountains
and sparkling streams — to sharper details — hot dog wrappers,
broken beer bottles, and the rusted car fender on the sand bar. But
whatever method of organization you decide on, stick with it. The
rapid alternation of long shot and zoom, or flashes of the past stuck into
the present, may be all right for experimental movies, but they are
difficult to handle in written description. They *can* be handled, and
very effectively, as James Thurber does in "A Dime a Dozen"; but
considerable skill and patient construction are required.

MISS ABBOTT

Willie Morris

Willie Morris was born in Yazoo City, Mississippi in 1934. He has been editor of the Texas Observer *and from 1967 to 1971 was Editor-in-Chief of* Harper's. *His first book,* North Toward Home, *won the Houghton Mifflin Library Fellowship in 1967. The following sketch is taken from that autobiographical account.*

Terror lurked for me in that school. The name *Miss Abbott* brings back long dreary afternoons, weary recitations, secret rage, and wounded bafflement over my own unexpected failure. She was my fourth-grade teacher; I was nine, and for the first time my grades were erratic and my conduct report questionable. My own mother, who had pushed me onward as the nicest and brightest boy in the county, predicted I would never work out, and began blaming the social effects of Radical Reconstruction, always an ominous sign.

Miss Abbott had a pink nose and came from a small town in South Mississippi. She pronounced words like "night," "bright" and "sight" with the "i's" prolonged and nasal, a sure sign of hill-country origins. The only book she read through and through, she told us, was the Bible, and you lived to believe her, and to rue the day she got hold of that book. I myself had my own private relationship with God, which embraced the good old hymns and quiet mumbled prayers and holy vengeance when it was really deserved, and in that town and at that age you took God so much for granted that you knew he was keeping a separate ledger on you simply as a matter of course. But Miss Abbott's religion was Christianity by fear and by rote — so tenacious it got you by the extremities and never let go; it was a thing of interminable monologues, crazed soliloquies; she wanted you to believe she herself was in radio contact with the Deity, and had hung the moon for Him on day number six. When she talked about the time she had been saved, a moist glint began creeping into her eyes, which invariably meant the sermon was on its way. She learned to play a little plastic flute, the kind you could get in Woolworth's for a quarter, and she would play us rousing hymns and Christian marches, heedless of the saliva trickling down that instrument onto the floor. After the music she would preach us on sin and redemption, there being more of the former than the latter, or what the Old Testament said about niggers or Japs, or why we would all end up in hell if God caught us in a backfire. She would not drink Coca-Colas, she said, because of their alcoholic content. Sometimes she would lapse into a sweet, unexpected silence, and gaze out the nearest window for endless minutes. Her features would be bathed in gentle peace. Then I knew Miss Abbott was praying to herself.

Twice a day, in the morning when the class convened, and in the afternoon after lunch, she would call on each of us to pray. We would all begin by blessing our soldiers and then ripping into the Germans and the Japs. Once Bo, from Graball Hill, began his prayer by saying, "Dear Lord, thank you for the bombs that ain't fallin' on us," and then stopped. "What's wrong?" the teacher asked, and Bo said, "I just can't think of nuthin' else to say." The worst tortures were the Bible verses. Two hours each morning she had us recite the verses she had assigned us to learn by heart; when we forgot a verse, she would rap our palm with a twelve-inch ruler. Then out would come that flute again, and if she caught you drowsing, while she piped away on "Onward Christian Soldiers," or scratching at your weary tail, she would go to her "conduct book," and with a slight little flourish, write down a "5." 3

I made the mistake of correcting her one day, during one of the rare intervals in which we were doing schoolwork. The capital of Missouri, she said, was St. Louis. I held up my hand. 4

"What is it, Willie?" 5

"Miss Abbott, the capital of Missouri is Jefferson City." 6

"No, it's St. Louis." 7

"I bet it's Jefferson City," and then immediately regretted it, because of the scriptural attitude on gambling. 8

"Kay King," she snapped, "look in the book and show him it's St. Louis." 9

The little girl looked in the book and turned red. "Well," she said, "it says here Jefferson City," but obsequiously, like everyone in that ill-fated class, she added, "But Miss Abbott ought to — " 10

"We'll see," Miss Abbott snapped, and changed the subject. Later, during "silent study," I caught her glowering at me. Why couldn't those people in Missouri have settled on St. Louis? 11

At noon recess that spring, while the teacher sat on the grass with a group of fawning little girls around her, fetching things for her and scratching her back when it itched, giving her little compliments and practicing their Bible verses, holding her hand and looking for four-leaf clovers to put behind her red ears, we were playing softball nearby. 12

Honest Ed Upton hoisted a lazy foul that went high into the air behind third base; from shortstop I watched its slow descent with interest, with an almost fanatic regard, as it drifted earthward and smacked Miss Abbott on the head. She sprawled on the ground, with a moo like a milk cow's — out cold. *Oh joy of joys!* The other teachers picked her up and carried her away in a car. In our room later, supervised by the principal, all the little girls cried — silent little bawls — and even Honest Ed Upton shed tears. The boys scratched their heads and fiddled with pencils; such was the tyranny in that room, they dared not look into one another's eyes. Except Bo—he caught a glance of mine and puckered his lips, and before long a penciled note came over from him —"i wich the old bich got hit with a hardbal insted." I prayed that she would die.

But back she returned, risen on the third day, and on a Friday after- 13 noon, when she had stepped out of the room, I made a spitball and threw it two rows over at Kay King. *"William!"* The sound of Miss Abbott's voice sent terror to my soul. Each afternoon during that incomparable spring I had to "stay in" — two hours a day for six weeks, working long division. Miss Abbott would sit at her desk, reading the Bible or *Reader's Digest,* while the shadows got longer and the sound of boys' voices wafted in through the open window. And when that year ended, with the C on my report card in math, I had crossed, swum, waded the Sea of Galilee, and joyously entered the city limits of old Jerusalem.

SUBJECT

1. Morris provides only two minor details about Miss Abbott's physical appearance. Since these hardly give a photographic impression of Miss Abbott (we do not even know if she is thin or plump, raw–boned or petite), what justification is there for their inclusion?

2. Which aspect of Miss Abbott seems to be the "essential" one? Are the details conveying this impression more vivid, more numerous, or both?

3. Can you judge by the essay any lasting effects a teacher like Miss Abbott would have on her students? Consider Morris's implied attitude toward religion and mathematics, for instance. Does there seem to be a difference between the effects on the boys and on the girls in the class?

4. What does the argument over the capital of Missouri reveal about Miss Abbott? Does this impression fit with the description of her brand of religion in paragraph 2?

5. Does Morris give enough information for the reader to form a coherent (if incomplete) impression of Miss Abbott? Did you feel that certain other information should have been included?

STRUCTURE

1. Which descriptive details about Miss Abbott do you recall most vividly? Is your recollection due more to their concreteness or to something unusual about them?

2. The opening paragraph contains a considerable number of "interpretive" adjectives — *dreary, weary,* and *ominous* being the most obvious. Do you find these objectionable in the context? How frequently does Morris resort to such words in the remainder of the essay?

3. Clearly, Morris has tried to be selective as well as accurate in his use of detail. Do the details chosen seem adequate and appropriate to his purpose?

4. Note that some of the most telling details in this description seem at first glance matter-of-fact and almost irrelevant — for instance, "reading the Bible or *Reader's Digest,*" or "heedless of the saliva trickling down that instrument onto the floor." Discuss the qualities that make a descriptive detail effective?

5. What principle of organization directs the order in which descriptive details and characterizing incidents are included?

A DIME A DOZEN

James Thurber

James Thurber (1894–1961) is probably best remembered as a humor-
ist and cartoonist. But he was also a noted fiction writer, playwright,
satirist, and journalist. His long association with the New Yorker
prompted him to write a biographical memoir, The Years with Ross,
about the magazine's founder and first editor, Harold Ross. The prob-
lems facing Thurber in writing this description were that Ross had
been both his friend and his boss (a somewhat ambivalent relationship),
that Thurber knew enough about his subject to make selection of
details difficult, and that Ross was a man of apparent contradictions. As
Walcott Gibbs warned Thurber, "If you do get Ross down on paper,
nobody will believe it." Despite the difficulties, Thurber succeeded
amazingly well. What follows is from the opening chapter of The
Years with Ross *(1957).*

I first met Harold Ross in February, 1927, when his weekly was just two
years old. He was thirty-four and I was thirty-two. The *New Yorker* had
printed a few small pieces of mine, and a brief note from Ross had asked
me to stop in and see him some day when my job as a reporter for the
New York *Evening Post* chanced to take me uptown. Since I was getting only forty dollars a week and wanted to work for the *New Yorker,*
I showed up at his office the next day. Our meeting was to become for
me the first of a thousand vibrant memories of this exhilarating and
exasperating man.

You caught only glimpses of Ross, even if you spent a long evening
with him. He was always in midflight, or on the edge of his chair,
alighting or about to take off. He won't sit still in anybody's mind long
enough for a full-length portrait. After six years of thinking about it, I
realized that to do justice to Harold Ross I must write about him the way
he talked and lived — leaping from peak to peak. What follows here
is a monologue montage of that first day and of half a dozen swift and
similar sessions. He was standing behind his desk, scowling at a manuscript lying on it, as if it were about to lash out at him. I had caught
glimpses of him at the theater and at the Algonquin and, like everybody

else, was familiar with the mobile face that constantly changed expression, the carrying voice, the eloquent large-fingered hands that were never in repose, but kept darting this way and that to emphasize his points or running through the thatch of hair that stood straight up until Ina Claire said she would like to take her shoes off and walk through it. That got into the gossip columns and Ross promptly had his barber flatten down the pompadour.

He wanted, first of all, to know how old I was, and when I told him it set him off on a lecture. "Men don't mature in this country, Thurber," he said. "They're children. I was editor of the *Stars and Stripes* when I was twenty-five. Most men in their twenties don't know their way around yet. I think it's the goddam system of women schoolteachers." He went to the window behind his desk and stared disconsolately down into the street, jingling coins in one of his pants pockets. I learned later that he made a point of keeping four or five dollars' worth of change in this pocket because he had once got stuck in a taxi, to his vast irritation, with nothing smaller than a ten-dollar bill. The driver couldn't change it and had to park and go into the store for coins and bills, and Ross didn't have time for that.

I told him that I wanted to write, and he snarled, "Writers are a dime a dozen, Thurber. What I want is an editor. I can't find editors. Nobody grows up. Do you know English?" I said I thought I knew English, and this started him off on a subject with which I was to become intensely familiar. "Everybody thinks he knows English," he said, "but nobody does. I think it's because of the goddam women schoolteachers." He turned away from the window and glared at me as if I were on the witness stand and he were the prosecuting attorney. "I want to make a business office out of this place, like any other business office," he said. "I'm surrounded by women and children. We have no manpower or ingenuity. I never know where anybody is, and I can't find out. Nobody tells me anything. They sit out there at their desks, getting me deeper and deeper into God knows what. Nobody has any self-discipline, nobody gets anything done. Nobody knows how to delegate anything. What I need is a man who can sit at a central desk and make this place operate like a business office, keep track of things, find out where people are. I am, by God, going to keep sex out of this office — sex is an incident. You've got to hold the artists' hands. Artists never go anywhere, they don't know anybody, they're antisocial."

Ross was never conscious of his dramatic gestures, or of his natural gift of theatrical speech. At times he seemed to be on stage, and you half expected the curtain to fall on such an agonized tagline, as "God, how I pity me!" Anthony Ross played him in Wolcott Gibbs's comedy *Season in the Sun,* and an old friend of his, Lee Tracy, was Ross in a short-lived

51

play called *Metropole,* written by a former secretary of the editor. Ross sneaked in to see the Gibbs play one matinee, but he never saw the other one. I doubt if he recognized himself in the Anthony Ross part. I sometimes think he would have disowned a movie of himself, sound track and all.

He once found out that I had done an impersonation of him for a group of his friends at Dorothy Parker's apartment, and he called me into his office. "I hear you were imitating me last night, Thurber," he snarled. "I don't know what the hell there is to imitate — go ahead and show me." All this time his face was undergoing its familiar changes of expression and his fingers were flying. His flexible voice ran from a low register of growl to an upper register of what I can only call Western quacking. It was an instrument that could give special quality to such Rossisms as "Done and done!" and "You have me there!" and "Get it on paper!" and such a memorable tagline as his farewell to John McNulty on that writer's departure for Hollywood: "Well, God bless you, McNulty, goddam it." 6

Ross was, at first view, oddly disappointing. No one, I think, would have picked him out of a line-up as the editor of the *New Yorker.* Even in a dinner jacket he looked loosely informal, like a carelessly carried umbrella. He was meticulous to the point of obsession about the appearance of his magazine, but he gave no thought to himself. He was usually dressed in a dark suit, with a plain dark tie, as if for protective coloration. In the spring of 1927 he came to work in a black hat so unbecoming that his secretary, Elsie Dick, went out and bought him another one. "What became of my hat?" he demanded later. "I threw it away," said Miss Dick. "It was awful." He wore the new one without argument. Miss Dick, then in her early twenties, was a calm, quiet girl, never ruffled by Ross's moods. She was one of the few persons to whom he ever gave a photograph of himself. On it he wrote, "For Miss Dick, to whom I owe practically everything." She could spell, never sang, whistled, or hummed, knew how to fend off unwanted visitors, and had an intuitive sense of when the coast was clear so that he could go down in the elevator alone and not have to talk to anybody, and these things were practically everything. 7

In those early years the magazine occupied a floor in the same building as the *Saturday Review of Literature* on West 45th Street. Christopher Morley often rode in the elevator, a tweedy man, smelling of pipe tobacco and books, unmistakably a literary figure. I don't know that Ross ever met him. "I know too many people," he used to say. The editor of the *New Yorker,* wearing no mark of his trade, strove to be inconspicuous and liked to get to his office in the morning, if possible, without being recognized and greeted. 8

From the beginning Ross cherished his dream of a Central Desk at 9
which an infallible omniscience would sit, a dedicated genius, out of
Technology by Mysticism, effortlessly controlling and coördinating
editorial personnel, contributors, office boys, cranks and other visitors,
manuscripts, proofs, cartoons, captions, covers, fiction, poetry, and
facts, and bringing forth each Thursday a magazine at once funny,
journalistically sound, and flawless. This dehumanized figure, disguised
as a man, was a goal only in the sense that the mechanical rabbit
of a whippet track is a quarry. Ross's mind was always filled with dreams
of precision and efficiency beyond attainment, but exciting to
contemplate.

This conception of a Central Desk and its super-human engineer was 10
the largest of half a dozen intense preoccupations. You could see it
smoldering in his eyes if you encountered him walking to work, oblivious of passers-by, his tongue edging reflectively out of the corner of his
mouth, his round-shouldered torso seeming, as Lois Long once put it,
to be pushing something invisible ahead of him. He had no Empire
Urge, unlike Henry Luce and a dozen other founders of proliferating
enterprises. He was a one-magazine, one-project man. (His financial
interest in Dave Chasen's Hollywood restaurant was no more central to
his ambition than his onetime investment in a paint-spraying machine
— I don't know whatever became of that.) He dreamed of perfection,
not of power or personal fortune. IIe was a visionary and a practicalist,
imperfect at both, a dreamer and a hard worker, a genius and a plodder,
obstinate and reasonable, cosmopolitan and provincial, wide-eyed and
world-weary. There is only one word that fits him perfectly, and the
word is Ross.

When I agreed to work for the *New Yorker* as a desk man, it was with 11
deep misgivings. I felt that Ross didn't know, and wasn't much interested in finding out, anything about me. He had persuaded himself,
without evidence, that I might be just the wonder man he was looking
for, a mistake he had made before and was to make again in the case
of other newspapermen, including James M. Cain, who was just about
as miscast for the job as I was. Ross's wishful thinking was, it seems to
me now, tinged with hallucination. In expecting to find, in everybody
that turned up, the Ideal Executive, he came to remind me of the
Charlie Chaplin of *The Gold Rush,* who, snowbound and starving with
another man in a cabin teetering on the edge of a cliff, suddenly beholds
his companion turning into an enormous tender spring chicken, wonderfully edible, supplied by Providence. "Done and done, Thurber,"
said Ross. "I'll give you seventy dollars a week. If you write anything,
goddam it, your salary will take care of it." Later that afternoon he
phoned my apartment and said, "I've decided to make that ninety

dollars a week, Thurber." When my first check came through it was for one hundred dollars. "I couldn't take advantage of a newspaperman," Ross explained.

By the spring of 1928 Ross's young *New Yorker* was safely past finan- 12
cial and other shoals that had menaced its launching, skies were clearing, the glass was rising, and everybody felt secure except the skipper of the ship. From the first day I met him till the last time I saw him, Ross was like a sleepless, apprehensive sea captain pacing the bridge, expecting any minute to run aground, collide with something nameless in a sudden fog, or find his vessel abandoned and adrift, like the *Mary Celeste.* When, at the age of thirty-two, Ross had got his magazine afloat with the aid of Raoul Fleischmann and a handful of associates, the proudest thing he had behind him was his editorship of the *Stars and Stripes* in Paris from 1917 to 1919.

As the poet is born, Ross was born a newspaperman. "He could not 13
only get it, he could write it," said his friend Herbert Asbury. Ross got it and wrote it for seven different newspapers before he was twenty-five years old, beginning as a reporter for the Salt Lake City *Tribune* when he was only fourteen. One of his assignments there was to interview the madam of a house of prostitution. Always self-conscious and usually uncomfortable in the presence of all but his closest women friends, the young reporter began by saying to the bad woman (he divided the other sex into good and bad), "How many fallen women do you have?"

Later he worked for the Marysville (California) *Appeal,* Sacramento 14
Union, Panama *Star and Herald,* New Orleans *Item,* Atlanta *Journal,* and San Francisco *Call.*

The wanderer — some of his early associates called him "Hobo" — 15
reached New York in 1919 and worked for several magazines, including *Judge* and the *American Legion Weekly,* his mind increasingly occupied with plans for a new kind of weekly to be called the *New Yorker.* It was born at last, in travail and trauma, but he always felt uneasy as the R of the F-R Publishing Company, for he had none of the instincts and equipment of the businessman except the capacity for overwork and overworry. In his new position of high responsibility he soon developed the notion, as Marc Connelly has put it, that the world was designed to wear him down. A dozen years ago I found myself almost unconsciously making a Harold Ross out of one King Clode, a rugged pessimist in a fairy tale I was writing. At one point the palace astronomer rushed into the royal presence saying, "A huge pink comet, Sire, just barely missed the earth a little while ago. It made an awful hissing sound, like hot irons stuck in water." "They aim these things at me!" said Clode. "Everything is aimed at me." In this fantasy Clode pursues a fabulously swift white deer which, when brought to bay, turns into a

woman, a parable that parallels Ross's headlong quest for the wonder man who invariably turned into a human being with feet of clay, as useless to Ross as any enchanted princess.

Among the agencies in mischievous or malicious conspiracy to wear 16
Ross down were his own business department ("They're not only what's the matter with *me,* they're what's the matter with the country"), the state and federal tax systems, women and children (all the females and males that worked for him), temperament and fallibility in writers and artists, marriages and illnesses — to both of which his staff seemed especially susceptible — printers, engravers, distributors, and the like, who seemed to aim their strikes and ill-timed holidays directly at him, and human nature in general.

Harold Wallace Ross, born in Aspen, Colorado, in 1892, in a year and 17
decade whose cradles were filled with infants destined to darken his days and plague his nights, was in the midst of a project involving the tearing down of walls the week I started to work. When he outlined his schemes of reconstruction, it was often hard to tell where rationale left off and mystique began. (How he would hate those smart-aleck words.) He seemed to believe that certain basic problems of personnel might just possibly be solved by some fortuitous rearrangement of the offices. Time has mercifully foreshortened the months of my ordeal as executive editor, and only the highlights of what he called "practical matters" still remain. There must have been a dozen Through the Looking Glass conferences with him about those damned walls. As an efficiency expert or construction engineer, I was a little boy with an alarm clock and a hammer, and my utter incapacity in such a role would have been apparent in two hours to an unobsessed man. I took to drinking Martinis at lunch to fortify myself for the tortured afternoons of discussion.

"Why don't we put the walls on wheels?" I demanded one day. "We 18
might get somewhere with adjustable walls."

Ross's eyes lighted gloomily, in an expression of combined hope and 19
dismay which no other face I have known could duplicate. "The hell with it," he said. "You could hear everybody talking. You could see everybody's feet."

He and I worked seven days a week, often late into the night, for at 20
least two months, without a day off. I began to lose weight, editing factual copy for sports departments and those dealing with new apartments, women's fashions, and men's wear.

"Gretta Palmer keeps using words like introvert and extrovert," Ross 21
complained one day. "I'm not interested in the housing problems of neurotics. Everybody's neurotic. Life is hard, but I haven't got time for people's personal troubles. You've got to watch Woollcott and Long and Parker — they keep trying to get double meanings into their stuff to

55

embarass me. Question everything. We damn near printed a newsbreak about a girl falling off the roof. That's feminine hygiene, somebody told me just in time. You probably never heard the expression in Ohio."

"In Ohio," I told him, "we say the mirror cracked from side to side." 22

"I don't want to hear about it," he said. 23

He nursed an editorial phobia about what he called the functional: 24 "bathroom and bedroom stuff." Years later he deleted from a Janet Flanner "London Letter" a forthright explanation of the long nonliquid diet imposed upon the royal family and important dignitaries during the coronation of George VI. He was amused by the drawing of a water plug squirting a stream at a small astonished dog, with the caption "News," but he wouldn't print it. "So-and-so can't write a story without a man in it carrying a woman to a bed," he wailed. And again, "I'll never print another O'Hara story I don't understand. I want to know what his people are doing." He was depressed for weeks after the appearance of a full-page Arno depicting a man and a girl on a road in the moonlight, the man carrying the back seat of an automobile. "Why didn't somebody tell me what it meant?" he asked. Ross had insight, perception, and a unique kind of intuition, but they were matched by a dozen blind spots and strange areas of ignorance, surprising in a virile and observant reporter who had knocked about the world and lived two years in France. There were so many different Rosses, conflicting and contradictory, that the task of drawing him in words sometimes appears impossible, for the composite of all the Rosses should produce a single unmistakable entity: the most remarkable man I have ever known and the greatest editor. "If you get him down on paper," Wolcott Gibbs once warned me, "nobody will believe it."

I made deliberate mistakes and let things slide as the summer wore 25 on, hoping to be demoted to rewriting "Talk of the Town," with time of my own in which to write "casuals." That was Ross's word for fiction and humorous pieces of all kinds. Like "Profile" and "Reporter at Large" and "Notes and Comment," the word "casual" indicated Ross's determination to give the magazine an offhand, chatty, informal quality. Nothing was to be labored or studied, arty, literary, or intellectual. Formal short stories and other "formula stuff" were under the ban. Writers were to be played down; the accent was on content, not personalities. "All writers are writer-conscious," he said a thousand times.

One day he came to me with a letter from a men's furnishing store 26 which complained that it wasn't getting fair treatment in the "As to Men" department. "What are you going to do about that?" he growled. I swept it off my desk onto the floor. "The hell with it," I said. Ross didn't pick it up, just stared at it dolefully. "That's direct action, anyway," he said. "Maybe that's the way to handle grousing. We can't please everybody." Thus he rationalized everything I did, steadfastly refusing to perceive that he was dealing with a writer who intended to write or to be thrown out. "Thurber has honesty," he told Andy White, "admits his mistakes, never passes the buck. Only editor with common sense I've ever had."

I finally told Ross, late in the summer, that I was losing weight, my grip, and possibly my mind, and had to have a rest. He had not realized I had never taken a day off, even Saturday or Sunday. "All right, Thurber," he said, "but I think you're wearing yourself down writing pieces. Take a couple of weeks, anyway. Levick can hold things down while you're gone. I *guess.*"

It was, suitably enough, a dog that brought Ross and me together out of the artificiality and stuffiness of our strained and mistaken relationship. I went to Columbus on vacation and took a Scottie with me, and she disappeared out there. It took me two days to find her, with the help of newspaper ads and the police department. When I got back to the *New Yorker,* two days late, Ross called me into his office about seven o'clock, having avoided me all day. He was in one of his worst God-how-I-pity-me moods, a state of mind often made up of monumentally magnified trivialities. I was later to see this mood develop out of his exasperation with the way Niven Busch walked, or the way Ralph Ingersoll talked, or his feeling that "White is being silent about something and I don't know what it is." It could start because there weren't enough laughs in "Talk of the Town," or because he couldn't reach Arno on the phone, or because he was suddenly afflicted by the fear that nobody around the place could "find out the facts." (Once a nerve-racked editor yelled at him, "Why don't you get Westinghouse to build you a fact-finding machine?")

This day, however, the Ossa on the Pelion of his molehill miseries was the lost and found Jeannie. Thunder was on his forehead and lightning in his voice. "I understand you've overstayed your vacation to look for a dog," he growled. "Seems to me that was the act of a sis." (His vocabulary held some quaint and unexpected words and phrases out of the past. "They were spooning," he told me irritably about some couple years later, and, "I think she's stuck on him.") The word *sis,* which I had last heard about 1908, the era *skidoo,* was the straw that shattered my patience. Even at sixty-four my temper is precarious, but at thirty-two it had a hair trigger.

The scene that followed was brief, loud, and incoherent. I told him what to do with his goddam magazine, that I was through, and that he couldn't call me a sis while sitting down, since it was a fighting word. I offered to fight him then and there, told him he had the heart of a cast-iron lawn editor, and suggested that he call in one of his friends to

27

28

29

30

help him. Ross hated scenes, physical violence or the threat of it, temper and the unruly.

"Who would you suggest I call in?" he demanded, the thunder clearing from his brow. 31

"Alexander Woollcott!" I yelled, and he began laughing. 32

His was a wonderful, room-filling laugh when it came, and this was 33
my first experience of it. It cooled the air like summer rain. An hour
later we were having dinner together at Tony's after a couple of drinks,
and that night was the beginning of our knowledge of each other underneath the office make-up, and of a lasting and deepening friendship.
"I'm sorry, Thurber," he said. "I'm married to this magazine. It's all I
think about. I knew a dog I liked once, a shepherd dog, when I was a
boy. I don't like dogs as such, though, and I'll, by God, never run a
department about dogs — or about baseball, or about lawyers." His
eyes grew sad; then he gritted his teeth, always a sign that he was about
to express some deep antipathy, or grievance, or regret. "I'm running
a column about women's fashions," he moaned, "and I never thought
I'd come to that." I told him the "On and Off the Avenue" department
was sound, a word he always liked to hear, but used sparingly. It
cheered him up.

It wasn't long after that fateful night that Ross banged into my office 34
one afternoon. He paced around for a full minute without saying anything, jingling the coins in his pocket. "You've been writing," he said
finally. "I don't know how in hell you found time to write. I admit I
didn't want you to. I could hit a dozen writers from here with this ash
tray. They're undependable, no system, no self-discipline. Dorothy
Parker says you're a writer, and so does Baird Leonard." His voice rose
to its level of high decision. "All right then, if you're a writer, write!
Maybe you've got something to say." He gave one of his famous prolonged sighs, an agonized protesting acceptance of a fact he had been
fighting.

From then on I was a completely different man from the one he had 35
futilely struggled to make me. No longer did he tell White that I had
common sense. I was a writer now, not a hand-holder of artists, but a
man who needed guidance. Years later he wrote my wife a letter to
which he appended this postscript: "Your husband's opinion on a practical matter of this sort would have no value." We never again discussed
tearing down walls, the Central Desk, the problems of advertisers, or
anything else in the realm of the practical. If a manuscript was lost,
"Thurber lost it." Once he accused me of losing a typescript that later
turned up in an old briefcase of his own. This little fact made no difference. "If it hadn't been there," he said, "Thurber would have lost it."
As I become more and more "productive," another of his fondest words,

he became more and more convinced of my helplessness. "Thurber hasn't the vaguest idea what goes on around here," he would say.

I became one of the trio about whom he fretted and fussed continu- 36 ally — the others were Andy White and Wolcott Gibbs. His admiration of good executive editors, except in the case of William Shawn, never carried with it the deep affection he had for productive writers. His warmth was genuine, but always carefully covered over by gruffness or snarl or a semblance of deep disapproval. Once, and only once, he took White and Gibbs and me to lunch at the Algonquin, with all the fret and fuss of a mother hen trying to get her chicks across a main thoroughfare. Later, back at the office, I heard him saying to someone on the phone, "I just came from lunch with three writers who couldn't have got back to the office alone."

Our illnesses, or moods, or periods of unproductivity were a constant 37 source of worry to him. He visited me several times when I was in a hospital undergoing a series of eye operations in 1940 and 1941. On one of these visits, just before he left, he came over to the bed and snarled, "Goddam it, Thurber, I worry about you and England." England was at that time going through the German blitz. As my blindness increased, so did his concern. One noon he stopped at a table in the Algonquin lobby, where I was having a single cocktail with some friends before lunch. That afternoon he told White or Gibbs, "Thurber's over at the Algonquin lacing 'em in. He's the only *drinking* blind man I know."

He wouldn't go to the theater the night *The Male Animal* opened in 38 January, 1940, but he wouldn't go to bed, either, until he had read the reviews, which fortunately were favorable. Then he began telephoning around town until, at a quarter of two in the morning, he reached me at Bleeck's. I went to the phone. The editor of the *New Yorker* began every phone conversation by announcing "Ross," a monosyllable into which he was able to pack the sound and sign of all his worries and anxieties. His loud voice seemed to fill the receiver to overflowing. "Well, God bless you, Thurber," he said warmly, and then came the old familiar snarl: "Now, goddam it, maybe you can get something written for the magazine," and he hung up, but I can still hear him, over the years, loud and snarling, fond and comforting.

SUBJECT

1. How much information does Thurber give about Ross' physical appearance? Does it seem pertinent to an understanding of the man? What, for instance, does the hair-cut incident in Paragraph 2 tell about Ross? Or the story about the black hat in Paragraph 7?

2. How does Thurber account for the changes in his boss's attitude toward him over the years? Did Thurber himself change?

3. Do the generalizations at the end of Paragraph 11 represent a summary of the impression of Ross given thus far through specific detail? What might be Thurber's purpose in generalizing at this point?

4. Is there anything "patristic" about Ross' view of his writers? Compare the attitude of a benevolent slave owner toward his blacks.

5. What was Ross' notion of the ideal executive? Why does Thurber think this notion was tinged with hallucination?

6. Thurber's overall picture of Ross seems more amused than flattering. Does the description present a picture of a man who might have founded one of the century's most successful magazines?

STRUCTURE

1. Thurber begins his description within a narrative framework, but he frequently interrupts it and finally drops it. Does this lack of consistent structure have an effect on the picture of Ross which is presented?

2. Do you see any relationship between the style of this essay and the style Ross wanted for the *New Yorker?* Why does Thurber deliberately call attention to his word choice in Paragraph 17?

3. Note that Thurber draws almost exclusively on his personal experience with Ross, even though he must have known considerably more about him. Consider the advantages and disadvantages of such a procedure.

4. Is there any pattern in the arrangement of information which Thurber presents (such as a progression from physical qualities to actions to mental attitudes)? What principle does seem to govern Thurber's selection of details?

5. Does the anecdote in the final paragraph seem a suitable summary or conclusion for the chapter? Would a return to Thurber's first meeting with Ross have been more effective?

6. Would a consistent chronological arrangement of details from 1927 to 1951 have been a better way for Thurber to organize his material? Can you suggest a more useful method?

THE WAY TO
RAINY MOUNTAIN

N. Scott Momaday

N. Scott Momaday (born in 1934) is professor of comparative literature at University of California, Berkeley, a poet, and winner of the 1969 Pulitzer Prize for his novel House Made of Dawn. *He has also published books on American poetry and on Indian folktales.* "The Way to Rainy Mountain" *is interesting as description because Momaday attempts to characterize his grandmother by concentrating on her background and environment rather than on her physical characteristics.*

A single knoll rises out of the plain in Oklahoma, north and west of the   1
Wichita range. For my people, the Kiowas, it is an old landmark, and
they gave it the name Rainy Mountain. The hardest weather in the
world is there. Winter brings blizzards, hot tornadic winds arise in the
spring, and in summer the prairie is an anvil's edge. The grass turns
brittle and brown, and it cracks beneath your feet. There are green
belts along the rivers and creeks, linear groves of hickory and pecan,
willow and witch hazel. At a distance in July or August the steaming
foliage seems almost to writhe in fire. Great green and yellow grasshoppers are everywhere in the tall grass, popping up like corn to sting the
flesh, and tortoises crawl about on the red earth, going nowhere in the
plenty of time. Loneliness is an aspect of the land. All things in the plain
are isolate; there is no confusion of objects in the eye, but *one* hill or
one tree or *one* man. To look upon that landscape in the early morning,
with the sun at your back, is to lose the sense of proportion. Your
imagination comes to life, and this, you think, is where Creation was
begun.

I returned to Rainy Mountain in July. My grandmother had died in   2
the spring, and I wanted to be at her grave. She had lived to be very
old and at last infirm. Her only living daughter was with her when she
died, and I was told that in death her face was that of a child.

Reprinted by permission of the author from *The Reporter* (Jan. 26, 1967), pp. 41-43.

61

I like to think of her as a child. When she was born, the Kiowas were   3
living the last great moment of their history. For more than a hundred
years they had controlled the open range from the Smoky Hill River to
the Red, from the headwaters of the Canadian to the fork of the Arkansas and Cimarron. In alliance with the Comanches, they had ruled the
whole of the Southern Plains. War was their sacred business, and they
were the finest horsemen the world has ever known. But warfare for
the Kiowas was pre-eminently a matter of disposition rather than of
survival, and they never understood the grim, unrelenting advance of
the U.S. Cavalry. When at last, divided and ill provisioned, they were
driven onto the Staked Plains in the cold of autumn, they fell into panic.
In Palo Duro Canyon they abandoned their crucial stores to pillage and
had nothing then but their lives. In order to save themselves, they
surrendered to the soldiers at Fort Sill and were imprisoned in the old
stone corral that now stands as a military museum. My grandmother
was spared the humiliation of those high gray walls by eight or ten
years, but she must have known from birth the affliction of defeat, the
dark brooding of old warriors.

Her name was Aho, and she belonged to the last culture to evolve in   4
North America. Her forebears came down from the high country in
western Montana nearly three centuries ago. They were a mountain
people, a mysterious tribe of hunters whose language has never been
classified in any major group. In the late seventeenth century they
began a long migration to the south and east. It was a journey toward
the dawn, and it led to a golden age. Along the way the Kiowas were
befriended by the Crows, who gave them the culture and religion of the
Plains. They acquired horses, and their ancient nomadic spirit was
suddenly free of the ground. They acquired Tai-me, the sacred sun-
dance doll, from that moment the object and symbol of their worship,
and so shared in the divinity of the sun. Not least, they acquired the
sense of destiny, therefore courage and pride. When they entered upon
the Southern Plains they had been transformed. No longer were they
slaves to the simple necessity of survival; they were a lordly and dangerous society of fighters and thieves, hunters and priests of the sun. According to their origin myth, they entered the world through a hollow
log. From one point of view, their migration was the fruit of an old
prophecy, for indeed they emerged from a sunless world.

Though my grandmother lived out her long life in the shadow of   5
Rainy Mountain, the immense landscape of the continental interior lay
like memory in her blood. She could tell of the Crows, whom she had
never seen, and of the Black Hills, where she had never been. I wanted

to see in reality what she had seen more perfectly in the mind's eye, and drove fifteen hundred miles to begin my pilgrimage.

A dark mist lay over the Black Hills, and the land was like iron. At the top of a ridge I caught sight of Devil's Tower upthrust against the gray sky as if in the birth of time the core of the earth had broken through its crust and the motion of the world was begun. There are things in nature that engender an awful quiet in the heart of man; Devil's Tower is one of them. Two centuries ago, because of their need to explain it, the Kiowas made a legend at the base of the rock. My grandmother said: 6

"Eight children were there at play, seven sisters and their brother. Suddenly the boy was struck dumb; he trembled and began to run upon his hands and feet. His fingers became claws, and his body was covered with fur. There was a bear where the boy had been. The sisters were terrified; they ran, and the bear after them. They came to the stump of a great tree, and the tree spoke to them. It bade them climb upon it, and as they did so, it began to rise into the air. The bear came to kill them, but they were just beyond its reach. It reared against the tree and scored the bark all around with its claws. The seven sisters were borne into the sky, and they became the stars of the Big Dipper." From that moment, and so long as the legend lives, the Kiowas have kinsmen in the night sky. Whatever they were in the mountains, they could be no more. However tenuous their well being, however much they had suffered and would suffer again, they had found a way out of the wilderness.   7

My grandmother had a reverence for the sun, a holy regard that now is all but gone out of mankind. There was a wariness in her, and an ancient awe. She was a Christian in her later years, but she had come a long way about, and she never forgot her birthright. As a child she had been to the sun dances; she had taken part in that annual rite, and by it she had learned the restoration of her people in the presence of Tai-me. She was about seven when the last Kiowa sun dance was held in 1887 on the Washita River above Rainy Mountain Creek. The buffalo were gone. In order to consummate the ancient sacrifice — to impale the head of a buffalo bull upon the Tai-me tree — a delegation of old men journeyed into Texas, there to beg and barter for an animal from the Goodnight herd. She was ten when the Kiowas came together for the last time as a living sun-dance culture. They could find no buffalo; they had to hang an old hide from the sacred tree. Before the dance could begin, a company of soldiers rode out from Fort Sill under orders to disperse the tribe. Forbidden without cause the essential act of their faith, having seen the wild herds slaughtered and left to rot upon the ground, the Kiowas backed away forever from the tree. That was July   8

63

20, 1890, at the great bend of the Washita. My grandmother was there. Without bitterness, and for as long as she lived, she bore a vision of deicide.

Now that I can have her only in memory, I see my grandmother in   9
the several postures that were peculiar to her: standing at the wood stove on a winter morning and turning meat in a great iron skillet; sitting at the south window, bent above her beadwork, and afterwards, when her vision failed, looking down for a long time into the fold of her hands; going out upon a cane, very slowly as she did when the weight of age came upon her; praying. I remember her most often at prayer. She made long, rambling prayers out of suffering and hope, having seen many things. I was never sure that I had the right to hear, so exclusive were they of all mere custom and company. The last time I saw her she prayed standing by the side of her bed at night, naked to the waist, the light of a kerosene lamp moving upon her dark skin. Her long black hair, always drawn and braided in the day, lay upon her shoulders and against her breasts like a shawl. I do not speak Kiowa, and I never understood her prayers, but there was something inherently sad in the sound, some merest hesitation upon the syllables of sorrow. She began in a high and descending pitch, exhausting her breath to silence; then again and again — and always the same intensity of effort, of something that is, and is not, like urgency in the human voice. Transported so in the dancing light among the shadows of her room, she seemed beyond the reach of time. But that was illusion; I think I knew then that I should not see her again.

Houses are like sentinels in the plain, old keepers of the weather   10
watch. There, in a very little while, wood takes on the appearance of great age. All colors wear soon away in the wind and rain, and then the wood is burned gray and the grain appears and the nails turn red with rust. The window panes are black and opaque; you imagine there is nothing within, and indeed there are many ghosts, bones given up to the land. They stand here and there against the sky, and you approach them for a longer time than you expect. They belong in the distance; it is their domain.

Once there was a lot of sound in my grandmother's house, a lot of   11
coming and going, feasting and talk. The summers there were full of excitement and reunion. The Kiowas are a summer people; they abide the cold and keep to themselves, but when the season turns and the land becomes warm and vital they cannot hold still; an old love of going returns upon them. The aged visitors who came to my grandmother's

house when I was a child were made of lean and leather, and they bore themselves upright. They wore great black hats and bright ample shirts that shook in the wind. They rubbed fat upon their hair and wound their braids with strips of colored cloth. Some of them painted their faces and carried the scars of old and cherished enmities. They were an old council of warlords, come to remind and be reminded of who they were. Their wives and daughters served them well. The women might indulge themselves; gossip was at once the mark and compensation of their servitude. They made loud and elaborate talk among themselves, full of jest and gesture, fright and false alarm. They went abroad in fringed and flowered shawls, bright beadwork and German silver. They were at home in the kitchen, and they prepared meals that were banquets.

There were frequent prayer meetings, and nocturnal feasts. When I 12
was a child I played with my cousins outside, where the lamplight fell upon the ground and the singing of the old people rose up around us and carried away into the darkness. There were a lot of good things to eat, a lot of laughter and surprise. And afterwards, when the quiet returned, I lay down with my grandmother and could hear the frogs away by the river and feel the motion of the air.

Now there is a funeral silence in the rooms, the endless wake of some 13
final word. The walls have closed in upon my grandmother's house. When I returned to it in mourning, I saw for the first time in my life how small it was. It was late at night, and there was a white moon, nearly full. I sat for a long time on the stone steps by the kitchen door. From there I could see out across the land; I could see the long row of trees by the creek, the low light upon the rolling plains, and the stars of the Big Dipper. Once I looked at the moon and caught sight of a strange thing. A cricket had perched upon the handrail, only a few inches away. My line of vision was such that the creature filled the moon like a fossil. It had gone there, I thought, to live and die, for there, of all places, was its small definition made whole and eternal. A warm wind rose up and purled like the longing within me.

The next morning, I awoke at dawn and went out on the dirt road 14
to Rainy Mountain. It was already hot, and the grasshoppers began to fill the air. Still, it was early in the morning, and birds sang out of the shadows. The long yellow grass on the mountain shone in the bright light, and a scissortail hied above the land. There, where it ought to be, at the end of a long and legendary way, was my grandmother's grave. She had at last succeeded to that holy ground. Here and there on the dark stones were ancestral names. Looking back once, I saw the mountain and came away.

SUBJECT

1. The brief history of the Kiowa people is interesting in itself; does it also contribute to a better understanding of Momaday's grandmother?

2. What purpose is served by the contrasting descriptions of the Kiowa's former territories in the misty Black Hills country and the sun-baked plains to which they migrated?

3. How clear a picture do you get of Aho? From what is given, do you see anything physically unusual about her? Is Momaday using her as a "symbol"?

4. What is the "essential characteristic" of Aho that Momaday wants to convey?

5. Does the loud and talkative aspect of Aho in the company of other women seem out of character with the other aspects of her character?

6. Why is the essay called "The Way to Rainy Mountain"? Would "My Grandmother Aho" be more appropriate?

STRUCTURE

1. What principle of organization controls the order in which materials are presented? Does anything seem to be extraneous? (Consider, for instance, the legend about Devil's Tower and the paragraph on houses as "sentinels in the plain.")

2. Examine one of the more vivid descriptive passages — that of the family reunion, for instance. Would you say that the verbs, the adjectives, or the nouns do most of the work in creating a sense of vividness? Is your answer what you would have expected?

3. Particularly in the passages relating Kiowa history, Momaday employs interpretive adjectives fairly heavily, rather than letting the description indicate whether the Indians were lordly, terrified, or humiliated. Do you see any reason for this use, or would you judge it a flaw in the writing?

4. The reasons for the descriptive details about the Kiowas and about Aho in particular are apparent. But at least half of the details in this article are devoted to the landscape. Can you relate this heavy use of nature description to Momaday's purpose in writing the article?

THE DAY
KHRUSHCHEV VISITED
THE ESTABLISHMENT

John Kenneth Galbraith

John Kenneth Galbraith (born in 1908) is a professor of economics at Harvard, author of The Affluent Society *and numerous other writings, former U.S. Ambassador to India and economic advisor to Presidents Kennedy and Johnson. Since he was in a position to know the principals in the meeting he describes, but could not be identified with either side, Galbraith is an almost ideal observer of the confrontation. He did not agree with Khrushchev, but he was clearly embarrassed by the views of the multimillionaires. Note that the article is simultaneously a description of the meeting itself and of Khrushchev at the meeting.*

A few weeks ago Averell Harriman phoned to chat and ask my recollec- 1
tions of the visit Nikita Khrushchev paid to his Manhattan house on September 17, 1959 — a matter of eleven years and a few weeks ago. I happily complied; few occasions are etched more vividly on my memory. Then it occurred to me that others might be interested.

I did not remind Harriman how I happened to be present — it was 2
not an occasion at which I naturally belonged. Khruschev, having been first in Washington, had just arrived in New York at the beginning of his American tour. He had evinced a desire to meet the people who really run the United States. This to a Marxist (which Khrushchev did not omit to remind Americans he was) did not mean Dwight D. Eisenhower, Richard Nixon, John Foster Dulles, Ezra Taft Benson, J. Edgar Hoover, Carl Hayden, Lyndon Johnson, or Sam Rayburn and our other nominal rulers in Washington. These were only the Executive Committee of the bourgeois class. It meant the people who had the money or, at a minimum, held the purse strings. Harriman obliged and established the sensible criterion that, to be present, a man must own or control assets of (as a rough figure) $100 million or more. This was more than I could readily command.

From *Economics, Peace and Laughter,* by John Kenneth Galbraith. Originally from *Harper's* (February 1971). Copyright © 1971 by John Kenneth Galbraith. Reprinted by permission of the publisher, Houghton Mifflin Company.

However, the day before the meeting — the word confrontation   3
had not yet entered the language — Harriman phoned me to talk
about matters in general and to ask for some help on a speech. (Harriman's use of the telephone is beyond anything imagined by Lyndon
Johnson. Johnson always had something in mind although you often
couldn't be sure what it was. Harriman calls friends for no purpose but
to exchange information. That can occupy pleasantly an hour or more.)
I promised the speech and then guided the conversation to the affair
the next afternoon. He did not respond; it was obvious that I did not
qualify. I pressed the matter; perhaps one representative of the proletariat should be present. He still demurred; conceivably it was because
Thomas K. Finletter, who was only a lawyer, had already been asked
to attend in this capacity. But in the end he invited me. After some
hesitation and a little persuasion, I accepted.

Two years later, talking of the forthcoming meeting between Presi-   4
dent Kennedy and Premier Khrushchev in Vienna, Prime Minister
Nehru told me that Khrushchev had earlier confided in him that his
purpose in getting out of Russia and around the world was to erase the
unpleasant and fearsome impression that all countries had formed of
the Soviet Union from Stalin. I am sure this was so although during my
years in India I discovered that another reason heads of government
travel is that they love to travel. Dozens came to India for no conceiv-
able reason of state. But the guns, bands, banquets, parades, crowds,
cheers, speeches, and sights are a perquisite of high position; it is for
such that a man seeks or seizes office. And so often there is a warmth
and enthusiasm about foreign crowds that a man does not experience
at home. One thinks even of Mr. Nixon. Unfortunately, the leading
members of the Executive Committee then in Washington, Mr. Dulles
in particular, suspected Mr. Khrushchev of other and less innocent
ambitions — they thought he was here to make Cold War propaganda
at the expense of the United States and this was a contest, in those days,
that was very closely scored. There was also fear that he would somehow allay the very natural and justified suspicions of the American
people as to Communist wickedness. (A reporter asked President Eisenhower at his press conference on the day Khrushchev reached New
York if he didn't worry that millions of Americans would see the Soviet
leader on television and conclude that he was a pretty good fellow after
all. Ike discounted the danger. The *Washington Post* ran this news
front-page under an eight-column headline.) There was also concern
that Khrushchev would seize on some of the insignificant flaws in
American society to conclude that the country was ripe for revolution
— or that the Soviets had more support from the masses than was
conceded by the classes. These fears were liberally communicated to

the reporters, many of whom were fiercely involved in the Cold War battle tactics, where they added appreciably to the tension of the tour.

The Administration's fears were also communicated to Henry Cabot 5 Lodge, Jr., who was currently getting good notices for his philippics against the Soviets in the Security Council. He was told to remain by Khrushchev's side throughout the visit and to correct, promptly, any misinformation coming from, or accruing to, the Soviet leader. This did not add so much to tension as to a kind of inspired silliness. At a luncheon at the Waldorf given by Mayor Wagner on the day of the Harriman party, Ambassador Lodge thoughtfully advised Mr. Khrushchev that in New York people of every race, religion, and color lived side by side. He went on to say that "you may as well know that one American national trait which irritates many Americans and must be convenient for our critics is that we relentlessly advertise our imperfections." As an example Mr. Lodge turned to what the *New York Times* called the Negro problem. Conceding that "racial discrimination in the United States has not ended" he pledged that the day would come when "legal segregation would completely disappear." That evening at the Economic Club of New York he rose to even greater heights. He told (speaking a trifle carelessly) of our "strict laws" against monopoly and of our high taxes for welfare and advised the Soviet leader not again to refer to our system as "monopoly capitalism." "Economic humanism" was much more accurate, he said. While the new designation seems not to have caught on in the Communist world it so inspired his audience of economic humanists that night that they rose and, placing arms across chests, spontaneously sang "The Star-spangled Banner." In days following, Mr. Lodge continued his civics lectures, as they were called by the press, until in Los Angeles Mayor Poulson and others were so egregiously rude to Mr. Khrushchev that he threatened to go home. Mr. Lodge thereafter concentrated on being a good host and urged his companion to ignore the insults of, as he sensibly described Poulson and others "the provincial politicians."

The Harriman party was scheduled for 5:30 in the afternoon. I arrived at 16 East 81st Street at 5:15. It occurred to me that I could not be too early — I would be showing my eagerness to belong, letting down my side. I walked around the block and arrived back at the house at 5:20. It was still too early but someone was going in so I followed. Except for the Russians, I was the last to arrive.

The Harriman house was large and handsome and filled with lovely 7 pictures — the famous Harriman collection of Impressionists and Post-Impressionists — and we were marshaled into a large, somewhat elongated circle in the library on the second floor — with others, Frederick H. Ecker of Metropolitan Life; W. Alton Jones, head of Cities Service; George Woods, head of the First Boston Corporation; Dean Rusk, head of the Rockefeller Foundation, and John D. Rockefeller III. (It is possible that the Rockefellers had drawn lots.) Presently the Russians — Khrushchev, Ambassador Menshikov, and the interpreter — arrived. Harriman took them around the circle for introductions and it was evident before he was more than halfway around that the Soviet leader was well in command of the situation. He warmly embraced Herbert Lehman (there as a former Senator as well as for the Lehman millions) and called him "my boss." Although they had never met, Khrushchev, following World War II, had been in charge of UNRRA operations (United Nations Relief and Rehabilitation Administration) in the Ukraine. Lehman had been the head of the agency, in the work of which he had taken much pride, and it was clear that he was well pleased with the salutation. For some of the others present it might not have been completely reassuring, for Lehman was considered a rather damaging radical, his money notwithstanding. I was standing next to Henry Heald, the president of the Ford Foundation (several hundred millions and thus eminently qualified). Khrushchev, on being introduced, shook hands perfunctorily. Then his face lit up, somewhat in the manner of an indigent college president, and he shook hands again saying, "Oh, Mr. Heald of the *FORD* Foundation." Everybody shook hands. He then took a seat before the fireplace, beneath a large Picasso. Harriman and the interpreter were nearby. The scene — the very shapeless man in a rather shapeless suit with a very large pink head and very short legs beneath the Picasso — still shines in my memory. Harriman made the introductions pointing out that both Republicans and Democrats were present in the audience but omitting to add that it was somewhat less than a perfect cross section of the two parties. Then there was an interruption while he offered his guest a drink. All politicians feel they must cherish homegrown commodities and the cliché evidently transcends ideology. Krushchev asked for some Russian vodka. Harriman explained that he had none and then in a truly inspired political gesture offered Mr. Khrushchev a glass of New York State *(sic)* brandy. In an even more heroic gesture Khrushchev sipped it.

Over the past half century the most persistent as well as the most durable advocate in either country of closer Soviet-American relations has been Averell Harriman, but he has always moved in his own remarkable way his wonders to perform. It is the movers and shakers in both countries that he has sought to move. This he considers to require not attention-catching oratory, or flamboyance of any kind, but the extremes of tact. Capitalist and Communist ideologues alike, he feels, must be provided with a formula for getting along which they can reconcile with their deeper commitment to suspicion, dislike, intransigence, bad manners, and natural belligerence. That evening, resuming after his reference to the bipartisan character of the occasion, he went on to say that all present were united in the support of President Eisenhower's foreign policy. That brought approving nods from the audience — all took for granted that as a good American he was rallying to the support of Dulles and the tough line. Then came the Harriman touch. He said that this approval extended strongly to any steps President Eisenhower might take to relax tensions between the two great powers. Were the Democrats to win the Presidency in 1960, he assured his visitor, they would honor Republican agreements to this end. Everyone continued to nod more or less automatically. Mr. Khrushchev said a few unmemorable words about Democrats and Republicans and expressed his belief, possibly even his satisfaction, that those present did, if often through their agents, rule the United States. Somebody demurred but in perfunctory fashion. Then began the questions.

A week or so after the meeting Harriman wrote a brief account of it 9 for *Life.* Rereading this I find my memory to be reasonably accurate as to what was said but very different as to mood. Harriman's tact was in evidence, as ever, in telling of the performance of his American guests. Their questions were, in fact, incredible.

Almost all began with a disavowal of Communist sympathies and a 10 strong affirmation of faith in the American free-enterprise system. In light of the asset position of the speakers, neither disavowal nor avowal seemed absolutely essential. All of the questions were phrased to convey information, not elicit it. A Ring Lardner parent once responded to his offspring: " 'Shut up,' he explained." On that afternoon there was a slight variation. " 'I would like to tell you something,' they asked." However, the questions did not convey much information and not because they were brief. As he spoke each interrogator covertly eyed the others present to see whether he was making a decent impression.

The first question came, as a matter of official precedence, from John 11 J. McCloy who was present both in his asset capacity as chairman of the Chase Manhattan Bank and also as the current chairman of the Establishment itself. Many people have speculated over the years as to the source of Mr. McCloy's extraordinary eminence. I have always held that it owed much to the rocklike self-confidence that he has always brought alike to truth, error, and even nonsense. He was never better than on that afternoon. Wall Street, he assured Mr. Khrushchev in his question, was without influence in Washington; if it supported some legislation, that was the kiss of death. And it was a particular mistake to assume that anyone in Wall Street or anywhere else wanted the arms race to continue. Harriman afterward quoted him as saying that "No one among the American people is trying to preserve international tension for profits. No one in this room knows of any such person." This was in pretty healthy contrast to the kind of stuff that Khrushchev encountered in Communist propaganda.

In response to Mr. McCloy's question Mr. Khrushchev spoke sympa-   12
thetically of the helplessness of Wall Street — he referred to it as a poor relation of the United States. But he stuck discouragingly to his belief that arms were good for business, some business anyhow. Already there was indication that, while the questions might not be good, the answers would be better. They were succinct and improved by the extraordinarily apt translation provided by Oleg Troyanovsky, the good-looking, youthful, Quaker-educated son of the first Soviet Ambassador to the United States. Troyanovsky's eyes sparkled in harmony with Khrushchev's thrusts and, as Russian-speaking reporters had already discovered, he frequently toned down a riposte that he thought a bit too abrasive. After McCloy came Frank Pace, onetime Director of the Budget, onetime Secretary of the Army, and now Chairman of General Dynamics, a giant among the weapons producers. Pace's question involved a novel twist. He made a compelling case for the American system by recounting in detail what it had done for him — how it had facilitated his passage from an Arkansas farm (or some economic equivalent) to Washington and the Bureau of the Budget and the Pentagon, on to the leadership of one of the nation's greatest corporations. The nub of his question was that General Dynamics would gladly liquidate its military business, if circumstances only allowed, as a contribution to the peace of the world. It is possible that Pace was better on promise than he would have been on performance. As he spoke, the Convair division of General Dynamics was on the verge of reporting the largest losses in American corporate history as the result of an ill-managed venture into the civilian air-transport market. The company was saved from bankruptcy by its weapons business on which henceforth it concentrated. In the course of the salvation, Frank Pace got fired. Mr. Khrushchev expressed his appreciation of what capitalism had done for Mr. Pace and said that he well understood why Mr. Pace supported the system.

The next question I subsequently estimated at twenty minutes —   13
but this could have been an impression. It was put — perhaps one could better say composed — by the Chairman of the Radio Corporation of America, General David Sarnoff himself. Mr. Sarnoff's manner

(at least to Khrushchev) could best be described as imperial. He made it clear at the outset that no disagreement would be tolerated. He began with a detailed outline of the free American system of broadcasting. He continued with a warm tribute to its freedom — and some statistics on the number of stations currently on the air. This question was punctuated by some pounding of the Sarnoff breast. No mention was made of commercials. The question was itself a commercial. The General then depicted the refined and varied blessings that would accrue were Russia to adopt a similar system employing a maximum of American programming. When he finished there was silence — a total solemn silence. On this question Khrushchev rose to the greatest heights of the meeting, perhaps indeed of the entire visit. After a general word or two he said, "Things have changed in Minsk since you were a boy."

From this point all was downhill. Mr. McCloy reentered with a ques- 14 tion that was almost a question. Was the Soviet Union willing to give up the idea of revolution in the non-Communist world? Khrushchev's reply was indistinct. Dean Rusk remained silent. Harriman nodded to me and I came through with a question urging Khrushchev to accept the thesis of American Keynesians, such as myself, that the capitalist crisis was now under control. I developed the question with care and at considerable length for I had concluded that the other men present could do with a lecture on modern economics. Many were still very suspicious of Keynesian fiscal policy; they, as well as Mr. Khrushchev, needed to understand the true foundations of American well-being. As my question continued, I watched my audience out of the corner of my eye. I could see that they were following me closely. Presently I finished. Mr. Khrushchev replied that I was entitled to my views, that he was sure that I took them seriously and that he was glad I had confidence in the system. He added that economics is a subject that does not greatly respect one's wishes.

Outside it was still daylight, a lovely autumn evening, and a large 15 crowd of newspapermen and cameramen were waiting. I walked out with Tom Finletter. Several reporters sensed that we might be the soft underbelly of the Establishment and tried to pump us. We remained loyal — a sense of class solidarity is quickly acquired. But it was not quite complete. As we turned down 81st Street, Tom said, "Do you have any doubt as to who was the smartest man in there tonight?"

SUBJECT

1. Galbraith's "excuse" for writing this essay is that Harriman had recently reminded him of the incident described. But what is there

about the occasion to make Galbraith think it would be interesting to readers a dozen years after it happened?

2. Does Galbraith's description of Khrushchev do anything to alter the general — and doubtless vague — impressions people retain of the former Russian leader?

3. This account contains only one sentence (in Paragraph 7) of actual physical description of Khrushchev. Does that seem adequate for Galbraith's purposes? Would he have done better to omit physical description entirely?

4. With so little physical description, how does Galbraith manage to convey a clear impression of Khrushchev — considering that no other person present at the meeting emerges clearly?

5. Does the final sentence represent an additional piece of information (in the form of a rhetorical question) or a conclusion justified by the preceding account of Khrushchev's meeting with the establishment?

STRUCTURE

1. The essay is divided by double-spacing after paragraphs 5 and 8; do these spacings mark logical divisions in the organization of the material?

2. Does the attempt to describe both the meeting and Khrushchev in the same brief article cause any structural confusion?

3. The first section of the essay explains how Galbraith happened to be present at the meeting and how Americans were reacting to Khrushchev's visit. Are both these explanations necessary? Should they have been separated?

4. Several of the paragraphs (4 and 5, for example) are relatively long; can you make topic sentences for those two? Should they have been subdivided or rearranged?

5. Does Galbraith provide enough details to convey a sense of the "essential nature" of Khrushchev? Does he capture the essence of the meeting itself?

6. Since Galbraith is an economist, one might anticipate that he had formed a habit of using abstract language which has little direct appeal to the five senses. Examine his language here to see if this is indeed the case. Can you suggest sentences which might have been improved with more vivid language?

HELEN

Lillian Hellman

Lillian Hellman (born in 1905) is the most successful woman play-wright, at least of the twentieth century. Her best known plays are The Little Foxes *(1939),* Watch on the Rhine *(1941), and* Another Part of the Forest *(1946). The selection which follows is from her autobiography,* An Unfinished Woman *(1969). In this passage Miss Hellman is trying both to describe her maid, Helen, and to explain their attitudes toward one another. To do this, Miss Hellman has had to discuss the other black woman who figured prominently in her life, Sophronia. Rather than risk damaging the prose by excising the Sophronia passages, I have chosen to reprint the entire selection, even though parts of it are only indirectly related to the description of Helen.*

In many places I have spent many days on small boats. Beginning with   1
the gutters of New Orleans, I have been excited about what lives in water and lies along its edges. In the last twenty years, the waters have been the bays, ponds and ocean of Martha's Vineyard, and autumn, when most people have left the island, is the best time for beaching the boat on a long day's picnic by myself — other people on a boat often change the day into something strained, a trip with a purpose — when I fish, read, wade in and out, and save the afternoon for digging and mucking about on the edge of the shore. I have seldom found much: I like to look at periwinkles and mussels, driftwood, shells, horseshoe crabs, gull feathers, the small fry of bass and blues, the remarkable skin of a dead sand shark, the shining life in rockweed.

One night about six months ago, when I was teaching at Harvard, it   2
occurred to me that these childish, aimless pleasures — my knowl-edge of the sea has grown very little with time, and what interested me as a child still does — which have sometimes shamed me and often caused self-mocking, might have something to do with the digging about that occasionally happens when I am asleep. It is then that I awake, feeling that my head is made of sand and that a pole has just

been pulled from it with the end of the pole carrying a card on which there is an answer to a long-forgotten problem, clearly solved and set out as if it had been arranged for me on a night table.

On that night I was living in a rickety Cambridge house and went running down the steps at the sound of a crash. A heavy rainstorm had broken the cheap piece of modernity that had been lighting the ceiling and, as I stood looking at the pieces on the floor, I thought: Of course, one has been dead three years this month, one has been dead for over thirty, but they were one person to you, these two black women you loved more than you ever loved any other women, Sophronia from childhood, Helen so many years later, and it was all there for you to know two months ago when, poking about the beach, a long distance from the house Helen and I had lived in, I found a mangled watch, wondered where I had seen it, and knew a few hours later that it was the watch I had bought in the Zurich airport and that had disappeared a short time after I gave it to Helen. The answer now was easy. She never walked much because her legs hurt. Sam had brought it down to the beach and she didn't want to tell me that my dog, who loved her but didn't love me, could have done anything for which he could be blamed.

From the night of that rainstorm in Cambridge, for weeks later, and even now, once in a while, I have dreamed of Sophronia and Helen, waking up sometimes so pleased that I try to go on with a dream that denies their death, at other times saddened by the dream because it seems a deep time-warning of my own age and death. When that happens, in argument with myself, I feel guilty because I did not know about Sophronia's death for two years after it happened, and had not forced Helen into the hospital that might have saved her. In fact, I had only been angry at her stubborn refusal to go. How often Helen had made me angry, but with Sophronia nothing had ever been bad . . . But the answer there is easy: Sophronia was the anchor for a little girl, the beloved of a young woman, but by the time I had met the other, years had brought acid to a nature that hadn't begun that way — or is that a lie? — and in any case, what excuse did that give for irritation with a woman almost twenty years older than I, swollen in the legs and feet, marrow-weary with the struggle to live, bewildered, resentful, sometimes irrational in a changing world where the old, real-pretend love for white people forced her now into open recognition of the hate and contempt she had brought with her from South Carolina. She had not, could not have, guessed this conflict would ever come to more than the sad talk of black people over collard greens and potlikker, but now here it was on Harlem streets, in newspapers and churches, and how did you

3

4

76

handle what you didn't understand except with the same martyr discipline that made you work when you were sick, made you try to forgive what you really never forgave, made you take a harsh nature and force it into words of piety that, in time, became almost true piety. Why had these two women come together as one for me? Sophronia had not been like that.

I don't know what year Helen came to work for me. We never agreed 5 about the time, although when we felt most affectionate or tired we would argue about it. But it was, certainly, a long time ago. The first months had been veiled and edgy: her severe face, her oppressive silences made me think she was angry, and my nature, alternating from vagueness to rigid demands, made her unhappy, she told me years later. (She did not say it that way: she said, "It takes a searching wind to find the tree you sit in.")

Then one day, at the end of the first uncomfortable months, she said 6 she was grateful, most deeply. I didn't know what she meant, didn't pay much attention, except that I knew she had grown affectionate toward me, even indulgent. Shortly after, she brought me three hundred dollars done up in tissue paper with a weary former Christmas ribbon. I asked her what it was, she said please to count it, I counted it, handed it back, she handed it back to me and said it was the return of the loan for her daughter. I said I didn't know what she was talking about. Her face changed to angry sternness as she said, "I want no charity. I pay my just debts, Miss Hellman. Mr. Hammett must have told you I said that to him."

Hammett hadn't told me she said anything, but it turned out that one 7 night when he had come from the country to have dinner with me, and found he was too tired to return to the country — it was the early period of emphysema — he decided to spend the night in the library. He had been reading at about three in the morning when the phone rang and a frightened voice said there was an emergency, was it possible to call Helen? He had climbed four flights of steps to fetch her, and when she had finished with the phone she said her niece or her daughter or somebody-or-other had had a terrible accident and she would have to go immediately. He asked her if she needed money and, after the long wait she always took when pride was involved, she asked him for taxi money.

Hammett had said, "What about money for the hospital?" 8

She had said, "Black people don't have it easy in a hospital." 9

He had said, "I know. So a check won't do you any good. You'd better 10 have cash."

I said to Hammett, "But what's this got to do with me?" 11

He said, "It's your money she's returning. I took it out of the safe." 12

He told me how disturbed she had been when he had opened my safe 13
and so he had said, "Don't worry. It's O.K. There's no sense waking Miss
Hellman because she can't learn how to open the safe and that makes
her angry."

For many years after, whenever I tried to open the safe, she would 14
come as close to mirth as ever I saw her, saying always that I wasn't to
get disturbed, she thought my fingers were too thin for such work, and
then always reminding me of the night Hammett gave her the money,
"before he even knew me, that is a Christian man."

I said to him, "Helen thinks you're a Christian man." 15

"Sure. She's a convert to my ex-church. We teach 'em to talk like 16
that."

"I won't tell her that. She might not like you." 17

"I won't find that too tough." 18

"But I'm worried that she might think you don't like her." 19

"I don't like her." 20

He didn't like her and he was the only person I ever met who didn't. 21
Sometimes he would say it was because she spoke rudely to me. (He was
right: when she didn't feel well, she often did.) Sometimes he would say
he couldn't stand Catholic converts, or overbig women, or he would
complain that she was the only Negro in America who couldn't carry
a tune. Even through the last four and a half years of his life, when he
had come to live in the house and when she, a woman older than he
by a number of years I never knew, would climb the steps with endless
trays or mail or books or just to ask if there was anything he wanted,
he never said anything more to her than "Good morning," or "Thank
you," or, on special occasions, "It looks like a pleasant day." I think it
is possible that the two of them, obsessed with pride and dignity, one
of the more acceptable forms of self-love, but self-love nevertheless, had
come face to face with a reflection and one of them didn't like what he
saw in the mirror.

Other people always came, in time, to like her and admire her, 22
although her first impression on them was not always pleasant. The
enormous figure, the stern face, the few, crisp words did not seem
welcoming as she opened a door or offered a drink, but the greatest clod
among them came to understand the instinctive good taste, the high-
bred manners that once they flowered gave off so much true courtesy.
And, in this period of nobody grows older or fatter, your mummie looks
like your girl, there may be a need in many of us for the large, strong
woman who takes us back to what most of us always wanted and few
of us ever had.

It is difficult to date anything between people when they have lived   23
together long enough, and so I can't remember when I knew, forgot,
knew, doubted, and finally understood that her feelings for white people and black people were too complex to follow, because what had
been said on one day would be denied on the next. In the early years,
when she told me of the white family in whose house she had been
raised in Charleston, her mother having been the cook there, I would
dislike the Uncle-Tomism of the memories, and often when the newspapers carried a new indignity from the South we would both cluck about
it, but she would turn away from my anger with talk about good and
bad among white people, and she had only known the good. During the
University of Mississippi mess, I asked her what she meant by good
whites, good to her?

She said, "There's too much hate in this world."   24

I said, "Depends on where you carry the hate, doesn't it, what it's   25
made of, how you use it?"

She shrugged. "I ain't ever hated."   26

I said, too fast, "Yes, you have. You just don't know it — " and   27
stopped right before I said, You often hate me, I've known it for years
and let you have it as a debt I wouldn't pay anybody else but Sophronia.

Oh, Sophronia, it's you I want back always. It's by you I still so often   28
measure, guess, transmute, translate and act. What strange process
made a little girl strain so hard to hear the few words that ever came,
made the image of you, true or false, last a lifetime? I think my father
knew about that very early, because five or six years after I was separated from Sophronia by our move to New York, when I saw her only
during our yearly visits to New Orleans, he shouted at me one night,
"To hell with Sophronia. I don't want to hear about her anymore."

That night started in Montgomery, Alabama, although why or how   29
we got to Montgomery I no longer remember. My father had, among
other eccentricities, an inability to travel from one place to another in
a conventional line; if it was possible to change trains or make a detour,
he arranged it. And since we traveled a great deal between New York
and New Orleans, stopping for business or for friends, we were often
to be found in railroad stations waiting for a train that would take us out
of our way.

I had been sleeping on a bench that night in Montgomery, Alabama,   30
so I don't know when I first saw the three figures — a young, very
thin Negro girl, and two white men. The men were drunk, my father
said later, and maybe that accounted for the awkward, shaggy movements, their sudden twists and turns. The girl would move to a bench,
sit, rise as the men came toward her, move to a wall, rest, slide along

it as the men came near, try for another bench, circle it, and move fast when they moved fast. She was trying to stay within the station lights and, as the train came in, she ran down the platform toward it. But she miscalculated and ran outside the lights. I saw one of the men light matches and move in the darkness. When he caught the girl he put the lighted matches to her arm before he kissed her. The girl dropped her valise and there was the noise of glass breaking. I have no clear memory of the next few minutes until I heard my father say, "Let the girl alone." Then he hit the man and the other man hit my father, but he didn't seem hurt because he picked the girl up and shoved her up the steps of the train, came running back for me, shoved me up the steps of the train, got in himself and suddenly began to yell, "My God, where is your mother?" My mother was on the ground repacking the girl's valise. The two men were running toward her but she smiled and waved at my father and put up her hand in a gesture to quiet him. She had trouble with the lock of the valise but she seemed unhurried about fixing it. My father was halfway down the train steps when she rose, faced the two men and said, "Now you just step aside, boys, and take yourselves on home." I don't know whether it was the snobbery of the word "boys" or the accents of her native Alabama, but they made no motion as she came aboard the train.

The girl was invited to share our basket supper and she and my   31
mother spent the next few hours speaking about the nature of men. I
went into the corridor to find my bored father.

Like most other children, I had learned you usually got further by   32
pretending innocence. "What did those men want to do with the girl?"

When he didn't answer, I said, "Rape, that's what. You're a hero.   33
Sophronia will be pleased."

His voice was loud and angry. "To hell with Sophronia. I don't want   34
to hear about her anymore."

A few days later, sitting on a bench in Audubon Park, while the two   35
small boys she now nursed played near us, I told Sophronia the story.
When she didn't speak, I said, "Papa was brave, wasn't he?"

"Yep."   36

"What's the matter?"   37

"Things not going to get themselves fixed by one white man being   38
nice to one nigger girl."

I thought hard and long about that, as I thought about everything she   39
said, and by the next year's visit to New Orleans I had decided on a
course for myself. Sophronia and I had gone to the movies and were
returning home on a streetcar. We had always moved back to sit in the
Negro section of the car, but this time I sat in the front directly behind
the driver and pulled her down next to me. She whispered to me, I

whispered back, she half rose, I pulled her down, and she sat still for a minute waiting for me to grow quiet. The conductor had evidently been watching us, because he turned his head.

"Back." 40

I held so tight to her arm that she couldn't move. 41

He said, "Get back in the car. You know better than this." 42

I said, my voice high with fright, "We won't. We won't move. This 43
lady is better than you are — "

And the car came to a sudden jolt in the middle of the street. People 44
rose and an old woman moved toward us. The conductor opened the doors.

Sophronia got to her feet and I screamed, "Come back, Sophronia, 45
don't you dare move. You're better than anybody, anybody — " and the old lady slapped me as the conductor took my arm. I was carrying a book bag and I threw it at him, turned to push the old lady, turned back to find Sophronia. She had moved between me and the conductor, who looked more surprised than angry. Now she grabbed my arm and pulled me into the street.

I said, "Let's run." 46

She said, "You run. I'm past the runnin' age." 47

So we stood together, staring up at the streetcar, waiting for what we 48
did not know. Then the car started up and moved away from us. I was crying as we walked together toward my aunts' house.

After a while she said, "Crybaby." 49

"I did wrong?" 50

It was an old question and she had always had a song for it: 51
Right is wrong and wrong is right
And who can tell it all by sight?

I said, "Sophronia, I want to go away with you for always, right now. 52
I've thought a lot about it all year and I've made up my mind. I want to live with you the rest of my life. I won't live with white people anymore — "

She put her hand over my mouth. When she took it away, I knew she 53
was very angry. She said, "I got something to tell you, missy. There are too many niggers who like white people. Then there are too many white people think they like niggers. You just be careful."

She crossed the street and was gone before I could move. Sleepless 54
that night and miserable the next day, I went on the second day to find her in Audubon Park.

I said, "Aren't you going to see me anymore?" 55

She said, "I got a no good daughter and a no good son." 56

I had heard this from my mother, but I didn't know then, and I don't 57
know now, what no good meant to her, and so I waited. We sat without

speaking on the park bench watching one little red-haired brother push the other off a tricycle.

She called out, "Stanley. Hugh," and the fight stopped immediately.   58

After a while, I said, "Aren't you going to see me anymore?"   59

"You're growing up, a few years away. Time's approachin' to   60
straighten things out."

"You mean I'm no good, either?"   61

She turned her head and looked at me as if she were puzzled. "I mean   62
you got to straighten things out in your own head. Then maybe you
goin' to be some good and pleasure me. But if they keep on pilin' in silly
and gushin' out worse, you goin' to be trouble, and you ain't goin' to
pleasure me and nobody else."

Many years later, I came to understand that all she meant was that   63
I might blow up my life with impulsiveness or anger or jealousy or all
the other things that she thought made a mess, but that day, in my
thirteenth year, I shivered at the contempt with which she spoke. (And
there I was not wrong. I came to know as she grew older and I did, too,
that she did feel a kind of contempt for the world she lived in and for
almost everybody, black or white, she had ever met, but that day I
thought it was only for me.)

I got up from the bench in maybe the kind of pain you feel when a   64
lover has told you that not only does the love not exist anymore, but that
it possibly never existed at all.

I said, "You mean I am no good and you don't want to see me any-   65
more. Well, I won't hang around and bother you — "

She got slowly to her feet. "You all I got, baby, all I'm goin' to have."   66

Then she leaned down and kissed me. She hadn't kissed me, I think,   67
since I was three or four years old. Certainly I have had happier minutes
since, but not up to then. We shook hands and I went back to the park
bench the next day.

There has always been a picture of Sophronia in my house, all of them   68
taken with me as a young child. Some years after Helen came to work
for me, I came into the library to find her with one of the pictures in
her hand.

I said, "My nurse, my friend. Handsome woman, wasn't she?"   69

"You look like a nice little girl."   70

"Maybe I was, but nobody thought so. I was trouble."   71

"She didn't think so."   72

I took the picture from Helen and, for the first time in the forty years   73
since it had been taken, saw the affection the woman had for the child
she stood behind.

I said, "It takes me too long to know things."   74

"What?"   75

82

"Nothing. I hadn't seen her for two years before she died." 76
"You didn't go to the funeral?" 77
"I didn't know she died. Her daughter didn't tell me." 78
"She was a light-skinned woman?" 79
I know about that question, I've known about it all my life. 80
"Yes, very. But she didn't use it, if that's what you mean." 81
"How old was she?" 82
"In the picture? I don't know. I — my God. She couldn't have been 83
thirty. I can't believe it, but — "
"Black women get old fast." 84
"Yes," I said, "watching white women stay young." 85
"White women never been bad to me." 86
I was in a sudden bad humor, maybe because she wasn't Sophronia. 87
I said, "Colored women who cook as well as you do never had a bad
time. Not even in slavery. You were the darlings of every house. What
about the others who weren't?"
She said, "You mean the good house nigger is king boy." 88
I said, "I mean a house nigger pay no mind to a field hand." 89
She laughed at the words we had both grown up on. A half hour later 90
I went down to the kitchen for a cup of coffee. She was using an electric
beater and so neither of us tried to talk over the noise. Then she turned
the beater off and, I think for the first time in her life, raised her voice
in a shout.
"You ain't got no right to talk that way. No right at all. Down South, 91
I cook. Nothing else, just cook. For you, I slave. You made a slave of me
and you treat me like a slave."
I said, "Helen! Helen!" 92
"A slave. An old, broken slave." 93
"You're a liar," I said, "just a plain God-damned liar." 94
"God will punish you for those words." 95
"He is, right now." 96
She took a check from her apron pocket — her share of the last 97
royalties from *Toys in the Attic* — tore it up, and held out the pieces
to me.
"There. Take it. You think money and presents can buy me, you're 98
wrong."
I said, "I'm going up to Katonah. That will give you a few days to 99
move out."
That night, sitting on a pile of books that had become the only place 100
one could sit in the depressing little cottage filled with furniture broken
by the weight of phonograph records and books, ashtrays toppling on
the edges of manuscripts, a giant desk loaded with unopened mail that
had arrived that day or five years ago, facing a window that had been

splintered by the gun of somebody who didn't like his politics, I told Hammett about the afternoon.

He said, "Why do you talk to her about the South?" 101

"I didn't think she hated me." 102

"She doesn't. She likes you very much and that scares her, because 103 she hates white people. Every morning some priest or other tells her that's not Christian charity, and she goes home more mixed up than ever."

"I guess so. But I don't care about what she hates or doesn't. I care 104 about what I said to her. I'll wait until she has left and then I'll write and say I'm sorry I screamed liar."

He stared at me and went back to reading. After a while he said, "You 105 should have screamed at her years ago. But of course you never lose your temper at the right time. Then you feel guilty and are sure to apologize. I've always counted on that, it's never failed."

I said, "All these years, waiting to catch me out." 106

"Yep. And shall I tell you something else that goes hand in hand, kind 107 of?"

"I am, as you know, grateful for all high-class revelations." 108

"Well," he said, "when you start out being angry, you're almost al- 109 ways right. But anybody with a small amount of sense learns fast that if they let you go on talking you come around to being wrong. So after you've slammed the door, or taken a plane, or whatever caper you're up to, that fine, upright, liberal little old sense of justice begins to operate and you'll apologize not only for the nonsense part of what you've said but for the true and sensible part as well. It's an easy game — just a matter of patience."

I thanked him and went back to New York. It has long been my habit 110 to enter the house on the bedroom floor, and on that day I did not wish to see the kitchen without Helen, did not wish to face a life without her, so it was four or five hours before I went downstairs. Helen was sitting in a chair, her Bible on the table.

She said, "Good evening. Your hair is wet." 111

"Yes," I said, "I'm trying to curl it." 112

We did learn something that day, maybe how much we needed each 113 other, although knowing that often makes relations even more difficult. Our bad times came almost always on the theme of Negroes and whites. The white liberal attitude is, mostly, a well-intentioned fake, and black people should and do think it a sell. But mine was bred, literally, from Sophronia's milk, and thus I thought it exempt from such judgments except when I made the jokes about myself. But our bad times did not spring from such conclusions by Helen — they were too advanced, too unkind for her. They came, I think, because she did not think white people capable of dealing with trouble. I was, thus, an intruder, and in the autumn of 1963 she told me so.

I had gone down to Washington to write a magazine piece about the 114 Washington March. Through Negro friends, through former Harvard students, through a disciple of Malcolm X, I had arranged to meet the delegations from Louisiana and Alabama. Sophronia's grandson, whom I had never seen, was to arrive with the Alabama delegation. Many years before, I had had letters from his older sister, a teacher at Tuskegee. Now, when I wrote to ask if they would like to come to Washington, she had written back that they could not make the trip. Immediately after, I had a letter from Orin saying that he wanted to come if I would send the bus fare, but please not to tell his sister, because she did not approve. I had sent the money and, as far as I knew, he was on his way.

At seven o'clock on the morning of the March, I was sitting on the 115 steps of the Lincoln Memorial waiting for Orin, wondering if he looked like Sophronia, if he had brought me the photographs I had asked for, if his mother had ever told him much about her. At nine o'clock I went to look for the Alabama delegation. They had been in Washington for six hours, but nobody had heard of Orin and they were sure he had never been on the bus, never signed up to come.

It was, of course, a remarkable day. Two hundred thousand people 116 come to ask only what they thought had been promised, still calm, pleasant and gay in the face of the one-hundred-year-old refusal. But as the day wore on, I felt as if a respectable Madison Avenue funeral had gone on too long. When Martin Luther King rose to speak — and there was no question of the pride the audience felt in the man, no question that he represented all that was gentle and kind in this kindest of people — I remembered too many Negro preachers from my childhood and grew impatient with "I have a dream."

I wandered off looking for something to eat. I dropped my pocket- 117 book, spilled the contents, and was helped by a small colored boy who, when I thanked him, said, "O.K., lady, courtesy of the Commonwealth." I laughed and found that his companion, a tall young Negro, was laughing, too.

I said, "What's that mean, courtesy of the Commonwealth?" 118

"Nothing," said the young man. "Old George tries to learn a new 119 word every day. We were up around Boston last night so today it will be 'Commonwealth.'"

Old George turned out to be fourteen years old, small for his age, and 120 the young man's name was Gene Carondelet.

I said, "That's the name of a street in New Orleans." 121

He said, "Yep. That's why I took it." 122

Old George weaved in and out of the crowd, bringing frankfurters 123
and then coffee, while Carondelet told me he had been in jail seven
times for trying to register Negroes in Greenwood, Mississippi, and for
leading a march in Baton Rouge. He said he had never seen old George
before McComb, Mississippi, where a policeman had hit George over
the head and George's mother had hit the policeman. The next day
George's mother said, "Take the boy with you. He's in danger here.
Take him and teach him."

"He's been with me for eight months. That George can do, learn 124
anything. Makes a mighty fine speech. Make a speech for the lady."

George rose. "You folks better take your black behinds down to vote 125
your way to freedom. The first correlative to freedom — " At the
word "correlative" George grinned at me and sat down, saying he
didn't feel too well, he had his headache back again. Carondelet explained that in a few days they were coming to New York to see a doctor
about the headaches George had been having since he got hit over the
head by the policeman.

About a week later, I came in the house to find Carondelet, George, 126
and a gangly popeyed man of about twenty-four sitting in the living
room with Helen. Carondelet said they'd been waiting for an hour and
now they had to go because George was on his way to the doctor's. As
I took them to the elevator, I did not notice that the strange man was
still in the living room until George said, "You wanted him, you got
him."

"Who?" 127

"That Orin something." 128

Carondelet said, "He's silly stuff." 129

Orin was, indeed, a dull young man, sleepy, over-polite, as anxious as 130
I was to get the visit over with. He had been born long after Sophronia's
death, had no memory of his mother's ever having talked about her.
What about his uncle, Sophronia's son? Never heard of him. Where was
his mother? She'd skipped long ago, maybe dead, maybe still turning
a trick. Why hadn't he come to Washington with the Alabama delegation? They weren't his kind. He'd come to New York, been robbed, lost
my address, hadn't eaten, where was the men's room? I pointed toward
the kitchen, waited a long time, puzzled and sad that this man should
be Sophronia's grandson. When he did come back, I said I had to go to
work, and rose to shake his hand. He suddenly began to talk in a more
animated way, although the words were now slurred. I had become
Miss Hellmar or, more often, "man" in puzzling sentences like "Man,
this is some town and they can take me to it any time they got enough,
man," and "Man, where them two finkies I come here with, and where

is here, just where is here at?" After a while I said I'd get him some money for the trip back home if he wanted to make it, and he began to laugh as I went into the hall to find Helen standing by the door.

She said, "He took a shot in the toilet."   131

"What do you mean?"   132

"A no good punkie-junkie. Maybe heroin."   133

The words were so modern, so unlike her, that I stared, amused and   134 puzzled that there was a side of her I didn't know.

"I don't think so. He's just stupid, and uncomfortable with me."   135

When I came back down the steps, the phonograph was playing very   136 loudly and Orin was moving around the room. I couldn't hear what Helen said, but his voice was very loud.

"Lady man, I'm stayin' right where I fall, see?"   137

Helen said, "You a sick boy. You going for a cure, or you going to   138 hell."

"Lady man, hell's my place and you my girl, tired and old. Maybe   139 even have to send you on a little errand soon — "

She crossed to him, pulled his arms behind his back, and stepped to   140 one side as he tried to kick her. She held him easily, gracefully, as she pulled him toward a chair.

She said to me, "Go for a walk," and closed and locked the door.   141

The following morning she said, "You see, things happen to people."   142

I didn't answer her, and after an hour or so she appeared again —   143 an old habit, conversation without prelude, in space, from hours or days or months before — "I locked the door 'cause I wanted you out of trouble."

"No," I said. "You just didn't think I'd be any good at it."   144

"Time I told you what I ain't told you. My daughter, same way, same   145 thing."

After a while I said, "That shouldn't have happened to you."   146

"No good for colored people to come North, no good," she said. "Live   147 like a slummy, die like one. South got its points, no matter what you think. Even if just trees."

I was never to see or hear from Orin again, but when George got out   148 of the hospital he came to stay with us several times, appearing and disappearing without explanation. There was something odd about his relations with Helen, something teasing on his side, cautious on hers.

The next summer he came to stay with us for a few days on the   149 Vineyard. He was romping with the poodle on the lawn outside her window, while I read on the porch above their heads.

He said to her, "Hey, Mrs. Jackson, your poodle got fleas."   150

"Lot of people got fleas," she said.   151

After a long pause, George called out, "I've been thinking about what 152 you said, and I'm God-damned if I understand it."

"You been sleepin' here, Miss Hellman been sleepin' here. That's all 153 I got to say."

George screamed with laughter. "You mean *we* give the dog the 154 fleas? You some far-out lady, Mrs. Jackson." And a door slammed.

At dinner, a few weeks later, he said to Helen, "Could I have a piece 155 of your cornbread?"

"Where you see cornbread?" 156

"Why you hide it where you do?" 157

It had long been her habit to hide any food that was fattening on the 158 pretense that she ate very little and thus had inherited her "fat glands." Now she opened the stove, reached far back into the oven, and slammed down on the table a giant cornbread cake and a pot of greens and fatback.

"Can I have some," I said, knowing he had made a bad mistake — 159 "nothing in the world like potlikker and corn — "

She said to George, "What you do all day, besides snoopin'? You know 160 more about this island than we ever find out, or want to."

"Sure do," said George, "that my job. Got to find out before you 161 organize. You, for example. Find out all about you being like crazy with your money. You got so much money, give it to SNCC instead of wasting it on that no good Almira family down in town."

Helen said, softly, "Eat your dinner, son." 162

George said to me, "Old man Almira leave his family for a fourteen- 163 year-old girl, and Mrs. Jackson here, that makes her sad, so she send money all year round, *all year round,* to the wife and kiddies — "

Helen said, "No good men, that's what you all are." 164

George said, "And no good kiddies. You some fine picker, Mrs. Jack- 165 son. The Almira boy was the one set the fire last week and the girl whores all over the Cape."

"You lie, boy, and you a mighty dirty talker about your own people." 166

"First," said George, "they ain't my people 'cause they ain't all black, 167 they part Portuguese. Two, bums is bums, forget the color. Three, a revolutionary got no right to defend the baddies even of his own color, kind or faith. Otherwise it comes about — "

I said, "Oh, shut up, George," and Helen hit me on the arm, an old 168 sign of affectionate approval.

George came to visit us the next summer for a few days but I did not 169 see him at all in 1965, until the cold autumn day of Helen's funeral. That night, quite late, he rang the bell, a small suitcase in his hand.

He said, "I wouldn't have come like this, but I'm going back to 170 Atlanta, and I wanted to — Well, I don't know."

We talked for a while about what he'd been doing, where he'd been, 171
and then he said, "You're worried, Miss Hellman."

"Yes," I said, "if that's the word." 172

"About the funeral. They didn't come to you?" 173

"I guess that's part of it, but not much. No, they didn't come to me, 174
although they telephoned, the two nieces, and the daughter I'd never
heard from before. They asked me what kind of funeral I wanted, but
I didn't like to intrude, or maybe — I don't know."

"Stinking funeral." 175

I said, "It's hard to know what strong people would want. I've been 176
there before. You think they're trying to tell you something, forbid you
something, but you don't know — "

"Ah," he said, "the one thing they knew for sure was she didn't want 177
that coffin, all done up for a bishop, with brass. Seventeen hundred
dollars."

"My God, I didn't know that. What fools — Well, at least I talked 178
them into burying her in South Carolina. That I know she wanted."

"It's my birthday," George said, so we had two drinks. When he got 179
up to leave he said, "Don't worry about the funeral or the coffin. It's
done, done."

"That's not what's worrying me. She got sick on Monday. I wanted 180
her to go to the hospital. She wanted to go home. I was annoyed with
her and went for a walk. When I came back she was gone. I phoned the
next day and she said she was better, but might not be able to work for
a while, and then as if she wanted to tell me something. The next
morning she was dead."

"She did want to tell you something. She was getting ready to die." 181

I said, "You know too much, George, too much you're sure of. I don't 182
believe she knew she was going to die. I won't believe it. And how do
you know how much the coffin cost?"

"They told me," he said. "On Tuesday morning, Mrs. Jackson asked 183
me to come round."

"She asked you, she didn't ask me. I'm jealous, George." 184

"She had things for me to do, errands." 185

I said, "She always had people doing secret errands. I didn't know you 186
saw each other."

"Oh, sure, whenever I came up North, and then I always wrote to her. 187
My second operation, I stayed in her place till I was better."

"You didn't tell me you had a second operation." 188

He smiled. "Anyway, there I am on Tuesday. She shows me two 189
Savings Bank things and says they're for her grandchildren. Then she
give me orders to pack her clothes and take 'em to the post office, all
of them except one dress and shoes."

"Where did she send them?"   190

"Somebody in Augusta, Georgia. Then I take around the TV radio set 191
and I sell that for her. When I come back, she asked me to make her
a lemonade and said she wanted to sleep. I said I'd be back at night, but
she said not to come, she wanted rest. Then she gave me one hundred
dollars. Eighty-five for me, she said, or wherever I wanted to give it.
Fifteen for Orin when I found him."

Orin? Orin?"   192

"He's still hanging around. She always gave him a little money. But 193
he ain't going to get this fifteen, 'cause I ain't going to find him. She was
some far-out lady, Mrs. Jackson. Some far-out Christian lady."

"Sure was," I said.   194

"I hope you feel better," he said. "Next time I'm here, I'll come see 195
you."

But he never has come to see me again.   196

SUBJECT

1.   How is Hellman's past experience with Sophronia related to her
more recent experience with Helen? Does the story of Sophronia in
any way clarify the reader's view of Helen?

2.   Does a coherent picture of Helen emerge from this somewhat
rambling series of descriptions and anecdotes? Does anything important seem to be left out?

3.   What function does the shadowy character, Hammett, play in
our understanding of Helen?

4.   Does George's conclusion that Helen was "some far-out Christian lady" seem a fair summary of what we know of her, or a gross
oversimplification? Can you tell what George means by "Christian"?

5.   Judging by her relationship with Helen and Sophronia, to what
extent do you think the following statement by Hellman applies to
herself ? — "The white liberal attitude is, mostly, a well-intentioned
fake, and black people should and do think it a sell." (Clearly Hellman
thinks of herself as an exception.)

STRUCTURE

1.   A number of quite varied incidents and anecdotes are chosen for
this portrait of Helen; do you see any *principle of selection* operating
(other than random recollection) in the choice of details?

2.   Near the beginning of this essay, the description of Helen contains many "interpretive" adjectives — *stubborn, resentful, affectionate,* etc; toward the end the characterization is accomplished more

and more through quoted dialogue. Which method seems to make the strongest impact? Why?

3. What difference do you notice between the style of the expository passages and that of the dialogue? Is the difference appropriate? or should the entire essay have been written in a consistent style?

4. In this selection Hellman is trying to do more than characterize her maid. If you were asked to reduce it to a character sketch, doubtless you would omit some of the material; would you then rearrange the remaining passages, or leave them in their present order? *Is* there an "order" of arrangement at present?

POWERHOUSE

Eudora Welty

Eudora Welty (born in 1909) was born and still lives in Jackson, Missis-
sippi. As a novelist and short story writer, she has won numerous
awards and honors, especially for her novel, The Ponder Heart *(1955).*
Among her collections of short stories are A Curtain of Green *(1941),*
The Wide Net *(1943) and* The Golden Apples *(1949). Her most recent*
book is Losing Battles *(1970). A regionalist, Miss Welty combines*
homely details of life in Mississippi with strange fantasies and dream-
like occurrences. Katherine Anne Porter said that she exhibits "the
waking faculty of daylight reason recollecting and recording the crazy
logic of the dream." "Powerhouse" is a good example of that faculty;
it also shows Miss Welty's fine ability to establish character through
carefully selected descriptive details.

Powerhouse is playing! 1

He's here on tour from the city — "Powerhouse and His Keyboard" 2
— "Powerhouse and His Tasmanians" — think of the things he calls
himself! There's no one in the world like him. You can't tell what he is.
"Nigger man"? — he looks more Asiatic, monkey, Jewish, Babylonian,
Peruvian, fanatic, devil. He has pale gray eyes, heavy lids, maybe horny
like a lizard's, but big glowing eyes when they're open. He has African
feet of the greatest size, stomping, both together, on each side of the
pedals. He's not coal black — beverage colored — looks like a
preacher when his mouth is shut, but then it opens — vast and obscene. And his mouth is going every minute: like a monkey's when it
looks for something. Improvising, coming on a light and childish melody
— *smooch* — he loves it with his mouth.

Is it possible that he could be this! When you have him there perform- 3
ing for you, that's what you feel. You know people on a stage — and
people of a darker race — so likely to be marvelous, frightening.

This is a white dance. Powerhouse is not a show-off like the Harlem 4
boys, not drunk, not crazy — he's in a trance; he's a person of joy, a
fanatic. He listens as much as he performs, a look of hideous, powerful
rapture on his face. Big arched eyebrows that never stop traveling, like

a Jew's — wandering-Jew eyebrows. When he plays he beats down piano and seat and wears them away. He is in motion every moment — what could be more obscene? There he is with his great head, fat stomach, and little round piston legs, and long yellow-sectioned strong big fingers, at rest about the size of bananas. Of course you know how he sounds — you've heard him on records — but still you need to see him. He's going all the time, like skating around the skating rink or rowing a boat. It makes everybody crowd around, here in this shadowless steel-trussed hall with the rose-like posters of Nelson Eddy and the testimonial for the mind-reading horse in handwriting magnified five hundred times. Then all quietly he lays his finger on a key with the promise and serenity of a sibyl touching the book.

Powerhouse is so monstrous he sends everybody into oblivion. When any group, any performers, come to town, don't people always come out and hover near, leaning inward about them, to learn what it is? What is it? Listen. Remember how it was with the acrobats. Watch them carefully, hear the least word, especially what they say to one another, in another language — don't let them escape you; it's the only time for hallucination, the last time. They can't stay. They'll be somewhere else this time tomorrow. 5

Powerhouse has as much as possible done by signals. Everybody, laughing as if to hide a weakness, will sooner or later hand him up a written request. Powerhouse reads each one, studying with a secret face: that is the face which looks like a mask — anybody's; there is a moment when he makes a decision. Then a light slides under his eyelids, and he says, "92!" or some combination of figures — never a name. Before a number the band is all frantic, misbehaving, pushing, like children in a schoolroom, and he is the teacher getting silence. His hands over the keys, he says sternly, "You-all ready? You-all ready to do some serious walking?" — waits — then, STAMP. Quiet. STAMP, for the second time. This is absolute. Then a set of rhythmic kicks against the floor to communicate the tempo. Then, O Lord! say the distended eyes from beyond the boundary of the trumpets, Hello and good-bye, and they are all down the first note like a waterfall. 6

This note marks the end of any known discipline. Powerhouse seems to abandon them all — he himself seems lost — down in the song, yelling up like somebody in a whirlpool — not guiding them — hailing them only. But he knows, really. He cries out, but he must know exactly. "Mercy! ... What I say! ... Yeah!" And then drifting, listening — "Where that skin beater?" — wanting drums, and starting up and pouring it out in the greatest delight and brutality. On the sweet pieces 7 such a leer for everybody! He looks down so benevolently upon all our faces and whispers the lyrics to us. And if you could hear him at this moment on "Marie, the Dawn is Breaking"! He's going up the keyboard with a few fingers in some very derogatory triplet-routine, he gets higher and higher, and then he looks over the end of the piano, as if over a cliff. But not in a show-off way — the song makes him do it.

He loves the way they all play, too — all those next to him. The far 8 section of the band is all studious, wearing glasses, every one — they don't count. Only those playing around Powerhouse are the real ones. He has a bass fiddler from Vicksburg, black as pitch, named Valentine, who plays with his eyes shut and talking to himself, very young: Power-house has to keep encouraging him. "Go on, go on, give it up, bring it on out there!" When you heard him like that on records, did you know he was really pleading?

He calls Valentine out to take a solo. 9

"What you going to play?" Powerhouse looks out kindly from behind 10 the piano; he opens his mouth and shows his tongue, listening.

Valentine looks down, drawing against his instrument, and says with- 11 out a lip movement, " 'Honeysuckle Rose.' "

He has a clarinet player named Little Brother, and loves to listen to 12 anything he does. He'll smile and say, "Beautiful!" Little Brother takes a step forward when he plays and stands at the very front, with the whites of his eyes like fishes swimming. Once when he played a low note, Powerhouse muttered in dirty praise, "He went clear downstairs to get that one!"

After a long time, he holds up the number of fingers to tell the band 13 how many choruses still to go — usually five. He keeps his directions down to signals.

It's a bad night outside. It's a white dance, and nobody dances, except 14 a few straggling jitterbugs and two elderly couples. Everybody just stands around the band and watches Powerhouse. Sometimes they steal glances at one another, as if to say, Of course, you know how it is with *them* — Negroes — band leaders — they would play the same way, giving all they've got, for an audience of one. . . . When somebody, no matter who, gives everything, it makes people feel ashamed for him.

Late at night they play the one waltz they will ever consent to play 15 — by request, "Pagan Love Song." Powerhouse's head rolls and sinks like a weight between his waving shoulders. He groans, and his fingers drag into the keys heavily, holding on to the notes, retrieving. It is a sad song.

"You know what happened to me?" says Powerhouse.   16

Valentine hums a response, dreaming at the bass.   17

"I got a telegram my wife is dead," says Powerhouse, with wandering   18
fingers.

"Uh-huh?"   19

His mouth gathers and forms a barbarous O while his fingers walk up   20
straight, unwillingly, three octaves.

"Gypsy? Why how come her to die, didn't you just phone her up in   21
the night last night long distance?"

"Telegram say — here the words: Your wife is dead." He puts 4/4   22
over the 3/4.

"Not but four words?" This is the drummer, an unpopular boy named   23
Scoot, a disbelieving maniac.

Powerhouse is shaking his vast cheeks. "What the hell was she trying   24
to do? What was she up to?"

"What name has it got signed, if you got a telegram?" Scoot is spitting   25
away with those wire brushes.

Little Brother, the clarinet player, who cannot now speak, glares and   26
tilts back.

"Uranus Knockwood is the name signed." Powerhouse lifts his eyes   27
open. "Ever heard of him?" A bubble shoots out on his lip like a plate
on a counter.

Valentine is beating slowly on with his palm and scratching the   28
strings with his long blue nails. He is fond of a waltz, Powerhouse
interrupts him.

"I don't know him. Don't know who he is." Valentine shakes his head   29
with the closed eyes.

"Say it again."   30

"Uranus Knockwood."   31

"That ain't Lenox Avenue."   32

"It ain't Broadway."   33

"Ain't ever seen it wrote out in any print, even for horse racing."   34

"Hell, that's on a star, boy, ain't it?" Crash of the cymbals.   35

"What the hell was she up to?" Powerhouse shudders. "Tell me, tell   36
me, tell me." He makes triplets, and begins a new chorus. He holds
three fingers up.

"You say you got a telegram." This is Valentine, patient and sleepy,   37
beginning again.

Powerhouse is elaborate. "Yas, the time I go out, go way downstairs   38
along a long cor-ri-dor to where they puts us: coming back along the
cor-ri-dor: steps out and hands me a telegram: Your wife is dead."

"Gypsy?" The drummer like a spider over his drums.   39

"Aaaaaaaaa!" shouts Powerhouse, flinging out both powerful arms for 40
three whole beats to flex his muscles, then kneading a dough of bass
notes. His eyes glitter. He plays the piano like a drum sometimes —
why not?

"Gypsy? Such a dancer?" 41

"Why you don't hear it straight from your agent? Why it ain't come 42
from headquarters? What you been doing, getting telegrams in the
corridor, signed nobody?"

They all laugh. End of that chorus. 43

"What time is it?" Powerhouse calls. "What the hell place is this? 44
Where is my watch and chain?"

"I hang it on you," whimpers Valentine. "It still there." 45

There it rides on Powerhouse's great stomach, down where he can 46
never see it.

"Sure did hear some clock striking twelve while ago. Must be 47
midnight."

"It going to be intermission," Powerhouse declares, lifting up his 48
finger with the signet ring.

He draws the chorus to an end. He pulls a big Northern hotel towel 49
out of the deep pocket in his vast, special-cut tux pants and pushes his
forehead into it.

"If she went and killed herself!" he says with a hidden face. "If she 50
up and jumped out that window!" He gets to his feet, turning vaguely,
wearing the towel on his head.

"Ha, ha!" 51

"Sheik, sheik!" 52

"She wouldn't do that." Little Brother sets down his clarinet like a 53
precious vase, and speaks. He still looks like an East Indian queen,
implacable, divine, and full of snakes. "You ain't going to expect people
doing what they says over long distance."

"Come on!" roars Powerhouse. He is already at the back door, he has 54
pulled it wide open, and with a wild, gathered-up face is smelling the
terrible night.

Powerhouse, Valentine, Scoot and Little Brother step outside into the 55
drenching rain.

"Well, they emptying buckets," says Powerhouse in a mollified voice. 56
On the street he holds his hands out and turns up the blanched palms
like sieves.

A hundred dark, ragged, silent, delighted Negroes have come around 57
from under the eaves of the hall, and follow wherever they go.

"Watch out Little Brother don't shrink," says Powerhouse. "You just 58
the right size now, clarinet don't suck you in. You got a dry throat, Little
Brother, you in the desert?" He reaches into the pocket and pulls out

a paper of mints. "Now hold 'em in your mouth — don't chew 'em. I don't carry around nothing without limit."

"Go in that joint and have beer," says Scoot, who walks ahead. 59

"Beer? Beer? You know what beer is? What do they say is beer? 60
What's beer? Where I been?"

"Down yonder where it say World Café — that do?" They are in 61
Negrotown now.

Valentine patters over and holds open a screen door warped like a 62
sea shell, bitter in the wet, and they walk in, stained darker with the
rain and leaving footprints. Inside, sheltered dry smells stand like
screens around a table covered with a red-checkered cloth, in the center of which flies hang onto an obelisk-shaped ketchup bottle. The
midnight walls are checkered again with admonishing "Not Responsible" signs and black-figured, smoky calendars. It is a waiting, silent, limp
room. There is a burned-out-looking nickelodeon and right beside it a
long-necked wall instrument labeled "Business Phone, Don't Keep
Talking." Circled phone numbers are written up everywhere. There is
a worn-out peacock feather hanging by a thread to an old, thin, pink,
exposed light bulb, where it slowly turns around and around, whoever
breathes.

A waitress watches. 63

"Come here, living statue, and get all this big order of beer we fixing 64
to give."

"Never seen you before anywhere." The waitress moves and comes 65
forward and slowly shows little gold leaves and tendrils over her teeth.
She shoves up her shoulders and breasts. "How I going to know who you
might be? Robbers? Coming in out of the black of night right at midnight, setting down so big at my table?"

"Boogers," says Powerhouse, his eyes opening lazily as in a cave. 66

The girl screams delicately with pleasure. O Lord, she likes talk and 67
scares.

"Where you going to find enough beer to put out on this here table?" 68

She runs to the kitchen with bent elbows and sliding steps. 69

"Here's a million nickels," says Powerhouse, pulling his hand out of 70
his pocket and sprinkling coins out, all but the last one, which he makes
vanish like a magician.

Valentine and Scoot take the money over to the nickelodeon, which 71
looks as battered as a slot machine, and read all the names of the records
out loud.

"Whose 'Tuxedo Junction'?" asks Powerhouse. 72

"You know whose." 73

"Nickelodeon, I request you please to play 'Empty Bed Blues' and let 74
Bessie Smith sing."

97

Silence: they hold it like a measure. 75

"Bring me all those nickels on back here," says Powerhouse. "Look 76
at that! What you tell me the name of this place?"

"White dance, week night, raining, Alligator, Mississippi, long ways 77
from home."

"Uh-huh." 78

"Sent for You Yesterday and Here You Come Today" plays. 79

The waitress, setting the tray of beer down on a back table, comes up 80
taut and apprehensive as a hen. "Says in the kitchen, back there putting
their eyes to little hole peeping out, that you is Mr. Powerhouse. . . .
They knows from a picture they seen."

"They seeing right tonight, that is him," says Little Brother. 81

"You him?" 82

"That is him in the flesh," says Scoot. 83

"Does you wish to touch him?" asks Valentine. "Because he don't 84
bite."

"You passing through?" 85

"Now you got everything right." 86

She waits like a drop, hands languishing together in front. 87

"Little-Bit, ain't you going to bring the beer?" 88

She brings it, and goes behind the cash register and smiles, turning 89
different ways. The little fillet of gold in her mouth is gleaming.

"The Mississippi River's here," she says once. 90

Now all the watching Negroes press in gently and bright-eyed 91
through the door, as many as can get in. One is a little boy in a straw
sombrero which has been coated with aluminum paint all over.

Powerhouse, Valentine, Scoot and Little Brother drink beer, and 92
their eyelids come together like curtains. The wall and the rain and the
humble beautiful waitress waiting on them and the other Negroes
watching enclose them.

"Listen!" whispers Powerhouse, looking into the ketchup bottle and 93
slowly spreading his performer's hands over the damp, wrinkling cloth
with the red squares. "Listen how it is. My wife gets missing me. Gypsy.
She goes to the window. She looks out and sees you know what. Street.
Sign saying Hotel. People walking. Somebody looks up. Old man. She
looks down, out the window. Well? . . . *Sssssst! Plooey!* What she do?
Jump out and bust her brains all over the world."

He opens his eyes. 94

"That's it," agrees Valentine. "You gets a telegram." 95

"Sure she misses you," Little Brother adds. 96

"No, it's night time." How softly he tells them! "Sure. It's the night 97
time. She say, What do I hear? Footsteps walking up the hall? That him?

Footsteps go on off. It's not me. I'm in Alligator, Mississippi, she's crazy.
Shaking all over. Listens till her ears and all grow out like old music-box
horns but still she can't hear a thing. She says, All right! I'll jump out
the window then. Got on her nightgown. I know that nightgown, and
her thinking there. Says, Ho hum, all right, and jumps out the window.
Is she mad at me! Is she crazy! She don't leave *nothing* behind her!"

"Ya! Ha!" 98

"Brains and insides everywhere, Lord, Lord." 99

All the watching Negroes stir in their delight, and to their higher 100
delight he says affectionately, "Listen! Rats in here."

"That must be the way, boss." 101

"Only, naw, Powerhouse, that ain't true. That sound too *bad.*" 102

"Does? I even know who finds her," cries Powerhouse. "That no-good 103
pussyfooted crooning creeper, that creeper that follow around after
me, coming up like weeds behind me, following around after me everything I do and messing around on the trail I leave. Bets my numbers,
sings my songs, gets close to my agent like a Betsybug; when I going out
he just coming in. I got him now! I got my eye on him."

"Know who he is?" 104

"Why, it's that old Uranus Knockwood!" 105

"Ya! Ha!" 106

"Yeah, and he coming now, he going to find Gypsy. There he is, 107
coming around that corner, and Gypsy kadoodling down, oh-oh, watch
out! *Sssst! Plooey!* See, there she is in her little old nightgown, and her
insides and brains all scattered round."

A sigh fills the room. 108

"Hush about her brains. Hush about her insides." 109

"Ya! Ha! You talking about her brains and insides — old Uranus 110
Knockwood," says Powerhouse, "look down and say Jesus! He say, Look
here what I'm walking round in!"

They all burst into halloos of laughter. Powerhouse's face looks like 111
a big hot iron stove.

"Why, he picks her up and carries her off!" he says. 112

"Ya! Ha!" 113

"Carries her *back* around the corner. . . ." 114

"Oh, Powerhouse!" 115

"You know him." 116

"Uranus Knockwood!" 117

"Yeahhh!" 118

"He take our wives when we gone!" 119

"He come in when we goes out!" 120

"Uh-huh!" 121

"He go out when we comes in!" 122

"Yeahhh!" 123

"He standing behind the door!" 124

"Old Uranus Knockwood." 125

"You know him." 126

"Middle-size man." 127

"Wears a hat." 128

"That's him." 129

Everybody in the room moans with pleasure. The little boy in the fine 130
silver hat opens a paper and divides out a jelly roll among his followers.

And out of the breathless ring somebody moves forward like a slave, 131
leading a great logy Negro with bursting eyes, and says, "This here is
Sugar-Stick Thompson, that dove down to the bottom of July Creek and
pulled up all those drownded white people fall out of a boat. Last
summer, pulled up fourteen."

"Hello," says Powerhouse, turning and looking around at them all 132
with his great daring face until they nearly suffocate.

Sugar-Stick, their instrument, cannot speak; he can only look back at 133
the others.

"Can't even swim. Done it by holding his breath," says the fellow 134
with the hero.

Powerhouse looks at him seekingly. 135

"I his half brother," the fellow puts in. 136

They step back. 137

"Gypsy say," Powerhouse rumbles gently again, looking at *them,* 138
" 'What is the use? I'm gonna jump out so far — so far. . . .' *Sssst — !*"

"Don't, boss, don't do it again," says Little Brother. 139

"It's awful," says the waitress. "I hates that Mr. Knockwoods. All that 140
the truth?"

"Want to see the telegram I got from him?" Powerhouse's hand goes 141
to the vast pocket.

"Now wait, now wait, boss." They all watch him. 142

"It must be the real truth," says the waitress, sucking in her lower lip, 143
her luminous eyes turning sadly, seeking the windows.

"No, babe, it ain't the truth." His eyebrows fly up, and he begins to 144
whisper to her out of his vast oven mouth. His hand stays in his pocket.
"Truth is something worse, I ain't said what, yet. It's something hasn't
come to me, but I ain't saying it won't. And when it does, then want
me to tell you?" He sniffs all at once, his eyes come open and turn up,
almost too far. He is dreamily smiling.

"Don't, boss, don't, Powerhouse!" 145

"Oh!" the waitress screams. 146

"Go on git out of here!" bellows Powerhouse, taking his hand out of 147
his pocket and clapping after her red dress.

The ring of watchers breaks and falls away. 148

"*Look* at that! Intermission is up," says Powerhouse. 149

He folds money under a glass, and after they go out, Valentine leans 150
back in and drops a nickel in the nickelodeon behind them, and it lights
up and begins to play "The Goona Goo." The feather dangles still.

"Take a telegram!" Powerhouse shouts suddenly up into the rain over 151
the street. "Take a answer. Now what was that name?"

They get a little tired. 152

"Uranus Knockwood." 153

"You ought to know." 154

"Yas? Spell it to me." 155

They spell it all the ways it could be spelled. It puts them in a wonder- 156
ful humor.

"Here's the answer. I got it right here. 'What in the hell you talk- 157
ing about? Don't make any difference: I gotcha.' Name signed:
Powerhouse."

"That going to reach him, Powerhouse?" Valentine speaks in a mater- 158
nal voice.

"Yas, yas." 159

All hushing, following him up the dark street at a distance, like old 160
rained-on black ghosts, the Negroes are afraid they will die laughing.

Powerhouse throws back his vast head into the steaming rain, and a 161
look of hopeful desire seems to blow somehow like a vapor from his own
dilated nostrils over his face and bring a mist to his eyes.

"Reach him and come out the other side." 162

"That's it, Powerhouse, that's it. You got him now." 163

Powerhouse lets out a long sigh. 164

"But ain't you going back there to call up Gypsy long distance, the 165
way you did last night in that other place? I seen a telephone. . . . Just
to see if she there at home?"

There is a measure of slience. That is one crazy drummer that's going 166
to get his neck broken some day.

"No," growls Powerhouse. "No! How many thousand times tonight I 167
got to say No?"

He holds up his arm in the rain. 168

"You sure-enough unroll your voice some night, it about reach up 169
yonder to her," says Little Brother, dismayed.

They go on up the street, shaking the rain off and on them like birds. 170

Back in the dance hall, they play "San" (99). The jitterbugs start up 171
like windmills stationed over the floor, and in their orbits — one circle, another, a long stretch and a zigzag — dance the elderly couples
with old smoothness, undisturbed and stately.

When Powerhouse first came back from intermission, no doubt full 172
of beer, they said, he got the band tuned up again in his own way. He
didn't strike the piano keys for pitch — he simply opened his mouth
and gave falsetto howls — in A, D and so on — they tuned by him.
Then he took hold of the piano, as if he saw it for the first time in his
life, and tested it for strength, hit it down in the bass, played an octave
with his elbow, lifted the top, looked inside, and leaned against it with
all his might. He sat down and played it for a few minutes with outrageous force and got it under his power — a bass deep and coarse as a
sea net — then produced something glimmering and fragile, and
smiled. And who could ever remember any of the things he says? They
are just inspired remarks that roll out of his mouth like smoke.

They've requested "Somebody Loves Me," and he's already down 173
twelve or fourteen choruses, piling them up nobody knows how, and it
will be a wonder if he ever gets through. Now and then he calls and
shouts, " 'Somebody loves me! Somebody loves me, I wonder who!' "
His mouth gets to be nothing but a volcano. "I wonder who!"

"Maybe . . ." He uses all his right hand on a trill. 174

"Maybe . . ." He pulls back his spread fingers, and looks out upon the 175
place where he is. A vast, impersonal and yet furious grimace transfi-
gures his wet face.

". . . Maybe it's you!" 176

SUBJECT

1. Why do you suppose Miss Welty chose such an unlikely-sounding
name as Alligator, Mississippi as the setting for this story?

2. Why doesn't Powerhouse tell his band about the telegram until
half-way through the concert? Does anyone else ever see the
telegram?

3. Do you think Powerhouse really believes his wife is dead? Are
there any clues that he is more shaken than he acts? Why doesn't he
telephone home to find out the truth, as his drummer suggests?

4. Does Powerhouse know who Uranus Knockwood is? Do the
other band members?

5. Note that Powerhouse treats his band members almost as children; does his mother-hen quality seem in character with the rest of
his artistic temperament? What kind of a man *is* Powerhouse?

STRUCTURE

1. Does Miss Welty capture an "essential nature" of Powerhouse? Does she emphasize more than one aspect of the man's personality?

2. Is there a correlation between the organization of the story and the points of view from which it is told? Do you find the shift in point of view distracting?

3. The opening paragraphs contain numerous concrete descriptive details; they also contain several interpretive words ("obscene," "hideous," "monstrous"). Do these adjectives seem appropriate to the description? What do they tell you about the anonymous describer?

4. Are the descriptive details selected to convey a consistent, unified view of Powerhouse, or do they strike you as random observations?

5. Do you find in the description appeals to senses other than sight? Are there places in the story where the author could have used such appeals more effectively?

MR. FLOOD'S PARTY

E. A. Robinson

Edwin Arlington Robinson (1869–1935) was born in Maine. He dropped out of Harvard after two years to become a poet. In 1905, Theodore Roosevelt rescued him from poverty by appointing him to a post in the Customs House in New York. From then on, his prestige as a poet rose rapidly, and he won Pulitzer Prizes in 1922, 1925, and 1928. Although much of his talent was spent on long narrative poems, these are seldom read today. His fame rests on a series of brilliant verse characterizations of typical New Englanders and embittered people whom life had passed by — people like Richard Cory and Miniver Cheevy. Robinson's lasting influence has been most obvious recently in the songs of Simon and Garfunkel. "Mr. Flood's Party" is one of the most touching of his verse characterizations.

Old Eben Flood, climbing alone one night   1
Over the hill between the town below
And the forsaken upland hermitage
That held as much as he should ever know
On earth again of home, paused warily.
The road was his with not a native near;
And Eben, having leisure, said aloud,
For no man else in Tilbury Town to hear:

"Well, Mr. Flood, we have the harvest moon   2
Again, and we may not have many more;
The bird is on the wing, the poet says,
And you and I have said it here before.
Drink to the bird." He raised up to the light
The jug that he had gone so far to fill,
And answered huskily: "Well, Mr. Flood,
Since you propose it, I believe I will."

Alone, as if enduring to the end   3
A valiant armor of scarred hopes outworn,
He stood there in the middle of the road
Like Roland's ghost winding a silent horn.

Below him, in the town among the trees,
Where friends of other days had honored him,
A phantom salutation of the dead
Rang thinly till old Eben's eyes were dim.

Then, as a mother lays her sleeping child   4
Down tenderly, fearing it may awake,
He set the jug down slowly at his feet
With trembling care, knowing that most things break;
And only when assured that on firm earth
It stood, as the uncertain lives of men
Assuredly did not, he paced away,
And with his hand extended paused again:

"Well, Mr. Flood, we have not met like this   5
In a long time; and many a change has come
To both of us, I fear, since last it was
We had a drop together. Welcome home!"
Convivially returning with himself,
Again he raised the jug up to the light;
And with an acquiescent quaver said:
"Well, Mr. Flood, if you insist, I might.

"Only a very little, Mr. Flood —   6
For auld lang syne. No more, sir; that will do."
So, for the time, apparently it did,
And Eben evidently thought so too;
For soon amid the silver loneliness
Of night he lifted up his voice and sang,
Secure, with only two moons listening,
Until the whole harmonious landscape rang —

"For auld lang syne." The weary throat gave out;   7
The last word wavered, and the song was done.
He raised again the jug regretfully
And shook his head, and was again alone.
There was not much that was ahead of him,
And there was nothing in the town below —
Where strangers would have shut the many doors
That many friends had opened long ago.

SUBJECT

    1. Eben Flood's "excuse" for talking to himself is that he is drunk;
what is his "reason" for doing so?

2.   There is some physical description of the setting, but none of Eben Flood himself; how is it that Robinson is able to characterize him?

3.   What is the "essence" of Mr. Flood that Robinson wants to convey?

4.   When Flood sings his song there are "only two moons listening." There was one moon at the beginning of the poem; what has happened?

5.   What indication do you have that this is not the first of Eben Flood's "parties"?

STRUCTURE

1.   Robinson several times resorts to explanation rather than letting the description convey the meaning — as in the final four lines. Do these interpretations strengthen or weaken the poem? Are they needed?

2.   What rhyme scheme does the poem employ? Is it appropriate to the tone and subject? (Suppose Robinson had made all the lines rhyme; would the effect have been different?)

3.   In stanzas 3 and 4, Robinson uses similes of a medieval knight in armor and of a mother with her child. Are they appropriate to the context? What effect is achieved by juxtaposing such unlike comparisons?

4.   What does the moonlit setting do for the poem? Would a cloudy day, or a sunrise, have done just as well? How would the selection of descriptive details have had to be changed in a daylight setting?

5.   Examine the words which Eben Flood speaks to himself; to what extent is his conversation characterizing of him? (Note that he does not say anything especially profound.)

3

THE MOVIES

Comparison and Contrast

Comparison and contrast are perhaps the most natural of all methods of establishing or clarifying an attitude. They are the product of man's important ability to see relationships and differences where none would be apparent to other animals. All of us utilize this ability daily, sometimes in making important decisions, sometimes in situations so insignificant that we are not even aware of employing comparison and contrast. We use it in deciding whether to sleep late or get up in time for breakfast, whether to sign up for biology or chemistry. But this ability to see likenesses and differences is the basis of what may be man's most significant capacity, evaluation. Before one can say, "Professor X is a better teacher than Professor Z," he must, of course, recognize that important differences exist between the two men or between their methods of presenting material.

Frequently in writing expository prose, a student finds it necessary to employ the methods of comparison and contrast in order to clarify either his subject or his attitude toward it. If he were writing a paper on socialism, for instance, he would almost surely want to point out the similarities and differences between socialism and communism. He would probably also want to compare and contrast two or more existing types of socialism — English, French, and Mexican, perhaps. Although writing comparison and contrast is not as difficult as some other writing assignments, it does require meticulous care, and the student should remember a few basic rules.

In the first place, the writer must *establish a clear basis for comparison.* Particularly in dealing with broad concepts or with groups of people, he may have to choose from a number of possible bases for comparison, and it would not do for him to confuse those bases or switch from one to another without warning. Suppose he wishes to compare socialism and communism; to consider and cover all possible bases for comparison would require a large volume. If he is writing a short paper he will probably have to limit his investigation to only one area — the extent of arbitrary political control by the government in power, perhaps, or the similarities and differences in economic theory and practice, the use of secret police and other methods of coercion to prevent internal resistance, or the degree of control over communications media. Once he has selected his basis of comparison, the writer should stick with it, developing it fully and clearly through both sides of the comparison. It would hardly be cricket, for instance, to discuss communism's totalitarian political system and then switch to socialism's economic system.

If the topic on which the student is writing is sufficiently limited there is, of course, no reason that he can't utilize several bases of comparison in the same essay — as long as he treats each one separately and fully before going on to the next. In a paper on the adequacy of preparation for college given by public high schools and private preparatory schools, the writer would probably consider outside reading assignments, research paper writing, and intellectual stimulation from fellow students as well as actual classroom preparation. But there would be no point in dragging in other comparisons which might occur to the writer — social life, or athletic programs, for instance.

A second rule is that the writer must *observe accurately.* Quite often minute details will be the most important, particularly since they are the ones an average observer is likely to miss. A good writer will never dismiss distinctions without examining them or be so careless as to claim, for instance, that "communism and fascism are really just two names for the same thing." Both terms may imply totalitarian governments and police states, but there must be some reason for the mutual hatred between fascist and communist. A closer examination would reveal such vital differences as the attitudes toward class structure and toward racial integration.

Obviously, then, the writer must also have an *adequate knowledge* of his subject. A passing acquaintance, half-hearted guesswork, or simply a vivid imagination will not do: the really important similarities and differences between two types of skin rash will only be apparent to a person trained in dermatology. The student who tries to write comparison and contrast without familiarizing himself with his subject is merely wasting the reader's time as well as his own. If he has an interest in the subject but not full knowledge of it, he can make good use of the college library.

The preceding three rules, though applicable to all comparison, are virtually useless without a fourth. Far more frequently than chance would justify, composition teachers are disappointed by students who hand in "comparison" papers somewhat like the one on which the following summary is based:

> As I look out my window I cannot help noticing the staunch old oak tree which stands so majestically beside the dormitory. . . . In many ways, it seems to me that this oak tree is very like my religion. . . .
>
> In the first place, the oak has its roots deep in a firm foundation, from which it receives material sustenance. The roots of my religion, too, are deep. . . .
>
> Secondly, the oak has a mighty trunk which is not shaken by the winds of chance. In the same way, my faith is unshakable. . . .
>
> And finally, the branches of the tree reach up to heaven, whence comes eternal light. The aim of my religion, similarly, is to reach up to heaven. . . .

Such a "comparison" may give a connotative indication of the firmness of the writer's faith and perhaps an appreciation of his ingenuity. But it does not give the reader any specific information about trees, about the exact nature of the writer's religious beliefs, or about any real relationship between the two. It is, in short, not true comparison at all, but analogy.

Comparison shows likenesses between things in the same class, while analogy points out a similarity between things in different classes. "The cloud from an atomic blast is shaped like a mushroom" is an analogy, since atomic clouds and mushrooms have little in common except shape. Analogy usually compares the unfamiliar with the familiar, not in order to establish relationships but to clarify the less familiar. Comparison, on the other hand, seeks both to clarify and to demonstrate relations. In other words, something is said about both objects or ideas being compared, and the points of comparison, while generally more subtle than those in analogy, are at the same time more significant. "Jeffersonian democracy was similar to modern liberal Republicanism" is the beginning of a comparison, for the two concepts are in the same general class. Clearly such a comparison, to be worthwhile, must be developed much more carefully than a simple analogy. And something must be said about both Jeffersonian Democrats and liberal Republicans if the comparison is to be meaningful. Would they have the same views on states' rights, or on civil liberties, for instance? It is not enough to say merely that both are "mildly conservative" by modern standards.

In comparing two concepts the writer should remember to look for significant points of comparison which are not commonly recognized. To dwell on the obvious would be a waste of time for reader and writer alike. On the other hand, the writer should not strain for comparison where there is only a remote and unimportant similarity, if any. Comparison should never be merely an exercise in ingenuity.

Most of the rules for comparison also apply to its opposite, contrast: the things or ideas must be in the same class, the differences developed at length should be significant but not boringly obvious, and the writer should never search for differences for their own sake, regardless of whether or not they are worth mentioning. It is possible, however, to develop fully only one side of a contrast if the writer can assume that his reader is already familiar with the other side.

Since contrast is only useful if the concepts being contrasted have many aspects in common or are frequently confused, comparison and contrast are usually employed in the same essay. If a student were to write a paper on "My High School and College Math Classes," he would want to point out both similarities and differences. He would not dwell on such obvious distinctions as "College courses are harder than the ones I had in high school," but would concentrate on similarities in methods of explaining abstract laws, perhaps, or differences in methods of integrating algebra and trigonometry.

Combining comparison and contrast is likely to be a matter of intellectual honesty. A writer who devotes a paper to proving that "Democracy and communism are in *all* respects unalterably opposed" or that "Democrats and Republicans really have identical beliefs" is either misguided or dishonest. Democracy and communism are not "unalterably opposed" on such issues as the liberation of African colonies from European domination or foreign aid for underdeveloped countries; and Democrats and Republicans hardly agree *en masse* on excess profits taxes or federal power projects.

The student who intends to write a comparison and contrast paper must first limit his subject to something he can treat in depth and with some insight. The title "High School and College Compared" would probably be much too broad for a short paper: the writer would be tempted to dwell on obvious differences — "College is harder than high school," "Students at college are more serious," "Most college students live away from home for the first time." A more useful subject might be "Using the Library: High School and College" or "Classroom Discussion in High School and College." Remember that writing should never be a mere exercise: the writer should learn something, at least by clarifying his views, and the reader should gain insight into both the subject and the ways in which different people view the same subject.

Comparison and contrast may be employed both as the chief method of development and the primary aim of an essay; or they may be used to furnish background information necessary for some further purpose. Alexander Knox, in "Acting and Behaving," wants not only to explain the difference between two acting styles but to make a plea for one style by showing its advantages over the other. In "Film Has Nothing to Do With Literature," Ingmar Bergman uses contrast to elucidate his own method of making pictures. But James Agee, al-

110

though he wants to point out that "they don't make movies the way they used to," has organized his essay so that the chief purpose is comparison and contrast itself. He treats in turn the best actors of the silent comedies, showing the skills and weaknesses of each, and comparing them with one another. But in each of these selections the basic principles are observed: the basis of the comparison is made clear, and distinctions and similarities pointed out are real and significant, neither blatantly obvious nor merely clever.

The writer will encounter some problems in organizing a comparison and contrast paper, for he must organize his materials in two ways at once — by the divisions of the subject matter and by the two concepts which he is comparing. Depending on the length of the paper and the complexity of the subject, he can select from three possible methods of organization: (1) present all the points about one side of the comparison, and then in the same order all the points about the other side; (2) alternate paragraphs about side A and side B according to subject divisions; or (3) alternate sentences about side A and side B within a paragraph. Suppose the writer were comparing and contrasting public high schools with private preparatory schools. If his paper were fairly short, so that the reader could keep the first half in mind while reading the second half, his outline might look something like this:

I. High Schools
   A. Classroom preparation
   B. Library assignments
   C. Research paper writing
   D. Intellectual environment
II. Private Schools
   A. Classroom preparation
   B. Library assignments
   C. Research paper writing
   D. Intellectual environment

If, on the other hand, the paper were to be rather long and the writer had a number of facts on each basis for comparison, he would probably do well to alternate paragraphs. His outline would then look like this:

I. Classroom Preparation
   A. High schools
   B. Private schools
II. Library Assignments
   A. High schools
   B. Private schools
III. Research paper Writing
   A. High schools
   B. Private schools

IV. Intellectual Environment
A. High schools
B. Private schools

The third possibility, alternating sentences about high school and preparatory school within a paragraph on classroom preparation, etc., while sometimes employed, is generally satisfactory only for very brief and relatively simple papers or when time is a factor — as in essay examinations or in-class themes. But regardless of which method the writer chooses, he should employ it consistently throughout the paper. Careful planning always pays in better grades and time saved; the writer who "waits for an inspiration" will waste hours and perhaps never get his inspiration.

FILM HAS NOTHING TO DO WITH LITERATURE

Ingmar Bergman

*Ingmar Bergman, Swedish play director and film-maker, is one of the
very best — and surely the most fortunate — among modern motion
picture directors. He is free to do virtually as he pleases at Swedish
Film Industries, and he has a permanent technical crew and a resident
troupe of actors, so that he always knows the abilities and limitations
of the people working with him. The result has been a series of almost
perfect films, classics such as* The Seventh Seal *and* Wild Strawberries.
*In the following passage, Bergman tries to communicate the complex
process by which a film is conceived, and he makes the startling assertion that "film has nothing to do with literature" — startling in view
of the hundreds of Hollywood movies adapted from novels.*

A film for me begins with something very vague — a chance remark   1
or a bit of conversation, a hazy but agreeable event unrelated to any
particular situation. It can be a few bars of music, a shaft of light across
the street. Sometimes in my work at the theatre I have envisioned
actors made up for yet unplayed roles.

These are split-second impressions that disappear as quickly as they   2
come, yet leave behind a mood — like pleasant dreams. It is a mental
state, not an actual story, but one abounding in fertile associations and
images. Most of all, it is a brightly colored thread sticking out of the dark
sack of the unconscious. If I begin to wind up this thread, and do it
carefully, a complete film will emerge.

This primitive nucleus strives to achieve definite form, moving in a   3
way that may be lazy and half asleep at first. Its stirring is accompanied
by vibrations and rhythms which are very special and unique to each
film. The picture sequences then assume a pattern in accordance with
these rhythms, obeying laws born out of and conditioned by my original
stimulus.

If that embryonic substance seems to have enough strength to be   4
made into a film, I decide to materialize it. Then comes something very

complicated and difficult: the transformation of rhythms, moods, atmosphere, tensions, sequences, tones and scents into words and sentences, into an understandable screenplay.

This is an almost impossible task. 5

The only thing that can be satisfactorily transferred from that original 6
complex of rhythms and moods is the dialogue, and even dialogue is a sensitive substance which may offer resistance. Written dialogue is like a musical score, almost incomprehensible to the average person. Its interpretation demands a technical knack plus a certain kind of imagination and feeling — qualities which are so often lacking, even among actors. One can write dialogue, but how it should be delivered, its rhythm and tempo, what is to take place between lines — all this must be omitted for practical reasons. Such a detailed script would be unreadable. I try to squeeze instructions as to location, characterization and atmosphere into my screenplays in understandable terms, but the success of this depends on my writing ability and the perceptiveness of the reader, which are not always predictable.

Now we come to essentials, by which I mean montage, rhythm and 7
the relation of one picture to another — the vital third dimension without which the film is merely a dead product from a factory. Here I cannot clearly give a key, as in a musical score, nor a specific idea of the tempo which determines the relationship of the elements involved. It is quite impossible for me to indicate the way in which the film "breathes" and pulsates.

I have often wished for a kind of notation which would enable me to 8
put on paper all the shades and tones of my vision, to record distinctly the inner structure of a film. For when I stand in the artistically devastating atmosphere of the studio, my hands and head full of all the trivial and irritating details that go with motion-picture production, it often takes a tremendous effort to remember how I originally saw and thought out this or that sequence, or what was the relation between the scene of four weeks ago and that of today. If I could express myself clearly, in explicit symbols, then this problem would be almost eliminated and I could work with absolute confidence that whenever I liked I could prove the relationship between the part and the whole and put my finger on the rhythm, the continuity of the film.

Thus the script is a very imperfect *technical* basis for a film. And 9
there is another important point in this connection which I should like to mention. Film has nothing to do with literature; the character and substance of the two art forms are usually in conflict. This probably has something to do with the receptive process of the mind. The written word is read and assimilated by a conscious act of the will in alliance with the intellect; little by little it affects the imagination and the emo-

tions. The process is different with a motion picture. When we experience a film, we consciously prime ourselves for illusion. Putting aside will and intellect, we make way for it in our imagination. The sequence of pictures plays directly on our feelings.

Music works in the same fashion; I would say that there is no art form 10 that has so much in common with film as music. Both affect our emotions directly, not via the intellect. And film is mainly rhythm; it is inhalation and exhalation in continuous sequence. Ever since childhood, music has been my great source of recreation and stimulation, and I often experience a film or play musically.

It is mainly because of this difference between film and literature that 11 we should avoid making films out of books. The irrational dimension of a literary work, the germ of its existence, is often untranslatable into visual terms — and it, in turn, destroys the special, irrational dimension of the film. If, despite this, we wish to translate something literary into film terms, we must make an infinite number of complicated adjustments which often bear little or no fruit in proportion to the effort expended.

I myself have never had any ambition to be an author. I do not want 12 to write novels, short stories, essays, biographies, or even plays for the theatre. I only want to make films — films about conditions, tensions, pictures, rhythms and characters which are in one way or another important to me. The motion picture, with its complicated process of birth, is my method of saying what I want to my fellow men. I am a film-maker, not an author.

Subject

1. In Paragraph 4, Bergman lists the ingredients which he combines to make a screenplay. Note that "story" or "plot" is not in this list; do you think this is an oversight or that Bergman deliberately omitted it?

2. Why does Bergman think that written dialogue is "almost incomprehensible to the average person"? The dialogue of a stage play is usually comprehensible; what is the difference?

3. What is "artistically devastating" about a film studio for Bergman?

4. Considering the number of novels which have been made into successful motion pictures — from *Gone With the Wind* to *Catch 22* — would you agree with Bergman that "film has nothing to do with literature"? What is Bergman's reasoning behind this statement? Does it help explain the frequency with which movie-goers complain, "the picture was nothing like the book"?

5. What does Bergman mean by the "irrational dimension" of a film or a book?

6. Bergman several times compares film to music; what connection does he see between the two art forms?

STRUCTURE

1. Bergman does not arrive at his contrast between film and literature until more than halfway through the passage; is what goes before vital to the contrast?

2. What is the *basis of comparison* between film and literature? Is the same basis employed when Bergman explains why books should not be made into films?

3. Does the basis on which Bergman compares film to music seem adequate? Is this comparison or analogy?

4. The language with which Bergman explains the creative process in the first three paragraphs is in some ways closer to that of poetry than of expository prose. Is it appropriate to the subject? As the remainder of the essay demonstrates, Bergman writes a very clear prose style; why doesn't he use it in these opening paragraphs?

5. Bergman several times refers to the "rhythm" of a film as its most important aspect. Does he make clear by definition or by context what he means by "rhythm" as it applies to film-making rather than music?

116

ACTING
AND BEHAVING

Alexander Knox

Alexander Knox was an actor both on Broadway and in Hollywood. At his best in character parts, he is remembered in film histories for his excellent portrayal of Woodrow Wilson (1944). In this article, first given as a talk at the Conference on American-Russian Cultural Exchange at UCLA in 1945, Knox is pleading that film actors be allowed to contribute their interpretive talents to the total effect of a picture — as they do in stage productions. In making this plea, he is flying in the face of such formidable theorists as Sergei Eisenstein, who felt that films should have as little resemblance as possible to stage plays and that people, not star actors, should be given primary attention. But Knox is also objecting to the Hollywood habit of making stars be "themselves" so that the audience never forgets it is watching Brando rather than Napoleon, Newman rather than Hud.

In this paper I propose to discuss actors, and to discuss them as if they had a contribution to make to the joy of living and to society. On the stage and on the screen there are two kinds of actors — actors who *behave* and actors who *act*. I hope to convince you that there is a difference between acting and behaving on the screen, and that acting is richer than behaving. 1

I start off under a certain difficulty: I am an actor myself; and the most powerful critic in the country, Mr. George Jean Nathan, has admitted that no one can have respect for a man who always has to go to his work up an alley. It is of stage actors, whom he respects, that he makes this unkind comment, and he declares that a screen performance bears the same relation to a stage performance that a hiccup bears to Camille's tuberculosis. If I make any attempt to answer back, Nathan asserts with finality: "Coquelin is the only actor who ever lived who proved that he had a critical mind in the appraisal of acting." However, the published words of Minnie Maddern Fiske and William Gillette, and some of the 2

117

comments of George Arliss, Ellen Terry, and others, seem to me to indicate that Nathan's statement is a trifle sweeping, so I will not allow it to scare me into silence. . . .

Behaving is a form of acting which is much admired in Hollywood 3
and elsewhere, mainly on the grounds that it holds the mirror up to nature. It is natural. But two very good critics have uttered certain warnings about behaving. Every young and revolutionary group of actors in the history of the theatre — and I think this applies with equal force in the shorter history of the movies — has seemed more natural than its predecessors. I have no doubt that, as John Mason Brown says, "Burbage would have thought Betterton too mild, that Betterton would have missed strength in Garrick, that Garrick would have been disappointed in Kean, Kean in Irving, Irving in Gielgud, and Booth in Barrymore."

John Mason Brown's word of warning about "behaving" begins, "Ac- 4
tors are commonly supposed to be good actors if they do not seem to be acting at all," and he continues, later, "To admire their performances as being the kind of art which conceals art is one thing, and a just cause for admiration. But to mistake their acting for not being acting, to applaud them for this very reason, is not only to insult the actors in question but to commit the final insanity of slovenly thinking. One of the pleasantest sensations they can afford us is for them to make us feel, however mildly, that what is done is done with a reason and by people who know what they are doing, so that no one mistakes the mirror that is held up to nature for nature herself."

And Mr. Bernard Shaw, another good critic, puts the same point more 5
concisely. "The one thing not forgivable in an actor is *being* the part instead of *playing* it."

These two strong statements are in direct opposition to a great deal 6
of Hollywood thinking. The men who made the statements are neither of them thoughtless men, nor are they men who enjoy the dreadful scent of old boiled Ham.

Behaving, at its best, is the kind of art which conceals art. Edward 7
Dmytryk, a brilliant director who has helped a number of actors to give excellent performances, has complained bitterly about Hollywood Ham-worship, which he alleges to be rife, and he says, "If a man hasn't quite perfected the technique of naturalness, we say he underplays, but when he has perfected the technique we say he is only playing himself." To some, it may seem that Mr. Dmytryk is tilting against a straw man, since the point he makes is fairly well accepted and a number of actors who have perfected the technique of naturalness in Hollywood get a great deal of credit.

118

In fact, behaving, when it is perfectly done, has always been the most   8
profitable form of acting, and the form which inspires most confidence.
Behaving makes use of intelligent observation and an alert contemporary mind. Its power is the power of reality, and without it no mummer
has the right to call himself an actor.

But behaving is capable of abuse. Behaving is a form of acting which   9
can be used to display the same kind of empty idealizations that fill
some of the popular magazines and pass for human beings. The result
is that a completely unreal creation, a man who never did exist on land
or sea, is made real by the misuse of an actor's skill. The process is one
of selection. Whatever imaginary type happens to be the wishful dream
of society at the moment is built up of segments of a human psyche, and
all those which would contradict or make diffuse the single effect of the
whole are conveniently omitted. . . .

Is acting any different? What is it? What can it do? Acting seems to   10
me to be *behaving plus interpretation.* The difference between acting
and behaving is the difference between Menuhin and the first violin,
the difference between Van Gogh and Sargent, between William
Shakespeare and Ben Jonson. The ability to paint photographically is
probably a necessary part of a painter's equipment, but it does not make
a painter. The ability to play every note in perfect pitch, volume, and
tempo is a necessary part of a violinist's equipment, but it does not make
a Menuhin. The ability to be just like the man next door is a necessary
part of an actor's equipment, but it does not make a Chaplin.

Now I am going to attempt the impossible. I am going to try to tell   11
you what I think acting is. I'm going to hang onto the beard of the
prophet Shaw till I find my balance. Shaw is speaking about Henry
Irving, whom he did not like. He says, "Irving was utterly unlike anyone
else: he could give importance and nobility to any sort of drivel that was
put into his mouth; and it was this nobility, bound up with an impish
humour, which forced the spectator to single him out as a leading figure
with an inevitability that I never saw again in any actor until it rose from
Irving's grave in the person of a nameless cinema actor who afterwards
became famous as Charlie Chaplin. Here, I felt, is something that leaves
the old stage and its superstitions and staleness completely behind, and
inaugurates a new epoch."

This is a comment by Shaw on Duse. He is explaining to Ellen Terry   12
how to become an actress — an occupation most men would have
thought rather impertinent, but Shaw didn't mind, and neither did Miss
Terry. "At first you try to make a few points and don't know how to
make them. Then you do know how to make them, and you think of
a few more. Finally the points all integrate into one continuous point,

which is the whole part in itself. I have sat watching Duse in Camille, analyzing all her play into the million or so of points of which it originally consisted, and admiring beyond expression the prodigious power of work that built it all up. *Now* the actress seems to make no points at all. This rare consummation Duse has reached."

Here is the poet W. B. Yeats speaking of a performance of Björnson's 13 *Beyond Human Power* by Mrs. Patrick Campbell: "Your acting had the precision and delicacy and simplicity of every art at its best. It made me feel the unity of the arts in a new way."

Charles Lamb wrote of Bensley, "He seized the moment of passion 14 with the greatest truth, he seemed to come upon the stage to do the poet's message simply — he threw over the part an air of loftiness which one catches only a few times in a lifetime."

Samuel Taylor Coleridge said of Kean, "To see Kean act is like read- 15 ing Shakespeare by flashes of lightning."

And Hazlitt, one of the most objective and astute of critics, who held 16 that Shakespeare needed no actors, that his own imagination was sufficient, when he had seen Mrs. Siddons and Kean at different times, admitted that each of them had "raised our imagination of the parts they acted." And some time later, when Kean played Hamelt, he declared that certain scenes in the production were "the finest commentary that was ever made on Shakespeare."

I have chosen these quotations because they understate the case. 17 There are many more fulsome comments on actors of the past and present, many comments which are foolish in their abandonment to a momentary enthusiasm. The comments I have quoted were made by men of taste, each superb in his own profession, each critical, and each well provided with standards of comparison, and I suggest that these comments were made on an art which is *more than behaving* — an art which has the power to shock and to excite, an art which has a function and a life and a purpose of its own, an art which is difficult to understand and even to detect because of its evanescent nature, an art which is a deep intellectual and emotional experience, and which leaves the psyche of the person who has been in contact with it subtly changed.

And if this seems to be a spasm of mystical nonsense, I would suggest 18 that whoever feels that way about it should suspend judgment until he has tried to define for himself the higher reaches of some other art as well. It is not easy.

The inevitable comment will now be made: "These actors were stage 19 actors. Even supposing there is a certain amount of validity in your mystical nonsense, how does that apply to the screen?"

And I have to confess that, with the exception of Chaplin, I have not   20
seen a sustained performance on the screen to which I would be inclined to apply similar words. But although sustained performances on
this level may not exist on the screen, we have all seen short bits of film
in which "acting" in this high sense has been caught and held. And
when we think of acting in this way, it is well to remember that at best
it is an interpretative art, and is dead the year after next; it is dead
because the manners of the people have changed. It is dead, but that
does not mean it has never been alive.

I can, from my own memory of films, list a number in which there   21
were passages of great beauty created solely by the actor. There is not
time to go into these in detail. Many of you will remember them also.
There were superb moments of performance in Cagney's *Yankee Doo-
dle,* and in an inferior film, *Dr. Jekyll and Mr. Hyde,* Spencer Tracy had
moments of peculiar effectiveness. Greta Garbo in *Camille,* Rosalind
Russell in *Craig's Wife,* Laurence Olivier in *Wuthering Heights,* a
scene of curious terror in *Alice Adams,* where Miss Katharine Hepburn
was trying to entertain *you* at dinner as well as the boy in the film.
Several sustained passages in Paul Muni's two fine performances, *Zola*
and *Pasteur.* Barrymore's *Bill of Divorcement,* Raimu in *La Femme du
boulanger,* Nikolai Cherkasov-Sergeyev in *General Suvarov,* and a
scene in the same film where an actor whose name I do not know —
he plays an old soldier — by telling a lying story of his old campaigns
creates the kind of excitement that acting alone can give.

Miss Patricia Collinge played in *The Little Foxes* in New York, and   22
she played the same part in the film version with Miss Bette Davis. Miss
Davis' performance was excellent, but the fact that interested me concerns the scene, almost a monologue, where Birdie (Miss Collinge) lets
her niece know that she has been a secret drinker for some years. It is
a ticklish scene, sometimes on the verge of laughter. I saw the film three
times, at long intervals, and each time there was a curious attempt at
scattered applause at the end of that scene. The performance was
exquisitely skillful, and in a strange way the film suddenly spoke with
unusual eloquence and I felt that I was watching and listening to something very close to a "great moment."

The last of these recollections of mine is more recent, and you will   23
probably all recall it. This performance, which, in my opinion, more
nearly touched the quality of the Keans and the Duses than most, was
given by Barry Fitzgerald in *Going My Way.* I saw Mr. Fitzgerald give
this performance, in its beginnings, about fifteen years ago, and it was
a great performance then. I am told that Mr. McCary, whose skill is
unrivaled, told Mr. Fitzgerald on many occasions that the camera

would keep on turning until he finished acting, that he was to do what he felt like, and that he was not to worry about wasting film. I imagine there are few people who saw the film who will not carry with them for the rest of their lives some vivid recollection of Mr. Fitzgerald.

The point about this long recital of memorable bits is an answer to   24
the widely held belief that acting may be valuable on the legitimate stage, but only behaving is useful in movies.

Is acting of any use to the screen?   25

It seems obvious to me that the high qualities of fine actors of the past   26
are not confined to the past; it is equally obvious that the essential quality that is acting has too seldom been caught in any sustained way on film. But it *has been caught.* If it can be caught in bits, there seems to me no good reason why it should not be caught more often as a sustained performance.

If it is to be caught, it will have to be caught as acting, not as behaving.   27
I believe that a thorough study of the customs and techniques of the sound stage might indicate the reasons of the somewhat disproportionate preponderance of behaving. To refer again to John Mason Brown's warning against slovenly thinking, one form of slovenly thinking, which is particularly difficult to combat, I have noticed more frequently in some of the younger writers and directors who are vastly impressed with the power of their medium but whose occasional comments indicate that they literally don't know how an actor works. The present custom of preventing writers from working on the set and from meeting actors has something to do with this, but it is not the whole reason. Pride in the power of the medium persuades many people to think that the contribution of an actor is very slight, and anyone who knows the history of the movies at all can point to certain fine films in which the contribution of an actor was almost nonexistent. But the fact that such films have been made does not suggest that no other kind of film can be made, and I believe that as the industry matures the contribution of the actor will become more important.

Great plays provide great parts, great parts discover great actors.   28
There are no great parts without passion, and there is no passion without belief. Passion is the emotional expression of a deep conviction. Without conviction, which is partly intellectual, passion becomes hysteria. Hysteria and the absence of emotion cannot substitute for passion and restraint.

In the complicated mechanism of a film studio, in the tremendous   29
costs of production, it is at present impossible to give the necessary time to acting. Behaving, when an actor has practiced it for years, becomes a finished product, a performance that can be turned on and off with less nervous strain than acting, which must always give what William

Gillette called "the impression of the first time." But if the distinction between acting and behaving is understood, I believe it is possible that improved techniques of the camera may make acting a steadily more valuable component of films.

Mr. Edward Dmytryk, whom I quoted before, said he had never seen 30 anyone succeed in changing himself into a different individual on the screen. "The insecurity of the actor," he continues, "trying to portray an individual who springs from a completely unfamiliar environment, is sure to be picked up by the searching eye of the camera. Result, a self-conscious performance."

If this is true, it may be due to a number of causes. Mr. Charles 31 Laughton played Captain Bligh one year and Ruggles of Red Gap another. I did not find the performances self-conscious. I thought each fitted its frame about as perfectly as anyone has a right to ask. Nikolai Cherkasov played Gorki in *Lenin* and Alexander Nevsky in the film of that name. Gorki seemed to me a beautifully simple and subtle performance, with a curious and telling awkwardness of movement which helped to make me believe that the actor was the man. M. Cherkasov played Nevsky in a wide, heroic manner, impossible for an untrained actor, as if he were a Russian Galahad. The effect was not one of either insecurity of self-consciousness.

I have met Mr. Charles Chaplin, Mr. Barry Fitzgerald, and M. Raimu, 32 and I have not found them "just like" any of the parts I have seen them play in films. Many of the parts I have seen them play were characters which sprang from a completely unfamiliar environment; but the camera did not record any insecurity, it recorded fragments of what to me was a fine and sensitive work of imaginative creation. Some of these "characterizations" take years to perfect; some take minutes, just as Van Gogh spent a month on one of his self-portraits and a day on one of the canvases of "A Garden at Arles"; but the time required to do the work has little to do with its quality. The fact is, the "searching eye of the camera" picks up what is there, and if a self-conscious performance takes place in front of it, that's what it records. It is the job of the writer and the director and the actor to see that the performance is not insecure or self-conscious. It is a special ability of the actor, if he has suitable material, to provide, first, "the illusion of the first time," and second, a sense of physical, intellectual, and emotional life which is more vivid than life itself.

One could cite examples of acting for hours, but I am reasonably 33 certain that the trouble is not with the ability of the actor, but with the mechanism of the studio.

The most powerful barrier against acting on the screen rises from the 34 fact that film is only about forty years old, and the happy writers, cameramen, and directors are still discovering new things about it. This will be, in the long run, all to the good, but just at present it makes it awkward for the actor. Tricky cinematography, from writers, cameramen, and directors, can destroy illusion faster than anything else I know.

A film, like a novel or a play, shows character in action. Anything that gets in the way of the action of that character is dramatically bad, but the boys who are expert at cinematography delight in yanking the audience off to contemplate a mountain or a goat, the immediate symbolic meaning of which is clear to everyone, but the dramatic value of which is not clear to anyone. These tricks are evidences of growing pains, but they are definitely *pains* nonetheless.

Actors are frequently asked questions such as, "Don't you find tricks of direction, photography, writing, and cutting helpful to the character you are playing?" And the answer must be a strong affirmative. But there is a great difference between clarifying a "character" and helping the actor. The invention of the tractor was a great help to the plowhorse — it put him out of work. Too often, in film making, trickiness is used not as a help to the actor but as a substitute for acting, and the man who knows his craft is therefore deprived of the advantages which he has a right to assume that knowledge of his craft will give him.

Actually, most of the tricks of the kind I mean are well conceived and add tremendously to the effectiveness of film, but there are some which are not well conceived, and add only to confusion. The difficulty is traceable, as are most difficulties, to the economic necessities of the industry and the present stage of mechanical development. Film will always be predominantly an intellectual medium. It consists in the fitting together of various pieces, one by one. This is done by means of the intellect, but it should be constantly subject to emotional suggestion. Unless the writer and the director treat film first emotionally, and then proceed to rationalize, we shall always see scenes such as the one in which Lenin, admirably played by Boris Shchukin, finishes ordering the execution of a batch of bread-hoarders and proving to Gorki that his harshness was warranted, and then meets a lost child in the corridor and proceeds to teach her to draw. The object of this scene was to show that Lenin was kind to children, but it succeeded in convincing me that the writer was writing his film from his mind and not his heart. If the two scenes had followed each other in a play, the first rehearsal would have convinced the author that the juxtaposition was too sudden, that a short transition was required. Lenin would not have been required awkwardly to truncate his emotions about bread-hoarders and be kind to the child. Or, if he were, he would have been aware of the awkwardness. The sequence, as it was cut together, prompted people to groan

35

36

37

124

"propaganda" when, if the emotions of a man in that situation had been more thoroughly explored by the *emotions* of the writer and not by his *mind,* the very abruptness of the juxtaposition could have been made effective.

Another bit of trickiness which irritated me and many others recently 38 came in the very successful picture *Spellbound.* Miss Bergman kissed the doctor, and shortly afterward a series of three doors opened, apparently without help from human hands. This, my reason told me, symbolized the dawn of love in Miss Bergman, the beginning of brighter things — the opening of doors — a literal translation of a literary cliché to the screen. Personally, I have complete faith in Miss Bergman's ability to convince me that doors are opening in her soul, if she is given adequate material to do it with, and, frankly, I'd rather look at her opening the doors than see Mr. Hitchcock do it — or see them open by themselves.

These are just a few of the things that make acting difficult on the 39 screen, and, correspondingly, make behaving easy. Actors, as George Jean Nathan says, are popinjays, but they have something to contribute. Does anyone want that contribution? If the films can use it, I have no doubt they will, but it will need quite a bit of careful study. Acting will never bring in the money that behaving will bring in, and acting is many times more expensive to buy.

SUBJECT

1. What are the primary differences between acting and behaving? What is Knox's objection to behaving?

2. Look at John Mason Brown's criticism of behaving in paragraph 4. Would you prefer, in watching a film, to feel that the actor is "acting" or "being himself"? What difference does it make to an audience?

3. Can you recall any film during which the audience applauded? What motivates such applause (obviously the actors cannot hear it)?

4. "I believe that as the industry matures the contribution of the actor will become more important." Has Knox's prophecy proved correct? Do you think the film industry has "matured" since Knox made the statement?

5. What kind of photographic "tricks" does Knox claim get in the way of the actor's art?

6. Examine Knox's objection to the unconvincing juxtaposition of scenes involving Lenin (paragraph 37). Knox argues that neither on stage nor in real life could a person make the rapid shift in emotions called for. But film is neither life nor stage drama; do you think the objection is still valid?

STRUCTURE

1. Does Knox establish a clear basis of comparison between acting and behaving? If so, what is it?

2. Does the author tell enough about each acting style so that the reader can follow him through the contrast? To which style does he give more space? Is there a good reason for the imbalance?

3. The opening paragraph gives a specific statement of the author's intent; does everything in the essay contribute to that intent? Is there ever any doubt about where it is going?

4. What is the purpose of the concluding remarks? Do they weaken the case Knox has built for acting? Might Knox have ended the essay in a better way?

5. Most of the supporting evidence Knox cites is about stage acting, not film acting. Is it thereby invalidated as evidence? Is Knox aware of a possible objection on this score?

FILMS, TELEVISION, AND TENNIS

Richard E. Peck

Richard E. Peck is a professor of English at Temple University. As a scholar, he has published a number of articles on American literature. He has also written numerous successful television scripts, and it is this experience which gives him his competence to discuss the subject of the following essay — the difference between films for cinema and for television. Anyone who has watched a "movie of the week" on television has been irritated by the untimely commercial interruptions, which seem perfectly timely in television dramas. Here, Peck explains why the two media are — and should remain — separate.

... Television programming has come full circle, returning for its most 1
characteristic success to sports or variety shows, the fare of the 1939
pioneer telecasts. Sportscasts and an occasional special remain almost
the only examples of live television. An insatiable public appetite for
entertainment became obvious early in the game, and television production moved toward film as the major vehicle. Even those few programs which may seem live, like NBC's *The Tonight Show,* are taped
for delayed broadcast. The advantages of tape or film are clear: re-runs
help amortize initial production costs, bloopers can be edited out, and
whole segments may be swapped between shows for better balance. It
is finally cheaper to film, hiring extras ("atmosphere people," in TV
jargon) for a single day's shooting, than to rehearse an entire cast for
weeks before a live production.

The overwhelming majority of prime-time televised drama is now 2
filmed. The halcyon days of *Omnibus* or *Playhouse Ninety's* error-
ridden live productions are long gone and longer lamented. Critics who
bemoan the loss of live televised drama, whatever its quality, and the
recent dominance of filmed drama do so out of noble motives. They see
two theatrical genres distinctively different in conception drifting toward one another in disappointing ways.

The similarities are unmistakable. In the most general terms techni- 3
cal production of a one-hour television drama differs little from that of
a full-length feature film. Cameras and sound equipment, lighting tech-

From *Man and the Movies,* edited by W. R. Robinson. Reprinted by permission of
Louisiana State University Press.

niques, processing methods in the lab, editing and scoring are identical. Even our home movies may get the same treatment. So the habit of discussing television and cinema in the same breath is understandable. Both offer a series of images which express a point of view or convey information. Actors move easily from one medium to the other. James Garner's success as Bret Maverick led to his work in motion pictures, and his apprenticeship in television gave him whatever acting skills he has. Richard Chamberlain moved from television to the Broadway stage. And Richard Burton's playing of Caliban in *The Tempest* some years back lacked nothing for its being performed before TV cameras rather than on "legitimate" boards. Directors more and more often break into cinematic work through television, a medium which demands of them precision and directness not so stringently required by the relatively leisurely pace of cinema direction. A filmed narrative does not change character because of the means of its distribution — wide screen or square box.

When one turns from the media's similarities to their differences, however, one finds that television influences cinema rather than being influenced. First, television is *not* minor league cinema. Granted, many of the same techniques apply; physical equipment and processing methods are similar, if not identical. The real distinction resembles that between free verse and the sonnet. Writing free verse is, in Robert Frost's famous phrase, like playing tennis with the net down. Like free verse, cinema is more nearly an open-ended form. The restrictions which control and limit the typical teleplay are stricter, more clearly prescribed, but not necessarily debilitating. A *Tom Jones,* perhaps even more a *Dear John,* reaches the screen as the director's creation, with the merits achieved by intricate cutting and editing, fine nuance of camera work, and a shuffling of constituent parts which is impossible in the short week available for the filming, editing, and scoring of an hour teleplay. But what arbiter decides that the enormous craft demanded in the creation of an hour teleplay should be demeaned in comparison? The contrast is ridiculous, rather like the question on an aptitude test that asks which one likes better, living in the country or in the summer. I opt for the craftsman, the man who stands facing a net raised high enough for volleyball and yet plays his tennis match without begging for a change in the rules.

To use the titles *Tom Jones* and *Dear John* as I have is to approach a new attitude toward an art only now fumbling its way into prominence. *Giles Goat-Boy* is characterized in several reviews as allegory, artifice, and even craft without content. The arrangement of the material figures in random discussions of that novel much more than the material itself: What is the allegory? How many levels of meaning obtrude? Such a concern with the artifice of art dominates *Tom Jones* as well. It is impossible not to notice the techniques: speeded-up film sequences, subtitles, ornate framing, shifts into and out of brilliant color. Albert Finney even reminds the audience forcefully that they are watching a filmed narrative by hanging his hat over the lens.

To oversimplify, one can generalize about the phenomenon by sug- 6
gesting that we who compose today's audience don't require "realism" any longer; we may not even respect it. Rather, we react to self-conscious art, to art forms which play with their own limitations and conventions. For that reason, television — that most stringently restricted of forms — sits perched securely atop what's happening. Perhaps by following a script from its birth as a vague idea in the writer's mind to the teleplay which results I can make my point, or at least suggest a new way of looking at a single hour of television drama.

The time necessary for revising, rewriting, editing, and correcting 7
flaws — time which is afforded a team at work on a cinematic production — is denied the television producer. When he gets a script, he needs it ready to go. It may later be polished, or even rewritten, but at the cost of an expensive, ulcer-producing delay. Thus the whole process of shaping the final product for television falls more urgently into the writer's hands. He must follow a methodical plan. One of the best writers I know — "best" as opposed to "prolific" — employs the same series of steps for every script. He submits to the producer a five- or six-page "story treatment," a condensed plot. Given an OK for the idea, he moves on to a fifteen-page "step outline" in which he indicates breakdown into act and scene divisions, perhaps even a bit of dialogue for the flavor it will give his finished script. His work once more approved, he gets down to business.

Writing the finished teleplay, he finds himself entangled in the net 8
I mentioned. There is no denying it — TV is formulaic; it has its own logic and rhetoric. Each show opens with a two- to five-minute "teaser," that capsule of drama which flashes on the screen to prevent our switching to Ed Sullivan or Lawrence Welk. In this brief span of time, the writer *must:* (1) Get our attention with a "hook" of unexplained action, striking character conflict, or a question important enough to make us eagerly await the answer; and (2) introduce the star or guest star for this particular episode. If he knows his business, he should also (1) introduce two or three other principal players, (2) distinguish the setting and historical period, (3) hint faintly at a secondary problem in the story to follow, and (4) conceal behind bright, forceful dialogue the fact that he is doing all this. If he is really good — and look to the all-too-rare scripts by names like Silliphant, Rose, McNeely, Mittleman, or the pseudonymous John Thomas James for examples — he will also make

us laugh at, cry with, or hate a character on the screen. All this in the teaser, before the credits roll past and give permission for a quick trip to the pantry. A glassblower with hay fever has an easier job.

But the writer's problem has only begun. Ahead of him lies the crea- 9 tion of a four-act play whose acts average twelve to thirteen minutes. More, each act should ideally end as strongly as the teaser does, particularly the second, which coincides with the half-hour stroke of the clock and a viewer's recurrent impulse to catch at least the jugglers and the rock-and-roll band on the second half of Sullivan's spectacular. Once the viewer has switched channels he's gone to stay. He must be kept hooked, this time principally through effective dialogue. Each line of dialogue gets tested: Does it: (1) Define character? (2) Advance the plot? (3) Evoke emotional reaction from the audience? If it does not, out it comes. In the best scripts each line will achieve at least two of these ends.

Assuming that his muse does not desert him, the writer finishes in a 10 matter of days — or weeks. But he has only a play, not a teleplay, and television differs even more from legitimate theater than from the cinema. The writer must now become director, sound technician, special effects man, even lighting and casting director. His completed script will contain comments unheard by any audience beyond the production staff. General camera directions are left to the director, but shots essential to creating a desired mood must be explicitly described in the script. The writer indicates essential sound cues, dramatically effective lighting, transitions between scenes — direct cut, slow dissolve, whatever paces his drama to best advantage. He includes with his script a summary description of sets and characters, perhaps even "typing" the characters according to what particular actor he might envision in each role.

And when he finally drops his pencil or leans back to let the type- 11 writer cool, he has a first draft, sixty typewritten pages. Then another test: Read it aloud. To his wife, or a friend, a tape recorder, his shaving mirror, someone critical yet sympathetic. Test it. Check it. Then rewrite. And rewrite. The final version handed the director offers a full blueprint of the entire hour, subject to whatever minor changes may occur to this harried man in his tight shooting schedule.

Even after the play is filmed, editing and scoring require more time. 12 Thus it becomes essential that a writer's ideas be explicit and readily translatable into action. Television is no medium for the improvisor who fondles and nurtures his creation to maturity; Bergman is a poor candidate for a job directing television drama. The time element assumes such major importance that a series may occasionally change because of it, shifting radically from the producer's original conception.

I understand that the crew of *Maverick* found it impossible to complete episodes for that show in anything less than eight or ten days. Brother Bret, the Garner role, appeared in relief of Jack Kelly's Bart Maverick. With two production units at work on separate scripts it then became possible to meet weekly deadlines and to relieve pressure on the original company. And to many fans the show became Garner's, not Kelly's.

Given all these restrictions — time limits, formulaic act structure, economic limitations (about $140,000 for a single episode as compared with about $3,000,000 for a feature film) — television is forced into a mold. The writer exercises his craft as well as he can; an intelligent audience watches him at work, fully aware of the rhetoric he employs. 13

Unfortunately, that mythical "intelligent audience" does not always include men in the *business* of television or cinema. No one in the audience seriously believes any longer that feature films come off well on TV. The necessity for commercial interruptions and station breaks destroys the original tempo and mood of the film. Yet some have tried to solve the problem by writing feature-length film-scripts specifically geared to the requirements of commercial television. They do both industries a disservice. *Fame is the Name of the Game* recently fared well enough as a televised movie, but, transported into a theater as it will inevitably be, it must fail as cinema. An audience can hardly be expected to enjoy jolting through 100-plus minutes of plot in which a crisis leaps out at them every thirteen minutes to announce a commercial which never appears. And so the producers of that film define themselves as part of the group which persists in equating, and confusing, two distinct theatrical forms. 14

If cinema buffs complain that television turns leftover movies into Hollywood hash by mixing in liberal quantities of commercials and interruptions, how will they justify Hollywood's creating the same hash, to order? Which is now the dominant medium, cinema or television? More of these half-caste creations are promised. Perhaps their flaws will finally illustrate to all concerned that the media are essentially different. As cinema, television drama is poor stuff; just as certainly, cinema fails as television drama because it lacks the merits of conciseness, of direct and precise craftsmanship, where nothing else will serve. To consider each as *sui generis* is to recognize the merits, and shortcomings, of each. Even more, it is to admit that by confusing them one loses the virtues of both and is left with rubbish. 15

The formal differences between these genres begin to disappear as television extends its influence. A new sort of audience has been trained, a generation of viewers accustomed to certain technical devices and structural patterns which dominate television drama. More recently television's influence has begun to alter the rhetoric of cinema, 16

131

either because producers and directors of cinema are themselves part of that great audience and succumb to a pressure they may not recognize, or because these same men *do* recognize and pander to the audience's new-found tastes. Everyone has noticed, perhaps without remarking on it, how audience reaction to a motion picture differs from that to a glowing television screen. The psychology of audience reaction is a study in itself, yet worth a brief comment here. Having paid his money and found a seat in a darkened theater, Mr. Average Cinemaddict is free to laugh or cry in general anonymity. People seated near him — all strangers — behave similarly; a great communion takes place. I laugh, you laugh, he laughs. But the same man ensconced in his favorite chair at home, in the glaring light of his living room and surrounded by his wife and kids, is reluctant to display his emotions; he feels foolish laughing alone. Understanding such a feeling, television moguls attempt to reproduce the conditions of the theater by providing accompaniment in the form of the comforting laugh track.

But this viewer's solitary reactions developed at home go with him 17 on his next visit to a theater. He has been acclimated to technical devices and rhetorical traditions alien to cinema in its halcyon days of pre-television monopoly. To this man's mind slow dissolves from one scene to another no longer deepen mood so effectively; they presage a commercial. A transition through a gray or black screen may lose his attention completely. Witness the restless murmur that accompanies such a transition the next time you watch a feature film in a theater. Leisurely movement prevails no longer in any but the most consciously "arty" pieces.

The close-up, once reserved to give potent impact, has become such 18 a common shot in many recent films that its virtues are lost. Within the brief span of an hour-long television drama a close-up allows the craftsman to say, "Look. This is important. Don't ignore it." He need underline a symbolic action or object only once, rather than repeating it as he might with more time available. But the fact that close-range camera work dominates TV seems little reason for its appearance in cinematic technique. *Gengis Khan* fairly screams at the viewer with close-ups of faces, spears, hands, swords, even maps and pointers: "Look. This is where we are now." I can stand a 21-inch screen full of face; thirty feet of forehead and mascaraed eyelashes overpowers unnecessarily. The influence seems clear.

Within the past half-dozen years cinema has adopted the teaser, a 19 device essential to the peculiarities of television but worse than useless in the theater. It's not uncommon to find eight to ten minutes of plot preceding the credits on a wide screen, certainly to the detriment of the film's structural integrity. Nothing can account for such a manner-

ism except its accepted presence on the TV tube and the possibility of
a television-trained director's having learned his lessons too well. In a
theater the audience is already "hooked," has paid, and expects to be
entertained. No one would consider leaving during the initial credits;
no one can switch channels. A teaser under these circumstances satisfies
expectations aroused in the audience not by the nature or traditions of
cinema but by hours and hours of that other medium. Cinema, once
blamed for too slavishly following a three-act structure inherited from
the legitimate stage, deserves no less criticism for its currently frequent
and illogical turn to the teaser-four-act structure of television.

"Don't give us a filmed stage play," critics once complained. And   20
cinema moved outdoors to frolic in scenery, settings, and mobility un-
available onstage. But the public's insatiable demand for more and
more televised drama forced TV producers back to the pattern of a
small cast and few sets. Economics demands it; the audience accepts it,
perhaps even considering it a new convention. But — once more —
what law requires that cinema play follow-the-leader? *The Apartment*
employs such a pattern. Only the opening sequence of a football game
saves *The Fortune Cookie* from deserving the same criticism. The new
traditions of television seem to sanction a return to theatrical patterns
once happily discarded. For cinema it's a step backward, but one that
offers an out to film producers: an audience which accepts filmed stage
plays is also obviously more willing to accept talky drama, the too-
frequently exercised option of repeating a pattern from the Greek
theater — action offstage discussed onstage. Second-rate cinema runs
the risk of becoming third-rate television by falling back on dialogue in
place of action.

Let each do what it can do best. If TV deserves any attack in this   21
circular mass of confusion, it is not because it too nearly approaches
cinema but because it returns to formulas of the stage which film should
long ago have overthrown. More, it leads cinema down the same garden
path.

The influence of television, then, is pervasive, affecting certainly   22
movies, if not *the film* — that common distinction of the culturati.
Let me suggest, finally, that even *the film* benefits from the fact of
television's very existence. Hollywood's self-congratulation for cinema's
new maturity is misdirected praise. "Adult films" of today would have
given the censors apoplexy not too long ago. Honesty is rampant. Illicit
love affairs in vivid detail, frank language, visible brutality — all mark
the new maturity. But it takes no cynic to suggest that all this "honesty"
is also profitable. Television, as the family medium, has staked its claim
on subject matter long the staple of Hollywood's output. I can see on
TV more situation comedy than a normal stomach will take; Andy

133

Hardy will never come back in a wide-screen version. Westerns abound on television. Detectives chase criminals from network to network. Film producers who expect cash customers to pay for longer versions of the same scripts misunderstand the audience and soon become agents instead of producers. Only insofar as films surpass television drama in frankness, or brutality, or "honesty" can they attract a mass audience. Whatever credit cinema claims for its honesty should be laid instead at TV's door. This is the final influence: if movies are better than ever, television made them so.

It all has to do with that net. When one recognizes that *the film* and *television* are different games, he can appreciate them both without resorting to comparisons which only cloud their differences. Let cinema play in its own backyard where television hasn't a chance to compete. And the next time you watch an hour teleplay pay attention to the net that gets in the TV playwright's way. It forces him to stretch a bit, to stay on his toes, a metaphorical exercise that might benefit all writers. A point harder won deserves more admiration. On its own court television serves up plenty of aces.

SUBJECT

1. Does Peck seem to think that the taping of television drama is an improvement over live drama, or only a necessary evil?

2. What are the chief differences between the making of a TV drama and of a feature film? What are the differences in audience expectation?

3. Peck suggests that going to the cinema is a communal experience, like going to church or to a rock festival, while at home before a TV set each member of the audience retains his individuality. Would you agree? Do you think TV dramas make less embarrassing appeals to the emotions than films do?

4. What influences, according to Peck, has television had on cinema? Would it be fair to say that the good influences are those which emphasize the difference between the two media, and that the harmful influences are those which make cinema more like television?

5. Peck does not suggest ways in which cinema has influenced television. Do you think the recent tendency to expand half-hour shows into 60-minute dramas reflects such an influence? What happens when television shows are expanded? Is there twice as much action, or is the plot twice as involved?

6. Have you noticed that movies tend more and more to resemble television drama, as Peck complains? If so, do you find it objectionable?

7. In what direction *should* movies be going, according to Peck?

STRUCTURE

1. In paragraph 4, Peck employs an analogy between cinema and free verse and between television drama and sonnet. Is the analogy a fair one? Does it help clarify the difference between the two media?

2. On what bases does Peck distinguish between the two media? Does he rely on these same bases when he discusses the influence of television on cinema?

3. As a television writer, Peck naturally has considerably more to say about the way TV dramas are made than about the making of feature films. Does this cause any difficulties in establishing the contrast?

4. Consider the appropriateness of the title to this essay. Is it misleading, or "catchy"? How does Peck use the tennis analogy as a unifying device?

MOVIES FROM
BEHIND
THE BARRICADES

Stephen Farber

Stephen Farber is the Los Angeles editor of Film Quarterly, *probably
the best American journal devoted to film-making as an intellectual
and artistic endeavor. In this review of a group of movies about campus
riots, Farber employs comparison and contrast, cause and effect analysis, and evaluation to explain why the films were box office failures, to
compare and contrast their aims and techniques, and to analyze their
individual merits and faults. To attempt this much in one essay requires, among other things, skillful organization. The reader is asked
to pay particular attention to the way Farber puts his materials
together.*

The fickleness of commercial decision-makers in Hollywood has never   1
been more strikingly in evidence, and it must discourage anyone who
is concerned about the future of the American film. Just a year ago there
was reason to be hopeful. Hollywood had discovered the youth audience. The success of *Midnight Cowboy, Easy Rider, Alice's Restaurant*
had convinced the executives that escapism was out of fashion, and,
anxious to tap the gigantic new market, they gave unprecedented freedom to film-makers who wanted to deal with the problems that touched
youth and inflamed them. Almost no movies with college settings had
been made during the sixties; even *The Graduate,* the most sucessful
youth movie of the decade, and set partly in Berkeley, concentrated on
sex and romance but curiously avoided any details that would suggest
what it was like to be in college two years after FSM. But all at once
the men who were trying to predict the future of the business decided
that young people wanted to see movies about their own experiences
— and what more logical subject for exploitation than campus rebellion and student protest? By late 1969, within a few months of the
phenomenal success of *Easy Rider,* several movies about college and
revolution were in preparation — *The Strawberry Statement* (based

to some extent on James Simon Kunen's book about the Columbia disturbances but relocated in Hayakawa country), *Getting Straight, The Magic Garden of Stanley Sweetheart, The Pursuit of Happiness, The Revolutionary, Up in the Cellar* (a quickie from American International). MGM had Antonioni's *Zabriskie Point* ready for release, and they were counting on the film to save their dying studio. Soon Stanley Kramer, always quick to pick up on a commerical social problem, proposes *RPM* to explore the issue of student rebellion from the other side of the generation gap, with Anthony Quinn scheduled to play Stanley Kramer, the aging, discarded liberal. The campus riot became the stock scene of 1970 films.

Now all these movies are in release. Only *Getting Straight* is a commercial success, and that appears to be more because of Elliott Gould's presence than because of the subject matter. The other movies are not just failures, they are commercial disasters. What went wrong? The question deserves some intensive analysis, because as a result of the failure of these movies, and the huge simultaneous success of *Airport,* the direction of American movie-making looks as if it is about to be reversed. Political films are being cancelled. "The day of the student film-maker and the youth movie is over," I heard an agent say recently. ("It's only *lasted* about a day," I wanted to protest, but to whom?) Studio executives, helplessly trying to understand the audience, and totally bewildered by the box-office receipts, are looking for safe entertainment, for "uplifting" pictures. On a television forum in Los Angeles recently, the head of production at MGM said he thought the audience was tired of "downers." Unfortunately, with the blooming of the Nixon Era, he may be right. 2

The critics probably did not foresee all of this when they blasted the opportunism of the campus pictures earlier in the year. Certainly few American movies have aroused more critical indignation than *Getting Straight* and *The Strawberry Statement.* Timing worked against the films. Both were released shortly after the student deaths at Kent State and Jackson; people had been shaken by a recognition of the gravity of student-police conflict on campus, and they were not about to tolerate any cynical Hollywood profiteers hawking slick, fashionable slogans of dissent and rebellion in the marketplace. *Newsweek* wrote: "While college students are being shot to death and colleges are fighting for their own lives in the real world, the unprincipled fools of the movie business rush in with *Getting Straight,* a violent varsity comedy in which light-hearted kids tear up a university and blow kisses to each other across the embattled campus." When these movies were planned, it was modish to attack the university as an instrument of the military-industrial complex; but by the time they were released the university 3

137

once again seemed a possible haven of reason and sanity in an increasingly repressive society.

Topical movies are clearly a dangerous enterprise, unless they can be produced and released much more quickly than the American studio system presently allows. But there are other reasons why these films have failed to attract the young audience. For one thing, they are probably *too* close to the experience of young people. Especially to young people committed to radical university reform or full-scale social revolution, the very *idea* of a Hollywood movie on the subject is bound to be offensive. And in an even more basic sense, young people have an easier time recognizing false touches in a movie drawn from a world that is familiar to them than they would in a movie about male prostitution in New York or turn-of-the-century Western bandits in South America. These student protest movies are dealing with material in which a large segment of the audience considers itself expert. (One veteran of the Columbia disturbance who was angry at *The Strawberry Statement* told me, "You don't wear your glasses during a bust.") 4

But these movies are not so much inaccurate as incomplete. Cultural historians in the future, who look to American films for some reflection of larger social attitudes, will find a striking vacuum in the movies of the sixties. No major American movie acknowledges what was taking place from about 1964 to 1968, the period of growing social involvement among the young and the awakening of national consciousness to the moral implications of the war in Vietnam, racism in American society, pollution of the environment, corruption and bureaucratic inefficiency within all major institutions in America — from the Pentagon to the university itself. Movies like *Bonnie and Clyde* and *The Graduate, Easy Rider* and *Alice's Restaurant* captured something of the spirit of young people in more indirect and archetypal terms; only *Medium Cool* tried to deal with the real social disturbances of those years within the frame of the fiction film. In the early sixties some talented American moviemakers had turned out a group of interesting political melodramas — *Advise and Consent, The Manchurian Candidate, Dr. Strangelove, Fail Safe, Seven Days in May, The Best Man* — dealing mainly with Cold War tensions and the threat of the Bomb. But throughout the last half of the sixties, our movies determinedly avoided political themes. 5

Now suddenly, in these student protest movies, all those years in which the conscience of a generation was formed, all those agonized internal struggles and fiery political debates are *taken for granted;* what propels the films of 1970 is the assumption of a youth culture socially and politically alert and dissatisfied, but in the movies at least, we have no record at all of how young people arrived at this point of concern. And the new movies themselves do not dramatize — sometimes do 6 not even *mention* — the issues that have enraged students and brought them to the point of throwing rocks at cops and at buildings. So there is an eerie sense of dislocation we feel in watching them. Both Richard Rush's *Getting Straight* and Robert Mulligan's *The Pursuit of Happiness* take as their heroes young men who, according to expository dialogue in the films, have already spent several years in active forms of social protest — Selma, anti-war marches, the McCarthy campaign, Chicago 1968 — and have grown frustrated and disillusioned with the dream of social involvement. Those political activities of the mid-sixties have never been presented on screen; while we are still waiting to see an American movie hero who comes to believe in the urgency of social involvement — a SNCC worker, a campus leader, a draft resister — we are already asked to understand characters who are *disillusioned* with the new politics, who *reject* any kind of peaceful political activism, self-consciously withdrawing from society or turning to violence as a last expression of outrage and despair. This bitterness is an accurate enough reflection of the mood of many American youth in 1970, but our movies haven't earned the right to take such a despairing, nihilist stance; their pose of radicalism seems much too glibly asserted.

It may be unfair to score the new movies because of the failures of other movie-makers; but we are so starved for challenging movies about political tensions that we cannot help resenting the intellectual emptiness of the "revolution" films. Even the best of them, *The Strawberry Statement,* is a bad joke if you try to take it as a serious, realistic movie about the issues that pertain to campus rebellion. The level of political thought in the movie can be found in the chants that the protagonist hears (or imagines he hears) at strike rallies: "Strike because you hate cops . . . Strike because you hate war . . . Strike because there is poverty . . . Strike because there's no poetry in your lectures . . . Strike because classes are a drag . . ." I think these slogans are deliberately exaggerated to suggest the nature of a boy's incipient political awareness; they are not meant as a documentary record of the quality of debate on the campuses. But there is no more sophisticated dialogue anywhere in the film. The strike is already on when *The Strawberry Statement* begins, and although we are told that it has something to do with the university taking possession of a playground used by black children and turning it into an ROTC center (based loosely on the situation at Columbia), the issues are never seriously explored or even explained. The meager details provided by the film are meant to clue in the knowing members of the audience; presumably we're all on the right side of the barricades.

The state of siege is also the *donnée* in *RPM.* ("They're occupying the administration building again," someone tells the board of trustees at the very beginning of the film, and their blasé acceptance of the fact is unintentionally amusing.) We have no clear idea why the students are protesting — we can catch a couple of references to Inner City scholarships and university business holdings in South Africa — but the movie-makers don't feel this is a crucial point to establish; they assume we're all hip enough to read the signals and fill in the background for ourselves. The plot of *RPM* turns on three student demands which are supposed to be unreasonable: the students want control over the curriculum, and even over the hiring and firing of faculty and the granting of degrees. To people who don't know anything about the debates that have been taking place on college campuses for most of a decade, these demands may indeed sound ludicrous — proof of the students' childishness and unwillingness to compromise. The young people are portrayed throughout as insensitive, intolerant extremists, and this is certainly one possible interpretation; but I think a movie that comes to this conclusion at least has an obligation to explain *why* the students have grown impatient with the conventional liberal representatives of the university. Those student demands might not seem so presumptuous if the movie allowed us to hear some intelligent student-faculty debates about the role of the university in a troubled world — debates which any student radical has taken part in. At least *Getting Straight* gives a few indications of where orthodox liberal education has lost touch with young people's concerns. *RPM* offers no glimpses of education in progress, no suggestion of the kind of curriculum student radicals would like to see, no fair representation of their ideal of a free, open university; so its anti-student bias seems cheap, insular, irresponsible.

American movies have, of course, never been strong on ideas. But in these films *about* student politics, this characteristic deficiency is particularly damaging. The hero of *RPM* is supposed to be a brilliant liberal sociologist; but although he drops a few of the right names in conversation, he never articulates any of his own philosophy of nonviolence or his ideas about the function of the university and the inequities in the society, so we have to take his credentials entirely on faith. One of these new movies, Paul Williams's *The Revolutionary,* even tries to define the maturation of a contemporary revolutionary without identifying the social setting in which his ideas develop ("somewhere in the free world," an opening title coyly informs us) or any of the specific social and political injustices he wants to fight. The film tries to build an abstract, generalized portrait that comes across only hollow and vague; the idea of doing a movie about radicalism shorn of a concrete social context for radical acts seems almost perversely evasive.

I believe the absence of genuine political thought in these movies, the failure to dramatize the full nature of involvement and protest, may have alienated many of the young people toward whom these films are ostensibly geared. And yet by ignoring these films, the young are missing some imaginative film-making, some interesting, challenging characterizations, and perhaps most simply, some crude, lively entertainment. I have emphasized the political and intellectual emptiness of these movies because I think that reveals something interesting — and depressing — about mass culture in America, but I do not mean to suggest that the movies are artistically invalidated merely by their political simplifications. In fact, nothing less than the provocative and important question of the relationship of politics to art is raised by this new group of films.

The critics, perhaps anxious to woo the young with a sign of solidarity, have simplified the issue by attacking the films in moral terms. Dotson Rader defined the high moral tone of this criticism in his review of *The Strawberry Statement* for the Sunday *New York Times.* Without bothering to analyze what the film was attempting, he blasted it as "a cheap attempt at the commercial co-option and exploitation of the anguish of a generation," but at least he identified himself as "having been a part of the Columbia Liberation of 1968," so I can understand his outrage, even though I find it largely irrelevant to any reasonable evaluation of the film *as film.* Other critics who did not take part in the Columbia Liberation may have less excuse for denouncing the film as a betrayal of the radical cause. Their objections to the new films, like those of Rader, often sound surprisingly naive: the movies are contemptible because they are not "real" and because they are not "sincere" — and because the studios releasing the films hope to make money from them. But "sincerity" — which may be an admirable quality in a friend or relative — has always been a pretty unreliable criterion for appraising a work of art. Part of the nature of art is to be playful, irresponsible, irreverent, which is not to say that it cannot treat serious themes; but art always serves itself first, the revolution second. *The Strawberry Statement* may have a radical statement to make, but it also exists *for its own sake:* Stuart Hagmann, the director, takes pleasure in *how* he makes his statement, in the beauty of his images, in an inventive structuring of scenes that can suggest an interior point of view; in dramatic confrontation and surprise. Perhaps that concern with technique is a form of self-indulgence, of bourgeois decadence, but no one, not even Godard, has yet explained how art — as opposed to journalism or propaganda — can survive without it.

The difficulty of sorting out aesthetic from ideological, political, and moral responses is most acute in *Getting Straight,* a film which exploits serious issues (the enervation of university bureaucracy, student and police violence) and uses familiar contemporary figures toward whom

11

12

141

an audience has very strong, sometimes ambivalent feelings — the black militant, the zonked-out hippie, the reactionary college president, the WASP-coed-turned-radical — to create a galley of eccentrics in a wacky screwball farce. "Ideas and characters are seldom protected from gags, for ideas and characters are expendable and gags aren't." Vincent Canby wrote of the campus movies. But although Canby's terms are loaded, I'm not sure these are the wrong priorities. The jokes in *Getting Straight* are indeed more important than the political message; so it follows that there can be jokes even on the heroes of the counter-culture — on the hippie who turns super-patriot when confronted with his draft board, on the sheltered liberal girls who are sexually stimulated by rioting, on the humorless, intense students who want to hear about Nat Turner's hemorrhoids in black history class. Are these jokes signs of corruption, Hollywood expediency, lack of true commitment, as Vincent Canby seems to suggest, or are they signs of a genuinely anarchic satire, a refreshing willingness to offend even the young audience toward whom the film is supposedly directed? Probably there is something of both courage and calculation in *Getting Straight's* wild, erratic, indiscriminately irreverent comedy.

The audience takes *Getting Straight* as a fanciful cartoon. I think they recognize the exaggerations and distortions and enjoy them; they respond to the colorful, amusing caricatures, and to the fantasy of defiance and revolt against the tired, repressive academic tradition. No one who has ever suffered through a pedantic lecture or seminar could possibly resist the outrageous climactic scene of Harry's MA oral exam, in which — goaded by a fanatical professor trying to push his own theory about Fitzgerald's homosexuality — Harry literally freaks out and explodes the polite complacency of his questioners with a barrage of obscenities. Liberal critics have been too solemn about the movie; like crusaders for decency during the thirties, they imagine a simple relationship between art and life — people imitate whatever they see on the screen. Kids do cheer the moment when Harry picks up a rock and heaves it at a university window in *Getting Straight's* final scene, but that doesn't mean they are going to go out and bomb their classrooms, any more than the blacks who cheer the murder of the white policeman at the end of *The Liberation of L. B. Jones* are likely to go out and start shooting at passing cops. These are only movies, after all, and part of their appeal is that they allow audiences to toy with some socially forbidden fantasies within the safety of the darkened theater, where no one can be held responsible for his dreams.

The main trouble with *Getting Straight* is a formal problem; it keeps changing tone — at one moment content to be an up-to-date screwball comedy with a campus setting, at the next straining after Signifi-

142

cance. The unreality is set by the outrageously stylized conversations shouted across the quad, by Harry's crazy, broken-down jalopy, which goes through more special-effects contortions than one of those cars invented for James Bond, by the ghoulish free drink of hot water, crushed crackers, and catsup that he prepares for himself. In the slickly fashioned scenes in which Harry debates his girlfriend Jan and her square doctor friend, the university PR man, or the radical activists, we aren't really interested in the content of the debates, we're interested in Harry's flamboyant style and the witty, theatrical repartee. The ideas are subordinated to the effect. And that's perfectly acceptable as long as the film remains comic and fantastic. When it turns serious, it turns sour. In Harry's pompous exchange with the president about the validity of student demands, or in the grossly sentimental scene when he explains how he turned a student on to *Don Quixote,* the crudely oversimplified, pandering "message" cinema is much more offensive than any of the jokes. The first riot sequence, complete with tear gas, police clubbing students and students kicking back, is one of the cheapest pieces of audience exploitation I have ever seen: aesthetically revolting because it is so completely gratuitous. It has nothing to do with the comic character study the film has been sketching; in fact, it goes on for five minutes before Harry, who has been our focus throughout the film, even makes an appearance. In this somber scene the film is crassly titillating its audience, playing with serious issues, and it seems ugly. (On these grounds the film can be contrasted with Ted Flicker's *Up in the Cellar,* a flip satire on university bureaucracy and repression that never makes the mistake of turning solemn. When Flicker wants to make a strong comment on the direction of American society, he does it *within* the comic frame he has established — as in one brilliant single-shot scene in which the hero and his girlfriend discuss their romance, while in the background a group of agitators are marched off by the police, apparently to a concentration camp. Flicker knows how to keep things in perspective, and his film is all the more mordant as a result.)

Perhaps the reason *Getting Straight* is such a mess is that the writer, 15 Robert Kaufman, has confused two different stories from two different historical periods. The satire on academic insularity and bureaucracy has a genial, light-hearted flavor that places it before the period of extreme student militancy. Similarly, the central theme of a fellow trying to get his teaching certificate, constantly frustrated by the pettiness of the university administrators, simultaneously battling with his girlfriend over her suburban middle-class fantasies, has been reworked in literature several times since the fifties (Kingsley Amis's *Lucky Jim* is probably the archetype). But this slightly nostalgic story is told against

143

a background of student radicalism and violence of the late sixties; the issues and characters don't really belong together. Kaufman and Rush, who are in their thirties, understand Harry Bailey well enough, but they have set him in an environment they seem to know only from second-hand reports.

The major significance and interest of the movie is its success in discovering a protagonist who is at once genuinely contemporary and representative, and absolutely original. Kaufman and Rush focus on an unlikely figure — the pushy Jewish intellectual — and turn him into a new-style hero for comic melodrama. It is a classic star turn, in which all of the qualities that make Elliott Gould so distinctive as a movie personality — his rudeness, his boorishiness, his self-satisfaction, his quick, alert, aggressive mind — are highlighted and glamorized, so that his portrait of Harry takes on an almost-mythical structure. The characterization is conceived in rather grand romantic terms, but it is closely observed too. A former radical, Harry is now contemptuous of the pettiness and naivete of radical demands, committed to the achievement of a limited private goal — the attainment of a teaching certificate — and quite ruthless in his determination to satisfy himself even at the expense of the movement. His cynicism is comprehensive — he is equally skeptical of both the students and administrators. The scenes between him and his girlfriend are especially well-drawn; Philip Roth would understand the mixture of passion and hostility in the relationship of this rough, unwashed Jew to the beautiful, complacent, unattainable WASP goddess, Candice Bergen. The character has roots in recognizable experience; as with the best movie characters, we can imagine a past for him, a life that stretches beyond his screen life. Unfortunately, Rush and Kaufman have had trouble imagining his future. They end the film too early — as Harry and Jan begin to make love on a stairway, while the riot goes on around them. But this facile fantasy conclusion leaves too much unsettled; we want to know where Harry will turn now, how he will use his energy and his intelligence once he has recognized the impossibility of creating a meaningful life within conventional boundaries. In other words, Rush and Kaufman have enough talent to create a valid, exciting, eccentric modern hero, but they have not tested themselves — or Harry — as searchingly as they might have; they lack the vision to foresee how this kind of man will make his way in the world.

A number of these films demonstrate the same ability to create interesting, offbeat characters, and the same inability to place those characters in the challenging dramatic situations that they deserve. Even Kramer's *RPM* has a potentially fascinating hero, a character through whom Kramer has tried to express some of his own doubts and angers and frustrations. F. W. J. Perez is in a classic liberal dilemma — a man who spent his life fighting repression suddenly finds himself repudiated by the radical young, who are unable to distinguish him from the most reactionary trustee. Anthony Quinn sensitively captures his humiliation at the contemptuous way the radicals treat him, his revulsion from violence and ultimate self-revulsion when he is forced to ally himself with the police; the material is here for a complex moral study. But Erich Segal's script, which delights in glib one-liners, utterly fails to develop or illuminate the theme. Without any incisive confrontation of the liberal and radical sensibility, without any effective visual or dramatic expression of the hero's inner life, all that we *can* respond to is the idea.

In *The Revolutionary* Jon Voight is given a little more to work with, 18 and he brings all of his craft and conviction as an actor to the sketchy, difficult role of "A," the young revolutionary-in-the-making. He fashions an expert, delicate portrait of the awkward, intense student intellectual, in its homely way probably much closer to reality than the gargoyle animated by Elliott Gould in *Getting Straight.* Voight is particularly good at capturing the would-be revolutionary's fussiness and solemnity. He conceives the character in comic terms, but the comedy grows out of affection; and although the movie ignores most of the dramatic possibilities of its subject, the writing and performance of the central role help to give a little texture and humanity to a curiously pale treatise.

The role written (by Sidney Carroll) for Michael Sarrazin in *The* 19 *Pursuit of Happiness* is even more intriguing; this is one of the first films that seriously tries to examine the background and unspoken motivations of today's rootless, disaffected young. Like other youth films, *The Pursuit of Happiness* emphasizes the repressiveness and dishonesty of respectable society — the bigotry of William's upper class family, the duplicity of his uncle, a successful lawyer, the hypocrisy of the courts, the brutality of our prisons. But this is no simple celebration of youth against the Establishment. William, our sensitive, alienated hero, a weary veteran of the antiwar movement, is clearly limited and inadequate in his own way. The film establishes this immediately by showing his obsession with toy boats, and then goes on to dramatize his helplessness and irresponsibility through a variety of adventures. Again and again, when in a bind, he turns back to his family and relies on their money and professional expertise to extricate him. At the very end William uses his grandmother's money to buy his way out of the country, but he bungles even that. He hopes to go to Canada, but the shifty pilot takes all his money and then tells him he is flying to Mexico on this round. It is too late to back down, and long past the point of caring

145

where he goes or what he does, William accepts the ride; as far as we can tell, his life is over. Trying to justify his lack of commitment, he says the country is having a "nervous breakdown," and although what the film shows us of the American system of justice would bear out his charge of ineradicable corruption, we feel William is only another victim of the society, hardly a victor over its hypocrisies. The film traces his carelessness, his lazy disillusionment, his casual disregard for authority to his easy, spoiled childhood; by asking us to see the relationship between the dull, comfortable upbringing of today's university rebels and the passive, tired style of much of their protest, *The Pursuit of Happiness* provocatively undercuts sentimentalization of the young — without going to the other extreme and trying to whitewash the decadent institutions of American society. This characterization gives the film an unusual point of view, but most everything else about it is undistinguished or simply false: Most of the other characterizations and performances are on a caricature level, and there is a good deal of shoddy contrivance in the plot; the result is that a very believable three-dimensional character is placed in a series of extremely unbelievable situations.

One of the chief difficulties with these socially conscious youth movies is deciding whom they are designed for. Are they propaganda films made to convert older people to the student cause? Are they new mass-audience entertainments simply to exploit the fantasies and fears of the young audience? Or can they be called works of art, created to satisfy the film-makers themselves? All of these movies have either crassly or confusedly hedged on their intentions, and perhaps that is why they seem to be fully satisfying to no one. *The Strawberry Statement* is the most cogent and unified of all of them, but even it is not entirely clear in its aims. The writer, Israel Horovitz, and the director Stuart Hagmann, seem to share their critics' insistence on social relevance as the major criterion in evaluating art; they want their movie to be a respectable radical-liberal document as well as a work of cinematic art. But the two aims may be irreconcilable. Hagmann has already made two significant cuts in the film — a comic fellatio scene that wittily mocked some of the young people's fantasies about violence, and a flashback montage at the very end — probably in the mistaken belief that those scenes compromised the seriousness of the political message. Hagmann and Horovitz have both said that they believe the film's main importance lies in what it tells middle America about student dissent: "We've got a very small ambition: to show those who still need showing that every protesting student is not insane..." Fortunately, the film is not that easily summarized and dismissed. In spite of its confusions of intention, its political and intellectual

20

inadequacies, *The Strawberry Statement* is one of the finest movies about young people ever made in America, an extraordinary lyric of childhood's end and the agonized awakening of a radical sensibility.

The Strawberry Statement has angered some people because, like *Getting Straight,* it has an impudent, skeptical sense of humor about young people and their movement. Simon joins the strike primarily because he is interested in a girl he meets there. Once inside the occupied administration building, he seems more anxious to use the president's bathroom and to watch *Mutiny on the Bounty* on television than to take part in the radicals' debate about slanted news coverage and war research on campus; he even lies about how he received a bloody nose because he wants to impress the hard-core activists with firsthand evidence of police brutality. Does the film's psychological astuteness really demean the radical cause? Only the most self-righteous of young people would deny that part of their reason for joining the movement is the simple thrill of rebellion and the promise of fraternal solidarity — and maybe a few even consider the possibility of sex behind the barricades. But in any case, Simon's initial apathy is what sets the conversion story in motion. *The Strawberry Statement* is told from the perspective of a boy who *isn't* involved, who is confused in his responses to radical rhetoric, who plays at revolution and sneaks into a student strike as if he were embarking on a forbidden adventure in a new kind of wonderland.

Stuart Hagmann's visual style has been generally derided as a mélange of TV commercial effects, but nonetheless it seems to me remarkably appropriate to capturing the quality of Simon's imagination. For Simon conceives his life in romantic terms, with extravagant flourishes borrowed from "lyrical" TV commercials and other movies. We are seeing the world through Simon's eyes (a simple fact that has somehow eluded almost all of the critics), and he tries to hold life off, see it with aesthetic distance. Reared on the media, he is uncomfortable without his radio or his Super 8 movie camera in his hand. One of the first times he takes note of the movement is when he comes upon a mime troupe enacting the beating of a student — revolution seen as dramatic performance. The original version of the film emphasized the secondhand nature of Simon's perceptions even more strongly: in the fellatio scene, when the girl in the xerox room took off her sweater to initiate Simon after his beating, Hagmann provided flash cuts of her breasts that were very obviously meant as a parody of the seduction scene in *The Graduate.* (Simon even asked the girl, as he gaped at her, "Did you see *The Graduate?*")

Simon's perspective on life is enchanted by movie and TV memories, the flair and beauty of art; but that enchantment is a kind of protective

147

blindness too. (It is no accident that Simon becomes aroused to a sense of social injustice for the first time when a group of blacks accost him in the park and, for no clear reason, smash his movie camera.) Hagmann deliberately calls attention to his visual style, for he means to comment on it: one of the film's most important themes is the magical power and the irresponsibility of art, and the distortions that arise when life begins to imitate art.

Like this scene in the park, most of the film works on a metaphorical, wittily allusive level, not a literal one. Hagmann uses recurring symbolic images — the crew teams rowing in harmony through the beautiful clear water, oblivious to the blighted urban landscape just out of eyeshot — as a kind of poetic refrain. And in the second half of the film he makes some startling experiments in blurring fantasy and reality that have gone virtually unnoticed by the people outraged over the film's commercial gloss. *The Strawberry Statement* takes an important step toward refining cinematic language. Simon's adventures in and out of the administration building, back at crew practice, swinging around the city with his girl, are a free-form fantasy trip, a combination of memory and projection, imagination and reality that is not exactly comparable to anything I have seen in films before.

Most of these scenes are probably part of an imagined drama, not a real one. They are all shot through with a crazy, uninhibited kind of whimsical poetry. Transitions are illogical, unpredictable jumps in time and place disorient us. There are witty, outrageous, absurdist fantasies — the sequence in which Simon is reverently whispered over, introduced to a black militant, and carefully photographed when he comes in boasting that he was attacked by pigs, or the abrupt conversion of Simon's enemy George, the All-American Jock, into a committed revolutionary. Other, more realistic scenes are shaded with subtle, unsettling surrealistic touches — an old man in a café where Simon is daydreaming sits staring at the miniature stuffed animals spread out on the table before him; a Negro woman holding an umbrella on a sunny day rocks back and forth with laughter as students are dragged away from a demonstration; Linda leaves Simon, saying, "I have to get the bus," and a moment later, in the background, we see her rising in a glass elevator. In his imagination Simon can experiment with revolutionary activity, curiously, timidly, roguishly; he and the other students torment the police on a playground, all very genially, and when they are hauled off to jail, Simon tries to see what it would feel like to litter from the back of the paddy wagon. And during all of this, while the strike and the occupation continue, Simon even imagines he has time to live out a full-length romantic melodrama: Linda rejects him for another activ-

148

ist (what he calls an "extrarevolutionary relationship"), he mopes around for a while, and she finally returns to him (in a scene that I think contains a deliberate parody of the reunion of Audrey Hepburn and Albert Finney in *Two for the Road*). The love scenes, though tender and charming, are not presented quite straight; they seem to be placed in quotation marks. They are meant to be seen as a slightly over-ripe stylistic convention, capsulizing a way of life that is already corrupt.

What is most poignant is the sense of compression and unreality in 26 these scenes — as if an entire boyhood romance were being squeezed into a few days, an entire dream of growing up absurd accelerated, apprehended only in fragments that seem to shatter before our eyes. This lyrical fantasy, in which "Up against the wall!" is no more than a challenge to masculine bravado — a kaleidoscope of images taken from romantic art and charged with all the passion and imagination that a boy can bring to ordinary experience — is a projection of the youth Simon wants to live, the youth he might have lived if he were only allowed a little more time to grow up. The strongest impulse behind the film is a nostalgia for lost innocence, a lament for a less urgent time when young people still had the leisure to spin dreams in which they might play the romantic hero.

Only at the film's climax — the elaborate, nightmarish sequence of 27 the police bust — are these feelings clearly focused for us; there is a delicate sense of self-irony throughout many of the early sections of the film, but the climax turns a grotesque distorting mirror on the romantic images, makes us reexamine all that had come before from a shocking new perspective. In this vision of the forces of the state turning their weapons against the children of their society, Simon is finally compelled to confront reality firsthand, denied the protection of fantasy. Revolution is no longer part of the game of growing up absurd; Simon has no more time to play or to dream. He is, at last, deeply involved and totally committed.

With this terrifying conclusion, *The Strawberry Statement* unques- 28 tionably presents a serious political statement about the inhumanity of our society and the radicalization of a boy scourged and purified by the horror of police brutality. But what makes the film so moving is its genuine affection for the boyhood dreams that the camera lingers over in the early sections. The movie is ironic about Simon's fantasies of romance and revolution, but it is also deeply attracted to his exuberant, playful, uncommitted vision of the world. In the last analysis, the film reminds us of the staggering sacrifice our age demands; we cannot help but mourn Simon's freewheeling imagination, a youthful spirit of abandon that can never be reclaimed. Perhaps the doubts and ambiguities of the film prevent it from being effective as a revolutionary document; but I would put it another way — *The Strawberry Statement* is remarkable because it transcends its "message"to make us *feel* the anguish that accompanies radical political commitment in our world. Yeats's great poem about the Irish rebellion of Easter 1916 sums up the transformation of ordinary men into revolutionaries — "All changed, changed utterly:/ A terrible beauty is born" — showing his awareness of the human costs of a cause he believed in. "A terrible beauty is born": the words would be an appropriate way of describing our feelings at the end of *The Strawberry Statement* too. Dotson Rader, that veteran of the Columbia Liberation, calls the film's attention to the complexities of human feeling "counterrevolutionary." And in a way, he may be right. But it seems the reason many of us regularly turn from politics back to art is that we are still searching for an illumination of the imaginative and emotional truths that any movement necessarily ignores. If the wave of campus rebellion movies has clarified this one crucial matter for film-makers and audiences, it will have served, in the long run, a useful purpose.

SUBJECT

1. Why, according to Farber, were most of these films box-office failures?

2. On what basis does Farber argue that the films are worth seeing?

3. Why does Farber think *The Strawberry Statement* is a better film than *Getting Straight,* even though the latter was more successful economically? Why, according to Farber, did *Getting Straight* make money?

4. As a professional critic, Farber has the objectivity to see a film as an artistic success even though it fails as political propaganda; do you think the average movie-goer could make the same separation? (If you have seen any of these films, judge by your own reaction.)

5. Were there places in the essay where you had the feeling that Farber saw things in a film — parodies and subtle ironies, for instance — which the film-maker himself might not have been conscious of? If so, would Farber's reading be negated? (Frost once claimed that a poet is entitled to any interpretation a reader gets out of his poem.)

6. Farber laments the fact that no film was ever made showing the process by which students became disillusioned with society during the second half of the sixties. Do you think it is too late now for such a film to be made — or *has* one been made that Farber misses?

STRUCTURE

1. Try making an informal outline of this review. How carefully is it put together? Should Farber have made some kind of summary statement at the end instead of stopping with a discussion of *The Strawberry Statement?*

2. When he explains the economic failure of these movies, Farber draws a contrast between what the films did and what they should have done. Is the same basis of comparison employed in each case?

3. In his extended discussion of four movies, upon what basis (or bases) does Farber compare them? Does he point out similarities as well as differences?

4. Farber cannot expect his readers to have seen all — if any — of the films he compares; does he give enough specific information about each so that the reader can tell what he is getting at? (We cannot, of course, expect him to provide a detailed plot summary of each film!)

5. Many writers on theory of film baffle the average reader either with technical terminology or with abstract philosophical disquisition. Does Farber successfully avoid both these dangers?

AFTERTHOUGHTS
ON MONTAGE

Sergei Eisenstein

Sergei Eisenstein (1898–1948) was the first great Russian film director. Three of his works, The Battleship Potemkin *(1925),* Ten Days that Shook the World *(1928), and* Alexander Nevsky *(1938), are still considered among the classic films of the century. In 1930, Eisenstein was invited to Hollywood to make movies, but Hollywood could not adjust to his techniques, he was publicly attacked as a Communist propagandist, and finally he was sent home without having completed a picture. His book,* The Film Sense *(1942) is generally considered the most difficult and the most knowledgeable work on film theory. The following passage, though tough going, gives a fair idea of Eisenstein's chief concerns as a director. It is an attempt to explain what went wrong with his earlier theory that montage is the most important aspect of film-making. (Montage is the art of cutting and splicing different shots to achieve special effects.)*

There was a period in Soviet cinema when montage was proclaimed   1
"everything." Now we are at the close of a period during which montage has been regarded as "nothing." Regarding montage neither as nothing nor everything, I consider it opportune at this juncture to recall that montage is just as indispensable a component feature of film production as any other element of film effectiveness. After the storm "for montage" and the battle "against montage," we must approach its problems simply and afresh. This is all the more necessary because in the period of "renunciation" of montage, its most incontrovertible aspect, the one really immune to challenge, was also repudiated. The point is that the creators of a number of films in recent years have so completely "discarded" montage that they have forgotten even its basic aim and function: that role set itself by every work of art, *the need for connected and sequential exposition of the theme, the material, the plot, the action,* the movement within the film sequence and within the film drama as a whole. Aside from the *excitement* of a story, or even

its logic or continuity, the simple matter of telling *a connected story* has often been lost in the works of some outstanding film masters, working in various types of films. What we need, of course, is not so much an individual criticism of those masters, but primarily an organized effort to recover the montage culture that so many have lost. This is all the more necessary since our films are faced with the task of presenting not only a narrative that is *logically connected,* but one that contains a *maximum of emotion and stimulating power.*

Montage is a mighty aid in the resolution of this task. 2

Why do we use montage at all? Even the most fanatical opponent of 3 montage will agree that it is not merely because the film strip at our disposal is not of infinite length, and consequently, being condemned to working with pieces of restricted lengths, we have to stick one piece of it on to another occasionally.

The "leftists" of montage saw it from the opposite extreme. While 4 playing with pieces of film, they discovered a certain property in the toy which kept them astonished for a number of years. This property consisted in the fact *that two film pieces of any kind, placed together, inevitably combine into a new concept, a new quality, arising out of that juxtaposition.*

This is not in the least a circumstance peculiar to the cinema, but is 5 a phenomenon invariably met with in all cases where we have to deal with juxtaposition of two facts, two phenomena, two objects. We are accustomed to make, almost automatically, a definite and obvious deductive generalization when any separate objects are placed before us side by side. For example, take a grave, juxtaposed with a woman in mourning weeping beside it, and scarcely anybody will fail to jump to the conclusion: *a widow.* It is precisely on this feature of our perception that the following miniature story by Ambrose Bierce bases its effect. It is from his *Fantastic Fables* and is entitled "The Inconsolable Widow":

> A Woman in widow's weeds was weeping upon a grave.
> "Console yourself, madam," said a Sympathetic Stranger. "Heaven's mercies are infinite. There is another man somewhere, besides your husband, with whom you can still be happy."
> "There was," she sobbed — "there was, but this is his grave."

The whole effect of this is built upon the circumstance that the grave 6 and the woman in mourning beside it lead to the inference, from established convention, that she is a widow mourning her husband, whereas in fact the man for whom she is weeping is her lover.

The same circumstance is often found in riddles — for example, this 7 one from international folk-lore: "The raven flew, while a dog sat on its tail. How can this be?" We automatically combine the juxtaposed elements and reduce them to a unity. As a result, we understand the query as though the dog were sitting on the tail of the raven, while actually, the riddle contains two unrelated actions: the raven flies, while the dog sits on its own tail.

This tendency to bring together into a unity two or more indepen- 8 dent objects or qualities is very strong, even in the case of separate words, characterizing different aspects of some single phenomenon.

An extreme instance of this can be found in that inventor of the 9 "portmanteau word," Lewis Carroll. His modest declaration of his invention, of "two meanings packed into one word like a portmanteau," concludes his introduction to *The Hunting of the Snark:*

> For instance, take the two words "fuming" and "furious." Make up your mind that you will say both words, but leave it unsettled which you will say first. Now open your mouth and speak. If your thoughts incline ever so little towards "fuming," you will say "fuming-furious"; if they turn, by even a hair's breadth, towards "furious," you will say "furious-fuming"; but if you have that rarest of gifts, a perfectly balanced mind, you will say "frumious."

Of course, in this instance we do not gain a new concept, or a new 10 quality. The charm of this "portmanteau" effect is built upon the sensation of duality residing in the arbitrarily formed single word. Every language has its "portmanteau" practitioner — the American language has its Walter Winchell. Obviously, the greatest manipulation of the portmanteau word is to be found in *Finnegans Wake.*

Essentially, therefore, Carroll's method is a *parody* of a natural phe- 11 nomenon, a part of our common perception — the formation of qualitatively new unities; hence it is a basic method of building comic effects.

This comic effect is achieved through the perception of both the new 12 result and its two independent parts — all at the same time. Instances of this kind of wit are innumerable. I shall cite here only three such examples that one can find — in Freud:

> During the war between Turkey and the Balkan States, in 1912, *Punch* depicted the part played by Roumania by representing the latter as a highwayman holding up the members of the Balkan alliance. The picture was entitled: *Kleptoroumania.* . . .

> A naughty jest of Europe has rebaptized a former potentate, Leopold, into *Cleopold* because of his relation to a lady surnamed Cleo. . . .

> In a short story . . . one of the characters, a "sport," speaks of the Christmas season as the *alcoholidays.* By reduction it can be easily seen that we have here a compound word, a combination of *alcohol* and *holidays.* . . .

I think it is apparent that the phenomenon we are discussing is more than widespread — it is literally universal. 13

Hence there is nothing surprising in the circumstance that a film audience also draws a definite inference from the juxtaposition of two strips of film cemented together. 14

We are certainly not criticizing all these facts, nor their noteworthiness, nor universality, but simply the false deductions and conclusions that have been drawn from them. On this basis it will be possible to make the necessary corrections. 15

Of what omission were we guilty when we first remarked the undoubted importance of the above phenomenon to an understanding and mastery of montage? What was true, and what false, in our enthusiastic declarations at that time? 16

The basic fact was true, and remains true to this day, that the juxtaposition of two separate shots by splicing them together resembles not so much a simple sum of one shot plus another shot — as it does a *creation*. It resembles a creation — rather than a sum of its parts — from the circumstance that in every such juxtaposition *the result is qualitatively* distinguishable from each component element viewed separately. At this late date no one need really be reminded that quantity and quality are not two different properties of a phenomenon but only different aspects of the same phenomenon. This law of physics is just as true in other spheres of science and in art. Of the many fields to which it can be applied, Professor Koffka's application of it to the field of behavior is apropos to our discussion: 17

> It has been said: The whole is more than the sum of its parts. It is more correct to say that the whole is something else than the sum of its parts, because summing is a meaningless procedure, whereas the whole-part relationship is meaningful.

The woman, to return to our first example, is a representation, the mourning robe she is wearing is a representation — that is, both are *objectively representable*. But *"a widow,"* arising from a juxtaposition of the two representations, is objectively unrepresentable — a new idea, a new conception, a new image. 18

What was the "distortion" in our attitude at that time to this indisputable phenomenon? 19

The error lay in placing the main emphasis on the possibilities of juxtaposition, while less attention seemed to be paid to the problem of *analyzing* the *material* that was juxtaposed. 20

My critics did not fail to represent this as a lack of interest in the 21
content of the film shot-pieces, confusing *research* in one aspect of a
problem with the attitude of the researcher to the representation of
reality.

I leave them to their consciences. 22

The trouble arose from my having been charmed primarily with that 23
newly revealed feature of the film strips — that, no matter how unrelated they might be, and frequently despite themselves, they engendered a "third something" and became correlated when juxtaposed
according to the will of an editor.

Hence I was preoccupied by a potentiality untypical in normal film 24
construction and film composition.

Operating at the outset with such material and such occurrences, it 25
was natural to speculate principally upon the potentialities of juxtaposition. Less attention was given to an *analysis* of the actual nature of the
pieces juxtaposed. Such attention would not have been sufficient in
itself. History has proven that such attention, directed solely to the
content of single shots, led in practice to a decline of montage to a level
of "special effects," "montage sequences," etc., with all the consequences this involved.

What should have been the proper emphasis, what should have re- 26
ceived the principal attention, in order that neither element would be
unduly exaggerated?

It was necessary to turn to that fundamental basis which equally 27
determines both the content enclosed by single frames and the compo-
sitional juxtaposition of these separate contents with each other, i.e., to
the content of the *whole,* of the general and *unifying* needs.

One extreme consisted in distraction with problems of the technique 28
of unification (the methods of montage), the other — with the unified
elements (the content of the shot).

We should have occupied ourselves more with an examination of the 29
nature of the *unifying principle* itself. This is precisely that principle
which should determine both the content of the shot and that content
which is revealed through a given *juxtaposition of these shots.*

But with this in mind it was necessary for the researcher's interest to 30
be turned primarily not in the direction of paradoxical cases, where this
whole, general, final result is not *foreseen* but emerges unexpectedly.
We should have turned to those cases where the shot-pieces are not only
not unrelated to each other, but where this *final,* this *general,* this
whole result is not merely foreseen, but itself predetermines both the
individual elements and the circumstances of their juxtaposition. Such
cases are normal, generally accepted and frequent in occurrence. In
such cases the whole emerges perfectly as "a third something." The full

picture of the whole, as determined both by the shot and by montage, also emerges, vivifying and distinguishing both the content of the shot and the content of the montage. It is cases of this kind that are typical for cinematography.

With montage considered in this light, both single shots and their 31 juxtaposition fall into a correct mutual relationship. In addition to this, the very nature of montage not only ceases to be divorced from the principles of realistic film delineation, but serves as one of the most coherent and practical resources for realistic narration of film content.

What is essentially involved in such an understanding of montage? In 32 such a case, each montage piece exists no longer as something un-related, but as a given *particular representation* of the general theme that in equal measure penetrates *all* the shot-pieces. The juxtaposition of these partial details in a given montage construction calls to life and forces into the light that *general* quality in which each detail has par-ticipated and which binds together all the details into a *whole,* namely, into that generalized *image,* wherein the creator, followed by the spec-tator, experiences the theme.

If *now* we consider two pieces of film placed together, we appreciate 33 their juxtaposition in a rather different light. Namely:

Piece *A* (derived from the elements of the theme being developed) 34 and piece *B* (derived from the same source) in juxtaposition give birth to the image in which the thematic matter is most clearly embodied.

Expressed in the imperative, for the sake of stating a more exact 35 working formula, this proposition would read:

Representation A and representation B must be so selected from all 36 the possible features within the theme that is being developed, must be so sought for, that their *juxtaposition* — that is, the juxtaposition of *those very elements* and not of alternative ones — shall evoke in the perception and feelings of the spectator the most complete *image of the theme itself.*

SUBJECT

1. Eisenstein does not explain why some directors had "re-nounced" montage; can you tell from the context what their objections were? Judging by recent movies you have seen, do modern directors employ or reject montage as a technique?

2. What is the difference between the effects of montage and of Lewis Carroll's "portmanteau" words?

3. What relationship is there between the theory of montage and the "Marxist dialectic"? Would this relationship explain why Russian directors — along with contemporary American "underground" film-

makers — are more devoted to montage than are most other directors?

4. What is the difference between the way Eisenstein did use montage and the way he thinks he *should* have used it? (It is interesting to note that the film which best exemplifies Eisenstein's new view, *Ivan the Terrible* (1946), got him into deep trouble with the Stalin government.)

5. Eisenstein's new theory is based on the assumption that the director has a "point" he wants to make — that is, that the film is essentially didactic. Does it follow that a "pointless" movie would have little use for montage? (Perhaps it does not matter what a pointless movie does. Do you think the best movies do have a message?)

STRUCTURE

1. Eisenstein cites a number of examples of what he is talking about — in fact, he overexplains a time or two. Why, then, is the writing as a whole so difficult? Is it that the subject is hard to explain, or that Eisenstein has not explained it as well as he might have?

2. What is the *basis of comparison* Eisenstein uses to establish the contrast between his past practice and the way he should have proceded? Does the repetition of his new principle "in the imperative" at the end make the contrast clearer?

3. A secondary contrast is set up between the use of montage and of "portmanteau" words; what is the basis of comparison in this instance? Are the things contrasted in the same class?

4. If you were grading Eisenstein's paper as an English composition, how would you advise him to revise it? Give specific suggestions.

COMEDY'S
GREATEST ERA

James Agee

James Agee (1910–1955) was one "literary" man who was not seriously frustrated by the restrictions of Hollywood script-writing. Best known today as a poet and author of the unfinished novel A Death in the Family, *Agee was also a film critic and one of the best of the Hollywood writers. Although he wrote and adapted filmscripts for numerous successful pictures, the classic is probably that for the Hepburn-Bogart* African Queen. *Agee's success was due partly to his intense love of film and partly to his recognition that its requirements and aims are very different from those of prose fiction. (See the Bergman essay that appeared earlier in this book.) As the following essay shows, Agee had a clear sense of what works and what doesn't work on film.*

In the language of screen comedians four of the main grades of laugh 1
are the titter, the yowl, the belly laugh and the boffo. The titter is just
a titter. The yowl is a runaway titter. Anyone who has ever had the
pleasure knows all about a belly laugh. The boffo is the laugh that kills.
An ideally good gag, perfectly constructed and played, would bring the
victim up this ladder of laughs by cruelly controlled degrees to the top
rung, and would then proceed to wobble, shake, wave and brandish the
ladder until he groaned for mercy. Then, after the shortest possible
time out for recuperation, he would feel the first wicked tickling of the
comedian's whip once more and start up a new ladder.

The reader can get a fair enough idea of the current state of screen 2
comedy by asking himself how long it has been since he has had that
treatment. The best of comedies these days hand out plenty of titters
and once in a while it is possible to achieve a yowl without overstrain-
ing. Even those who have never seen anything better must occasionally
have the feeling, as they watch the current run or, rather, trickle of
screen comedy, that they are having to make a little cause for laughter
go an awfully long way. And anyone who has watched screen comedy
over the past ten or fifteen years is bound to realize that it has quietly

but steadily deteriorated. As for those happy atavists who remember silent comedy in its heyday and the belly laughs and boffos that went with it, they have something close to an absolute standard by which to measure the deterioration.

When a modern comedian gets hit on the head, for example, the most   3
he is apt to do is look sleepy. When a silent comedian got hit on the head he seldom let it go so flatly. He realized a broad license, and a ruthless discipline within that license. It was his business to be as funny as possible physically, without the help or hindrance of words. So he gave us a figure of speech, or rather of vision, for loss of consciousness. In other words he gave us a poem, a kind of poem, moreover, that everybody understands. The least he might do was to straighten up stiff as a plank and fall over backward with such skill that his whole length seemed to slap the floor at the same instant. Or he might make a cadenza of it — look vague, smile like an angel, roll up his eyes, lace his fingers, thrust his hands palms downward as far as they would go, hunch his shoulders, rise on tiptoe, prance ecstatically in narrowing circles until, with tallow knees, he sank down the vortex of his dizziness to the floor and there signified nirvana by kicking his heels twice, like a swimming frog.

Startled by a cop, this same comedian might grab his hatbrim with   4
both hands and yank it down over his ears, jump high in the air, come to earth in a split violent enough to telescope his spine, spring thence into a coattail-flattening sprint and dwindle at rocket speed to the size of a gnat along the grand, forlorn perspective of some lazy back boulevard.

Those are fine clichés from the language of silent comedy in its in-   5
fancy. The man who could handle them properly combined several of the more difficult accomplishments of the acrobat, the dancer, the clown and the mime. Some very gifted comedians, unforgettably Ben Turpin, had an immense vocabulary of these clichés and were in part so lovable because they were deep conservative classicists and never tried to break away from them. The still more gifted men, of course, simplified and invented, finding out new and much deeper uses for the idiom. They learned to show emotion through it, and comic psychology, more eloquently than most language has ever managed to, and they discovered beauties of comic motion which are hopelessly beyond reach of words.

It is hard to find a theater these days where a comedy is playing; in   6
the days of the silents it was equally hard to find a theater which was not showing one. The laughs today are pitifully few, far between, shallow, quiet and short. They almost never build, as they used to, into something combining the jabbering frequency of a machine gun with

160

the delirious momentum of a roller coaster. Saddest of all, there are few comedians now below middle age and there are none who seem to learn much from picture to picture, or to try anything new.

To put it unkindly, the only thing wrong with screen comedy today   7
is that it takes place on a screen which talks. Because it talks, the only comedians who ever mastered the screen cannot work, for they cannot combine their comic style with talk. Because there is a screen, talking comedians are trapped into a continual exhibition of their inadequacy as screen comedians on a surface as big as the side of a barn.

At the moment, as for many years past, the chances to see silent   8
comedy are rare. There is a smattering of it on television — too often treated as something quaintly archaic, to be laughed at, not with. Some two hundred comedies — long and short — can be rented for home projection. And a lucky minority has access to the comedies in the collection of New York's Museum of Modern Art, which is still incomplete but which is probably the best in the world. In the near future, however, something of this lost art will return to regular theaters. A thick straw in the wind is the big business now being done by a series of revivals of W. C. Fields's memorable movies, a kind of comedy more akin to the old silent variety than anything which is being made today. Mack Sennett now is preparing a sort of potpourri variety show called *Down Memory Lane* made up out of his old movies, featuring people like Fields and Bing Crosby when they were movie beginners, but including also interludes from silents. Harold Lloyd has re-released *Movie Crazy*, a talkie, and plans to revive four of his best silent comedies, *Grandma's Boy, Safety Last, Speedy* and *The Freshman.* Buster Keaton hopes to remake at feature length, with a minimum of dialogue, two of the funniest short comedies ever made, one about a porous homemade boat and one about a prefabricated house.

Awaiting these happy events, we will discuss here what has gone   9
wrong with screen comedy and what, if anything, can be done about it. But mainly we will try to suggest what it was like in its glory in the years from 1912 to 1930, as practiced by the employees of Mack Sennett, the father of American screen comedy, and by the four most eminent masters: Charlie Chaplin, Harold Lloyd, the late Harry Langdon and Buster Keaton.

Mack Sennett made two kinds of comedy: parody laced with slap-   10
stick, and plain slapstick. The parodies were the unceremonious burial of a century of hamming, including the new hamming in serious movies, and nobody who has missed Ben Turpin in *A Small Town Idol,* or kidding Erich von Stroheim in *Three Foolish Weeks* or as *The Shriek*

161

of Araby, can imagine how rough parody can get and still remain subtle and roaringly funny. The plain slapstick, at its best, was even better: a profusion of hearty young women in disconcerting bathing suits, frisking around with a gaggle of insanely incompetent policemen and of equally certifiable male civilians sporting museum-piece mustaches. All these people zipped and caromed about the pristine world of the screen as jazzily as a convention of water bugs. Words can hardly suggest how energetically they collided and bounced apart, meeting in full gallop around the corner of a house; how hard and how often they fell on their backsides; or with what fantastically adroit clumsiness they got themselves fouled up in folding ladders, garden hoses, tethered animals and each other's headlong cross-purposes. The gestures were ferociously emphatic; not a line or motion of the body was wasted or inarticulate. The reader may remember how splendidly upright wandlike old Ben Turpin could stand for a Renunciation Scene, with his lampshade mustache twittering and his sparrowy chest stuck out and his head flung back like Paderewski assaulting a climax and the long babyish back hair trying to look lionlike, while his Adam's apple, an orange in a Christmas stocking, pumped with noble emotion. Or huge Mack Swain, who looked like a hairy mushroom, rolling his eyes in a manner patented by French romantics and gasping in some dubious ecstasy. Or Louise Fazenda, the perennial farmer's daughter and the perfect low-comedy housemaid, primping her spit curl; and how her hair tightened a good-looking face into the incarnation of rampant gullibility. Or snouty James Finlayson, gleefully foreclosing a mortgage, with his look of eternally tasting a spoiled pickle. Or Chester Conklin, a myopic and inebriated little walrus stumbling around in outsize pants. Or Fatty Arbuckle, with his cold eye and his loose, serene smile, his silky manipulation of his bulk and his satanic marksmanship with pies (he was ambidextrous and could simultaneously blind two people in opposite directions).

The intimate tastes and secret hopes of these poor ineligible dunces were ruthlessly exposed whenever a hot stove, an electric fan or a bulldog took a dislike to their outer garments: agonizingly elaborate drawers, worked up on some lonely evening out of some Godforsaken lace curtain; or men's underpants with big round black spots on them. The Sennett sets — delirious wallpaper, megalomaniacally scrolled iron beds, Grand Rapids *in extremis* — outdid even the underwear. It was their business, after all, to kid the squalid braggadocio which infested the domestic interiors of the period, and that was almost beyond parody. These comedies told their stories to the unaided eye, and by every means possible they screamed to it. That is one reason for the India ink silhouettes of the cops, and for convicts and prison bars and their shadows in hard sunlight, and for barefooted husbands, in tigerish pajamas, reacting like dervishes to stepped-on tacks.

The early silent comedians never strove for or consciously thought of anything which could be called artistic "form," but they achieved it. For Sennett's rival, Hal Roach, Leo McCarey once devoted almost the whole of a Laurel and Hardy two-reeler to pie throwing. The first pies were thrown thoughtfully, almost philosophically. Then innocent bystanders began to get caught into the vortex. At full pitch it was Armageddon. But everything was calculated so nicely that until late in the picture, when havoc took over, every pie made its special kind of point and piled on its special kind of laugh.   12

Sennett's comedies were just a shade faster and fizzier than life. According to legend (and according to Sennett) he discovered the tempo proper to screen comedy when a green cameraman, trying to save money, cranked too slow.[1] Realizing the tremendous drumlike power of mere motion to exhilarate, he gave inanimate objects a mischievous life of their own, broke every law of nature the tricked camera would serve him for and made the screen dance like a witches' Sabbath. The thing one is surest of all to remember is how toward the end of nearly every Sennett comedy, a chase (usually called the "rally") built up such a majestic trajectory of pure anarchic motion that bathing girls, cops, comics, dogs, cats, babies, automobiles, locomotives, innocent bystanders, sometimes what seemed like a whole city, an entire civilization, were hauled along head over heels in the wake of that energy like dry leaves following an express train.   13

"Nice" people, who shunned all movies in the early days, condemned the Sennett comedies as vulgar and naïve. But millions of less pretentious people loved their sincerity and sweetness, their wild-animal innocence and glorious vitality. They could not put these feelings into words, but they flocked to the silents. The reader who gets back deep enough into that world will probably even remember the theater: the barefaced honky-tonk and the waltzes by Waldteufel, slammed out on a mechanical piano; the searing redolence of peanuts and demirep perfumery, tobacco and feet and sweat; the laughter of unrespectable people having a hell of a fine time, laughter as violent and steady and deafening as standing under a waterfall.   14

Sennett wheedled his first financing out of a couple of ex-bookies to whom he was already in debt. He took his comics out of music halls,   15

---

[1]Silent comedy was shot at twelve to sixteen frames per second and was speeded up by being shown at sixteen frames per second, the usual rate of theater projectors at that time. Theater projectors today run at twenty-four, which makes modern film taken at the same speed seem smooth and natural. But it makes silent movies fast and jerky.

burlesque, vaudeville, circuses and limbo, and through them he tapped in on that great pipeline of horsing and miming which runs back unbroken through the fairs of the Middle Ages at least to ancient Greece. He added all that he himself had learned about the large and spurious gesture, the late decadence of the Grand Manner, as a stage-struck boy in East Berlin, Connecticut, and as a frustrated opera singer and actor. The only thing he claims to have invented is the pie in the face, and he insists, "Anyone who tells you he has discovered something new is a fool or a liar or both."

The silent-comedy studio was about the best training school the movies have ever known, and the Sennett studio was about as free and easy and as fecund of talent as they came. All the major comedians we will mention worked there, at least briefly. So did some of the major stars of the '20s and since — notably Gloria Swanson, Phyllis Haver, Wallace Beery, Marie Dressler and Carole Lombard. Directors Frank Capra, Leo McCarey and George Stevens also got their start in silent comedy; much that remains most flexible, spontaneous and visually alive in sound movies can be traced, through them and others, to this silent apprenticeship. Everybody did pretty much as he pleased on the Sennett lot, and everybody's ideas were welcome. Sennett posted no rules, and the only thing he strictly forbade was liquor. A Sennett story conference was a most informal affair. During the early years, at least, only the most important scenario might be jotted on the back of an envelope. Mainly Sennett's men thrashed out a few primary ideas and carried them in their heads, sure that better stuff would turn up while they were shooting, in the heat of physical action. This put quite a load on the prop man; he had to have the most improbable apparatus on hand — bombs, trick telephones, what not — to implement whatever idea might suddenly turn up. All kinds of things did — and were recklessly used. Once a low-comedy auto got out of control and killed the cameraman, but he was not visible in the shot, which was thrilling and undamaged; the audience never knew the difference.

Sennett used to hire a "wild man" to sit in on his gag conferences, whose whole job was to think up "wildies." Usually he was an all but brainless, speechless man, scarcely able to communicate his idea; but he had a totally uninhibited imagination. He might say nothing for an hour; then he'd mutter, "You take . . ." and all the relatively rational others would shut up and wait. "You take this cloud . . ." he would get out, sketching vague shapes in the air. Often he could get no further; but thanks to some kind of thought transference, saner men would take this cloud and make something of it. The wild man seems in fact to have functioned as the group's subconscious mind, the source of all creative energy. His ideas were so weird and amorphous that Sennett can no

16

17

164

longer remember a one of them, or even how it turned out after rational processing. But a fair equivalent might be one of the best comic sequences in a Laurel and Hardy picture. It is simple enough — simple and real, in fact, as a nightmare. Laurel and Hardy are trying to move a piano across a narrow suspension bridge. The bridge is slung over a sickening chasm, between a couple of Alps. Midway they meet a gorilla.

Had he done nothing else, Sennett would be remembered for giving   18
a start to three of the four comedians who now began to apply their sharp individual talents to this newborn language. The one whom he did not train (he was on the lot briefly but Sennett barely remembers seeing him around) wore glasses, smiled a great deal and looked like the sort of eager young man who might have quit divinity school to hustle brushes. That was Harold Lloyd. The others were grotesque and poetic in their screen characters in degrees which appear to be impossible when the magic of silence is broken. One, who never smiled, carried a face as still and sad as a daguerreotype through some of the most preposterously ingenious and visually satisfying physical comedy ever invented. That was Buster Keaton. One looked like an elderly baby and, at times, a baby dope fiend; he could do more with less than any other comedian. That was Harry Langdon. One looked like Charlie Chaplin, and he was the first man to give the silent language a soul.

When Charlie Chaplin started to work for Sennett he had chiefly to   19
reckon with Ford Sterling, the reigning comedian. Their first picture together amounted to a duel before the assembled professionals. Sterling, by no means untalented, was a big man with a florid Teutonic style which, under this special pressure, he turned on full blast. Chaplin defeated him within a few minutes with a wink of the mustache, a hitch of the trousers, a quirk of the little finger.

With *Tillie's Punctured Romance,* in 1914, he became a major star.   20
Soon after, he left Sennett when Sennett refused to start a landslide among the other comedians by meeting the raise Chaplin demanded. Sennett is understandably wry about it in retrospect, but he still says, "I was right at the time." Of Chaplin he says simply, "Oh well, he's just the greatest artist that ever lived." None of Chaplin's former rivals rates him much lower than that; they speak of him no more jealously than they might of God. We will try here only to suggest the essence of his supremacy. Of all comedians he worked most deeply and most shrewdly within a realization of what a human being is, and is up against. The Tramp is as centrally representative of humanity, as many-sided and as mysterious, as Hamlet, and it seems unlikely that any dancer or actor can ever have excelled him in eloquence, variety or poignancy of motion. As for pure motion, even if he had never gone on

to make his magnificent feature-length comedies, Chaplin would have made his period in movies a great one singlehanded even if he had made nothing except *The Cure,* or *One* A.M. In the latter, barring one immobile taxi driver, Chaplin plays alone, as a drunk trying to get upstairs and into bed. It is a sort of inspired elaboration on a soft-shoe dance, involving an angry stuffed wildcat, small rugs on slippery floors, a Lazy Susan table, exquisite footwork on a flight of stairs, a contretemps with a huge, ferocious pendulum and the funniest and most perverse Murphy bed in movie history — and, always made physically lucid, the delicately weird mental processes of a man ethereally sozzled.

Before Chaplin came to pictures people were content with a couple   21 of gags per comedy; he got some kind of laugh every second. The minute he began to work he set standards — and continually forced them higher. Anyone who saw Chaplin eating a boiled shoe like brook trout in *The Gold Rush,* or embarrassed by a swallowed whistle in *City Lights,* has seen perfection. Most of the time, however, Chaplin got his laughter less from the gags, or from milking them in any ordinary sense, than through his genius for what may be called *inflection* — the perfect, changeful shading of his physical and emotional attitudes toward the gag. Funny as his bout with the Murphy bed is, the glances of awe, expostulation and helpless, almost whimpering desire for vengeance which he darts at this infernal machine are even better.

A painful and frequent error among tyros is breaking the comic line   22 with a too-big laugh, then a letdown; or with a laugh which is out of key or irrelevant. The masters could ornament the main line beautifully; they never addled it. In *A Night Out* Chaplin, passed out, is hauled along the sidewalk by the scruff of his coat by staggering Ben Turpin. His toes trail; he is as supine as a sled. Turpin himself is so drunk he can hardly drag him. Chaplin comes quietly to, realizes how well he is being served by his struggling pal, and with a royally delicate gesture plucks and savors a flower.

The finest pantomime, the deepest emotion, the richest and most   23 poignant poetry were in Chaplin's work. He could probably pantomime Bryce's *The American Commonwealth* without ever blurring a syllable and make it paralyzingly funny into the bargain. At the end of *City Lights* the blind girl who has regained her sight, thanks to the Tramp, sees him for the first time. She has imagined and anticipated him as princely, to say the least; and it has never seriously occurred to him that he is inadequate. She recognizes who he must be by his shy, confident, shining joy as he comes silently toward her. And he recognizes himself, for the first time, through the terrible changes in her face. The camera just exchanges a few quiet close-ups of the emotions which shift and intensify in each face. It is enough to shrivel the heart to see, and it is the greatest piece of acting and the highest moment in movies.

Harold Lloyd worked only a little while with Sennett. During most 24 of his career he acted for another major comedy producer, Hal Roach. He tried at first to offset Chaplin's influence and establish his own individuality by playing Chaplin's exact opposite, a character named Lonesome Luke who wore clothes much too small for him and whose gestures were likewise as un-Chaplinesque as possible. But he soon realized that an opposite in itself was a kind of slavishness. He discovered his own comic identity when he saw a movie about a fighting parson: a hero who wore glasses. He began to think about those glasses day and night. He decided on horn rims because they were youthful, ultravisible on the screen and on the verge of becoming fashionable (he was to make them so). Around these large lensless horn rims he began to develop a new character, nothing grotesque or eccentric, but a fresh, believable young man who could fit into a wide variety of stories.

Lloyd depended more on story and situation than any of the other 25 major comedians (he kept the best stable of gagmen in Hollywood, at one time hiring six); but unlike most "story" comedians he was also a very funny man from inside. He had, as he has written, "an unusually large comic vocabulary." More particularly he had an expertly expressive body and even more expressive teeth, and out of his thesaurus of smiles he could at a moment's notice blend prissiness, breeziness and asininity, and still remain tremendously likable. His movies were more extroverted and closer to ordinary life than any others of the best comedies: the vicissitudes of a New York taxi driver; the unaccepted college boy who, by desperate courage and inspired ineptitude, wins the Big Game. He was especially good at putting a very timid, spoiled or brassy young fellow through devastating embarrassments. He went through one of his most uproarious Gethsemanes as a shy country youth courting the nicest girl in town in *Grandma's Boy*. He arrived dressed "strictly up to date for the Spring of 1862," as a subtitle observed, and found that the ancient colored butler wore a similar flowered waistcoat and moldering cutaway. He got one wandering, nervous forefinger dreadfully stuck in a fancy little vase. The girl began to try to identify that queer smell which dilated from him; Grandpa's best suit was rife with mothballs. A tenacious litter of kittens feasted off the goose grease on his home-shined shoes.

Lloyd was even better at the comedy of thrills. In *Safety Last*, as a 26 rank amateur, he is forced to substitute for a human fly and to climb a medium-sized skyscraper. Dozens of awful things happen to him. He gets fouled up in a tennis net. Popcorn falls on him from a window above, and the local pigeons treat him like a cross between a lunch wagon and St. Francis of Assisi. A mouse runs up his britches leg, and the crowd below salutes his desperate dance on the window ledge with wild applause of the daredevil. A good deal of this full-length picture hangs thus by its eyelashes along the face of a building. Each new floor is like a new stanza in a poem; and the higher and more horrifying it gets, the funnier it gets.

In this movie Lloyd demonstrates beautifully his ability to do more than merely milk a gag, but to top it. (In an old, simple example of topping, an incredible number of tall men get, one by one, out of a small closed auto. After as many have clambered out as the joke will bear, one more steps out: a midget. That tops the gag. Then the auto collapses. That tops the topper.) In *Safety Last* Lloyd is driven out to the dirty end of a flagpole by a furious dog; the pole breaks and he falls, just managing to grab the minute hand of a huge clock. His weight promptly pulls the hand down from IX to VI. That would be more than enough for any ordinary comedian, but there is further logic in the situation. Now, hideously, the whole clockface pulls loose and slants from its trembling springs above the street. Getting out of difficulty with the clock, he makes still further use of the instrument by getting one foot caught in one of these obstinate springs.

A proper delaying of the ultrapredictable can of course be just as funny as a properly timed explosion of the unexpected. As Lloyd approaches the end of his horrible hegira up the side of the building in *Safety Last,* it becomes clear to the audience, but not to him, that if he raises his head another couple of inches he is going to get murderously conked by one of the four arms of a revolving wind gauge. He delays the evil moment almost interminably, with one distraction and another, and every delay is a suspense-tightening laugh; he also gets his foot nicely entangled in a rope, so that when he does get hit, the payoff of one gag sends him careening head downward through the abyss into another. Lloyd was outstanding even among the master craftsmen at setting up a gag clearly, culminating and getting out of it deftly, and linking it smoothly to the next. Harsh experience also taught him a deep and fundamental rule: Never try to get "above" the audience.

Lloyd tried it in *The Freshman.* He was to wear an unfinished, basted-together tuxedo to a college party, which would gradually, fall apart as he danced. Lloyd decided to skip the pants, a low-comedy cliché, and lose just the coat. His gag men warned him. A preview proved how right they were. Lloyd had to reshoot the whole expensive sequence,

27

28

29

build it around defective pants and climax it with the inevitable. It was one of the funniest things he ever did.

When Lloyd was still a very young man he lost about half his right 30 hand (and nearly lost his sight) when a comedy bomb exploded prematurely. But in spite of his artificially built-out hand he continued to do his own dirty work, like all of the best comedians. The side of the building he climbed in *Safety Last* did not overhang the street, as it appears to. But the nearest landing place was a roof three floors below him, as he approached the top, and he did everything, of course, the hard way, i.e., the comic way, keeping his bottom stuck well out, his shoulders hunched, his hands and feet skidding over perdition.

If great comedy must involve something beyond laughter, Lloyd was 31 not a great comedian. If plain laughter is any criterion — and it is a healthy counterbalance to the other — few people have equaled him, and nobody has ever beaten him.

Chaplin and Keaton and Lloyd were all more like each other, in one 32 important way, than Harry Langdon was like any of them. Whatever else the others might be doing, they all used more or less elaborate physical comedy; Langdon showed how little of that one might use and still be a great silent-screen comedian. In his screen character he symbolized something as deeply and centrally human, though by no means as rangily so, as the Tramp. There was, of course, an immense difference in inventiveness and range of virtuosity. It seemed as if Chaplin could do literally anything, on any instrument in the orchestra. Langdon had one queerly toned, unique little reed. But out of it he could get incredible melodies.

Like Chaplin, Langdon wore a coat which buttoned on his wishbone 33 and swung out wide below, but the effect was very different: he seemed like an outsized baby who had begun to outgrow his clothes. The crown of his hat was rounded and the brim was turned up all around, like a little boy's hat, and he looked as if he wore diapers under his pants. His walk was that of a child which has just got sure on its feet, and his body and hands fitted that age. His face was kept pale to show off, with the simplicity of a nursery school drawing, the bright, ignorant, gentle eyes and the little twirling mouth. He had big moon cheeks, with dimples, and a Napoleonic forelock of mousy hair; the round, docile head seemed large in ratio to the cream-puff body. Twitchings of his face were signals of tiny discomforts too slowly registered by a tinier brain; quick, squirty little smiles showed his almost prehuman pleasures, his incurably premature trustfulness. He was a virtuoso of hesitations and of delicately indecisive motions, and he was particularly fine in a high wind, rounding a corner with a kind of skittering toddle, both hands nursing his hatbrim.

He was as remarkable a master as Chaplin of subtle emotional and 34
mental process and operated much more at leisure. He once got a good three hundred feet of continuously bigger laughs out of rubbing his chest, in a crowded vehicle, with Limburger cheese, under the misapprehension that it was a cold salve. In another long scene, watching a brazen show girl change her clothes, he sat motionless, back to the camera, and registered the whole lexicon of lost innocence, shock, disapproval and disgust, with the back of his neck. His scenes with women were nearly always something special. Once a lady spy did everything in her power (under the Hays Office) to seduce him. Harry was polite, willing, even flirtatious in his little way. The only trouble was that he couldn't imagine what in the world she was leering and pawing at him for, and that he was terribly ticklish. The Mata Hari wound up foaming at the mouth.

There was also a sinister flicker of depravity about the Langdon 35
character, all the more disturbing because babies are premoral. He had an instinct for bringing his actual adulthood and figurative babyishness into frictions as crawly as a fingernail on a slate blackboard, and he wandered into areas of strangeness which were beyond the other comedians. In a nightmare in one movie he was forced to fight a large, muscular young man; the girl Harry loved was the prize. The young man was a good boxer; Harry could scarcely lift his gloves. The contest took place in a fiercely lighted prize ring, in a prodigious pitch-dark arena. The only spectator was the girl, and she was rooting against Harry. As the fight went on, her eyes glittered ever more brightly with blood lust and, with glittering teeth, she tore her big straw hat to shreds.

Langdon came to Sennett from a vaudeville act in which he had 36
fought a losing battle with a recalcitrant automobile. The minute Frank Capra saw him he begged Sennett to let him work with him. Langdon was almost as childlike as the character he played. He had only a vague idea of his story or even of each scene as he played it; each time he went before the camera Capra would brief him on the general situation and then, as this finest of intuitive improvisers once tried to explain his work, "I'd go into my routine." The whole tragedy of the coming of dialogue as far as these comedians were concerned — and one reason for the increasing rigidity of comedy ever since — can be epitomized in the mere thought of Harry Langdon confronted with a script.

Langdon's magic was in his innocence, and Capra took beautiful care 37
not to meddle with it. The key to the proper use of Langdon, Capra always knew, was "the principle of the brick." "If there was a rule for

170

writing Langdon material," he explains, "it was this: His only ally was God. Langdon might be saved by the brick falling on the cop, but it was *verboten* that he in any way motivate the brick's fall." Langdon became quickly and fantastically popular with three pictures, *Tramp, Tramp, Tramp, The Strong Man* and *Long Pants;* from then on he went downhill even faster. "The trouble was," Capra says, "that high-brow critics came around to explain his art to him. Also he developed an interest in dames. It was a pretty high life for such a little fellow." Langdon made two more pictures with highbrow writers, one of which *(Three's a Crowd)* had some wonderful passages in it, including the prize-ring nightmare; then First National canceled his contract. He was reduced to mediocre roles and two-reelers which were more rehashes of his old gags; this time around they no longer seemed funny. "He never did really understand what hit him," says Capra. "He died broke [in 1944]. And he died of a broken heart. He was the most tragic figure I ever came across in show business."

Buster Keaton started work at the age of three and a half with his parents in one of the roughest acts in vaudeville ("The Three Keatons"); Harry Houdini gave the child the name Buster in admiration for a fall he took down a flight of stairs. In his first movies Keaton teamed with Fatty Arbuckle under Sennett. He went on to become one of Metro's biggest stars and earners; a Keaton feature cost about $200,000 to make and reliably grossed $2 million. Very early in his movie career friends asked him why he never smiled on the screen. He didn't realize he didn't. He had got the deadpan habit in variety; on the screen he had merely been so hard at work it had never occurred to him there was anything to smile about. Now he tried it just once and never again. He was by his whole style and nature so much the most deeply "silent" of the silent comedians that even a smile was as deafeningly out of key as a yell. In a way his pictures are like a transcendent juggling act in which it seems that the whole universe is in exquisite flying motion and the one point of repose is the juggler's effortless, uninterested face.

Keaton's face ranked almost with Lincoln's as an early American archetype; it was haunting, handsome, almost beautiful, yet it was irreducibly funny; he improved matters by topping it off with a deadly horizontal hat, as flat and thin as a phonograph record. One can never forget Keaton wearing it, standing erect at the prow as his little boat is being launched. The boat goes grandly down the skids and, just as grandly, straight on to the bottom. Keaton never budges. The last you see of him, the water lifts the hat off the stoic head and it floats away.

171

No other comedian could do as much with the deadpan. He used this   40
great, sad, motionless face to suggest various related things: a one-track
mind near the track's end of pure insanity; mulish imperturbability
under the wildest of circumstances; how dead a human being can get
and still be alive; an awe-inspiring sort of patience and power to endure,
proper to granite but uncanny in flesh and blood. Everything that he
was and did bore out this rigid face and played laughs against it. When
he moved his eyes, it was like seeing them move in a statue. His short-
legged body was all sudden, machinelike angles, governed by a daft
aplomb. When he swept a semaphorelike arm to point, you could almost
hear the electrical impulse in the signal block. When he ran from a cop
his transitions from accelerating walk to easy jog trot to brisk canter to
headlong gallop to flogged-piston sprint — always floating, above this
frenzy, the untroubled, untouchable face — were as distinct and as
soberly in order as an automatic gearshift.

Keaton was a wonderfully resourceful inventor of mechanistic gags   41
(he still spends much of his time fooling with Erector sets); as he ran
afoul of locomotives, steamships, prefabricated and overelectrified
houses, he put himself through some of the hardest and cleverest punishment ever designed for laughs. In *Sherlock Jr.,* boiling along on the
handlebars of a motorcycle quite unaware that he has lost his driver,
Keaton whips through city traffic, breaks up a tug-of-war, gets a shovel-
ful of dirt in the face from each of a long line of Rockette-timed
ditchdiggers, approaches at high speed a log which is hinged open by
dynamite precisely soon enough to let him through and, hitting an
obstruction, leaves the handlebars like an arrow leaving a bow, whams
through the window of a shack in which the heroine is about to be
violated, and hits the heavy feet first, knocking him through the opposite wall. The whole sequence is as clean in motion as the trajectory of
a bullet.

Much of the charm and edge of Keaton's comedy, however, lay in the   42
subtle leverages of expression he could work against his nominal deadpan. Trapped in the side wheel of a ferryboat, saving himself from
drowning only by walking, then desperately running, inside the accelerating wheel like a squirrel in a cage, his only real concern was,
obviously, to keep his hat on. Confronted by Love, he was not as deadpan as he was cracked up to be, either; there was an odd, abrupt motion
of his head which suggested a horse nipping after a sugar lump.

Keaton worked strictly for laughs, but his work came from so far   43
inside a curious and original spirit that he achieved a great deal besides,
especially in his feature-length comedies. (For plain hard laughter his
nineteen short comedies — the negatives of which have been lost —
were even better.) He was the only major comedian who kept senti-

ment almost entirely out of his work, and he brought pure physical comedy to its greatest heights. Beneath his lack of emotion he was also uninsistently sardonic; deep below that, giving a disturbing tension and grandeur to the foolishness, for those who sensed it, there was in his comedy a freezing whisper not of pathos but of melancholia. With the humor, the craftsmanship and the action there was often, besides, a fine, still and sometimes dreamlike beauty. Much of his Civil War picture *The General* is within hailing distance of Mathew Brady. And there is a ghostly, unforgettable moment in *The Navigator* when, on a deserted, softly rolling ship, all the pale doors along a deck swing open as one behind Keaton and, as one, slam shut, in a hair-raising illusion of noise.

Perhaps because "dry" comedy is so much more rare and odd than "dry" wit, there are people who never much cared for Keaton. Those who do cannot care mildly.   44

As soon as the screen began to talk, silent comedy was pretty well finished. The hardy and prolific Mack Sennett made the transfer; he was the first man to put Bing Crosby and W. C. Fields on the screen. But he was essentially a silent-picture man, and by the time the Academy awarded him a special Oscar for his "lasting contribution to the comedy technique of the screen" (in 1938), he was no longer active. As for the comedians we have spoken of in particular, they were as badly off as fine dancers suddenly required to appear in plays.   45

Harold Lloyd, whose work was most nearly realistic, naturally coped least unhappily with the added realism of speech; he made several talking comedies. But good as the best were, they were not so good as his silent work, and by the late '30s he quit acting. A few years ago he returned to play the lead (and play it beautifully) in Preston Sturges' *The Sin of Harold Diddlebock,* but this exceptional picture — which opened, brilliantly, with the closing reel of Lloyd's *The Freshman* — has not yet been generally released.   46

Like Chaplin, Lloyd was careful of his money; he is still rich and active. Last June, in the presence of President Truman, he became Imperial Potentate of the A.A.O.N.M.S. (Shriners). Harry Langdon, as we have said, was a broken man when sound came in.   47

Up to the middle '30s Buster Keaton made several feature-length pictures (with such players as Jimmy Durante, Wallace Beery and Robert Montgomery); he also made a couple of dozen talking shorts. Now and again he managed to get loose into motion, without having to talk, and for a moment or so the screen would start singing again. But his dark, dead voice, though it was in keeping with the visual character, tore his intensely silent style to bits and destroyed the illusion within   48

173

which he worked. He gallantly and correctly refuses to regard himself as "retired." Besides occasional bits, spots and minor roles in Hollywood pictures, he has worked on summer stages, made talking comedies in France and Mexico and clowned in a French circus. This summer he has played the straw hats in *Three Men on a Horse.* He is planning a television program. He also has a working agreement with Metro. One of his jobs there is to construct comedy sequences for Red Skelton.

The only man who really survived the flood was Chaplin, the only one 49 who was rich, proud and popular enough to afford to stay silent. He brought out two of his greatest nontalking comedies, *City Lights* and *Modern Times,* in the middle of an avalanche of talk, spoke gibberish and, in the closing moments, plain English in *The Great Dictator,* and at last made an all-talking picture, *Monsieur Verdoux,* creating for that purpose an entirely new character who might properly talk a blue streak. *Verdoux* is the greatest of talking comedies though so cold and savage that it had to find its public in grimly experienced Europe.

Good comedy, and some that was better than good, outlived silence, 50 but there has been less and less of it. The talkies brought one great comedian, the late, majestically lethargic W. C. Fields, who could not possibly have worked well in silence; he was the toughest and the most warmly human of all screen comedians, and *It's a Gift* and *The Bank Dick,* fiendishly funny and incisive white-collar comedies, rank high among the best comedies (and best movies) ever made. Laurel and Hardy, the only comedians who managed to preserve much of the large, low style of silence and who began to explore the comedy of sound, have made nothing since 1945. Walt Disney, at his best an inspired comic inventor and teller of fairy stories, lost his stride during the war and has since regained it only at moments. Preston Sturges has made brilliant, satirical comedies, but his pictures are smart, nervous comedy-dramas merely italicized with slapstick. The Marx Brothers were sidesplitters but they made their best comedies years ago. Jimmy Durante is mainly a night-club genius; Abbott and Costello are semi-skilled laborers, at best; Bob Hope is a good radio comedian with a pleasing presence, but not much more, on the screen.

There is no hope that screen comedy will get much better than it is 51 without new, gifted young comedians who really belong in movies, and without freedom for their experiments. For every one who may appear we have one last, invidious comparison to offer as a guidepost.

One of the most popular recent comedies is Bob Hope's *The Paleface.* 52 We take no pleasure in blackening *The Paleface;* we single it out, rather, because it is as good as we've got. Anything that is said of it here could be said, with interest, of other comedies of our time. Most of the laughs in *The Paleface* are verbal. Bob Hope is very adroit with his lines and now and then, when the words don't get in the way, he makes a good beginning as a visual comedian. But only the beginning, never the middle or the end. He is funny, for instance, reacting to a shot of violent whisky. But he does not know how to get still funnier (i.e., how to build and milk) or how to be funniest last (i.e., how to top or cap his gag). The camera has to fade out on the same old face he started with.

One sequence is promisingly set up for visual comedy. In it, Hope and 53 a lethal local boy stalk each other all over a cow town through streets which have been emptied in fear of their duel. The gag here is that through accident and stupidity they keep just failing to find each other. Some of it is quite funny. But the fun slackens between laughs like a weak clothesline, and by all the logic of humor (which is ruthlessly logical) the biggest laugh should come at the moment, and through the way, they finally spot each other. The sequence is so weakly thought out that at that crucial moment the camera can't afford to watch them; it switches to Jane Russell.

Now we turn to a masterpiece. In *The Navigator* Buster Keaton 54 works with practically the same gag as Hope's duel. Adrift on a ship which he believes is otherwise empty, he drops a lighted cigarette. A girl finds it. She calls out and he hears her; each then tries to find the other. First each walks purposefully down the long, vacant starboard deck, the girl, then Keaton, turning the corner just in time not to see each other. Next time around each of them is trotting briskly, very much in earnest; going at the same pace, they miss each other just the same. Next time around each of them is going like a bat out of hell. Again they miss. Then the camera withdraws to a point of vantage at the stern, leans its chin in its hand and just watches the whole intricate superstructure of the ship as the protagonists stroll, steal and scuttle from level to level, up, down and sidewise, always managing to miss each other by hairbreadths, in an enchantingly neat and elaborate piece of timing. There are no subsidiary gags to get laughs in this sequence and there is little loud laughter; merely a quiet and steadily increasing kind of delight. When Keaton has got all he can out of this fine modification of the movie chase he invents a fine device to bring the two together: the girl, thoroughly winded, sits down for a breather, indoors, on a plank which workmen have left across sawhorses. Keaton pauses on an upper deck, equally winded and puzzled. What follows happens in a couple of seconds at most: Air suction whips his silk topper backward down a ventilator; grabbing frantically for it, he backs against the lip of the ventilator, jackknifes and falls in backward. Instantly the camera cuts back to the girl. A topper falls through the ceiling and lands tidily, right side up, on the plank beside her. Before she can look more than startled, its owner follows, head between his knees, crushes the topper, breaks the plank with the point of his spine and proceeds to the floor. The breaking of the plank smacks Boy and Girl together.

It is only fair to remember that the silent comedians would have as 55 hard a time playing a talking scene as Hope has playing his visual ones, and that writing and directing are as accountable for the failure as Hope himself. But not even the humblest journeymen of the silent years would have let themselves off so easily. Like the masters, they knew, and sweated to obey, the laws of their craft.

Subject

1. At the beginning of this essay, Agee seems to say that it was the invention of sound which ruined comedy's greatest era; at the end, he appears to blame the decline on incompetent acting and directing. Is he contradicting himself, or do these two causes go together?

2. If you had never seen a silent comedy, could you get a fair idea of how the old stars worked by Agee's description?

3. As Agee discusses each of the four great silent stars, the reader is likely to get the idea that *this* one was the best; does Agee make clear in what *way* each was best?

4. This essay was written 20 years after the advent of talking pictures, but still more than 20 years ago. Do you think comedy has improved since Agee lamented its decline? Have any truly great comic actors emerged recently? If you can think of some, are any of them American?

5. Agee seems to miss an important reason for the decline of the kind of comedy he liked in the silent films: why is it impossible for talking pictures to generate sustained laughter in the audience?

Structure

1. This essay contains both a contrast between silent comedy and "modern" comedy, and a comparison of four great silent-film stars. On what basis does Agee contrast silent with talking comedy? How is he able to account for the fact that W. C. Fields made great talkies?

2. On what basis (or bases) does Agee compare Chaplin, Lloyd, Keaton, and Langdon? Does he make clear their similarities as well as their differences?

3. Agee cannot expect his readers to be familiar with all the films and actors he discusses; it is his responsibility then to provide vivid concrete examples to support his comparisons. Does he do this consistently?

4. Agee provides one direct contrast between two ways of handling a similar situation, one by Bob Hope and one by Buster Keaton. Does the example clearly establish the superiority of the silent version? Why has Agee put this example almost at the end of his article?

5. Compare the style of this essay with that of others in this section. This is the only one written for a very general audience, the readers of *Life;* is there any noticeable difference in the level of language?

A PATRIOTIC SHORT

F. Scott Fitzgerald

F. Scott Fitzgerald (1896–1940) was a literary lion of the 1920s and early 30s. But because he wanted to live the image of the roaring twenties, he always spent money faster than he could earn it. His best books, The Great Gatsby *(1925) and* Tender is the Night *(1934), could not sustain the kind of life he wanted. Finally he went to Hollywood as a script writer in 1937, but his genius was channeled into comparatively mundane tasks, at which he was no better than many another lesser talent. Disillusioned, ill, with rapidly dwindling fortunes, he turned again to alcohol and drugs. Although Fitzgerald controlled this problem eventually, he was never again to enjoy the steady, high-salaried work which took him to Hollywood. During the last 15 months of his life, Fitzgerald supported himself largely by writing for* Esquire *seventeen stories about Pat Hobby, a down-and-out Hollywood writer. While Hobby can hardly be taken as a representation of the author, clearly Fitzgerald did invest these stories with some of his own frustrations and disappointments. The story included here draws an interesting contrast between the Pat Hobby of the good old days and the indigent hack-writer of 1939.*

Pat Hobby, the writer and the man, had his great success in Hollywood during what Irvin Cobb refers to as "the mosaic swimming-pool age — just before the era when they had to have a shinbone of St. Sebastian for a clutch lever." 1

Mr. Cobb no doubt exaggerates, for when Pat had his pool in those fat days of silent pictures, it was entirely cement, unless you should count the cracks where the water stubbornly sought its own level through the mud. 2

"But it *was* a pool," he assured himself one afternoon more than a decade later. Though he was now more than grateful for this small chore he had assigned him by producer Berners — one week at two-fifty — all the insolence of office could not take that memory away. 3

He had been called in to the studio to work upon an humble short. 4
It was based on the career of General Fitzhugh Lee who fought for the
Confederacy and later for the U.S.A. against Spain — so it would
offend neither North nor South. And in the recent conference Pat had
tried to co-operate.

"I was thinking — " he suggested to Jack Berners " — that it might 5
be a good thing if we could give it a Jewish touch."

"What do you mean?" demanded Jack Berners quickly. 6

"Well I thought — the way things are and all, it would be a sort of 7
good thing to show that there were a number of Jews in it too."

"In what?" 8

"In the Civil War." Quickly he reviewed his meager history. "They 9
were, weren't they?"

"Naturally," said Berners, with some impatience, "I suppose every- 10
body was except the Quakers."

"Well, my idea was that we could have this Fitzhugh Lee in love with 11
a Jewish girl. He's going to be shot at curfew so she grabs a church bell
— "

Jack Berners leaned forward earnestly. 12

"Say, Pat, you want this job, don't you? Well, I told you the story. You 13
got the first script. If you thought up this tripe to please me you're losing
your grip."

Was that a way to treat a man who had once owned a pool which had 14
been talked about by —

That was how he happened to be thinking about his long lost swim- 15
ming pool as he entered the shorts department. He was remembering
a certain day over a decade ago in all its details, how he had arrived at
the studio in his car driven by a Filipino in uniform; the deferential bow
of the guard at the gate which had admitted car and all to the lot, his
ascent to that long lost office which had a room for the secretary and
was really a director's office . . .

His reverie was broken off by the voice of Ben Brown, head of the 16
shorts department, who walked him into his own chambers.

"Jack Berners just phoned me," he said. "We don't want any new 17
angles, Pat. We've got a good story. Fitzhugh Lee was a dashing cavalry
commander. He was a nephew of Robert E. Lee and we want to show
him at Appomattox, pretty bitter and all that. And then show how he
became reconciled — we'll have to be careful because Virginia is
swarming with Lees — and how he finally accepts a U.S. commission
from President McKinley — "

Pat's mind darted back again into the past. The President — that 18
was the magic word that had gone around that morning many years
ago. The President of the United States was going to make a visit to the

lot. Everyone had been agog about it — it seemed to mark a new era in pictures because a President of the United States had never visited a studio before. The executives of the company were all dressed up — from a window of his long lost Beverly Hills house Pat had seen Mr. Maranda, whose mansion was next door to him, bustle down his walk in a cutaway coat at nine o'clock, and had known that something was up. He thought maybe it was clergy but when he reached the lot he had found it was the President of the United States himself who was coming . . .

"Clean up the stuff about Spain," Ben Brown was saying. "The guy 19
that wrote it was a Red and he's got all the Spanish officers with ants in their pants. Fix up that."

In the office assigned him Pat looked at the script of *True to Two* 20
Flags. The first scene showed General Fitzhugh Lee at the head of his cavalry receiving word that Petersburg had been evacuated. In the script Lee took the blow in pantomine, but Pat was getting two-fifty a week — so, casually and without effort, he wrote in one of his favorite lines:

LEE: (*to his officers*)

Well, what are you standing here gawking for? DO *something! 6.*
Medium Shot. Officers pepping up, slapping each other on back, etc.

Dissolve to:

To what? Pat's mind dissolved once more into the glamorous past. On 21
that happy day in the twenties his phone had rung at about noon. It had been Mr. Maranda.

"Pat, the President is lunching in the private dining room. Doug 22
Fairbanks can't come so there's a place empty and anyhow we think there ought to be one writer there."

His memory of the luncheon was palpitant with glamor. The Great 23
Man had asked some questions about pictures and had told a joke and Pat had laughed and laughed with the others — all of them solid men together — rich, happy and successful.

Afterwards the President was to go on some sets and see some scenes 24
taken and still later he was going to Mr. Maranda's house to meet some of the women stars at tea. Pat was not invited to that party but he went home early anyhow and from his veranda saw the cortège drive up, with Mr. Maranda beside the President in the back seat. Ah he was proud of pictures then — of his position in them — of the President of the happy country where he was born . . .

Returning to reality Pat looked down at the script of *True to Two* 25
Flags and wrote slowly and thoughtfully: *Insert: A calendar — with*

the years plainly marked and the sheets blowing off in a cold wind, to show Fitzhugh Lee growing older and older.

His labors had made him thirsty — not for water, but he knew better than to take anything else his first day on the job. He got up and went out into the hall and along the corridor to the water-cooler. 26

As he walked he slipped back into his reverie. 27

That had been a lovely California afternoon so Mr. Maranda had taken his exalted guest and the coterie of stars into his garden, which adjoined Pat's garden. Pat had gone out his back door and followed a low privet hedge keeping out of sight — and then accidentally come face to face with the Presidential party. 28

The President had smiled and nodded. Mr. Maranda smiled and nodded. 29

"You met Mr. Hobby at lunch," Mr. Maranda said to the President. "He's one of our writers." 30

"Oh yes," said the President, "you write the pictures." 31

"Yes I do," said Pat. 32

The President glanced over into Pat's property. 33

"I suppose — " he said, " — that you get lots of inspiration sitting by the side of that fine pool." 34

"Yes," said Pat, "yes, I do." 35

. . . Pat filled his cup at the cooler. Down the hall there was a group approaching — Jack Berners, Ben Brown and several other executives and with them a girl to whom they were very attentive and deferential. He recognized her face — she was the girl of the year, the It girl, the Oomph girl, the Glamour Girl, the girl for whose services every studio was in violent competition. 36

Pat lingered over his drink. He had seen many phonies break in and break out again, but this girl was the real thing, someone to stir every pulse in the nation. He felt his own heart beat faster. Finally, as the procession drew near, he put down the cup, dabbed at his hair with his hand and took a step out into the corridor. 37

The girl looked at him — he looked at the girl. Then she took one arm of Jack Berners' and one of Ben Brown's and suddenly the party seemed to walk right through him — so that he had to take a step back against the wall. 38

An instant later Jack Berners turned around and said back to him, "Hello, Pat." And then some of the others threw half glances around but no one else spoke, so interested were they in the girl. 39

In his office, Pat looked at the scene where President McKinley offers a United States commission to Fitzhugh Lee. Suddenly he gritted his teeth and bore down on his pencil as he wrote: 40

LEE

Mr. President, you can take your commission and go straight to hell.

Then he bent down over his desk, his shoulders shaking as he thought   41
of that happy day when he had had a swimming pool.

SUBJECT

1.   Why does Hobby attach so much importance to a cracked swimming pool?

2.   What indications do you have that Hobby is not simply unlucky but that he no longer merits the high pay and steady work he once had? Does Hobby seem to recognize this?

3.   Can you tell from the sketchy information about *True to Two Flags* under what kinds of restriction Hollywood writers were forced to work?

4.   In 1939, Lee's directive "go straight to hell" would not have been allowed in a movies (*Gone With the Wind* was the first picture to get by with "damn"). Why does Hobby insert this line into the script he's working on?

STRUCTURE

1.   How is the incident of the "It" girl toward the end structurally related to the rest of the story?

2.   Consider the role played by repetition (of words and themes) in the unity of this story.

3.   The chief basis for comparison between the good old days and the present is not, as one might expect, money — or even swimming pools. What is it?

4.   Examine the devices by which Fitzgerald gets Hobby into and back out of his reveries. Which ones work most smoothly? Could you suggest improvements for others? Do the successful ones operate by some formula not employed in the weaker ones?

4

WORK IN AN ALIENATED SOCIETY

Cause and Effect

Probably ninety per cent of scientific — and research paper — writing employs two methods of presentation: analysis of cause and effect and of process. The two can be distinguished quite easily: cause and effect analysis answers the question, "*Why* does something work or happen?" and process analysis answers the question, "*How* does it work or happen?" A study of the principles of physics which cause an internal combustion engine to operate would be analysis of cause and effect; an explanation of how an engine is constructed would be process analysis. The reason so much writing is of these two types is probably apparent. Although the first duty of a scientist is to observe accurately, the isolated facts he collects are meaningless until some relationships or applications are worked out. Cause and effect and process analysis show these relations and applications.

The immediate difficulty confronting the analyzer of cause and effect relations is the possibility of a "multiplicity of causes." Seldom in nature or in society does a one cause-one effect relationship occur; normally a number of factors contribute to any one result, and one cause such as the atom bomb can have any number of after-effects. If a chemical reaction will not take place except under pressure, at a certain temperature, and in the presence of a catalyst, then pressure, temperature, and catalyst must be considered along with the chemicals actually involved in the reaction as "causes" of the reaction. In the social sciences the problems are even more complicated, and the observer who fails to expect many causes or effects is almost certain to distort his analysis. Gibbon in his great work, *The Decline and Fall of*

183

the Roman Empire, failed to see the multiplicity of economic and political causes involved when he tried to show that the Roman Empire fell primarily because of the rise of Christianity.

Another danger in cause and effect analysis is the possible presence of incidental factors which are not really a part of the cause but which may appear to be so because of their very presence. "This must be a good theme — I spent six hours on it" or "I knew he'd fail that test: he went off on a pledge trip the previous week end" are common examples of too-hasty assumption of a cause and effect relationship. A less obvious example would be this: "No wonder I failed the test — I had a bad headache that day." The headache might, of course, have been a partial cause, but the student might also have done just as badly without the headache. Certainly it would be a mistake to assume a one cause-one effect relationship here.

In spite of these difficulties of false cause and multiplicity of causes, analysis of cause and effect can be a profitable endeavor, even by the student untrained in the intricacies of logical analysis. Take the question, "Why did I come to college?" Perhaps the student has never really thought about an answer to this question, but if he considers it objectively he can probably discover the causes for his coming to college: a pure interest in learning, desire for a better job, parental pressure, desire to keep up with his friends, unreadiness to face the world on his own, and so on. Although he may miss a few causes his answer is likely to tell him something about himself which he hadn't realized before. Or take one more example: John asks himself, "Why do I love Jane?" Probably he will either invent a few likely-sounding reasons (rationalize) or quickly put the question out of his head unanswered. But if he honestly and objectively tries to answer it, he may find that his love has a sounder basis than he suspected — or he may realize that he is being "taken."

At any rate, since students are constantly being called upon to analyze cause and effect relationships ("Why did Hamlet refuse to kill the king at prayers?" "Why does this painting seem to have more depth than that one?" "What factors influence juvenile delinquency rates?"), it is well to know some of the basic principles involved.

The primary requirement is an objective, unprejudiced approach. One must never make the mistake of assuming he knows the cause beforehand and then looking for supporting evidence. This is what happens when a tobacco company employs an "impartial" scientist to prove that there is no cause and effect relation between smoking and lung cancer. At best his chances of arriving at "truth" are cut in half before he even starts.

Another requirement, then, is that the analyzer gather all the facts available and consider all possible explanations, or causes, for an effect. If Joe asks Henrietta to go water skiing with him and she refuses, he cannot immediately conclude that Henrietta is either a snob or a fool. To arrive at the real cause or causes for this effect, Joe needs to collect as much pertinent evidence as he can, formulate various hypotheses from these facts, and then test each hypothesis to see if it might be the cause, or part of the cause, of Henrietta's refusal. Perhaps she doesn't like water skiing; she may have a cold; she may have several important tests coming up; she may be engaged to another man; or she may not like Joe. If Joe tests each of these possibilities and finds that Henrietta is healthy, loves water skiing, does not have another boy friend but does date, then Joe may suspect — but not yet definitely conclude — that Henrietta does not like him.

But how can he find out for certain? His next step would be a controlled experiment to check his remaining hypothesis. He might try asking Henrietta to a different social function, say a concert, on a different day. If she accepts gladly, Joe must go back and check on other possible causes of the water skiing fiasco. If on the other hand she still refuses, he has further corroborating evidence for his hypothesis that Henrietta doesn't like him. But it may be that she doesn't like concerts and refused the second date on that account. So Joe must test a bit further. He might induce his friend Jim to ask Henrietta to go water skiing at the same time and place Joe had suggested to her. If she accepts Joe can be fairly certain that *he* is at least partly the cause for Henrietta's refusal. As a final check, he could have a second friend ask Henrietta to the concert. If she accepts that date, too, Joe can start looking for greener pastures — or girl friends.

But suppose Joe is interested only in Henrietta and wants to know *why* she doesn't like him. Then he must begin a whole new series of analyses. He must gather the facts about himself and Henrietta which might be pertinent to their relationship, and from these formulate hypotheses which could explain the effect. There may be a basic personality clash; she may be a foot taller than Joe; she may not like his taste in clothing; or perhaps he needs a better toothpaste. The point is that Joe must again employ the same principles of objective analysis and testing which he used in arriving at the first conclusion.

The same procedures apply for any analysis of cause and effect. Since the facts and circumstances will be different in different problems, no more specific advice than this can be given here. Tracking down cause and effect relations may sometimes seem frustrating, but it can be a fascinating search. It is what provides the excitement in almost any research project. If the student who attempts a cause and effect analysis will remember to be unprejudiced, to collect as many pertinent facts as possible, and to test each hypothesis, he should be able to make some significant contribution, at least to his own self-knowledge.

THE PROTEST
OF YOUNG
FACTORY WORKERS

Herbert J. Gans

Herbert J. Gans is professor of sociology and planning at M. I. T. and faculty associate of the MIT-Harvard Joint Center for Urban Studies. He is the author of The Urban Villagers *(1962),* The Levittowners' Ways of Life *(1967),* People and Plans *(1968), and a new book on national news media.*

When students at Berkeley and other elite campuses first began to demonstrate against the university — and against the Establishment — many observers explained their behavior as the consequences of being affluent and elite. Indeed, the myth of Middle America and its Silent Majority that emerged in response to student unrest postulates a basic difference between the "classes," suggesting that the former are satisfied with American society and only the snobs are unhappy.

It should be clear from the articles in this issue of *New Generation,* however, that this simple dichotomy is just not true; some blue-collar workers are at least as critical of the factory as students are of the multiversity. While they have not often resorted to media covered demonstrations and confrontations, they have probably been more effective in disrupting the assembly line than students, the university, through high rates of absenteeism and turnover, wild-cat strikes, deliberately shoddy workmanship and occasional acts of sabotage.

From the limited journalistic and sociological research so far available, it would appear that a yet unknown number of blue-collar workers, particularly on the assembly line, complain, like the students, that their work is inauthentic and their workplace, dehumanizing. They do not use these terms, of course, but they find the work boring; they have no control over the job; they must obey arbitrary decisions by their foremen and they cannot take time off for personal business or even a phone call. In short, they are veritable prisoners of the assembly line and the people who run it.

Work: Old Feelings and New Expectations

Any explanation of the current blue-collar protest must begin with   4
the fact that the feelings behind it are by no means new; indeed, discontent with working conditions is as old as the Industrial Revolution itself. Until fairly recently, the discontent was voiced publicly mainly by middle class social critics, novelists and film-makers (remember Charlie Chaplin's classic critique of the assembly line, "Modern Times"), for the workers themselves could not easily protest about working conditions. Job insecurity was still rampant, and besides, their first priority was to achieve a living — and rising — wage. Still there is no doubt that the writers and film-makers expressed many of the workers' feelings. For example, Eli Chinoy's sociological study, *Automobile Workers and the American Dream,* published in 1955, concluded that the assembly line workers only endured the work to earn enough money for achieving their American dream: to buy a gas station or garage. When I studied a Boston working class neighborhood in the late 1950's, I heard many of the same complaints that workers are making today, but the West Enders, for whom even garage ownership was unachievable, had resigned themselves to the working conditions they could not change, and sought their satisfactions in family and peer group life.

Today, age-old feelings are being translated into action, mainly by   5
some young workers, and especially the better educated among them. They are not saving up to buy a garage but are going to night school to become eligible for a white-collar job, and since they do not expect to spend the rest of their lives in the factory, they can express their discontent or quit when the work becomes unbearable.

Moreover, these young workers do not accept the traditional working   6
class belief that the major purpose of the job is to finance the non-work parts of life. Whether or not they practice middle class life styles, many have embraced the expectation, common in the middle class, that the job itself should provide some satisfaction, and this is hard to find on the assembly line. But even for the men who are not looking forward to better jobs, the line no longer provides the same rewards it offered their fathers. When most blue-collar work was unskilled, the line was at least a gold-plated sweatship, as Walter Reuther put it. Today even the money is not that good anymore; there is less prestige than in skilled work, and opportunities for promotion are rare. Why else would blacks have been allowed on the line, and in such large numbers? (Today, over 60% of Detroit's assembly line workers are black.)

Still, the status of the assembly line has been declining for some time   7
now; other reasons must explain why the protest has only surfaced in the last couple of years. First, younger men are an ever more important

part of the work force; 40 percent of the current UAW members are under thirty. Second, some are increasingly unhappy with the union, which is more responsive to older workers — and *they* are naturally more interested in pensions than working conditions. Also, as B. J. Widick wrote recently in the *Nation,* "The old-timers think of the UAW as an organization that protects them from company abuse. Young workers think of the UAW as an outfit that had better get them what they think they deserve, and now. The young are not burdened with memories of the miseries of the past or the struggles of two decades ago." A third factor is the current recession. During more affluent years, dissatisfied assembly line workers could find better jobs outside the factory; now, these jobs are scarcer and the men feel trapped on the line.

Fourth, the blue-collar protest has erupted now because dissatisfied   8
workers, like other protesters, have learned from the civil rights and peace movements that demonstrations and confrontations are frequently more successful in bringing about change than traditional grievance procedures. To be sure, it has taken the workers some years to learn this, partly because such methods have only just become respectable in the politically conservative world of the working class, partly because the number of protesters had to reach a critical mass before they could act with impunity. But now that these conditions have been met, it is likely that the protest will spread.

Nevertheless, the prime reason for the protest comes from beyond   9
the factory, for the discontented workers are expressing a nation-wide upgrading of expectations about how life should be lived which is taking place in many levels and sectors of American society. Although what is happening is often described as a politico-cultural revolution or a youthful rebellion, the diverse new expectations also have in common a demand for more equality in America's principal institutions, and I prefer to label the change as the "equality revolution." As a result, one finds similar dissatisfactions and demands in many places: for example, among blacks who want equality with whites, and women, with men; among journalists who question the absolute power of editors, and enlisted men, that of officers; among professional athletes who resent being owners' chattel, clients who doubt the monopoly on wisdom of professionals, consumers who oppose the practices of manufacturers and merchants, adolescents who want the sexual privileges heretofore reserved for adults, and students who seek more power in their schools.

As in the factory, the feelings underlying the discontent are old; what   10
is new is the belief that the time has come to act on them, and all across the societal board. Young people are saying that age should be a lesser justification of authority than it has been; lower income groups, that

income and status should not be the sole sources of rights and privileges; the less skilled, that expertise is not limited to experts; and citizens, that not all decisions should be made by politicians and bureaucrats. Seen in the light of the larger equality revolution, then, the blue-collar discontent is a demand for more of the satisfactions and rights of white-collar and even professional workers.

SUBJECT

1. What historical causes does Gans suggest for the unrest of factory workers?

2. What new causes have brought this latent unrest to the surface?

3. One hears much less about worker disruption of assembly lines than about student disruption of universities. Does Gans suggest a reason for this?

4. Gans places the dissatisfaction of factory workers into a more general category, the "equality revolution." Would you agree that the aims of young factory workers are essentially the same as the aims of dissenting college students?

5. Although factory workers are of course not construction workers, would it be fair to say that the much-publicized "hard-hat" confrontations with college students weakens Gans's assessment of the extent of worker protest?

STRUCTURE

1. This brief article represents more a summary of causes than a full cause and effect analysis. Given that limitation, does Gans succeed in showing a necessary relation between worker unrest and the causes he suggests for it?

2. Has Gans adequately considered the probability of a multiplicity of causes? Does his placing worker unrest into a more general movement, the "equality revolution," represent an oversimplification?

3. Does the explanation of why "the protest has only surfaced in the last couple of years" seem convincing? Can you think of other possible causes?

4. Compare the style of Gans's article with that of books and articles you have read by other sociologists. Would you say this essay is aimed at a general audience or at other sociologists? Does Gans ever lapse into sociological jargon?

COMMUNES AND
THE WORK CRISIS

Lewis M. Andrews

Lewis M. Andrews is a television producer and free lance writer. He is the author of two books, Requiem for Democracy *(1971) and* Venice: A World Cultural Guide *(1971). The following article first appeared in* The Nation.

Until recently, work has enjoyed a good reputation. For most Americans who grew up during the depression, work and life were synonymous. Finding a job, any job, was the prime directive. Liberals and radicals criticized the capitalist economy, but their aim was to "humanize" work, to make it "fulfilling," not to eliminate it. 1

Now, however, work has fallen into disrepute, especially among young adults. Whereas it was once a solution to life's problems — were they as straightforward and fundamental as survival or as elusive as the need for self-expression — work is now in itself a problem. The question, "Plastics?," from the film *The Graduate* symbolizes an entire generation's disenchantment with the job options offered by the most diversified society in the world. The famous identity crisis, which is intimately bound up with occupational goals, is becoming a major problem for school guidance counselors. (Almost 65 percent of students who consult school psychologists and guidance counselors present themselves as vocationally confused.) A recent study of Stanford and Berkeley undergraduates found that vocational choice is seen by students as a threat instead of an opportunity. 2

Increasingly, the reaction of the young to the establishment work scene is to drop out. For some this means revolutionary political activism, for others it means "taking a few years off" to find themselves, and for still others it means an irrevocable break with "straight" society. Many bright college graduates become taxi drivers, waiters and supermarket checkers, in order to "keep themselves together" with a minimum of effort. Others go off to join one of the 300 known (and myriad unknown) hippie communes which have sprouted up across rural America during the past five years. [See "Living Together in Cali- 3

Reprinted from *The Nation* (November 9, 1970) by permission of the publisher.

fornia" by Maitland Zane, *The Nation,* October 19, 1970.] For obvious reasons, no one knows exactly how many are dropping out, but sociologists agree that the number is accelerating geometrically, with estimates ranging as high as 20,000 per year. More significant, however, is the fact that the dropouts are often among the most intelligent and best educated young people. Communes have been founded by renegades from Yale, Princeton, Stanford, Dartmouth and Berkeley.

This rebellion against the work ethic has potential dangers which   4
even the dropout recognizes. A completely work-free society is impossible to attain. Even if we could mechanize or eliminate all the menial, superficial and redundant jobs, society would still require doctors, programmers, teachers, technicians, firemen, maintenance men, supervisors and other skilled professionals. (I leave out lawyers and police on the premise that such a society would be free of conflict — a dubious assumption.) Unfortunately, the more leisure-oriented our society becomes, the more unevenly the work load is distributed. The burden of servicing an advanced technology falls upon its most intelligent and technically competent members — those very bright young people who are most ready to drop out! In short, the rebellion against the work ethic, if it continues, could lead to a bizarre economic situation: we may find ourselves dependent upon a complex technology that nobody can or will run. Dr. Stanley F. Yolles, former director of the National Institute of Mental Health, sees "serious dangers that large proportions of current and future generations will reach adulthood embittered towards the larger society, unequipped to take on parental, vocational and other citizen roles."

But even if society can successfully convince — that is, bribe — in-   5
telligent young people to assume the burdens of technology management, as most economists believe it can, work alienation still presents a major social problem. Dissatisfaction with work is a growing source of emotional illness. Psychiatrist Salvatore Maddi finds that people who see themselves as mere players of social roles and who have an acute awareness of superficiality, two symptoms of work dissatisfaction, are highly susceptible to what he calls "existential neurosis"; that is, feelings of chronic meaninglessness, aimlessness and apathy, culminating in severe depression.

Why has work fallen into disrepute among the young? There are   6
legitimate reasons which by now have become clichés: work seems meaningless in a redundant economy that creates needless wants through advertising; work seems meaningless in a society that ignores real problems of poverty and pollution; the nine-to-five routine saps

191

spontaneity and precludes the evolution of individual life styles, etc. But none of these reasons justifies the complete rejection of work. A doctor, lawyer, teacher, even a businessman, can always find work that is meaningful and flexible, *if he wants to find it.* To understand the work crisis, we must explore several illusions that have become axioms to many young Americans.

The first illusion is that work should be a continuous experience of intellectual and emotional delight. Synonyms: self-actualizing and self-fulfilling. Television has undoubtedly played a major role in cultivating this particular illusion. Marcus Welby, M.D., performs at least one medical miracle each week, while over at NBC *The Bold Ones* are resolving crucial social issues at the same rate. And those TV characters who opt for a meaningful family life never have job problems. Did Jim Anderson (*Father Knows Best*) ever stay up late working on his client's insurance policies? Ever see Donna Reed's doctor husband lift as much as a tongue depressor? And who could figure out what Ozzie Nelson did for a living?   7

Educators also bear responsibility for supporting this particular illusion. They spend so much time preparing students for future work that they forget to explain what the word *work* represents. Our neolithic ancestors were hardly concerned with "the quality of life." For them work — hunting, fishing, farming — was existence. Civilization offers three work advantages: it can make working conditions more pleasant, it can reduce the work load and, by dividing labor, it can offer individuals a choice among more or less satisfying jobs. But even the most rewarding work has its drawbacks. Doctors hate to read medical journals, psychologists dislike treating alcoholics, writers resent deadlines, and so on. Work does not promise Nirvana. That's why people are paid for their labor.   8

The illusion that work must be an orgasm leads to the corollary illusion that people should be drawn to work by some calling, irrepressible commitment or mystical force. True, a few people know what they want to do at the age of 10, and follow this inspiration for the rest of their lives. Most of us, however, have to be introduced to a subject before we become interested in it. How many people who are happy in their present jobs have ever said, "I never thought I'd end up doing this!"?   9

The work ethic is further depreciated by two seemingly divergent pseudo-philosophies gaining popularity among the nation's young. The first is a neo-Puritanism which holds that each man must justify his existence by forsaking personal gain and doing something socially constructive. This frequently means ghetto teaching, working in a free   10 clinic, or community organizing. As Edward Banfield cogently observes in *The Unheavenly City,* self-justification has become a growth industry. Dedication to solving social ills is an admirable quality, but neo-Puritanism has had the effect of demeaning any form of work which is done for money, which includes about 99 percent of all existing jobs. As a result, many college graduates are ashamed to say they are working *just* for a living.

In opposition to neo-Puritanism among the young is a neo-Freudianism, which also depreciates work but for different reasons. Popularized by Norman Brown (*Life Against Death*), Herbert Marcuse (*Eros and Civilization*), neo-Freudianism strives for the resurrection of what Freud called the Pleasure Principle. According to Brown, civilization represses the Pleasure Principle by instilling a sense of guilt which we literally work out in our respective jobs. The more guilty and repressed we are, the harder we work. The solution, writes Theodore Roszak, is the evolution of a "counter culture" that will turn our mundane work existence into a joyous festival, a spontaneous "celebration of life."   11

Neo-Freudianism has obvious merits. The fact that psychosomatic illnesses are so prevalent among society's most "successful" members demonstrates a partial validity to Freud's theory of cultural repression. However, neo-Freudianism is grossly misinterpreted, especially by social malcontents who equate liberation with anarchy. Freud himself recognized that a certain degree of repression is necessary in order to buy freedom from a primitive existence. Furthermore, many modern psychologists disagree sharply with the premise of neo-Freudianism, arguing that discipline and acquisition of skills are highly satisfying activities. One psychologist has argued that the drive for competence, like the sex drive, is an innate motivation.   12

The young are not to be blamed for their susceptibility to illusion. They have nothing else to trust. The young are, in a sense, the most victimized generation in history. "Manipulated for goals they cannot believe in," writes Paul Goodman, "the young are alienated." They have been exploited by status-conscious parents ("It's for your own good, my dear"), by businessmen eager to sap the youth market for dad's last penny, and by ambitious politicians, Left and Right. Even the most independent jobs demand a degree of trust that many members of the new paranoid generation are unwilling to give.   13

How is the work crisis to be resolved? In theory, the solution is simple; a little realism would do the trick. The young must recognize that work is necessary for survival and, further, that any form of work necessarily involves discipline and sacrifice. At the same time, adult champions of the work ethic must learn what they already feel — that the good life is more than an impressive financial statement. Unfortunately, people   14

193

would rather create illusions to justify their past actions than confront reality. Many dropouts support what youth psychologist Kenneth Keniston has called "the fallacy of romantic regression" — that is, an idealized vision of primitive living which never has and never will exist.

Similarly, "successful" businessmen and professionals extol ulcer-producing work and competition as Christ-like virtues. These fantasies are supported and enriched by media that specialize in what their audiences want to hear. Underground papers such as the Berkeley *Barb,* the Los Angeles *Free Press,* and the New York *Rat* weekly herald the decline of the decadent establishment, while the respectable press gives us front-page stories about hippie teen-agers (especially girls from wealthy families) who come to a bad end as a result of drugs and shiftless commune living.   15

A few businesses have tried to solve the work crisis with token gestures. Many law firms, for example, encourage young attorneys to spend part of their workday doing poverty law. People who work in television, advertising and other communications industries are allowed liberal dress, liberal hours and frequent leaves of absence for educational purposes. But tokenism wears thin. If the aspiring lawyer wants to stay with the firm, he works overtime to finish the firm's work. And the copywriter is still responsible for servicing the soap account.   16

A more successful approach to the work crisis is the rapidly growing phenomenon of the "work commune." Unlike the hippie commune which is organized around a simple life style, the work commune is organized around a professional skill or interest. Members strive for a secure income while, at the same time, advancing each person's independence and work satisfaction.   17

One such commune is the Farallones Institute, an architecture commune, founded in Berkeley by two University of California graduate students. Members develop their own environmental design projects and then seek financial assistance to carry them off. The commune's first paycheck came from a government grant. (Work communes have few qualms about taking government money.) Assistance now comes from the Berkeley High School system, which is interested in the commune's ideas about new educational environments. In neighboring Sausalito is another architecture commune which calls itself the Ant Farm. Founded by two former architecture students, Chip Lord from Tulane and Doug Michaels from Yale, the Ant Farm currently specializes in building plastic "inflatables," balloon-type environments which are used at rock festivals and on children's playgrounds. The Berkeley area   18 also includes numerous legal communes. Some specialize in reform projects; others simply seek a relaxed legal practice.

Work communes are not limited to professional skills. The Portola 19 Institute of Menlo Park, Calif., is a thriving commune of full-time dilettantes. Billed as "a nonprofit co-operative to encourage, organize, and conduct innovative educational projects," it is actually a group of creative people, ranging in education from Ph.D. to high school dropout, whose common bond is the desire to play for a living. Current projects of the Portola Institute include maintaining a playroom for creative high school students, developing a teacher-training laboratory, exploring music theory, and publishing the *Whole Earth Catalog,* which provides the reader with information about books and tools and "enables him to shape his environment, internal and external." Because the *Catalog* has been so successful (circulation 140,000), the institute is under pressure to expand, but members prefer to keep it small. "When people come to us with new ideas," says member Sam Yanes, "we often tell them to start their own institute. We're happy staying about our present size." The institute has encouraged several projects which now function as independent work communes in other parts of California.

California, especially the San Francisco Bay area, has the largest 20 concentration of work communes, but the phenomenon is spreading. The Communications Company, in Columbus, Ohio, publishes a handbook on alternative life styles. The Meeting, in Minneapolis, Minn., is an experimental school. New York City's East Village houses numerous film communes and group-run psychedelic shops. The growing number of free universities and underground newspapers are also part of the work commune movement.

Work communes provide a promising model for a realistic balance 21 between society's need for productive work in order to sustain itself, and the individual's need for autonomy. Yanes, for example, has no illusions about economics. "Frankly, I'm a capitalist," he admits. "I need the bread to live, and working here at the [Portola] Institute is better than planting my own garden." But given the necessity of working for a living, Yanes places paramount emphasis on the freedom to live as he chooses. "This is the best place to work because I can do what I like. I couldn't work anywhere else for more money or for anything."

However, not all dropouts are enthusiastic about the work commune 22 movement. Phil Trounstein, a Stanford radical, refers to the Portola Institute as a "Fascist organization" in disguise. "No matter how they dress or act, they still exploit people with their products." A lot of hippies are also critical, but their reasons are more personal than political. "It's still work and routine," remarked one Berkeley nomad.

The fact that rebels from the traditional work ethic disagree among   23
themselves is probably more significant than any particular viewpoint.
The work crisis will not be resolved by black-white distinctions between
glorified Puritanism and unbridled hedonism. The young must feel free
to experiment with new life styles to find their own solutions to the
problem of work.

SUBJECT

1.   Judging from your own observation, do you agree with Andrews
that people least willing to join the work force are among the most
intelligent and best educated of our youth?

2.   Assuming that those who do not choose to work are the very
ones most capable of finding work in a technological society, what
"bizarre economic situation" does Andrews predict if the trend continues? Wouldn't this necessarily mean a return to a less complicated
civilization?

3.   In addition to the usual reasons given for the disrepute into
which work has fallen, Andrews suggests three or four common "illusions" as contributing causes. Do you agree that these are illusions?
What is the difference between an illusion and a delusion?

4.   What hope does Andrews offer of a solution to the work crisis?
How widespread would such a movement need to be in order to
comprise a satisfactory solution? What factors work against such a
solution?

5.   Does the final paragraph strike you more as an appropriate summary or as a cop-out?

6.   What is "the fallacy of romantic regression"?

STRUCTURE

1.   The average reader would probably think of "the work crisis" as
high unemployment; does Andrews make clear the sense in which he
is using the phrase? Does he offer convincing evidence that there *is*
such a crisis?

2.   In paragraph 6, Andrews mentions three commonly accepted
causes for the current disillusionment with work. Although he says
there are inadequate explanations, he does not reject them as partial
causes; should he then have analyzed them to show that they are
indeed partial causes?

3.   How convincing a case does Andrews make for the common "illusions" as causes? Should he have explained the rather complicated
neo-Freudian concept in greater detail? (That is, does Andrews assume

more familiarity with the subject than the average reader is likely to have?)

4. Is Andrews trying to explain the work crisis to the young, to an older generation, or to both? What indications are there of any assumption by Andrews about the nature of his audience?

5. Andrews says that because attempts by business to solve the work crisis have failed, youth "must find their own solutions to the problem of work." What is the fallacy in his reasoning here?

WEAR AND TEAR IN THE COMMUNES

Albert Solnit

Albert Solnit has written widely on development and social change in American university communities, Amazon Indian villages, Peruvian barriadas, New Mexico's Spanish highlands, and Appalachian coal towns. Currently he is Chief of Advanced Planning for Marin County, California — a position which in view of the very large number of communes there, particularly qualifies Mr. Solnit to discuss the subject of communes.

Now that *The New York Times, Look, Time* and even *Redbook* have   1
discovered communes to be symbols of "the new social rebellion" and "the green revolution," and "a challenge to the survival of the American family," it is time to take a cooler look at what's been going on. To begin with, "leaving home" is an old American institution. Joining the services, going off to college, getting a job, or getting married used to be the ways out for middle-class children who wanted to cut their dependence on their parents. For today's Aquarians, the services have fallen into disrepute, college residences are often considered extensions of parental control, and initial jobs at the non-menial level are rarer than ever for the high school graduate. That leaves marriage. While boys and girls still believe in love, they more than ever balk at being pushed into a legal commitment. Instead they contract informal partnerships, living in a holding pattern with no strings, but with all the intimacy and emotional support of a marriage.

Like-minded couples and a few single friends are the usual founders   2
of an urban commune. However, their experiments in cooperative living are perhaps as much a result of economic necessity as of ideals. And their economic needs are considerable, because they are generally the first generation to grow up in post-World War II suburbia. Suburbia was sold to their parents as an approximation of utopia that combined country living with all the modern conveniences and access to urban facilities. If the location of communes in the San Francisco Bay Area is any indication, the communards also look for country living, but not too far out to miss their own kind of amenities. That would explain why lush, wealthy Marin County is a location more favored than the Oakland

Reprinted from *The Nation* (April 27, 1971) by permission of the publisher.

black ghetto or the blue-collar areas of Richmond or San Francisco, where housing is cheaper.

If a young couple wishes to live together in Marin, they will find that inexpensive single-family houses have almost disappeared from the market. The era of the inexpensive tract house for the couple just starting out ended in Marin about 1960. New homes are all priced at $30,000 or more. Most new construction has been in apartments, but at least two-thirds of apartment house owners will not rent to couples with children, and probably even fewer will sign a lease with a pair of unmarried long hairs.

Therefore, a common way to meet the housing shortage has been for several couples or singles to pool their incomes and rent large, expensive houses in the better neighborhoods. During World War II, service and war-industry families beat the lack of housing by doubling up, a practice that was countenanced by their neighbors as being part of a temporary wartime situation. Today, it doesn't look as though the housing shortage would be solved by winning a war, and many residents are becoming notably eager to force cooperative living groups out of their single-family districts. Where local politicians have responded, the favorite anti-commune ploy has been that all-around tool of exclusivity, the local zoning ordinance. Many cities around the nation have officially defined what a family is by limiting occupancy of single-family homes to no more than four or five persons unrelated by blood, marriage or legal adoption. It is said that a house occupied by more than four or five people not so related creates fire and health hazards, traffic congestion, crowding and noise that are not present when the same house is lived in by a traditional family. While it is almost impossible to enforce an ordinance based on whether or not the occupants of a house are related, it does allow officials to harass communal groups when the neighbors complain.

Thus zoning definitions of this sort strike at the communal life style itself, rather than at the assumption of undesirable behavior or conditions that lies behind the ordinance. The commune people have fought back by seeking to have their groups officially recognized as legal families. At a Marin County public hearing, the American Civil Liberties Union put the issue this way:

> In reviewing similar cases throughout the country, we see these ordinances as vague and of constitutional uncertainty. Under this concept six airline stewardesses or six college students could not occupy a single house of whatever size even if they owned it.
>
> The ordinance is probably discriminatory and a violation of the Fourteenth Amendment. It deals with social problems through a zoning ordinance. There are other existing methods to solve social prob-

199

lems. It appears to be class legislation aimed at the young and the poor. If the Board [of Supervisors] should pass this, it would create hostility in the young . . . and give rise to a series of test cases.

The first test case to produce a result was that of the *Palo Alto Tenants* 6 *Union v. George Morgan, et. al.* Judge Albert C. Wollenberg of the U.S. District Court for Northern California upheld a zoning ordinance defining a "family" as limited to "a group not exceeding four persons living as a single housekeeping unit" in single-family residential zones.

The judge's decision made the following distinction between commu- 7 nal families and traditional families:

> There is a long recognized value in the traditional family relationship which does not attach to the "voluntary family." The traditional family is an institution reinforced by biological and legal ties which are difficult or impossible to sunder. It plays a role in educating and nourishing the young which far from being voluntary is often compulsory. . . .
>
> The communal living groups represented by the plaintiffs share few of the above characteristics. They are voluntary, with fluctuating memberships who have no legal obligations of support or cohabitation. They are in no way subject to the state's vast body of domestic relations law. They do not have the biological links which characterize most families.

The battle line between communards and the Establishment was 8 never more clearly framed than in the judge's choice of words like compulsory roles, legal ties and legal obligations. If there is anything the communal groups seem united in rejecting, it is compulsory roles such as being parent-client to a public school system, or being the sole economic or emotional support of a mate or child. More often than not, the goal of the commune is to replace the legal ties and obligations of the traditional family with something freely given and centered in the group for as long as the individual member of the group wants to belong and contribute. Freedom to split is basic to the creed.

One other important aim found in most communes is withdrawal 9 from participation in consumership, by which they mean the getting and spending that for them characterizes straight society. For many, this means first removing oneself from career-building employment, or in some cases from any kind of steady, confining work. To avoid compromising the ideal of being free to "do your own thing," they support themselves with temporary jobs, craft sales, food stamps and minor marijuana dealing. Ownership of property is another middle-class value that is rejected, not so much for its materialistic connotations but because, like legal marriage, it ties one down. The communards evince a rootlessness and mobility that insure only a short-term commitment to any place or group. For many the style they seek is expressed in *Easy Rider* or *Alice's Restaurant.*

Yet none of this is really new. Some of the best American traditions 10
and folklore are based on the pathfinders, the trappers and the pioneers
who settled for a spell and then moved on in search of greener pastures.
There are today probably as many elderly wanderers in camper trucks
and trailers as there are hippie gypsies in second-hand school busses.

Nor is the ideal of living outside the mass-production system a recent 11
invention. In 1931, Ralph Borsodi urged in *Flight From the City* withdrawal to the countryside in cooperative communities dedicated to
domestic production to insure independence from the coils of the ur-
ban-industrial system. A number of such communities were established
before World War II, the most notable being "The School of Living" in
Suffern, N.Y.

Compare the following statement of philosophy from the School's 12
November 1938 *Homestead Bulletin* with the goals of the readers of
today's back-to-the-land bible, *The Whole Earth Catalog:*

> To carry out the program of independence and self-sufficiency recom-
> mended by the School ... will require these families to set up new
> ideals, new standards, new objectives. But these are supremely worth
> their while, and for most of them represent the only way in which they
> can become genuinely free and independent — free not only from
> the financial worries that now trouble most of them but also indepen-
> dent of the changes and the ups and downs of modern industry.
>
> The School believes that every family which produces for its own
> consumption and serves its own needs as far as it can on a modern
> organized, labor saving basis approaches the only proper ideal for the
> American people — *the ideal of the spiritual liberty and the eco-
> nomic self-sufficiency of the family.*

Much of the time this quest for group self-sufficiency in meeting 13
physical and emotional needs means a greater surrender of individuality and a greater break with the world at large than the participants
may have anticipated. The odyssey of one couple who found this to be
so points up the problem of fitting personal needs into the idealized
pattern of group living.

Dennis and Jean are an interracial couple with a new baby. When 14
they first met, they lived together with Jean's people in the Fillmore
(San Francisco's Harlem), but the crime, the police, and all the other
problems of ghetto life forced them to move to Berkeley. There they
lived in an old school bus fixed up with beds and a hot plate, parking
it outside a friend's house and using his bathroom. But Berkeley got to
be too much of a hassle too, what with the rioting, the tear-gassing, and
the police sweeps. Their next move was to an old house in a predominantly black section of Oakland. Although they lived there coopera-

201

tively with a number of other people, they described it as "just an economic trip, because everyone just took up their own space and didn't really mean anything to each other." So Dennis, Jean and about a dozen friends decided to find a place where they could give one another the love and support they'd missed in their families, schools and jobs.

They wound up in a Mill Valley home in the redwoods. Like many others, they found the "vibes" right in this Marin County community, because it was close in to San Francisco, had a natural setting, and up to then a relatively tolerant attitude toward the long hairs who were settling in. Their commune, a year after its founding, was housed in a four-story hillside building that resembled a ski lodge. The place had twelve rooms, about eighteen residents, including two babies, a few itinerant guests, two dogs and two cats. The monthly rent was $500.

Outside were a number of old cars and two school busses, one of which was Dennis and Jean's original home on wheels. The house was furnished with thrift-shop and homemade furniture. Sleeping bags on top of a dining table were used for the babies' naps. In the kitchen were signs pleading, "Please keep animals in the kitchen or outside" and "Papers only please," above the waste baskets. However the prevailing impression was one of disorder on the brink of chaos.

This commune was seen as a refuge from a world that programs you for joyless work, irrelevant schooling and loveless family life. Here members of the group would be open and loving, and find enlightenment together. Money, however, was a nagging problem. Only four or five members, including Dennis and Jean, brought it in regularly. The phone had been removed only the week before for nonpayment of bills. The previous month Dennis had contributed his whole paycheck to meet the rent. None of the transient guests had been asked to leave, even though they rarely helped with either work or money. The commune also had permanent members who had not worked either for money or around the house; but this was accepted because it was considered more important to "be sympathetic with their problems."

Dennis had been acting as leader since last summer. He still hoped that the commune would be a success — if they could all get it together with Scientology. "Once you get the crap out of your head, you can see what's correct." Then the group could "get a gig together," a means of making money through a business; or maybe they would move to a farm where they could grow their own organic food. (The commune's diet was vegetarian, heavy on beans and rice.)

Jean felt that she and Dennis, who worked in retail stores all week, were carrying too many nonworkers on their backs. She had been raised in a black ghetto and the middle-class affluence the white mem-

202

bers were rejecting was foreign to her. On the other hand, she *was* used to overcrowding and poverty, and the daily life of the commune was no joyous new experience. She was especially unhappy about Dennis' practice of casual sex with other girls in the commune.

At last Jean and Dennis decided that their survival as a couple and their baby's welfare were more important than struggling on with the group. They got back into their school bus and parked it at the home of Jean's employer across town. Last fall they drove to Santa Barbara and are living at the home of Dennis' straight sister. He now sells clothes in a trendy shop and shows every sign of becoming a good provider for Jean and the baby, even though at last report they were not married. 20

The Mill Valley commune still struggles on, led by an older couple who are legally married and veterans of a rural commune. Other members appear ready to drop out because of the emotional strain of having to work out "meaningful relationships" with more than a dozen people at once. 21

Mill Valley will soon have its own anti-commune ordinance and the Nixon Administration has cut off food stamps for households made up of unrelated individuals. Agriculture Department officials concede that the new amendment is intended to deny food stamps to "unrelated youths following the hippie family life style." Many citizens now blame long-haired youth for the rise in welfare costs, crime, drug abuse in the schools, the spread of V.D., and the wave of bombings. The only attempt to pin down the fact behind all this fuss was made recently in Santa Cruz County by Environmental Operations Research of Los Gatos. They set out to find that great beast, "The Undesirable Transient Element." They discovered that: 22

> From information at hand, it is evident that the long-haired group is the seat of the agitation of the community. It is not quite so evident that this group is the major instigator and perpetrator of all crime. It is perhaps best to say that the group is both the source and focus of the irritation and the fears of the community and indeed "asks" for a lot of the hassling it gets. . . .

What seems to be going on with communes per se is some social experimenting that is neither as new nor as widespread as the media feature writers would have us believe. As for finding a sizable portion of the next generation in communes, with the family a dying institution, the evidence is still lacking. 23

However, something very ominous that is going on is often overlooked in all the chatter about the sex and psychology of the communes. 24

And that is that the communes are only the most visible focal point for an alarming amount of the kind of hate mongering, stereotyping and discriminatory class legislation that was once reserved for blacks, but is now spreading to "the long hairs" or hippies. Most of them do not live in communes, but like blacks, they're visually different and culturally separate. Anti-loitering laws specifically directed at hippies by the cities of Carmel and San Rafael were recently struck down by the California courts. [See editorial, "Hippies Have Rights," *The Nation,* March 15.] While they were being enforced, U.S. citizens were being rousted from public places because of their appearance. Thoughtful people began to wonder if the Old South's Jim Crow had been resurrected as the totem of law and order in the West. As the polarization and social alienation between long-haired youth and the straight community grows, should the long hairs be relegated to a ghetto of their own? Will they then burn their way toward equal civil rights as the blacks did in Watts, or does someone in power have a better idea?

SUBJECT

1. Why, according to Solnit, are so many people turning to communal living? Do you think residents of communes would resent being placed in "the old American institution" of "leaving home"? What about the comparison to "elderly wanderers in camper trucks"?

2. Why are communes subjected to so much external harrassment? Is what goes on in the house next door any business of a neighbor?

3. What seems to be Solnit's purpose in the lengthy section showing that neither rootlessness nor communal living are anything new in American society?

4. For what reasons, according to Solnit, are communes generally unable to achieve the ideals for which they were formed?

5. Solnit does not seem especially hopeful about the future of communes; would you say he is antagonistic toward them? Toward whom are the strongest statements in the article directed?

STRUCTURE

1. There are really three related but different cause and effect analyses in this article; what are they? Has Solnit organized the essay so that their separation is made clear?

2. Is the final sentence a rhetorical question or a genuine query? Do you think such a question is an effective way to end the essay?

3. Solnit cannot logically generalize from a single example — that of Dennis and Jean. Of what use, then, is this one example?

4. Considering the many different kinds of communes which have been formed, are the reasons given for people joining communes adequate to explain them all? Has Solnit considered the possibility of a multiplicity of causes?

5. Can you think of reasons other than those suggested by Solnit that a neighborhood would want to keep communes out? Does Solnit recognize that there may be a difference between stated reasons and *real* reasons?

6. For many people of the "youth culture," motives for action are often in terms of "Why not?" rather than "Why?" Does Solnit make the mistake of assuming that people who join communes do so because they have a conscious and valid "reason"?

THE BLACKS
AND THE UNIONS

Bayard Rustin

Bayard Rustin is executive director of the Randolph Institute in New York. For the past twenty-five years he has been an active organizer for civil rights and peace movements. He was a chief organizer of that grandfather of many marches on Washington since, the 1963 black Freedom March (at which Martin Luther King gave his famous "I have a dream" speech). The intricately organized article which follows bases its argument on a causal relationship known in logic as "concomitant variations." (If the results of a chemical reaction always vary when the temperature is raised or lowered, then temperature is part of the cause of the reaction.) Here, Rustin wants to show that variations in the status of unions bear a causal relationship to the welfare of blacks.

One of the main articles of faith in liberal dogma these days is that the interests and objectives of the American trade-union movement are in fundamental conflict with the interests and objectives of black America. One can hardly pick up any of the major journals of liberal opinion without reading some form of the statement that the white worker has become affluent and conservative and feels his security to be threatened by the demand for racial equality. A corollary of this statement is that it is a primary function of the labor movement to protect the white worker from the encroaching black. Furthermore, the argument runs, since there are no signs that the blacks may be letting up in their struggle for economic betterment, a hostile confrontation between blacks and the unions is not only inevitable but necessary.

It may well be that historians of the future, recording the events of the past five years, will conclude that the major effect of the civic turbulence in this period has been in fact to distract us from the real and pressing social needs of the nation. And perhaps nothing illustrates the point more vividly than the whole question of the relations between blacks and the unions.

Reprinted by permission from *Harper's* (May 1971).

This question itself, however, cannot be properly understood except   3
in the larger context of the history of the civil-rights movement. Negro
protest in the Sixties, if the movement is in its turn to be properly
understood, must be divided into two distinct phases. The first phase,
which covered something like the first half of the decade, was one in
which the movement's clear objective was to destroy the legal foundations of racism in America. Thus the locale of the struggle was the South,
the evil to be eliminated was Jim Crow, and the enemy, who had a
special talent for arousing moral outrage among even the most reluctant sympathizers with the cause, was the rock-willed segregationist.

Now, one thing about the South more than any other has been ob-   4
scured in the romantic vision of the region — of ancient evil, of defeat, of enduring rural charm — that has been so much of our literary
and intellectual tradition: for the Negro, Southern life had precisely a
quality of clarity, a clarity which while oppressive was also supportive.
The Southern caste system and folk culture rested upon a clear, albeit
unjust, set of legal and institutional relationships which prescribed roles
for individuals and established a modicum of social order. The struggle
that was finally mounted against that system was actually fed and
strengthened by the social environment from which it emerged. No
profound analysis, no overriding social theory was needed in order both
to locate and understand the injustices that were to be combated. All
that was demanded of one was sufficient courage to demonstrate against
them. One looks back upon this period in the civil-rights movement
with nostalgia.

During the second half of the Sixties, the center of the crisis shifted   5
to the sprawling ghettos of the North. Here black experience was radically different from that in the South. The stability of institutional relationships was largely absent in Northern ghettos, especially among the
poor. Over twenty years ago, the black sociologist E. Franklin Frazier
was able to see the brutalizing effect of urbanization upon lower-class
blacks: ". . . the bonds of sympathy and community of interests that held
their parents together in the rural environment have been unable to
withstand the disintegrating forces in the city." Southern blacks migrated north in search of work, seeking to become transformed from a
peasantry into a working class. But instead of jobs they found only
misery, and far from becoming a proletariat, they came to constitute a
Lumpenproletariat, an underclass of rejected people. Frazier's pro-
phetic words resound today with terrifying precision: ". . . as long as the
bankrupt system of Southern agriculture exists, Negro families will continue to seek a living in the towns and cities of the country. They will
crowd the slum areas of Southern cities or make their way to Northern

cities, where their family life will become disrupted and their poverty will force them to depend upon charity."

Out of such conditions, social protest was to emerge in a form peculiar to the ghetto, a form which could never have taken root in the South except in such large cities as Atlanta or Houston. The evils in the North are not easy to understand and fight against, or at least not as easy as Jim Crow, and this has given the protest from the ghetto a special edge of frustration. There are few specific injustices, such as a segregated lunch counter, that offer both a clear object of protest and a good chance of victory. Indeed, the problem in the North is not one of social injustice so much as the results of institutional pathology. Each of the various institutions touching the lives of urban blacks — those relating to education, health, employment, housing, and crime — is in need of drastic reform. One might say that the Northern race problem has in good part become simply the problem of the American city — which is gradually becoming a reservation for the unwanted, most of whom are black. 6

In such a situation, even progress has proved to be a mixed blessing. During the Sixties, for example, Northern blacks as a group have made great economic gains, the result of which being that hundreds of thousands of them were able to move out of the hard-core poverty areas. Meanwhile, however, their departure, while a great boon to those departing, only contributed further to the deterioration of the slums, now being drained of their stable middle and working class. Combined with the large influx of Southern blacks during the same period, this process was leaving the ghetto more and more the precinct of a depressed underclass. To the segregation by race was now added segregation by class, and all of the problems created by segregation and poverty — inadequate schooling, substandard and overcrowded housing, lack of access to jobs or to job training, narcotics and crime — were greatly aggravated. And again because of segregation, the violence of the black underclass was turned in upon itself. 7

If the problems of the ghetto do not lend themselves to simple analyses or solutions, then, this is because they cannot be solved without mounting a total attack on the inadequacies endemic to, and injustices embedded in, all of our institutions. It is perhaps understandable that young Northern blacks, confronting these problems, have so often provided answers which are really non-answers; which are really dramatic statements satisfying some sense of the need for militancy without even beginning to deal with the basic economic and political problems of the ghetto. Primary among these non-answers is the idea that black 8 progress depends upon a politics of race and revolution. I am referring here not to the recent assertions of black pride — assertions that will be made as long as that pride continues to be undermined by white society — but to the kind of black nationalism which consists in a bitter rejection of American society and vindicates a withdrawal from social struggle into a kind of hermetic racial world where blacks can "do their thing." Nationalists have been dubbed "militants" by the press because they have made their point with such fervent hostility to white society, but the implication of their position actually amounts to little more than the age-old conservative message that blacks should help themselves — a thing that, by the very definition of the situation, they have not the resources to do.

The same is true of black proposals for revolution. For to engage in   9
revolutionary acts in contemporary America — where, despite a lot of inflammatory rhetoric, there is not even a whisper of a revolutionary situation — not only diverts precious energies away from the political arena where the real battles for change must be fought, but might also precipitate a vicious counterrevolution the chief victims of which will be blacks.

The truth about the situation of the Negro today is that there are   10
powerful forces, composed largely of the corporate elite and Southern conservatives, which will resist any change in the economic or racial structure of this country that might cut into their resources or challenge their status; and such is precisely what any program genuinely geared to improve his lot must do. Moreover, these forces today are not merely resisting change. With their representative Richard Nixon in the White House, they are engaged in an assault on the advances made during the past decade. It has been Nixon's tragic and irresponsible choice to play at the politics of race, not, to be sure, with the primitive demagoguery of a "Pitchfork Ben" Tillman, say, but nevertheless with the same intent of building a political majority on the basis of white hostility to blacks. So far he has been unsuccessful, but the potential for the emergence of such a reactionary majority does exist, especially if the turbulence and racial polarization which we have recently experienced persists.

What is needed, therefore, is not only a program that would effect   11
some fundamental change in the distribution of America's resources for those in the greatest need of them, but also a political majority that will support such a program. In other words, nothing less than a program truly, not merely verbally, radical in scope would be adequate to meet the present crisis; and nothing less than a politically constituted majority, outnumbering the conservative forces, would be adequate to carry it through. Now, it so happens that there is one social force which, by virtue both of its size and its very nature, is essential to the creation

of such a majority — and so in relation to which the success or failure of the black struggle must finally turn. And that is the American trade-union movement.

Addressing the AFL-CIO convention in 1961, Martin Luther King observed: "Negroes are almost entirely a working people. There are pitifully few Negro millionaires and few Negro employers. Our needs are identical with labor's needs — decent wages, fair working conditions, livable housing, old-age security, health and welfare measures, conditions in which families can grow, have education for their children and respect in the community." 12

Despite the widely held belief that the blacks and the unions have not the same, but rather irreconcilable, interests — and despite the fact that certain identifiable unions do practice discrimination — King's words remain valid today. Blacks *are* mostly a working people, they continue to need what labor needs, and they must fight side by side with unions to achieve these things. 13

Of all the misconceptions about the labor movement that have been so lovingly dwelt on in the liberal press, perhaps none is put forth more often and is farther from the truth than that the unions are of and for white people. For one thing, there are, according to labor historian Thomas R. Brooks, between 2,500,000 and 2,750,000 black trade unionists in America.* If his figures are correct, and other estimates seem to bear them out, the percentage of blacks in the unions is a good deal higher than the percentage of blacks in the total population — 15 percent as compared with 11 percent, to be precise. And since the vast majority of black trade unionists are members of integrated unions, one can conclude that the labor movement is the most integrated major institution in American society, certainly more integrated than the corporations, the churches, or the universities. 14

Moreover, blacks are joining unions in increasing numbers. According to a 1968 report by *Business Week,* one out of every three new union members is black. The sector of the economy which is currently being most rapidly unionized is that of the service industries, and most particularly among government employees, such as hospital workers, sanitation workers, farm workers, and paraprofessionals in educational and social-welfare institutions. This category of worker is, of course, both largely nonwhite and shamefully underpaid. 15

Like other workers, blacks have gained from the achievements of their unions in the way of higher wages, improved working conditions, 16

*"Black Upsurge in the Unions," *Dissent* (March-April, 1970).

and better fringe benefits. To be sure, in some unions whites still possess a disproportionate number of the higher-paying jobs and there is not yet adequate black representation at the staff level and in policy-making positions. But the question of what continues to account for the perpetuation of such inequities cannot properly be answered by the fashionable and easy reference to racial discrimination in the unions. Statistical surveys have shown that the participation of blacks in the work force is no higher in nonunionized occupations than in unionized ones. Indeed, as Derek C. Bok and John T. Dunlop have pointed out in their remarkably informed and comprehensive study, *Labor and the American Community,* even in the automotive and aero-space industries, where the unions have been known for dedication to racial justice, the percentage of blacks, particularly in the skilled jobs, is not appreciably higher than in other industries.

There have, therefore, to be far more fundamental social and economic reasons for present inequalities in employment. Primary among these reasons are certain underlying changes within the entire society which are being reflected in the evolving character and composition of the work force itself. The upsurge of union organization of minority-group workers in the fields of education, sanitation, and health care, for instance, is the result of the rapid expansion of the service sector of the economy. 17

Another crucial factor here is government economic policy. The tremendous growth in the economy from 1960 to 1968 increased nonwhite employment by 19 percent, 4 percent higher than the increase for whites, and during the same period the unemployment rate for nonwhite adult men dropped from 9.6 to 3.9 percent. A large number of these new black workers entered unions for the simple reason that they had jobs. And now many of them are out of jobs, not because of union discrimination, but because the Nixon Administration's economic policies have so far caused a sharp increase in unemployment. 18

All of which is not to exonerate the entire labor movement of any possible charge of wrongdoing. It is rather to put the problem of economic inequality into some useful perspective. The inequalities which persist within the unions must of course be corrected. They are in fact being corrected through the work of the labor movement itself — the role of the Civil Rights Department of the AFL-CIO is particularly noteworthy here — the civil-rights activities of the federal government, and the efforts of black trade unionists who are taking over leadership positions in their locals and are playing more of a role in determining union policy. The union drive against discrimination was exemplified by 19

211

the fight made by the AFL-CIO to have a Fair Employment Practices section written into the 1964 Civil Rights Act. Both President Kennedy and Robert Kennedy were opposed to including an FEPC section because they thought it would kill the bill, but George Meany pressed for it. He did so for a simple reason. The AFL-CIO is a federation of affiliates which retain a relatively high degree of autonomy. The parent body can urge compliance with its policies, but the decision to act is left up to the affiliates. Meany felt that the only way the AFL-CIO could deal effectively with unions practicing discrimination would be to demand compliance with the law of the land. He testified before the House Judiciary Committee that the labor movement was calling "for legislation for the correction of shortcomings in its own ranks." And the passage of the 1964 Civil Rights Act greatly speeded the process of this correction.

Most labor leaders, I believe, are opposed to discrimination against 20 the blacks on moral grounds. But they also have highly practical grounds for their position. They understand that discrimination hurts the entire labor movement as much as it hurts blacks. They know from long experience as unionists that anything which divides the workers makes it more difficult for them to struggle together for the achievement of common goals. Racial antagonisms have undermined solidarity during strikes and have been exploited by management as a means of weakening unions. The following passage from the classic study, *The Black Worker,* written in 1931 by Sterling D. Spero and Abram L. Harris, may not be typical of every company's approach to its work force, yet it describes a practice commonly in use till this very day:

> The Negro is now recognized as a permanent factor in industry and large employers use him as one of the racial and national elements which help to break the homogeneity of their labor force. This, incidentally, fits into the program of big concerns for maintaining what they call "a cosmopolitan force," which frees the employer from dependence upon any one group for his labor supply and also thwarts unity of purpose and labor organization.

People no longer lend much credence to the idea that management 21 continues to think and operate in such convoluted terms. But it does, and so does labor. Indeed, such terms as "labor solidarity" or "labor disunity" are standard tools of the trade in labor-management relations. A further error is to imagine that unions might from such reasoning increase unity within their ranks by excluding blacks. On the contrary, given the character of the American working class, the *only* possibility for genuine labor solidarity is for the blacks to be fully integrated into every level of the trade-union movement. If they are not, then they will continue to exist outside the unions as a constant source of cheap labor exploitable by management to depress wages or to break strikes.

Another notion which has passed into vogue among some blacks as 22 well as some whites is that the whole problem of integration can be finessed by organizing the workers into dual unions. This is not a new idea; nor is its feasibility any greater today than was evidenced by a record of impossibility in the past. For were there to be racially separate unions, it would naturally follow that the interests of blacks would be diametrically opposed to those of whites, with whom they would be in competition. And once again, no matter how innocently or unintentionally, the blacks would remain in the role of being a reserve army that could be called into action whenever companies felt the white workers needed a good kick in the pants.

Of course, the blacks would also be victims in this situation since they 23 would be at the beck and call of management only if they were chronically unemployed. Thus, exploitation is as much the effect of poverty as its cause. It is only the poor, those who are needy and weak, who can be manipulated at the whim of the wealthy. This introduces another notion concerning the welfare of black and white workers about which there has grown up a misplaced skepticism — namely, the function of the supply of labor. Put very simply, it is in the interests of employers for the supply of labor to be greater than the demand for it. This situation obtains when there is high unemployment or what is often called a "loose" labor market. Under these conditions, the bargaining position of the unions is weakened since labor, which is after all the product unions are selling, is not in high demand, and also because there are a lot of unemployed workers whom the companies can turn to if the unions should in any way prove recalcitrant. Generally speaking, an excess of supply over demand for labor exerts a downward pressure on wages, and, vice versa, there is an upward pressure on wages when the demand for labor outpaces the supply. In addition, this dynamic of supply and demand affects the level of racial antagonism within the work force. If supply exceeds demand, i.e., if there is a high level of unemployment, there will be tremendous competition for jobs between white and black workers, and racial tensions will increase. Under conditions of relative full employment, there will be little job competition and greater racial harmony. As George Lichtheim recently pointed out: "If economic conflict as a source of political antagonism is ruled out . . . the residual cultural tensions . . . need not and doubtless will not fall to zero; but they can be held down to a tolerable level."*

*"What Socialism Is and Is Not," *The New York Review of Books* (April 9, 1970).

These ideas shape the conceptual universe as well as the behavior of   24
many of the principal actors in our country's economic conflicts. The
fact that they tend to be ignored in so much current discussion of blacks
and unions is as much a testimony to the naïveté of liberal journalists
as it is to the public-relations skills of corporations. A good example of
what I mean is the press treatment accorded the terrible racial conflict
in the building trades and the Administration's policies in this area.

Racial discrimination exists in the building trades. It is unjustifiable   25
by any moral standard, and as to the objective of rooting it out there
can be no disagreement among people of good will. How truly to
achieve this objective is another matter. An important distinction here
is often overlooked. One cannot set varying moral standards in judging
the performance of institutions; the same standard must be applied
equally to all — to the unions, the corporations, the churches, etc. But
beyond the realm of moral judgment is the crucial question of social
utility. Blacks could attack Jim Crow in the South without regard to the
welfare of the lunch counters, the hotels, or whatever, because they had
little or no stake in them. This is not the case with the trade-union
movement, a social force in which blacks *do* have a stake. If blacks
attack the unions in such a way as to damage them irreparably, they will
ultimately harm themselves. As it happens, certain presently self-styled
friends of the Negro are in fact not at all averse to such a possible
development.

Writing in the *New York Times,* Tom Wicker reflected the views of   26
many liberals when he described the Nixon Administration's strong and
forthright position on the building-trades issue as "remarkable." Wicker's analysis, however, never advances beyond this point. He never asks
why the Nixon Administration — particularly Attorney General
Mitchell, and most particularly given other Administration policies —
would suddenly take such an interest in the welfare of blacks. The
question is neither gratuitous nor idle. Why, in fact, would a President
who has developed a "Southern strategy," who has cut back on school-
integration efforts, tried to undermine the black franchise by watering
down the 1965 Voting Rights Act, nominated to the Supreme Court
men like Haynsworth and Carswell, cut back on funds for vital social
programs, and proposed a noxious crime bill for Washington, D.C. —
which is nothing less than a blatant appeal to white fear — why indeed would such a President take up the cause of integration in the
building trades?

To begin with, Mr. Nixon's Philadelphia Plan — which requires   27
contractors to make a commitment to hire a certain quota of black
workers on a job where over $500,000 of federal funds are involved
— actually does nothing for integration. In order to meet this com-

mitment, a contractor could shift the required number of black workers in an area onto a particular job, a procedure known in the trade as checker-boarding. He would thus satisfy federal requirements *for that job,* but no new jobs would be created for blacks and no Negroes would be brought into the building trades. In fact, the contractor can even achieve compliance simply by making an effort of good faith, such as contacting certain people in the area who are concerned about black participation in the building trades. If those people do not produce any workers, the contractor has done his job and can get the federal money. The Philadelphia Plan makes no provision for training, nor does it provide a means for blacks to attain the security of journeyman status within the unions. It is geared only to temporary jobs, and even in this area it is deficient. It is designed primarily to embarrass the unions and to organize public pressure against them.

In simple truth, the plan is part and parcel of a general Republican attack on labor. The same Administration which designed it (as well as the Southern strategy), has also sent to Congress a measure that would increase federal control over internal union political affairs. Republican Senators and Representatives have introduced dozens of antilabor bills: one of which, for example, would create a right-to-work law for federal employees; another would restrict labor's involvement in political activities. Moreover, the Administration has turned the heat on labor at the same time that it has cooled pressure against discrimination by the corporations. 28

The advantages to the Republicans from this kind of strategy should be obvious. Nixon supports his friends among the corporate elite and hurts his enemies in the unions. He also gains a convenient cover for his anti-Negro policies in the South, and above all, he weakens his political opposition by aggravating the differences between its two strongest and most progressive forces — the labor movement and the civil-rights movement. 29

The Philadelphia Plan and related actions are also part of the Administration's attempt to pin onto labor the blame for inflation in construction costs. The *Wall Street Journal* has suggested that contractors welcome the thrust for integration in the building trades since this "might slow inflation in construction by increasing the supply of workers." There is reason to believe that Mr. Nixon thinks in these same terms. It will be remembered that on almost the very day he proposed the Philadelphia Plan, he also ordered a 75 percent reduction in federal construction — thereby reducing the number of jobs available in the industry and producing the twofold effect of exerting a deflationary pressure on wages and increasing competition among workers over scarce jobs. When Nixon finally freed some of the construction funds 30 some months later (a move no doubt designed to improve the economic picture for the 1970 elections), he warned that "a shortage of skilled labor runs up the cost of that labor." He said he would issue directives to the Secretaries of Defense; Labor; and Health, Education, and Welfare to train veterans and others toward the goal of "enlarging the pool of skilled manpower."

It should be pointed out in passing that the President's approach to the problem of inflation in construction costs cannot succeed since he has made the typical businessman's error of identifying wages as the major inflationary factor. According to the Bureau of Labor Statistics, on-site labor costs as a percentage of total construction costs decreased between 1949 and 1969 from 33 percent to 18 percent. During the same period, the combined cost of land and financing rose from 16 percent to 31 percent of the total cost. Thus land and financing, not labor, have been the major causes of inflation in construction. Nevertheless, the President continues his crusade against "wage inflation." 31

The concern with increasing the supply while reducing the cost of labor is what motivated the Nixon Administration's most recent act in the construction field — the suspension of the 1931 Davis-Bacon Act. Here the "deflationary" intention is more evident than in the case of the Philadelphia Plan, but the similarity between the two moves is striking, particularly with regard to the anti-union role envisioned for the unorganized Negro worker. 32

The Davis-Bacon Act requires contractors on federal or federally assisted projects to pay all workers, union or nonunion, the prevailing union wage rates. The suspension of the Act will not directly affect the wages of unionized workers who are protected by their contract. It will, however, enable contractors to cut the wages of nonunion workers, and this, in turn, should encourage the employment of these workers instead of the higher paid unionists. Thus, there will be fewer jobs for organized workers (there is already an 11 percent unemployment rate in the construction industry), and the bargaining power of the unions will be weakened. Since many of the unorganized workers are nonwhite, it might be argued that this is a boon to their fortunes since they will be more likely to find work. Aside from the fact that they will be working for lower wages, the question is again raised whether it is in the interests of blacks to let themselves be used by employers to hurt unions. I do not think that it is. Their interests lie in becoming part of the trade-union movement. Ironically, the current attack on labor may speed the process of their entrance into the labor movement, for in situations where union standards have been threatened by open shops, unions have been spurred on to fully organize their industry. 33

216

It should be emphasized that this would only encourage changes that   34
have already been taking place for a number of years as a result of
pressure from civil-rights groups and union leaders.

Seventy-nine Outreach programs now operate in as many cities and   35
have placed over 8,000 minority-group youngsters in building-trades
apprenticeship training programs. Sixty percent have been placed in
the highest paying trades — the plumbers, electricians, sheet-metal
workers, carpenters, pipe fitters, and iron workers. This is far from
sufficient, of course, but within the past two years, these programs have
expanded by over 400 percent, and they are continuing to grow. The
role of civil-rights activists should be to continue to see that they grow.

The blacks have a choice. They can fight to strengthen the trade-   36
union movement by wiping out the vestiges of segregation that remain
in it, or they can, knowingly or unknowingly, offer themselves as pawns
in the conservatives' games of bust-the-unions.

The choice must be made on the basis of a critical assessment of the   37
current economic plight of blacks. More than any single factor, the
Nixon Administration's policies of high interest rates, "fiscal responsibility," and economic slowdown are undermining the gains which blacks
made during the past decade. Dr. Charles C. Killingsworth, a leading
manpower economist, predicted some months ago that within a year
the unemployment rate is likely to go up to 8 percent. We could expect
the rate for blacks to be twice as high. Nixon's managed recession may
calm the fears of businessmen, but it will do so at terrible cost to blacks
and to all other working people. There are, no doubt, many well-mean-
ing people who are concerned about the plight of unemployed workers
under Nixon, but it is only the labor movement that is fighting every
day for policies that will get these workers back on the job.

Thus, it is clear why unions are important to black workers. What may   38
perhaps seem less obvious and must also be sharply emphasized is that
the legislative program of the trade-union movement can go a long way
toward satisfying the economic needs of the larger black *community*.
The racial crisis, as we have seen, is not an isolated problem that lends
itself to redress by a protesting minority. Being rooted in the very social
and economic structure of the society, it can be solved only by a comprehensive program that gets to the heart of why we can't build adequate housing for everybody, why we must always have a "tolerable"
level of unemployment, or why we lack enough funds for education. In
this sense the racial crisis challenges the entire society's capacity to
redirect its resources on the basis of human need rather than profit.

Blacks can pose this challenge, but only the federal government has the power and the money to meet it. And it is here that the trade-union movement can play such an important role.

The problems of the most aggrieved sector of the black ghetto cannot 39 and will never be solved without full employment, and full employment, with the government as employer of last resort, is the keystone of labor's program. One searches in vain among the many so-called friends of the black struggle for a seconding voice to this simple yet far-reaching proposition. Some call it inflationary, while to others, who are caught up in the excitement of the black cultural revolution, it is pedestrian and irrelevant. But in terms of the economic condition of the black community, nothing more radical has yet been proposed. There is simply no other way for the black *Lumpenproletariat* to become a proletariat. And full employment is only one part of labor's program. The movement's proposals in the areas of health, housing, education, and environment would, if enacted, achieve nothing less than the transformation of the quality of our urban life. How ironic that in this period when the trade-union movement is thought to be conservative, its social and economic policies are far and away more progressive than those of any other major American institution. Nor — again in contrast to most of the other groups officially concerned with these things — is labor's program merely in the nature of a grand proposal; there is also an actual record of performance, particularly in the area of civil rights. Clarence Mitchell, the director of the Washington Bureau of the NAACP and legislative chairman of the Leadership Conference on Civil Rights, a man more deeply involved in Congressional civil-rights battles than any other black in America, has said, "None of the legislative fights we have made in the field of civil rights could have been won without the trade-union movement. We couldn't have beaten Haynsworth without labor, and the struggle against Carswell would not have been a contest."

Labor's interest in progressive social legislation naturally leads it into 40 the political arena. The Committee on Political Education of the AFL-CIO, the Political Action Committee of the UAW, and the political arm of the Teamsters were active in every state in the last election registering and educating voters and getting out the vote. This year trade unionists were more politically active than they have ever been during an off-year election. The reason for this is clear. With so many liberal Senators up for reelection, and with political alignments in great flux, 1970 presented itself as a year that would initiate a new period in American politics — a period which would see the regrouping of liberal forces or the consolidation of a conservative majority.

218

One of the important factors determining the kind of political align- 41
ments that will emerge from this period of instability will be the relationship between the trade-union movement and the liberal
community, and today this relationship is severely strained. Differences
over the war in Vietnam are frequently cited as a major cause of this
division, but there has been a great deal of misunderstanding on this
issue. The house of labor itself is divided over the war, and even those
labor leaders who support it have enthusiastically backed dove Congressional candidates who have liberal domestic records, among them
such firm opponents of the war as Mike Mansfield, Edward Kennedy,
Vance Hartke, Philip Hart, Howard Metzenbaum, and Edmund
Muskie.

A better understanding of the trade-union movement by liberals may 42
be developing, but for the present the antagonistic attitudes that exist
cast an ideological pall over the chances for uniting the democratic Left
coalition. It must be said that the vehement contempt with which the
liberals have come to attack the unions bespeaks something more than
a mere political critique of "conservatism." When A. H. Raskin writes
that "the typical worker — from construction craftsman to shoe clerk
— has become probably the most reactionary political force in the
country"; or when Anthony Lewis lumps under the same category the
rich oilmen and "the members of powerful, monopolistic labor unions";
or when Murray Kempton writes that "the AFL-CIO has lived happily in
a society which, more lavishly than any in history, has managed the care
and feeding of incompetent white people," and adds, "Who better
represents that ideal than George Wallace"; or when many other liberals casually toss around the phrase "labor-fascists," one cannot but inevitably conclude that one is in the presence not of political opposition but
of a certain class hatred. This hatred is not necessarily one based on
conflicting class interests — though they may play a role here — but
rather a hatred of the elite for the "mass." And this hatred is multiplied
a thousandfold by the fact that we live in a democratic society in which
the coarse multitude can outvote the elite and make decisions which
may be contrary to the wishes and values, perhaps even the interests
and the prejudices, of those who are better off.

It is difficult not to conclude that many liberals and radicals use 43
subjective, rather than objective, criteria in judging the character of a
social force. A progressive force, in their view, is one that is alienated
from the dominant values of the culture, not one which contributes to
greater social equality and distributive justice. Thus today the trade-
union movement has been relegated to reactionary status, even though
it is actually more progressive than at any time in its history — if by

219

progressive we mean a commitment to broad, long-term social reform in addition to the immediate objectives of improving wages and working conditions. At the same time, the most impoverished social group, that substratum which Herbert Marcuse longingly calls "the outcasts and the outsiders," has been made the new vanguard of social progress. And it is here that liberals and New Leftists come together in their proposal for a new coalition "of the rich, educated, and dedicated with the poor," as Eric F. Goldman has admiringly described it, or in Walter Laqueur's more caustic phraseology, "between the *Lumpenproletariat* and the *Lumpenintelligentsia.*"

This political approach, known among liberals as New Politics and among radicals as New Leftism, denotes a certain convergence of the Left and the Right, if not in philosophy and intent, then at least in practical effect. I am not referring simply to the elitism which the intellectual Left shares with the economic Right, but also to their symbolic political relationship. Many of the sophisticated right-wing attacks on labor are frequently couched in left-wing rhetoric. Conservative claims that unions are anti-black, are responsible for inflation, and constitute minorities which threaten and intimidate the majority reverberate in the liberal community and are shaping public opinion to accept a crackdown on the trade-union movement. 44

While many adherents of the New Politics are outraged by Nixon's Southern strategy, their own strategy is simply the obverse of his. The potential for a Republican majority depends upon Nixon's success in attracting into the conservative fold lower-middle-class whites, the same group that the New Politics has written off. The question is not whether this group is conservative or liberal, for it is both, and how it acts will depend upon the way the issues are defined. If they are defined as race and dissent, then Nixon will win. But if, on the other hand, they are defined so as to appeal to the progressive economic interests of the lower middle class, then it becomes possible to build an alliance on the basis of common interest between this group and the black community. The importance of the trade-union movement is that it embodies this common interest. This was proved most clearly in 1968 when labor mounted a massive educational campaign which reduced the Wallace supporters among its membership to a tiny minority. And the trade-union movement remains today the greatest obstacle to the success of Nixon's strategy. 45

The prominent racial and ethnic loyalties that divide American society have, together with our democratic creed, obscured a fundamental reality — that we are a class society and, though we do not often talk 46 about such things, that we are engaged in a class struggle. This reality may not provide some people with their wished-for quotient of drama, though I would think that the GE strike or the UAW strike against GM are sufficiently dramatic, and it may now have become an institutionalized struggle between the trade-union movement and the owners and managers of corporate wealth. Yet it is a struggle nonetheless, and its outcome will determine whether we will have a greater or lesser degree of economic and social equality in this country. As long as blacks are poor, our own struggle will be part of this broader class reality. To the degree that it is not, black liberation will remain a dream in the souls of an oppressed people.

SUBJECT

1. What change does Rustin say has taken place in the civil rights movement since the early sixties? Why are the new problems more difficult to solve?

2. What is the basis of Rustin's argument that there must be a coalition between blacks and the labor movement? What does he think they could accomplish together?

3. What efforts does Rustin think are being made to prevent such a coalition?

4. What is economically wrong with the idea of blacks establishing their own, "separate but equal" unions?

5. Why, according to Rustin, have liberals become disenchanted with the labor movement?

6. What does Rustin think can be done to get blacks and white unionists to vote together? Doesn't a large majority of these two groups consistently vote Democratic, anyway?

STRUCTURE

1. How does Rustin establish a causal relationship between the success of unions and the welfare of blacks? Does he ignore any significant differences in aims which might counterbalance the similarities?

2. In paragraphs 22 and 23, Rustin predicts what would happen if blacks formed separate unions. This is of course a *hypothetical* cause and effect relationship; does Rustin base it adequately on *known* labor economics to make his prediction at least reasonable if not inevitable?

3. Examine the explanation of why liberals no longer strongly support unions. Are the causes assigned shown to be "necessary" or merely "probable"?

4. Would you say that Rustin is aiming his article chiefly at blacks, at white unionists, or at some other group? Why would he choose to publish the essay in *Harper's*?

5. How would you characterize the style of this writing? Does Rustin seem to be deliberately avoiding the "black idiom" of many black (and New Left white) leaders?

WORK IN AN
ALIENATED SOCIETY

Erich Fromm

Dr. Erich Fromm was born in Germany in 1900. His training and his chief interest have been in social psychology. Since coming to the United States in 1934 to escape the Nazi persecution of Jews, Fromm has taught at Columbia, Bennington, Michigan State, N.Y.U., and in Mexico, where he now lives. His books include the classic Escape from Freedom *(1941), which is still widely read in college classes,* Man for Himself *(1947),* The Art of Loving *(1956),* May Man Prevail? *(1961),* The Heart of Man *(1964), and* You shall Be as Gods *(1966). The following passage is from* The Sane Society *(1955), one of the "sacred texts" of many who seek to avoid the alienation of living in a technological society by joining communes and other life style experiments. What Fromm argues for in this book is a "Humanistic Communitarian Socialism."*

What becomes the meaning of *work* in an alienated society? 1

We have already made some brief comments about this question in 2
the general discussion of alienation. But since this problem is of utmost importance, not only for the understanding of present-day society, but also for any attempt to create a saner society, I want to deal with the nature of work separately and more extensively in the following pages.

Unless man exploits others, he has to work in order to live. However 3
primitive and simple his method of work may be, by the very fact of production, he has risen above the animal kingdom; rightly has he been defined as "the animal that produces." But work is not only an inescapable necessity for man. Work is also his liberator from nature, his creator as a social and independent being. *In the process of work, that is, the molding and changing of nature outside of himself, man molds and changes himself.* He emerges from nature by mastering her; he develops his powers of cooperation, of reason, his sense of beauty. He separates himself from nature, from the original unity with her, but at the same time unites himself with her again as her master and builder. The

more his work develops, the more his individuality develops. In molding nature and re-creating her, he learns to make use of his powers, increasing his skill and creativeness. Whether we think of the beautiful paintings in the caves of Southern France, the ornaments on weapons among primitive people, the statues and temples of Greece, the cathedrals of the Middle Ages, the chairs and tables made by skilled craftsmen, or the cultivation of flowers, trees or corn by peasants — all are expressions of the creative transformation of nature by man's reason and skill.

In Western history, craftsmanship, especially as it developed in the 4 thirteenth and fourteenth centuries, constitutes one of the peaks in the evolution of creative work. Work was not only a useful activity, but one which carried with it a profound satisfaction. The main features of craftsmanship have been very lucidly expressed by C. W. Mills. "There is no ulterior motive in work other than the product being made and the processes of its creation. The details of daily work are meaningful because they are not detached in the worker's mind from the product of the work. The worker is free to control his own working action. The craftsman is thus able to learn from his work; and to use and develop his capacities and skills in its prosecution. There is no split of work and play, or work and culture. The craftsman's way of livelihood determines and infuses his entire mode of living."[1]

With the collapse of the medieval structure, and the beginning of the 5 modern mode of production, the meaning and function of work changed fundamentally, especially in the Protestant countries. Man, being afraid of his newly won freedom, was obsessed by the need to subdue his doubts and fears by developing a feverish activity. The outcome of this activity, success or failure, decided his salvation, indicating whether he was among the saved or the lost souls. *Work, instead of being an activity satisfying in itself and pleasureable, became a duty and an obsession.* The more it was possible to gain riches by work, the more it became a pure means to the aim of wealth and success. Work became, in Max Weber's terms, the chief factor in a system of "inner-worldly asceticism," an answer to man's sense of aloneness and isolation.

However, work in this sense existed only for the upper and middle 6 classes, those who could amass some capital and employ the work of others. For the vast majority of those who had only their physical energy to sell, work became nothing but forced labor. The worker in the eighteenth or nineteenth century who had to work sixteen hours if he did not want to starve was not doing it because he served the Lord in this way, nor because his success would show that he was among the

[1] C. W. Mills, *White Collar,* Oxford University Press, New York, 1951, p. 220.

"chosen" ones, but because he was forced to sell his energy to those who had the means of exploiting it. The first centuries of the modern era find the meaning of work divided into that of *duty* among the middle class, and that of *forced labor* among those without property.

The religious attitude toward work as a duty, which was still so preva- 7 lent in the nineteenth century, has been changing considerably in the last decades. Modern man does not know what to do with himself, how to spend his lifetime meaningfully, and he is driven to work in order to avoid an unbearable boredom. But work has ceased to be a moral and religious obligation in the sense of the middle-class attitude of the eighteenth and nineteenth centuries. Something new has emerged. Ever-increasing production, the drive to make bigger and better things, have become aims in themselves, new ideals. Work has become alienated from the working person.

What happens to the industrial worker? He spends his best energy for 8 seven or eight hours a day in producing "something." He needs his work in order to make a living, but his role is essentially a passive one. He fulfills a small isolated function in a complicated and highly organized process of production, and is never confronted with "his" product as a whole, at least not as a producer, but only as a consumer, provided he has the money to buy "his" product in a store. He is concerned neither with the whole product in its physical aspects nor with its wider economic and social aspects. He is put in a certain place, has to carry out a certain task, but does not participate in the organization or management of the work. He is not interested, nor does he know why one produces this, instead of another commodity — what relation it has to the needs of society as a whole. The shoes, the cars, the electric bulbs, are produced by "the enterprise," using the machines. He is a part of the machine, rather than its master as an active agent. The machine, instead of being in his service to do work for him which once had to be performed by sheer physical energy, has become his master. Instead of the machine being the substitute for human energy, man has become a substitute for the machine. *His work can be defined as the performance of acts which cannot yet be performed by machines.*

Work is a means of getting money, not in itself a meaningful human 9 activity. P. Drucker, observing workers in the automobile industry, expresses this idea very succinctly: "For the great majority of automobile workers, the only meaning of the job is in the pay check, not in anything connected with the work or the product. Work appears as something unnatural, a disagreeable, meaningless and stultifying condition of getting the pay check, devoid of dignity as well as of importance. No wonder that this puts a premium on slovenly work, on slow-downs, and on other tricks to get the same pay check with less work. No wonder

225

that this results in an unhappy and discontented worker — because a pay check is not enough to base one's self-respect on."[2]

This relationship of the worker to his work is an outcome of the whole 10 social organization of which he is a part. Being "employed,"[3] he is not an active agent, has no responsibility except the proper performance of the isolated piece of work he is doing, and has little interest except the one of bringing home enough money to support himself and his family. Nothing more is expected of him, or wanted from him. He is part of the equipment hired by capital, and his role and function are determined by this quality of being a piece of equipment. In recent decades, increasing attention has been paid to the psychology of the worker, and to his attitude toward his work, to the "human problem of industry"; but this very formulation is indicative of the underlying attitude; there is a human being spending most of his lifetime at work, and what should be discussed is the *"industrial problem of human beings," rather than "the human problem of industry."*

Most investigations in the field of industrial psychology are concerned 11 with the question of how the productivity of the individual worker can be increased, and how he can be made to work with less friction; psychology has lent its services to "human engineering," an attempt to treat the worker and employee like a machine which runs better when it is well oiled. While Taylor was primarily concerned with a better organization of the technical use of the worker's physical powers, most industrial psychologists are mainly concerned with the manipulation of the worker's psyche. The underlying idea can be formulated like this: if he works better when he is happy, then let us make him happy, secure, satisfied, or anything else, provided it raises his output and diminishes friction. In the name of "human relations," the worker is treated with all devices which suit a completely alienated person; even happiness and human values are recommended in the interest of better relations with the public. Thus, for instance, according to *Time* magazine, one of the best-known American psychiatrists said to a group of fifteen hundred Supermarket executives: "It's going to be an increased satisfaction to our customers if we are happy. . . . It is going to pay off in cold dollars and cents to management, if we could put some of these general principles of values, human relationships, really into practice." One speaks of "human relations" and one means the most in-human relations, those between alienated automatons; one speaks of happiness

[2]Cf. Peter F. Drucker, *Concept of the Corporation,* The John Day Company, New York, 1946, p. 179.

[3]The English "employed" like the German *angestellt* are terms which refer to things rather than to human beings.

and means the perfect routinization which has driven out the last doubt
and all spontaneity.

The alienated and profoundly unsatisfactory character of work results 12
in two reactions: one, the ideal of complete *laziness;* the other a deep-
seated, though often unconscious *hostility* toward work and everything
and everybody connected with it.

It is not difficult to recognize the widespread longing for the state of 13
complete laziness and passivity. Our advertising appeals to it even more
than to sex. There are, of course, many useful and labor saving gadgets.
But this usefulness often serves only as a rationalization for the appeal
to complete passivity and receptivity. A package of breakfast cereal is
being advertised as *"new — easier to eat."* An electric toaster is advertised with these words: "... the most distinctly different toaster in
the world! Everything is done *for* you with this new toaster. You need
not even bother to lower the bread. Power-action, through a unique
electric motor, *gently takes the bread right out of your fingers!"* How
many courses in languages, or other subjects are announced with the
slogan "effortless learning, no more of the old drudgery." Everybody
knows the picture of the elderly couple in the advertisement of a life-
insurance company, who have retired at the age of sixty, and spend
their life in the complete bliss of having nothing to do except just travel.

Radio and television exhibit another element of this yearning for 14
laziness: the idea of "push-button power"; by pushing a button, or
turning a knob on my machine, I have the power to produce music,
speeches, ball games, and on the television set, to command events of
the world to appear before my eyes. The pleasure of driving cars certainly rests partly upon this same satisfaction of the wish for push-button
power. By the effortless pushing of a button, a powerful machine is set
in motion; little skill and effort is needed to make the driver feel that
he is the ruler of space.

But there is far more serious and deep-seated reaction to the mean- 15
inglessness and boredom of work. It is a hostility toward work which is
much less conscious than our craving for laziness and inactivity. Many
a businessman feels himself the prisoner of his business and the commodities he sells; he has a feeling of fraudulency about his product and
a secret contempt for it. He hates his customers, who force him to put
up a show in order to sell. He hates his competitors because they are
a threat; his employees as well as his superiors, because he is in a
constant competitive fight with them. Most important of all, he hates
himself, because he sees his life passing by, without making any sense
beyond the momentary intoxication of success. Of course, this hate and
contempt for others and for oneself, and for the very things one produces, is mainly unconscious, and only occasionally comes up to aware-

227

ness in a fleeting thought, which is sufficiently disturbing to be set aside as quickly as possible.

Subject

1. Why, according to Fromm, has work changed from a basic and self-satisfying need to a loathsome task?

2. If craftsmanship provided happiness and security, why don't dissatisfied workers simply quit their jobs and become craftsmen once more?

3. Why would renaissance man have been "afraid of his newly won freedom" (paragraph 5)?

4. When work becomes merely a "means of getting money," what are the effects (a) on production and (b) on attitudes toward work? Which of these does Fromm consider most serious?

5. Do you think modern man has become lazy, as Fromm suggests, or that he expends his energy in other directions (fishing, for instance)?

6. What basic mistake have industrial psychologists made in dealing with worker dissatisfaction? Have you any personal experience that would support Fromm's assessment of the problem?

Structure

1. In his historical cause and effect analysis, Fromm says that "the meaning of work divided into that of *duty* among the middle class, and that of *forced labor* among those without property." From this point on, Fromm discusses effects on the laboring class — until the final paragraph, where without warning he changes his example to the resentment of a middle-class businessman. Does this shift constitute a flaw in his analysis?

2. In the closing paragraphs, Fromm discusses two results of unsatisfactory working conditions. One of these, laziness, is supported by numerous references to commercial advertising. Might there be other reasons for the advertising of labor saving gadgets?

3. Examine the analysis of "what happens to the worker" in paragraph 8; would you class this as valid cause and effect analysis, a personal judgment, or the results of a cause and effect analysis without a full explanation?

4. Three complete sentences in this essay are cast in italic type; what is the relationship among them? Why are they in italics? Would their function be more clear if Fromm had not italicized words and phrases elsewhere in the essay?

5. Fromm clearly has tried to avoid the specialized jargon of social psychology. Specialists often point out that the danger in doing this is oversimplification — perhaps even unintentional falsification — of a scientifically defensible analysis. Do you think Fromm's essay might be faulted on this score?

BLOODSTAINS

Joyce Carol Oates

Joyce Carol Oates was born in western New York in 1938. One of our most prolific young writers, she has already published three collections of short stories, By the North Gate *(1963),* Upon the Sweeping Flood *(1965), and* The Wheel of Love *(1970); two volumes of poetry,* Anonymous Sins *(1969) and* Love and Its Derangements *(1970); two plays, and four novels,* With Shuddering Fall *(1964),* A Garden of Earthly Delights *(1967),* Expensive People *(1968), and* Them *(1969). The latter, a kind of modern gothic novel, won the National Book Award for fiction in 1970. Miss Oates currently lives in Canada, where she is a professor of English at the University of Windsor. In her fiction, her chief interest seems to be in characters struggling in an environment they can neither understand nor control. As one critic, Alfred Kazin, puts it, "They are caught up in the social convulsion and move unheedingly, compulsively, blindly, through the paces assigned to them by the power god." "Bloodstains" first appeared in* Harper's *(August, 1971).*

He sat. He turned to see that he was sharing the bench with a young   1
mother who did not glance around at him. The park they were in was
a small noisy island around which traffic moved in a continual stream.
Aged, listless men sat on other benches — a few women shoppers,
pausing to rest, their eyes eagle-bright and their gloved fingers tugging
at the straps of shoes or at hemlines — a few children, Negro and
white, urchins from the tenement homes a few blocks off this wide main
street. Great untidy flocks of pigeons rose and settled again and rose,
startled, scattering. Lawrence Pryor looked at everything keenly. He
knew that he was out of place here; he had come down from his office
because his eleven o'clock appointment had canceled out; he was free
for half an hour. The only place to sit had been beside this pretty young
mother, who held her baby up to her face and took no interest at all in
the pigeons or the chattering children or Lawrence himself. He was
sitting in a patch of sunlight that fell upon him through the narrow
channel between two tall buildings, as if singling him out for a blessing.

All these women shoppers! He watched them cross quickly to the 2
island, and quickly over to the other curb, for they rarely had the time
to sit and rest. They were in a hurry. Because of them, hurrying across
the street, traffic was backed up waiting to make right-hand turns. Out
of the crowd of shoppers he saw a blond woman appear, walking briskly
and confidently. She hurried against a red light and a horn sounded.
How American she was, how well-dressed and sure of herself! Lawrence found himself staring at her, imagining the face that might reveal
itself to him if he were to approach her — startled and elegant and
composed, seeing by his face that he was no danger to her, no danger.

She did not cross the little park but took the sidewalk that led around 3
it. Avoiding the benchsitters and the pigeons. Lawrence was disappointed. And then, watching her, he saw that the woman was familiar
— her brisk, impatient walk, her trim blue coat — and, indeed, he
knew her well, the woman was his own wife! He tapped his jaw with
the tips of his fingers in a gesture of amused surprise. Of course! Beverly!
As if acting out embarrassment for an audience, he smiled up toward
the sky . . . and when he looked back, his wife was already hurrying
across the street, moving bravely against the light while buses and
taxicabs pressed forward.

He got to his feet to follow her. But an extraordinarily tall man got 4
in front of him, walking quickly, and then a small crowd of women
shoppers, everyone hurrying now that the light had turned green.
Something held Lawrence back. The tall man was hurrying as if to catch
up with Beverly. He was strangely tall, freakishly tall, with silver-gray
hair that was bunched around his head in tight little curls, like grapes.
He wore a dark coat, and on the back of his neck there was a vivid red
birthmark, a stain in the shape of a finger. The shoppers moved forward,
in front of Lawrence, and the tall man and Lawrence's wife moved into
the distance. All this motion made Lawrence feel slightly dizzy.

The legend about him was his fanaticism about work: Beverly com- 5
plained of this, she worried about it, she was proud of it. He was a doctor
and his patients were sacred to him. And so he had better not run after
his wife, because she would be alarmed to see him out on the street at
this time of day, and because it might be ten or fifteen minutes before
he could get away again. She might want him to have lunch with her.
She might want him to go into stores with her. Better to stay behind,
to stay hidden. So he watched her disappear — his wife hurrying into
the midst of the city — and he sat down again, feeling oddly pleased
and excited. He felt as if something secret had been revealed to him.

Beside him the young woman was leaning her face to her child, 6
whispering. She had a pale, angular face, illuminated by love, or by the

child's reflecting face, or by the narrow patch of sunlight that was moving slowly from Lawrence and onto her. Women, seen like this, were gifts to men.

He considered smiling at her. But no, that might be a mistake — this was not a city in which people smiled freely at one another. 7

Herb Altman came into the office, striding forward with his head slightly lowered. Bald, but only forty-five. He had a portly, arrogant body and his clothes were always jaunty — today he wore a bright yellow necktie that jumped in Lawrence's vision. 8

Shaking hands. 9

"How are you?" 10

"Not well. I can't sleep. I never sleep, you know that," Altman said. 11

He sat and began to talk. His voice was urgent and demanding. As he spoke he shook his head so that his cheeks shivered. Altman's wife Connie was a friend of Lawrence's wife. It seemed to Lawrence that the women in their circle were all close friends; in a way they blended into one another. The husbands, too, seemed to blend into one another. Many of them had several lives, but the lives were somehow shared. They lived in one dimension but turned up in other dimensions — downtown late in the afternoon, or in downriver suburbs. Their expensive homes and automobiles and boats could not quite contain them. Too much energy. Urgent, clicking, demanding words. While Altman talked angrily about his insomnia and switched onto the complaints of his wife and then onto the complaints of his girl, Lawrence saw again his own wife in the distance of his imagination, a dream he had dreamt while awake, moving freely and happily along the sidewalk of this massive city. 12

What mystery was in her, this woman he had lived with for so long? They had one child, a daughter. They had known each other for two decades. And yet, seeing her like that, Lawrence had been struck by the mystery of her separateness, her being. . . . 13

Altman said in a furious whisper, "I'm going to have her followed!" 14

"Your wife?" 15

"Evie. *Evelyn.* Twenty-five years old, a baby, and she tells me the plans she dreams up! She wants me to marry her next year!" 16

The numerals of Lawrence's watch were greenish-white, glowing up out of a dark face. They were supposed to glow in the dark but they glowed in the light as well. 17

"All right," Altman said, seeing Lawrence look at his watch, "so I'm wasting your time with this. So. Check my heart, my blackened lungs, 18 tap me on the back to see if I have echoes inside, to see what's hollowed out — I'm a sick man, we both know that. Here I am."

In the end Lawrence did as he always did: refilled Altman's prescrip- 19 tion for barbiturates. It was for six refills, and Altman would be back again in a few weeks.

At the door Altman paused dramatically. His white shirt front bulged. 20

"Why do they keep after me?" he said. "Larry, what is it? Why are 21 they always after me? I can't sleep at night. I'm planning a trip in my mind but when I get up I can't remember it — I don't sleep but I don't remember what I think about. Why are they always after me, those women? What are they doing to me?"

Lawrence and his wife and daughter lived in a brick home that had 22 been painted white, a few blocks from the lake. The house glowed in the air of twilight. It had the ghostly weightless look of something at the bottom of a lake, made perfect. It was a place in which Lawrence might sleep soundly, as he had never slept in his parents' oversized, combative home in Philadelphia. No more of that life! He had blocked out even the memory of that life.

Behind him in the city were his patients and the unhappy memories 23 of his patients. Ten, sometimes twelve hours of ailments — the shame of being sick, of being weak, of uttering words better left unsaid. Office hours were worse than hospital hours. During the day Lawrence's hand turned shaky and reluctant,writing out so many prescriptions, smiling with his prescribed smile, a forty-year-old face that was in danger of wearing out. His patients had too many faces. They were blotched or sullen or impatient or, like Altman's, familiar but eerily distant, de- manding something Lawrence could not give and could not under- stand.

Many of the ailments were imaginary. They existed, yes, but they 24 were imaginary; how to cure them?

The telephone was ringing as he entered his home. He had the idea 25 that it had been ringing for some time. When he went to answer it, in the kitchen, it stopped ringing and he stood with his hand out, a few inches above the receiver, listening to the silence of the house.

His mother is coming to visit, due the next morning on the nine-thirty 26 flight from Philadelphia.

Beverly and Edie are going out again; they get in each other's way 27 by the closet. Edie, fourteen years old and taller than her mother, sticks her arms angrily into her coat. The coat is khaki-colored and lined with fake wool, years old; Edie will not give it up in spite of her mother's pleas. Lawrence stands with the evening newspaper, watching them. It is six-thirty. "Do you have to go out now?" he says.

"I forgot to get new towels. I wanted to get new towels for your 28 mother, I can't let her use those old ones," Beverly says.

"New towels? You're going out now for new towels?" 29

"Everything is sleazy. It isn't good enough for her." 30

Beverly's jaws are hardening. Her eyes are bright, alert, restless. Edie 31 is shiny-faced and almost pretty, but always in a hurry, always bumping into things. It is obvious to Lawrence that his wife and daughter have been arguing about something. Edie knocks against a chair in the foyer and screws up her face. "God!" she winces.

"Did you go shopping downtown today?" Lawrence asks his wife. 32

She is frowning into her purse, looking for something. "No." 33

"I thought I saw you." 34

"Saw me? When?" 35

"A little before noon." 36

She stares at him, closing her purse. There is a cold, bright look 37 around her eyes, a look Lawrence cannot understand. Then she smiles. "Oh, yes, I was downtown . . . I just drove down and back, looking for some things I couldn't get out here. . . . I've been running around all day. I had to pick Edie up at school and take her to the dentist and now . . . now I have to go out again."

"You're making too much out of it. My mother doesn't expect you to 38 fuss over her."

She shakes her head and avoids his eye. He thinks of the tall, silver- 39 haired man with the birthmark, hurrying along after her as if to catch up with her.

His mother. The airport. They have met his mother like this many 40 times and each time they say the same things; it seems that the same crowds are at the airport. His mother begins at once to tell him about the news at home and she will continue to tell him of funerals and weddings, births, illnesses, surgery, surprises, all the way home, though she has written him about these things in her weekly letters.

"Oh, look at this!" she says in disgust. She holds up her hands for them 41 to see her white gloves, which are soiled and even stained with something that looks like rust or blood, a very faint red-brown color.

"I'll wash them out for you, Mother," Beverly says at once. 42

"Traveling is so dirty. Filthy," Lawrence's mother says. 43

He recalls her having said that before. 44

While his mother and his wife talk, Lawrence drives in silence. He's 45
happy that his mother is visiting them. She comes often, several times
a year. Lawrence has the idea that she blames him for having left
Philadelphia and coming to this city of strangers, where he has no
relatives. The letters they write to each other do not seem to express
them. Beneath his neat, typed lines, and beneath her slanted lines in
their lavender ink, there seems to be another dimension, a submerged
feeling or memory, that the two of them can only hint at but cannot
express.

They are approaching Lawrence's home. "I like that house," his 46
mother says flatly, as she always does. This seems to settle something.
Lawrence and Beverly both feel relieved.

The old family home had been white also. Now Lawrence's mother 47
lives in an apartment favored by other widows, but for decades of her
life she lived in a house the size of a municipal building. In his dreams
Lawrence sometimes climbs the stairway to the third floor, which had
been closed off, to look through the stacks of his father's old medical
journals, as he did when he was a child. There were bundles of journals.
Small towers. He spent many hours looking through them, fascinated.

His mother's presence in his house, his own house, makes Lawrence 48
feel a little displaced. It seems to him that time is confused. His own age
is uncertain. But he is a good host to her, helping Beverly out; he is
gallant to her. After dinner that night they look through snapshots,
another ritual. The snapshots are passed around. Then, leaning toward
him, in a sudden stiff motion that makes him realize how his mother is
corseted — his wife, also, her body slim and deft but smoothly hard to
the touch — she hands him a photograph that had been taken years
ago. That photograph again! It is Lawrence, Larry Jr., sitting on a spotted pony at some forgotten fair, a rented pony, Lawrence's dark hair
combed down onto his forehead in a way that makes him look like a
moron, his stare startled and vacuous, his mouth too timid to smile.
Lawrence stares at the photograph. Why does his mother treasure it so
much? Why does she always bring it along with the more recent snapshots, as if she doesn't remember she has shown it to him on her last
visit?

"Look at that, isn't that darling? A darling boy?" she says stubbornly. 49

Lawrence stares down at his own face, which is blank and stark in the 50
photograph. It was a face that might have become anything. Any personality might have inhabited it. It *was so blank, that face — anything
could inhabit it.*

He stands suddenly. His mother and his wife stare at him in alarm. 51

"Larry? What's wrong?" Beverly says. 52

He passes his hand over his eyes. He sits down again.   53
"Nothing."   54
"Did you hear something in the house?"   55
"No. Nothing."   56
Two evenings later he is driving home when a car veers out around   57
him, passing him with its horn blaring. The car is filled with kids —
boys and girls — and he thinks he sees Edie in with them. His heart
jumps. But he cannot be sure.
When he gets home it is nearly dark. His mother kisses him on the   58
side of the face. She is powdery and yet hard, a precise, stubborn little
woman. What do they talk about all day, women? His mother and his
wife? They are telling him now about what they have done today. Their
chatter is like music, rising in snatches about them, airy and incomplete.
It never quite completes itself; it has to continue.
"Is Edie home yet?" he says.   59
"No, not yet," says Beverly.   60
"Where is she?"   61
"She had something after school — choir practice — "   62
"All this time?"   63
"No, not all this time. She's probably at someone's house. She'll be   64
home in a few minutes."
"But you don't know where she is?"   65
"Not exactly. What's wrong? Why are you so angry?"   66
"I'm not angry."   67
When she comes in he will find out nothing from her. Nothing. She   68
will move her body jerkily through the kitchen and to the front closet,
she will take off her coat, she will sit slouching at dinner and stare down
into her plate or stare dutifully up at him, and he will find out nothing
about her, nothing. His heart pounds angrily. Once Beverly said of Edie,
"She has all that stuff on her face but you should see her neck — she
never washes! I could roll the dirt off her neck with my fingers!"
His mother asks him about his day. Did he work hard? Is he tired?   69
answers her vaguely, listening for Edie to come in. But when she does   70
come in he will find out nothing from her. His mother switches to
another topic — complaints about one of his aunts — and he can't
follow her. He is thinking of Edie, then he is thinking of his wife. Then
he finds himself thinking of one of his patients, Connie Altman. She
wept in his office that morning. "I need something to help me sleep at
night. I lie awake thinking. Then in the morning I can't remember what
I was thinking about. I'm so nervous, my heart pounds, can you give me
something stronger to help me sleep? Everything is running out . . ."
This puzzled him. "What do you mean, everything is running out?"   71

"There isn't any point. I don't see it. We are all running out, people   72
our age, things are running out of us . . . draining out of us . . . I will have
to live out my life in this body . . ."

She is a woman of beauty, very small, with childish wrists and ankles.   73
But her face has begun to harden in the past few years.

"I need something to help me sleep. Please. I know that in the other   74
room *he* is awake, he can't sleep either, it drives me crazy! I prefer the
nights he stays out. At least he isn't in the house, lying awake like me,
I don't care who he's with . . . I need something to help me sleep, please.
I can't stand my thoughts all night long."

His daughter's room. Saturday afternoon. The house is empty for a   75
few hours and he may walk through it, anywhere, because it is his house
and all the rooms are his, his property.

Edie's room is piled with clothes, school books, shoes, junk. Two of the   76
three dresser drawers are pulled out. The top of the dresser is cluttered.
Lawrence's reflection moves into the mirror and he looks at himself in
surprise — is that really him, Dr. Pryor? He is disappointed. He is
even a little angry. His soul is neat, neatly defined as the many cards
he carries in his wallet, and as neat as the curve of his haircut against
his neck; neat as his files at the office and as his car, which he takes pride
in. But his body looks untidy — the shirt rumpled, though he has put
it on fresh only that morning — his face sallow, edgy, his hands
strangely empty. Is that really Dr. Pryor, that man? How has it happened that he must wake in the morning to this particular face and
body, always, this particular human being?

He goes to the dresser, avoiding his own eyes in the mirror, and tugs   77
at the first drawer. A jumble of stockings, black tights, wool socks of
various colors, filmy, gauzy things. A spool of white thread rolls harm-
lessly around. He starts to close the drawer and then remembers that
it was partly open. Good. It is good he remembered that. He pulls out
the second drawer — underclothes of various colors, pink and yellow
and green, things jumbled together, releasing to him an air of fresh,
clean laundry. He stares into this drawer. What if it falls out? What if
the underclothes fall out and he can't put them back in order again? But
they are not in any order, everything is a jumble. He smiles.

He has never come into this room alone in his memory. Never. But   78
being here this afternoon, so close to his daughter and yet safe from her
fourteen-year-old's curious, sarcastic eye, he feels oddly pleased. She is
very real to him at this moment: She might be standing close behind
him, about to break into one of her greetings — "Hiya, buddy!" has

been a commonplace remark of hers this past month — or about to hum into his ear one of her slangy, mysterious, banal little tunes.

He finds himself looking through the silky underclothes. Things stick   79 together; there is the crackle of minor electricity. He holds up a half-slip of mint green with tiny white bows on it. Pretty! It is very pretty. He wants to rub it against his face. And now a kind of despair rises in him as he thinks of his daughter and these clothes, his daughter out running around this afternoon at the shopping center with her girlfriends, and these clothes which are now in his possession, here in this room, safe. It is a mystery, his having a daughter. He cannot quite comprehend it. He looks through the drawer farther, this sense of despair rising strongly in him ... Rolled up in a ball, stuck back in a corner of the drawer, are a pair of white underpants. He picks them up. They have several bloodstains on them, thick and stiff, almost caked. He stares. Why bloodstains? Why here? For a moment he feels nothing, he thinks nothing. He is not even surprised. Then it occurs to him that his daughter was ashamed to put these soiled underpants in the wash, that she had meant to wash them herself but had forgotten, and weeks, maybe months have gone by ... the blood grown old and hard, the stains impossible to get out ... she has forgotten about them ... balled up, rolled up, and stuck in the corner of the drawer, forgotten ...

His mother is talking with some friends of theirs who have dropped   80 in. An ordinary Sunday afternoon. Beverly is handing drinks around. In the mirror above the fireplace his mother's bluish-white hair bobs weightlessly. Long white candlesticks in holders of silver, on the mantel; the wicks perfectly white, never burnt. What are they talking about so earnestly? Lawrence tries to listen. Beverly is chiding him gently for working so hard — it is a familiar pattern, almost a tune, the words of his mother to his father years ago — and he nods, smiles, he is Dr. Pryor, who works hard. The fact is that he has done nothing all day except sit in his study, at his desk, leafing through medical journals. He has not been able to concentrate on anything.

Ted Albrecht, a friend of many years, is talking in his usual fanciful   81 manner. He is a stockbroker but thinks of himself as a social critic. A short man, with glasses and lively eyebrows; he is considered a friend of Lawrence's, and yet the two men have never talked together, alone together. They always meet at parties, in someone's living room, with groups of other people around.

Ted says, "I guarantee you, a vehement hot time is coming for this   82 nation!"

238

Lawrence has not been able to concentrate on the conversation. He 83
thinks that he may not be able to endure this minute, this very minute.

Voices ring around him. It is a ring of concentric rings, a ring of voices 84
and breaths and bright glances, circling him. Like music, the voices do
not come to rest. They pause shrilly; they pause in expectation. Lawrence accepts a drink from his wife, a woman whose face looks oddly
brittle. The ice cubes in his glass make him think of the Arctic —
pure crystal, pure colorless ice and air, where no germs survive. It is
impossible, this minute. Impossible to stand with these people. He does
not know what is wrong and yet he understands that it has become
impossible, that his body is being pushed to the breaking point, that to
contain himself — his physicalness, his being — would take the
strength of a wrestler, a man not himself.

The minute expands slowly. Nothing happens. 85

Again, the airport. The reversal of the meeting last week: now she is 86
going home. The airliner will draw up into it a certain number of
people, Lawrence's mother among them, and then it will be gone. Now
there is a rush of words. Things to be said. His mother complains bitterly
of one of his aunts — he nods in agreement, embarrassed that she
should say these things in front of Beverly — he nods yes, yes; he will
agree to anything. "What could she know? She was never married!"
Lawrence's mother says, twisting her mouth. Of Lawrence's father,
who died in a boating accident when Lawrence was eighteen, she does
not ever speak, exactly; she speaks around him, around that solitary
mysterious event, alluding to it with petulant jerks of her stiff little
body. Lawrence's father died on the lake, alone. He drowned, alone.
The boat must have capsized and he drowned, alone, with no one to
witness the death or to explain it.

Lawrence's mother begins to cry. She will back off from them, crying, 87
and then at a certain point she will stop crying, collecting herself, and
she will promise to telephone them as soon as she lands in Philadelphia.
The visit is concluded.

Though it was a weekday evening, they went to Dorothy Clair's art 88
gallery, where a young sculptor was having an opening. Dorothy Clair
was a widow some years older than the Pryors, a wealthy woman on the
periphery of their social group. It was a champagne opening. Lawrence
and his wife were separated, drawn into different groups; Lawrence
was not really taking part in the conversation, but he appeared en-

thusiastic. The champagne went to his head. His mother had stayed with them for nearly a week, the visit had gone well, everything was over. Good. It was a weekday evening but they had gone out as if to reward themselves.

Next to Lawrence there was a piece of sculpture — a single column 89 of metal, with sharp edges. It looked dangerous. A woman seemed about to back into it and Lawrence wondered if he should warn her. He could see his own reflection in its surface, blotchy and comic. All the pieces of sculpture were metallic. Some hung from the ceiling, heavily; others hung from the walls. Great massive hulks — not defined enough to be shapes — squatted on the floor. People drifted around the sculpture, sometimes bumping into it. A woman stooped to disentangle her skirt from some wire, a thick ball of wire that had been sprayed with white paint.

What were these strange forms? They were oppressive to Lawrence. 90 But no one else seemed to be uneasy. He went to examine the wire — it looked like chicken wire — and he could make no sense of it. Elsewhere in the crowded room there were balls of metal that were distorted, like planets wrenched out of shape. Their shiny surfaces reflected a galaxy of human faces, but the faces were not really human. They were cheerful and blatant and flat, as if there were no private depths to them. . . . How they were all chattering away, those faces! No privacy at all, nothing but the facial mask of flesh: no private depths of anguish or darkness or sweetness, nothing. The faces were all talking earnestly to one another.

Lawrence looked for his wife. He saw her across the room, talking to 91 a tall man with silvery hair. It was the man he had seen downtown! Astonished, Lawrence could not move. He stood with his drink in his hand, as metallic and fixed as the pieces of sculpture. These columns punctuated the gallery, each reaching to the ceiling, with flat, shiny surfaces and edges that appeared razor-sharp. They made him think suddenly of the furniture in his parents' house that he had stood up on end, as a child — allowed by his mother to play with the furniture of certain rooms, upending tables and chairs so that he could crawl under them and pretend they were small houses, huts. He had crouched under them, peering out past the legs of tables and chairs. Sometimes his mother had given him a blanket to drape over the piece of furniture.

The man with the silver hair turned and Lawrence saw that it was 92 not the stranger from downtown after all — it was someone he'd known for years. Yet he felt no relief. He was still paralyzed. Beverly, not seeing him, was looking around cautiously, nervously. The man was about to drift into another conversation and leave her. He had a big, heavy, handsome head, his silver-gray hair curly and bunched, his face florid and generous and a little too aggressive, too sure of itself. Lawrence felt a sudden dislike for him. And yet he was grateful that he had not become that man — grateful that, in the moment of paralysis and panic, his soul had not flown out of him and into that man, into that other body. It might have happened. Anything might happen!

He went out. He walked quickly out of his building and into the 93 midday crowd, in a hurry, and once on the sidewalk he stayed near the curb so that he could walk fast. The day was cold and overcast. He walked several blocks to the end of the street and across the street to the riverfront. There were few people down here, only the most hardy of tourists. No shoppers bothered to come this far. There were no stores here, only concrete and walls and a ferry landing and the water, the grim cold water. He leaned over a railing. He stared down at the lapping water. It was not very clean; there were long streaks of foam in it, as long as six or eight feet, bobbing and curling and twisting like snakes.

The discontent of the past two weeks rose in his mind. What was 94 wrong? What had happened? It had begun on that sunlit day when he'd seen his wife from a distance. His wife. His mother arrived the following morning; they picked her up at the airport as always. And his daughter — there had been something about his daughter as well — but he could not remember. In the dirty, bouncy water he saw Edie's face, grinning up at him. But she did not really see him. There was nothing there. He was alone. He thought in a panic of himself and the river: the fact of being alone like this, with the river a few yards beneath him.

There was a sensation of deadness around his eyes. His eyes had 95 become hardened, crusted over, like crusts of blood; the wounds where eyes had once been. And now they might fall off . . .? Another face was pushing its way through. He must scratch at the scabs of his eyes and scratch them off, to make way for the new face, digging the crusts of blood away with his nails. He must tear at himself. He must do it now, this minute . . . for at this minute his body could no longer contain itself, it was like a wrestler with superbly developed muscles bursting through his clothing, tearing his clothing with anger and joy!

The river beneath him was a river of souls: the murky, sour, rebellious 96 souls of all the children he had been meant to father, flowing out of him and helplessly, ferociously downstream. He stared at the water. All of these his children! Sons and daughters of his body! He had been meant to father these thousands, these thousands of millions of souls, and yet he was on the concrete walk, leaning against the guardrail, and the children of his body were flowing by him, bouncing, lapping noisily against the abutment, becoming lost.

For some time he stood in silence. His eyes did ache. He tried to think of what he must do — had he planned something? Why had he come down here? If he were to drown, perhaps scenes of his past life would flash to him. He would see the upended furniture again — the clumsy gold-covered chair with its curved legs and its gauzy bottom, the springs visible through the dark gauze — he would crawl between the legs again, drawing his knees up to his chest, hiding there, sly and safe. He would see the big house, he would see the piles of magazines and he would smell the acrid, lovely odor of loneliness on the third floor of that house; he would pass into that room and live out his life there chastely and silently. But perhaps he would fall into the water screaming. He would thresh his arms and legs — he would sink at once, screaming — and no one could save him. People might come to gawk, but they could not save him. And perhaps he would see nothing at all, no visions, no memories, perhaps it was only a lie about a drowning man living his life again and he would see nothing, nothing, he would drown in agony and be washed downstream, lost. 97

He glanced at his watch. After one. 98

He hurried back to his office. The receptionist, a pretty Negro woman, chided him for walking in the rain. She took his trench coat from him, shook it, hung it up. In the waiting room — he could see through two partly opened doors — a few people were sitting and had been sitting for a while. He went into his private office. In a few minutes the nurse showed in his first patient of the afternoon: Herb Altman. 99

"I'm back a little faster this time but everything is the usual. Diagnosis the usual," Altman said flatly. He wore a stylish, wide green tie, mint green. There were tiny white streaks in it that bothered Lawrence's vision. 100

Shaking of hands. 101

"Maybe somebody should just shoot me. I should croak, eh?" Altman laughed. "Anyway I still can't sleep, Larry. The same damn thing. Give me something strong to help me sleep, eh? And did you hear about that bastard, that investigator, I got to follow Evie? He was a friend of hers! It turned out he was a friend of hers! He told her everything, he tipped her off. I fired him and I'm dumping her, believe you me, I think even she and my wife are comparing notes on me and laughing and it's no goddam wonder I can't sleep. Maybe I should just croak, eh? Make things easier for everybody? What's your opinion?" 102

242

"Let me do just a routine examination," Lawrence said. "You do look 103 a little agitated."

Subject

1. What seems to be bothering Lawrence Pryor? Does *he* know what is bothering him?

2. Would it be fair to say that this is a story in which nothing happens? Does inaction seem valid subject matter for a short story? How does Oates make it interesting?

3. How many of Lawrence's friends are mentioned in the story? How close is he to them? Is he close to his family?

4. How did Lawrence's father die? Does Oates seem to imply that the death was suicidal? Can you tell from the story whether the father's life was happier than the son's — or very different?

5. Read the final paragraph of Fromm's "Work in an Alienated Society"; does the description of an alienated man seem to apply to Lawrence? Is he alienated from society? from himself?

6. At the end, Lawrence seems to be carrying on his work very much as at the beginning; do you think he has made any adjustment?

Structure

1. The incident of the bloodstains is a minor one in the story, one which Lawrence can't even remember at the end. Why do you suppose Oates chose this for the title?

2. The story is composed of half a dozen such minor incidents; how does Oates tie them all together?

3. What does the business about Herb Altman have to do with the story about Lawrence Pryor? Why does Oates bring it up again at the end?

4. Nothing ever comes of Lawrence's suspicions about his wife; what function does the incident play in the story? Does it matter whether or not the reader thinks she is unfaithful?

5. Although Lawrence is alone three times, Oates arranges the story so that most of his thoughts and daydreams occur in the presence of other people — when he ought, perhaps, to be carrying on a conversation. How does this arrangement strengthen the point of the story? (Note particularly Lawrence's detached observations about the people he is with.)

THE DAY
OF TRIALS

Albert Lebowitz

Albert Lebowitz was born in St. Louis, Missouri in 1923 and still lives there. He is a graduate of Washington University and Harvard Law School, now practicing law by day and writing by night. He has published two novels, Laban's Will *(1966) and* The Man Who Wouldn't Say No *(1969), as well as several short stories. He has just finished a third novel.*

— I do not choose to run. 1

One of our Presidents said that and to show the quality of my mind 2
I don't remember who it was. I, with an excellent memory, don't bother
to remember most names, including those of witnesses in trials I conduct. Waller, my friend and law partner, says it's because I play too hard
at being aristocratic. His statement, meant to annoy, pleases me. Pa-
tronization of trivial people is what makes a champion. It permits him
to concentrate his energies on the main chance. I have had Trudy for
three whole months while Waller is half crazy with frustration. The
President's remark. It shows the quality of *his* mind: spare, firm. Impressive. A lean mixture of will and rectitude. Calvinistic, and I remember. Hardly memorable to the college student I defend for murder in
the second degree but with a memorable phrase to his credit. One
Aaron Farrelly likes to use: I do not choose to fight in an imperialistic
war. I do not choose to listen or be polite to my elders. I do not choose
to consider law of the slightest importance. I do not choose.

I hold Farrelly in contempt but not for the reasons you might think. 3
Not even for his indifference to the law. I hate his corrupt idea of
nobility. Farrelly was tried for murder because he defended his wife,
which is hardly noble. He's a muddy thinker attacking a social institution by defending another.

I run all of the time. I am running now, stride for stride, with Waller, 4
who also chooses to run. It keeps us spare, lean, hard-bellied — our
choice. More important, it tests our right to Trudy sitting on the grass

beside the cinder track. She waits for the winner which is as it should be.

Farrelly is wrong. His crowd occupies police stations like they used to crowd into telephone booths. Community sing. Follow the dancing ball. I go it alone, in the courtroom, in my jousts with Waller, and for no silly abstractions like justice or truth or morality. I do it for Trudy. Waller does it for Trudy. For her we will fight, asking for and giving no quarter. Farrelly is soft and heroism is merciless.

I correctly judge Waller's temper. He was too anxious and started the two-mile run at too fast a pace. I lag behind for the first mile, pull abreast at a mile-and-a-half and am ready to make my move. I push ahead of the whistle in his lungs and cross the finish line a good twenty yards ahead. It was certain that Trudy would be mine for another week since I do not lose in push-ups, the next test, and all I need is two out of three. We won't even get to arm-wrestling. I trotted over to Trudy and got my fine, hard kiss on the mouth. Waller nods, grim in defeat. He is in a terrible mood after three months of abstinence. I cupped my hand around Trudy's familiar breast before I stood up and Waller has to look because that is the rule. Neither of us dreams of breaking our rules. Farrelly must learn there was no honor without rules.

We shower together in our apartment, another rule. As the winner of the race, I am privileged to soap Trudy's body. I lingered at her breasts and belly and buttocks and Waller must watch.

Afterward, nude, we go into the living room and begin the push-ups. On the day of trials, Sunday, we remain naked in the apartment until the next morning. We were permitted to hide nothing from each other, not even the ache of the loser. One of our responsibilities was to face defeat openly. We don't need to count push-ups. The last man up won. My mind is free to refresh the memory of my special victory that leads to three months of Trudy. The winner of the lost cause got three months and in our year together only I won a lost cause. I disprize what Farrelly stands for but he is the instrument of my greatest triumph. And when I beat Waller at push-ups I keep Trudy for another week.

— I want to make it perfectly clear so that we understand each other. I cannot condone what you did or the circumstances that led you to be there. To be brutally frank, I cannot say that I find you particularly palatable. Having told you this, I want you to know that I will defend you to the best of my ability. I can promise you that.

I say this to the long-haired, foul-fleshed boy. He looked at me with his self-communing grin and said — Peace, man.

— I hope you will be as frank with me as I am with you. You will have no reason to regret it. I will never betray your trust. Whatever you say will be held in the strictest confidence. You killed a police officer and

245

they throw the book at you. In all modesty you have one chance —
me.

— The good book? 12

— Please pay attention. They crack you like an egg. I can't suffi- 13
ciently emphasize the gravity of your situation. If you were ever serious
in your life it should be now. When this nightmare's over, with the help
of God I hope we'll have some laughs together. I can have a good time
as well as the next guy. Meanwhile you must help me to help yourself.

— Do you really think that God is on my side? What can I say? 14

— Start anywhere and in your own words just tell me what hap- 15
pened. I'll be the judge of what is important.

— Yes, I think you will be. Why don't I start at the beginning? I 16
have a hunch you'd like that.

I know he thinks I am a fool and I waited impassively. I want him to 17
know I know.

— My father is president of a nuts and bolts company. My mother 18
is a graduate of Bryn Mawr.

I look at him. I know the value of blue eyes. Hard as steel. Hard as 19
my muscles. I look at his scraggly beard, his hair to his shoulders like
a watered-down Sir Lancelot, his brown eyes soft and sticky as semen.

— I am acquainted with your father and admire him very much. 20
But Freud is no defense in a court of law. Not for cop-killing.

And he laughs, flashing beautiful, white teeth that look out of place 21
in his tangled beard. I was pleased to have him know I could be as
smart-ass as he.

— Iodine 131 comprises a specific fraction of the total fission prod- 22
uct. If iodine 131 is in the grass, and the grass is in the cow, and the milk
is in the child, is it 175 or 1200 rads of radiation? What matter of degree
is it?

— Murder in the second degree could mean imprisonment for a 23
term of ten to life. They see you coming. They stick things in your rear
end you can't dream of. What have you told the police?

— Both hard and soft detergents are clearly toxic to goldfish and 24
mosquito fish, which indicates a similar toxicity to other fish which are
omnivorous like the goldfish — carp, suckers, catfish, et cetera — and
carnivorous like the mosquito fish — bass, trout, et cetera.

— Have I said that I am a very patient man? Anyway, I am. I have 25
my own reasons for defending you. Sooner or later I think you'll realize
you're not on a picnic. They carve guys like you up for breakfast. They
feed on you with their carp and trout. If you're trying to annoy me into
dropping the case, be advised it won't work. I have too much respect
for your father and for myself to do that. Sooner or later you'll get

awfully worried about what's going to happen to you. Whether you like it or not, you're no different from anybody else. I can wait. Go ahead. You talk and I'll listen. I have reasons of my own.

— You keep saying that and it's very impressive. May I inquire as 26 to your own reasons? My father's money?

— No, and my reasons are no concern of yours. I'm sure they 27 would only bore you.

— I'm sure they wouldn't but that's neither here nor there, is it? 28 All right, then. To begin at the beginning, which is where it all started, the question before us is one of survival.

— I couldn't have put it better myself. Bearing that in mind, did 29 you confess to the police?

— I'm afraid I did. I confessed that the normal cleansing mech- 30 anism of the lung is interfered with by irritant gases from industrial wastes, cigarette smoke, automobile exhausts and coal fumes so that the bronchial passages are narrowed and the mucus blanket thickened, that each of us to survive still needs his twelve to fifteen thousand daily liters of filtered air.

— I hope you told them that. Did you tell them why you killed the 31 cop?

— I like to think so but they wouldn't listen. They weren't inter- 32 ested in anything I said. It's a problem of communication.

I stood up. 33

— I see what you mean. I certainly do. I have to leave but don't 34 worry, I'll be back. I find your conversation very stimulating and I'm ready to listen at any time. I think I mentioned that you are in serious trouble and that you are lucky to have a patient man defending you. Whether or not you care to lift a finger, I intend to leave no stone unturned. I intend you to be found not guilty even though you confess that the moon is made of yellow cheese. Meanwhile, say whatever you like to the police. That isn't my usual advice but why should I be selfish? They might as well profit along with me in your thoughtful observations.

— I appreciate your interest, he says. I really do. 35

— Just remember I have reasons of my own as well as a few pro- 36 fundities like, shave off your beard. Cut your hair. Take a bath. Do Canadian Air Force exercises. You might also consider a few of the deeper implications of the jury system.

— I'll certainly take your suggestions under advisement. But, I 37 must confess, only for reasons of my own.

— Do. I'll appreciate it. In the meantime, I'll talk to your wife. If 38 she's anything like you, I'm sure it will be an entertaining experience.

I would hope she doesn't want a broom handle stuck up your behind.

— I am humbly grateful to have you defend me despite my long 39
hair and all. Give my wife my love.

I look at him, I think of Trudy and I say — You don't know the 40
meaning of the word.

He gave me that hairy-assed smile and suddenly, to believe it I had 41
to be there, his eyes filled with tears. These kids.

I confess that my arms were getting tired. I watch Waller from the 42
corner of my eye. He gave no sign of weakening. His body is stiff as a
bar of steel, according to the rule, and he has never before lasted this
long. Trudy, out of my range of vision, was silent. None of us speaks until
the trials are over and the victor reaps his reward. This is the rule.
Waller and I knew the value of silence. It stood a lawyer in good stead
and it exemplifies our manliness. Waller never won at push-ups but he
seems to be inspired. If he makes it in push-ups it was a stand-off and
everything depends on arm-wrestling which is anybody's guess. Arm-
wrestling is the unpredictable one. Either of us may win. Ignoble
thoughts assail me: perhaps I grow soft with success. Three months
open, exclusive, notorious possession of Trudy weakens my moral fibre.
Three months was not ideal. Or I waste time rehashing my triumph
with Farrelly. I dissipated my powers of concentration. My arms twitch
like severed worms and I must not lose my head. I needed my muscles
for arm-wrestling. I must begin to concentrate on that, save myself for
that. I eased to the floor and lay there with my face buried in the rug.
I lose the push-ups. I heard the sharp drawing of breath behind me and
frown because Trudy violated the rule. I store up the memory of this.
Trudy must be chastized. She knew that as well as we do.

Waller and I stand up and I nod in defeat which is the rule. I like to 43
think that my face is as grim as his. Our blue eyes search for hints of
weakness. I find none in his nor he in mine. I was strong again. I
concentrated all my energies on arm-wrestling. I allow no other
thought to contaminate my mind. This is my edge. Waller was desperate to win. He *must* win and I only want to with all of my heart.

We settled into place at the table. Trudy sits nearby in my field of 44
vision. I shake my head and frown. She violated another rule and she
jumps and moved away. I erase the irritation from my mind. Waller and
I touch, grasp hands. We lock into place and the pressure begins. Immediately he is rash and I know I will win. He realizes his mistake and
lets up too late. We both knew I am now stronger than he. I looked into
his eyes and saw the fatal traces of doubt. We notice together that
Waller's arm was bent a fraction. It is the beginning of the end. I saw
no reason to delay and began his downward movement. It was over.
Trudy was mine for another week.

Waller stares at his vanquished arm on the table and I wait. He said   45
nothing and I began to get angry at the violation of the rule. Finally he
mumbles — I am your servant to do with as you will.

— Thank you, I say not without annoyance.   46

He was in bad shape to play with the rules. And Trudy's transgres-   47
sions leave something to be desired. She sat leaning forward, breasts
pointing downward as if she had nothing better to do. But finally she
says as she must — Alex has proved his love and has won my heart.
Let him fuck me.

I do not hide my displeasure at her tardiness. We went into the   48
bedroom and I climb into bed with Trudy while Waller watches as is
the rule. I notice that Trudy lies limp as she has been known to do
before. I decided to punish her infractions and thought of other things
to avoid an erection. She lay there and Waller watched. Patience is
always my ally.

Wanda Farrelly was even more beautiful than Trudy. I can't believe   49
my eyes. She was graceful and fragile with the bones of a bird. She is
dressed in a humble cotton garment. Her blond hair of the finest silk
falls below her delicate shoulders and I think of the dirty, scratchy body
of Farrelly crushing her with his corrupt weight. It was another instance
of marriage yoking beasts with beauties. I am proud of my lean, hard,
immaculate body and I beg her indulgence while I remove my jacket
and arrange it carefully on a chair. She looked at my muscular torso and
I am thankful she has a moment with a real man. I informed her that
I would defend her husband to the best of my ability. I do not tell her
that she will be better off if he goes to jail. I do not tell her that I defend
him for reasons of my own. When I put my pen to legal pad, she tells
me her story.

— Aaron is on the steering committee of the Student Non-Violent   50
Coordinating Committee and local organizer of Students For a Democratic Society. He is active in CORE and ACTION and W. E. B. DuBois
and the WAR RESISTERS, took part in the Washington, D.C. Peace
March, the Selma, Alabama Peace March and attended three sessions
of a Communist Party school which was held last winter in this city.

— He's a busy boy, I say. And you?   51

— I am his wife, she said and I nodded with a sympathetic ripple of   52
my jaw muscles.

— We gathered at the police station lobby to protest the arrest of   53
some of our group for demonstrating at the hotel where the President
was giving his speech. I brought a thirty-cup silver coffee urn and
plugged the cord into the lobby electric outlet. There were thirty of us
sitting on the lobby floor. Six uniformed policemen were there and two
superior officers, one a Captain Brimm who addressed us informing us

he was a police officer and that we were creating a security problem. That we were interfering with the normal business of the Police Department by blocking the normal flow of traffic. He ordered us to disperse and vacate the lobby. If we failed to comply with his order, we would be arrested on charges of public peace disturbance and interfering with a police officer. He repeated the statement twice more but we did not move. The policemen formed a line near the elevators at the rear of the lobby and advanced toward us to make us leave the building through the front doors. Captain Brimm told us we were under arrest and to get up and walk to the booking desk. We did not move. They began picking us up and carrying us out to the detention cell. Aaron and I were the last ones left. A policeman, Bradley Barrett, pulled me up with one hand. In his other he held his night stick which he raised above his head. I don't know why he did this. Aaron broke loose from the two policemen hauling him out, grabbed Bradley Barrett's night stick and struck him on the back of the neck. Bradley Barrett fell to the floor with a broken neck and died. That is how it happened. A policeman hit Aaron between the eyes with his fist and Aaron fell down. That is the story.

— I have it all down, I say flexing my fingers. Here is how it is. 54 Your husband's situation is extremely grave. For reasons of my own I will do whatever I can to save him. Will you do the same?

She looks at me with eyes fully open to the light. — Yes. 55

I admire her devotion. She was a worthy object of adoration if I was 56 not already committed.

— Good. You must take the stand and tell your story. You must 57 brace yourself for the ordeal.

— Of course, she says. I will do anything I can. I will die if it will 58 help.

I am impressed by her devotion to such a loathsome creature but I 59 wish to show her she might have someone better, someone worthy of fidelity. I threw my shoulders back and expanded my chest.

— The killing of an officer of the law attempting to make a lawful 60 arrest ordinarily cannot be justified as self-defense. *State vs. Bronson.* Though homicide was committed in resisting the illegal arrest of accused's son, if it was committed with express malice, it sustained a conviction of second-degree murder. *State vs. Gallatin.* However, the statutes provide that homicide is justifiable in the lawful defense of a wife when there shall be reasonable cause to apprehend immediate danger of some great personal injury to her. Your husband, we must admit, killed a cop perhaps overzealous in the doing of his duty. Nobody likes a cop-killer. Nobody likes a cop-killer's wife. This is a certified, bona fide lost cause, no sense pulling punches, but for reasons of my own

I intend to prevail. It's in my lap and it's all up to me. I must choose the right jury, I must make the right argument and it won't be easy. Nobody can say it will be easy. I'll need all the help I can get and a little more.

— I will do anything to save Aaron, said Wanda. *Anything.* 61

Trudy gets restive. She examines my male organ. She pummeled it, 62
kissed it. I allowed her to make amends for her sins of omission. Waller looks away which is not permitted. I tired of the sport and finished off the exercise in a quick, explosive burst. Trudy lay beneath me with her eyes closed. I stand up and confront them.

— Trudy. You drew a deep breath when I lost the push-ups. You 63
sat in my field of vision during arm-wrestling. When I won, you delayed in honoring me. John. You delayed in certifying my victory. You looked away during sexual intercourse.

They are silent. They must do penance. It is the rule. 64

— Alex, said Trudy. It's all over with us. Waller and I are in love. 65
We want to get married. I'm sincerely sorry that we've failed to live up to your standards. I wish there were some way to make amends, some words that would make it easier.

I waited for Waller and he nodded. — You won and earned a week. 66
We can't let you have it. We let you have Trudy once more for old time's sake and you must realize how painful it was for two people in love. You must realize how painful it is to break our vows. I'm sorry but that's the way it is.

My selection of the jury is what did it. I selected conservatives, home- 67
owners, Chamber of Commerce, American Legion. I choose the believ-ers in the law, defenders of the faith. I struck the bedeviled bleeders and question-begging liberals. My jury found the defendant not guilty. Justifiable homicide in the killing of a man in blue. They bent over backward to be fair. They would not use their emotions to sway the law. I pay them with my respect. Farrelly is another story. The foreman says he is not guilty but I know he is and he knows that I know. He looks at me his soup-stained smile and attempts to hide behind a — Thanks, but no thanks. My unyielding glance forced his graceless gratitude behind his beard and, lifting my chest, I stand clear of him and accept the token of Wanda's weeping. He knew the victory was mine, not his, and that it will be ever so.

I don't mind in the least what Waller and Trudy have decided to do. 68
I am very sorry for them and they know I am because they can't look at me. To be perfectly truthful, I was relieved. Three months with Trudy is an awfully long time and not once do I break the rules.

— I wish you all the luck in the world. You have my blessings, you 69
really do. You two keep the apartment, of course. I imagine you have a lot to talk about.

And I leave without another word. I dress and leave them to the 70
codeless, clamorous language of love.

Subject

1. Alex says that he "has his own reasons" for defending the hippie
cop-killer, but he never tells his client what those reasons are. What are
they?

2. Alex does not seem to be hopelessly in love with Trudy; why is
he so determined to keep his monopoly on her?

3. What does Alex's concern for the rules tell you about him? Can
you tell by the story whether the "rules of the game" were thought up
by Alex and Waller together or by Alex alone?

4. After Alex has gone to so much trouble to win Trudy again, does
it seem out of character for him to be so unconcerned when Waller and
Trudy announce their intention to marry?

5. What does Alex think makes a man deserving of a woman? (Note
his behavior with Aaron Farrelly's wife.)

Structure

1. Discuss the appropriateness of the title to the story. Does it apply
in more than one way?

2. Does Lebowitz give enough information about his central character so that we can understand why he acts as he does? (Cause-and-
effect analysis of a single person — even a fictional one — is
particularly tricky; witness Shakespeare's difficulties with Hamlet.)

3. One danger in this kind of cause and effect analysis is oversimplification — concentrating so much on one aspect of a person's character that he seems unreal. Has Lebowitz successfully avoided this
danger?

4. Does Lebowitz integrate the constant flashbacks to the Aaron
Farrelly trial, three months earlier, so that the reader is not confused
by the time sequences?

5. Why does Lebowitz interject the passing thoughts about ecology
— iodine and detergent pollution — into Alex's interview with Aaron
Farrelly? Is a special purpose served by these thoughts, or should
Lebowitz have left them out?

6. Examine the few passages in which Alex speaks directly to someone; how does his own language differ from that in which the rest of
the story is told?

5

PROBLEMS OF POSTCIVILIZATION

Process

Process refers to the explanation, step by step, of the way in which something happens or operates. It does not, like cause and effect, have to tell *why* the phenomenon occurs, but only *how* it happens. Thus a recipe for devil's food cake is a simple process analysis. Such questions as "Why does yeast make dough rise?" do not need to be answered (although cause and effect analysis is frequently combined with process). If the process is followed correctly, the dough *will* rise, whether or not we understand why it does.

Generally speaking, there are two kinds of process analysis, mechanical and historical, though such a division overlaps to some degree. Mechanical process explains the steps by which a thing is put together or operates. The instructions for setting up an experiment in chemistry lab are an example of mechanical process; so, in coded form, is the score for playing Mozart's "Jupiter" symphony. More complicated mechanical processes would be an analysis of how sea gulls fly and an explanation of how a linear accelerator is constructed.

Historical process analysis is the same sort of procedure, except that it represents a description of the steps by which an event or series of events took place historically. Of this type would be a logistical account of the Battle of Bull Run — the deployment of troops, position of artillery, steps in the attack procedure, and so on. A geological account of the formation of the Hawaiian Islands would also be an historical process, as would a description of the way in which Macbeth attained the throne.

Writing process papers is ordinarily somewhat easier than is analysis of cause and effect. Some processes, of course, are extremely complicated, but even so you do not have to worry about such problems as multiplicity of causes. If you understand the process clearly, then you have only to worry about writing carefully.

There are two important rules to keep in mind when writing a process paper. In the first place, the steps in any process must be kept in exact order. If you do not do this, a simple chemistry experiment can destroy both laboratory and experimenter. If you reverse the steps "add 2/3 cup milk" and "simmer 20 minutes," the result can be a plate of fudge best attacked with hammer and chisel.

This rule of exact order is obvious and hardly needs to be dwelled upon. More important for a writer to remember is the rule of clarity; if one step in a process involving fifty steps is not clearly explained, the whole process is useless to the reader. Forty-nine clear explanations out of fifty is a good average, but in process it will not do. Every girl who has made a dress probably knows the frustration of trying to decipher a step not clearly explained on the pattern, as does the builder of a foreign-made radio lab kit with directions written by an unskilled translator. Even the simplest process demands clarity in each step; the more complicated ones you will have to write as a college student — lab reports, research papers, case histories, and engineering reports — require even closer attention to clarity.

Many of the processes mentioned above are of the least complicated variety, simple sets of directions. But the processes you will write in college frequently will not allow an explanation of steps in uninterrupted 1-2-3-4 order. One problem is that the subject is likely to demand descriptions and explanations which are not part of the process itself. Another is that in a complicated process several things may be happening simultaneously. Consequently, you may have to proceed by stages or subdivisions. Even in a purely mechanical process like the operation of an automobile engine, subdivisions would be necessary: the carburetion system; the ignition system; the piston, rod, and valve assembly and operation; and the transmission. (The steps in each subdivision, of course, must still be kept in order.) In such fields as biology and psychology, the processes may be even more complicated. Your problem then will be to find a way of organizing the material in such a way that the reader can understand all the factors involved and still see clearly the steps or stages of the process.

It is because of the absolute necessity for clarity that process writing is such useful practice for students in freshman composition. Process analysis can develop the habit of making certain that your reader will understand what you are trying to communicate. When you write a process paper, you should test your explanations by reading the first draft to someone who is not familiar with the process being explained. Any steps which he does not understand you can then rewrite and explain in greater detail. In extremely complicated processes, you may find diagrams useful in explaining some of the steps.

THE PETER PRINCIPLE

Raymond Hull

Raymond Hull is the collaborator with Dr. Lawrence J. Peter on the book The Peter Principle *(1969).*

Bunglers are always with us and always have been. Winston Churchill 1
tells us, in his history of World War II, that in August, 1940, he had to
take charge personally of the Armed Forces' Joint Planning Committee
because, after almost twelve months of war, the Committee had not
originated a single plan.

In the 1948 Presidential election, the advance public-opinion polls 2
awarded an easy victory to Thomas E. Dewey. In the Fifties, there was
the Edsel bungle. In 1965, Houston's domed baseball stadium opened
and was so ill-suited to baseball that, on sunny days, fielders could not
see fly balls against the blinding glare from the skylight.

We have come to expect incompetence as a necessary feature of 3
civilization. We may be irked, but we are no longer amazed, when our
bosses make idiotic decisions, when automobile makers take back thousands of new cars for repairs, when store clerks are insolent, when law
reforms fail to check crime, when moon rockets can't get off the ground,
when widely used medicines are found to be poisons, when universities
must teach freshmen to read, or when a hundred-ton airliner is brought
down by a duck.

We see these malpractices and mishaps as unconnected accidents, 4
inevitable results of human fallibility.

But one man says, "These occurrences are not accidents; they are 5
simply the fruits of a system which, as I have shown, *develops, perpetuates and rewards incompetence.*"

The Newton of incompetence theory is a burly, black-haired, slow- 6
spoken Canadian philosopher and iconoclast, Dr. Laurence J. Peter,
who made his living as Assistant Professor of Education at the University of British Columbia until recently, when he moved down the coast
to become a Professor of Education at the University of Southern
California.

There is nothing incompetent about Dr. Peter. He is a successful 7
author: his *Prescriptive Teaching* is a widely used text on the education
of problem children. He built a house with his own hands, makes his
own wine, is an expert cook, a skilled woodcarver, and an inventor. (He
created a new tool rack for school woodwork shops and perfected an
apparatus for marking fifty exam papers at once.) Yet his chief claim to
fame may be his founding of the science of hierarchiology.

> Hierarchiology [he says,] is the study of hierarchies. "Hierarchy" origi-
> nally meant "church government by clergy graded into ranks." The
> term now includes any organization whose members or employees are
> arranged by rank or grade.
>
> Early in life, I faced the problem of occupational incompetence. As
> a young schoolteacher I was shocked, baffled, to see so many knotheads
> as principals, inspectors and superintendents.
>
> I questioned older teachers. All I could find was that the knotheads,
> earlier in their career, had been capable, and that was why they had
> been promoted.
>
> Eventually I realized that the same phenomenon occurs in all trades
> and professions, because the same basic rule governs the climb
> through every hierarchy. A competent employee is eligible for promo-
> tion, but incompetence is a bar to promotion. So an employee's final
> position must be one for which he is incompetent!
>
> Suppose you own a drug-manufacturing firm, Perfect Pill Incor-
> porated. Your foreman pill-roller dies of a perforated ulcer; you seek
> a replacement among the rank-and-file pill-rollers. Miss Cylinder, Mrs.
> Ellipse and Mr. Cube are variously incompetent and so don't qualify.
> You pick the best pill-roller, Mr. Sphere, and promote him to foreman.
>
> Suppose Sphere proves highly competent in this new job: later,
> when deputy-works-manager Legree moves up one step, Sphere will
> take his place.
>
> But if Sphere is incompetent as foreman, he won't be promoted
> again. He has reached what I call his *level of incompetence* and there
> he will stay till he retires.

An employee may, like Mr. Cube, reach his level of incompetence at 8
the lowest rank: he is never promoted. It may take one promotion to
place him at his level of incompetence; it may take a dozen. But, sooner
or later, he does attain it.

Dr. Peter cites the case of the late General A. Jacks.* His hearty 9
manner, informal dress, scorn for petty regulations and disregard for
personal safety made him the idol of his men. He led them from victory
to victory.

*It is Dr. Peter's usual practice to employ fictitious names in his case histories.

Had the war ended sooner, Jacks might have retired, covered in glory. But he was promoted to the rank of field marshal. Now he had to deal, not with fighting men, but with politicians of his own country, and with two punctilious Allied field marshals.

He quarreled with them all and took to spending whole days drunk, sulking in his trailer. The conduct of the war slipped out of his hands and into those of his subordinates.

The final promotion had brought him from doing what he *could* do, to attempting what he could not do. He had reached his level of incompetence.

The Jacks' case exemplifies the Peter Principle, the basic theorem of   10 hierarchiology. *In a hierarchy each employee tends to rise to his level of incompetence: every post tends to be occupied by an employee incompetent to execute its duties.*

How is it, then, that any work is done at all? Peter says, "Work is done   11 by people who have not yet attained final placement at their level of incompetence."

And how is it that we occasionally see a competent person at the very   12 top of the hierarchy? "Simply because there are not enough ranks for him to have reached his level of incompetence: in other words, *in that hierarchy* there is no task beyond his abilities."

> As a rule, such a prodigy of competence eventually sidesteps into another hierarchy — say from the Armed Forces into industry, from law to politics, from business to government — and there finds his level of incompetence. A well-known example is Macbeth, a successful general, but an incompetent king.

In an unpublished monograph, *The Pathology of Success: Morbidity*   13 *and Mortality at the Level of Incompetence,* Peter expands his theory to take in matters of health.

> Certain physical conditions are associated with the final placement: peptic ulcers, high blood pressure, nervous disorders, migraine headaches, alcoholism, insomnia, obesity and cardiovascular complaints. Obviously such symptoms indicate the patient's constitutional incompetence for his level of responsibility.
>
> Edgar Allen Poe, a highly competent writer, proved incompetent when raised to the rank of editor. He became "nervous in a very unusual degree," took to drink and then to drugs in a vain search for relief.
>
> Such ailments, usually appearing two or more together, constitute the Final Placement Syndrome.
>
> Medication and surgery are often prescribed for F.P.S. patients, but they miss the root cause of the condition. Psychoanalysis fails for the same reason. The analyst is probing into the patient's subconscious for

Oedipus complex, castration-complex, penis-envy or whatnot, when the trouble really lies outside, in the patient's hierarchal placement.

Is there no escape? Must every worker reach his level of incompe- 14 tence, suffer the miseries of Final Placement Syndrome and become a laughing stock for his behavioral or temperamental symptoms?

Peter describes two escape routes. The first is for a man who realizes 15 that he has reached his level of incompetence, yet still wants to preserve health, self-respect and sanity.

> Many an employee adjusts to final placement by the process of Substitution. Instead of executing his proper duties, he substitutes a set of irrelevant duties, and these self-imposed tasks he carries out to perfection.
>
> A. L. Tredwell, assistant principal of a secondary school, was intellectually competent and maintained good relationships with teachers, students, and parents. He was promoted to principal. Soon it became clear that he lacked the finesse to deal with newspaper reporters, school-board members, and the district superintendent. He fell out of favor with the officials, and his school lost community support. Realizing consciously or subconsciously — it doesn't matter which — that he was incompetent for the proper duties of a principal, Tredwell *Substituted.* He developed an obsessive concern with the movement of students and staff about the school.
>
> He drew complex plans of traffic-flow, had white lines painted on floors and arrows on walls, spent hours prowling the building looking for violations of his rules, and bombarded professional journals with articles about his scheme.
>
> Tredwell's Substitution is a great success. He is active and contented now, and shows no sign of the Final Placement Syndrome.

Peter's alternate escape route is for the employee who is capably and 16 happily doing his work and who wants to avoid ever reaching his level of incompetence.

Merely to *refuse* promotion seldom leads to happiness. It annoys 17 one's superiors, rouses suspicion among one's peers, and shames one's wife and children. Few people can endure all that. So one must contrive never to be offered promotion.

The first step is to avoid asking, or seeming to ask, for it. The oft-heard 18 complaint, "My job lacks challenge," is usually understood as showing desire for promotion. So don't give voice to such complaints!

The second step is described by Peter in his lecture, Creative In- 19 competence: "I have found some employees who are contented in their work, and who seem to be using effective means of maintaining their position."

Adam Greenaway, a gardener, happily tends the landscaped grounds of the Ideal Trivet Company. He is competent in all aspects of his work but one: He keeps losing delivery slips for goods received. He gives vague explanations such as "I must have planted the papers with the shrubs." Most important, he concealed the fact that he wanted to avoid promotion.

Lack of delivery slips so upset the accounting department that, when a new maintenance foreman was needed, Greenaway was not considered for the post.

Thus he could stay indefinitely at a level of competence and enjoy the keen personal satisfaction of regularly accomplishing useful work. Surely this offers as great a challenge as the traditional drive for higher ranks!

By his Darwinian Extension Theorem, Peter applies his Principle to the whole human race. Man may go the way of the dinosaur and the sabre-tooth tiger. Those beasts were destroyed by excessive development of the qualities — bulk and fangs — that had originally favored their survival. Man's cleverness was originally a survival characteristic, but now he has become clever enough to destroy himself. If he takes that step, he will achieve his ultimate level of incompetence, in proving himself unfit to live. 20

"Man's one hope," says Peter, "lies in hierarchiology. I feel that it will soon be recognized as the supreme science. Earlier sociological studies have insufficiently recognized man's hierarchal nature." 21

A knowledge of the Peter Principle becomes more and more important as hierarchal systems become stronger. Government and education are prime examples. Both already swollen, both expanding their demands for money and manpower, both extending their influence as more people stay longer in school, and as government controls more functions of life. Even industry, once a stronghold of individualism, is largely an aggregation of hierarchies. My point is that man ought to be using the hierarchal system for his benefit. But he can't possibly use it unless he understands it, and to do that he must understand the Peter Principle. Failing such understanding, the system will destroy the individuals who comprise it.

Many people accept the Peter Principle on first hearing. It sounds so obvious, so like common sense; it explains so aptly a group of hitherto mystifying phenomena. 22

In academic circles, however, the Principle has made little impression. A few of Peter's subordinates when he was at the University of British Columbia grasped it, but none of his superiors. Some of them saw it as a humorous trifle, others as sociological heresy. Said Peter at the time: "I'm neither primarily funny or unfunny. I study society 23 scientifically because I must live in it. I present my findings to you because they describe the world you live in."

> Anyway, I'm too busy to worry much about what others think of me. I teach future schoolteachers how to work with handicapped and disturbed children. I'm pursuing two fascinating lines of research: into autism, a profound emotional disorder in which children have no sense of self, and no ability to learn by experience; and into developmental dyslexia, an inability to recognize printed words that often, tragically, pins a "mentally retarded" label on a genuinely intelligent child. It's all deeply satisfying: I'm about as happy in my work as anyone I know.

The thought then occurred that Peter's hierarchiology might, just 24 might, be *his* form of Creative Incompetence — a means of making himself slightly suspect, and so avoiding an unwanted academic promotion.

"No, no! Of course not!" said the doctor. "But even if it were, of 25 course I wouldn't admit it!"

SUBJECT

1.   Test your understanding of the Peter Principle by applying it to a hierarchy not considered in detail in this essay.

2.   Do you agree that the Peter Principle operates in every organization having a hierarchal structure? Can you think of any in which it does not apply?

3.   If Peter believes that his principle applies to all organizations, why doesn't he advocate the abolition of hierarchies?

4.   Criticize the following application of the Peter Principle: "The United Nations General Assembly accomplishes little because it is composed of formerly able statesmen who were promoted to their level of incompetence."

5.   How, according to Peter, can a person avoid reaching his level of incompetence? How has Peter himself avoided it?

6.   Can you suggest ways by which a hierarchy — say a school system or a business corporation — could avoid filling all its executive positions with incompetents?

7.   Does the process which Peter calls "Substitution" strike you as a satisfactory way to avoid "Final Placement Syndrome"? Is it prevalent, judging from your own observation?

STRUCTURE

1.   Several separate processes are explained in this essay, including the historical process of how Peter arrived at his principle. Does in-

cluding more than one process in the same article cause any confusion? Do they all belong here?

2.   Professor Peter explains his principle with two illustrations, the cases of Mr. Sphere and General A. Jacks. Does this procedure give a clear idea of the process? Why must Peter resort to particular examples instead of outlining the steps in general?

3.   Do you think Hull created a structural problem for himself by trying to ·tell his readers about Professor Peter and about the Peter Principle both in the same essay? Does one lead naturally into the other? How does Hull tie them together at the end?

4.   Peter says that "man ought to be using the hierarchal system for his benefit." Does this essay make clear how man can do this, considering Peter's contention that his principle invariably operates at present? Should the essay have been expanded at this point? or should the statement have been omitted?

PARKINSON'S LAW

C. Northcote Parkinson

*C. Northcote Parkinson (born in 1909), teacher and public lecturer,
first devised his "law" when he was a professor of history at the University of Malaya. It occurred to him as a result of research into certain
agencies of the British government. But his book,* Parkinson's Law *(of
which the selection here is the first chapter), argues that the law and
its corollaries apply to all administrations, whether in government,
education, or private enterprise.*

Work expands so as to fill the time available for its completion. General 1
recognition of this fact is shown in the proverbial phrase "It is the
busiest man who has time to spare." Thus, an elderly lady of leisure can
spend the entire day in writing and dispatching a postcard to her niece
at Bognor Regis. An hour will be spent in finding the postcard, another
in hunting for spectacles, half an hour in a search for the address, an
hour and a quarter in composition, and twenty minutes in deciding
whether or not to take an umbrella when going to the mailbox in the
next street. The total effort that would occupy a busy man for three
minutes all told may in this fashion leave another person prostrate after
a day of doubt, anxiety, and toil.

Granted that work (and especially paper work) is thus elastic in its 2
demands on time, it is manifest that there need be little or no relationship between the work to be done and the size of the staff to which it
may be assigned. A lack of real activity does not, of necessity, result in
leisure. A lack of occupation is not necessarily revealed by a manifest
idleness. The thing to be done swells in importance and complexity in
a direct ratio with the time to be spent. This fact is widely recognized,
but less attention has been paid to its wider implications, more especially in the field of public administration. Politicians and taxpayers
have assumed (with occasional phases of doubt) that a rising total in the
number of civil servants must reflect a growing volume of work to be
done. Cynics, in questioning this belief, have imagined that the multi-
plication of officials must have left some of them idle or all of them able

to work for shorter hours. But this is a matter in which faith and doubt seem equally misplaced. The fact is that the number of the officials and the quantity of the work are not related to each other at all. The rise in the total of those employed is governed by Parkinson's Law and would be much the same whether the volume of the work were to increase, diminish, or even disappear. The importance of Parkinson's Law lies in the fact that it is a law of growth based upon an analysis of the factors by which that growth is controlled.

The validity of this recently discovered law must rest mainly on statistical proofs, which will follow. Of more interest to the general reader is the explanation of the factors underlying the general tendency to which this law gives definition. Omitting technicalities (which are numerous) we may distinguish at the outset two motive forces. They can be represented for the present purpose by two almost axiomatic statements, thus: (1) "An official wants to multiply subordinates, not rivals" and (2) "Officials make work for each other." 3

To comprehend Factor 1, we must picture a civil servant, called A, who finds himself overworked. Whether this overwork is real or imaginary is immaterial, but we should observe, in passing, that A's sensation (or illusion) might easily result from his own decreasing energy: a normal symptom of middle-age. For this real or imagined overwork there are, broadly speaking, three possible remedies. He may resign; he may ask to halve the work with a colleague called B; he may demand the assistance of two subordinates, to be called C and D. There is probably no instance in history, however, of A choosing any but the third alternative. By resignation he would lose his pension rights. By having B appointed, on his own level in the hierarchy, he would merely bring in a rival for promotion to W's vacancy when W (at long last) retires. So A would rather have C and D, junior men, below him. They will add to his consequence and, by dividing the work into two categories, as between C and D, he will have the merit of being the only man who comprehends them both. It is essential to realize at this point that C and D are, as it were, inseparable. To appoint C alone would have been impossible. Why? Because C, if by himself, would divide the work with A and so assume almost the equal status that has been refused in the first instance to B; a status the more emphasized if C is A's only possible successor. Subordinates must thus number two or more, each being thus kept in order by fear of the other's promotion. When C complains in turn of being overworked (as he certainly will) A will, with the concurrence of C, advise the appointment of two assistants to help C. But he can then avert internal friction only by advising the appointment of two more assistants to help D, whose position is much the same. With this 4

263

recruitment of E, F, G, and H the promotion of A is now practically certain.

Seven officials are now doing what one did before. This is where 5 Factor 2 comes into operation. For these seven make so much work for each other that all are fully occupied and A is actually working harder than ever. An incoming document may well come before each of them in turn. Official E decides that it falls within the province of F, who places a draft reply before C, who amends it drastically before consulting D, who asks G to deal with it. But G goes on leave at this point, handing the file over to H, who drafts a minute that is signed by D and returned to C, who revises his draft accordingly and lays the new version before A.

What does A do? He would have every excuse for signing the thing 6 unread, for he has many other matters on his mind. Knowing now that he is to succeed W next year, he has to decide whether C or D should succeed to his own office. He had to agree to G's going on leave even if not yet strictly entitled to it. He is worried whether H should not have gone instead, for reasons of health. He has looked pale recently — partly but not solely because of his domestic troubles. Then there is the business of F's special increment of salary for the period of the conference and E's application for transfer to the Ministry of Pensions. A has heard that D is in love with a married typist and that G and F are no longer on speaking terms — no one seems to know why. So A might be tempted to sign C's draft and have done with it. But A is a conscientious man. Beset as he is with problems created by his colleagues for themselves and for him — created by the mere fact of these officials' existence — he is not the man to shirk his duty. He reads through the draft with care, deletes the fussy paragraphs added by C and H, and restores the thing back to the form preferred in the first instance by the able (if quarrelsome) F. He corrects the English — none of these young men can write grammatically — and finally produces the same reply he would have written if officials C to H had never been born. Far more people have taken far longer to produce the same result. No one has been idle. All have done their best. And it is late in the evening before A finally quits his office and begins the return journey to Ealing. The last of the office lights are being turned off in the gathering dusk that marks the end of another day's administrative toil. Among the last to leave, A reflects with bowed shoulders and a wry smile that late hours, like gray hairs, are among the penalties of success.

From this description of the factors at work the student of political 7 science will recognize that administrators are more or less bound to multiply. Nothing has yet been said, however, about the period of time likely to elapse between the date of A's appointment and the date from which we can calculate the pensionable service of H. Vast masses of statistical evidence have been collected and it is from a study of this data that Parkinson's Law has been deduced. Space will not allow of detailed analysis but the reader will be interested to know that research began in the British Navy Estimates. These were chosen because the Admiralty's responsibilities are more easily measurable than those of, say, the Board of Trade. The question is merely one of numbers and tonnage. Here are some typical figures. The strength of the Navy in 1914 could be shown as 146,000 officers and men, 3249 dockyard officials and clerks, and 57,000 dockyard workmen. By 1928 there were only 100,000 officers and men and only 62,439 workmen, but the dockyard officials and clerks by then numbered 4558. As for warships, the strength in 1928 was a mere fraction of what it had been in 1914 — fewer than 20 capital ships in commission as compared with 62. Over the same period the Admiralty officials had increased in number from 2000 to 3569, providing (as was remarked) "a magnificent navy on land." These figures are more clearly set forth in tabular form.

TABLE 1

Admiralty Statistics

	Year		Increase or decrease
	1914	*1928*	
Capital ships in commission	62	20	–67.74%
Officers and men in R.N.	146,000	100,000	–31.5%
Dockyard workers	57,000	62,439	+9.54%
Dockyard officials and clerks	3249	4558	+40.28%
Admiralty officials	2000	3569	+78.45%

The criticism voiced at the time centered on the ratio between the numbers of those available for fighting and those available only for adminstration. But that comparison is not to the present purpose. What we have to note is that the 2000 officials of 1914 had become the 3569 of 1928; and that this growth was unrelated to any possible increase in their work. The Navy during that period had diminished, in point of fact, by a third in men and two-thirds in ships. Nor, from 1922 onward, was its strength even expected to increase; for its total of ships (unlike its total of officials) was limited by the Washington Naval Agreement of that year. Here we have then a 78 percent increase over a period of fourteen years; an average of 5.6 percent increase a year on the earlier total. In fact, as we shall see, the rate of increase was not as regular as

8

that. All we have to consider, at this stage, is the percentage rise over a given period.

Can this rise in the total number of civil servants be accounted for 9 except on the assumption that such a total must always rise by a law governing its growth? It might be urged at this point that the period under discussion was one of rapid development in naval technique. The use of the flying machine was no longer confined to the eccentric. Electrical devices were being multiplied and elaborated. Submarines were tolerated if not approved. Engineer officers were beginning to be regarded as almost human. In so revolutionary an age we might expect that storekeepers would have more elaborate inventories to compile. We might not wonder to see more draughtsmen on the payroll, more designers, more technicians and scientists. But these, the dockyard officials, increased only by 40 percent in number when the men of Whitehall increased their total by nearly 80 percent. For every new foreman or electrical engineer at Portsmouth there had to be two more clerks at Charing Cross. From this we might be tempted to conclude, provisionally, that the rate of increase in adminstrative staff is likely to be double that of the technical staff at a time when the actually useful strength (in this case, of seamen) is being reduced by 31.5 percent. It has been proved statistically, however, that this last percentage is irrelevant. The officials would have multiplied at the same rate had there been no actual seamen at all.

It would be interesting to follow the further progress by which the 10 8,118 Admiralty staff of 1935 came to number 33,788 by 1954. But the staff of the Colonial Office affords a better field of study during a period of imperial decline. Admiralty statistics are complicated by factors (like the Fleet Air Arm) that make comparison difficult as between one year and the next. The Colonial Office growth is more significant in that it is more purely administrative. Here the relevant statistics are as follows:

1935	1939	1943	1947	1954
372	450	817	1139	1661

Before showing what the rate of increase is, we must observe that the 11 extent of this department's responsibilities was far from constant during these twenty years. The colonial territories were not much altered in area or population between 1935 and 1939. They were considerably diminished by 1943, certain areas being in enemy hands. They were increased again in 1947, but have since then shrunk steadily from year to year as successive colonies achieve self-government. It would be rational to suppose that these changes in the scope of Empire would be reflected in the size of its central administration. But a glance at the figures is enough to convince us that the staff totals represent nothing but so many stages in an inevitable increase. And this increase, although related to that observed in other departments, has nothing to do with the size — or even the existence — of the Empire. What are the percentages of increase? We must ignore, for this purpose, the rapid increase in staff which accompanied the diminution of responsibility during World War II. We should note rather, the peacetime rates of increase: over 5.24 percent between 1935 and 1939, and 6.55 percent between 1947 and 1954. This gives an average increase of 5.89 percent each year, a percentage markedly similar to that already found in the Admiralty staff increase between 1914 and 1928.

Further and detailed statistical analysis of departmental staffs would be inappropriate in such a work as this. It is hoped, however, to reach a tentative conclusion regarding the time likely to elapse between a given official's first appointment and the later appointment of his two or more assistants. 12

Dealing with the problem of pure staff accumulation, all our researches so far completed point to an average increase of 5.75 percent per year. This fact established, it now becomes possible to state Parkinson's Law in mathematical form: In any public administrative department not actually at war, the staff increase may be expected to follow this formula — 13

$$x = \frac{2k^m + l}{n}$$

k is the number of staff seeking promotion through the appointment of subordinates; l represents the difference between the ages of appointment and retirement; m is the number of man-hours devoted to answering minutes within the department; and n is the number of effective units being administered. x will be the number of new staff required each year. Mathematicians will realize, of course, that to find the percentage increase they must multiply x by 100 and divide by the total of the previous year, thus:

$$\frac{100 \, (2k^m + l)}{yn} \%$$

where y represents the total original staff. This figure will invariably prove to be between 5.17 percent and 6.56 percent, irrespective of any variation in the amount of work (if any) to be done.

The discovery of this formula and of the general principles upon which it is based has, of course, no political value. No attempt has been made to inquire whether departments *ought* to grow in size. Those who hold that this growth is essential to gain full employment are fully 14 entitled to their opinion. Those who doubt the stability of an economy based upon reading each other's minutes are equally entitled to theirs. It would probably be premature to attempt at this stage any inquiry into the quantitative ratio that should exist between the administrators and the administered. Granted, however, that a maximum ratio exists, it should soon be possible to ascertain by formula how many years will elapse before that ratio, in any given community, will be reached. The forecasting of such a result will again have no political value. Nor can it be sufficiently emphasized that Parkinson's Law is a purely scientific discovery, inapplicable except in theory to the politics of the day. It is not the business of the botanist to eradicate the weeds. Enough for him if he can tell us just how fast they grow.

SUBJECT

1. Since Parkinson is obviously interested in administration, why does he begin with the illustration of a lady sending a postcard?

2. Parkinson shows how the law works by giving specific examples of it in operation; although this is not a process of the "how to bake a pie" variety, is it possible to give an abstract outline of the steps involved?

3. Do you know of any local or national offices whose administrative staff has increased while that which it "administers" has decreased — as in Parkinson's examples of the British Navy and Colonial Offices? While the Congress of the United States has increased only slightly in size in the past twenty years, its staff has increased tremendously; would you say that this growth reflects added duties of Congress, or the operation of Parkinson's Law?

4. Why do you suppose Parkinson makes the disclaimer in the final paragraph? If the law does indeed operate, isn't it obvious that something should be done about it?

STRUCTURE

1. Parkinson is clearly describing a process; yet it differs from other processes described in this section. In what ways?

2. If the aim of this passage is satire, why does Parkinson maintain such a deadpan tone?

3. The mathematical formulae at the end are of course useless; why does Parkinson include them?

4. Try to find the organizational scheme for this essay. Do the last two paragraphs fit into the scheme?

THE INTERLAKE AFFAIR

Alexander Polikoff

Alexander Polikoff is executive director of Businessmen for the Public Interest. "The Interlake Affair" is an excerpt from Mr. Polikoff's forthcoming book on the pollution of Lake Michigan. The essay is included here not to pick on one company involved in water pollution — Polikoff himself admits that Interlake may well be a leader in pollution control efforts. Rather, the concern here is with an incredible amount of government red tape. In one sense, the essay represents a negative process — how pollution control failed. In another sense, it is a historical process analysis showing how seven different government agencies managed to make an impossible tangle in prosecuting an obvious violation of the Refuse Act.

In June, 1968, a steel worker was crossing a river on a railroad bridge on his daily walk to work. From the bridge he saw a pipe, extending from the steel plant, spewing a black discharge into the river. He telephoned the U.S. Coast Guard to report what he had seen.

So began a skirmish in the fight to save Lake Michigan, sixth largest of the world's fresh water lakes, but well on its way to the degradation of Lake Erie. What has happened in the two-and-a-half years since that phone call is the ire-raising story of how our antipollution agencies turn themselves off while the remaining years of Lake Michigan's life slip inexorably away.

The steel company is Interlake, Inc. It has been around for 65 years. Its $355 million of property includes plants on the Grand Calumet River in Chicago and on the Little Calumet River in suburban Riverdale, Illinois. Stockbrokers call Interlake a "fully integrated steelmaker" and the "largest factor" in the pig-iron market. It makes steel stripping, pipe, storage rack systems, and much more. It owns 90 percent of a Belgian producer and is a partner with French and German firms. In 1969 its sales were $325 million and its operating income over $42 million.

Interlake prides itself on being a leader in the fight against pollution. In one of his speeches on that subject Interlake's president, Reynold C.

MacDonald, said it seemed "mighty important" to him that industry "demonstrate by deeds, as well as words and desires, a willingness to ... take the actions necessary to meet its [pollution] obligations. Obviously," he added, "our first job must be to clear up our own company's pollution."

MacDonald described how Interlake went at the problem through a pollution control project team of specialists, and he told of one of Interlake's proudest achievements in pollution control: 5

> ... a technique we developed with DuPont to neutralize waste hydrochloric acid pickle liquor. ... This latest development completely eliminates all pollutants from waste pickle liquor.

MacDonald also talked of honesty:

> Every company must act candidly and openly, in this, and all areas. If we in industry are to generate the confidence, trust, and goodwill that we must have from our partners in this massive campaign, we have to be honest and open. Interlake's public policy is to report both good and bad news with dispatch. I wouldn't have it any other way.

Interlake, it seemed, was an anti-pollution exemplar for all of industry.   6

The steelworker is Frank Jacklovich, 29, who lives with his wife and three children on the Chicago side of the Little Calumet River, an eight-minute walk from Interlake's Riverdale plant. The river, an important shipping artery, flows into or out of Lake Michigan a few miles away, depending on whether the O'Brien locks, just up the river from Interlake's plant, are open or closed.   7

The route that Jacklovich walked to work every morning took him across the quarter-mile-wide Little Calumet River on a railroad bridge leading into Interlake's sprawling Riverdale plant. From the bridge he could see, quite plainly, a large pipe, over two feet in diameter, extending from Interlake's mill and overhanging the river. He could also see, quite plainly, the steady coal-black stream which poured from the pipe and fell to the river three feet below. And Jacklovich began to report what he saw to the Coast Guard.   8

Gunk Goes to Court

The Coast Guard is the first of the many government agencies involved in this story. One of the Guard's duties is to check on violations of the venerable Refuse Act, a criminal law passed in 1899. The Refuse Act was originally designed to deal with harbor and navigation matters.   9

But with the emergence of environmental concerns, the Supreme Court interpreted the act to cover pollution problems as well. With Biblical simplicity, the Refuse Act says, in effect, Thou shalt not dump refuse in navigable waters.

The Coast Guard did check up on Jacklovich's reports. On June 3, 1968, the Guard took water samples from the pipe near the bridge (officially called Interlake Outfall No. 18) and delivered them to the Chicago District Office of the U.S. Army Corps of Engineers. The Corps, which is the principal administering agency under the Refuse Act, in turn had the samples analyzed by a private laboratory. The results were positive — or maybe negative, depending on the point of view. The samples showed that oil and mill scale (flaked steel particles produced in the steel-making process) were spewing from Outfall No. 18. The deposit of cither substance in the river is a violation of the Refuse Act, so the Corps passed its information on to the U.S. Attorney in Chicago, the local official responsible for legal enforcement of the act. In December, 1968, just three months after President MacDonald's industry responsibility speech, the U.S. Attorney charged Interlake with violating the Refuse Act. The case was assigned to Chief Judge Edwin Robson of the Federal District Court in Chicago.

Interlake pleaded not guilty, and its lawyer, Henry Pitts, first vice president of the Illinois State Bar Association and a senior partner in a large and prestigious Chicago law firm, attacked the whole idea of prosecuting Interlake. Pitts said that the U.S. Attorney couldn't bring the law suit because he hadn't been asked to by the Corps. (The Refuse Act says U.S. Attorneys should "vigorously" enforce the prohibition against dumping, but Pitts argued that the U.S. Attorney could do nothing unless somebody else asked him to.)

Pitts also argued that the Refuse Act was "superseded" by a newer law (even though the newer statute expressly said it was not to "affect or impair" the Refuse Act). Finally, Pitts said the U.S. Attorney shouldn't be allowed to proceed against a defendant who was "all the while in compliance with the modern, up-to-date standards for water pollution control set by another arm of government." He was referring to standards set by an agency of the state of Illinois, the Sanitary Water Board, and his argument implied that Interlake was meeting those standards. (The fact was that Interlake was not. Indeed, the next year the Water Board would ask the Illinois Attorney General to sue Interlake for *not* meeting its standards.)

In March, 1969, Chief Judge Robson brushed Pitts' arguments aside and ordered Interlake to go on trial on May 26, 1969. Precisely on that date, with the trial ready to go on, Interlake changed its plea to *nolo contendere,* meaning it wouldn't fight the charges but neither would

271

it plead guilty. Interlake also filed an affidavit by Frank Armour, its vice president of engineering, saying, yes, Interlake had discharged mill scale into the Little Calumet River from Outfall No. 18 on June 3, 1968, but that it was all an accident. Armour said that Interlake's system removed mill scale and oil before discharging water into the river but that a drain leading to Outfall No. 18 had broken open and the break had caused the accident. The affidavit also said that the drain problem had been corrected "by reblocking the drain with a heavy steel plate sealed into place and supported by the pouring of a concrete base and providing additional bulkheading." Armour added, "This installation has correctd the problem, as evidenced by the fact that there have been no further incidents."

The affidavit also advised the court that Interlake was in the midst of   14 a $30 million pollution abatement program, that it was co-developer of the "pickle liquor" treatment process for handling waste acids to which President MacDonald had referred, and that Interlake was "attempting to cooperate fully with all federal, state, and local pollution control agencies." MacDonald's speech was included as an exhibit to the affidavit, along with an Izaak Walton League citation for "great progress" in water pollution abatement which called Interlake "an outstanding example of industry in action and forward motion." Also included was a letter Interlake had received from the Cook County Clean Streams Committee. The committee's letter said it had been "very disturbed" to read of the charges against Interlake since Interlake was "the Chicago area leader" in progress against pollution.

Despite all this, Judge Robson found Interlake guilty and fined it   15 $500, the minimum permitted by the Refuse Act (the maximum is $2,500). He also ordered that Jacklovich be paid $250 because the Refuse Act says half the fine should be paid to a citizen who supplies information which leads to conviction.

A Shifty System

At this point, everybody seemed to be happy and one would have   16 thought the system was working well. The U.S. Attorney had obtained a conviction, showing he was interested in enforcing the antipollution laws. The laws themselves had been strengthened by Judge Robson's opinion. Jacklovich had played a useful citizen's role and had received $250 for his effort. And Interlake, although convicted, had gotten off with a minimum fine. (It had also had a chance to protect its corporate image by publicly expressing its concern about pollution and making the point that the incident for which it had been convicted was acciden-

tal and would not be repeated.) But that was what one would have
thought.

As it turned out, everybody was not happy and the system was not 17
working well. The mill scale and oil continued to flow from Outfall No.
18 even after the drain was blocked (notwithstanding Interlake's affidavit that the seeping had been a one-time accident). Pollution continued
to flow from other Interlake outfalls too, including the one from the
highly touted "pickle liquor" facility.

In his daily walks across the bridge Jacklovich saw what was happen- 18
ing and continued to phone the Coast Guard and Corps of Engineers.
He called in June, one month after the conviction, and he called many
times in July, in August, and in September.

After one such complaint, which Jacklovich made on September 3, 19
1969, the Corps made arrangements to use the Coast Guard's 17-foot
fiberglass speedboat to take water samples from the river alongside
Interlake's plant. The results of the sample proved, as usual, that Interlake was polluting the river.

Finally, more than five months later, the Corps got around to report- 20
ing the results, and on February 12, 1970, Charles W. Wyant, district
counsel in Chicago, stated that the incident appeared to be a violation
of the Refuse Act, and concluded: "Prosecution is recommended."

Wyant's report then went through channels: to Wyant's superior in 21
Chicago, then to his superior in the general counsel's office of the Chief
of Engineers in Washington, and then, presumably, to the Department
of Justice in Washington, which should in turn have told the U.S. Attorney in Chicago to prosecute. Once again, nothing happened.

Why? It was the same kind of pollution for which Interlake had been 22
convicted just a few months earlier (swearing it was a one-time accident
— a misstatement about which apparently nobody even probed Interlake), and it came from exactly the same outfall. Nor was the September
4 incident just another accident; there were all those other Jacklovich
phone calls, many of which had been investigated and confirmed by the
Coast Guard and Corps. Finally, the Corps had recommended prosecution. Why, then, didn't the U.S. Attorney prosecute Interlake?

A Deferment for Refuse

The precise answer is shrouded in bureaucratic mystery, but a clue 23
may be found in the attitude of the Justice Department in Washington.
In early 1970, the Justice Department began to develop its "deference"
policy: the policy of deferring in pollution matters to another federal
agency, the Federal Water Quality Administration (FWQA). FWQA

was set up under the Federal Water Pollution Control Act (FWPCA, passed in 1948 and since amended several times) as the federal agency to develop and enforce water quality standards in cooperation with state antipollution agencies. The mechanism for doing this under the FWPC Act is called the "enforcement conference," which is a Rube Goldberg administrative nightmare in which federal and state officials are supposed to sit down together and agree on water quality standards and how to enforce them. There is an ultimate right to go to court to force polluters to adhere to the standards, but the administrative procedure which must precede court action is so time-consuming and involved that court action has hardly even been used in the history of the FWPC Act.

The first federal-state enforcement conference with respect to Lake 24 Michigan wasn't even convened until 1965. By that time the peril to Lake Michigan was not exactly a secret, especially with the grim reminder of Lake Erie only a few hundred miles away.

Five-and-a-half years and thousands of pages of enforcement confer- 25 ence proceedings later, a report was issued in November, 1970, by a technical committee of the conference. The report contained high praise for all that everybody had accomplished in the previous five-and-a-half years. Buried in the praise were two questions and answers: First, what had happened to water quality in the five-and-a-half years of enforcement conference work? Answer: in most places no better and in many places "deteriorated." Second, what would be the water quality when the conference's clean-up programs were completed? Answer: The waters would still be polluted.

This was the agency and procedure to which the Justice Department 26 was going to "defer" in pollution matters. A concerned Congressman who got wind of the new policy, Henry Reuss of Wisconsin, immediately wrote to Attorney General John Mitchell to find out what was going on.

Gnarled in the Outfall

Reuss got his answer on June 2, 1970, in a letter from Mitchell's 27 assistant, Shiro Kashiwa. In bureaucratese Kashiwa told Reuss that the Department was *not* going to "vigorously enforce" the Refuse Act as Congress had said it should, but would "defer" to FWQA and the states. "The policy of the executive," Kashiwa declared, would be to "fit" the Refuse Act into the "regulatory scheme devised by Congress to combat pollution. . . ." This meant, said Kashiwa, that the Refuse Act was not to be enforced where it would have "a disruptive or devitalizing effect upon programs designed or approved" by FWQA, or where a company was spending "significant amounts of money" to abate pollution under a FWQA program.

An incensed Reuss responded, "The law doesn't exempt polluters 28 who spend money to clean up their mess. . . . The Justice Department should obey the law." Reuss also said, "If the Justice Department winks at the industrial polluter who violates the 1899 Refuse Act, there will be no incentive to . . . comply with water quality standards as the law requires."

But Reuss was ignored and on July 10, 1970, the Attorney General 29 issued "guidelines" to all U.S. Attorneys which in effect told them not to enforce the Refuse Act against industrial pollution "of a continuing nature resulting from the ordinary operation of a manufacturing plant." The guidelines acknowledged that such pollution posed "the greatest threat to the environment" but said that the FWQA had been created to handle that kind of pollution. (The guidelines failed to mention that the law creating FWQA had said it was not to "affect or impair" the Refuse Act.)

The result of all this was that the Refuse Act was to be substantially 30 a dead letter with respect to continuous industrial pollution — the field was to be left to FQWA and the states — and Jacklovich got no action from all of his phone calls. Angrily, Reuss called the Attorney General "a scofflaw where water pollution is concerned," and said that according to the Justice Department's "absurd doctrine" a polluter could continue to violate the Refuse Act if someday he were going to abate his pollution under a program of the FWQA.

Although FWQA's performance hardly seemed to warrant benching 31 the Refuse Act through the "deferencé policy," perhaps the Refuse Act could stay in the ball game to "coordinate" part of the enforcement scheme. In April, 1970, Jack B. Schmetterer, then first Assistant U.S. Attorney in Chicago, told the Chicago Bar Association that the U.S. Attorney's office had reviewed its position on pollution enforcement and had decided that an aggressive prosecution policy under the Refuse Act "would prove a powerful incentive to corporate managers and officers" to cooperate with FWQA.

Schmetterer said that his office had received permission from Wash- 32 ington to proceed with an "incentive" program and had received excellent cooperation from the Coast Guard and the Corps of Engineers. He went on:

> I regret to report to you, however, that the one federal agency that has sophisticated technical staff and information sufficient to help us move forward against major water problems . . . has refused to give us that

aid. . . . [The] absolute refusal of the Interior Department to permit the Federal Water Pollution Control Administration office [as FWQA was then called] to supply us any information or technical advice defies understanding.

Schmetterer said that his requests for specific information on specific companies had gone unanswered, that his requests for general advice as to which companies posed the most critical problems had gone unanswered, and that his final request for "just such information as would be made available to any member of the public" had not been complied with. "Perhaps," he concluded, "that attitude is due to the view of an Interior Department official who called me from Washington to ask why I wanted to prosecute 'those nice people.'" 33

Schmetterer's speech might have had some effect, for on paper at least FWQA in Chicago agreed that continuous discharges would be prosecuted under the Refuse Act where a firm was not in compliance with FWQA standards. 34

But it was not to be so. To illustrate, in September, 1970, a Jacklovich complaint was sent over to FWQA by the Corps after the Corps had been told to get FWQA recommendations. Further action, said the Corps, would be held in abeyance pending FWQA's advice. 35

An FWQA staff member was assigned to review the file. He concluded the evidence showed, as usual, that periodic discharges from Interlake's Riverdale plant violated the Refuse Act. His report said that prosecution under the Refuse Act "might be helpful in persuading the company to eliminate their remaining problems promptly." His written recommendation to that effect made its way to the desk of the FWQA boss in Chicago, Francis Mayo. At this writing it is still there. The Corps request, now over four months old, is still unanswered, and action (on an incident now over nine months old) is still held in "abeyance." Schmetterer had left office after a change in administration and there was no one around, apparently, to remind Mayo of his agreement that if a firm were "not in good cooperation" with FWQA schedules, it was a "fit" subject" for Refuse Act prosecution. 36

Highly Coordinated Waste

Could it be that all this federal inaction was justified because Illinois was taking good care of the Interlake problem? (That wouldn't have been an excuse for non-enforcement of the Refuse Act which Congress had said was to be "vigorously enforced" but FWQA might legitimately take a back seat if a state were really doing an effective job.) 37

276

Way back in September, 1968, the Metropolitan Sanitary District of 38
Chicago issued an order giving Interlake until September 30, 1969, to
comply with its antipollution rules. That day came and went and Interlake was not in compliance, so the Sanitary District filed a suit which
sounded as if it meant business. The lawsuit said that the District's
efforts to bring voluntary compliance had failed and that Interlake's
pollution posed a "grave, ever-present and great danger and immediate
threat to the health, safety, and well-being" of the people of Illinois. The
suit asked that Interlake be ordered to stop violating the Sanitary District rules and be fined.

Brave words ... followed by no action. Interlake's lawyer, Henry 39
Pitts, filed a motion which said that the Sanitary District had no right
to sue Interlake at all (for the reason, among others, that it was itself a
polluter!). The district did nothing to get the motion decided by the
judge to whom the case was assigned and for a full year took no action
at all. Then, on September 30, 1970, something was finally done —
the Sanitary District requested a *delay* because "the case is not ready
for trial." When asked about the suit in the fall of 1970, District officials
said they hadn't pushed their law suit because they had "understood"
Interlake was correcting the problems (although they couldn't be specific about exactly what was being done and what effect it would have).
But, they said, they had now become disillusioned with Interlake's lack
of progress and were going to push their law suit vigorously.

Meanwhile, another state agency had gone after Interlake. The Il- 40
linois Sanitary Water Board had also ordered Interlake to comply with
its water quality rules by September 30, 1969. Interlake failed to comply, so the Water Board asked the Illinois Attorney General, William
Scott, to sue Interlake.

Scott's suit was filed on March 2, 1970, five months after the Water 41
Board's deadline date. A curious fact was that Scott's office didn't file a
summons for five more months, meaning that Interlake wasn't formally
notified of the suit until July, 1970, 10 months after the Water Board's
deadline date.

At that point Interlake's lawyer, Henry Pitts, filed another motion 42
which, among other things, questioned Scott's right to sue Interlake
(nobody, it seemed, had that right) and also argued that Illinois law had
been changed during the time Scott had neglected to have a summons
served so that Scott was now operating under the wrong law.

Once again Pitts' motion went unanswered. This time, however, 43
Judge Nathan Cohen, to whom the case was assigned, called for a
"progress report." A new Illinois agency, the Environmental Protection
Agency, prepared the report, which included the Riverdale plant as

well as the others. The report, dated November 10, 1970, said that Interlake was making some progress but that all five of the outfalls at Riverdale were discharging pollutants in violation of the Agency's rules. The pickle liquor outfall in particular was a major offender, discharging visible amounts of oil and solids, including lead and zinc.

Judge Cohen entered an order requiring that a "final report" be filed on December 14, 1970. Ten days before then, on December 3, Pitts' law firm went to a different judge and asked that the Scott suit be "consolidated" with the moribund Sanitary District suit. It was; the case was taken from Judge Cohen; and to this date that "final report" has not been filed. The latest word at this writing is that the staff of the Environmental Protection Agency had talked to Interlake and reached the less than earth-shaking conclusion that "We don't think they've solved the problem yet." Similarly, a Sanitary District official reported that Interlake was "still having problems." (Note that the official felt it was Interlake, not the Sanitary District, or the people of Illinois, that was having the problems.) 44

So the circle of inaction was complete. The Refuse Act was not enforced out of "deference" to FWQA and the states. FWQA's enforcement of the law against Interlake consisted of learning that the Metropolitan Sanitary District had sampled Interlake. The Sanitary District and Attorney General Scott couldn't even get up enough steam to argue Henry Pitts's motions, and neither talked to the other about their respective law suits. When a judge did get tough, and one of the law suits finally seemed about to move forward, it was quickly consolidated with the suit that was going nowhere. This consolidation occurred exactly two-and-one-half years after the incident for which Interlake was convicted under the Refuse Act and more than two years after the deadline dates Interlake had been given by the Sanitary District and the Water Board — hardly prompt attention to the "immediate threat to the health, safety, and well-being" of the people of Illinois. 45

Nixon Chooses Effluent

There was, however, one effort to break out of the circle. On July 30, 1970, the Corps announced a new policy — permits would be required for all industrial discharges into navigable waters. Under the new policy Interlake would need a Corps permit to discharge any refuse and couldn't get one without Sanitary District and Water Board approvals. Presumably these agencies would decline to give approvals until Interlake complied with their orders. 46

The new policy looked promising on paper, and Congressman Reuss 47
congratulated the Corps on its "progressive step," adding a hope that
the Corps would implement its new policy promptly and not just issue
a press release. But again it was not to be so.

Congress only appropriated half the money that the Corps had re- 48
quested for its new program. On top of that there was yet another
jurisdictional struggle with the recently created President's Council on
Environmental Quality. At a meeting in late 1970 to try to resolve the
issues, Justice Department lawyers objected to the proposed Corps
program and — incredibly — walked out when the Corps insisted that
the program proceed promptly. And if that weren't enough, another
new agency (yes, still another), the Environmental Protection Agency,
felt that it, not the Corps, should control the new program.

So even though President Nixon's announcement on December 23, 49
1970, of "more activist utilization of the Refuse Act" sounded good, as
usual, it seemed to mean simply that one more program would be
trapped in the FWQA-type administrative maze.

Nixon's statement seemed promising. He said that Corps permits 50
would be immediately required for any new discharges on navigable
waters and that industry would have to file for permits on existing
discharges by July 1, 1971. "In the meantime," the President said,
"violators of water quality standards would not be exempt from prosecution under the Refuse Act."

Moreover, Nixon referred to requiring "effluent data" for industrial 51
discharges, a key point. If enforcement of a permit system were tied to
exactly what came out of the end of a discharge pipe, it would be a lot
more precise than under water quality standards — applicable to the
condition of the receiving waters as a whole. One Illinois official, referring to water quality standards, said, "Because of this trick, and that's
all it is, we've got U.S. Steel dumping 150 pounds of cyanide per day
into the lake. ...."

The Pickle Liquor Pipe

But implementing the permit program was a different matter, as we 52
shall see. Accompanying the Nixon statement was an order which assigned administrative responsibility to the Corps, but also said the
Corps should accept the determinations of the Environmental Protection Agency on water quality matters. On the last day of 1970, the Corps
published its proposed permit regulations and allowed a 45-day public
comment period, after which the regulations might be made final.

Comment was not long in coming. Reuss, who had gotten a draft of 53
the regulation before it was made public, said the draft was inadequate
and inconsistent with existing law. There followed 14 single-spaced
pages of detailed objections. He suggested the proposed permit regulation be revised.

It was not. Two leading environmental organizations, Friends of the 54
Earth and the Natural Resources Defense Council, also objected. They
said the proposed administration program would actually hinder water
pollution abatement. They objected to the fact that the Administration
had violated one of its own environmental protection laws in the very
issuance of the new regulations in that it did not prepare and submit
to the public an "environmental impact statement" as required by law.

More importantly, said the Defense Council, the new program was 55
susceptible to administrative delay, EPA's role was vague, effluent standards were not mentioned, there was no clear-cut method to insure
compliance with permit conditions, and public participation provisions
were vague. The permit program seemed designed to transform the
simple, effective Refuse Act into another Rube Goldberg, FWQA-type
administrative maze.

A proposed memorandum of understanding between the Corps and 56
the Environmental Protection Agency spelled out the role of the two
agencies a little more but did not change the proposed regulations in
any significant respect. There was still no suggestion that Refuse Act
court actions would be used as the enforcement mechanism. The Justice Department was not even mentioned.

Meanwhile, back at Interlake's Riverdale plant, nothing has hap- 57
pened except that Jacklovich was fired and the Little Calumet River
continues to receive Interlake's discharges. On May 26, 1970, one year
to the very day after Interlake's conviction, Interlake discharged, according to Corps files, "an orange liquid at the rate of 500 gallons per
minute which covered approximately 300 feet in length and half the
width of the Little Calumet River." Samples and photographs were
taken, and the Corps report says that the facts showed a violation of the
Refuse Act. A copy of the report was mailed to the U.S. Attorney.
Presumably out of "deference," nothing was done. The discharge was
from the waste pickle liquor outfall.

On November 19, 1970, a weary Jacklovich himself sued Interlake. 58
His theory was that since the Refuse Act entitled him to half the fine,
and the U.S. Attorney wasn't doing anything, he was entitled to bring
a citizen's action to recover his half of the fine and enforce the Act.

As might have been expected, Henry Pitts vigorously opposed Jack- 59
lovich's right to sue. It remains to be seen what the court will do with
Jacklovich's theory. And what the people will do with John Mitchell's.

Friends Can Be Poison

What conclusions can be drawn from the Jacklovich Interlake story? 60
Interlake may be one of the *better* companies in dealing with pollution.
Although its concern with its corporate image has led it to be less than
candid, and although it has been painfully slow in remedying its pollution problems, it may still — incredible though it seems — have
moved faster than many if not most companies. It is difficult to fault
Interlake for not being willing to spend pollution control dollars faster
than its competitors are required to, and they were not, of course,
forced to comply with the law any more effectively than was Interlake.

The result has been that literally years have gone by without ade- 61
quate enforcement of existing antipollution laws — years during
which increments of Interlake pollution have been added to the public's waters long after the pollution should have ended. Uncounted
dollars and hours of government time have been spent in useless activity and buck-passing. Letters, reports, conferences, sampling, lawsuits, more conferences — everything has happened except the one
thing that would have been effective: an injunction order under the
Refuse Act. The Coast Guard, the Corps, the Justice Department, the
FWQA, the Sanitary District, the Water Board, the Illinois Attorney
General — all have been involved in one way or another, largely
without cooperation, or even communication, and indeed frequently
justifying their own inaction because of what other agencies were supposed to be doing.

Meanwhile, the life of Lake Michigan is edging toward irreversible 62
degradation. Three years ago, then Secretary of the Interior Steward
Udall said, "Delay means death to Lake Michigan." One year ago, a
scientist working under an FWQA grant said that the lake was at the
"break point" of drastic changes in the ecosystem.

There should be no "deference" to anybody unless and until the 63
states and FWQA (now called the Office of Water Quality and a part of
the Environmental Protection Agency) impose specific and adequate
pollution-ending requirements and set firm dates for compliance. Until
then, the Refuse Act should be "vigorously" enforced, as Congress said.
The injunctive power should be used to impose specific, pollution-
ending schedules on a plant-by-plant basis. If and when the states and
FWQA get around to imposing adequate schedules, the Refuse Act
should be used to enforce them. A comply-or-close-down court order
will deliver a much clearer message than a dozen FWQA enforcement
conferences.

Until some such program is worked out, we can anticipate continua- 64
tions and repetitions of the Interlake story, and worse. Lake Michigan

might still be saved from its enemies if given half a chance. The question is whether it can survive its friends.

SUBJECT

1. Do you see any relationship between the Interlake affair and "Parkinson's Law"?

2. Of the seven government agencies involved in the Interlake litigation, do any of them seem actually desirous of obstructing justice? What prevented action from being taken?

3. Granting that Interlake did not seem overeager to correct this particular pollution problem, do you see reasons that they might have difficulty complying with pollution control laws in any case?

4. A number of politicians are fond of saying, "You can't legislate morality." Does pollution control seem to be an area where this statement applies?

5. Can you see in the jumble of mistakes in the handling of this case what *could* have been done under existing law?

STRUCTURE

1. Does Polikoff succeed in writing *about* confusion without letting his own account become confusing?

2. Were there any places where you felt Polikoff was being unfair in his analysis of what happened?

3. Would it be possible to abstract from this account an outline (or recipe) for how the Interlake affair got into the tangle it is in where Polikoff leaves it?

4. Explanation of a process frequently includes some cause and effect analysis as a matter of necessity. How much do you find here? Could Polikoff have eliminated it without losing clarity in his process analysis?

5. The opening paragraphs set the stage and introduce the contestants much in the way an announcer might at a championship boxing match or football game. What advantages — or weaknesses — are there in this kind of introduction? Does Polikoff "overdramatize"?

OLD WEAPONS
ARE BEST

Kevin P. Shea

Kevin P. Shea is Scientific Director for Environment, *published by the*
Committee for Environmental Information. The journal's purpose, as
illustrated by Shea's article, is to provide accurate "scientific informa-
tion relevant to political and social issues," on the assumption that
considerable heat and not enough light has been generated on the
subject of environmental quality. Here Shea suggests some pest
control methods which are both scientifically sound and ecologically
beneficial.

Of the hundreds of thousands of species of insects and plants that are 1
potentially damaging to man's agricultural activities only a few hundred are considered to be pests. The great majority are part of an
ecological system of checks and balances which keeps their numbers
below the level at which they become economically injurious. Inevitably, increased mobility of human populations and the mass application
of agricultural technology have, in some cases, upset the natural regulation of both plants and insects and have created serious problems of pest
control. For the most part, the response has been a unilateral attack
with an enormous variety of synthetic chemicals in the hope that
agriculture would find "salvation at the end of a spray nozzle."[1]

Unfortunately, the result has been less than satisfying. As the use of 2
chemicals increased, new pests were created, old ones became resistant, and the entire global environment has been contaminated with
long-lasting, biologically active synthetic chemicals.

At the same time, however, scientists have been learning to manipu- 3
late some of the elements of the natural ecosystem in order to restore
the balance that once existed and thereby reduce pest populations to
the point where the use of chemicals is greatly reduced or even eliminated. As we shall see, this more ecologically oriented approach to pest
control has proved highly successful.

Reprinted from *Environment* (June 1971) by permission of *Environment.* Copyright
© 1971 by Committee for Environmental Information.

283

In 1887 a burgeoning new citrus industry in California was on the   4
verge of collapse from the ravages of an insect pest known as the
cottony cushion scale. Three years later, after the introduction from
Australia of a voracious little lady beetle that feeds exclusively on the
pest, shipments of citrus from Los Angeles County groves leaped from
700 to 2,000 cars. With this remarkably dramatic demonstration of the
value of natural enemies in controlling insect pests, the science of biological control was launched fullscale. It has since become a highly
sophisticated application of ecological and biological principles which
has enjoyed enormous success in many parts of the world.

The notion of controlling insect pests by manipulating their own   5
natural enemies was not a new one even in the late 1800s. As with many
other ideas, the practice of biological control can be traced to ancient
China, where citrus growers purchased and placed in their groves the
nests of a predaceous ant which they felt was valuable in reducing the
number of foliage-feeding insects in their trees. A similar practice was
reported in 1775 to occur among date growers in Yemen, and certainly
the beneficial habits of lady beetles have been known for centuries.[2]

During the nineteenth century many naturalists both here and   6
abroad noted the role of natural enemies of insects in maintaining pest
populations at noninjurious levels. In England, Erasmus Darwin wrote
of a small ichneumonfly that helped control the cabbage caterpillar. In
Austria, Vincent Kollars's work on the natural enemies of insects was
published at the command of Emperor Francis I of Austria for the
benefit of farmers, foresters, and gardeners of that country.[3] In this
country, the renowned entomologist, Asa Fitch, was, in 1856, probably
the first to suggest the purposeful introduction of the natural enemies
of insect pests from a foreign country.[4]

But it wasn't until the startling success in Southern California with   7
the cottony cushion scale that the full potential of biological control
became known to the world. The story of the introduction of the Vedalia beetle *(Rhodolia cardinalis)* to control the cottony cushion scale is
an interesting one in that it demonstrates a number of principles that
still hold in modern day programs of biological control. It also demonstrates that not a little bit of luck was involved.

In April of 1887, with destruction of citrus groves at its peak, the   8
Convention of Fruit Growers met in Riverside, California. They invited
as their principal speaker Charles Valentine Riley, who was at the time
chief of the Division of Entomology of the United States Department
of Agriculture (USDA).

It was during this speech that Riley suggested the possibility of send-   9
ing an entomologist to the native home of the pest for the purpose of
collecting and sending back to California any promising natural ene-

mies that might be discovered.[5] Riley suggested that the state, or even the county, should appropriate $2,000 for the purpose he outlined, and sadly admitted that, as chief U.S. entomologist, he would not have hesitated to furnish the money had it been available. "But," said Riley, "the mere suggestion that I wanted $1,500 to $2,000 for such a purpose would be more apt to cause laughter and ridicule on the part of the average committee in Congress than serious and earnest consideration."[6]

With Riley's idea planted in their minds, the California citrus growers 10 began to lobby their representatives in Washington. Norman J. Coleman, commissioner of agriculture in California, in a letter to Representative Felton, suggested that, even though the Division of Entomology was restricted to travel in the United States, there was to be an Exposition in Melbourne in which the U.S. government was to participate. He further suggested that "this exposition in many ways would further the investigation referred to in your memorial." As luck would have it, the Honorable Frank McCoppin of San Francisco was appointed U.S. Commissioner to the exposition and it was he who arranged for the travel funds to support an entomologist to accompany the U.S. delegation, ostensibly to represent the Department of Agriculture. Thus it was that the Department of State played a major role in the advancement of biological control.

Riley appointed Albert Koebele, his able associate who had been 11 working in California, to make the trip to Australia, and soon the shipments of various species began to arrive in California. Correspondence between Koebele and Riley pointed out something that even today is considered foolhardy, that is, trying to predict the success of an imported natural enemy. In October 1888 Koebele wrote to Riley that he had found several species of promising natural enemies, among them a small coccinellid (the first mention of the Vedalia beetle). Riley replied, "the sending of the coccinellids of course is desirable, but I think we have much more to hope from the *Crytochaetum* [a parasitic fly]."[5] The rest of the story is entomological history. It was this auspicious beginning that led to many more successful programs of biological control in more than sixty countries around the world.

In the past few years a number of innovative techniques have been 12 devised for controlling insect pests. Some, like the sterile male technique, have been very successful in controlling insects in specific kinds of situations. Others, like the use of sex-attractants, are still in various stages of development, but hold great promise. None of these are, strictly speaking, biological controls. As defined by the practitioners of the science, biological control is "the action of parasites, predators or pathogens [disease-causing agents] on a host or prey population which produces a lower general equilibrium position than would prevail in the absence of these agents."[7] In plain language, this means that the presence of the natural enemies permanently reduces the general abundance of the host or prey population.

Vincent Kollar stated the idea much more eloquently in 1837:   13

> Besides mammalia, birds, and amphibious animals, nature, to restore the equilibrium among her creatures, and particularly to prevent the preponderance of some sorts of insects, makes use chiefly of insects themselves, namely those which feed upon others, and which by degrees obtain a superiority over those which are hurtful to us.[3]

From the experience with the Vedalia beetle and from many more   14
case histories since, it became clear that the most likely candidates for biological control are those pests introduced into a country from a foreign land. Pests of various kinds have been stowaways in man's transportation systems for hundreds of years. In the case of insects, more often than not a pest is introduced into an alien land without its normal complement of natural controls. If it finds the climate to its liking, its population can grow in a nearly unrestricted way. The idea, then, is to determine the native land of the pest, as was done with the cottony cushion scale, and then search its home for those natural enemies which usually limit its population. In 1856 Asa Fitch had this to say of the wheat midge, a European species that was then spreading across the United States:

> Why is it so severe and unremitting a pest in our country when it is so slight and transitory in its native land? There must be a cause for this remarkable difference. What can that cause be? I can impute it to only one thing. We here are destitute of nature's appointed means for repressing and subduing this insect. Those other insects which have been created for the purpose of quelling this species and keeping it restrained within its appropriate sphere have never yet reached our shores. We have received the evil without the remedy.[8]

This, then, has been one of the guiding principles upon which biologi-   15
cal control programs have been based. Successful programs, however, are not restricted to introduced pests, as will be discussed later. The entire process sounds relatively simple and the story of the Vedalia beetle makes it appear simple. In the past 70 years, however, entomologists have found that repeating the Vedalia success is anything but easy. In the first half of the twentieth century, hundreds of parasites and predators were shipped to and from a variety of countries in the hope of controlling any number of pests. Many never became established in their new homes, and many that did become established were unable

to check their hosts (the pests) sufficiently and were consequently not worthwhile. But even in the "release and pray" days of this fast-developing science, an impressive number of successes were recorded.

Information on Insects' Habits Necessary

What quickly became obvious was that success, if luck was not to be 16 trusted, depended upon a great amount of information about both the insect to be controlled and the natural enemies chosen to do the job. The enormous variability among predators and parasites, both between species and within species, gives some idea of why ignorance of such characteristics as their ability to survive in different climates, the rate at which they can find their hosts, and the number of progeny they produce, can lead to failure in attempts to use them in programs of biological control.

It might be well here to describe what is meant by predators and 17 parasites of insects. A predator is any organism which preys upon or consumes another organism. In entomological terms the definition is somewhat modified to designate insects which consume other insects — lady beetles, for example, that feed on aphids or other plant-feeding insects. Many other orders of insects have members which are predaceous, such as some flies whose larvae are predaceous. Besides, there are birds, amphibians, fish, and mammals that are effective predators of insects. In entomological terms, parasites are those insects which deposit their eggs or larvae in, on, or near the body of another insect (host); the developing parasite larva derives its entire nourishment from a single host — and in the process kills it. The most important insect parasites are in the order Hymenoptera. They are tiny- to medium-sized, wasp-like insects.

Ignorance of the sometimes bizarre habits of these highly specialized 18 insects has probably, more often than not, been the major reason for some of the failures of biological control.

An outstanding example of how entomologists can be led astray by 19 incomplete knowledge is that of attempts to introduce a promising parasite of another citrus pest, the California red scale. The parasite, *Casca chinensis,* was originally discovered attacking red scale on citrus in south China in 1906.[9] Observations made at that time and in subsequent years indicated that it might be an ideal controlling agent for red-scale in California: it seemed able to find its host at very low densities; the climate of the two areas (California and south China) seemed similar; and its development appeared to be limited to citrus red scale only. Furthermore, it was able to produce more than one progeny on a single scale insect. Between 1906 and 1954 six different attempts were made at establishing the parasite in California citrus orchards; each was a failure. The most vexing problem encountered was that of determining how the males of the species were produced so that laboratory colonies could be established. (Most parasitic Hymenoptera reproduce in accordance with Dzierzon's Law — that is, mated females produce only *female* progeny while unmated females produce only *male* progeny. Sex determination in honey bees is regulated by this mechanism.) It was noted on numerous occasions that mated females would readily lay their eggs in host scale, and the resulting generation would be all females. These unmated females would then lay their eggs in fresh host scale, but no progeny would result. For some unknown reason the scale insect was a suitable host for the development of females (from fertilized eggs), but not for males (from unfertilized eggs). Because of political conditions in mainland China, attempts to introduce the parasite were abandoned in the middle 1950s. To this day, entomologists in the United States are unable to explain how the males of *Casca chinensis* develop.

This case illustrates only one of an almost unlimited number of curi- 20
ous biological habits of some of the parasites of insects. Some parasites never come into direct contact with their hosts, but deposit their eggs on plants which their victims frequent. In these species the host contacts the parasite. But even this can vary. In one case, that of a parasitic fly which attacks the silk worm (from man's standpoint this could not be called a beneficial insect), the adult female fly deposits its tiny eggs on the leaves of mulberry. When feeding on such foliage, the silkworm ingests the egg, whereupon the parasitic larva hatches within the gut of the silkworm and eventually grows and kills it.[10] A variation on this method of development occurs in some parasitic wasps which attack species of carpenter ants. The adult wasps deposit their eggs on the leaves of trees visited by the ants. After hatching on the leaves, the specialized larvae of these wasps await the arrival of adult ants to whose bodies they attach themselves. Eventually they are carried back to the nest, where they leave the adult ants and attack the developing ant larvae in the galleries of the nest.[11]

If it is true that detailed knowledge of the life history and habits of 21
both pests and natural enemies is a necessary beginning to planning a successful program of biological control, it is also true that this kind of knowledge has been useful in dispelling some widely held beliefs that are of little or no help in controlling a pest.

As mentioned earlier, the beneficial habits of lady beetles have been 22
known for centuries, and have even been praised in poetry. On some occasions, however, their prowess has been somewhat exaggerated, so

much so that some private collectors of the convergent lady beetle *(Hippodamia convergens)* in the western United States have been able to make a comfortable living by selling the beetles by the gallon (70,000 individuals per gallon have sold for as high as ten dollars, and some "beetle brokers" sell as many as 10,000 gallons per year). A detailed study of the life history of the convergent lady beetle has cast considerable doubt on the efficacy of this method of biological control.[12] There is no question that under some conditions the beetles are excellent predators of a variety of noxious insects, but whether or not the purchaser of a gallon of convergent lady beetles really gets his money's worth is another matter. The lady beetles migrate from the hot valleys in California in early summer to the western slopes of the Sierra Nevada Mountains. As the beetles work their way up the slopes, they eventually settle in their winter aggregation sites, and it is here that they can be easily collected in large numbers. Some of the sites cover an area of several hundred square feet, and the beetles attain a depth of several inches: wall-to-wall lady beetles! Some collectors have even constructed large vacuum collectors with which they gather the beetles in early spring before their migratory flights back to the valleys. Before settling in their winter sites, however, the beetles store a large amount of fat in their bodies to sustain them on their westward flight back to the valleys in the spring. Furthermore, they do not eat until this fat reserve is used up. After being given a free ride to the valley and then being released in alfalfa fields to control, for example, spotted alfalfa aphid, the first instinct of the beetles is to fly. And that is exactly what they do. It is doubtful that this practice has a harmful effect; in fact, its overall effect may be good. Farmers who have paid ten dollars a gallon for the beetles are not likely to spray haphazardly. This might be considered a kind of psychological control.

Successes in Biological Control of Insects

In spite of the complicated nature of biological control programs, entomologists around the world have recorded an impressive list of successes. The cottony cushion scale alone has been completely controlled in 25 different countries, the first being the United States in 1890 and the last, Venezuela in 1941.[13] Some of the most outstanding successes have occurred during the past two decades. The importation into Israel from Hong Kong in 1955 of a parasite to control a major pest of citrus, the Florida red scale, resulted in complete control of that pest by 1959. In Mexico, the citrus blackfly was likewise completely controlled by importing four parasites from the Orient. More recently in the United States, a serious pest of commercial olive plantings, the olive

23

scale, has been brought under control by the action of two parasites, one imported from Persia and the other from Pakistan.[14]

The olive scale was first discovered in Fresno, California in 1934. It 24 soon spread to nearly the entire length and breadth of the Sacramento and San Joaquin valleys, attacking not only olives, but a wide variety of other fruits and ornamental trees, including peach, apricot, plum, and almond. In 1953 a species of parasite known as the Persian *Aphytis* was first established in olive groves in California. Although the early observations on the effectiveness of this parasite were indeed promising, it was soon obvious that it could not be relied upon to give good commercial control year after year. The scale has two generations of young per year, one in the spring that matures in late summer, and another in late summer that is dormant over the winter and matures in the spring. The Persian *Aphytis,* although able to parasitize the overwintering generation to a substantial degree, has trouble surviving the hot, dry California summers, with the result that the adult scales from the spring generation are able to reproduce largely unhindered in the fall. To supplement the work of the Persian *Aphytis,* another parasite *(Coccophagoides utilis)* was introduced from Pakistan in 1957. The Pakistan parasite, because of its closer synchrony with the host and its ability to withstand the hot, dry California summers, has contributed greatly to the overall biological control of the olive scale.

One interesting aspect of these studies was the method employed to 25 evaluate the effectiveness of the parasites working together. Trees were sprayed with DDT in two orchards in which the parasites were actively controlling the scale, with the idea of deliberately killing the parasites. Before the spraying, a count was made to determine the number of unparasitized scales per twig (the sampling technique used for the entire study). In one orchard there were no unparasitized scale, while in the other there was 0.04 per twig. After the spraying, which was carefully timed to kill both species of parasites, the unparasitized scale had increased to 107.54 per twig and the other to 149.33 per twig, clearly demonstrating that the parasites were achieving a high degree of control before the DDT was applied.

The olive scale project further adds empirical evidence to one side 26 of an argument that biological control theorists have been debating for years. This centers on the question of whether or not two or more natural enemy species that compete for the same host have the overall effect of interfering with each other and reducing their collective effectiveness below what a single parasite could achieve. Some theorists have argued for first, exhaustive studies of parasites — before any introductions are made — to determine which species has the greatest potential for control, and second, introduction of only that species.

290

Although from theoretical considerations the argument has some merit, there is empirically little evidence to indicate that competition between species would actually reduce the effectiveness of two parasites. Should competition occur between two parasites, it is likely that one would eventually displace the other in some or all of the habitat they both occupy. This has been demonstrated in field studies. A parasite of California red scale *(Aphytis chrysomphali)* was eliminated from nearly its entire range (4,000 square miles) over a ten-year period by another species *(Aphytis lignanensis)*. Still another species *(Aphytis melinus)* displaced *A. lignanensis* from an area of 500 square miles where climatic conditions were more favorable to *A. melinus* than to *A. lignanensis.* [15]

It would have been most difficult to predict these adjustments to habitat, but it is obviously possible to select parasites and predators that best suit the area for which they are needed. But as stated earlier, any prediction is little better than an educated guess. The control of the Eucalyptus snout weevil in South Africa was accomplished by a parasite imported from a subtropical area in Australia. It subsequently was able to establish itself in the temperate areas of its new home. The same is true for two other parasites of the California red scale introduced from a much more amenable subtropical climate to a more rigorous climate in California. 27

One might get the impression that only introduced pests can be controlled by biological control methods, and, indeed, the prospects for introduced pests are much greater. However, there have been a few examples of native pests being brought under control. One instance of this kind occurred in Fiji, where the coconut leafmining beetle, a native pest of coconut, was controlled within a year after the introduction of a parasite from Java. The coconut moth, another native species, was likewise controlled in Fiji by an imported parasite, this one from Malaya. 28

Not all biological control programs are established in the hope that permanent control can be achieved. Many projects, instead, involve the delivery to the field of large numbers of insectary-reared parasites, or predators which can overwhelm the existing pest population, but then do not remain to check the pest should resurgence occur. Releases must be repeated when it appears that a pest problem is redeveloping. Although this is expensive, it is sometimes economically competitive with the application of insecticides and causes far less disruption of natural control of other pests which may be present in low densities. Several species of *Trichogramma,* a tiny wasp that can be produced by the millions, are sometimes used in this manner. The mealybug destroyer *(Cryptolaemus montrouzieri)* has been used in a similar but slightly 29

291

different way to control mealybugs in orchards in both California and the Soviet Union. Rather than trying to overwhelm the pest, periodic "inoculative releases" are made in orchards to coincide with the peak abundance of the mealybug. In this case, it is the second generation of the released adults which gives control. Releases of ten beetles per tree are made periodically from April to September. Certain other parasites and predators are used in a similar way.[16]

Biological Control of Unwanted Plants

Alien weeds have also been successfully controlled by the introduc- 30 tion of their natural enemies. In fact, some of the most encouraging results in biological control have been obtained in weed control projects. The problems associated with the biological control of weeds, however, are much different than those encountered in controlling insect pests, and programs of this kind are approached in a much more conservative way. For the most part an insect which feeds on other insects is not likely to become a pest. (There are some exceptions, like the many natural enemies of beneficial insects.) However, the chance of an insect-feeding insect developing a taste for a crop plant is most unlikely. The possibility has been likened to that of a leopard developing a taste for, and being able to survive on, lettuce. With a plant-feeding insect the possibility is not so farfetched, and exhaustive tests must be first conducted in the native home of the insect before it can safely be introduced into a new habitat.

Another difficulty is that a plant may be considered a weed in one 31 area and a valuable plant in another. When a plant-feeding insect is released in a continental area, there must be full agreement as to the desirability of controlling its host, as there is no guarantee that the insect will be limited only to the area where the plant is considered a weed.

Among the most interesting and thoroughly successful cases of bio- 32 logical control of weeds is that involving the control of several species of prickly pear (*Opuntia* spp.) in Australia. By 1925, several species of this cactus, all of which were alien to Australia, had managed to invade 60 million acres of rangeland, and some of the stands had become so dense as to be impenetrable by man and large animals. Since the native range of *Opuntia* extends from the southwestern U.S. through Mexico into Central America, Australian explorers were sent to this area and South America to search out insects that might help to control the cactus in Australia. Twelve cactus-feeding candidates were chosen, among them a moth *(Cactoblatis cactorum)* whose larvae feed on the cactus pads. By 1930 huge areas of cactus were being destroyed by the moth, but today the cacti are no longer considered pests except in very local areas. The unusual aspect of this case is that the moth was found in Argentina, a country in which the cacti are *not* endemic.[17]

An interesting sidelight to the *Opuntia* story was the series of complications that occurred in Mauritius (an island in the Indian Ocean east of Madagascar) in the late 1930s.[18] In 1927 a cactus-feeding insect *(Dactylopius tomentosus)* was introduced from Ceylon in an attempt to control the weed. In 1938 a predaceous beetle *(Cryptolaemus montrouzieri)* was also colonized in Mauritius for an entirely different purpose, the control of the pineapple mealybug. Since *Dactylopius* is among those species upon which the newly introduced beetle feeds, it soon became apparent that control of the cactus was being impeded by *Cryptolaemus.* Subsequently, however, the *Cactoblastis* moth was introduced; the cactus is now fairly well suppressed.

Cactoblastis has never been introduced into the U.S. because in many parts of the west *Opuntia* spp. are considered beneficial. They are said to be a source of food and moisture for livestock on the arid ranges of the Southwest. An attempt has been made to control two species of *Opuntia* on Santa Cruz Island, 30 miles off the coast of southern California.[19] But in this case, only natural enemy species that were native to southwestern North America were introduced to the island.

Klamath weed *(Hypericum perforatum)* has been the target of intensive biological control efforts. The plant is of European origin and now occurs widely in temperate areas throughout the world. The initial work on biological control of this weed actually began in Australia in 1917, where the weed was even then considered a pest of great importance. Two species of plant-feeding beetles were found in England and France and colonized in Australia, where some control has been obtained.

In North America, success in controlling Klamath weed on California rangelands equaled that of *Opuntia* in Australia. The weed is thought to have been introduced around the Klamath River in northern California about 1900 and soon spread to about two million acres in California alone and another three million in the states of Idaho, Oregon, Montana, and Washington.[20] The weed is not only aggressive in taking over ranges of annual grasses, but an oil in the plant sensitizes the areas of white skin on cattle; when exposed to sunlight, these skin areas can become ulcerous.

It wasn't until 1944 that importations of the natural enemies of Klamath weed began in California and, because of the wartime conditions, the insects were brought from Australia rather than Europe and England. Arrangements to deliver the two most important leaf-feeding beetles *(Chrysolina quadrigemina and Chrysolina hyperici)* were made with the cooperation of the United States Army Transport Command, but only after exhaustive studies were made to determine that the beetle would starve rather than eat numerous important plants. Those tested were sugar beets, flax, hemp, sweet potato, and cotton. One of the first problems encountered when the beetle arrived in California was that of synchronizing the life cycle of the beetles to the growth of the Klamath weed in the northern hemisphere. Since Australian seasons are opposite of those in California, the beetle arrived in a dormant stage. In their homeland dormancy is terminated by autumn rains, so by spraying the beetles with a fine mist of water, their dormancy was broken, and within three weeks the beetles had adjusted to the northern hemisphere. Within two years of the initial field release no more importations were necessary, and within ten years the Klamath weed had been eaten back to about 1 percent of its former range in California. In other states the beetles have attained a considerable degree of control, but none as spectacular as that in California. So happy were the citizens of Humboldt County, California with the work of the *Chrysolina* beetle that in 1958 they erected a plaque in its honor in the city of Eureka.

Raising Insects for Biological Control

Rearing large numbers of insects under artificial conditions is an 38 essential part of biological control and has become a science in itself. The silkworm industry was probably the first to engage in such activity and, compared to present day rearing of predators and parasites, it seems relatively easy since there is only one insect involved. In the culture of entomophagus insects (insect-eating insects) there must be at least two insects — the natural enemy and its host. The idea, of course, is to rear as many insects as possible in the shortest amount of time and at the least expense. To accomplish this, the habits of both host and parasite must be carefully studied under the conditions in which they are reared.

This is one of the undertakings of the USDA Biological Control of 39 Insects Research Laboratory in Columbia, Missouri (see "Know Your Enemy," this issue). Here, huge numbers of the egg parasite *Trichogramma* are needed for field experiments, so there is a great interest in the techniques of production. *Trichogramma,* like many other parasites, has a wide host range — it attacks, and develops in the eggs of, a variety of host insects. As a result, the progeny may not always be the same, at least in some important biological characteristics. For example, those that develop on one host may be a bit larger, more robust, longer lived, and more fertile than those developed on another. On the other hand, the host that produces the best *Trichogramma* (in the biological sense) may be the most difficult to rear under artificial conditions. Choice of an insect host then may be the most important aspect of mass production of parasites.

The habits of the parasite may also influence production methods. For example, scientists at the Columbia, Missouri laboratory found that when *Trichogramma minutum* adults were exposed to cabbage looper eggs that were laid less than eleven hours earlier, the parasites killed 100 percent of the eggs, but only 15 percent were killed when the eggs were 27 hours old. Mortality inflicted by the parasites increased again to 95 percent when the eggs were 60 hours old.[21] Information of this kind is of the utmost importance in the efficient production of parasites and predators.

As stated earlier, a parasite may be adaptable in the laboratory to conditions quite unlike those it will encounter in the field. The rearing of olive scale for the production of its parasites is one such case. Obviously, growing olive trees to produce the scale would not be possible in the laboratory. Luckily however, the scale will also develop quite nicely on potato tubers, so potatoes were substituted for olive trees in the insectary (where insects are bred). But even then, there were problems. Consider, for example, the description of the pedigrees of the potatoes needed for this purpose.

> The success of the program depended basically on the ability of the potatoes to bear an increasingly heavy burden of scales for as long as 180 days. The standard specifications were that they should be Grade A Russet (netted) variety, having a very light matrix; that they be smooth and of uniform shape, weighing from 6 to 8 ounces each; that they had been grown in a relatively disease-free and tubermoth-free region such as Oregon or Idaho; and that neither the tubers nor their containers had been treated with a pesticide. The White Rose variety is a better host than the Russet, but since the former is more susceptible to bacterial rot it could not be used safely over the long period of rigorous stresses to which the host is subjected in this project.[22]

Use of Disease Organisms

Another aspect of biological control which is only now beginning to come into prominence (see *Environment,* October 1969 and January/February 1970) is that of employing disease organisms for pest control. Like most other plants and animals, insects are, on occasion, afflicted with a variety of fatal diseases. The scientific literature reports over 1,000 insect diseases, and unquestionably, hundreds more are still to be discovered. Among the most promising are some bacterial and viral

diseases, although researchers are also studying insect-infesting proto-
zoans, fungi, and nematodes.

Early naturalists were quite aware that insects suffered from a variety   43
of maladies. The first scientific account of such a disease was that done
by the great French naturalist, de Réaumur, who reported and illustrated a fungus disease of a moth in 1726.[23] It is noteworthy that another Frenchman, Louis Pasteur, entered the field of microbiology and
gained great fame for his historic work on the diseases of the silkworm.
His studies of these diseases and the development of techniques to
control them literally saved the French silk industry in the late nineteenth century.

Early work in the actual field use of insect diseases centered around   44
interest in the use of fungi for controlling insects. In the late 1870s, a
Russian microbiologist, Elie Metchnikoff, performed some field experiments, and later another Russian, Isaah Krassilstschik, established a
small plant to produce the spores of a fungus with which he attempted
to control a pest of sugar beets.

In the United States several scientists became interested in another   45
fungus *(Beauvaria bassiana)*, which they felt might aid in controlling the
chinch bug. In 1888 the Kansas state legislature established an experiment station at the University of Kansas for the purpose of propagating
and distributing the *Beauvaria* fungus.

It wasn't until the middle 1940s, however, that attention was drawn   46
to the real possibility of microbial insect control. A large-scale coloniza-
tion program in which milky disease bacteria were distributed throughout the northeastern United States for the control of the Japanese
beetle clearly demonstrated the usefulness of bacterial agents in insect
control. Soon afterward another bacterium, *Bacillus thuringiensis*,
aroused interest because of its ability to control a number of lepidopter-
ous larvae. Techniques have been worked out to produce the spores of
the bacteria in commercial quantities, and the material is now available
for some uses.

More recently, viruses have come into prominence (see *Environ-*   47
ment, January/February 1971) and one, the Heliothis virus, has been
registered by the USDA for experimental use. The development of virus
materials has been slowed by the fact that they must be produced in the
tissue of the host insect, whereas some bacteria can be produced in
great quantity by using artificial media in a fermentation process.

For many reasons microbial control has advanced at a much slower   48
rate, as far as its practical application is concerned, but as more information is compiled and new techniques of production are developed,
disease agents will no doubt assume a greater role in insect control.

Effective Methods of Control

With the production of powerful, broad-spectrum insecticides begin-   49
ning in the middle 1940s, the development of biological control
programs became more difficult. The new poisons, unlike their predecessors, were able to penetrate the body covering of insects and kill
them simply by contact, whereas the older materials had to be eaten
by the pest in order to kill. This was a very important difference, since
the nonplant-eating species (parasites and predators) were for the most
part spared by the so-called stomach poisons and remained in the environment to do their work. The newer chemicals make no distinction
and kill a broad spectrum of insects. This has resulted in the appearance
of new pests, that is, insects that were always present, but never in large
enough numbers to become pests because they were suppressed by
their natural enemies. But the destruction of their natural enemies
created a vacuum in which they could erupt. So, instead of there being
characteristically one or two serious pests on a single crop, there are
now four or five or more. This, of course, makes biological control far
more complicated. Furthermore, some pests which were under substantial biological control are again becoming pests because their natural enemies have been decimated by the use of modern chemicals.

Because of this situation and the fact that some of the persistent   50
chemicals are causing a variety of other unintended side effects, entomologists are now working toward an integrated system of pest management. The idea is to employ all methods of control — biological,
cultural, microbial, and chemical — in programs that cause minimum
disruption to the ecosystem. In such a program, timing of the application of an insecticide so as not to interfere with the existing biological
controls is extremely important. This has been demonstrated, for example, in alfalfa fields in California. By using a relatively selective chemical, and applying it at just the right time, aphid populations were
reduced without a substantial reduction in predator populations. The
predators were then able to reproduce to the point where they suppressed the remaining aphid population below the level at which economic injury occurred for the remainder of the season.[24] In other
words, the chemical was used in such a manner as to bring the predator
and its prey into a favorable ratio.

Because pest control has become much more complicated, entomolo-   51
gists are more and more coming to the realization that chemical and
biological control are not necessarily separate alternatives, but can in
fact be used to augment each other. To accomplish this, the right
chemicals — that is, short-lived, selective materials that will cause

minimal disruption of the ecosystem — must be available. Also, a knowledge of the population dynamics, and life histories of the pests is essential. Just as important, however, is knowing the level at which pest insects actually cause sufficient economic injury to the crop to justify the cost of chemical control measures. Because this level has not been known for many crops, pest control has been both wasteful and damaging to the environment far beyond what has actually been necessary.

Even though the emphasis in pest control is becoming increasingly centered on integrated programs, there is no question that the introduction and manipulation of parasites, predators, and pathogens will continue to be of major importance in pest control. In fact, since most programs of this kind develop around the manipulation of populations of parasites and predators, there would be no integrated control without natural enemies. There are still many opportunities to effect substantial biological control, and in many of these cases integrated control will be unnecessary. In any event, it is now clear that the use of broad-spectrum insecticides, especially those which are persistent, is not the ultimate answer to safe and effective insect control. Alternative methods will have to be used, and among these biological control is one of the most important. 52

Notes

1. Jacob, F. H., "Some Modern Problems in Pest Control," *Science Progress,* 181: 30-45, 1958.

2. Debach, Paul, editor, *Biological Control of Insect Pests and Weeds,* Reinhold Press, 1964, p. 22.

3. Debach, *ibid.,* p. 24.

4. Compere, H., "The Red Scale and Its Insect Enemies," *Hilgardia,* Volume 31, No. 7, November 1961.

5. Doutt, R. L., "Vice, Virtue and Vedalia," *Bulletin of the Entomological Society of America,* Vol. 4, No. 4, December 1958.

6. Debach, *op. cit.,* p. 34.

7. Stern, V. M., et al., "The Integration of Chemical and Biological Control of the Spotted Alfalfa Aphid," *Hilgardia,* Vol. 29, No. 2, October 1959.

8. Debach, *op. cit.,* p. 26.

9. Flanders, S. E., et al., "*Casca chinensis,* an Internal Parasite of California Red Scale," *Hilgardia,* Vol. 28, No. 3, November 1958.

10. Debach, *op. cit.,* p. 224.

11. Clausen, C. P., "The Immature Stages of the Eucharidae." Proceedings of the Entomological Society, Washington, 42:161-170, 1940.

12. Hagen, K. S., "Biology of the Predaceous *Coccinellidae,*" *Annual Review of Entomology,* Vol. 7, 1962.

13. Debach, *op. cit.,* p. 690.

298

14.   Huffaker, C. B. and C. E. Kennett, in "Studies of Two Parasites of Olive Scale," *Hilgardia,* Vol. 37, No. 9, 1966.

15.   Debach, Paul, and R. A. Sundby, "Competitive Displacement between Ecological Homologues," *Hilgardia,* Vol. 34, No. 5, April 1963.

16.   Debach, *op. cit.,* p. 441.

17.   Huffaker, C. B., "Biological Control of Weeds with Insects," *Annual Review of Entomology,* 4:251-276, 1959.

18.   Debach, *op. cit.,* p. 265.

19.   Goeden, R. D., et al., "Biological Control of Prickly Pear Cacti on Santa Cruz Island, California," *Hilgardia,* Vol. 38, No. 16, November 1967.

20.   Huffaker, "Biological Control of Weeds with Insects," *op. cit.,* p. 266.

21.   Marston, N., and L. R. Ertle, "Host Age and Parasitism by Trichogramma minutum (Hymenoptera: Trichogramatidae)," *Annals of the Entomological society of America,* Vol. 62, No. 6.

22.   Finney, G. L., in "Studies of Two Parasites of the Olive Scale," *Hilgardia,* 37(9): 339.

23.   Steinhaus, E. A., "Microbial Control — The Emergence of an Idea," *Hilgardia,* Vol. 26, No. 2, October 1956.

24.   Stern, V. M., et al., "The Integration of Chemical and Biological Control of the Spotted Alfalfa Aphid," *Hilgardia,* Vol. 29, No. 2, October 1959.

SUBJECT

1.   What went wrong with agriculture's grand plan to find "salvation at the end of a spray nozzle"?

2.   Describe the process by which insect pests are controlled biologically rather than chemically. What special problems have to be considered?

3.   What possible problems must be anticipated in biological control of unwanted plants (weeds and cactus, for instance)?

4.   The title and the thrust of the article suggest that Shea is against use of chemical pesticides; then in the closing three paragraphs, Shea calls for "integrated" control programs. Is this a cop-out or a valid compromise?

STRUCTURE

1.   Why is it necessary for Shea to give extended examples of the particular processes he describes?

2.   More than one process is analyzed in this article; does Shea make clear the relations and differences among them, or is the total effect merely more confusing than if he had developed only one process?

3.   Shea is attempting both to be scientifically accurate and to write for a general audience. Does he succeed in the latter aim? Could he have improved readability without sacrificing accuracy?

4. Is the section on "Raising Insects for Biological Control" properly a part of the process on biological control, or a separate process in itself? Does it belong in this essay?

5. Consider Shea's insertion of subheadings — what he uses them for, whether they correspond to logical divisions of the material, whether they are helpful to the reader.

THE POPULATION TRAP

Kenneth Boulding

*Kenneth E. Boulding (b. 1910), is professor of economics and codirec-
tor of the Center for Research in Conflict Resolution at the University
of Michigan. English by birth, he has lived in the United States since
1937. He has written many books on the technological revolution,
including* The Meaning of the Twentieth Century *(1964), from which
the following essay was taken.*

One of the most difficult problems facing mankind in the present his-   1
torical era is the control of its own population. The problem has two
aspects: an immediate short-run aspect involving the relation of population growth to the dynamics of a developing society, and a long-run
aspect involving the ultimate population equilibrium. Both these problems are of great importance and both of them are fundamentally
unsolved.

The short-run aspect of the problem is largely the result of the sudden   2
introduction of malaria control and other public health measures in
tropical societies which previously have had a high rate of infant mortality. We can regard this if we like as the incursion of certain postcivilized
techniques into what are essentially societies in the stage of classical
civilization. The results are usually dramatic. With the aid of DDT, it
has been possible to reduce the crude death rate from its "civilized"
level of about twenty-five per thousand down to nine or ten in a matter
of a year or two. The exact physiological causes of this phenomenon are
still imperfectly understood. The eradication of malaria seems to be the
main contributing factor, though probably not the sole cause. Whatever
the cause, however, the facts are clear and the results, alas, can easily
be disastrous. There is no more tragic irony than this, that a sudden
improvement in the health of the people and especially in the health
of children could prove to be a disaster. Nevertheless in the absence of
an equally sharp decline in the birth rate these societies may easily find

themselves faced with an unmanageable problem which may actually prevent their economic development altogether.

The problem arises because a sudden change in infant mortality, 3 without a corresponding change in the birth rate, results in a shift in the age distribution of the society toward the younger ages with great rapidity, so that they have an unusually large proportion of children. This means correspondingly that the proportion of the population of working age is diminished. Thus in 1955 the proportion between the ages of fifteen and fifty-nine was an almost uniform 61 percent in Europe, North America, and Oceania — that is, the developed part of the world — whereas in tropical Africa it was only 49 percent, and in Asia about 55 percent. This is in spite of the fact that in the developed part of the world there is a much larger proportion of old people. In Africa and Southeast Asia 43 percent of the population were under the age fifteen. In part this is due to adult mortality, so that a smaller proportion of the population lives to be sixty. In part it is also a result of the tremendous decline in infant mortality which hit most of these countries in the late 1940's.

This situation, in which infant mortality declines without a corre- 4 sponding decline in the birth rate, and before an expansion of adult longevity, is a recipe for demographic and economic disaster. A constantly declining proportion of the population of the working age has to support the constantly increasing proportion of population of nonworking age, and the ability of the society to spare resources for a growth industry is correspondingly impaired. The problem is made doubly difficult because a major element in the growth industry itself is the education of the young. When there is a very large proportion of children and young people, it becomes increasingly difficult to provide the resources for the kind of education which is necessary if the society is to pass over into the modern world.

One of the essential differences between civilized and postcivilized 5 society is that in civilized society a relatively small proportion of resources of the adult working population need to be devoted to the upbringing and education of the young. Children are raised and educated in the casual spare time of their mother, whose time mainly has to be devoted to the productive work of the peasant farm, the small shop, or the industrial household. In a postcivilized society the amount of learning which must be performed by the average individual is so great that the task of education cannot possibly be done by the family. There therefore has to be an increasing proportion of resources devoted to formal education, and as we move toward postcivilization we move toward a society in which virtually every child and young person receives formal education for the first twenty years or so of his life. This deliberate investment in the human resource is the main key to the transition from civilized to postcivilized society. And in those civilized societies which are suffering the great demographic upheaval the problem of the transition is enormously intensified because of the burden of the large proportion of children.

For the developed countries the dynamic problem of the demo- 6 graphic upheaval is not so severe, though even in many of these countries the remarkable upsurge in the birth rate from about 1940 on has created a serious problem for education. All countries, however, whether developed or undeveloped, face the problem of long-run equilibrium of population. There is no country in the world whose population is stationary. The average rate of increase of the world population at a very modest estimate is about 1.6 percent a year, and over the next forty years this may be 2 percent a year. This means a doubling of the world population in something under forty years. It is little wonder that the present century is called the age of population explosion. In the whole of its history the human population has never expanded at this rate, and it is clear that this rate of expansion cannot go on for very long. At present rates of population expansion it will take only a little over three hundred years for the whole land area of the world to become a single city. It takes only seven or eight hundred years before we have standing room only over the whole face of the planet! Just in case anyone thinks we can solve the problem by shooting people to outer space, it would take only about eight thousand years at the present rate of population increase before the whole astronomical universe, two billion light years in diameter, is packed solid with humanity!

A generation ago it seemed reasonable to suppose that this problem 7 would solve itself with the increase in income. It was observed that the richer countries had lower birth rates than the poorer countries and that the richer classes within each country had a lower birth rate than the poorer classes. The recipe for the control of population then seemed merely to be to make everybody rich. Then it was argued that people would become aware of the high cost of having children and would automatically restrict their families to the numbers which would not diminish their income. In the 1930's, indeed, there were many areas in Europe and many sections of the population in North America where the net reproduction rate was so low that there was a fear of race suicide. The net reproduction rate may be roughly thought of as the ratio of each generation to the numbers of its parents. If this ratio is one, then each generation as it dies off leaves an exactly equal generation to replace it. If it is more than one, the population is bound to increase; if it is less than one, the population is bound to diminish. In the 1930's in many parts of the developed societies the net reproduction rate was actually less than one. In the 1940's, however, there was a change, perhaps caused by rising incomes, coupled with a more favorable attitude toward children. This may signify a retreat into the family as the one island of security in a world in which the state has become a monster incapable of providing security or of attracting true affection. Whatever the reasons, the facts are clear. In almost all societies today, the net reproduction ratio is much greater than one. At its present rate of increase, for instance, the United States will reach a billion people in a little over a hundred years. It is therefore quite possible that our great-grandchildren will look back on this as a golden age of spacious living and will inhabit a planet in which there is no room to move and no place to go.

Mankind is therefore faced with a hideous problem in terms of sheer 8 arithmetic. It is an arithmetic, moreover, which cannot be denied even though we nearly all try to deny it. The arithmetic is simply this: *any* positive rate of growth whatever eventually carries a human population to an unacceptable magnitude, no matter how small the rate of growth may be, unless the rate of population growth can be reduced to zero before the population reaches an unacceptable magnitude. There is a famous theorem in economics, one which I call the dismal theorem, which states that if the only thing which can check the growth of population is starvation and misery, then the population will grow until it is sufficiently miserable and starving to check its growth. There is a second, even worse theorem which I call the utterly dismal theorem. This says that if the only thing which can check the growth of population is starvation and misery, then the ultimate result of any technological improvement is to enable a larger number of people to live in misery than before and hence to increase the total sum of human misery. These theorems can of course be restated in a cheerful form — that if something other than starvation and misery can check the growth of population before it reaches an unacceptable magnitude, then the population does not have to grow until it is miserable and starved. The cheerful forms of these theorems, however, require work and conscious effort and social organization. In the absence of these, the dismal theorems take over.

For the theorems to be cheerful we must face another piece of arith- 9 metic. This is, that in an equilibrium population the birth rate and death rate must not only be equal, but must be equal to the reciprocal of the average age at death — or what is the same thing, of the average expectation of life at birth. If the average age at death is twenty-five, then the birth rate and the death rate will be forty per thousand in an equilibrium population. If the average age of death is seventy, as it will be in a post-civilized society, then the birth rate and the death rate cannot be more than about fourteen. If there is no birth control — that is, the limitation of the number of births below the natural limit of fecundity — then there can be no death control. If the birth rate is allowed to rise to the limit of natural fecundity, which is something between forty and fifty per thousand, the death rate will also eventually rise to this level, and this means that the average age at death will be only twenty-five years or even less. This indeed is the typical condition of classical civilization. If we want to have death control, and if we want to raise the average age of death to seventy, then we must face the limitation of birth. Any moral principle which states otherwise is false morality, for no morality can be true which attempts to deny the sheer fact of arithmetic.

Having said this, we must hasten to add that there are many different 10 methods of achieving limitation of births. Contraception is one method and an important one but by no means the only one, and indeed it is almost certainly not sufficient. As in the case of economic development, the motto in population control seems to be "where there's a will there's a way." The will is all-important, the way is secondary. Many of the ways, however, which are most effective are also unpleasant and indeed unacceptable. Infanticide and abortion are probably still the most certain methods of population control. Infanticide is repugnant to a developed moral sensitivity and can hardly be practiced without destroying certain intangible values which are important to a high quality of human life. Abortion is undoubtedly preferable to infanticide, though we know too little about the physiological and psychological damage which it may cause to recommend it without serious qualms. If this is the only method for successful population control, however, the moral prejudice against it may have to be waived in the light of the unmitigated human misery which will result from inability to control population altogether. This is one place where we have to reckon the moral cost against the moral returns.

Contraception certainly seems preferable to abortion, and indeed the 11 moral objection to contraception in principle seems to be confined to a single major branch of the Christian church. Even here the difference in practice between this church and the rest of society is much smaller than the difference in precept. Contraception, however, also has its problems, and it is by no means an automatic solution to the problem of population control. Even with full knowledge and practice of contraception parents may still decide, voluntarily, to have more children, on the average, than are required to keep the population in a stable equilibrium. Furthermore existing methods are by no means certain in operation, and even if, for instance, most parents decide to have two children but end up by accidentally having a third, this is enough to upset the population equilibrium.

The fact that we must recognize is that it is social institutions which 12 are dominant in determining the ability of society to control its population, not the mere physiology of reproduction. A classic example of this proposition is Ireland. The Irish learned the Malthusian lesson the hard way. In 1700 they had a population of about two million. They were living in misery on small grains. Then someone introduced the potato, which was a great technical improvement, enabling a larger amount of food to be grown per acre, and indeed per man, than before. For a while the standard of life of the Irish improved, infant mortality declined, and there was a great increase in population. By 1846 there were eight million people living in misery on potatoes. Hardly any better example of the utterly dismal theorem can be found. Then came the failure in the potato crop and the great famine. Two million people died of starvation. Two million emigrated and the four million who remained had learned a lesson. The population of Ireland has increased very little in over a hundred years, partly as a result of continued emigration, but more as a result of limitation of births. In this case the limitation was achieved through late marriages and the imposition of a strongly puritan ethic upon the young people which seems to have the effect of strongly limiting the number of children born out of wedlock. It is striking that one of the most successful examples of population control should have taken place in a Roman Catholic country, one, however, in which Catholicism takes an unusually puritanical form.

But the great variety of possible solutions to this problem becomes 13 apparent when we look at Japan, which is almost the only other country where the deliberate limitation of population growth has had much success. Here the machinery of population control seems to have been abortion rather than late marriages. The precariousness of these solutions, however, is indicated first by the fact that neither of them has been totally successful, for in neither Ireland nor Japan has the net reproduction rate actually been reduced to one, and in the second place even the existing solutions can easily break down under the impact of social change or economic development.

On a world scale this whole problem is enormously complicated by 14 the different rates of population growth of different regions and nations. The first fruits of the technological revolution were enjoyed by Europe, and the period from 1500 to the early twentieth century can well be regarded as dominated by the expansion of European power and European populations to other parts of the world. The entire continents

306

of North and South America and Australia were in fact populated largely from Europe, at least in their temperate regions. The mosquito saved most of tropical Africa from European immigration, and Asia was already reasonably full of people at the beginning of the era. We now find ourselves in the twentieth century with this period of expansion come to an end and very few open spaces left in the world. The geographical distribution of the world population is probably set for a long time to come, excluding wars of biological extermination.

Under these circumstances the problem of migration as a solution to the population problem becomes one of great difficulty. It is clear that migration is no longer a general solution for the population problem, and indeed on a world scale may actually intensify it. A region which is under genuine Malthusian pressure, for instance, can easily become a perpetual source of emigrants. If the population is really being limited by the food supply, then every person who emigrates releases food which enables another child or even two to survive. Even in the relatively short run, migration then provides very little alleviation of severe population pressure. Furthermore emigration often has a bad qualitative effect on the society which is losing people in this way, for it is usually the young, the ambitious, and the energetic who migrate. Hence in a society which has a substantial volume of emigration it is the old, the children, the sick, and the unambitious who remain behind not only to carry on the work of the society but also to produce the next generation. A society or a region which has a long-continued emigration therefore becomes depleted in human resources. It usually lacks leadership and sometimes becomes completely incapable of reorganizing itself. The southern Appalachian region in the United States is a good case in point. In these societies even the education system often turns into a funnel to drain off all the best young people, and so benefits the society which is receiving the migrants rather than the one that is educating and then losing them. The tragic truth of the principle that "to him that hath shall be given" is dramatically illustrated by this principle. The rich areas or the rich countries tend to attract the abler people from poorer areas, and this perpetuates or even increases the disparities of income.

The different rates of growth of different populations also comprise an important long-run force producing international and internal political tension. The idea of population pressure as a cause of war is too crude to be taken very seriously. Population pressure itself is a result of a large number of social factors some of which may increase and some of which may diminish the propensities to make war. Nevertheless differential rates of population growth unquestionably increase the difficulty of the problem of stable peace. The unwillingness of many countries and many sub-groups within countries to face the problem of population control is closely connected with their unwillingness to seem to weaken their relative position in the world. The inability of the United Nations, for instance, even to get this problem on its agenda is a reflection of the fact that the fears of relative changes in population are sufficient to prohibit any rational discussion of the total problem.

Ability to handle this problem intelligently is further handicapped by the fact that there are some short-run exceptions to the principles outlined above. The example of Puerto Rico, for instance, suggests that in a poor, small country which is already suffering from severe population pressure the ability to find a temporary outlet for its surplus population can be an important aid in its development. Certainly if Puerto Rico had not been able to send over half a million people to the mainland of the United States its development over the last twenty-five years would have been much more difficult. It is therefore hard to say to a country like Haiti or Indonesia or even China, "You must not export your surplus population, for this will do you no good in the long run." Indeed if a process of internal reorganization is going on, this proposition may not be true. It is not even always true that an increase in population is an enemy of development. There are some societies indeed in which population increase is the first step toward development. A decline in infant mortality upsets the old family structure, tends to destroy the extended family, provides a labor force for new cities, and may indeed provide precisely the disequilibrating influence which will throw the society off its old equilibrium of stable poverty and create an ongoing process of development.

It is very hard to avoid a certain pessimism in this area. Nowhere are such strong forces laid against the learning of realistic images of the future of mankind. All existing solutions to this problem are either disagreeable or unstable, and yet solutions must be found if postcivilized society is not to end in disaster and if our great technological accomplishments are not to result in enormous increase in the total sum of human misery. There is need to devote a substantial intellectual resource to this problem, and this we are not doing. We need to expand our knowledge of physiology, psychology, sociology, economics, and ethics in this whole area. There is a strong temptation for "folk wisdom" to refuse to face this problem or to try to brush it off with partial solutions. The Communist and the Catholic are curiously alike, though for different ideological reasons, in this particular respect, and they both seem to be almost incapable of developing a realistic appraisal of the nature of the problem and the need for its solution. On this particular point my perception of truth requires me to say that I think both the Communist and the Catholic are, at present, enemies of man's future, although I think it is also possible for both of them to reform and to take a more realistic attitude. I am deeply conscious furthermore that the "liberal" attitude toward the subject, while it may recognize its importance, has contributed very little toward its solution. We are all guilty of ignorance, frivolity, and blindness, and the accusing fingers of billions of the unborn are pointed angrily toward us.

I have only one positive suggestion to make, a proposal which now 19 seems so farfetched that I find it creates only amusement when I propose it. I think in all seriousness, however, that a system of marketable licenses to have children is the only one which will combine the minimum of social control necessary to the solution to this problem with a maximum of individual liberty and ethical choice. Each girl on approaching maturity would be presented with a certificate which will entitle its owner to have, say, 2.2 children, or whatever number would ensure a reproductive rate of one. The unit of these certificates might be the "decichild," and accumulation of ten of these units by purchase, inheritance, or gift would permit a woman in maturity to have one legal child. We would then set up a market in these units in which the rich and the philoprogenitive would purchase them from the poor, the nuns, the maiden aunts, and so on. The men perhaps could be left out of these arrangements, as it is only the fertility of women which is strictly relevant to population control. However, it may be found socially desirable to have them in the plan, in which case all children both male and female would receive, say, eleven or twelve decichild certificates at birth or at maturity, and a woman could then accumulate these through marriage.

This plan would have the additional advantage of developing a 20 long-run tendency toward equality in income, for the rich would have many children and become poor and the poor would have few children and become rich. The price of the certificate would of course reflect the general desire in a society to have children. Where the desire is very high the price would be bid up; where it was low the price would also be low. Perhaps the ideal situation would be found when the price was naturally zero, in which case those who wanted children would have them without extra cost. If the price were very high the system would probably have to be supplemented by some sort of grants to enable the deserving but impecunious to have children, while cutting off the desires of the less deserving through taxation. The sheer unfamiliarity of a scheme of this kind makes it seem absurd at the moment. The fact that it seems absurd, however, is merely a reflection of the total unwillingness of mankind to face up to what is perhaps its most serious long-run problem.

SUBJECT

1. Why, according to Boulding, is a sudden shift in population distribution toward the younger ages more disastrous for underdeveloped countries than for the developed countries?

2. If Boulding's dire predictions in Paragraph 6 are correct, population control is perhaps our most pressing problem. Why, then, do you think most people fail to be actively concerned — or to do anything about it?

3. Do you see any way around Boulding's contention that checking population growth is the only way to keep the "dismal" and the "utterly dismal" theorems from taking over?

4. Boulding poses an embarrassing question regarding population control: Which is less moral, practicing birth control and abortion, or letting the human race increase its misery until it eventually extinguishes itself? How would you answer the question? Do you agree that it is necessary to make a choice?

5. What have been the ways of handling population problems in the past? Why won't they work any longer?

6. What solution does Boulding offer? Does it seem to you "absurd," as he suggests it will? Do you think it would work? What are the side benefits to such a plan? What might be some problems in application?

STRUCTURE

1. This essay illustrates the close working relationship between cause-and-effect and process analysis, especially in scientific writing. The whole essay is not exposition of *a process;* rather, Boulding uses process as one method of development. What are some of the related processes which he analyzes?

2. What is the organizational plan of the essay? How does Boulding indicate the divisions without using numerals or subtitles?

3. Try reconstructing the "recipe for demographic and economic disaster" discussed in Paragraph 4. Is the process all contained in that paragraph?

4. Does the context give sufficient clue to the meaning of the specialized vocabulary? What is a "postcivilized society," for instance?

5. Should the discussion of the Irish famine be placed three paragraphs earlier, after the statement of the "utterly dismal theorem" which it illustrates? Examine the intervening paragraphs to discover why Boulding didn't place it there.

6.   In Paragraph 17, Boulding cites several exceptions to the dismal process he has described earlier. Do these exceptions weaken his case? Should he have included them?

7.   Is the proposed process for regulating the birth rate in the last two paragraphs made clear? Does anything seem to be left out?

THE AGE
OF OVERBREED

Julian Huxley

Sir Julian Huxley, born in 1897, is the grandson of the famous 19th century defender of Darwinism, Thomas Henry Huxley, and he is the brother of the novelist Aldous Huxley. A world-famous biologist, he has received numerous awards and held several important professorships; in 1946, he was appointed the first Director-General of UNESCO. Huxley has written dozens of books on man's place and his future in the world. As early as the 1920s, he was campaigning for population control and eugenics programs. Huxley has consistently tried to define man's position and goals in terms of the biological facts of his existence, even arguing against war on the grounds that it is against man's biological nature. His most famous books, Man Stands Alone *and* On living in a Revolution, *were written during World War II; their ideas are only now gaining currency.*

The most bewildering characteristic of the present moment of history 1 is that things are happening faster and faster. The pace of change in human affairs, originally so slow as to be unnoticed, has steadily accelerated, until today we can no longer measure it in terms of generations. Major changes now take place every few years, and human individuals have to make several drastic adjustments in the course of their working lives. Where are these breathless changes taking us? Is change synonymous with progress, as many technologists and developers would like us to believe? Is there any main direction to be discerned in present-day human life and affairs? The answer at the moment is no. Change today is disruptive; its trends are diverging in various directions. What is more, many of them are self-limiting or even self-destructive — think of the trend to explosive population increase, to overgrown cities, to traffic congestion, to reckless exploitation of resources, to the widening gap between developed and underdeveloped countries, to the destruction of wild life and natural beauty, to cutthroat competition in economic growth, to Galbraith's private affluence and public squalor, to overspecialization and imbalance in science and technology, to monotony, boredom and conformity, and to the proliferation of increasingly expensive armaments.

What is to be done? Before attempting an answer, we must look at the problem in a long perspective — indeed in the longest perspective of all, the perspective of evolution. The process of evolution on this planet has been going on for five billion years or so. First of all, it was only physical and chemical — the formation of the continents and oceans and the production of increasingly complex chemical compounds. Then, nearly three billion years ago, this purely physicochemical phase of evolution was superseded by the biological phase — the evolution of living matter, or "life." The threshold to this was crossed when one of the numerous organic chemical compounds built up by ultraviolet radiation in the world's warm, soupy seas became capable of reproducing itself. This compound is a kind of nucleic acid, called DNA for short; its complex molecule is built in the form of a double helix, like a spirally twisted ladder whose complementary halves are joined by special chemical rungs. In favorable conditions, the two halves sooner or later break apart, and both build themselves into new wholes by incorporating organic compounds from the surrounding medium. DNA also has the capacity to build up special enzymes and many other proteins out of its chemical surroundings, with the final result of producing a primitive cell with DNA as its core. 2

DNA is thus self-reproducing and self-multiplying matter. It is also self-varying, since now and again it undergoes a small change in part of its structure as a result of radiation or some chemical agency (or sometimes spontaneously), and then reproduces itself in this changed form. In modern terms, it mutates, and the mutation is hereditary. And very soon, the sexual process multiplies the variation manyfold by recombining mutations in every possible way. 3

As a result of these two properties of self-multiplication and self-variation, there results a "struggle for existence" between the different variants, and this in turn results in what Darwin called *natural selection* — a shorthand phrase for the results of the differential death, survival and reproduction of variants. 4

Crossing the threshold must have been a relatively slow business, taking perhaps ten million years or more, but once it was crossed, the whole process of evolution was enormously speeded up, major changes taking place at intervals to be measured in hundred-million-year instead of billion-year units. And, as Darwin pointed out over a century ago, and as has become clearer ever since, major change was inevitably progressive, headed in the direction of improvement — improving 5

313

the organization of plants and animals in relation to their environment, enabling them to surmount more of its dangers and make better use of its resources.

Each major change in biological evolution involved the step-by-step crossing of a critical threshold, leading to the formation of a new dominant type. This is followed by a rapid flowering of the new type and its further improvement along many divergent lines, usually at the expense of its parent and predecessor type. Sooner or later, the process reveals itself as self-limiting: The type as a whole comes up against a limit, and further progress can only be realized by one or two lines slowly achieving a new and improved pattern of organization, and stepping across the threshold barrier to give rise to quite new dominant types. 6

Thus the amphibians broke through the barrier from water to land, though they still had to live in water as tadpoles or larvae in the early stages of their development, but after about 100,000,000 years, they were succeeded by a new and fully terrestrial dominant type, with shelled eggs containing private ponds to develop in — the reptiles, which, as everyone knows, produced an astonishing variety of specialized lines — crocodiles and tortoises, marine ichthyosaurs and plesiosaurs, aerial pterosaurs and the splendid array of terrestrial dinosaurs. 7

But after nearly 150,000,000 years, they, too, reached their limit. A new type of organization was produced, involving hair, warm blood, milk and prolonged development within the mother, and broke through to dominance in the shape of the placental mammals, while most reptilian lines became extinct. This new type again radiated out, to produce all the familiar mammal groups — carnivores and ungulates, rats and bats, whales and primates. Once more, after 50,000,000 years or so, their evolution seems to have reached its limits and got stuck. Only one line among the primates took all the steps — to erect posture, tool and weapon making, increased brain size, and capacity for true speech — that led, a mere 100,000 or so years back, to the emergence of man as the new dominant type, and took life across the threshold from the biological to the psychosocial phase of evolution. 8

This works by cumulative tradition rather than by genetic variation, and is manifested in cultural and mental rather than in bodily and physical transformation. Yet evolving human life progresses in the same sort of way as animal life — by a succession of improved dominant types of organization. However, these are not organizations of flesh and blood and bodily structure but of ideas and institutions, of mental and social structure — systems of thought and knowledge, feeling and belief, with their social, economic and political accompaniments. We may call them psychosocial systems. With the emergence of each new sys- 9 tem, man radically changes his ideas about his place, his role and his job in nature — how to utilize natural resources, how to organize his societies, how to understand and pursue his destiny.

Up to the present there have been five such dominant psychosocial systems, five major progressive stages, involving four crossings of a difficult threshold to a new way of thinking about nature and coping with existence. First the crossing from the stage of food gathering by small groups to that of organized hunting and tribal organization. Then the step, first taken some ten thousand years ago, across to the neolithic stage, based on the idea of growing crops and domesticating animals, associated with fertility rites and priest-kings, and leading to food storage and settled life in villages and small towns. Third, nearly six thousand years ago, the radical step to civilization, with organized cities and trading systems, castes and professions, including a learned priesthood, with writing or other means of nonvocal communication, and leading to large and powerful societies (and eventually to empires), always with a religious basis. And fourth, less than five hundred years ago, the even more decisive step, marked by the Renaissance, the Reformation and the beginnings of organized objective inquiry, over the threshold to the stage of exploration — geographical, historical, religious and, above all, scientific: in a word, the stage of science. This was associated with increasingly secular representative government, with the idea of progress based on ever increasing knowledge and wealth, and led to a profit-based economic system, industrialization and competitive nationalism.

What, you may ask, has all this to do with our present troubles? The answer is that they portend a new threshold to be crossed to a new dominant system and a new stage of human advance. During each previous dominant stage, mankind differentiated into competing groups, with divergent trends of thought and action. These were in the long run self-limiting, self-defeating, disruptive or just hampering. But they contained seeds of self-correction. As their unhelpful nature became obvious, this provoked new thinking and new action to reduce their harmful effects, and eventually to make clear the need to attempt the difficult passage into a new stage based on a radically new system. To take but one case, abuses of ecclesiastical power provoked the Reformation, backward-looking and hairsplitting scholasticism helped on the new birth of the Renaissance and of modern science, and the reaction against the Church's ban on "usury" or charging interest on a loan, coupled with the urgent need for large-scale trade ventures, stimulated the birth of the capitalist system.

The same sort of thing is at work today. The population explosion is stimulating birth control, monolithic overplanning in the U. S. S. R. and

315

its satellites is producing liberalizing reactions, while the doctrinaire freedom of enterprise and expression of the U. S. A. and its acolytes is forcing the acceptance of some degree of discipline and planning; the gap between rich and poor nations is stimulating increased aid and assistance, while racial injustice is stimulating campaigns for integration. The inadequacy of our educational systems has called forth efforts for their expansion and reform; the reckless exploitation and careless destruction of the world's varied resources is leading to a multitude of separate attempts to conserve them; traffic congestion and the other frustrations of city life are leading to transportation planning and schemes of urban renewal; in reaction against the conformity and boredom of modern mechanized existence, a whole crop of new outlets for life is sprouting, in sport and art, in adventure and dedicated projects, while to fill the vacuum caused by the enfeeblement of traditional religious belief and expression, new adventures of spiritual and mental exploration are being undertaken. And the giant wars of this most destructive of centuries have provoked a reaction against war itself and generated a general desire for peace and a crop of projects for preserving and fostering it.

But all this is not enough — all these are negative attempts, actions *against* something, instead of positive efforts *for* something. What is needed is a new over-all pattern of thinking and willing that will give us a new vision and a constructive purpose, providing meaning for our lives and incentives for our actions. Only this can bring together the separate reactions against the divergent threats that beset us and harness them (and all our reserves of suppressed good will) in a single-minded team.   13

A new vision has been revealed by post-Darwinian science and learning. It gives us a new and an assured view of ourselves. Man is a highly peculiar organism. He is a single joint body-mind, not a body plus a separate mind or soul, but with mind on top, no longer subordinate to body, as in animals. By virtue of this, he has become the latest dominant type in the solar system, with three billion years of evolution behind him and (if he doesn't destroy himself) a comparably long period of evolution before him. Certainly no other organism could oust him from his position. He would quickly become aware of any challenge, whether from rat, termite or ape, and would be able to nip it in the bud. His role, whether he wants it or not, is to be the leader of the evolutionary process on earth, and his job is to guide and direct it in the general direction of improvement.   14

To do this, he must redefine his aims. In the past, most human groups and most human individuals have aimed at wealth or pleasure or pride   15 of power, though with a sizable minority seeking salvation in a future life, and a smaller minority seeking spiritual satisfactions or creative outlets in this life. During the long march of prehuman evolution, dominant types have split into a multitude of separate biological organizations termed species. Dominant man has also split, but into separate psychosocial and often competing organizations that Konrad Lorenz calls pseudospecies — tribes and nations, empires and religions (though this tendency toward diversity and disunity has been partially offset by an increasing tendency toward convergence and unity).

Clearly, our first aim must be to demote these pseudospecies and   16
recognize the unity of the real species *Homo sapiens* — in other words, the oneness of mankind. And, *pari passu* with that, to construct more effective organs of his unity, in the shape of really effective international (or preferably supranational) institutions, to think, plan and act on behalf of the human species as a whole. A supporting aim must be to increase man's understanding of this new vision of himself, of his destiny and responsibility, of the limitless possibilities of improvement. And to convert understanding into action, he must improve his instruments for actually getting on with the job — new knowledge and new skills, new technological achievements, new social and political mechanisms.

But his most important instrument is his mind; accordingly, one of his   17
most urgent tasks is to improve his own mental and psychological organization. As anthropologist Loren Eiseley has said, ancestral man entered his own head; ever since, he has been trying to adapt to what he found there. What he found there, of course, was a lot of myths and mumbo jumbo, witchcraft and wish fulfillment, the results of primitive thinking trying to cope with his own profound ignorance, with the civil war of conflicting passions inside and with the constricting forces of nature outside.

Man's primitive or fantasy thinking is always projecting his own ideas,   18
his own guilt and his own secret wishes, onto someone or something else; its unconscious cunning is always inventing justifications for his own passions — supernatural justification like shifting the blame for his actions onto God, moral justifications like ascribing wickedness to his enemies or proclaiming his own group as divinely inspired or chosen.

In the natural sciences, man has learned the technique of "reality   19
thinking" — of accepting the facts and phenomena of external nature and trying to understand them objectively, without bias. But he still has to tackle the more difficult task of abandoning primitive for reality thinking in dealing with the facts of his own nature and his own psychosocial creations, like religions and arts, laws and customs, social

organizations and political institutions, and all the myths and rationalizations concerning them. In a word, man must improve his mechanisms for thinking about himself.

An obvious aim is to find out further how best to avoid conflict by 20 transcending or transforming it, both internally, within our heads, and externally, in the physical and social world. Another is to ensure that the new pattern of thought and belief (and therefore of potential action) shall not be self-destructive but capable of constructive growth, not self-limiting but open-ended. And the aim of aims must be to provide truly satisfying goals for human beings everywhere, so as to energize our species, to stimulate it to move and to ensure that it moves in the right direction. This involves planning for greater fulfillment for human individuals and greater achievement by human societies, and for fuller realization of man's varied possibilities, both personal and collective. It means aiming at quality rather than quantity — quality of life and personality instead of quantity of people, wealth and material goods. The time is ripe for a new approach to destiny, a new look at human life through the telescope of comprehensive vision of wholes instead of the microscope of analysis into separate parts.

Now I want to take another brief look at some of the unpleasant and 21 threatening trends I spoke of at the outset, to see how the countermeasures we obviously must take against them may help us in planning the practical steps needed to achieve these new integrated ends.

First, population. The world's population is increasing by over sixty 22 million a year — the equivalent of a good-sized town every day of the year, and of nearly twelve baseball teams (with coach) every minute of the day. Its compound-interest rate of increase has also increased, from under ½ percent per annum to over 1¾ percent today, and is still increasing a good deal. This applies just as much to Western countries like Britain or Sweden with a slow increase rate or the U. S. A. with a medium rate as to Asian or Latin American countries with a high rate.

Whatever we do, the world's population will double by the turn of the 23 century. If we do nothing now, life for our grandchildren and great-grandchildren will be much more unpleasant than it is for us, which is saying a good deal. If we go on doing nothing, man will lose his chance of being the beneficent guide of evolution and will become the cancer of the planet, ruining it and himself with it.

A prerequisite for further human progress is immediate and universal 24 birth control as an instrument of national and international policy, with the immediate aim of reducing man's rate of increase to manageable

318

proportions, well below 1 percent a year, and the ultimate aim of reducing the total number of human beings in the world.

This means publicizing the need for birth control, incorporating 25 family planning in national health services, adjusting family allowances and taxation systems to discourage overlarge families, and providing birth-control appliances and trained personnel to fit them, in all programs of aid and technical assistance. This means rethinking the whole problem of population, in terms of higher quality of life instead of increasing quantity of people. It also means rethinking the problem of resources, in terms of long-term conservation based on scientific ecology instead of quick exploitation based on mechanized technology.

Next there is the problem of cities. In the last half-century, more and 26 more metropolitan areas have grown to monstrous size, up to 12,-000,000, 14,000,000 even 16,000,000 in Tokyo, Greater London or Greater New York. If you take as your yardstick the city proper, the central area without its suburban tentacles, the number of cities with over a million inhabitants has grown from thirty at the end of World War Two to over eighty today. And meanwhile, the population of automobiles is growing twice as fast as that of people. As a result, cities are suffering from traffic thrombosis and their inhabitants from severe vital frustration. We know from experiment that overcrowding in animals leads to distorted, neurotic and downright pathological behavior. We can be sure that the same is true in principle for people. City life today is definitely leading to mass mental disease, to growing vandalism and possible eruptions of mass violence.

Existence in cities must be made not merely tolerable but life- 27 enhancing, as it has so often been in the past. To do this, we must forcibly restrict any further expansion of overbig cities, while undertaking planned and limited expansion of smaller ones; we must create new towns in strategic locations (as is already being done in Britain) to accommodate the overspill of the nation's population; and we must rigorously prevent the horrible unplanned spread of what is neither city nor suburb nor country town, but "slurb" — a compound of slum, suburbia and urban sprawl, which has already blighted southern California and much of the Atlantic seaboard.

And we must be ready to devote a great deal of money and a great 28 deal of skilled effort to something much bigger and more constructive than what often passes for urban renewal — the conversion of cities from being victims of their own size, ugly or infinitely dreary monuments of profiteering development and general unplanning, or even parasites of the automobile like Los Angeles, into what they should be by definition: organs for civilized existence; places in which their in-

319

habitants enjoy living, instead of being turned into neurosis fodder; generators of fulfillment instead of frustration.

Science is exploding even more violently than population. Scientists 29 (including technologists) are multiplying over three times as fast as ordinary people. The one million or so scientists now at work constitute over 90 percent of all the scientists who have ever lived, and their numbers may well go up to 20,000,000 or even 30,000,000 by A.D. 1999. The number of scientific journals has increased from one in 1665 — *The Philosophical Transactions of the Royal Society* — to about 1000 in 1865, to over 50,000 in 1965, in which nearly 5,000,000 separate articles are published each year, and the rate of increase is itself increasing. If nothing is done about it, science itself runs the risk of drowning in this torrent of paper; specialization will make scientists in one field more ignorant of work in other fields; and man's advance will be stifled in the mounting mass of unassimilable knowledge that he himself has accumulated.

The situation is made worse by the gross lack of balance between 30 different fields of research. Billions of dollars are spent every year on outer-space research — much of it merely for the sake of prestige, in an effort to get to Mars before somebody else — as against a few millions on exploring the "inner space" of the human mind; billions on weapons research as against a few millions on the sociology of peace; hundreds of millions on "death control" through medical science as against four or five millions on birth control and reproduction. Biological research has given us the tools for real eugenic improvement, in the shape of artificial insemination with the deep-frozen sperm of outstanding male donors, even after their death, and the speedy prospect of grafting ova from admired female donors — but nothing (except words) has been spent on any such project.

The situation is also made worse by the lack of balance between 31 scientific progress in different countries and regions. There is a big scientific and technological "brain drain" from Britain and Europe to the U. S. A. and Canada, and this is producing an equally big one to Britain and Europe from underdeveloped countries like those of Southeast Asia, the Middle East and Africa. In consequence, the gap between rich and poor nations is widening scientifically as well as economically.

What is to be done? The torrential flow of scientific printed matter 32 could be reduced if the scientific reputation of a man or a department did not depend so much on the number of scientific papers published. This leads, among other things, to postgraduate students being pushed to undertake researches where publishable results rather than scientific importance are the prime consideration. (This holds with even greater force in the humanities, which too often pretend to be "scientific," flooding the learned market with Ph.D. theses crammed with unimportant literary or historical details.)

But what is mainly necessary is a change in approach. Instead of all 33 the separate sciences, like inorganic chemistry or astronomy or systematic botany, pushing on and on along their own divergent lines, and individual scientists competitively striving for new discoveries (or just for publishable facts), more and more scientific man power should be mobilized to converge on problems that can only be solved by cooperative teamwork between different branches of natural and human science — problems of land use and city planning, of resource use and conservation, of human behavior and health, of communication and education. Beyond all, we need a science of human possibilities, with professorships in the exploration of the future.

Tentative beginnings on a world basis are being made along these 34 lines, like the very successful I. G. Y., or International Geophysical Year, and now the International Biological Program, or I. B. P., and I am sure that they will increase and multiply in regional, national and professional affairs as well. At the same time we must do our best to get rid of the present imbalance between different branches of science and integrate them in a framework of common effort. This is a necessary step toward a greater goal — the integration of science with all other branches of learning into a single comprehensive and open-ended system of knowledge, ideas and values relevant to man's destiny. This might even lure professional philosophers out of their linguistic burrows and metaphysical towers to take part in rebuilding a genuine philosophy of existence. But before this can happen, we must repudiate our modern idolatry of science and technology, and dethrone them from the exaggerated pedestals on which we have set them. After all, "science" is only the name for a particular system of knowledge, awareness and understanding acquired by particular methods; it must come to terms with other systems acquired by other methods — aesthetic and historical, intuitive and subconscious, imaginative and visionary. A prerequisite for this is the creation of a real science of psychology in place of the array of conflicting heresies at present occupying the field. I venture to prophesy that this will find its root in ethology, the science dealing with the analysis and evolution of animal mind and behavior.

One of technology's most exciting but also alarming achievements is 35 the computer, which is pushing technologically advanced countries like America into an era of computerized automation. I say *alarming* because computerized automation coupled with population increase must tend to split a country into two nations, to use Disraeli's phrase about mid-Victorian Britain. In late twentieth-century America, the two nations will not be the rich and the poor but the employed and the nonemployed, the minority with assured jobs and high incomes, the majority with no jobs and only unemployment pay. Even though automation can ensure increased production of all kinds of goods, this would be a socially disastrous and politically intolerable situation. Somehow or other, the technologically advanced countries will have to rethink the whole concept of work and jobs. One kind of work that will certainly expand is teaching; another is learning — teaching and learning how to live.

The problems of adjustment will be formidable, and the methods for 36 achieving it will need not only hard thinking but time to work out. Meanwhile, we may be driven to providing everyone, even if they have no job in the customary sense, with a really adequate income to tide them over the period of adjustment.

In regions of dense population and rapid industrial growth, science 37 and technology are producing an alarming increase in pollution and ecological degradation. The volume of solid matter discharged annually into the world's waters amounts to over sixty-five cubic miles — equivalent to a mountain with twenty-thousand-foot vertical sides and a flat top of over sixteen square miles. This includes so much sewage that bathing in many lakes, including even the Lake of Geneva, and on numerous sea beaches has become either disgusting, dangerous to health, or both. Our vaunted Affluent Society is rapidly turning into an Effluent Society. Meanwhile, rubbish dumps and used automobiles are polluting the land; automobile exhausts, domestic smoke and industrial fumes are polluting the air; and pesticides and herbicides are killing off our birds, our wild flowers and our butterflies. The net result is that nature is being wounded, man's environment desecrated, and the world's resources of enjoyment and interest demolished or destroyed.

Here is an obvious case where quality of life and living must take 38 precedence over quantity of production and profit. Compulsory measures against pollution, whatever they may cost, are as necessary as are compulsory vaccination or compulsory quarantine against disease. Meanwhile, science can be set to find better methods of pest control, and technology put to work to reduce effluents, to render them innocuous (or even beneficial, as are some forms of sewage treatment) and to recover any valuable components for future use. Both science and technology must also be called in to reduce the really shocking gap in standards of living and quality of existence between rich and poor countries. If this goes on widening, it will split the world economically into two hostile halves. It will inevitably stir up "envy, hatred, malice, and all uncharitableness," as The Litany puts it, in the poor countries, all too probably combined with racial animosity and with a threat of violence lurking under the surface.

It is all too clear that our present methods of aid and assistance are 39 pitifully inadequate to reduce the gap to below the danger point, let alone close it. To take a single example: The losses inflicted on the countries of Latin America by the falling prices of their primary export products during the Fifties were greater than all the aid they received in the same period. During the present so-called Development Decade, they may well become less instead of more developed.

We have to rethink the whole system. The very idea of aid and 40 assistance, with its implications of charity, of a man satisfying his conscience by giving a beggar half a dollar, must be dropped; for it we must substitute the idea of cooperation in world development, with rich and poor in active though complementary partnership.

This will involve large changes, both in attitude and in practice. First, 41 we must take into account the raw fact that an underdeveloped country cannot be industrialized if its rate of population increase is too high. Too much of the capital and skills required is used up in feeding, housing, educating and generally taking care of the excess crop of human infants; it goes down the drain — the baby drain. Thus, expert inquiry has made it clear that unless the Indian birth rate is halved within a generation, it will be impossible for India to break through to modernized economy. Accordingly, all plans for aid must take account of what may be called the recipient country's demographic creditworthiness; if this is too low, some of the aid must go to help the country control its rate of increase, by providing contraceptives and training personnel in their use, and by sending expert advisors.

Secondly, we must somehow transform our international economic 42 system — trade and barter, loans and grants and technical assistance — from the outdated shackles of "free" enterprise and competitive profitability. It is not for a noneconomist to suggest remedies, beyond obvious ones like making loan terms as easy as possible and stabilizing commodity prices. But clearly the job is urgent and demands a high degree of economic and political statesmanship, in nations, foundations and international bodies.

Both science and automation link up with education. Dorothy Parker 43 once acidly remarked that education consisted in casting sham pearls before real swine. Omitting all questions of the swinishness of its recipients or victims, we must admit that many of its pearls *are* false, flawed or misshapen and, to change the metaphor, that it often involves the forcible feeding of its pupils on unsuitable, unhealthy or even poisonous diets. Just as education in Hitler's Germany was based on stuffing children's brains with National Socialist dogma and anti-Jewish indoctrination, in many Roman Catholic countries it is based on Catholic dogma and anti-Communist and antihumanist indoctrination; and in China, the U. S. S. R. and its satellites, it is based on Communist dogma and anticapitalist and antireligious indoctrination. Meanwhile, educational systems in the Western world, and I regret to say in India and most emergent nations in Africa and Southeast Asia, are suffering from the complaint that has been called *examinotosis* — cramming pupils with facts and ideas that are to be regurgitated at appropriate intervals, in subjects that can be marked or graded by the examination process, with the ultimate idea of awarding certificates, diplomas and degrees that will help the examinees in obtaining jobs.

In addition, the world's poor countries suffer grievously from un- 44 dereducation at all levels. One result of this is that adult illiteracy is actually increasing. A UNESCO survey has shown that between 1952 and 1962, thirty-five million adults were added to the over one billion of the world's illiterates, and the figure is growing yearly. In many countries, only 25, 15, or even 10 percent of the male population is literate, and the illiteracy of women is considerably higher. Meanwhile, surveys have demonstrated that literacy is an indispensable basis for vigorous national life in the world of today and that 40 percent literacy is the minimum needed for achieving appreciable economic, techno-logical or cultural success. The Shah of Iran has suggested that all na-tions should contribute 2 percent of their annual military budgets to a world campaign against illiteracy, and there are numerous other pro-jects for promoting literacy.

Many efforts are also being made to free the examination-ridden 45 educational systems of developed countries from their restrictive prac-tices and liberate them from their true goals — of transmitting hu-man culture in all its aspects and enabling the new generation to lead fuller and more rewarding lives.

The first thing is to reform the curriculum so that, instead of separate 46 "subjects" to be "taken" piecemeal, growing minds are offered a nutri-tious core of human knowledge, ideas, techniques and achievements, covering science and history as well as the arts and manual skills. The key subject must be ecology, both biological and human — the science of balanced interaction between organisms and their environ-ment (which of course includes other organisms) — together with its practical applications in the conservation of the world's resources, ani-mal, vegetable and mineral, and human. Education must prepare grow-ing human beings for the future, not only their own future but that of their children, their nation and their planet. For this, it must aim at varied excellence (including the training of professional elites) and at the fullest realization of human possibilities.

324

This links up with the rethinking of religion — a vital task, but one 47 I can only touch on in summary fashion. It is clear that the era of mutually exclusive and dogmatic religions, each claiming to be the sole repository of absolute and eternal truth, is rapidly ending. If mankind is to evolve as a whole, it must have a single set of beliefs in common; and if it is to progress, these beliefs must not be self-limiting but open-ended, not rigid barriers but flexible guidelines channeling men in the general direction of improvement and perfection. Already an effort is being made to find common ground between the world's various religions and churches, and we can be sure that necessity will drive them further in this direction. But this is not enough. In the light of our new and comprehensive vision, we must redefine religion itself. Religions are not necessarily concerned with the worship of a supernatural God or gods, or even with the supernatural at all; they are not mere superstition nor just self-seeking organizations exploiting the public's superstitions and its belief in the magical powers of priests and witch doctors.

The ultimate task will be to melt down the gods, and magic, and all 48 supernatural entities, into their elements of transcendence and sacred power and then, with the aid of our new knowledge, build up these raw materials into a new religious system that will help man to achieve the destiny that our new evolutionary vision has revealed. Meanwhile, we must encourage all constructive attempts at reformulating and rebuilding religion. My personal favorite is Evolutionary Humanism, but there are many others tending in the same general direction, like Yoga and Zen, ethical and meditative systems, and the cults of release through psychedelic drugs or bodily rituals.

How does this all add up? It adds up to a meaningful whole, some- 49 thing greater than the sum of its parts. We need no longer be afflicted with a sense of our own insignificance and helplessness, or of the world's nonsignificance and meaninglessness. A purpose has been revealed to us — to steer the evolution of our planet toward improvement — and an encouragement has been given us, in the knowledge that steady evolutionary improvement has actually occurred in the past, and the assurance that it can continue into the future.

It is especially encouraging to know that biological improvement has 50 been born of struggle, and that conflict has often been disinfected of open violence and sometimes even converted into cooperative bonding; and it is especially significant that the most vital of all improvements has been the improvement of mind — awareness, knowledge and understanding — coupled with ability to learn and profit from experience. What is more, improvements in the human lot, in man's ways of coping with the problems of existence, have always depended on improvements in his awareness, knowledge and understanding; and today the explosive increase of knowledge has given us a wholly new understanding of our role in the universe and wholly new hopes of human improvement. We are still imprisoned in a mental cage, whose walls are made of the forces of nature as we have experienced them, whose bars are the constructions of our own primitive thinking — about destiny and salvation, enjoyment and ethics, guilt and propitiation, peace and war.

Today the individual man or woman need not feel himself a meaning- 51 less insect in the vast spaces of the cosmos, nor an insignificant cog in a huge, impersonal social machine. For one thing, the individual human is the highest and most wonderful organization we know of. In developing his own personality, he is making his own unique contribution to the evolution of the universe.

Secondly, he is a unit of mankind, and mankind is the highest type 52 in the solar system, the only organism we know of in whom mind has broken through to dominate existence. Mankind is not only a product of past evolution but an active agent in its future course. The human individual can help mankind shoulder this responsibility.

Our first objective is to clarify the new vision of our evolution. The 53 next is to define the tasks required to carry out our responsibilities. Our over-all aim is improvement. Our immediate tasks are to achieve the peaceful unity and cooperative development of mankind, to encourage varied excellence and greater achievement, to think in terms of ecology and to practice conservation, and to build a fulfillment society underpinned by some new system of beliefs. The final aim will be the eugenic transformation of man's genetic nature, coupled with the cultural transformation of his social environment. Meanwhile, all can help in understanding and spreading the new revelation of human destiny.

SUBJECT

1. Why does each major improvement in the evolutionary process prove to be "self-limiting"? (Might not the dinosaurs, for instance, have continued to be dominant even though mammals developed?) What are the "limits" in our own stage of development?

2. What is the "psychosocial phase of evolution"? Do you think it can legitimately be called a phase of biological evolution?

3. Examine Huxley's five stages of psychosocial evolution (paragraph 10). Would you say these are obviously correct, or arbitrarily selected, divisions?

4.   Does Huxley present convincing evidence that we are on the threshold of a new evolutionary phase? How can he be sure that we will not go the way of the dinosaurs?

5.   At a time when many thinkers are giving up on science as the hope for the future, does Huxley seem a little backward to put his faith in it? What does he think science can do for man?

6.   Huxley criticizes the *examinotosis* of modern education; does he make clear what kind of educational system should replace it?

7.   Huxley does not believe in the existence of a god; why, then, is he so anxious to establish a world religion? Is he particular about what kind of religion it ought to be?

STRUCTURE

1.   Huxley obviously cannot explain in detail every stage of biological evolution. Does he at least manage to make clear in a general way how the historical process operated? Is there anything which should have been explained more fully?

2.   Try to make an outline of the mechanical process beginning in paragraph 15. Can the material be arranged in satisfactory outline form?

3.   Does Huxley make clear the steps that must be taken to properly redefine man's aims? Are these procedures to be carried out simultaneously or in some regular order?

4.   Paragraph 21 begins a rather complex portion of the essay: Huxley describes six related processes — population control, etc. — to see how these measures "may help us in planning the practical steps needed to achieve" the ends he has just described. How does he manage to tie all this together at the end?

5.   There are at least eight processes explained in this essay — a tall order even for a writer of Huxley's ability. What would you say are the chief weaknesses in what he has written? Could they have been avoided had he attempted less?

THE UNKNOWN CITIZEN

W. H. Auden

Wyston Hugh Auden was born in England in 1907. He has published some 25 volumes of poetry, five plays, five volumes of criticism, five translations, and edited 27 other volumes. Auden has won numerous awards for poetry, including Pulitzer and Bollingen prizes and the King's Gold Medal (1937). Although "The Unknown Citizen" should be judged primarily as a poem, it is also an interesting kind of double process analysis: it shows how the unknown citizen "got processed" by his society, and it is a recipe for cooking up a model citizen according to accepted standards. The poem was composed in 1940, but Auden might have written something not very different today.

*(To JS/07/M/378
This Marble Monument
Is Erected by the State)*

He was found by the Bureau of Statistics to be
One against whom there was no official complaint,
And all the reports on his conduct agree
That, in the modern sense of an old-fashioned word, he was a saint,
For in everything he did he served the Greater Community.   5
Except for the War till the day he retired
He worked in a factory and never got fired,
But satisfied his employers, Fudge Motors Inc.
Yet he wasn't a scab or odd in his views,
For his Union reports that he paid his dues,   10
(Our report on his Union shows it was sound)
And our Social Psychology workers found
That he was popular with his mates and liked a drink.
The Press are convinced that he bought a paper every day
And that his reactions to advertisements were normal in every way.   15

Policies taken out in his name prove that he was fully insured,
And his Health-card shows he was once in hospital but left it cured.
Both Producers Research and High-Grade Living declare
He was fully sensible to the advantages of the Instalment Plan
And had everything necessary to the Modern Man,   20
A phonograph, a radio, a car and a frigidaire.
Our researchers into Public Opinion are content
That he held the proper opinions for the time of year;
When there was peace, he was for peace; when there was war, he
    went.
He was married and added five children to the population,   25
Which our Eugenist says was the right number for a parent of his
    generation,
And our teachers report that he never interfered with their
    education.
Was he free? Was he happy? The question is absurd:
Had anything been wrong, we should certainly have heard.

SUBJECT

1. Is there any way to tell whether the citizen acted from his own chosen values or because he had been perfectly programmed? (How does Auden make clear, in other words, that his intent is satire?)

2. In what sense can the citizen be called a "saint"? If he is a saint, why is he "unknown"?

3. "And our teachers report that he never interfered with their education"; what is implied by the choice of the pronoun "their"?

4. Do all the statistics on the unknown citizen add up to a coherent portrait? Is anything missing? (Note that his religion is not mentioned; should it be?)

5. Assuming that Auden's portrait is approximately what the establishment encourages — whether consciously or not — as a model, what would the result be if it succeeded in getting everyone to conform to that model? How would such a society differ from that pictured in Huxley's *Brave New World?*

STRUCTURE

1. Try working out the rhyme scheme of the poem. Is there any regular rhythm (iambic pentameter, e.g.)? Do you think Auden was trying to write an "unpoetic poem"? Would there have been any advantage, given the subject, to making the meter and rhyme scheme monotonously regular?

2.   The poem makes clear all the ingredients of the establishment's recipe for a model citizen; are they arranged in any logical order? Should they be?

3.   Do you think the last two lines are really necessary to the poem? What effect do they have? Are they out of character with the rest of the inscription on the monument?

SHELLFISH

Richard Brautigan

Richard Brautigan is a now-generation writer with an awesome disregard for traditional forms and aims of literature. More famous as a writer of novels (or anti-novels) than as a poet, his best known books are Trout Fishing in America, In Watermelon Sugar, *and* The Pill Versus the Springhill Mine Disaster. *Although widely read by the younger generation and touted by other new writers, Brautigan is universally ignored in biographical dictionaries. The poem included here is from* Rommel Drives on Deep Into Egypt.

Always spend a penny
as if you were spending a dollar
and always spend a dollar
as if you were spending
a wounded eagle and always
spend a wounded eagle as if
you were spending the very sky itself.

SUBJECT

1. On the surface this poem represents the simplest kind of process: a mere set of directions. But the unusual nature of the directions indicates a deeper meaning behind them; can you tell what Brautigan is getting at?

2. Is Brautigan recommending a tight fiscal policy or personal frugality ("a penny saved is a penny earned")? What relationship is there between the spending of money and the spending of wounded eagles?

3. Except perhaps for credit cards, the dollar sign may be as good a symbol as we have for contemporary civilization; what effect is achieved by the juxtaposition of "unnatural" money with "the sky itself"?

STRUCTURE

1. Critics debate whether a poem needs to have a paraphrasable content, but they are agreed that it ought to have an emotional impact beyond the mere logic of *what* is said. The paraphrasable content of "Shellfish" is almost simplistic; how does Brautigan give his poem a deeper, "emotional" meaning?

2. What relationship is there, if any, between the title and the subject of this poem? Would a title such as "Eagle" or "Wounded Eagle" have limited the implications of the poem in a way that "Shellfish" does not?

3. Do you think this poem would have benefited in any way from a more formal structure, or even a more logical division into poetic lines?

6

WORKS OF THE IMAGINATION

Definition

Most students have been taught — and properly — to go to the dictionary if they cannot tell the meaning of a work from its context. And the development of the modern, carefully compiled dictionary within the last century has been invaluable in furthering communication. Unfortunately, however, the dictionary has its limitations. Consider for a moment how a dictionary goes about defining a word. Normally, it puts the word into a more general classification and then limits its description of that larger class until the definition can refer only to the one word being defined. Thus, "Cocker spaniel: any of a breed of small spaniels having short legs, long floppy ears . . ." or "tamale: a native Mexican food having. . . ." This procedure is useful if the general classification is more recognizable than the particular member of it being defined. If the reader has a fair idea of what the general class, "Mexican food" is like, he is enlightened by the definition of tamale as a "native Mexican food" having certain special characteristics.

But suppose the word to be defined is a very general or abstract concept like "love" or "bravery." The dictionary might classify such a concept as "an emotion" or "an attitude," but its doing so does not tell us much, even if we know what "an atittude" is. Adequate definitions of these broad concepts need much more space than a dictionary can devote to them.

Serious misunderstandings seldom occur from the use of specific or concrete terms like cocker spaniel. If a reader does not know what the word means, he can use his dictionary to find out. But an abstract term may cause two kinds of difficulty. First, if the reader does not know the term, he will get little help from his dictionary. And if he does know the term his understanding of it may still be quite different from the meaning intended in any particular context. The peace talks in Korea were reportedly prolonged because of a misunderstanding of the word "aggressor." To the Americans representing the United Nations in the talks, the North Koreans were the aggressors because they had invaded a territory not their own. To the Chinese, the U.N. forces were the aggressors, for the Chinese understood the word to mean "a foreigner who attacks"; when Koreans were fighting Koreans, there was civil war but not aggression, for no "foreigners" were involved until the U.N. forces arrived.

Most abstract terms have only a general *area* of meaning, not a particular meaning upon which all can agree. This is because the concept has been abstracted from — drawn out of — a great many particular situations which are considerably varied in their details. Suppose, for instance, a South Pacific tribe witnesses, on three successive days, a tribesman killing a shark to save his friend, another rescuing some children from a burning hut, and a warrior killing seven enemies in one battle. To all of these acts they apply a word meaning "courage." Clearly, though, the deeds have little in common except this abstraction, courage. "Courage," then, does not mean "saving children from a burning hut"; the word has a much more general *area* of meaning.

Since no two people have identical sets of experiences, and since the meaning of an abstract concept is derived from experience, both firsthand and vicarious, it follows that an abstract term cannot mean exactly the same to any two people. The meanings of some terms may vary so slightly from person to person that we can use them without fear of serious misunderstanding. Other terms have such an infinite variety of meanings that no one really expects to know quite what someone else means by them. We make a kind of tacit agreement, for instance, that no one will inquire in too much detail what another person means by "love." We simply allow the word so much flexibility that it is possible for a person to express a "love" for mashed potatoes. In between these relatively harmless extremes, however, are a great many terms which are used as though they had a fairly specific and commonly accepted meaning. Not only do serious misunderstandings result from such careless use of abstract words and terms, but important differences in meaning are often obscured. One is likely to hear this type of argument, for example: "The Democratic and Republican parties both believe in the American Way of Life; so there isn't really any significant difference between them." The statement, of course, ignores the fact that "American Way of Life" does not mean the same for both parties — or even for various members of one party. Frequently such statements reflect a deliberate attempt to deceive, as when military leaders cover a disastrous defeat with the phrase "strategic withdrawal."

A student should watch for careless use of abstractions in print and try to discover as nearly as possible from the context what the writer means by his terms. Perhaps more important, he should be aware of what *he* means by terms when he uses them, for such careless usage invariably leads to sloppy thinking. The student should also make clear in his own writing his meaning of abstract concepts, either by the context in which he uses them or, if necessary, by definition. This does not mean that every paper should be prefaced with the awkward and formal "definition of terms" paragraph so common in student themes. For the reader, remember, learns nothing by "According to Webster, courage means. . . ."

But if one cannot give an adequate dictionary definition, the reader may fairly ask, how does he go about making clear the meaning of his terms? The key is to keep in mind that the meaning of an abstract concept is the sum total of one's experiences which have that concept in common. The best way, then, to define the term is to put it back into specific context by giving typical and relevant examples from the writer's own experience. The easiest way to define "book" is to point to one and say, "*This* is a book." The same is true of abstract terms: to define "courage," point out examples of it. Enough instances, however, must be given so that the area of meaning is established.

If one cannot conveniently give sufficient illustrations from his own experience there are other methods of defining which can be employed. These are the same as the methods of presenting material which have been illustrated thus far in this book: comparison and contrast, description, cause and effect, and process. Suppose, for instance, a writer needed to define "alcoholic." Certainly a description of a typical alcoholic would help — a personal acquaintance would be best. But it would also be helpful to discuss various theories concerning the *cause* of alcoholism, or its social consequences (*effects*). The writer might want to show the *process* by which a person develops into an alcoholic. Or perhaps, through *comparison and contrast,* he would show the difference between a "drinker" and an "alcoholic." It would be possible for a writer to use all of these methods in a single extended definition. The important consideration is that the reader come to an understanding of the term as nearly as possible like that of the writer. The writer's definition may vary considerably from the reader's, but if the reader sees clearly this difference communication will be effected.

Extended definition is one of the most difficult types of writing; but it can be accomplished if the writer will remember to put the term into specific contexts. He needs only to watch out for two traps into which students frequently fall. (1) It is not necessary to establish a definition which will be valid for all men in all time. The writer's task is only to convey clearly what *he* means by the term. (2) The student should beware of writing about the term as though it were already defined, *i.e.,* of assuming that the reader really knows from the beginning what

335

the writer means by the term. He cannot possibly know exactly, and the slight differences are significant.

The essays in this section are all attempted definitions of the abstract concept "art," or of one of the fine arts. The reader will see that they reflect a variety of approaches to the problem of definition and that the authors have achieved varying degrees of success. Picasso almost despairs of accomplishing such a task. MacLeish tries to give insight into the nature of poetry by employing apparent contradictions. Mill, on the other hand, tries a more objective, logical approach. The variety of definitions which these writers have produced should make clear the point that there is no one meaning and no satisfactory "dictionary definition" for an abstract concept like art.

A NOTE ON THE WORK
OF THE IMAGINATION

Denise Levertov

Denise Levertov, born in England in 1923, has published a dozen books of poetry since migrating to the United States in 1948. She has won numerous awards, and has been visiting lecturer in poetry writing at several universities, including Vassar, M. I. T., and Berkeley. She held a Guggenheim Fellowship in 1962.

The *work* of the imagination, its far-reaching and faithful permeation of those details that, in a work of art, illuminate the whole, was recently illustrated for me in a dream with particular clarity. 1

I had been dreaming of a large house, set in a flat landscape, and of its history, which is not relevant here. At a certain point I half awoke; and when I returned to the dream I was conscious that I was dreaming. Still close to the threshold of waking, I knew very well that I was lying down for an afternoon nap, in my son's room, because there the street noises would hardly reach me; that though I had a blanket over me I was cold; and that he would soon be home from school and I must get up. But all this was unimportant: what gripped me was the knowledge that I was dreaming, and vividly. A black, white and gray tiled pavement I crossed — how "real" it felt under my feet! To see, as I saw the poplar avenue, and the bluish misty fields around the large buildings, was good — but at no time is it hard to call up scenes to the mind's eye; it was the sensations of touch — the pavement felt through the ball of the foot, the handle of a door in my hand — and of space — the outdoors sensation first, then the spaces of rooms and of the confinement of corridors and of turns in the corridors when I re-entered the house — that interested me, in being so complete even though I knew I was dreaming. 2

At length I came into a small bedroom fitted with a washbasin and mirror and the idea came to me of looking in the mirror as a test of how far in fidelity the dream would go; but I was afraid. I was afraid the mirror would show me a blank, or a strange face — I was afraid of the 3 fright that would give me. However, I dared: and approached the mirror. It was rather high on the wall, and not tilted, so that what first appeared, as I slowly drew near, was the top of my head. But yes, surely something was wrong — a misty whiteness glimmered there!

I crept nearer still, and standing straight, almost on tiptoe, now saw   4 my whole face, my usual face-in-the-glass — pale, the dark eyes somewhat anxious, but in no way changed, or lacking or causing me fear. What then was the radiant glimmer that had startled me just before?

Why! — in the dark, somewhat fluffy hair was a network of little   5 dew or mist diamonds, like spiders' webs on a fall morning! The creative unconscious — the imagination — had *provided,* instead of a fright, this exquisitely realistic detail. For hadn't I been walking in the misty fields in the dewfall hour? Just so, then, would my damp hair look. I awoke in delight, reminded forcibly of just what it is we love in the greatest writers — what quality above all others, surely, makes us open ourselves freely to Homer, Shakespeare, Tolstoi, Hardy — that *following through,* that *permeation* of detail — relevant, illuminating detail — which marks the total imagination, distinct from intellect, at work. "The mind's tongue, working and tasting into the very rock heart!" as Ruskin wrote of Turner. The feared Hoffmanesque blank — the possible monster or stranger — would have illustrated the work of Fancy, that *"by invisible wires puts marionettes in motion, and pins butterflies to blotting-paper, and plays Little-Go among the Fairies"* (Landor, in *Imaginary Conversations*). And mere Reason can put two eyes and a nose where we suppose them to be. But it was Imagination put seed pearls of summer fog in Tess Durbeyfield's hair (and *"an intenser little fog amid the prevailing one,"* as a friendly cow breathed out in recognition of her approach) — and it was the same holy, independent faculty that sprinkled my hair with winter-evening diamonds.

We sigh — or I do — for the days when whole cultures were infused   6 with noble simplicity; when though there was cruelty and grief there was no ugliness; when King Alcinous himself stowed the bronze pots for Odysseus under the rower's benches; when from shepherd's pipe and warrior's sandal to palace door and bard's song, all was *well-made.* Any culture worth the name, in fact, though "noble simplicity" may be partially an illusion, has the quality of harmony; the blood stream flows right to the fingertips and the toes; no matter how complex the structure, the parts accord with the whole. Our age appears to me a chaos and our environment lacks the qualities for which one could call it a culture. But by way of consolation we have this knowledge of power that perhaps no one in such a supposed harmonious time had: what in the greatest poets is recognizable as Imagination, that breathing of life into the dust, is present in us all embryonically — manifests itself in the life of dream — and in that manifestation shows us the possibility: to permeate, to quicken, all of our life and the works we make. What joy to be reminded by truth in dream that the Imagination does not arise from the environment but has the power to create it!

SUBJECT

1. Does Miss Levertov intend to suggest that her entire dream was the work of the imagination, or only that touch of mist on her hair? Was it necessary for her to be *aware* that she was dreaming in order for the imagination to function?

2. Do you think the imagination is a faculty separate from reason and fancy?

3. Judging by Miss Levertov's example, does "the creative unconscious" (paragraph 5) seem a just synonym for "imagination"?

4. What does the digression on "noble simplicity" in past ages have to do with the definition of imagination? Can you think of any reason why the assumption that great cultures of the past had noble simplicity might be misguided?

5. On what grounds does Miss Levertov think people of modern times have greater powers of imagination? Do you think her thought is a valid one?

6. Of what special use is imagination in a time when "Our age appears . . . a chaos and our environment lacks the qualities for which one could call it a culture"?

STRUCTURE

1. What method of development is chiefly employed in this definition? (Note that Miss Levertov must define by use and function rather than physical characteristics of imagination, since an attempt to locate the imagination in some portion of the brain would be of little help.)

2. Does she make clear her distinction between the function of imagination, and reason and fancy?

3. Paragraph 5 contains the only abstract statements about imagination; how does Miss Levertov ground these in the particular?

4. Are the concluding statements about possible uses of the imagination part of the definition?

5. Comment on the effectiveness of Miss Levertov's starting with a lengthy illustration instead of the abstraction that it illustrates.

WRITING

Norman Podhoretz

Norman Podhoretz (born in 1930), is editor-in-chief of Commentary *magazine and a frequent contributor to* Partisan Review, New Yorker, Harper's *and* New Republic. *His books include* Doings and Undoings: the 50's and After in American Writing *(1964) and* Making It *(1968), from which the following brief digression on the creative process was taken.*

Writing is among the most mysterious of human activities. No one, least   1
of all the psychoanalysts, knows the laws by which it moves or refuses
to move. And yet the whole phenomenon obviously falls within the
domain of psychoanalytic theory. The poem, the story, the essay, and
even something so apparently inconsequential as a book review (I mean
one which is approached with seriousness), is already *there,* much in
the way that Socrates said mathematical knowledge was already there,
before a word is ever put to paper; and the act of writing is the act of
finding the magical key that will unlock the floodgates and let the flow
begin.

As every writer can testify, the Muses once invoked by poets are a   2
reality, except that the ancients were probably wrong in thinking that
they reside in the heavens. More likely they are located in reaches of
the mind which are accessible or not according to their own sweet
volition. Unless he is writing mechanically, the writer does not experience his writing as an act of creation; he experiences it as an act of
discovery: it *comes* or *happens* or is *given* to him, and when it does,
he *recognizes* it at once for his own. It is not within the power of his
will to summon it forth if it refuses to come; nor is he capable of resisting
it for long when it starts to demand release. What, according to Saint
Augustine, the penis is to the body — he said it was the only limb or
"member" which defied the control of the will, which, that is, actually
had a will of its own, rising and falling of its own accord and not, like
the arms or the legs, at the dictates of "owner's" will — the act of
writing is to the mind. In fact, so closely connected in some obscure way

are the two phenomena, with the ability to write resembling the feeling of a ready sexual potency and the inability to write resembling the experience of sexual impotence, that many men have a strong impulse to masturbate when they are about to start on a piece of writing, as though to persuade themselves that they *are* in control, that they can get it up and make it come.

But if the act of writing cannot be controlled by the will, it can be 3 controlled by that magical key of which I have already spoken. The key, I believe, is literally a key in that it is musical (which, if I may indulge in a bit of fanciful etymologizing à la Heidegger, is perhaps why it was to the *Muses* that the ancient poets appealed): it is the tone of voice, the only tone of voice, in which this particular piece of writing will permit itself to be written. To find that tone is to unlock the floodgates. Yet the unconscious, or the Muse, or whatever it is, often exacts a sacrifice from the writer before it will allow him to hit upon the right tone, the key. It may specify a certain number of hours or days or months of agony so intense that fantasies of suicide inevitably arise. (Conrad's wife used to lock him in a room to write; he would writhe on the floor and bang on the door, begging to be let out.) It may, on the other hand, decide to give him a break, possibly because he has accumulated a large enough balance of suffering to entitle him temporarily to a free ride.

In that blessed case, the writer will enter into a state of bliss such as 4 exists nowhere else on earth, and probably not in heaven either. He will be in touch with himself and in command of all his powers to a degree that would gratify the greatest narcissist (and being a writer he will invariably be a greater narcissist than anyone except singers and actors) while paradoxically freeing him from self-preoccupation (the disease D. H. Lawrence described as "falling from the hands of God") to a degree that would gratify the most ambitious saint. In this beatific condition, he will sit with a pen or at a typewriter and watch, in delight and amazement, sentences mysteriously shaping themselves into rhythms he *knows* to be right and then giving birth by parthenogenesis to successive generations of sentences which flow into paragraphs which in turn by seamless transition flow gently into other paragraphs which in their turn begin to shape themselves into an organically coherent pattern that miraculously corresponds — only better, much better — to the dim vision he had had of it and which had driven him in the first place to the desk. He will find that he has not only been permitted to uncover things he did not know he knew, but that he has also been allowed for the first time to say many things he knew he knew and had never been able to get onto a page because they never *fitted* anywhere and only what fits is allowed.

Finished, he will be exhausted and exhilarated, all anxieties gone; he 5
will feel that everything in the world makes sense after all, that there
is an order to things, and that he himself is part of that order. For that,
at bottom, is what he wants — coherence and order, coherence with
himself and order in the world. (Not for nothing, then, do writers slip
so easily into paranoia. The paranoid fantasy, a drama in which the
minutest details all hang together in a perfect fit, with oneself as the
menaced hero, would naturally be the occupational hazard of a narcissist questing for order.)

I have, of course, been describing the process as it must look in an 6
ideal state — with Shakespeare, say, who according to Ben Jonson
"never blotted a line," or with Mozart, who could write a whole symphony while riding in a carriage along a bumpy road. The reality with
lesser mortals is likely, as usual, to fall considerably short. Thus even
when the flow is true, when the piece is writing itself, it may not be
entirely true, and the writer's will then has to intervene to blot a line
or two or ten or a hundred: to correct, to polish, to reorganize, to
perfect. At this point exhilaration gives way to self-doubt. Was the
whole thing, now beyond reach and the floodgates slammed shut, an
illusion? Sometimes the doubt is justified: it may be, flow or not, that
what the writer had to say was not especially worth saying, what he had
to do not especially worth doing.

But even if it was not an illusion, even if he has just produced a 7
masterpiece, the writer may find himself full of loathing for it. Instead
of being better than his original dim vision, it is, he is certain, a betrayal
of it and defective past redemption. So, for example, T. E. Lawrence,
after finishing *The Seven Pillars of Wisdom,* very nearly burned the
manuscript, explaining to George Bernard Shaw: "There's a lot of half-
baked thinking, some cheap disgust and complaint . . .: in fact, the sham
stuff you have spent your life trying to prick. . . . My own disgust with
it is so great that I no longer believe it worth trying to improve (or
possible to improve)."

In other less-than-ideal instances, the writer may have been driven 8
by desperation into the delusion that he has found the key, and he may
in that case force something onto paper that a perceptive critic can
recognize as "willed." Or the flow, having truly started, may suddenly
decide to stop, and the writer may nevertheless push desperately ahead
with a willed pen, refusing to acknowledge his loss of the flow. Yet even
here the matter is not so simple. The Augustinian analogy to a willed
piece of writing would be an orgasm achieved by masturbation, and just
as masturbation does in fact produce an orgasm (a point which puritans
invariably forget to mention), so force-fed writing can sometimes work
a momentary opening of the floodgates: a minute ago the mind was

dead and all at once it comes alive, only to die again a minute later. This kind of writing (which is very precisely described in Dan Jacobson's novel, *The Beginners*) the critic will recognize as "uneven" or "unrealized." It differs from mechanical or hack writing in deriving from the ambition to attain to the real thing, and from the real or "realized" thing in not attaining to that quality of organic coherence which Coleridge rightly identified as the mark of a living work of the Imagination (his upper case, not mine).

Where all the Coleridgeans among us go wrong, I think, is in their assumption that this quality of Imagination can exist only in poems or stories. The truth is that it can and does exist, demonstrably so, in any form of writing, however humble or trivial that form may be by the evanescent or even the legitimate standards of a given moment. Writing always involves a man sitting with an implement and an inchoate idea before a blank sheet of paper and in terror at the answering blankness of his own mind. Consequently, if one is speaking of the experience of being a writer, the only defensible distinction is between writers who are willing to accept the risks of suffering entailed by the effort to tap their inner potentialities of organic coherence, and those who are unable or unwilling to take such risks.

Because misunderstanding on the point is very widespread indeed, it is important to stress that a writer's motives are relevant to the quality of his work *only* to the extent that they relate to his willingness or the lack of it. "No man but a blockhead ever wrote except for money," said Dr. Johnson. Well, he was wrong, but not in the way the kind of purists he was trying to shock by the statement are pleased to think. There are other forms of worldly currency, such as attention, admiration, and fame, for which men have always written, and there cannot have been many men in history who have written in total disregard of these things. But the issue of motives is simply irrelevant, having arisen in the first place from a confusion between art and religion and a misguided consequent campaign to erect the artist into a substitute for the saint. It may well be true of the saint that he not only refrains from physically committing adultery but also refrains from lusting after his neighbor's wife in his heart; or, to extend the Pauline image, he not only refrains from devoting himself to the pursuit of worldly goods but transcends his natural desire for them. But artists have rarely if ever been notable for transcending the desire for worldly goods. There is indeed no reason why they should cultivate this curious ambition unless conditions absolutely force them into it (which, of course, conditions in the modern world have frequently enough done), and many reasons, directly affecting the vitality of their work, why they should not. A writer, it seems necessary to say in the face of his mistaken romantic identity as a saint,

343

is a man, and being such his motives, in writing as in everything else, are likely to be mixed.

More than that, even, the narcissism which is an invariable and indispensable element of his very being as a writer is bound to leave him with an unusually strong appetite for success, and as many forms of it as he can get. So long, however, as his aim in the *act* of writing is to find the key to the quality of organic coherence locked within the reaches of his mind — and this, to put it with maximum plainness, is what "giving his all" really means — he must be deemed a serious writer, whether he is writing "for" money, sex, invitations to parties, or any other unseemly objective.

11

Subject

1.   Podhoretz is attempting to define "writing" — not the finished product but the act itself. Since writers differ considerably in the way they go about their work, he must find in their varied activities some common ingredients which will adequately characterize the activity. Does he succeed in doing this?

2.   Note that Podhoretz neither quotes a dictionary nor tries to give a dictionary definition; should he have done one or the other? Look up "writing" in your dictionary.

3.   Does Podhoretz try to establish a universal "meaning," or does he try to make us see what "writing" means to him?

4.   To define the abstract, a writer should put the term into specific contexts, both first and second hand. Does Podhoretz do so? What parts of the essay stick best in the memory?

5.   Would Podhoretz subscribe to the notion that "writing is 5 percent inspiration, 95 per cent perspiration"? What kind of "suffering" must the writer go through? Does his description correspond to your own experience?

6.   How much effect do motives for writing have on the finished product, according to Podhoretz?

Structure

1.   Can you discover any organizational plan to this essay, or is it simply a collection of random thoughts? (This selection is not a separate, formal essay, but a digression inserted into an autobiographical account.)

2.   Podhoretz's chief method of development is not a detailed example but an elaborate analogy between writing and masturbation.

Admittedly, the analogy seems far-fetched; how successfully does Podhoretz use it to clarify his notion of the act of writing? Should he have concentrated on some other method?

3.   The final two paragraphs employ the method of cause and effect analysis. What relationship does Podhoretz develp? Is it pertinent to his definition?

THE VATIC VOICE

Donald Hall

Donald Hall (born in 1916) is a professor of English at the University of Michigan. The essay which follows was originally a speech given at the Conference on Creativity of the National Council of Teachers of English, November, 1968.

Today, I want to talk about the first moment of the creative process — the excited flash of insight, coming in the shape of images, a rush of words before which one often feels like a passive observer — rather than talk about elaboration — getting the words right, learning how to cross out the wrong words, learning how to stimulate the secondary inspiration of revision. I am talking in terms of poetry, but I think my terms apply to other endeavors also. 1

A premise: within every human being there is the vatic voice. *Vates* was the Greek word for the inspired bard, speaking the words of a god. To most people, this voice speaks only in dream, and only in unremembered dream. The voice may shout messages into the sleeping ear, but a guard at the horned gate prevents the waking mind from remembering, listening, interpreting. It is the vatic voice (which is not necessarily able to write good poetry, or even passable grammar) which rushes forth the words of excited recognition, which supplies what we call inspiration. And inspiration, a breathing-into, is a perfectly expressive metaphor: "Not I, not I, but the wind that blows through me!" as Lawrence says. Or Shelley's "Ode to the West Wind." We are passive to the vatic voice, as the cloud or the tree is passive to the wind. 2

Just this month I have had an odd experience with a student who is trying to write poems. I let him into the writing class liking part of his examples, but not convinced of his talent. The first poems he showed me were wordy, explanatory, sincere, and dull. Then I happened to tell the whole class an anecdote about Hart Crane, who sometimes stimulated first-drafts by listening to Ravel, very loud, and about Gertrude Stein, who wrote while parked at Parisian intersections with all the horns beeping. They were using sound to clear away the tops of their 3

Reprinted by permission of the author.

minds. A week later my student came to office hours excited. He had been trying something. He had been listening to music, earphones clapped to his head and volume turned way up, and writing, "Whatever came into my head." He had a series of small fragments of astonishingly new and original imagery. The lines weren't finished, the rhythm wasn't very good, here and there was a cliché or a dead metaphor. But there was astonishing originality in each poem; some corner of new light, and what I can only call an extraordinary original intelligence. I think that in his case the apparatus of the ordinary intelligence had conspired to make his old poems pedestrian. When he was able to remove the top of his mind by this external stimulus of noise, the vatic voice broke through. He still has a way to go to learn to make his imaginings into good poems, but that is another matter.

I make up the phrase, "the vatic voice," not because I am especially in love with it — it sounds pretentious — but because I am trying to avoid using words that have acquired either more precise meanings, or more precise affectations of meaning, like "the unconscious mind." Anyway, the unconscious mind does not talk directly to us.   4

Two characteristics that distinguish the vatic voice from normal discourse are that it is always original, and that we feel passive to it. We are surprised by it, and we may very well, having uttered its words, not know what we mean.   5

We must find ways to let this voice speak. We want to get loose, we want to regress in the service of the ego, we want to become as children. We want to do this not only to make poems, or to invent a new theory of linguistics, but because it feels good, because it is healthy and therapeutic, because it helps us to understand ourselves and to be able to love other people. I think, I truly think, that to clear the passageway to the insides of ourselves, to allow the vatic voice to speak through us, is the *ultimate* goal to which men must address themselves. It is what to live for, it is what to live by.   6

Poetry is evidence of the vatic speech, but it is also typically an exhortation toward the vatic condition. Never to hear this voice in remembered night dream, or in day dream, or in moments of transport, is to be a lamentable figure, a lamentable figure frequent on college campuses. Children all hear it. This is a romantic cliché, and it is an observable truth. "There is another world that lives in the air." Most bad poetry — that which is not mere technical incompetence, technical competence can be acquired — is a result of defective creative process, which is a result of neurosis. That is, bad poetry is largely the result of being a lamentable man.   7

Sometimes I have tried to keep in touch with this vatic voice by sleeping a lot. Taking short naps can be a great means of keeping the   8

347

channel open. There is that wonderful long, delicious slide or drift down heavy air to the bottom of sleep, which you touch for only a moment, and then there is the floating up again, more swiftly, through an incredible world of images, sometimes in bright colors. I come out of these fifteen or twenty minute naps, not with phrases of poetry, but wholly refreshed, with the experience of losing control and entering a world of total freedom. I wake with great energy. On occasion, I remember phrases or scenes from dreams, either night dreams, or nap dreams, or waking fantasy dreams — and take these phrases or images directly into a poem. That happens, but it is not the only virtue of dream. Dream is the spirit dying into the underworld, and being born again.

There is also the deliberate farming of daydream. There is a way in which you can daydream quite loosely, but also observe yourself. You watch the strange associations, the movements. These associations are frequently trying to tell us something. The association is always there for some reason. Listen. When you hum a tune, remember the words that go with the tune and you will usually hear some part of your mind commenting on another part of your mind, or on some recent action. 9

There is something I want to call peripheral vision, and I don't mean anything optical. If you talk about a dream with an analyst, and there is an old battered table in the dream that you casually mention, he may well say, "What about this table? What did it look like?" Often these little details are so important. When I am listening to something passively speaking out to me, I don't attempt to choose what is most important, I try to listen to all of it. I never know what is going to be the most important message until I have lived with it for a while. Very frequently, the real subject matter is something only glimpsed, as it were out of the corner of the eye. Often the association which at first glance appears crazy and irrelevant, ultimately leads to the understanding, and tells what we did not know before. I don't know how to stimulate peripheral vision. But one can train the mind to observe the periphery rather than to ignore it. Remember: if you are thinking about something, and you have one really crazy, totally irrelevant, nutty, useless, unimaginably silly association, listen hard; it's the whole point, almost without a doubt. 10

Mostly, when the vatic voice speaks through me, I have not stimulated its appearance in any way. I do not know how to make it happen. I know that it comes frequently when I have been busy on other materials. The way I am living now, poetry, and new ideas in general, are apt to come out of a busy schedule, as a kind of alternative to, relief from, or even infidelity to more conventional duties. But I do not mean to 11 generalize; this will not be true of all people, or even true of me six months from now.

I do know that as you grow older you can learn better how to listen   12
to this voice inside yourself. You can learn better not to dismiss it, you can learn not to be frightened of it. You can learn to stay loose enough to let it keep talking and yet attentive enough to remember and record it. When the voice is silent one can only wait. One can only try to keep the channels open, to stay ready for the voice, which will come when it chooses to come. Staying ready for the voice involves not being frightened, hung up tight, mature, intellectual, reasonable, or otherwise neurotic.

SUBJECT

1. Why does Hall invent a new term rather than using one such as "inspiration" or "creative imagination"?

2. In talking about a creative process, Hall often uses the word "passive"; aren't "creative" and "passive" contradictory notions? If you have experienced the "vatic voice," did you find it a passive experience?

3. The vatic voice must be either divinely inspired or the production of our own brains. While Hall does not explicitly endorse the ancient Greek notion of *Vates* as the "voice of a god," he seems to think of it as something not ourselves which we should "listen to." What difference does it make whether it is an inspiration or an invention of the brain?

4. Judging by what Hall says in Paragraph 6, do you think he would approve of experiments with "mind-expanding" drugs? Or would he insist that the mind can be "expanded" without drugs?

5. What is so important about the vatic voice that Hall should feel it to be "the *ultimate* goal to which men must address themselves"?

6. Do you think it is possible to write good poems — or themes and research papers — without hearing the vatic voice?

7. In his concluding sentence, Hall implies that being mature or intellectual is being "neurotic"; in what sense does he mean that?

STRUCTURE

1. Does Hall give enough concrete instances of the vatic voice for the reader to understand the term?

2. What particular difficulty would you expect Hall to have in defining a term of his own invention? What advantage?

3.   What rhetorical techniques other than example does the author employ?

4.   Does Hall make clear the relationship between the "vatic voice" and "peripheral vision"? How could he have improved his transition in Paragraph 10?

ARTISTIC ART

Jose Ortega y Gasset

Ortega y Gasset, (1883–1955) Spanish philosopher, newspaperman, professor, politician, and critic, has been one of the most influential thinkers of our century. As early as 1930, in Revolt of the Masses, *he was telling the world that the new concept of mass man (even in a welfare state) would be stifling to individual genius — a prediction which would not become apparent to some until the student riots of the late sixties. In* The Dehumanization of Art, *from which the following passage is taken, Ortega y Gasset applies his political theory to art and literature.*

... If the new art is not accessible to every man this implies that its 1 impulses are not of a generically human kind. It is an art not for men in general but for a special class of men who may not be better but who evidently are different.

One point must be clarified before we go on. What is it the majority 2 of people call aesthetic pleasure? What happens in their minds when they "like" a work of art; for instance, a theatrical performance? The answer is easy. A man likes a play when he has become interested in the human destinies presented to him, when the love and hatred, the joys and sorrows of the personages so move his heart that he participates in it all as though it were happening in real life. And he calls a work "good" if it succeeds in creating the illusion necessary to make the imaginary personages appear like living persons. In poetry he seeks the passion and pain of the man behind the poet. Paintings attract him if he finds on them figures of men or women whom it would be interesting to meet. A landscape is pronounced "pretty" if the country it represents deserves for its loveliness or its grandeur to be visited on a trip.

It thus appears that to the majority of people aesthetic pleasure 3 means a state of mind which is essentially undistinguishable from their ordinary behavior. It differs merely in accidental qualities, being perhaps less utilitarian, more intense, and free from painful consequences.

From "Artistic Art," in Jose Ortega y Gasset, *The Dehumanization of Art and Other Essays on Art, Culture, and Literature* (revised edition copyright © 1968 by Princeton University Press; Princeton Paperback, 1968), pp. 8-14. Reprinted by permission of Princeton University Press.

But the object towards which their attention and, consequently, all their other mental activities are directed is the same as in daily life: people and passions. By art they understand a means through which they are brought in contact with interesting human affairs. Artistic forms proper — figments, fantasy — are tolerated only if they do not interfere with the perception of human forms and fates. As soon as purely aesthetic elements predominate and the story of John and Mary grows elusive, most people feel out of their depth and are at a loss what to make of the scene, the book, or the painting. As they have never practiced any other attitude but the practical one in which a man's feelings are aroused and he is emotionally involved, a work that does not invite sentimental intervention leaves them without a cue.

Now, this is a point which has to be made perfectly clear. Not only 4 is grieving and rejoicing at such human destinies as a work of art presents or narrates a very different thing from true artistic pleasure, but preoccupation with the human content of the work is in principle incompatible with aesthetic enjoyment proper.

We have here a very simple optical problem. To see a thing we must 5 adjust our visual apparatus in a certain way. If the adjustment is inadequate the thing is seen indistinctly or not at all. Take a garden seen through a window. Looking at the garden we adjust our eyes in such a way that the ray of vision travels through the pane without delay and rests on the shrubs and flowers. Since we are focusing on the garden and our ray of vision is directed toward it, we do not see the window but look clear through it. The purer the glass, the less we see it. But we can also deliberately disregard the garden and, withdrawing the ray of vision, detain it at the window. We then lose sight of the garden; what we still behold of it is a confused mass of color which appears pasted to the pane. Hence to see the garden and to see the windowpane are two incompatible operations which exclude one another because they require different adjustments.

Similarly a work of art vanishes from sight for a beholder who seeks 6 in it nothing but the moving fate of John and Mary or Tristan and Isolde and adjusts his vision to this. Tristan's sorrows are sorrows and can evoke compassion only in so far as they are taken as real. But an object of art is artistic only in so far as it is not real. In order to enjoy Titian's portrait of Charles the Fifth on horseback we must forget that this is Charles the Fifth in person and see instead a portrait — that is, an image, a fiction. The portrayed person and his portrait are two entirely different things; we are interested in either one or the other. In the first case we "live" with Charles the Fifth, in the second we look at an object of art.

But not many people are capable of adjusting their perceptive ap- 7
paratus to the pane and the transparency that is the work of art. Instead
they look right through it and revel in the human reality with which
the work deals. When they are invited to let go of this prey and to direct
their attention to the work of art itself they will say that they cannot
see such a thing, which indeed they cannot, because it is all artistic
transparency and without substance.

During the nineteenth century artists proceeded in all too impure a 8
fashion. They reduced the strictly aesthetic elements to a minimum and
let the work consist almost entirely in a fiction of human realities. In this
sense all normal art of the last century must be called realistic. Beethoven and Wagner were realistic, and so was Chateaubriand as well as
Zola. Seen from the vantage-point of our day Romanticism and Natural-
ism draw closer together and reveal their common realistic root.

Works of this kind are only partially works of art, or artistic objects. 9
Their enjoyment does not depend upon our power to focus on transpar-
encies and images, a power characteristic of the artistic sensibility; all
they require is human sensibility and willingness to sympathize with
our neighbor's joys and worries. No wonder that nineteenth century art
has been so popular; it is made for the masses inasmuch as it is not art
but an extract from life. Let us remember that in epochs with two
different types of art, one for minorities and one for the majority, the
latter has always been realistic.[1]

I will not now discuss whether pure art is possible. Perhaps it is not; 10
but as the reasons that make me inclined to think so are somewhat long
and difficult the subject better be dropped. Besides, it is not of major
importance for the matter in hand. Even though pure art may be
impossible there doubtless can prevail a tendency toward a purification
of art. Such a tendency would effect a progressive elimination of the
human, all too human, elements predominant in romantic and naturalistic production. And in this process a point can be reached in which
the human content has grown so thin that it is negligible. We then have
an art which can be comprehended only by people possessed of the
peculiar gift of artistic sensibility — an art for artists and not for the
masses, for "quality" and not for hoi polloi.

That is why modern art divides the public into two classes, those who 11
understand it and those who do not understand it — that is to say,
those who are artists and those who are not. The new art is an artistic
art.

[1]For instance in the Middle Ages. In accordance with the division of society in the two
strata of noblemen and commoners, there existed an aristocratic art which was "conventional" and "idealistic," and a popular art which was realistic and satirical.

I do not propose to extol the new way in art or to condemn the old. 12
My purpose is to characterize them as the zoologist characterizes two
contrasting species. The new art is a world-wide fact. For about twenty
years now the most alert young people of two successive generations
— in Berlin, Paris, London, New York, Rome, Madrid — have found
themselves faced with the undeniable fact that they have no use for
traditional art; moreover, that they detest it. With these young people
one can do one of two things: shoot them, or try to understand them.
As soon as one decides in favor of the latter it appears that they are
endowed with a perfectly clear, coherent, and rational sense of art. Far
from being a whim, their way of feeling represents the inevitable and
fruitful result of all previous artistic achievement. Whimsical, arbitrary,
and consequently unprofitable it would be to set oneself against the new
style and obstinately remain shut up in old forms that are exhausted and
the worse for wear. In art, as in morals, what ought to be done does not
depend on our personal judgment; we have to accept the imperative
imposed by the time. Obedience to the order of the day is the most
hopeful choice open to the individual. Even so he may achieve nothing;
but he is much more likely to fail if he insists on composing another
Wagnerian opera, another naturalistic novel.

In art repetition is nothing. Each historical style can engender a 13
certain number of different forms within a generic type. But there
always comes a day when the magnificent mine is worked out. Such, for
instance, has been the fate of the romantico-naturalistic novel and theater. It is a naïve error to believe that the present infecundity of these
two genres is due to lack of talent. What happens is that the possible
combinations within these literary forms are exhausted. It must be
deemed fortunate that this situation coincides with the emergence of
a new artistic sensibility capable of detecting other untouched veins.

When we analyze the new style we find that it contains certain closely 14
connected tendencies. It tends (1) to dehumanize art, (2) to avoid living
forms, (3) to see to it that the work of art is nothing but a work of art,
(4) to consider art as play and nothing else, (5) to be essentially ironical,
(6) to beware of sham and hence to aspire to scrupulous realization, (7)
to regard art as a thing of no transcending consequence.

SUBJECT

1. Does the assessment of what art means to the average person
seem to you reasonably accurate? If this is what art means to most
people, shouldn't it be the correct definition (as a dictionary defines
words according to common usage)?

2. "Preoccupation with the human content of the work is in principle incompatible with aesthetic enjoyment proper." On what grounds does Ortega y Gassett make this claim? Wouldn't it be possible to enjoy art on both levels simultaneously?

3. Would you agree that "an object of art is artistic only in so far as it is not real"? (The ancient Greeks and Romans defined art as "an imitation of life.")

4. If art is "transparency and without substance" rather than the object or situation portrayed, what is the viewer supposed to look at — or for?

5. Do you see any tendency among artists since this essay was written (in 1925) to move closer to "pure art"? Does your generalization hold for novels, films, and music as well as for painting?

6. In "epochs with two different types of art, one for minorities and one for the majority, the latter has always been realistic." Consider the applicability of this statement to modern music — classical and popular. Is the popular more "realistic"?

Structure

1. Ortega y Gassett makes clear what people look for when they view art from the wrong perspective; should he have explained in closer detail what they *ought* to be looking at? What reasons might he have had for not doing so?

2. Does the elaborate comparison in paragraph 5 seem to you a false analogy or a valid one? Recall that analogy can only be used to clarify, never to prove, a point; does Ortega y Gassett employ this one properly?

3. The author protests his intention to be as "objective as a zoologist." To what extent does he succeed? Do you find evidence that his analysis is colored by personal preferences?

4. Does the list of seven "tendencies" in paragraph 14 strike you as a good beginning for a definition of modern art? (Ortega y Gassett goes on in the book to explain each in some detail.)

5. Compare Ortega y Gassett's definitions of popular art and artistic art; which is the better definition? Why?

WHAT IS POETRY?

John Stuart Mill

With the possible exception of Aristotle, John Stuart Mill (1806–1873) was probably the most intelligent man who ever lived. Mill "had no childhood": he was writing poetry in English, Latin, and Greek by age eight; studying algebra and logic by ten; philosophy and economics by twelve. His interests remained varied throughout his life, and he wrote important works on philosophy, history, economics, logic, women's liberation, governmental reform, and religion. His autobiography is one of the finest in the language; his Essay on Liberty *has become a classic of political philosophy. The definition of poetry reprinted here, while clearly a product of the age, is the most incisive and rational one arrived at by the nineteenth century. It is complicated reading, but it may serve as a correction to the notion that genius is characterized by careless thinking.*

It has often been asked, What is Poetry? And many and various are the answers which have been returned. The vulgarest of all — one with which no person possessed of the faculties to which poetry addresses itself can ever have been satisfied — is that which confounds poetry with metrical composition; yet to this wretched mockery of a definition many have been led back by the failure of all their attempts to find any other that would distinguish what they have been accustomed to call poetry from much which they have known only under other names. 1

That, however, the word "poetry" imports something quite peculiar in its nature; something which may exist in what is called prose as well as in verse; something which does not even require the instrument of words, but can speak through the other audible symbols called musical sounds, and even through the visible ones which are the language of sculpture, painting, and architecture, — all this, we believe, is and must be felt, though perhaps indistinctly, by all upon whom poetry in any of its shapes produces any impression beyond that of tickling the ear. The distinction between poetry and what is not poetry, whether explained or not, is felt to be fundamental; and, where every one feels a difference, a difference there must be. All other appearances may be 2 fallacious; but the appearance of a difference is a real difference. Appearances too, like other things, must have a cause; and that which can cause any thing, even an illusion, must be a reality. And hence, while a half-philosophy disdains the classifications and distinctions indicated by popular language, philosophy carried to its highest point frames new ones, but rarely sets aside the old, content with correcting and regularizing them. It cuts fresh channels for thought, but does not fill up such as it finds ready-made: it traces, on the contrary, more deeply, broadly, and distinctly, those into which the current has spontaneously flowed.

Let us then attempt, in the way of modest inquiry, not to coerce and confine Nature within the bounds of an arbitrary definition, but rather to find the boundaries which she herself has set, and erect a barrier round them; not calling mankind to account for having misapplied the word "poetry," but attempting to clear up the conception which they already attach to it, and to bring forward as a distinct principle that which, as a vague feeling, has really guided them in their employment of the term. 3

The object of poetry is confessedly to act upon the emotions; — and therein is poetry sufficiently distinguished from what Wordsworth affirms to be its logical opposite; namely, not prose, but matter of fact, or science. The one addresses itself to the belief; the other, to the feelings. The one does its work by convincing or persuading; the other, by moving. The one acts by presenting a proposition to the understanding; the other, by offering interesting objects of contemplation to the sensibilities. 4

This, however, leaves us very far from a definition of poetry. This distinguishes it from one thing; but we are bound to distinguish it from every thing. To bring thoughts or images before the mind, for the purpose of acting upon the emotions, does not belong to poetry alone. It is equally the province (for example) of the novelist: and yet the faculty of the poet and that of the novelist are as distinct as any other two faculties; as the faculties of the novelist and of the orator, or of the poet and the metaphysician. The two characters may be united, as characters the most disparate may; but they have no natural connection. 5

Many of the greatest poems are in the form of fictitious narratives; and, in almost all good serious fictions, there is true poetry. But there is a radical distinction between the interest felt in a story as such, and the interest excited by poetry; for the one is derived from incident, the other from the representation of feeling. In one, the source of the emotion excited is the exhibition of a state or states of human sensibility; in the other, of a series of states of mere outward circumstances. Now, all minds are capable of being affected more or less by representations 6

357

of the latter kind, and all, or almost all, by those of the former; yet the two sources of interest correspond to two distinct and (as respects their greatest development) mutually exclusive characters of mind.

At what age is the passion for a story, for almost any kind of story, merely as a story, the most intense? In childhood. But that also is the age at which poetry, even of the simplest description, is least relished and least understood; because the feelings with which it is especially conversant are yet undeveloped, and, not having been even in the slightest degree experienced, cannot be sympathized with. In what stage of the progress of society, again, is story-telling most valued, and the story-teller in greatest request and honor? In a rude state like that of the Tartars and Arabs at this day, and of almost all nations in the earliest ages. But, in this state of society, there is little poetry except ballads, which are mostly narrative, — that is, essentially stories, — and derive their principal interest from the incidents. Considered as poetry, they are of the lowest and most elementary kind: the feelings depicted, or rather indicated, are the simplest our nature has; such joys and griefs as the immediate pressure of some outward event excites in rude minds, which live wholly immersed in outward things, and have never, either from choice or a force they could not resist, turned themselves to the contemplation of the world within. Passing now from childhood, and from the childhood of society, to the grown-up men and women of this most grown-up and unchildlike age, the minds and hearts of greatest depth and elevation are commonly those which take greatest delight in poetry: the shallowest and emptiest, on the contrary, are, at all events, not those least addicted to novel-reading. This accords, too, with all analogous experience of human nature. The sort of persons whom not merely in books, but in their lives, we find perpetually engaged in hunting for excitement from without, are invariably those who do not possess, either in the vigor of their intellectual powers or in the depth of their sensibilities, that which would enable them to find ample excitement nearer home. The most idle and frivolous persons take a natural delight in fictitious narrative: the excitement it affords is of the kind which comes from without. Such persons are rarely lovers of poetry, though they may fancy themselves so because they relish novels in verse. But poetry, which is the delineation of the deeper and more secret workings of human emotion, is interesting only to those to whom it recalls what they have felt, or whose imagination it stirs up to conceive what they could feel, or what they might have been able to feel, had their outward circumstances been different.

Poetry, when it is really such, is truth; and fiction also, if it is good for any thing, is truth: but they are different truths. The truth of poetry is to paint the human soul truly: the truth of fiction is to give a true picture

358

of life. The two kinds of knowledge are different, and come by different ways, — come mostly to different persons. Great poets are often proverbially ignorant of life. What they know has come by observation of themselves: they have found within them one highly delicate and sensitive specimen of human nature, on which the laws of emotion are written in large characters, such as can be read off without much study. Other knowledge of mankind, such as comes to men of the world by outward experience, is not indispensable to them as poets: but, to the novelist, such knowledge is all in all; he has to describe outward things, not the inward man; actions and events, not feelings; and it will not do for him to be numbered among those, who, as Madame Roland said of Brissot, know man, but not *men.*

All this is no bar to the possibility of combining both elements, poetry and narrative or incident, in the same work, and calling it either a novel or a poem; but so may red and white combine on the same human features or on the same canvas. There is one order of composition which requires the union of poetry and incident, each in its highest kind, — the dramatic. Even there, the two elements are perfectly distinguishable, and may exist of unequal quality and in the most various proportion. The incidents of a dramatic poem may be scanty and ineffective, though the delineation of passion and character may be of the highest order, as in Goethe's admirable "Torquato Tasso"; or, again, the story as a mere story may be well got up for effect, as is the case with some of the most trashy productions of the Minerva press: it may even be, what those are not, a coherent and probable series of events, though there be scarcely a feeling exhibited which is not represented falsely, or in a manner absolutely commonplace. The combination of the two excellences is what renders Shakespeare so generally acceptable, — each sort of readers finding in him what is suitable to their faculties. To the many, he is great as a story-teller; to the few, as a poet. 9

In limiting poetry to the delineation of states of feeling, and denying the name where nothing is delineated but outward objects, we may be thought to have done what we promised to avoid, — to have not found, but made, a definition in opposition to the usage of language, since it is established by common consent that there is a poetry called descriptive. We deny the charge. Description is not poetry because there is descriptive poetry, no more than science is poetry because there is such a thing as a didactic poem. But an object which admits of being described, or a truth which may fill a place in a scientific treatise, may also furnish an occasion for the generation of poetry, which we thereupon choose to call descriptive or didactic. The poetry is not in the object itself, nor in the scientific truth itself, but in the state of mind in which the one and the other may be contemplated. The mere delinea- 10 tion of the dimensions and colors of external objects is not poetry, no more than a geometrical ground-plan of St. Peter's or Westminister Abbey is painting. Descriptive poetry consists, no doubt, in description, but in description of things as they appear, not as they are; and it paints them, not in their bare and natural lineaments, but seen through the medium and arrayed in the colors of the imagination set in action by the feelings. If a poet describes a lion, he does not describe him as a naturalist would, nor even as a traveller would, who was intent upon stating the truth, the whole truth, and nothing but the truth. He describes him by imagery, that is, by suggesting the most striking likenesses and contrasts which might occur to a mind contemplating a lion, in the state of awe, wonder, or terror, which the spectacle naturally excites, or is, on the occasion, supposed to excite. Now, this is describing the lion professedly, but the state of excitement of the spectator really. The lion may be described falsely or with exaggeration, and the poetry be all the better: but, if the human emotion be not painted with scrupulous truth, the poetry is bad poetry; i.e., is not poetry at all, but a failure.

Thus far, our progress towards a clear view of the essentials of poetry 11 has brought us very close to the last two attempts at a definition of poetry which we happen to have seen in print, both of them by poets, and men of genius. The one is by Ebenezer Elliott, the author of "Corn-law Rhymes," and other poems of still greater merit. "Poetry," says he, "is impassioned truth." The other is by a writer in "Blackwood's Magazine," and comes, we think, still nearer the mark. He defines poetry, "man's thoughts tinged by his feelings." There is in either definition a near approximation to what we are in search of. Every truth which a human being can enunciate, every thought, even every outward impression, which can enter into his consciousness, may become poetry, when shown through any impassioned medium; when invested with the coloring of joy, or grief, or pity, or affection, or admiration, or reverence, or awe, or even hatred or terror; and, unless so colored, nothing, be it as interesting as it may, is poetry. But both these definitions fail to discriminate between poetry and eloquence. Eloquence, as well as poetry, is impassioned truth; eloquence, as well as poetry, is thoughts colored by the feelings. Yet common apprehension and philosophic criticism alike recognize a distinction between the two: there is much that every one would call eloquence, which no one would think of classing as poetry. A question will sometimes arise, whether some particular author is a poet; and those who maintain the negative commonly allow, that, though not a poet, he is a highly eloquent writer. The distinction between poetry and eloquence appears to us to be equally fundamental with the distinction between poetry and narrative, or between poetry and description, while it is still farther from having been satisfactorily cleared up than either of the others.

Poetry and eloquence are both alike the expression or utterance of   12
feeling: but, if we may be excused the antithesis, we should say that eloquence is *heard;* poetry is *over*heard. Eloquence supposes an audience. The peculiarity of poetry appears to us to lie in the poet's utter unconsciousness of a listener. Poetry is feeling confessing itself to itself in moments of solitude, and embodying itself in symbols which are the nearest possible representation of the feeling in the exact shape in which it exists in the poet's mind. Eloquence is feeling pouring itself out to other minds, courting their sympathy, or endeavoring to influence their belief, or move them to passion or to action.

All poetry is of the nature of soliloquy. It may be said that poetry   13
which is printed on hot-pressed paper, and sold at a bookseller's shop, is a soliloquy in full dress and on the stage. It is so; but there is nothing absurd in the idea of such a mode of soliloquizing. What we have said to ourselves we may tell to others afterwards; what we have said or done in solitude we may voluntarily reproduce when we know that other eyes are upon us. But no trace of consciousness that any eyes are upon us must be visible in the work itself. The actor knows that there is an audience present; but, if he act as though he knew it, he acts ill. A poet may write poetry, not only with the intention of printing it, but for the express purpose of being paid for it. That it should *be* poetry, being written under such influences, is less probable, not, however, impossible; but no otherwise possible than if he can succeed in excluding from his work every vestige of such lookings-forth into the outward and every-day world, and can express his emotions exactly as he has felt them in solitude, or as he is conscious that he should feel them, though they were to remain for ever unuttered, or (at the lowest) as he knows that others feel them in similar circumstances of solitude. But when he turns round, and addresses himself to another person; when the act of utterance is not itself the end, but a means to an end, — viz., by the feelings he himself expresses, to work upon the feelings, or upon the belief or the will of another; when the expression of his emotions, or of his thoughts tinged by his emotions, is tinged also by that purpose, by that desire of making an impression upon another mind, — then it ceases to be poetry, and becomes eloquence.

Poetry, accordingly, is the natural fruit of solitude and meditation;   14
eloquence, of intercourse with the world. The persons who have most feeling of their own, if intellectual culture has given them a language in which to express it, have the highest faculty of poetry: those who best understand the feelings of others are the most eloquent. The persons

and the nations who commonly excel in poetry are those whose character and tastes render them least dependent upon the applause or sympathy or concurrence of the world in general. Those to whom that applause, that sympathy, that concurrence, are most necessary, generally excel most in eloquence. And hence, perhaps, the French, who are the least poetical of all great and intellectual nations, are among the most eloquent; the French also being the most sociable, the vainest, and the least self-dependent.

If the above be, as we believe, the true theory of the distinction   15
commonly admitted between eloquence and poetry, or even though it be not so, yet if, as we cannot doubt, the distinction above stated be a real *bonâ-fide* distinction, it will be found to hold, not merely in the language of words, but in all other language, and to intersect the whole domain of art.

Take, for example, music. We shall find in that art, so peculiarly the   16
expression of passion, two perfectly distinct styles, — one of which may be called the poetry, the other the oratory, of music. This difference, being seized, would put an end to much musical sectarianism. There has been much contention whether the music of the modern Italian school, that of Rossini and his successors, be impassioned or not. Without doubt, the passion it expresses is not the musing, meditative tenderness or pathos or grief of Mozart or Beethoven; yet it is passion, but garrulous passion, — the passion which pours itself into other ears, and therein the better calculated for dramatic effect, having a natural adaptation for dialogue. Mozart also is great in musical oratory; but his most touching compositions are in the opposite style, — that of soliloquy. Who can imagine "Dove sono" *heard*? We imagine it *over*heard.

Purely pathetic music commonly partakes of soliloquy. The soul is   17
absorbed in its distress; and, though there may be bystanders, it is not thinking of them. When the mind is looking within, and not without, its state does not often or rapidly vary; and hence the even, uninterrupted flow, approaching almost to monotony, which a good reader or a good singer will give to words or music of a pensive or melancholy cast. But grief, taking the form of a prayer or of a complaint, becomes oratorical: no longer low and even and subdued, it assumes a more emphatic rhythm, a more rapidly returning accent; instead of a few slow, equal notes, following one after another at regular intervals, it crowds note upon note, and often assumes a hurry and bustle like joy. Those who are familiar with some of the best of Rossini's serious compositions, such as the air "Tu che i miseri conforti," in the opera of "Tancredi," or the duet "Ebben per mia memoria," in "La Grazza Ladra," will at once understand and feel our meaning. Both are highly tragic and passionate: the passion of both is that of oratory, not poetry. The

like may be said of that most moving invocation in Beethoven's "Fidelio," —

> Komm, Hoffnung, lass das letzte Stern
> Der Müde nicht erbleichen, —
> [Come, Hope, let not the last star of
> sorrow turn pale.]

in which Madame Schröder Devrient exhibited such consummate powers of pathetic expression. How different from Winter's beautiful "Paga fui," the very soul of melancholy exhaling itself in solitude! fuller of meaning, and therefore more profoundly poetical, than the words for which it was composed; for it seems to express, not simple melancholy, but the melancholy of remorse.

If from vocal music we now pass to instrumental, we may have a 18 specimen of musical oratory in any fine military symphony or march; while the poetry of music seems to have attained its consummation in Beethoven's "Overture to Egmont," so wonderful in its mixed expression of grandeur and melancholy.

In the arts which speak to the eye, the same distinctions will be found 19 to hold, not only between poetry and oratory, but between poetry, oratory, narrative, and simple imitation or description.

Pure description is exemplified in a mere portrait or a mere land- 20 scape, — productions of art, it is true, but of the mechanical rather than of the fine arts; being works of simple imitation, not creation. We say, a mere portrait or a mere landscape; because it is possible for a portrait or a landscape, without ceasing to be such, to be also a picture, like Turner's landscapes, and the great portraits by Titian or Vandyke.

Whatever in painting or sculpture expresses human feeling, — or 21 character, which is only a certain state of feeling grown habitual, — may be called, according to circumstances, the poetry or the eloquence of the painter's or the sculptor's art: the poetry, if the feeling declares itself by such signs as escape from us when we are unconscious of being seen; the oratory, if the signs are those we use for the purpose of voluntary communication.

The narrative style answers to what is called historical painting, 22 which it is the fashion among connoisseurs to treat as the climax of the pictorial art. That it is the most difficult branch of the art, we do not doubt, because, in its perfection, it includes the perfection of all the other branches; as, in like manner, an epic poem, though, in so far as it is epic (i.e., narrative), it is not poetry at all, is yet esteemed the greatest effort of poetic genius, because there is no kind whatever of poetry which may not appropriately find a place in it. But an historical picture as such, that is, as the representation of an incident, must necessarily, as it seems to us, be poor and ineffective. The narrative powers of painting are extremely limited. Scarcely any picture, scarcely even any series of pictures, tells its own story without the aid of an interpreter. But it is the single figures, which, to us, are the great charm even of an historical picture. It is in these that the power of the art is really seen. In the attempt to narrate, visible and permanent signs are too far behind the fugitive audible ones, which follow so fast one after another; while the faces and figures in a narrative picture, even though they be Titian's, stand still. Who would not prefer one "Virgin and Child" of Raphael to all the pictures which Rubens, with his fat, frouzy Dutch Venuses, ever painted? — though Rubens, besides excelling almost every one in his mastery over the mechanical parts of his art, often shows real genius in *grouping* his figures, the peculiar problem of historical painting. But then, who, except a mere student of drawing and coloring, ever cared to look twice at any of the figures themselves? The power of painting lies in poetry, of which Rubens had not the slightest tincture, — not in narrative, wherein he might have excelled.

The single figures, however, in an historical picture, are rather the 23 eloquence of painting than the poetry. They mostly (unless they are quite out of place in the picture) express the feelings of one person as modified by the presence of others. Accordingly, the minds whose bent leads them rather to eloquence than to poetry rush to historical painting. The French painters, for instance, seldom attempt, because they could make nothing of, single heads, like those glorious ones of the Italian masters with which they might feed themselves day after day in their own Louvre. They must all be historical; and they are, almost to a man, attitudinizers. If we wished to give any young artist the most impressive warning our imagination could devise against that kind of vice in the pictorial which corresponds to rant in the histrionic art, we would advise him to walk once up and once down the gallery of the Luxembourg. Every figure in French painting or statuary seems to be showing itself off before spectators. They are not poetical, but in the worst style of corrupted eloquence.

SUBJECT

1. Would you agree that the appreciation of poetry requires greater intellectual powers than the appreciation of novels?

2. "The lion may be described falsely or with exaggeration, and the poetry be all the better; but, if the human emotion be not painted with scrupulous truth, the poetry is bad poetry." Would you agree with the first half of the statement? Keats, in his sonnet, "On First Looking into Chapman's Homer," credits Cortez with the discovery of the Pacific.

Should the poet be excused for such an error in fact, or does it spoil the poem?

3.   Mill makes a precise distinction between external fact and "feeling." Is such a clear-cut distinction realistic? Could an artist really paint a landscape without including something of his feelings about the landscape?

4.   On what grounds does Mill dislike French painting?

5.   Does Mill's discussion of "the poetry of music" and "the poetry of painting" destroy the usefulness of his definition of poetry? Would you say that he is really trying to define all art rather than one type, poetry? Would the definition of poetry be satisfactory as a definition of art?

STRUCTURE

1.   Comment on the style of this essay. Is precision necessarily synonymous with clarity? Mill studied logic extensively and wrote a famous textbook on it; does his logical approach aid or hinder his definition of art?

2.   Mill's chief rhetorical techniques in this essay are comparison and contrast. From what does he wish to distinguish poetry?

3.   What differences does Mill point out between poetry and fiction? Are these real and observable differences? Is Mill being fair to the novelist?

4.   What differences does Mill point out between poetry and "eloquence"? Are the distinctions clear? How might Mill have given this section greater clarity?

ARS POETICA

Archibald MacLeish

Archibald MacLeish was born in 1892 in Illinois. He began his career as a lawyer, but went to France in 1923 to become a poet. He has since taught at Cambridge and at Harvard, was librarian at the Library of Congress, and was the first chairman of the American delegation to UNESCO. Although he has won Pulitzer prizes in both poetry and drama, his most influential work may be a book on political liberty, Freedom Is the Right to Choose *(1951).*

A poem should be palpable and mute   1
As a globed fruit,

Dumb
As old medallions to the thumb,

Silent as the sleeve-worn stone   5
Of casement ledges where the moss has grown —

A poem should be wordless
As the flight of birds.

A poem should be motionless in time
As the moon climbs,   10

Leaving, as the moon releases
Twig by twig the night-entangled trees,

Leaving, as the moon behind the winter leaves,
Memory by memory the mind —

A poem should be motionless in time   15
As the moon climbs.

A poem should be equal to:
Not true.

From *Collected Poems of Archibald MacLeish 1917–1952*. Reprinted by permission of the publisher, Houghton Mifflin Company.

For all the history of grief
An empty doorway and a maple leaf.   20

For love
The leaning grasses and two lights above the sea —

A poem should not mean
But be.

SUBJECT

1. A poem is composed of words. How, then, can it be "wordless"? Might MacLeish be implying the same meaning which Mill stated directly, that poetry deals not with facts but with reactions to facts?

2. In the second part, MacLeish says that a poem "should be motionless in time as the moon climbs." But the moon is not motionless. Does this contradiction in fact hurt the poem? Does a person who "experiences" the moon see it as moving?

3. Consider these two explanations of the second part: First, a poem should be universal and moving, yet valid for all time. Second, a poem should have movement, but should proceed from image to image, so that the mind stops to contemplate one image, then goes on to the next instead of "moving" steadily through the poem. Which, if either, of these interpretations do you think MacLeish intended?

4. Can an "empty doorway" symbolize "all the history of grief"? Is a poet obligated to universalize his private experience? Doesn't this statement contradict the final statement that a "poem should not mean but be"?

5. Consider the last statement. To say that a poem "should not mean" is to make it "mean" something. That this poem does say something is so obvious that MacLeish could hardly have contradicted himself inadvertently. What, then, might he mean by his final lines? Might he be implying that a poem means much more than a mere prose paraphrase of it — or to put it another way, that the totality of a poem is an indivisible entity meaning much more than an explanation of its parts?

STRUCTURE

1. Rather than proceeding by logical statements as does Mill, MacLeish suggests meanings; he wants the reader to feel what a poem is. Look at the similes in the first part. What overtones of meaning (connotations) are suggested by "globed fruit," "old medallions," "sleeve-worn stone" and "the flight of birds"?

367

2. What does the poet mean when he says that a poem is not true but "equal to"? Recall Mill's distinction between poetry and science.

3. Read the poem again in its entirety. Is it an adequate definition of poetry? How does it compare with Mill's? (It might be observed that "Ars Poetica" certainly satisfies the requirement that the abstract concept being defined be put back into concrete instances.)

4. If poetry really does contain elements which prose cannot reach, could you say that the best definition of poetry *must* be a poem?

TEN DEFINITIONS
OF POETRY

Carl Sandburg

Carl Sandburg (1878–1967), Illinois poet, folksinger, and biographer of Abraham Lincoln, has always been more admired by the public than by the critics. And that is as he would wish, for he said of himself, "I am the people — the mob — the crowd — the mass." Before his death, the former hobo had won almost every prize a writer can receive. In Good Morning, America *(1928), he wrote thirty-eight definitions of poetry, of which the following ten are typical.*

1. Poetry is a projection across silence of cadences arranged to break that silence with definite intentions of echoes, syllables, wave lengths.

2. Poetry is a journal of a sea animal living on land, wanting to fly the air.

3. Poetry is a series of explanations of life, fading off into horizons too swift for explanations.

4. Poetry is a search for syllables to shoot at barriers of the unknown and the unknowable.

5. Poetry is a theorem of a yellow-silk handkerchief knotted with riddles, sealed in a balloon tied to the tail of a kite flying in a white wind against a blue sky in spring.

6. Poetry is the silence and speech between a wet struggling root of a flower and a sunlit blossom of that flower.

7. Poetry is the harnessing of the paradox of earth cradling life and then entombing it.

8. Poetry is a phantom script telling how rainbows are made and why they go away.

9. Poetry is the synthesis of hyacinths and biscuits.

10. Poetry is the opening and closing of a door, leaving those who look through to guess about what is seen during a moment.

SUBJECT

1. What are the "echoes" and "wave lengths" referred to in definition 1?

2. In 2, what is the "sea animal"? Does Sandburg mean to imply that the poet is spokesman for the species?

3. Shelley called poets "the unacknowledged legislators of the world"; do you think Sandburg would endorse this statement?

4. Whether or not they "define" poetry for the reader, most of Sandburg's images can at least be visualized. Are there any that cannot? If so, do they injure the poem?

5. Which of the comparisons tells you most about poetry? Which tells you least? Is there any relationship between the effectiveness of an image and its quality (simple or complex, vivid or vague, specific or general)?

STRUCTURE

1. Do you think these stanzas are intended to be ten separate and self-sufficient definitions, or should they be taken as various facets of one definition?

2. The first definition suggests four ingredients with which the poet is primarily concerned: cadences, echoes, syllables, wave lengths. Are there other important characteristics Sandburg has omitted?

3. How many of the definitions are concerned with what the poet is attempting to do, and how many with the poetry-reader's experience of the poem? Should they all be from the same point of view?

4.   What is the primary method used by Sandburg in developing his definitions? What advantage accrues to using the same method more than once?

5.   Are Sandburg's metaphors comparisons or analogies? Can you suggest a reason for this?

6.   Examine the use of repeated sounds in definition 9. Does the line itself achieve a "synthesis of hyacinths and biscuits"?

ART IS NOT MADE
TO BE UNDERSTOOD

Pablo Picasso

Pablo Picasso, the most successful artist (perhaps the greatest) of the 20th century, was born in Spain in 1881. His fame began after he moved to Paris in 1903, and has grown until today his signature alone has sold for several thousand dollars. Picasso, always an experimenter, was the beginner or a leader of many of the important art movements during this century — post-impressionism, cubism, surrealism, and abstract expressionism. Although known mainly as a painter, Picasso has created masterpieces in almost every medium, from pencil sketches to ceramic plates. In fairness to Picasso, it should be noted that the extract printed here is from an interview with M. Zervos. Consequently, it cannot be expected to have the close organization and coherence of a written essay on painting. Perhaps it demonstrates the fact that definition of an abstract concept cannot be accomplished without careful thought and planning — not even by Picasso himself.

A painter paints to unload himself of feelings and visions. People seize on painting to cover up their nakedness. They get what they can wherever they can. In the end I don't believe they get anything at all. They've simply cut a coat to the measure of their own ignorance. They make everything, from God to a picture, in their own image. That is why the picture-hook is the ruination of a painting — a painting which has always a certain significance, at least as much as the man who did it. As soon as it is bought and hung on a wall, it takes on quite a different kind of significance, and the painting is done for. 1

Academic training in beauty is a sham. We have been deceived, but so well deceived that we can scarcely get back even a shadow of the truth. The beauties of the Parthenon, Venuses, Nymphs, Narcissuses, are so many lies. Art is not the application of a canon of beauty but what the instinct and the brain can conceive beyond any canon. When we love a woman we don't start measuring her limbs. We love with our desires — although everything has been done to try and apply a canon even to love. The Parthenon is really only a farmyard over which 2

Reprinted by permission of the publisher from "Conversation avec Picasso," *Cahiers d'Art,* X:10 (1935).

someone put a roof; colonnades and sculptures were added because there were people in Athens who happened to be working, and wanted to express themselves. It's not what the artist *does* that counts, but what he *is*. Cézanne would never have interested me a bit if he had lived and thought like Jacques Emile Blanche, even if the apple he painted had been ten times as beautiful. What forces our interest is Cézanne's anxiety — that's Cézanne's lesson; the torments of Van Gogh — that is the actual drama of the man. The rest is a sham.

Everyone wants to understand art. Why not try to understand the   3
song of a bird? Why does one love the night, flowers, everything around one, without trying to understand them? But in the case of a painting people have to *understand*. If only they would realize above all that an artist works of necessity, that he himself is only a trifling bit of the world, and that no more importance should be attached to him than to plenty of other things which please us in the world, though we can't explain them. People who try to explain pictures are usually barking up the wrong tree. Gertrude Stein joyfully announced to me the other day that she had at last understood what my picture of the three musicians was meant to be. It was a still life!

How can you expect an onlooker to live a picture of mine as I lived   4
it? A picture comes to me from miles away: who is to say from how far away I sensed it, saw it, painted it; and yet the next day I can't see what I've done myself. How can anyone enter into my dreams, my instincts, my desires, my thoughts, which have taken a long time to mature and to come out into the daylight, and above all grasp from them what I have been about — perhaps against my own will?

SUBJECT

1. What objection does Picasso have to people who buy and hang pictures? Since the artist depends on these people for his livelihood, might Picasso simply be expressing a natural resentment?

2. In what sense is "academic training in beauty . . . a sham"? Would Picasso want to eliminate courses in art and music appreciation? Would he advocate *no* training in beauty?

3. Examine the statements concerning the relative importance of painter and painting. Is there a contradiction among these statements?

4. Picasso objects to people who try to understand art. What does he mean by "understand"? Is there more than one way to understand art?

5. Picasso implies that people cannot presume to know "what I have been about — perhaps against my own will." Does he mean that some of his paintings are deliberately obscure? Is an artist justified

in resenting people who delve into his life — perhaps even try to psychoanalyze him — through his paintings? Or should he be more willing to accept "the curse of fame"?

6.   Many artists admit that they have little respect for critics but great need of them. Does Picasso appear to feel this way? (Christian Zervos, who recorded this interview, was a critic and editor of an art magazine.) Do critics have a useful function even though artists themselves may object to that function?

STRUCTURE

1.   Picasso's explanation of art is not strictly "logical" in its approach. Is it thereby a failure as definition? Is the connotative definition clearer than the denotative meaning?

2.   Is the analogy between painting and love helpful? (Remember that analogy tries to clarify a point, not to prove it.) Are love and art comparable?

3.   How does Picasso support his abstract definition, "Art is not the application of a canon of beauty but what the instinct and the brain can conceive beyond any canon"?

4.   Picasso's complaint in the closing paragraph is about precisely the same problem pointed out in the introduction to this section regarding the difficulty of defining abstractions. We have suggested ways of getting around the difficulty; has Picasso himself managed, in some degree, to accomplish what he says can't be done?

HOW WE LISTEN

Aaron Copland

*Aaron Copland, born in Brooklyn in 1900, is probably the most famous
of American classical composers. Best known for tone poems such as*
Billy the Kid *and* Appalachian Spring, *he has also done outstanding
work on musical scores for films — among them* The Red Pony, of
Mice and Men, Our Town, *and* The Heiress *(for which he won an
Oscar). He has won almost every award given to composers, including
the Freedom Medal in 1964. The essay printed here is a chapter from
Copland's book,* What to Listen for in Music *(rev. 1957).*

We all listen to music according to our separate capacities. But, for the   1
sake of analysis, the whole listening process may become clearer if we
break it up into its component parts, so to speak. In a certain sense we
all listen to music on three separate planes. For lack of a better terminology, one might name these: (1) the sensuous plane, (2) the expressive plane, (3) the sheerly musical plane. The only advantage to be
gained from mechanically splitting up the listening process into these
hypothetical planes is the clearer view to be had of the way in which
we listen.

The simplest way of listening to music is to listen for the sheer plea-   2
sure of the musical sound itself. That is the sensuous plane. It is the
plane on which we hear music without thinking, without considering
it in any way. One turns on the radio while doing something else and
absent-mindedly bathes in the sound. A kind of brainless but attractive
state of mind is engendered by the mere sound appeal of the music.

You may be sitting in a room reading this book. Imagine one note   3
struck on the piano. Immediately that one note is enough to change the
atmosphere of the room — proving that the sound element in music
is a powerful and mysterious agent, which it would be foolish to deride
or belittle.

The surprising thing is that many people who consider themselves   4
qualified music lovers abuse that plane in listening. They go to concerts
in order to lose themselves. They use music as a consolation or an
escape. They enter an ideal world where one doesn't have to think of

the realities of everyday life. Of course they aren't thinking about the music either. Music allows them to leave it, and they go off to a place to dream, dreaming because of and apropos of the music yet never quite listening to it.

Yes, the sound appeal of music is a potent and primitive force, but you must not allow it to usurp a disproportionate share of your interest. The sensuous plane is an important one in music, a very important one, but it does not constitute the whole story. 5

There is no need to digress further on the sensuous plane. Its appeal to every normal human being is self-evident. There is, however, such a thing as becoming more sensitive to the different kinds of sound stuff as used by various composers. For all composers do not use that sound stuff in the same way. Don't get the idea that the value of music is commensurate with its sensuous appeal or that the loveliest sounding music is made by the greatest composer. If that were so, Ravel would be a greater creator than Beethoven. The point is that the sound element varies with each composer, that his usage of sound forms an integral part of his style and must be taken into account when listening. The reader can see, therefore, that a more conscious approach is valuable even on this primary plane of music listening. 6

The second plane on which music exists is what I have called the expressive one. Here, immediately, we tread on controversial ground. Composers have a way of shying away from any discussion of music's expressive side. Did not Stravinsky himself proclaim that his music was an "object," a "thing," with a life of its own, and with no other meaning than its own purely musical existence? This intransigent attitude of Stravinsky's may be due to the fact that so many people have tried to read different meanings into so many pieces. Heaven knows it is difficult enough to say precisely what it is that a piece of music means, to say it definitely, to say it finally so that everyone is satisfied with your explanation. But that should not lead one to the other extreme of denying to music the right to be "expressive." 7

My own belief is that all music has an expressive power, some more and some less, but that all music has a certain meaning behind the notes and that that meaning behind the notes constitutes, after all, what the piece is saying, what the piece is about. This whole problem can be stated quite simply by asking, "Is there a meaning to music?" My answer to that would be, "Yes." And "Can you state in so many words what the meaning is?" My answer to that would be, "No." Therein lies the difficulty. 8

Simple-minded souls will never be satisfied with the answer to the second of these questions. They always want music to have a meaning, and the more concrete it is the better they like it. The more the music 9 reminds them of a train, a storm, a funeral, or any other familiar conception the more expressive it appears to be to them. This popular idea of music's meaning — stimulated and abetted by the usual run of musical commentator — should be discouraged wherever and whenever it is met. One timid lady once confessed to me that she suspected something seriously lacking in her appreciation of music because of her inability to connect it with anything definite. That is getting the whole thing backward, of course.

Still, the question remains, How close should the intelligent music 10 lover wish to come to pinning a definite meaning to any particular work? No closer than a general concept, I should say. Music expresses, at different moments, serenity or exuberance, regret or triumph, fury or delight. It expresses each of these moods, and many others, in a numberless variety of subtle shadings and differences. It may even express a state of meaning for which there exists no adequate word in any language. In that case, musicians often like to say that it has only a purely musical meaning. They sometimes go farther and say that *all* music has only a purely musical meaning. What they really mean is that no appropriate word can be found to express the music's meaning and that, even if it could, they do not feel the need of finding it.

But whatever the professional musician may hold, most musical nov- 11 ices still search for specific words with which to pin down their musical reactions. That is why they always find Tschaikovsky easier to "understand" than Beethoven. In the first place, it is easier to pin a meaning-word on a Tschaikovsky piece than on a Beethoven one. Much easier. Moreover, with the Russian composer, every time you come back to a piece of his it almost always says the same thing to you, whereas with Beethoven it is often quite difficult to put your finger right on what he is saying. And any musician will tell you that that is why Beethoven is the greater composer. Because music which always says the same thing to you will necessarily soon become dull music, but music whose meaning is slightly different with each hearing has a greater chance of remaining alive.

Listen, if you can, to the forty-eight fugue themes of Bach's *Well* 12 *Tempered Clavichord.* Listen to each theme, one after another. You will soon realize that each theme mirrors a different world of feeling. You will also soon realize that the more beautiful a theme seems to you the harder it is to find any word that will describe it to your complete satisfaction. Yes, you will certainly know whether it is a gay theme or a sad one. You will be able, in other words, in your own mind, to draw a frame of emotional feeling around your theme. Now study the sad one a little closer. Try to pin down the exact quality of its sadness. Is it pessimistically sad or resignedly sad; is it fatefully sad or smilingly sad?

Let us suppose that you are fortunate and can describe to your own 13
satisfaction in so many words the exact meaning of your chosen theme.
There is still no guarantee that anyone else will be satisfied. Nor need
they be. The important thing is that each one feel for himself the
specific expressive quality of a theme or, similarly, an entire piece of
music. And if it is a great work of art, don't expect it to mean exactly
the same thing to you each time you return to it.

Themes or pieces need not express only one emotion, of course. Take 14
such a theme as the first main one of the *Ninth Symphony,* for example.
It is clearly made up of different elements. It does not say only one
thing. Yet anyone hearing it immediately gets a feeling of strength, a
feeling of power. It isn't a power that comes simply because the theme
is played loudly. It is a power inherent in the theme itself. The extraordinary strength and vigor of the theme results in the listener's receiving
an impression that a forceful statement has been made. But one should
never try to boil it down to "the fateful hammer of life," etc. That is
where the trouble begins. The musician, in his exasperation, says it
means nothing but the notes themselves, whereas the nonprofessional
is only too anxious to hang on to any explanation that gives him the
illusion of getting closer to the music's meaning.

Now, perhaps, the reader will know better what I mean when I say 15
that music does have an expressive meaning but that we cannot say in
so many words what that meaning is.

The third plane on which music exists is the sheerly musical plane. 16
Besides the pleasurable sound of music and the expressive feeling that
it gives off, music does exist in terms of the notes themselves and of their
manipulation. Most listeners are not sufficiently conscious of this third
plane. It will be largely the business of this book to make them more
aware of music on this plane.

Professional musicians, on the other hand, are, if anything, too con- 17
scious of the mere notes themselves. They often fall into the error of
becoming so engrossed with their arpeggios and staccatos that they
forget the deeper aspects of the music they are performing. But from
the layman's standpoint, it is not so much a matter of getting over bad
habits on the sheerly musical plane as of increasing one's awareness of
what is going on, in so far as the notes are concerned.

When the man in the street listens to the "notes themselves" with any 18
degree of concentration, he is most likely to make some mention of the
melody. Either he hears a pretty melody or he does not, and he generally lets it go at that. Rhythm is likely to gain his attention next, particularly if it seems exciting. But harmony and tone color are generally
taken for granted, if they are thought of consciously at all. As for music's

378

having a definite form of some kind, that idea seems never to have occurred to him.

It is very important for all of us to become more alive to music on its 19 sheerly musical plane. After all, an actual musical material is being used. The intelligent listener must be prepared to increase his awareness of the musical material and what happens to it. He must hear the melodies, the rhythms, the harmonies, the tone colors in a more conscious fashion. But above all he must, in order to follow the line of the composer's thought, know something of the principles of musical form. Listening to all of these elements is listening on the sheerly musical plane.

Let me repeat that I have split up mechanically the three separate 20 planes on which we listen merely for the sake of greater clarity. Actually, we never listen on one or the other of these planes. What we do is to correlate them — listening in all three ways at the same time. It takes no mental effort, for we do it instinctively.

Perhaps an analogy with what happens to us when we visit the the- 21 ater will make this instinctive correlation clearer. In the theater, you are aware of the actors and actresses, costumes and sets, sounds and movements. All these give one the sense that the theater is a pleasant place to be in. They constitute the sensuous plane in our theatrical reactions.

The expressive plane in the theater would be derived from the feel- 22 ing that you get from what is happening on the stage. You are moved to pity, excitement, or gayety. It is this general feeling, generated aside from the particular words being spoken, a certain emotional something which exists on the stage, that is analogous to the expressive quality in music.

The plot and plot development is equivalent to our sheerly musical 23 plane. The playwright creates and develops a character in just the same way that a composer creates and develops a theme. According to the degree of your awareness of the way in which the artist in either field handles his material will you become a more intelligent listener.

It is easy enough to see that the theatergoer never is conscious of any 24 of these elements separately. He is aware of them all at the same time. The same is true of music listening. We simultaneously and without thinking listen on all three planes.

In a sense, the ideal listener is both inside and outside the music at 25 the same moment, judging it and enjoying it, wishing it would go one way and watching it go another — almost like the composer at the moment he composes it; because in order to write his music, the composer must also be inside and outside his music, carried away by it and yet coldly critical of it. A subjective and objective attitude is implied in both creating and listening to music.

What the reader should strive for, then, is a more *active* kind of listening. Whether you listen to Mozart or Duke Ellington, you can deepen your understanding of music only by being a more conscious and aware listener — not someone who is just listening, but someone who is listening *for* something. 26

SUBJECT

1. Copland characterizes the sensuous plane as listening "for the sheer pleasure of the sound itself." How does this differ from the third or "sheerly musical plane"?

2. Probably the average listener is uncomfortably aware that he ought to appreciate Beethoven more than Ravel or Tschaikovsky, but he takes refuge in the claim that "what's good as far as I'm concerned, is what appeals to me. It's a matter of individual preference." Would you say that this type of person is listening largely on the sensuous plane?

3. If one can appreciate music on the sensuous plane alone, is it necessary that he consider it on the other two planes? Does Copland have any right to claim that "you must not allow [the sensuous plane] to usurp a disproportionate share of your interests"?

4. If, as Copland admits, many composers refuse to recognize the existence of an "expressive plane," why does Copland insist on including it? Does he mean to imply that these composers are mistaken?

5. Copland pokes fun at people who ask that music paint a picture or tell a story, but isn't doing so merely a logical extension of the expressive plane?

STRUCTURE

1. Instead of trying to define music with an abstract statement including such terms as harmony, rhythm, melody, and tone, Copland attempts to explain what music is by analyzing "the way in which we listen." Does he give the reader a better understanding of music by this method? What indications are there that Copland doubts a precise definition of music can be formulated?

2. What is Copland's chief rhetorical method in this chapter? Describe the three "planes" of listening.

3. Can you make a clear statement of what Copland means by the expressive plane? Why does he insist on it and at the same time insist on keeping it vague?

4. Copland supplements his primary method, division, with an analogy near the end of the chapter. Is it a false analogy or a valid one? Does it help to clarify Copland's meaning? (Analogy should always clarify; if it diverts the reader's attention to another subject it has been misused.)

5. Would you say that this essay is an adequate definition of music, a partial definition, or background for a definition? Was it worth writing?

7

WHERE THE
POWER IS

Argument

Argument as an essay form has little in common with the heated discussion which usually terminates a college bull session: it is not a technique for "outshouting" one's opponent in writing. By a devious route through Rome and Medieval Europe, its ancestor was the deliberative oration of ancient Athens. The deliberative oration, as taught by Aristotle and others, was a set form for speeches to be delivered before the Anthenian Senate on matters of public policy and proposed legislation. Its chief feature was its carefully controlled, logical approach: it was intended to convince the senators of the reasonableness of the speaker's position — not, in our common use of the term "argument," to engage in a verbal free-for-all. Although the speaker might feel strongly about his subject, his aim was to stimulate a spirit of free and serious inquiry, not to overwhelm with rhetoric or to provoke anger.

This same honest, objective, and logical approach characterizes the argument as a literary form today. Although a week or two spent studying argument in a composition course is hardly a substitute for a class in logic, the student can learn much by studying the various arguments presented in this section and by writing an argument himself. He will want to watch for careless logic both in the essays and in his own thinking. He should recognize, for instance, that an opinion, no matter how forcefully presented, is still opinion, not fact. In his own argument he should support his opinions with typical and relevant evidence — facts, observations, and reasons. Rather than slinging mud at possible opponents of his beliefs, the student should remember that the purpose of argument is to invite free discussion in the hope of arriving at a workable solution to the problem under consideration. If the writer of an argument firmly believes that his solution is "right," he should by all means argue it forcefully; but he can still have the open-minded attitude which allows him to change his position in the light of new evidence. His job is to search for truth, not obscure it with dogmatism.

Although the original Greek deliberative oration contained some frosting with which we can dispense, a good written argument will contain the four basic ingredients of the old recipe. First, there should be a brief but penetrating introduction to, or analysis of, the problem which needs a solution. This analysis ought to be as objective and honest as the writer can make it; if he starts with a slanted interpretation, the aims of argument are defeated at the outset.

The second ingredient is a clear, concise statement of the author's proposed solution. Normally, this immediately follows the analysis of the problem, and it is sometimes repeated in summary at the end of the argument. Or the writer may prefer to save it for the end, as a logical conclusion to his arguments. If possible it should be concentrated into a sentence or two, so that the reader can readily grasp it in its entirety.

The other parts of a good argument are a refutation of an opponent's arguments, if there are any, and a confirmation of the writer's own position. The refutation may be placed before or after the confirmation, or the two may be intermixed. (The writer should remember, however, to save his strongest point for the last, whether it be proof or disproof.) In refuting an opponent's arguments, one ought to recognize that seldom is one side completely right and the other completely wrong; usually, taking sides should be a matter of weighing merits and demerits, and then deciding which side has more advantages. If the writer has honestly done this he need have no fear of admitting a few merits of the other side or the disadvantages of his own position. In no case should he resort to mere name-calling instead of disproof. ("Of course we don't want a government-operated medical plan — that's socialism!" or "As any fool can plainly see. . . .")

Since a good argument should be mainly positive, the writer will want to concentrate most heavily on his proof. He should be prepared to include as much evidence as his experience and the word limit of his paper will allow. The more specific the evidence, of course, the better. There are two major traps to watch for: insufficient evidence and atypical evidence. As one swallow doesn't make a summer, so one example, no matter how detailed, doesn't justify a generalization. ("Polio vaccine is worthless. I heard of a child who contracted polio after having three shots.") Although the student may wish to concentrate on one piece of evidence, he ought at least to mention others

384

briefly to show that more is available. Secondly, there is always the danger of selecting from a number of available facts certain ones which will only appear to prove the writer's point. Anyone who has watched political debates on television has probably noticed how both opponents cite numerous statistics to "prove" that they are right. Since the purpose of the argument as an essay form is not to win elections at all costs but to deal honestly with a problem, the student will want to avoid either slanting his facts or selecting evidence which does not indicate the general trend of *all* the evidence. This is not always easy to do, but if the writer strives for integrity he will be much less likely to go wrong. Although he may not solve all the world's problems he will at least learn something about logical analysis and the objective search for truth.

POWER

John Cogley

John Cogley has been contributing editor and religion editor for several national journals, including Commonweal. *He has edited two collections of essays on religion,* Religion in America *(1958) and* Natural Law and Modern Society *(1963). He is currently editor of* Center Magazine, *the publication of the Center for the Study of Democratic Institutions. During 1971, the chief concern of* Center Magazine *was the subject of power — who has it, who ought to have it, the relationship of the individual to the state. In the following article, the editor inserted his own views on the subject. Despite its brevity, "Power" is a good example of the form for classic argument.*

"All power to the people!" is a dangerous slogan. It is particularly dangerous for the very persons who are most likely to be heard shouting it on the streets, for usually they represent unpopular minorities. If "the people" were taken in any numerical sense, they would have the most to lose from granting the fulness of power to the majority.

Even if "the people" means only the victims of injustice, there is no indication they would rally in any significant number around the revolutionary banners. It is extremely doubtful that the black community en masse would join the revolutionaries, nor would the majority of students, and the so-called working class would be the last to fall in line. "All power" in any of these hands would be employed to sustain the very system the sloganeers despise, though certain reforms might be expected, different ones from different groups.

Just who are "the people"? If the word is used as it is in the basic documents of the United States ("We the people . . ."), their power has already been claimed and is exercised through law. Not only is it exercised through law, it is modified and controlled by law.

"We the people," eschewing "all power," long ago bound ourselves by solemn compact to tolerate dissent from the reigning opinion, for example; we bound ourselves to provide a fair trial for our enemies; we bound ourselves to accept the decisions of the majority after the votes were counted; we set up a number of safeguards to protect the in-

Reprinted by permission from *The Center Magazine,* vol. IX, no. 1, a publication of the Center for the Study of Democratic Institutions in Santa Barbara, California.

dividual against any government that rules in our name. We turned down "all power" for ourselves because we knew how easily it could be abused.

At a time when "all power to the people!" has become a mindless slogan it may be a good idea to remind ourselves that no one, even the people, should have a claim on the plenitude of power. We are all aware of what omnipotent leaders have done; we are all familiar with the evils wrought by all-powerful elites. Totally empowering the people, supposing one could locate them, would be just as dangerous and perhaps even more so, since though there may be such things as benevolent dictators no one yet has ever discovered a benevolent mob — and a powerful populace uncontrolled by law is all too quickly turned into a mob.

Reinhold Niebuhr's most famous dictum is that "Man's capacity for justice makes democracy possible; but man's inclination to injustice makes democracy necessary." The statement incorporates both political and philosophical wisdom. These days one thinks of it again every time the demand for "all power to the people" rings in the air.

We know enough about men and societies to recognize the error in the slogan. We know, for example, that societies which have overemphasized human weakness have despaired of the ordinary citizen's capacity for self-government; we also know that those which have exaggerated human virtues have failed because they attributed to the "people" a mystical character, an innate nobility, and almost divine infalibility that the people do not have, no matter who is included in the phrase. In both cases the results have been tyrannical.

In the first instance, the tyranny was usually based on the notion that some few men — a hereditary sovereign, a chosen leader, a party, a race, a class, or a caste — have been ordained to rule over others. In the second, it was based on the idea that he who took it upon himself to speak for the mystic "people" had absolute power over the lonely individuals who stood out against popular opinion. We have learned from experience to beware of anyone who purports to be speaking for "the people" or who demands power in their name. In the first place, the people have not assigned any one or any group to speak for them. In the second, a grab for power, no matter how piously worded, remains just that, a grab for power.

All power, then, to no one.

SUBJECT

1. How might advocates of the slogan "All power to the people" answer Cogley's objection that "no one yet has ever discovered a benevolent mob"?

2. Why, according to Cogley, is power for the people "particularly dangerous" to the very people who are demanding it?

3. What objection might there be to the argument that "we the people" "long ago bound ourselves by solemn compact"? Does one generation have a right to "bind" the next to anything — even freedom?

4. Why does Cogley quote Niebuhr in paragraph 6? Does he mean to imply that those who want "all power to the people" do not want democracy? What are the implications of Niebuhr's statement?

5. Advocates of "power to the people" argue (rightly, if public opinion poles are to be trusted) that the government does not always act according to the wishes of the majority — witness the "unpopular" war in Vietnam. *Should* an elected representative always do what the majority wants? If the government were abolished, how would the people execute their power?

6. Should a minority be free to ignore the will of the majority? What kind of system best guarantees the rights of minorities?

STRUCTURE

1. In what order has Cogley placed the four traditional parts of argument? (See Introduction.)

2. In his final argument (paragraph 8), Cogley's supporting evidence is simply that "we have learned from experience"; should he have cited some specific examples, or do examples come readily to mind? (If so, there is little need for Cogley to waste time on examples.)

3. Does Cogley present his argument in the spirit of an open search for truth? (It is certainly allowable to dislike what one is arguing against, so long as that dislike is based on reason rather than prejudice.) Do you find any instances of "loaded" language?

4. To what group of people do you think this argument is addressed — revolutionaries, "the people," those who already dislike revolutionaries, those who are likely to be taken in by a phrase which sounds as equitable as "all power to the people"?

OF THE ENDS OF POLITICAL SOCIETY AND GOVERNMENT

John Locke

John Locke (1632–1704), English philosopher, physician, political scientist, theologian, and member of the Royal Society, was, probably more than any other writer, responsible for the faith in Reason which prevailed from his own time until very recently. His Essay Concerning Human Understanding, the Two Treatises of Civil Government, and Letter Concerning Toleration became the philosophical basis for the American Declaration of Independence and the Constitution. In an age of Puritan oligarchy and selfish monarchy under the later Stuarts, Locke held out for individual liberty and a government responsive to the will of the majority. His theory that man is born free and joins a political society for his own benefit is fairly well summarized in this chapter from the second Treatise of Civil Government.

If man in the state of nature be so free, as has been said, if he be absolute lord of his own person and possessions, equal to the greatest, and subject to nobody, why will he part with his freedom, this empire, and subject himself to the dominion and control of any other power? To which, it is obvious to answer, that though in the state of nature he hath such a right, yet the enjoyment of it is very uncertain, and constantly exposed to the invasions of others. For all being kings as much as he, every man his equal, and the greater part no strict observers of equity and justice, the enjoyment of the property he has in this state is very unsafe, very unsecure. This makes him willing to quit this condition, which, however free, is full of fears and continual dangers; and it is not without reason that he seeks out and is willing to join in society with others, who are already united, or have a mind to unite, for the mutual preservation of their lives, liberties, and estates, which I call by the general name, property. 1

The great and chief end, therefore, of men's uniting into common- 2
wealths, and putting themselves under government, is the preservation
of their property; to which in the state of nature there are many things
wanting.

First, There wants an established, settled, known law, received and 3
allowed by common consent to be the standard of right and wrong, and
the common measure to decide all controversies between them. For
though the law of nature be plain and intelligible to all rational creatures; yet men, being biased by their interest, as well as ignorant for
want of study of it, are not apt to allow of it as a law binding to them
in the application of it to their particular cases.

Secondly, In the state of nature there wants a known and indifferent 4
judge, with authority to determine all differences according to the
established law. For every one in that state, being both judge and
executioner of the law of nature, men being partial to themselves,
passion and revenge is very apt to carry them too far, and with too much
heat in their own cases, as well as negligence and unconcernedness, to
make them too remiss in other men's.

Thirdly, In the state of nature there often wants power to back and 5
support the sentence when right, and to give it due execution. They
who by any injustice offend, will seldom fail, where they are able by
force to make good their injustice; such resistance many times makes
the punishment dangerous, and frequently destructive to those who
attempt it.

Thus mankind, notwithstanding all the privileges of the state of na- 6
ture, being but in an ill condition, while they remain in it, are quickly
driven into society. Hence it comes to pass that we seldom find any
number of men live any time together in this state. The inconveniences
that they are therein exposed to by the irregular and uncertain exercise
of the power every man has of punishing the transgressions of others,
make them take sanctuary under the established laws of government,
and therein seek the preservation of their property. It is this makes
them so willingly give up every one his single power of punishing, to
be exercised by such alone, as shall be appointed to it amongst them;
and by such rules as the community, or those authorised by them to that
purpose, shall agree on. And in this we have the original right and rise
of both the legislative and executive power, as well as of the governments and societies themselves.

For in the state of nature, to omit the liberty he has of innocent 7
delights, a man has two powers.

The first is to do whatsoever he thinks fit for the preservation of 8
himself, and others within the permission of the law of nature, by which

law, common to them all, he and all the rest of mankind are of one community, make up one society, distinct from all other creatures. And were it not for the corruption and viciousness of degenerate men there would be no need of any other, no necessity that men should separate from this great and natural community, and associate into lesser combinations.

The other power a man has in the state of nature is the power to 9 punish the crimes committed against that law. Both these he gives up when he joins in a private, if I may so call it, or particular political society, and incorporates into any commonwealth separate from the rest of mankind.

The first power, viz., of doing whatsoever he thought fit for the 10 preservation of himself and the rest of mankind, he gives up to be regulated by laws made by the society, so far forth as the preservation of himself and the rest of that society shall require; which laws of the society in many things confine the liberty he had by the law of nature.

Secondly, The power of punishing he wholly gives up, and engages 11 his natural force (which he might before employ in the execution of the law of nature, by his own single authority as he thought fit), to assist the executive power of the society, as the law thereof shall require. For being now in a new state, wherein he is to enjoy many conveniences, from the labour, assistance, and society of others in the same community, as well as protection from its whole strength; he has to part also with as much of his natural liberty, in providing for himself, as the good, prosperity and safety of the society shall require; which is not only necessary but just, since the other members of the society do the like.

But though men when they enter into society give up the equality, 12 liberty and executive power they had in the state of nature into the hands of the society, to be so far disposed of by the legislative as the good of the society shall require; yet it being only with an intention in every one the better to preserve himself, his liberty and property (for no rational creature can be supposed to change his condition with an intention to be worse), the power of the society, or legislative constituted by them, can never be supposed to extend farther than the common good, but is obliged to secure every one's property by providing against those three defects above-mentioned that made the state of nature so unsafe and uneasy. And so whoever has the legislative or supreme power of any commonwealth is bound to govern by established standing laws, promulgated and known to the people, and not by extemporary decrees; by indifferent and upright judges, who are to decide controversies by those laws; and to employ the force of the community at home only in the execution of such laws, or abroad, to prevent or redress foreign injuries, and secure the community from inroads and invasion. And all this to be directed to no other end but the peace, safety, and public good of the people.

Subject

1. What does Locke mean by "property"? Would the intention of Locke's essay be changed if "property" were given its modern meaning?

2. Consider the three disadvantages in the state of nature which Locke says cause men to band together in civil society; do they seem to be valid and adequate reasons? Can you think of other advantages in joining a civil society?

3. Locke's argument depends largely on an undemonstrated basic premise: that "the corruption and viciousness of degenerate men" prevents their living together amicably in a state of nature. Is this a self-evident assumption, or should it be supported with evidence?

4. Most people in government would agree with Locke's statement of the aims and responsibilities of the peoples' representatives in government; how is it, then, that all the people do not seem to enjoy the "peace, safety, and public good" which should be their right? Are there practical considerations which Locke ignores?

5. If a manifesto of this sort were to be made today, would any basic changes need to be made in it?

Structure

1. Considering that it was written three centuries ago, Locke's essay is not really very different from modern writing in its choice of words; what does mark its style as not contemporary?

2. Locke's essay does not quite follow the standard form for argument; analyze the construction to see how he gets from the opening question to the conclusion of the final paragraph.

3. Does Locke take too much for granted? Can you suggest ways he might have strengthened his argument? (In fairness to Locke, it should be noted that this chapter is a kind of summary of a longer work.)

4. Would you class this argument as primarily deductive, or inductive (that is, does the conclusion follow from basic, undemonstrated assumptions, or is it a generalization from analysis of basic facts)?

THE MILITARY-
INDUSTRIAL COMPLEX

Dwight D. Eisenhower

Dwight D. Eisenhower (1890–1969) was the 34th President of the United States and, during World War II, Supreme Commander of the allied forces in Europe. As a member of the "military-industrial complex" for most of his career, Eisenhower was interestingly the first to use this now famous phrase publicly. In his farewell speech at the end of his eight years as President (1961), he here voices a warning which subsequent years have demonstrated was not sufficiently heeded.

My fellow Americans: 1

Three days from now, after half a century in the service of our coun-   2
try, I shall lay down the responsibilities of office as, in traditional and
solemn ceremony, the authority of the Presidency is vested in my
successor.

This evening I come to you with a message of leave-taking and fare-   3
well, and to share a few final thoughts with you, my countrymen.

Like every other citizen, I wish the new President, and all who will   4
labor with him, Godspeed. I pray that the coming years will be blessed
with peace and prosperity for all.

Relations with Congress

Our people expect their President and the Congress to find essential   5
agreement on issues of great moment, the wise resolution of which will
better shape the future of the nation.

My own relations with the Congress, which began on a remote and   6
tenuous basis when, long ago, a member of the Senate appointed me
to West Point, have since ranged to the intimate during the war and
immediate postwar period, and, finally, to the mutually interdependent
during these past eight years.

From *Weekly Report, Congressional Quarterly* (January 17, 1961). Reprinted by permission.

In this final relationship, the Congress and the Administration have, 7
on most vital issues, co-operated well to serve the national good rather
than mere partisanship, and so have assured that the business of the
nation should go forward. So, my official relationship with the Congress
ends in a feeling, on my part, of gratitude that we have been able to
do so much together.

We now stand 10 years past the midpoint of a century that has wit- 8
nessed four major wars among great nations. Three of these involved
our own country. Despite these holocausts, America is today the strongest, the most influential and most productive nation in the world. Understandably proud of this pre-eminence, we yet realize that America's
leadership and prestige depend, not merely upon our unmatched
material progress, riches and military strength, but on how we use our
power in the interests of world peace and human betterment.

Need for Balance

Throughout America's adventure in free Government, our basic pur- 9
poses have been to keep the peace, to foster progress in human achievement, and to enhance liberty, dignity and integrity among people and
among nations. To strive for less would be unworthy of a free and
religious people. Any failure traceable to arrogance, or our lack of
comprehension or readiness to sacrifice, would inflict upon us grievous
hurt both at home and abroad.

Progress toward these noble goals is persistently threatened by the 10
conflict now engulfing the world. It commands our whole attention,
absorbs our very beings. We face a hostile ideology — global in scope,
atheistic in character, ruthless in purpose and insidious in method.
Unhappily, the danger it poses promises to be of indefinite duration. To
meet it successfully there is called for, not so much the emotional and
transitory sacrifices of crisis, but rather those which enable us to carry
forward steadily, surely and without complaint the burdens of a prolonged and complex struggle — with liberty the stake. Only thus shall
we remain, despite every provocation, on our charted course toward
permanent peace and human betterment.

Crises there will continue to be. In meeting them, whether foreign 11
or domestic, great or small, there is a recurring temptation to feel that
some spectacular and costly action could become the miraculous solution to all current difficulties. A huge increase in newer elements of our
defenses; development of unrealistic programs to cure every ill in
agriculture; a dramatic expansion in basic and applied research —
these and many other possibilities, each possibly promising in itself,
may be suggested as the only way to the road we wish to travel.

But each proposal must be weighed in the light of a broader consider- 12
ation: The need to maintain balance in and among national programs
— balance between the private and the public economy; balance between cost and hoped-for advantages; balance between the clearly
necessary and the comfortably desirable; balance between our essential
requirements as a nation and the duties imposed by the nation upon the
individual; balance between actions of the moment and the national
welfare of the future. Good judgment seeks balance and progress; lack
of it eventually finds imbalance and frustration.

The record of many decades stands as proof that our people and their 13
Government have, in the main, understood these truths and have responded to them well, in the face of stress and threat. But threats, new
in kind or degree, constantly arise. I mention two only.

Effects of Armament

A vital element in keeping the peace is our military establishment. 14
Our arms must be mighty, ready for instant action, so that no potential
aggressor may be tempted to risk his own destruction.

Our military organization today bears little relation to that known by 15
any of my predecessors in peacetime, or indeed by the fighting men of
World War II or Korea.

Until the latest of our world conflicts, the United States had no arma- 16
ments industry. American makers of plowshares could, with time and
as required, make swords as well. But now we can no longer risk emergency improvisation of national defense; we have been compelled to
create a permanent armaments industry of vast proportions. Added to
this, 3.5 million men and women are directly engaged in the defense
establishment. We annually spend on military security alone more than
the net income of all United States corporations.

This conjunction of an immense military establishment and a large 17
arms industry is new in the American experience. The total influence
— economic, political, even spiritual — is felt in every city, every
statehouse, every office of the Federal Government. We recognize the
imperative need for this development. Yet we must not fail to comprehend its grave implications. Our toil, resources and livelihood are all
involved; so is the very structure of our society.

In the councils of Government, we must guard against the acquisition 18
of unwarranted influence, whether sought or unsought, by the military-
industrial complex. The potential for the disastrous rise of misplaced
power exists and will persist.

We must never let the weight of this combination endanger our 19
liberties or democratic processes. We should take nothing for granted.

Only an alert and knowledgeable citizenry can compel the proper meshing of the huge industrial and military machinery of defense with our peaceful methods and goals, so that security and liberty may prosper together.

Akin to, and largely responsible for the sweeping changes in our industrial-military posture, has been the technological revolution during recent decades. 20

In this revolution, research has become central; it also becomes more formalized, complex and costly. A steadily increasing share is conducted for, by, or at the direction of the Federal Government. 21

Today, the solitary inventor, tinkering in his shop, has been overshadowed by task forces of scientists in laboratories and testing fields. In the same fashion, the free university, historically the fountainhead of free ideas and scientific discovery, has experienced a revolution in the conduct of research. Partly because of the huge costs involved, a Government contract becomes virtually a substitute for intellectual curiosity. For every blackboard there are now hundreds of new electronic computers. 22

The prospect of domination of the nation's scholars by federal employment, project allocations, and the power of money is ever present — and is gravely to be regarded. 23

Yet, in holding scientific research and discovery in respect, as we should, we must also be alert to the equal and opposite danger that public policy could itself become the captive of a scientific-technological elite. 24

It is the task of statesmanship to mold, to balance and to integrate these and other forces, new and old, within the principles of our democratic system — ever aiming toward the supreme goals of our free society. 25

Another factor in maintaining balance involves the element of time. As we peer into society's future, we — you and I, and our Government — must avoid the impulse to live only for today, plundering, for our own ease and convenience, the precious resources of tomorrow. We cannot mortgage the material assets of our grandchildren without risking the loss also of their political and spiritual heritage. We want democracy to survive for all generations to come, not to become the insolvent phantom of tomorrow. 26

Disarmament Problem

Down the long lane of the history yet to be written, America knows that this world of ours, ever growing smaller, must avoid becoming a 27 community of dreadful fear and hate, and be, instead, a proud confederation of mutual trust and respect.

Such a confederation must be one of equals. The weakest must come 28
to the conference table with the same confidence as do we, protected
as we are by our moral, economic and military strength. That table,
though scarred by many past frustrations, cannot be abandoned for the
certain agony of the battlefield.

Disarmament, with mutual honor and confidence, is a continuing 29
imperative. Together we must learn how to compose differences, not
with arms, but with intellect and decent purpose. Because this need is
so sharp and apparent, I confess that I lay down my official responsibilities in this field with a definite sense of disappointment. As one who has
witnessed the horror and the lingering sadness of war — as one who
knows that another war could utterly destroy this civilization which has
been so slowly and painfully built over thousands of years — I wish I
could say tonight that a lasting peace is in sight.

Happily, I can say that war has been avoided. Steady progress toward 30
our ultimate goal has been made. But — so much remains to be done.
As a private citizen, I shall never cease to do what little I can to help
the world advance along that road.

Prayer for Peace

So — in this, my last "good night" to you as your President — I 31
thank you for the many opportunities you have given me for public
service in war and in peace. I trust that, in that service, you find some
things worthy; as for the rest of it, I know you will find ways to improve
performance in the future. You and I — my fellow citizens — need to
be strong in our faith that all nations, under God, will reach the goal of
peace with justice. May we be ever unswerving in devotion to principle,
confident but humble with power, diligent in pursuit of the nation's
great goals.

To all the peoples of the world, I once more give expression to Ameri- 32
ca's prayerful and continuing aspiration:

We pray that peoples of all faiths, all races, all nations, may have their 33
great human needs satisfied; that those now denied opportunity shall
come to enjoy it to the full; that all who yearn for freedom may experience its spiritual blessings; that those who have freedom will understand, also, its heavy responsibilities; that all who are insensitive to the
needs of others will learn charity; that the scourges of poverty, disease

and ignorance will be made to disappear from the earth, and that, in the goodness of time, all peoples will come to live together in a peace guaranteed by the binding force of mutual respect and love.

SUBJECT

1. The "hostile ideology" which Eisenhower says we must guard against is of course communism. In contrasting our goals with the aims of communism, does he assume that "peace and human betterment" are not also the ultimate goals of communism? (That is, does he confuse methods with goals here?)

2. In paragraphs 11 and 12, Eisenhower argues for "balance" and against crash programs. Is balance necessarily a virtue? Can you think of some areas in which a middle-of-the-road policy would not be good?

3. What do you think happened in the years since 1961 to allow the military-industrial complex to acquire "unwarranted influence," as Eisenhower feared? If that complex was necessary, as Eisenhower himself admitted, wouldn't it be unrealistic to expect such a complex to be without tremendous power?

4. To what extent do you think Eisenhower was justified in his warning about what might happen to the universities? Has any such trend reversed itself in recent years?

5. How does Eisenhower suggest that those dangers can be avoided? Should he have been more specific? What might he have *done* as outgoing President to ensure that the threats would not materialize?

6. Eisenhower argues that we must not give up the conference table in favor of the battlefield; yet the years since 1961 have produced marvelously little at the conference table — or on the battlefield, for that matter. Are there other alternatives to "peace, progress, and prosperity"?

STRUCTURE

1. The "clear statement of the problem" comes after several paragraphs of introductory remarks. Is the opening appropriate to the occasion? Does it have any relationship to the argument itself?

2. In the course of his argument, does Eisenhower anticipate and answer any opposing points of view, or is the body of the speech primarily confirmation of his own position?

3. Examine the style of this speech. Does there seem to be any conscious attempt to make it a "classic American speech," like the Gettysburg address?

4.   Politicians, great and mean, from President to precinct committeeman, have a tendency to use cliches in public speeches (as President Nixon overused "And so I say to you tonight" and "Let me make one thing perfectly clear," or as Johnson overused "My fellow Americans"). How many political cliches do you find in this speech?

5.   Is the concluding prayer for peace related to the argument within the farewell speech, or only to the farewell itself? Does it make a fitting conclusion? Or do you find it a bit hokey?

THE LIMITS
OF LAW AND ORDER

Robert M. Hutchins

Robert M. Hutchins (born in 1899) began his distinguished career as a lecturer at Yale law school. He was later president, then chancellor, of the University of Chicago (1929–1951), where he fostered many radical educational innovations — guaranteeing that every graduate had a humanistic education in the Great Books, for instance, and granting advanced placement — ideas which have since become standard at most universities. Hutchins has been chairman of Encyclopedia Britannica since 1943, and presently is chairman of the Center for the Study of Democratic Institutions in Santa Barbara, California, where he resides. Hutchins has been awarded at least a dozen honorary degrees, and has published many books on experiments in university education and education in a democratic society. "The Limits of Law and Order" first appeared in Center Magazine *(1971).*

During the campaign of 1968 Mr. Nixon told the country the big issue was Law and Order. Though the figures, such as they are, were showing no important increase in serious crimes, Mr. Nixon thought it his duty to warn us that our lives and property were in the gravest danger. He strongly hinted that the principal reasons for this alarming condition were the weakness of the Attorney General, Ramsey Clark, and the leniency of the courts.

We now have a new Attorney General, who talks very tough, and we are on the way to a new Supreme Court. The present Court has shown surprising liberality to some poor people in some respects. It has held Connecticut's fees in divorce cases unconstitutional for those who cannot pay them. It has invalidated laws requiring indigents to go to jail if they cannot pay their fines. This last decision suggests that the whole system of money bail is in contravention of due process and equal protection. If a poor man cannot be jailed after conviction because he is poor, how can he be held for that reason when he has not been tried and is presumed innocent?

Reprinted by permission from *The Center Magazine,* vol. III, no. 3, a publication of the Center for the Study of Democratic Institutions in Santa Barbara, California.

Otherwise the new justices have confirmed Mr. Nixon's expectations. 3
They have been lax about the confrontation required by the Sixth
Amendment, and they have sanctioned the use, for the purpose of
impeaching the credibility of the defendant, of statements obtained
from him in violation of the *Miranda* rules.[1]

It is unlikely that Mr. Mitchell's speeches and press releases or recent 4
Court decisions will have much effect on Law and Order. For example,
the principal result of admitting statements obtained in violation of the
Miranda rules for purposes of impeachment will be to keep defendants
off the stand. If they take it, they may find remarks inadmissible in chief
used to attack their veracity. No matter what the instructions are, the
jury is unlikely to make the distinction between guilt and falsehood.

But Mr. Nixon did not rely on changes in the Department of Justice 5
and the courts alone. He also sponsored a large number of bills dealing
with crime, often referred to as his Law and Order "package." These
bills have now become law. Apart from major improvements in the
judicial system of the District of Columbia, these laws are intended to
reduce crime by cracking down harder, more frequently, and in more
disagreeable ways on persons suspected of it. They are designed to shift
the balance in favor of the government and against the accused before
and during prosecution and after conviction. In view of the tremendous
imbalance that has always existed in favor of the government against
the accused, it seems likely that whatever reduction in crime is brought
about by this legislation will be purchased at the cost of justice.

One thing is fairly certain and that is that any reduction in crime 6
resulting from this legislation will be negligible. The reduction in civil
liberties is clear. "No-knock," preventive detention, wiretapping, etc.,
all restrict the freedom of the citizen. If the constitutionality of these
restrictions is upheld, but crime is not reduced, the argument will be
that these restrictions did not go far enough and that we need additional
restrictions on top of them. The outcome of this process is likely to be
unpleasant.

And what of the disillusionment that must ensue if the Administra- 7
tion's program, which has been presented as a panecea, has little or no
effect on crime? Mr. Nixon must be hoping that voters have in fact the
short memories often attributed to them.

The most persuasive argument against the Administration's program 8
is that it is diversionary. It turns attention away from the real problems
of crime and criminal justice and leads citizens to suppose that a little

[1]The *Miranda* rules pertain to the rights of a suspect to remain silent and to have a
lawyer present when being interrogated. See US Supreme Court decision, *Miranda v.
Arizona* (384 US 436).

tinkering here and there involving some slight risk to their civil liberties, or rather to the civil liberties of the poor and the black, will insure their safety. This means that the intellectual and financial effort we must make if we are really going to reduce crime will be still further postponed.

At the Center's Conference on Crime Control Legislation James V. 9 Bennett, former director of the United States Bureau of Prisons, estimated the cost of modernizing the penal institutions of the country at eighteen billion dollars. Nobody thought this figure was too high. Many of those present thought it was too low. Whatever the correct figure is, it is a fraction of what it would take to get a modern penal system, for Mr. Bennett was talking only about modernizing buildings. The cost of a well-trained staff in numbers and quality adequate to administer an enlightened program running from conviction through probation and parole would be many billions. More important, it would demand much intelligence, courage, and patience.

The same is true of every department of criminal justice. We need 10 more and better judges, more and better prosecutors, more and better public defenders, more and better police, more and better probation officers and parole boards, and all these groups need more and better facilities. Of course, what they need most of all is more and better ideas.

The demand for more personnel and more facilities would diminish 11 if the President, instead of ranting, would take up the one good idea he has in this field and educate the country to understand and accept it. This is the idea of "decriminalization," which became a sort of central theme of the conference at the Center and which the President referred to in a speech on March 11. As far as I can recall, it received unanimous support. Even Carl Rauh, of the Department of Justice, endorsed it. The reservations expressed about it had to do with details.

On the main point there was general agreement, and that was that 12 offenses that did not damage the person or property of others, where there was no victim and no complainant, should as far as possible be taken out of the system of criminal justice.

This would remove from the scope of the criminal law people for 13 whom that law can do nothing and who are now the principal burden upon it. Narcotics addicts and alcoholics cannot be helped by terms in the penitentiary. What they need is medical treatment. It was said at the Center's conference that sixty percent at least of all serious crime is drug-related and that alcoholics account for more than fifty percent of the arrests in the country. Although all statistics on crime are unreliable, these figures suggest what would happen if narcotics addicts and alcoholics were regarded as patients rather than criminals.

Some eight to ten million people in this country are said to be using 14
marijuana in open violation of the law. In some states an enormous part
of the apparatus of criminal justice is dedicated to detecting and con-
victing these people and to getting them locked up. If no convincing
evidence can be offered that marijuana is more harmful than alcohol or
tobacco, the possession and use of marijuana should be legalized. It
should follow that the sale of marijuana would be legal as well.

The criminal law cannot stop the traffic in "hard" drugs. As Troy 15
Duster pointed out at the Center's conference, the profits in the business are so large that dealers caught and jailed are immediately replaced. If criminal penalties were removed and the whole business
were regulated or owned by government, if something like the British
system were introduced, the resources now wasted in tracking down
those involved in the drug business could be devoted to the invention
of practical solutions to the problem.

Some form of gambling is legal everywhere. Some states have gone 16
so far as to set up state owned gambling institutions. If all restrictions
on gambling were removed, the strain it places on the system of criminal justice would be relieved. The hazards to civil liberties would be
reduced. The only argument advanced for "no-knock" and wiretapping
where "national security" is not involved is that in drug and gambling
cases these procedures are necessary to obtain and preserve evidence.
If there were no drug or gambling cases nobody would have the face
to advocate these procedures.

Drugs turn out to be, too, an important argument for preventive 17
detention: the addict out on bail must engage in crime in order to
support his habit. Taking addicts out of the criminal system would
minimize the demand to lock up people in order to protect the public
from them.

Every reader can make his own list of those acts, now called criminal, 18
which should be considered candidates for "decriminalization." Many
readers may differ with some of the examples I have used. This is not
material. The point is that the idea should be accepted and as many acts
covered by it as possible as soon as possible.

Where there is a social problem with which the system of criminal 19
justice is now vainly trying to deal, we do not solve the problem by
removing it from the scope of the criminal law. We merely abandon a
wasteful and futile attempt to cope with it. The problem remains.
Attempts to take mentally ill persons out of the reach of the criminal
law have been a dubious advantage to them. Most students of the
subject agree that a mentally ill defendant in a criminal case is better
off, in those jurisdictions which have civil commitment, if his illness is

not referred to during his trial. If he is sent to the penitentiary, he has at least some idea when he will get out. If he is civilly committed he may be detained for years and in the meantime get little more or better treatment than he would have in prison.

Civil commitment was thought to be a great step forward when it was   20
introduced. The reason that a noble, humanitarian effort has failed to produce better results is the same as that which must be given for the failure of the system of criminal justice. We as a people do not care to put the necessary intellectual and financial resources into the job. We are therefore an easy prey for snake-oil salesmen who tell us that if we will only stop "coddling criminals" we shall be secure.

Newsweek quotes Joe Olgiati, who runs a work-training program for   21
probationers in New York, as saying, "If you were to eliminate all cops, judges, parole officers, and courts, it would have a highly negligible effect on crime in the streets. In fact, it might even be better. You wouldn't just be trying to repair what we have now."

The thought does cross one's mind as one listens to the horrors recited   22
in a conference on crime control that it might be better if no criminal were ever caught. Everybody who is involved with the criminal law seems to be worse because of his contact with it. For example, the fifty-two percent of the jail population who are being detained pending trial must be more dangerous to society as a result of this experience than they were before.

Yet we cannot dispense with the criminal law. Although we know   23
very little about deterrence, it seems probable that the prospect of punishment does dissuade some people from the commission of some crimes. We should try to make the system of criminal justice work as swiftly, surely, and fairly as we can. As Ramsey Clark said at the Center's conference, safety and freedom are not incompatible; the thing to do is to enlarge both. Law and Order, in the modern interpretation of this slogan, will give us neither.

Subject

1. Why does Hutchins think the "law and order package" enacted under President Nixon will have little effect on law and order? Might there be political reasons for enacting such legislation even though it was known in advance that crime would not be reduced?

2. What adverse effects does Hutchins suggest will result from the legislation?

3. What advantages does Hutchins see in "decriminalization"? Does he give due recognition to the fact that ceasing to call an activity criminal does not eliminate that activity?

4.   Would you agree that the examples cited are likely areas for decriminalization? Can you suggest others?

5.   Do you agree with the statement by Joe Olgiati in paragraph 21? Does Hutchins? Is it possible that the system of law enforcement could cause more crime than it prevents?

STRUCTURE

1.   What kind of evidence does Hutchins provide to refute Nixon's solution to "crime in the streets"? How does he defend his own solution of decriminalization?

2.   Hutchins several times cites outside authorities — James Bennett and Troy Duster, for instance — to support his position. Appeals to authority can be one form of avoiding logic (Vida Blue uses this brand of after shave lotion). Is Hutchins' usage pertinent and reasonable?

3.   Do you find any evidence of name-calling or ridicule as a way of refuting the opposition?

4.   Does Hutchins' conclusion in the final paragraph follow logically from his argument? Should he have done more with "swiftness" of criminal justice?

5.   Would you say that Hutchins reveals an open or a closed mind in his search for solutions to crime in the streets? What influence does his attitude have on the effectiveness of the argument?

ON NOT BECOMING REVOLUTIONARY

Raymond Gozzi, Jr.

Raymond Gozzi, Jr. graduated from Harvard in 1967. After a summer registering voters in Mississippi, he went to Berkeley on a fellowship. After receiving his M. A. in history in 1968, he was forced to give up his fellowship because of the draft. He is now teaching school in California. This passage from his book, Ready for the Rain, *first appeared in* The Nation.

I've felt it happen to me, too. You lose that relaxed, easy feeling of being   1
free. Your vision focuses down on the narrow, bad, festering things and these become your world. Everything becomes politicized and nothing remains beautiful.

I spent two years in Berkeley and saw a lot of confrontations and saw   2
a lot of bad things come down on good people, and I must say I agreed more with the radicals than I did with the university administration, the police, the state or the federal government. I was also having draft problems, which eventually made me resign a five-year fellowship, and that did nothing to endear me to the *status quo.*

But I decided not to become a revolutionary. It was a possibility: it   3
would have given me a sense of immediacy and purpose that I don't have now, a feeling of involvement that I don't have now. But I made the right choice, for me. At first it was more than anything else an aesthetic choice.

I thought the radicals showed a lot of the same behavior as did affluent   4
America. I didn't like it in affluent America, and it didn't look any better with the radicals. Like everybody else in affluent America, the radicals seemed to follow fads. Whatever looked promising, they would hop on to, sometimes dropping other things a little ungracefully. Agitation for a professor, fired apparently for political reasons, suddenly disappeared when people got interested in a strike for Black Studies. The pamphlets had put it quite strongly: academic freedom was threatened, this was the first step toward political qualifications for professors, freedom of speech was being quashed. Quite important issues. And then the whole thing just disappeared — no more pamphlets, no more noon rallies,

no demonstrations — and everybody was off on the strike thing. All those issues, which had seemed so urgent, just gone.

I also thought there was a tendency to overadvertise, something like the Mustang ads that promise you masculinity if only you'll buy the car. The radicals were promising "self-fulfillment" and "finding yourself," simply by going to demonstrations or joining some organizations. It was a different version of the Marlboro Man.

During one strike the radicals used a new tactic: the "mill-in." The idea was that everybody would go into the Administration Building and just mill around, disrupting work, but staying mobile so they couldn't be arrested. They had a big rally and marched on Sproul Hall — I could see the people inside the building in their shirt sleeves, just watching this crowd of about 3,000 marching on the building. The administration stayed calm, nobody hassled the radicals, there was no violence on either side, work·stopped, people milled.

At a noon rally the next day, one of the leaders said: "They played it cool yesterday, all the secretaries sitting around being nice, everybody joking around. Well, we've got to show them that they aren't going to get off that easy. We've got to raise the cost to them of not considering our demands. We've got to escalate!"

Those were exactly the phrases Lyndon Johnson was using at the time to justify the bombing of North Vietnam — "raise the cost" of not doing what I say you should do. "Escalation" was what it was all about.

I am sure there are always persuasive reasons for escalating and raising the cost of aggression. Most of the people in the U.S. Government found many good reasons for escalating in Vietnam, and the radical critique at its best pointed out how, though this may have looked logical from the inside, it resulted in a grotesquely inappropriate, not to say dangerous, response. And now the radicals were doing the same thing. Escalating. Looking only at the internal logic of their situation and their short-range goals.

Then there was the time when radicals kept sending busloads of people down to the Oakland Induction Center, even though they knew the Oakland police were beating people up there, because it was their goal to have as big a demonstration as possible. If in fact your goal is to have as big a demonstration as possible, then that is logical behavior, but it means you must send people off into a situation where you know there is violence and they might be seriously injured. But of course the goal is the demonstration, not the people.

That, too, looked a little too much like LBJ shipping off more troops to fight *his* holy war in Vietnam for my taste. It seemed that there were people all around who wanted to use me for cannon fodder to prove their point. I didn't cotton to it, no matter who was doing it.

407

I think it's part of the general problem of being a *specialist*. You 12
become a policeman and learn how to use a billy club, and soon you
can't see any other solution to problems. You become a soldier and learn
how to shoot people, and soon you can't see any other solution. You
become a graduate student and read books and soon you can't discuss
anything else.

You become a reformer, and learn how to organize demonstrations, 13
and soon you can't think of anything else. When the reform doesn't
come, or comes very slowly, and all you see are mealy-mouthed politicians oozing out of your TV screens, you can get mighty, mighty unhappy. And if this has become your whole world, you might very easily
come to the conclusion that the world needs blowing up.

The trouble is that, being a specialist, what you think is the whole 14
world is only a narrow part of it. And what you think is the whole
solution is only a narrow part of it. (If any part of it at all — I've seen
too many specialists turn out dead wrong to take any specialist's word
on anything.) It seemed to me that the revolutionaries were suffering
from exactly the problems of every other specialist.

Would napalm convert you to democracy? It didn't work in Vietnam 15
and the radicals knew it wouldn't. Then why should a bomb in your
office convert you to the revolution? It sounds like the same logic the
U.S. Air Force used. "We'll bomb them back into the Stone Age," a U.S.
general said. Presumably that would break the will of the North Vietnamese. It didn't. Then why should bombing U.S. corporations break
their will?

So, as I say, I think it was the aesthetics of the thing that really did 16
it for me. The radicals reminded me too much of too many things that
I didn't like about American life. It all tasted a little sour, not really
beautiful. Of course I wasn't ready to insist on beauty. if things seemed
to be working. But the radicals' war seemed to be going about like LBJ's
— not too well, despite all the noise and the fury.

The hassle over Eldridge Cleaver on campus should show what I 17
mean. During that time I had some long talks with radical friends about
what would happen. This provided a test case, so to speak, of how well
the radical understanding of things — the radical ideology — worked.

The issues were whether or not Cleaver would be given a room to 18
lecture on campus, whether or not academic credit would be given for
the course, and whether or not the Berkeley academic senate would
resist the regents' ruling that official credit was not to be given for the
course. There were sit ins, mass picketing: some people even took over
a building — Moses Hall.

My radical friends and I got into a long argument about the whole 19
thing — I saying basically that taking over Moses Hall would not sway

408

the regents or the academic senate, that the action was premature anyway, since the academic senate hadn't had a chance to act fully, and there was a good chance credit would be allowed for the course. My friends said, No, all the faculty members want is peace and quiet, so they can do research; the university is implicated in the racism of this society so deeply that it can't rise above it; and anyway you are foolish to expect the faculty senate to do *anything, ever;* and the taking over of Moses Hall is necessary to help build a movement.

I think it is fair to say that I didn't win the argument, in that none 20 of my points were agreed to; but I think it is also fair to say that events bore out my position. The academic senate did defy the regents, they did allow Cleaver on campus, and months later — long after the radicals had lost interest and you didn't hear a thing about the issue from them — the academic senate even voted to let anyone graduate who had taken Cleaver's course, and was thus short of the credit that the regents would not grant. The faculty senate would grant them a diploma in lieu of the one withheld by the regents. A reasonably gutsy stand, I thought.

As for Moses Hall, the cops waited until early morning, when the 21 crowd was small, and then came in peaceably and arrested everybody nonviolently, and the whole thing *died.* (That might be a lesson for somebody, too.) A few months later, the student newspaper interviewed some of the leaders of the Moses Hall take-over, who were now involved in some court business, and they were all muttering about how the movement needed to be stronger so that when it made a mistake like taking over Moses Hall it wouldn't leave people — i.e., them — isolated. They themselves now admitted it had been a mistake, but at the time if you even suggested as much (I know, for I tried), all kinds of dark accusations were made against you: "What are you, some kindofa cop-out? Favoring racism? Where's your loyalty to your generation?"

The consumer-society radicals put down the Eldridge Cleaver issue 22 the way you'd put down a pizza pie that you didn't want to finish, and I was aware of no radical activity to help out any kids who took that course and stood on principle about the credit. I thought it was a bad show on the radicals' part, and that their categories of understanding had led them to predict the results of every major move just 180 degrees wrong. And this kind of thing happened all the time.

In Berkeley life, the emotions you feel are political emotions, which 23 are big, heavy, gross things. When people become too deeply politicized, I think they tend to see the world in terms of ideology rather than as it really is. Ideologies can be useful, but they seem to make their holders intolerant. My wife and I decided to work in the McCarthy campaign in the spring of 1968, and the amount of abuse we got from doctrinaire radicals surprised us. Some of the ugliest types reminded me of the good citizens of Mississippi.

When you'd try to say to someone, look we're all after the same thing; 24 several years of radical demonstrations haven't changed our policy in Vietnam; why can't you let me try this way and I'll let you try yours; we'll both be happy if either side wins — what you'd get in reply would be a philosophical tirade about imperialism and how both parties are the same and the system is corrupt. There was never any attempt to communicate on a personal level; it was always dialects and philosophy. And if I didn't agree with them, I was wrong.

When McCarthy came to Berkeley to speak, he started off by saying: 25 Well, when I first ran, some people said I was just putting up a trial balloon and was really working for Bobby Kennedy. "That's right," someone in the crowd bellowed. McCarthy went on: And then some other people said I was simply being a foil and was really working for Lyndon Johnson. "That's right," the same guy bellowed. "Mighty hard to be both at the same time," McCarthy said, and the guy quieted down. But after that speech my wife and I knew that Berkeley wouldn't be able to come together, and it made us sad.

I think the strongest part of radicalism is its criticism of the injustice, 26 dehumanization and absurdity in the modern world. I would hate to think of a future without a strong tradition of radical protest; bureaucrats seem to blunder into things without really questioning, and a responsible, nonviolent radicalism is important to keep those people from fouling us all up.

But there will be no radical tradition in the future if it gets wiped out 27 during this dark age. A quick glance at the history of the IWW, or the Red scare of 1919 — where hundreds of radicals were arrested without charges, held without being allowed lawyers, and deported without trials — or the Southern tradition of dealing with dissenters: lynch them — should convince anyone who didn't know it that Americans are capable of ruthless and unprincipled action against those who are seen as violently threatening.

When groups go underground, plotting dark deeds, they lay them- 28 selves open for illegal repression in the name of national security, and once a thing is declared to be in the interest of national security, it can be labeled Secret, and all hope for constitutional rights will be gone. Constitutional rights may not mean much, as the Chicago Seven trial graphically shows, but they *may* be the difference between freedom and jail, as the Oakland Seven trial proved. The government couldn't prove conspiracy to a jury of twelve Oaklanders and they went free. That's better than what Stalin's opponents got.

And another historical fact is that no government has ever been 29
overthrown by internal revolution if it has kept control over its police and military forces. As we know, the police and military are among the firmest ideological supporters of the American Way. As we also know, and as I saw in the streets of Berkeley, some police are not excessively scrupulous about other people's rights, and some politicians will back them up.

If the goal of radicalism is simply to create havoc and destruction, it 30
is perhaps doing fine. But if the goal of radicalism is actually to *help* other people, to try to reduce the effects of racism at home and mindless militarism abroad, I think those goals should be kept in mind and all actions tested against them. The goals will not be furthered if the radical movement in America allows itself to be smashed by a right-wing reaction to its violent attempt to bring on a hopeless revolution. And a lot of good people, who will be needed in the future, will be gone.

"We have waited 300 years, and we ain't gonna wait any longer!" The 31
fact that injustices have existed for centuries should warn us that they will not disappear simply because we may wish them gone. The world, it seems, was not made to spring to our every command. This does not mean that we should be passive, or despairing. It just means that we'll have to pick our shots carefully in our attacks on injustice: being in a strategic place at the right time; registering voters in Mississippi; working in primaries; marching; tutoring ghetto kids; teaching in rural summer schools. With the goal that individually you hope to make a difference in someone's life, and collectively make a difference in the society's life. There are a lot of people and there is lots to do.

It goes back, I guess, to that argument in Mississippi. Do you shoot for 32
the long-range goals and register voters, or do you insist on all the symbols and sit-in on the benches? My choice then was for the long-range goals. We were registering voters. That's what will make the most difference to the most people in the long run; let's not sweat the benches.

That is still my choice. It seems clear that, if we can only get through 33
the next ten years or so of this dark age, we should come out on the other side to a better world.

For instance, I think that a guaranteed annual income would do more 34
to wipe out the effects of racism in this country than would anything else, including The Revolution. (Friends who have been to Cuba say there is still racism there; you don't change people's minds as fast as you

411

change their government.) And I think that within ten or twenty years, probably sooner, we'll have a guaranteed annual income. When someone of the views of Richard M. Nixon proposes to Congress family income supplements, it is safe to say we're on the road. I don't care who does make it the law — I'll be happy, even, if it's Richard Nixon.

I think the guaranteed income can be sold to voters. When I was   35 speaking at a McCarthy meeting in a working-class district, I got some pointed questions about it. I said: Well under the present welfare system the incentive is not to work. Once you get a job, you're off welfare. Studies seem to show that the guaranteed income encourages people to work — you get a reduction of benefits on a sliding scale, but you are better off if you work. And nobody will sit around getting rich on it; this will just keep people from starving, give kids enough food, that kind of thing. The voters liked it; it made sense to them.

I also think that the plain facts of demography are for us. In the next   36 twenty years there will be how many million more Beatles fans as voters? You think the political system won't change? Just because Congress right now is dominated by septuagenarian relics from an earlier era, doesn't mean it will always be so, and a younger electorate should bring some changes. History, I think, is on our side.

SUBJECT

1.   Gozzi clearly did not object to the radical movement out of any "America, right or wrong" brand of patriotism; what were his objections?

2.   Gozzi's contention that the radicals used the same tactics as the establishment would probably not sit well with either radicals or establishment. Does he make a convincing case for this argument?

3.   What, according to Gozzi, is wrong with being a specialist? Do you think he means to include specialists in every area?

4.   What solution does Gozzi prefer to correct "injustice, dehumanization, and absurdity in the modern world"? Assuming that he would be pleased to have instant perfection, why does he choose the long-range plan?

5.   Does Gozzi seem too optimistic about the guaranteed annual income as a cure-all?

STRUCTURE

1.   The strongest part of Gozzi's essay is the refutation of revolutionary tactics; what makes this section strong?

2. What indications are there that Gozzi is trying to be fair to revolutionists? Could you say that the entire argument represents an open-minded search for truth?

3. The author assumes that much in the world needs changing; should he have taken the trouble to give examples of injustice?

4. The style of this argument is very informal, at times slangy. What advantages and disadvantages are there to this style? Should any of the clichés and slang expressions have been deleted?

5. Toward what group of readers do you think this argument is aimed? Is Gozzi trying to justify himself or to recruit support?

WHAT IS A
SOCIAL PROBLEM?

Neil H. Jacoby

Neil H. Jacoby, former dean and for many years a professor in the Graduate School of Business Administration at U. C. L. A., is an associate of the Center for the Study of Democratic Institutions. In this argument, which appeared in Center Magazine *for July/August, 1971, Professor Jacoby's conservative approach to social problems may prove a refreshing contrast to the more alarmist views expressed elsewhere in this book. In any case, his idea that a social problem is the gap between expectation and reality deserves consideration.*

It is widely believed that the American nation confronts serious social problems. Many hold that our society is being shaken by a succession of overlapping and interrelated crises, including population growth and concentration, environmental pollution, poverty, crime, drugs, racial enmity, malnutrition, urban blight, and the war in Southeast Asia. Most of those in the New Left aver that unresolved problems are mounting in intensity. Changes in social institutions are occurring too slowly, they say, to accommodate changes in the goals, beliefs, and expectations of the public. Hence, the potentiality of a political revolution — of a sudden drastic restructuring of our social institutions — is rising. Indeed, extremist groups like the Weathermen and the Black Panthers, along with such mentors as Professor Herbert Marcuse, are actively fomenting revolution. They deliberately reject the course of working peacefully within the social system to shape its development along desired lines. The mounting level of violence in American society throughout the sixties suggests that not a few persons have given credence to this line of thought.   1

It is therefore timely to examine the meaning of social problems. How do they arise? By what process do they escalate into crises? How can they be ameliorated or resolved?   2

A basic premise of our inquiry is that peaceful evolution is nearly always to be preferred to violent revolution as a path of social reform. Although revolution may in some circumstances be necessary, man's   3

Reprinted by permission from the July/August issue of *The Center Magazine,* a publication of the Center for the Study of Democratic Institutions in Santa Barbara, California.

history shows that it is an extremely wasteful mode of social change. Revolution destroys physical and social capital and leaves in its wake a large reservoir of wrongs and inequities that require generations to liquidate. Evolutionary social change can avoid these setbacks. It can steadily augment social justice and material well-being. It can yield progress without hiatus.

Let us consider the nature of a "social problem." In January, 1969, the distinguished Panel on Social Indicators appointed by the Secretary of Health, Education, and Welfare reported that, by nearly all measures, the well-being of the American people had improved materially since World War II. Yet it found that public disaffection had also risen markedly. The reason was, it wisely observed, that people's expectations had risen faster than reality could improve. 4

The phenomenon noted by the Panel on Social Indicators was the same as that observed by Toqueville in eighteenth-century France: "The evil which was suffered patiently as inevitable, seems unendurable as soon as the idea of escaping from it crosses men's minds. All the abuses then removed call attention to those that remain, and they now appear more galling. The evil, it is true, has become less, but sensibility to it has become more acute." 5

A social problem, then, may be defined as a gap between society's expectations of social conditions and the present social realities. Social expectations are the set of demands and priorities held by the people of a society at a given time. Social realities mean the set of laws, regulations, customs, and organizations, along with the pertinent economic, political, and social processes that prevail at a given time. 6

Social problems are created by public awareness of, or belief in, the existence of an expectation-reality gap. They are basically psychological phenomena — ideas held in the minds of people — about the disparity between what should be, and what is, in our society. Social problems are not definable solely in physical or biological terms, such as so many calories of food intake per day, or so many square feet of housing per capita. They must be defined in terms of the extent of the expectation-reality gap. 7

One may illustrate the independence of a social problem from any particular social condition by considering the example of poverty. Poverty is now perceived by Americans to be an important social problem in the United States, because in 1970 eleven percent of the population had incomes under the official poverty level (about $3,500 per year for a family of four), whereas Americans generally believe that no one should live under the poverty line. Poverty was not perceived to be an important social problem in 1947, although twenty-seven percent of the population then lived under the poverty line by 1970 standards. 8

Despite an astonishing gain in the real incomes of those in the lowest brackets, public expectations outraced realities. Hence the expectation-reality gap with respect to poverty is wider today than it was in 1947. The problem of poverty has become more serious at the same time that the incidence of poverty has been cut sixty percent and continues to decline.

Once the concept is grasped that a social problem is a gap between public expectations of social conditions and social realities, it becomes clear that our society, and especially its political leaders, must pay as much attention to the forces that determine public expectations as to those that shape social realities. They should seek to keep the gap at a tolerable size and thereby avoid violent or disruptive social behavior. 9

The expectation-reality gap is, of course, a dynamic system that changes through time. Public expectations change as a consequence of the expanding size and concentration of the human population, of rising affluence, or of technological advances. Thus, the high priority now assigned to the problem of environmental pollution reflects an elevation in the social expectations of clean air and water and other environmental amenities by a richer and more crowded population. Public expectations are also shaped by the flow of information, words, and pictures that they receive from the mass media of communication — newspapers, magazines, radio, and television. Expectations are likewise heavily influenced by publicly expressed views of political leaders. For example, President Eisenhower raised the nation's expectations for better highways with his support of the interstate highway system in the fifties; President Johnson boosted public expectations of an end to poverty with his "war on poverty" in the sixties. 10

Changes in social expectations require responsive changes in social realities, if a rise in social tensions — that is, in revolutionary potential — is to be avoided. For example, racial tensions have risen in the United States partly because the rising social expectation of racial integration of the public-school system, called for by the 1954 *Brown* decision of the Supreme Court, has not yet produced a commensurate shift in the racial structure of the educational system. As with the social problem of poverty, the realities of educational integration have improved, but have been outrun by the rise in public expectations. 11

Revolutionary potential — the degree of public frustration caused by a gap between expectations and realities — is also a function of time. It will rise as the time lapse lengthens between a given expectation and responsive change in social institutions and processes. The American Revolution of 1776 exploded when a sufficiently large num- 12 ber of colonials found that the gap between their long-reiterated demands for a larger voice in their own government and the intransigency of the British Crown was no longer endurable. Timely action by the British to delegate powers of self-government would have reduced the revolutionary potential and even possibly avoided a political revolution.

There have been periods in American history when popular expectations of social improvement have been extremely low. During the Great Depression, for example, the revolutionary potential was surprisingly weak. Public expectations of social improvement had become so deflated by 1933 that only a small gap separated them from the grim social realities of those times. President Roosevelt and his New Deal performed a magnificent act of political leadership in regenerating public expectations. 13

The mass media play an important role in the creation and magnification of social problems. They do this by increasing public awareness of gaps between social goals and current realities, and also by magnifying public perceptions of such gaps. Millions of Americans read about and see on their television screens crime on the streets, slums in the cities, deprivation in the ghettos, smog in the air, and sewage in the water. The American public was only remotely informed about these conditions fifty years ago. The mass media are frighteningly effective in widening public awareness of the chasms that separate man's expectations of peace, plenty, justice, and stability from the realities of the human condition. Thus they create social problems where none had existed before, and they escalate minor problems into major crises. 14

If the mass media operated simply as faithful transmitters of printed and pictorial images of society as it is, one could not complain about their effect on the public's perception of reality or the size of the expectation-reality gap. However, they are more than mere transmitters. They are selectors of the information and images presented to people. Because they thrive on the shocking, the extreme, the bizarre, they have little interest in conveying to their audiences the normal life or the quiet incremental progress of society. The mass media tend to screen out words and images that reveal normality, and to transmit those that show deprivation, injustice, suffering, and maladjustment, on the one hand, and those that depict wealth, extravagance, or conspicuous consumption, on the other. Thus they function as magnifiers or amplifiers of the expectation-reality gap that previously existed in the public's mind. Expectations of social improvement are elevated even higher; social realities are seen to be even worse than before. 15

Art Buchwald recently recounted how George III suppressed television in Britain during the latter eighteenth century, because TV pic- 16

417

tures of British mercenaries suppressing colonial Americans were inciting the British public to a state of rebellion against its colonial policies. Despite its humorous approach, the proposal has a serious point. Buchwald used this imaginary analogy to suggest that the U.S. government should suppress all television coverage of the war in Southeast Asia.

A recent example of journalistic distortion was the pronouncement 17 by *The New York Times* and the Washington *Post* that the police have killed twenty-eight Black Panthers since January 1, 1968. This "news" statement was widely copied, and followed by editorial speculation that the police were conspiring to wipe out Black Panther leadership. The Negro community reacted in anger. In a carefully researched article in the *New Yorker* of February 13, 1971, Edward J. Epstein showed that the source of this inflammatory statement was Charles R. Garry, counsel for the Panther organization, and that it was false. Ten of the twenty-eight Panthers had been killed by their own political opponents. With two possible exceptions about which the facts are unclear, a study of the other sixteen deaths showed that in every case the Panthers were armed, threatened the police and shot first. There was not a shred of evidence to support the conspiracy thesis.

If the mass media are a powerful instrument in the formation of 18 public attitudes and expectations, it becomes vitally important that they present accurate and balanced word-and-picture images of events within their proper historical contexts. No one would suggest governmental censorship of information flows to the public. What is proposed is self-disciplined objectivity so that the mass media will perform their function of accurate and objective transmission of information that can be the basis of rational and realistic public attitudes and expectations.

Our political system of representative democracy also tends to create 19 or to expand social problems by raising public expectations of social gains and by exaggerating gaps between expectations and realities. Politicians generally do not challenge the validity of existing public expectations, or seek to reduce them to realizable levels. The basic reason for their one-sided influence is clear enough. It is in the professional interest of the politician to inflate rather than deflate unrealistic expectations. Politicians are elected by "viewing with alarm" the empty records of their opponents in office and by leading the voters to believe that the incumbent scoundrels have prevented them from getting their share of the good things of life. If only the electorate turns the rascals out, change will bring great improvements. Of course, by the time of the next election the roles of politicians in the two parties are often reversed; the "great society" still has not been achieved and the people are more frustrated than ever. The expectation-reality gap has widened.

Intellectuals are also traditional "viewers with alarm" because any other attitude would compromise their professional reputations as social critics. They consider it a duty to decry gaps between the performance of the society and its potential. Otherwise their colleagues would believe that they had sold out to the Establishment or had lost their critical faculties. Given the strong propensity to hypercriticize in scholarly teaching and writing, and considering the now vast number of youths under academic influence in the higher educational system, it is no wonder that a rising fraction of the U.S. population has become alienated from society and its institutions. 20

Presidential Task Forces and Commissions and other public groups often generate or enlarge social problems by attention-getting public statements. Although such bodies are supposed to provide calm and objective assessments of social problems, their effort to compete with the tidal wave of information that daily inundates us all often leads them to make shocking statements that create distorted impressions or beliefs in the public mind. Because the whole truth is rarely dramatic, they tend to twist the truth or to convey partial truths in order to create shock value. 21

An instance of headline-grabbing by distortion is the 1968 Report of the National Advisory Commission on Racial Disorders, commonly known as the Kerner Report. Although this weighty document contained much wisdom, what stood out when it was issued was the inflammatory headlined statement that "this nation is moving toward two societies, black and white, separate and unequal." The vast majority of people who read this headline, but who did not read the whole report, concluded that the Kerner Commission found that racial inequality and separation in America was rising in all dimensions. The implications of the statement were extremely disruptive. By implying that the Establishment was failing to improve racial relations, and that the racial gap was widening, the Kerner Report added fuel to the fiery demands of militant groups for revolutionary changes. Seeds of bitterness were sown in the minds of the uninformed. Racial tensions were exacerbated at home. The nation was denigrated abroad. 22

Yet the truth is that our democratic political institutions and our market economy, despite imperfections, have been making steady progress in narrowing the economic, educational, political, and social inequalities between the races ever since World War II. The median 23 income of nonwhite families rose from fifty-five percent of that of white families in 1950 to sixty-three percent in 1968; and, according to figures cited by Daniel Moynihan, the incomes of black young married couples had become equal to those of white young married couples in 1970. The proportionate reduction in poverty since 1959 has been almost as great among blacks as among whites. Whereas in 1947 black adult Americans completed thirty-four percent fewer years of schooling than the entire population, by 1969 this difference had narrowed to nineteen percent; and, for persons in the age bracket from twenty-five to twenty-nine years, it had nearly vanished. The differences between the life expectancies at birth of the two races diminished significantly during the postwar era. The steadily rising proportion of black citizens that are registered and vote in elections and of blacks in public office shows a narrowing of the political gap. Blacks themselves overwhelmingly believe that conditions are improving for their race in this country, as sociologist Gary T. Marx reported in his book *Protest and Prejudice.* All these facts demonstrate impressive postwar progress of the American Negro toward economic and political equality, although many will understandably say "too little and too late." The correct conclusion to be drawn, however, is to keep public policy on the present course and to try to accelerate its pace.

The gravity of the nation's social problems is also enlarged by the teachings and writings of the liberal left. Much liberal left social thought is based upon illusory concepts of the nature of man and society, well described by Professor Harold Demsetz as the "Nirvana," "other grass is greener," "free lunch," and "people could be different" fallacies (*Journal of Law and Economics,* April, 1960). 24

The "Nirvana" approach to social policy presents a choice between a theoretical ideal never approached in man's history and existing conditions. The vast distance between the two naturally creates a social "crisis." The true choice, however, lies between existing conditions and others that are feasible in the sense of being capable of attainment. Because the expectation-reality gap in the latter case is usually small, the "crisis" is reduced to a manageable problem. 25

The "other grass is greener" illusion credits an alternative social condition, usually in some foreign country, with great virtues said to be lacking in American society. This atmospheric pollution is said to be the product of capitalistic enterprise, and its cure is to adopt state socialism. This idea is repeated by social critics who have not taken the trouble to ascertain that pollution levels in socialist countries have risen, along with their G.N.P.'s, even faster than in capitalist countries. 26

420

The "free lunch" fallacy is that there are costless remedies for social   27
ills. Since unemployment is an evil, say the critics, abolish it and reduce
the unemployment ratio to zero. They choose to ignore the heavy social
costs of such a policy in the form of restrictions on individual freedom,
lowered productivity, and price inflation. Every decision that produces
public benefits imposes costs, and the problem is to weigh both and
determine the balance.

The "people could be different" fallacy is that the Good Society can   28
be attained by radical changes in the moral and ethical behavior of
people. Thus the "new communist man," imbued with a totally altruis-
tic concern for the public welfare, was seen by the older Marxists as the
condition for the ultimate transformation of socialism into true communism. Unfortunately, he has not yet appeared in sufficient numbers to
make this possible; and he shows no sign of doing so. While moderate
changes in men's values and behavior can occur over time (indeed,
changes are essential if our society is to improve), sharp mutations in
human nature are a fantasy. In reforming our society, we are wise to
take human nature as a datum, and to design structures and processes
for imperfect men and women rather than for saints or philosophers.

In his report to the nation on U.S. foreign policy for the nineteen-   29
seventies, President Nixon observed: "No nation has the wisdom and
the understanding and the energy required to act wisely on all problems, at all times, in every part of the world." The statement is equally
true and important if we substitute "nation" for "world." The number
of different domestic problems that the people of a nation can cope with
effectively at any given time is limited, not only by the stock of popular
wisdom, energy, and understanding, but also by the available economic
resources of the society. In view of the fact that available economic
resources form a severe constraint upon national capability to improve
real social conditions, whereas public expectations of social improvement can soar at a virtually unlimited rate, it is far more likely that a
social problem will escalate into a "crisis" through an inordinate rise in
expectations than by a failure of real conditions to improve.

If national political and intellectual leaders ignore the resource con-   30
straints upon real social improvements, they may, by dramatizing one
social deficiency after another, stimulate public expectations so power-
fully that multiple social "crises" are created in the public mind. During
the Administration of President Johnson, for example, a "war on poverty" was followed by a "war on hunger" and a "war on slums" and so
on. Faced by a "war" on a new social front every few months without
having won any of those already in progress the American people

became progressively confused, frustrated, angered, and alienated from their government. Failure of the national political leadership to hold social expectations within the boundaries of national capabilities led to the violence and disruptive behavior that marked the last half of the sixties.

By the end of 1968 public frustration and social tensions in the United States had reached a dangerous level. Americans demanded a quantity and variety of social improvements far beyond the capacity of this or any other society to produce. People's energies were being dissipated in dropoutism, absenteeism, and irrelevant protest rather than utilized in constructive action — as shown by a catastrophic drop in productivity. Fortunately the succeeding Nixon Administration applied the remedies of "low profile" and "benign neglect," which succeeded in reducing many social "crises" into manageable problems by deflating exaggerated public expectations. 31

It is a mistaken view that real social progress only occurs after a "crisis" has been generated, or that a deflation of exaggerated public expectations is tantamount to foot-dragging in making necessary social reforms. On the contrary, there is a good deal of evidence that "crises" — especially if accompanied by violence — are inimical to long-run progress; and that the maintenance of a proper relation between expectations and realities avoids disruptive social behavior that retards real social progress. Thus, poverty in the United States was being rapidly reduced after World War II and there is no convincing evidence that the "war on poverty" launched in 1965 speeded up the process. 32

Our theory of social tensions helps to explain the almost pathological mood of self-criticism and self-deprecation that has descended upon Americans in recent years. William James said that an individual's self-esteem could be measured by the ratio of his success or achievement to his potential. By analogy, national self-esteem is the ratio of national achievement to national potential, as they are generally perceived by people. As national achievements (i.e., social realities) are depreciated, and national potentialities (i.e., social expectations) are exaggerated, the quotient of national self-esteem will fall to the vanishing point. 33

Our society is a dynamic system in which public values and expectations and social institutions and processes change through time. The central aims of public policy should be to maintain an optimal expectation-reality gap and to achieve an optimal rate of change in both social expectations and social realities. 34

An optimal expectation-reality gap is wide enough to preserve incentive and motive for beneficial changes in social institutions and processes. ("Man's reach should exceed his grasp, else what is Heaven for?") 35

Yet it is not so wide as to cause public frustration and diversion of energy from constructive action to inaction or to disruptive behavior. Public goals and expectations should advance through time, fast enough to maintain social flexibility and adaptability, but not so rapidly as to lose contact with realities.

The real conditions of life should also be improved through time, fast   36
enough to sustain a popular belief in progress but not so fast as to lead to malallocations of resources and social imbalances.

Because the rate of improvement in social conditions is determined   37
within a fairly narrow range by well-known constraints upon the growth of production, whereas the rate of increase in public expectations is virtually unlimited, it is likely that political leaders will more frequently find it necessary to moderate public expectations than to raise them in order to avoid dangerous gaps. This appears especially probable in our society which, as has been seen, is institutionally organized to magnify expectation-reality gaps and in which high achievement is the normal goal.

The general strategy for approaching the optimum gap between   38
expectations and realities will include the following elements: (1) accelerate desired institutional changes in the economic, political, and social systems to an optimum rate; (2) publicize the changes that are occurring in the society to reduce poverty, racial discrimination, crime, or to improve health, housing, and other conditions; (3) instruct the public in the political and economic processes of change and their time dimensions so that there will emerge a general appreciation of what is realistically possible; (4) develop through research more frequent and reliable indicators of social conditions and of the state of public expectations, and of their rates of change through time, as guides to social policymakers. Social scientists should also try to measure the sustainable rates of change in social institutions. Leonard Lecht's pioneering effort to measure the dollar costs of attaining U.S. national goals, and to compare it with national production capacity is a type of research that should be expanded (*Goals, Priorities, and Dollars.* New York: Free Press, 1966).

Managing public expectations has become a vital new dimension of   39
political leadership in the United States, of coördinate importance with the engineering of orderly reform of our social institutions. Political leaders need to observe expectation-reality gaps constantly in order to maintain the proper state of tension in society. The statesmen of the future will be those who know how to bring about orderly social change and also to keep public expectations in a productive relationship to realities. Thus they will enable our society to resolve successfully a constantly emerging set of new social problems.

SUBJECT

1. Examine Jacoby's definition of a social problem in paragraph 6. Is there any significant difference between this and the definition of a social problem as a "discrepancy between what is and what ought to be"?

2. Presumably Jacoby would have to say that a poverty-stricken primitive tribe, with no notion or expectation of a better life, does not have a "social problem." Would you agree? Would substandard existence in a voluntary commune be a "social problem"?

3. Is Jacoby suggesting that the way to reduce social problems is to convince people that they *aren't* problems?

4. What forces does Jacoby blame for raising expectations beyond realistic limits? Do you see a likelihood of change in approach from any of these forces?

5. What are the four "fallacies" promulgated by the liberal left? Does Jacoby show each to be indeed a fallacy?

6. Do you agree that the Nixon administration succeeded in deflating public expectations of reform? Is such deflation "fortunate," as Jacoby claims?

7. What is Jacoby's program for eliminating social crises? Do you think it could be successful? What obstacles might there be?

STRUCTURE

1. Does Jacoby's essay conform to the traditional four-part structure of argument? Is anything added or omitted?

2. In paragraph 3, Jacoby explains a basic premise of his argument; since the premise might be debatable, do you think it is good strategy to bring it out in the open?

3. How effectively does Jacoby employ statistics to support his argument? Does he use them more in refuting others or in supporting his own position? Do you see why?

4. Isolate points at which Jacoby seems to employ unfair tactics (loaded language, name-calling, etc.). Could he have made the same points without resorting to these tactics?

5. Does the four-point strategy proposed at the end of the essay materially strengthen Jacoby's argument? Suppose he had left it out?

6. Except in the concrete examples, Jacoby's language tends to be abstract. Does its abstractness interfere with communication — that is, is it good, or fuzzy, abstract language?

DANGERS OF
THE MILITARY SELL

J. William Fulbright

J. William Fulbright (born in 1905), a former Rhodes scholar and later president of the University of Arkansas, has been U. S. Senator from Arkansas since 1945. He has become known throughout the world as the author of the student and faculty exchange program which bears his name. Always an opponent of demagoguery and of misplaced power, he was the only senator who voted to deny funding to Senator Joseph McCarthy's infamous investigating committee. More recently, as chairman of the Foreign Relations Committee, Senator Fulbright has devoted his efforts to curtailing the takeover by the administration of congressional prerogatives in the areas of foreign policy and military deployment. The televised hearings of his committee's investigation of the Vietnam war did much to change majority opinion from approval to disapproval of the war. The essay below was taken from The Pentagon Propaganda Machine *(1970), an exposé of the extensive Pentagon lobbying and propaganda machinery set up to secure passage of the huge military budget bills.*

Although I cannot conceive of a single top-ranking officer in any of the 1
armed services who today would consider an attempt to overturn our constitutional government — in the manner of *Seven Days in May* fiction — militarism as a philosophy poses a distinct threat to our democracy. At the minimum, it represents a dangerously constricted but highly influential point of view when focussed on our foreign relations. It is a viewpoint that by its nature takes little account of political and moral complexities, even less of social and economic factors, and almost no account of human and psychological considerations.

Rarely does a general officer invoke the higher loyalty of patriotism 2
— his own concept of it, that is — over loyalty to civilian political authority, as General MacArthur did in his defiance of President Truman.* But if, as time goes on, our country continues to be chronically

* *The MacArthur Story,* a film version of the glamorous general's life made by the Office of Information for the Armed Forces, is available to the public in military film libraries.

at war, continues to neglect its domestic problems, and continues to have unrest in cities and on campuses, then militarism will surely increase. And even if the military itself does not take over the government directly, it could — because of increasing use in domestic crises — come to acquire power comparable to that of the German General Staff in the years before World War I. I hope this never comes to pass. It may not seem likely now, but it is by no means so inconceivable that we need not warn against it and act to prevent it.

I have often warned those students who talk of the need to revise our system by revolution that if such a revolution were to take place, the government that would emerge for our country would not be the one they seek. It would rather be authoritarian and controlled by the very forces who today promote military solutions to foreign policy problems. 3

The leadership of professional military officer corps stems from a few thousand high-ranking officers of unusual ability and energy that comes of single-mindedness. Marked as men of talents by their rise to the highest ranks through the rigorous competitiveness of the military services, they bring to bear a strength in conviction and a near unanimity of outlook that gives them an influence, in government councils and in Congress, on public policy disproportionate to their numbers. Disciplined and loyal to their respective services, with added prestige derived from heroic combat records, they operate with an efficiency not often found among civilian officials. 4

The danger to public policy arises from civilian authorities adopting the narrowness of outlook of professional soldiers — an outlook restricted by training and experience to the use of force. As we have developed into a society whose most prominent business is violence, one of the leading professions inevitably is soldiering. Since they are the professionals, and civilian bureaucrats refuse to challenge them, the military have become ardent and effective competitors for power in American society. 5

The services compete with each other for funds, for the control of weapons systems, and for the privilege of being "first to fight." Constantly improving their techniques for rapid deployment, they not only yearn to try them out but when opportunities arise they press their proposals on civilian authorities. The latter group all too often is tempted by the seemingly quick "surgical" course of action proposed by the military in preference to the long and wearisome methods of diplomacy. For a variety of reasons — from believing it the only course of action to testing equipment and techniques of counterinsurgency, or just to avoid the disgrace of being "left out" — all the military services were enthusiastic about the initial involvement in Vietnam. By now they should have had their fill, but they still push on, 6 trying out new weapons and new strategies — such as "destroying sanctuaries" in Cambodia.

The root cause of militarism is war, and so long as we have the one   7
we will be menaced by the other. The best defense against militarism is peace; the next best thing is the vigorous practice of democracy. The dissent against our government's actions in Southeast Asia, the opposition to the ABM and MIRV, and the increased willingness of many in the Congress to do something about the hitherto sacrosanct military budget are all encouraging signs of democracy being practiced. But there is much in American polity these days that is discouraging.

There seems to be a lack of concern among too many people about   8
the state of the nation, and a too easy acceptance of policies and actions of a kind that a generation ago would have appalled the citizenry. The apparent broad acceptance of the "volunteer army" idea comes to mind — a concept completely at variance with our historic development. Up to now, a blessing of our system has been that those who go into the military service, whether by enlistment or through the draft, could hardly wait to get out.* But today, because of the exigencies of the times, there is a chance that we may turn our back on this fundamental principle: a large, standing professional army has no place in this Republic.

Along with promoting militarism as part of our society, the mindless   9
violence of war has eaten away at our moral values as well as our sensitivity. Reporters covering the domestic aspects of the My Lai massacre story in the home area of Lieutenant Robert Calley were surprised to find loud support for the accused — not sympathy, which might be expected, but support. Among these people there seemed to be no recognition of possible wrongdoing or criminal act in the alleged massacre.

Beyond the discouragements — and even the disturbing things   10
such as the Cambodian adventure and our activities in Thailand and Laos — one has to hope, with reason drawn from our history, that the traditional workings of our system and the innate common sense of Americans will prevail. The task certainly is not going to be easy. We have been so stunned, almost desensitized — like Lieutenant Calley's supporters — by what has gone on during the recent past that it is almost possible to turn to total pessimism. History did not prepare the American people for the imperial role in which we find ourselves, and we are paying a moral price for it. From the time of the framing of our Constitution to the two world wars, our experience and values — if

*Despite attractive re-enlistment bonuses, the Army's rate of retention in 1969 of men finishing their first term is 14.6 percent for volunteers and 7.4 percent for draftees.

not our uniform practice — conditioned us not for the unilateral exercise of power but for the placing of limits upon it. Perhaps it was vanity, but we supposed that we could be an example for the world — an example of rationality and restraint.

Our practice has not lived up to that ideal but, from the earliest days 11 of the Republic, the ideal has retained its hold upon us, and every time we have acted inconsistently with it — not just in Vietnam and Cambodia — a hue and cry of opposition has arisen. When the United States invaded Mexico two former Presidents and a future one — John Quincy Adams, Van Buren, and Lincoln — denounced the war as violating American principles. Adams, the senior of them, is even said to have expressed the hope that General Taylor's officers would resign and his men desert. When the United States fought a war with Spain and then suppressed the patriotic resistance of the Philippines, the ranks of opposition numbered two former Presidents — Harrison and Cleveland — Senators and Congressmen, including the Speaker of the House of Representatives, and such distinguished — and differing — individuals as Andrew Carnegie and Samuel Gompers.

The incongruity between our old values and the new unilateral 12 power we wield has greatly troubled the American people. It has much to do, I suspect, with the current student rebellion. Like a human body reacting against a transplanted organ, our body politic is reacting against the alien values which, in the name of security, have been grafted upon it. We cannot, and dare not, divest ourselves of power, but we have a choice as to how we will use it. We can try to ride out the current convulsion in our society and adapt ourselves to a new role as the world's nuclear vigilante. Or we can try to adapt our power to our traditional values, never allowing it to become more than a means toward domestic societal ends, while seeking every opportunity to discipline it within an international community.

It is not going to help us to reach these ends to have a president 13 fearful that we are going to be "humiliated," nor for him to turn to the military as a prime source of advice on foreign affairs. In the case of Cambodia the President accepted military advice during the decision-making process, apparently in preference to that of the Department of State, thereby turning to an initial military solution rather than a diplomatic or political one. Of course the Senate was not consulted. Once the treaty power of the Senate was regarded as the only constitutional means of making a significant foreign commitment, while executive agreements in foreign affairs were confined to matters of routine. Today the treaty has been reduced to only one of a number of methods of entering binding foreign engagements. In current usage the term "commitment" is used less often to refer to obligations deriving from treaties than to those deriving from executive agreements and even simple, sometimes casual declarations.

Thailand provides an interesting illustration. Under the SEATO Treaty, the United States has only two specific obligations to Thailand: to act "in accordance with its constitutional processes" in the event that Thailand is overtly attacked, and to "consult immediately" with the other SEATO allies should Thailand be threatened by subversion. But the presence of 40,000 American troops, assigned there by the executive acting entirely on its own authority, creates a *de facto* commitment going far beyond the SEATO Treaty, a commitment largely based on military recommendations and desires. On March 6, 1962, Secretary of State Dean Rusk and Thai Foreign Minister Thanat Khoman issued a joint declaration in which Secretary Rusk expressed "the firm intention of the United States to aid Thailand, its ally and historic friend, in resisting Communist aggression and subversion." Obviously this goes far beyond the SEATO Treaty and omits any reference to Constitutional processes. 14

An even more striking illustration of the upgrading of a limited agreement into a *de facto* defense obligation is provided by the series of agreements negotiated over the past sixteen years for the maintenance of bases in Spain. Initiated under an executive agreement in 1953, the bases agreement was significantly upgraded by a joint declaration issued by Secretary Rusk and Spanish Foreign Minister Castiella in 1963 asserting that a "threat to either country" would be an occasion for each to "take such action as it may consider necessary within its constitutional processes." In strict constitutional law, this agreement, whose phrasing closely resembles that of our multilateral security treaties, would be binding on no one excepting Private Citizen Rusk; in fact it is what might be called the "functional equivalent" of a treaty ratified by the Senate. Acknowledging even more explicitly the extent of our *de facto* commitment to Spain, General Earle Wheeler, then Chairman of the Joint Chiefs of Staff, acting under instructions from Secretary Rusk, provided Spanish military authorities in 1968 with a secret memorandum asserting that the presence of American armed forces in Spain — like the ones who participated in *Exercise Pathfinder Express* described in chapter six — constituted a more significant security guarantee than would a written agreement. Again, as with the Thai commitment, strategic military considerations, arrived at by military commanders with the acquiesence of civilian authorities undoubtedly were the overriding factors in the political decision. 15

The Department of State is not alone among the agencies of government awed as well as outmanned, outmaneuvered, or simply elbowed aside by executive military decision-making. The Defense Department 16 has established a massive bureaucracy, like that at the Department of Commerce, the Atomic Energy Commission, the Department of Health, Education, and Welfare, and all the rest who protect their positions and interests within the mechanism of governmental power and appropriations.

When war was abhorrent to the American people, the military was 17 considered only as a tool to be used if needed. Today, with our chronic state of war, and with peace becoming the unusual, the military has created for itself an image as a comforting thing to have around. In reality, however, it has become a monster bureaucracy that can grind beneath its wheels the other bureaucracies, whatever their prescribed roles in the process of government and their legitimate needs.

One of the arms of the Defense Department monster bureaucracy is 18 the military public relations apparatus that today is selling the Administration's Southeast Asia policy, just as it sold the Vietnam policy of the previous Administration, with increasing emphasis on patriotic militarism and activity directed against its critics. The enthusiasm and dedication of the purveyors of the hard military line are such that their present course could easily be changed so as to direct attention to the removal of those in the Congress who question actions of the executive branch and the growth of military influence.

Considering the normal skepticism of the American citizen, such 19 overt political activity by the military would seem to have small chance of success. But I raise the point, nevertheless; the apparatus exists, and we of the Congress, in another context, have been put on notice that legitimate, and even constitutionally required questioning is viewed by some as interference with executive prerogatives.

It is interesting to compare American government's only *official* 20 propaganda organization, the U.S. Information Agency, with the Defense Department's apparatus. USIA is so circumscribed by Congress that it cannot, with the rarest of exceptions, distribute its materials within this country. Since much USIA output is composed of a filtered view of the United States and its policies, such a prohibition is eminently sensible. But the Defense Department, with more than twice as many people engaged in public relations as USIA has in all of its posts abroad, operates to distribute its propaganda within this country without control other than the executive, and floods the domestic scene with its special, narrow view of the military establishment and its role in the world.

Of course the military needs an information program. But it should 21 be one designed to inform, not promote or possibly deceive. There is no need for production of self-promotional films for public consumption. There is no need for flying private citizens about the country to demonstrate to them our military might. There is no need for sending speakers at taxpayers' expense anywhere from Pensacola, Florida, to Portland, Oregon, to talk to luncheon clubs and veterans organizations. There is no need for setting up expensive and elaborate exhibits at state and county fairs. There is no need for taking VIP's on pleasant cruises to Hawaii aboard aircraft carriers. There is no need for "Red," "White," and "Blue" teams criss-crossing the country, "educating" people about the dangers of communism, the need for patriotism, and the Gross National Product of newly independent lands. There certainly is no need for military production of television shows for domestic, commercial use showing "feature" aspects of the Southeast Asian war.

What can be done about the situation? 22

An obvious answer comes at once to mind — legislation that would 23 again set a ceiling on Defense Department public relations spending. It didn't work before, but perhaps this time it might be possible to require the Defense Department to report on a regular basis to the Congress and to the public on just what it is doing in the "information" field. Such legislation might also eliminate some of the activities that are far outside the military's proper role in our society — such as the "V-Series" films from Southeast Asia and the "educational" programs of the Industrial College of the Armed Forces. It also might require the State Department to enforce strict clearance of films, speeches, and other material involving foreign policy.

The passage of such legislation would be desirable, but only as a step 24 toward limiting the other activities in which the Pentagon is engaged far beyond the true mission assigned — of physically protecting the country.

The real solution to militarism, of course, requires a central attack on 25 the previously uncontrolled size of the military establishment. The growth of the military attitude began in perilous times when an implacable Stalin and world communism were a major threat to the noncommunist world recovering from a devastating war. But the growth of real Pentagon political power did not begin until we became increasingly involved in Vietnam seven years ago. Although the Congress these days is looking more coolly at the enormous defense budget than it has in the past, the surgical process of cutting back will be a difficult one — and not popular with many members to whose districts the military-industrial establishment has become of very great economic importance.

It may help if the public starts examining carefully attempts by the 26 military to sell them its point of view. The press, radio, and television might look more critically on the military's attempts to influence or use them. Not that the media have been remiss in their responsibilities. The exposure of the Starbird Memorandum, for example, was a very real

431

service, and frequently the press has been the only source of real information about what is going on in Southeast Asia and throughout the world. But there are some who allow themselves to be seduced by the military with free trips and VIP treatment, and even a few who are not much more than trained seals for the Pentagon. Also, there are editors who are not skeptical enough about the material fed to them by the military. Radio and television, as we have seen, are heavy users of the military's propaganda and public relations output. Perhaps some of their executives should devote more attention to filling their "public service" time examining the grave domestic problems besetting the country instead of using "V-Films" and the Army's "Big Picture."

Nearly ten years ago I made a speech to the National War College and   27
the Industrial College of the Armed Forces in Washington. I said:

> The effectiveness of our armed services depends upon the mainte-
> nance of their unique prestige and integrity. These will remain intact
> only so long as the services adhere to their tradition of nonpolitical
> professionalism. No group or institution can participate in political
> debate without itself becoming an object of partisan attack. It is pre-
> cisely because of its status as a nonpolitical institution that the military
> in the past has enjoyed the virtually unanimous support of the Ameri-
> can people and has thus been beyond partisan assault. . . . It is my hope
> that the armed services will never yield to misguided temptations
> which can only shatter the high esteem in which they are held. The
> preservation of that esteem is essential to the success of the armed
> forces in fulfilling their assigned mission and essential also, therefore,
> to the defense of the Republic.

Since I made that speech in 1961, the military has been dragged into   28
the political arena. President Johnson at one crisis point brought General Westmoreland from Saigon to address a joint session of the Congress, in order to counter critics in the Senate with an honored officer's
explanation as a means of selling administration policy. What troubles
me today is that some politicians want to use the military in such a role,
and will be loath to give it up.

An indication — let us say a hint — of some in the military's liking   29
that role is contained in the "Prize Essay 1970" printed in the March
1970 issue of *U.S. Naval Institute Proceedings,* a semi-official learned
journal on naval affairs printed in Annapolis, Maryland.

The prize essay, chosen presumably by a high-ranking group of naval   30
officers, is titled "Against All Enemies," and was written by Captain
Robert J. Hanks, USN, commander of a destroyer squadron who earlier
served in the Pentagon. The theme of his essay is that the military must
determine the nature and extent of external threats against our national
security, and must also determine the character of our response to
them. Captain Hanks also wrote that there are many individuals in the

country who want to curb the military, including a fair sampling of the Senate. He names Senators Clifford P. Case and Walter F. Mondale, who have questioned the need for more aircraft carriers, Mike Mansfield and Stuart Symington, who wonder about the size of our troop levels in Europe, Charles E. Goodell, who proposed withdrawal of our troops from Vietnam by December 1, 1970, and myself — people who he wrote, would, in effect, "so weaken this nation's defenses as to place the United States in the greatest jeopardy in its history."

Captain Hanks also came to the conclusion that "while the threat   31
from without remains, we now face an equally potent challenge from within. . . . In concentrating on the main task of the past 30 years — the external threat — some of us may have forgotten that we solemnly swore to support and defend the Constitution of the United States against all enemies, foreign *and domestic*" [Italics are Captain Hanks'.] And, "If the United States is to be protected against efforts of those who would place her in peril — through apathy, ignorance, or malice — we of the military cannot stand idly, silently by and watch it done. Our oath of office will not permit it."

A real hope in the fight against military influence, I believe, rests with   32
our young. War is abhorrent to them as it seemingly is not to many of us who have lived with slaughter for the past thirty years and made an apparent accommodation to the threat of nuclear destruction. The young remain unpersuaded that man is brought upon this earth solely to find his way to the grave. There is among them a vigorous affirmation of life, a love of life that is optimistic and confident of the future. The anti-life philosophy of militarism offends their minds and hearts.

An observation so widely cited that it is almost an axiom is that no one   33
hates war more than the professional soldier. I think de Tocqueville was closer to the mark when he wrote:

> . . . all the ambitious minds in a democratic army ardently long for war, because war makes vacancies [for promotion] available and at last allows violations of the rule of seniority, which is the one privilege natural to a democracy. We thus arrive at the strange conclusion that of all armies those which long for war most ardently are the democratic ones, but that of all peoples those most deeply attached to peace are the democratic nations. And the most extraordinary thing about the whole matter is that it is equality which is responsible for both these contradictory results.*

Beyond the ambition of which de Tocqueville wrote, there is even   34
more danger to our democracy from the dehumanizing kind of war we are fighting that produces among the military an insensitivity to life

*de Tocqueville, *Democracy in America,* pp. 622-623.

hard for the civilian to comprehend. We have fought many wars before, but none since our Revolution has lasted as long as the present one. Officers and noncoms go back to Southeast Asia for second and third tours of duty, to engage in second and third rounds of killing. Such long immersion in violence of the kind peculiar to this war cannot but brutalize many of those who go through it. *Harper's* magazine in its May 1970 issue ran an excerpt from Seymour M. Hersh's book on the My Lai massacre.*

Hersh wrote, "One brigade commander ran a contest to celebrate his   35
unit's 10,000th enemy kill. The winning GI received a week's pass to stay in the colonel's personal quarters. Many battalions staged contests among their rifle companies for the highest score in enemy kills, with the winning unit getting additional time for passes." I recall nothing during World War II that equals in callousness a statement that Hersh attributes to the colonel-son of a famous general: "I do like to see the arms and legs fly." Horrifying words, but no more so than the euphemisms "body count," "free-fire zone," and others the military use to camouflage their deadly business.

Perhaps there is something in the theory advanced by psychologist   36
Erich Fromm that in man there are polar attitudes toward life, "biophilia" (love of life) and "necrophilia" (love of death). Spinoza in his *Ethics,* Fromm says, epitomized the spirit of the biophile: "A freeman thinks of death least of all things and his wisdom is a dedication not of death but of life." The necrophile, on the other hand, has values precisely the reverse, for death, not life, excites and satisfies him. Hitler was a clear case of necrophilia, and Hitler and Stalin with their unlimited capacity and willingness to kill and destroy were loved by the necrophiles.

Fromm goes on to say that the necrophile, by extension in modern   37
society, might be labeled *homo mechanicus* who "has more pride in, and is more fascinated by, devices that can kill millions of people across several thousands of miles in minutes than he is depressed and frightened by the possibility of such mass destruction."

"If more people became aware of the difference between love of life   38
and love of death," Fromm goes on to say, "if they became aware that they themselves are already far gone in the direction of indifference or necrophilia, the shock alone could produce new and healthy reactions. ... Many might see through the pious rationalizations of the death lovers and change their admiration for them to disgust. Beyond this, our hypothesis would suggest one thing to those concerned with peace and survival: that every effort must be made to weaken the attraction of

My Lai 4: A Report on the Massacre and its Aftermath (New York: Random House, 1970).

death, and to strengthen the attraction of life. Why not declare that
there is only one truly dangerous subversion, the subversion of life?"
Why do not those who represent the traditions of religion and humanism speak up and say that there is no deadlier sin than love of death
and contempt for life?*

These are the kinds of questions the young are asking — not only   39
those who demonstrate and dissent but those, too, who go unwilling
aboard the jet aircrafts that daily fly from the West Coast to Saigon.
There are "bums" among them, of course, but on both sides — the
bomb makers and the droppers of excreta in college deans' offices on
one, and those who will turn their guns on frightened women and
children or make as much money as they can in the black market on
the other. But, by and large, the young of today are life-affirmers of a
seemingly new breed who may at last, I think, give meaning to the worn
phrases of generations of graduation speakers about their being "the
hope of the future."

However, the task of strengthening the "attraction of life," the core   40
of the American optimism that built this country, is in the hands of those
no longer young. It is my generation who must halt, then turn back the
incursions the military have made in our *civilian* system. These incursions have subverted or muffled civilian voices within the Executive
branch, weakened the constitutional role and responsibility of the Congress, and laid an economic and psychological burden on the public that
could be disastrous.

Subject

1. One might expect an opponent of the war in Vietnam to be an
opponent of the draft as well. What is Fulbright's objection to a volunteer army?

2. What seems to be the distinct advantage the military has in
getting its solutions to foreign problems accepted instead of peaceful,
diplomatic solutions?

3. How, according to Fulbright, have civilians aided the military in
its quest for power?

4. Does Fulbright's recommendation (paragraph 12), that we use
our power for domestic ends and severely limit it in foreign affairs,
mark him as an isolationist?

5. Consider the following proposition: "The existence of a Pentagon propaganda machine to get military budgets through Congress
indicates either that the military considers itself a better judge than

*"Creators and Destroyers," *Saturday Review,* January 4, 1964, pp. 22-25.

Congress of what is best for the country, or that bureaucracy strives to perpetuate itself, even beyond its usefulness."

6. Fulbright says the young are a "real hope — in the fight against military influence"; but later he says his own generation must do the job. Is he contradicting himself?

STRUCTURE

1. Although what Fulbright is arguing for (or against) is clear enough, the argument is long and rather loosely organized. Does the organization hurt the essay's effectiveness? Would some subheadings be helpful?

2. Consider Fulbright's use of supporting evidence; where is it most forceful? Are there any unsupported points which need evidence?

3. Fulbright is manifestly opposed to the military power grab; does he allow his position to influence the objectivity of his argument? Does he ever appear to be trying to be more than fair?

4. Is the "human body" analogy in paragraph 12 appropriate and forceful?

5. Why does Fulbright introduce the love-death theory of Erich Fromm toward the end of his essay? Does it seem an integral part of his argument? Is its primary appeal rational or emotional?

TACTICS FOR AMERICANS

Paul R. Ehrlich and
Richard L. Harriman

Paul Ehrlich, professor of biology and director of graduate studies at Stanford University, is a population biologist and ecologist. He is probably the most outspoken expert in these fields, having lectured at nearly 200 college campuses, testified at congressional hearings, and written many articles and several books on the threatened destruction of environment by overpopulation and careless consumption. His best-seller is The Population Bomb *(1968). Richard Harriman is a graduate student in political science at Stanford who has worked closely with Dr. Ehrlich on studies of the population crisis and its relationship to environmental deterioration. The argument which follows was taken from their book,* How to Be a Survivor *(1971).*

What specifically can average Americans do now to change the course 1 of their country and pave the way for the emergence of new men, new values, a new culture? The answer is, of course, that they must reclaim some of the power which has been gradually taken from them and vested in the corporate state. There is some debate at the moment about the exact nature of that state and precisely who holds how much power within it, but there is little dispute about the really crucial points. Power in the United States is almost as concentrated as wealth. As measured both by who makes the decisions and who benefits, very few people run the United States.

Whether the decision makers are mostly the extremely rich and those 2 they own and control or whether they include sizable numbers of more or less independent managers and technicians need not concern us here. At the moment, decisions are not made in any real sense by the people of the United States or by individuals who represent the best interests of the people at large. What is worse, the corporate state acts like a dinosaur rushing toward an abyss, too stupid or with too much momentum to turn aside. To put it another way, whoever is making the decisions is doing a very bad job.

What strategy is available, then, to divert the dinosaur before it takes us over the edge? The revolutionary or radical answer is to shoot it or blow it up. Only 3.5 percent of current college youth is categorized as revolutionary.[1] The liberal answer is to use the channels provided by the system to change the system.   3

The radical answer suffers from a great defect. It is difficult to stop a charging dinosaur with a BB gun or a firecracker, and, relative to the power of the corporate state, that is all the radicals have. The defect of the liberal answer is even greater. It has been tried, and it hasn't worked — you cannot stop a charging dinosaur by whispering in its ear, either.   4

We would like to suggest a multivalent approach to solving the problem, but first we would like to make one point crystal clear. There is no a priori reason why the dinosaur should *not* go over the edge. Contrary to widely-held American beliefs, everything does not always come out all right in the end. Individuals have difficulty imagining their own extinction; so do societies and species. We offer no sure solution, only directions in which to try.   5

Fundamentally, our approach is to use grassroots power. We have an elitist society with decisions in the hands of a few, and it is not working. We make no assumption that a more broadly based governmental structure automatically will lead to more intelligent decisions (although it could hardly avoid leading to greater equity). But we see no other choice except to try that route. We also see no choice but to attempt to wrest power from the special interests without destroying the technological apparatus of the nation. For, as we have indicated earlier, that apparatus is necessary if we are to save the world.   6

Charles Reich argues[2] that a fight to gain power is unnecessary, that all we have to do is await the emergence of the new men, of his "Consciousness III." He states: 7

> There is a great discovery awaiting those who choose a new set of values — a discovery comparable to the revelation that the Wizard of Oz was just a humbug. The discovery is simply this: there is nobody whatever on the other side. Nobody wants inadequate housing and medical care — only the machine. Nobody wants war except the machine. And even businessmen, once liberated, would like to roll in the grass and be in the sun. There is no need, then, to fight any group of

[1] Richard M. Scammon and Ben J. Wattenberg, *The Real Majority* (New York: Coward-McCann, Inc., 1970), p. 52.

[2] Charles Reich, *The Greening of America* (New York: Random House, 1970), Chapter 11.

438

people in America. They are all fellow sufferers. There is no reason to fight the machine. It can be made the servant of man. Consciousness III can make a new society.[3]

Reich might well be right; if we had the time, the new men might 8 gradually take over and all would be well. But we haven't got a generation — we only have a few years. And the people in power are, perhaps with the best of intentions, killing us all. Here is what James D. Reilly, a Vice President of Consolidated Coal Company, said in a speech at Pittsburgh on May 8, 1969:

> The conservationists who want strip miners to restore land are stupid idiots, Socialists, and Commies who don't know what they are talking about. I think it is our bounden duty to knock them down and subject them to the ridicule they deserve.[4]

If James Reilly is not an enemy, he will do until one comes along. Our 9 society is loaded with enemies, and we cannot merely wait for them to die off. And we cannot, as Reich suggests, hole up until the bad times are over. The bad times will probably kill us in our holes, and if they don't, they may well outlast us.

There is nothing extreme about our program for changing the direc- 10 tion of the corporate beast. Basically, we suggest that public education and consumer boycott should lay the groundwork for political action.

A number of things give us hope. The first is that survival itself is the 11 issue. Once people understand that, they will fight like hell for it — even the Mr. Reillys of the world. Many of the people with power are smart, some are liberal, and all want to survive. When *they* can be convinced that our current course is killing *them,* the course will be changed. The second hopeful thing is that it is becoming more and more difficult to avoid the truth. The situation is deteriorating on all sides, and the need for fundamental change is becoming increasingly apparent. The third reason for hope is the appearance of some new men, the development of Reich's New Consciousness, especially among some of our young. If these new men turn outward to help their fellow men, they may be a powerful engine for change.

Consumer Power

We need grassroots power, and one way to grassroots power is 12 through a consumer movement. Ralph Nader's Center for the Study of Responsive Law and John Banzhaf's group at the School of Law of

[3]Reich, p. 348.

[4]Quoted by Harry M. Caudill in "Are Conservation and Capitalism Compatible?" in H. W. Helfrich, Jr., *Agenda for Survival; The Environmental Crisis — 2* (New Haven: Yale University Press, 1970), p. 177.

George Washington University in Washington, D.C. are both doing good jobs in the area of legal reform of consumer protection legislation. Consumer's Union through their house publication, *Consumer's Report,* is doing a fine job of educating the consumer on which products are the best buy, but it does not advocate group action, nor does it of course suggest that purchasing be restricted in any way. Progress in this area is greatly impeded by the vested interests that wield multi-billion dollar influence in our government. The last thing they want to see is effectively organized consumer power. We already know that we must neutralize the influence of these special interest lobbies in some way — the question is "how?"

The answer would seem to lie in organizing a *national cooperative* 13 *movement* which will exercise great economic and political power. A buyers' cooperative committed to the realistic use of economic power could reorganize American business practices by boycotting and striking on a mass scale. It could pledge a fixed percentage of its sales income to supporting political action population-environment groups. Hopefully, it could form the basis for a mass movement. Not only will the consumer pay reduced prices for ecologically sound products, but also he will be indirectly supporting the population-environment groups which can really *do* something about changing our political institutions.

With the support of groups like Nader's Raiders, a truly national, 14 powerful Consumer's Union could force the American business community to exercise social responsibility toward their customers. The rationale is simple: *everyone* is a consumer — even the poorest individual is a consumer at least of food and housing. Labor has long been organized, but no one has proceeded systematically to organize the hundreds of billions of dollars of consumer purchasing power. Consumers must have a say in the production of the goods which are offered for sale if our society is to survive.

Can you imagine the impact if a national cooperative were to say, 15 "For the next two years we are not going to buy groceries at Safeway or automotive products from General Motors!" Obviously, this threat would be lifted if the corporation involved, whatever it might be, met some predetermined, specific performance requirements, such as buying only union-grown food; not selling products that come in nonbiodegradable wrappings or no-deposit, no-return containers; reducing the prices on certain items or not selling them at all; ceasing to produce major cosmetic automobile model changes year after year without much improvement of safety features; making more durable, smaller, less powerful and recyclable vehicles; reducing the prices of automotive products. If the boycotts were successful, the consumers' cooperative obviously would have to help support the workers unemployed because of boycotts by giving them additional food discounts and contributing to strike funds. But, hopefully, the large scale and impact of the boycotts would make them short-term affairs.

There are enough other places to buy goods in this country so that 16 corporate giants who refuse to participate in a competitive economy can be heavily penalized. Oligopolistic capitalism in this country has had its day; now it is time for the enforced consumer to become a user by choice.

The same sort of tactics may be applied to the housing situation. 17 Tenants' unions and strikes, if well organized and financially underwritten by consumer groups, could be extremely effective. The key to the entire strategy is organization and solidarity, just as it was in the labor union movement.

Once consumers have been organized, very potent political weapons 18 will reside in their confidence and economic power. Imagine what would happen if, say, two million taxpayers deducted 60 percent from their federal taxes, an amount proportional to their share of the military budget. Such massive group action would be a far different problem for the military-industrial complex than the scattered refusal to pay war taxes by such courageous individuals as Joan Baez. Most citizens do not like paying taxes anyway, so it might not take much to convince a large number of average taxpayers to withhold a sizable chunk of their taxes, especially when they knew that many other people were doing the same thing. Even if the taxpayers ultimately yielded to the pressure of governmental lawsuits and agreed to pay their taxes, the backlog of paperwork and the delay in receiving the taxes would cause financial havoc for the government programs. If the government tried to hold out on welfare, social security, or other popular disbursements in order to continue supporting the military, then people would really *feel* where their money was being spent.

Once a cooperative movement had gained momentum, it could also 19 engage in an enormous campaign to re-educate other consumers and to change their buying habits. The pitch might be: "Try to live below your means! It will be good for your family's economic situation, and it may also help to save the world." Not only would people be urged to buy less, but to buy better quality products, whenever there was a choice they could afford. They might also be asked to change their dietary habits for their own good health and for the health of the world-wide ecosystem. Much of the food sold to the American public in supermarkets is nutritionally sub-standard. Recent reports on breakfast cereals, bread that has most of the important nutrients removed, and on the deceptive practices used to treat meat to make it look fresher give some indication of the degree of responsibility that the food

441

industry feels toward its captive clientele. It is extremely difficult for an American to eat an adequately balanced diet, especially without taking in too many calories. Many food additives are of doubtful safety, and the highly saturated fats produced in our higher-yield meat industry may be extremely dangerous to health. An effective national consumer group could drive America's "plastic bread" and all of its sleazy relatives from the grocer's shelves.

Giant corporations must be shown that there is extreme public disap- 20 proval of their activities. Suggested tactics have ranged from shutting down industry switchboards through organized telephone campaigns to long term boycotts of one or more automobile manufacturer's products. Certainly, it would be no hardship for everyone who needed an automobile during the year to purchase a used car. But one must also weigh the effects of such a boycott on the employees of the automobile industry. It is encumbent, therefore, on boycotting organizations to include programs in their planning to alleviate the distress which may be experienced by some segments of the labor force.

We do not wish to denigrate the individual symbolic protest tactics 21 suggested in *The Environmental Handbook* and *Ecotactics* or the efforts of environmental groups such as Ecology Action. But they must be recognized for exactly what they are — symbolic protests. As we have indicated, changing individual attitudes and patterns of behavior as expressed through personal life styles is extremely important. But the larger institutions which limit the alternatives for individual behavior must also be changed before any really significant progress in solving the population-environment crisis can be made. And, before these basic institutions can be changed, we must gain the power to change them. This, of course, means gaining control of the political system.

A prerequisite, if this overall strategy is to have any chance of success, 22 is to enlist more people into the survival movement as soon as possible. A prime target should be the recruitment of the young. They must be reached before they fossilize into standard American consumers and polluters. Those of us who are over thirty must try to infiltrate the education process by teaching, participating in the local P.T.A., running for the school board in our communities, or by becoming involved with youth in other ways. You might, for instance, be able to help young people organize programs and ecology fairs by finding informed speakers for such meetings, or, even better, by becoming well-informed and speaking yourself.

Concerned people who are fortunate enough to be young can also 23 contribute. If you are a junior high, high school or college student, there are two effective tactics you can employ: talk to your parents and their friends, and bring social pressure to bear on your own friends and

acquaintances whose attitudes are contrary to environmental principles or who exhibit ecologically unsound behavior. Surprising as it may
seem, parents are listening to their children more and more.

Keep after your parents. Show your concern by becoming a walking   24
encyclopedia on population and environment. Give them books to
read. Start out with popular, straightforward books, such as *Moment in
the Sun* and *The Rich and the Super-Rich.* Discuss the issues with them;
tell them about the candidates who are strong on population-environment issues and discourage them from voting for old-style politicians
who do not understand the urgency of the crisis. You will have maximum impact on your parents and their friends if you are well informed,
stick to the issues, and remain patient and unemotional.

The same procedures hold true for friends of your own age. The only   25
difference is that you should make it clear that certain attitudes and
behavior are socially unacceptable. If one of your classmates expresses
a desire to have more than two natural children, inform him of the facts
and make sure that he understands the seriousness of the situation. If
one of your friends wants a big new car or buys lots of new clothes to
keep up with the new fashions being pushed by Madison Avenue, let
him know that his attitudes are not only ecologically destructive, but
repugnant to you. If one of your friends stops riding a bicycle to school
or work and begins driving a car, let him know that you disapprove; or
if he stops driving a car and starts riding a bicycle, let him know how
pleased you are. You will be surprised how much impact the opinion
of peers can have. Adults may have similar effects on their associates,
although the older one is, the more thoroughly entrenched consumer-
ism and other attitudes are likely to be.

These are just a few suggestions, but whatever you do (unless you are   26
already active in a national organization), start out on a local level and
work within the institutions most familiar to you. These are the places
where you will be most effective and where you can exert your maximum influence. Young or old, if you are a member of the J.C.'s, the Boy
Scouts or Girl Scouts, the Kiwanis Club, the Lions Club, Rotarians,
garden club, church group, Junior League, DAR, American Legion,
etc., work within your own organization to steer its activities and policies in the direction of survival. Almost everyone belongs to at least one
organization at school, at work, or in connection with sports, hobbies,
church, social activities, etc. If you are not affiliated with some such
group, join one and make your views known. Even if you do not completely convince anyone, at least you may expose others to your ideas
and to the issues involved.

Besides attacking on the local front, you may well want to participate   27
in the larger battle. There are several national action organizations

concerned with population-environmental issues with which you can affiliate. Most will give you assistance if you want to start a new chapter. At the present time, the formation of new national groups will only tend to divide the population-environment movement, and unity is going to be essential in the long, hard fight to come. We receive a great many letters describing groups that have just been formed and who are now soliciting financial assistance and public support. Although it is encouraging that so many people are interested, more consolidated effort is needed in order to apply a maximum amount of pressure on specific targets. Once some tangible victories have been chalked up, there will be more public support for a broader approach.

The very real danger of being divided and dissipating energy was 28 apparent at the First National Congress on Optimum Population and Environment held in Chicago in June, 1970. Unfortunately, much of the energy generated there by the 1200 delegates, representing hundreds of groups, was expressed as schisms between factions. Much time and effort was spent trying to achieve unity, instead of being directed outward toward common objectives. "Divide and conquer" is a time-honored defensive tactic that many special interest groups will be quick to employ against us.

Once you have affiliated with an organization, pick a specific local 29 project and get going. You may wish to support a "good guy" in a political race, boycott a polluter, or picket a hospital which will not perform legal abortions or sterilizations on demand. Remember, you can have the most impact on those issues which you and other members of your group know best. Remember also that time is short, and therefore political action should have top priority whenever possible.

Political Power

A great weakness of both our major political parties is that we never 30 hear from them except during election years, and, even then, only when they want something. A sustained campaign must be launched to inform large numbers of citizens of the issues and to keep these concerns in the forefront of their minds. In other words, we face the unenviable task of trying to educate and politicize millions of ordinarily apathetic citizens. But we have the best of circumstances under which to do so. The deteriorating environment will not go away. Its problems will thrust themselves on a public trained to feel entitled to the "best," until that public begins to ask *why*. It is only a question of time. The sooner we can get the question asked, the better. The short-term goal is to elect in 1972 an ecologically-oriented President and Vice-President, and to effect great personnel changes in Congress and in state and

444

local governments. This means working to elect public officials at all levels who understand the urgency of the population-environment crisis and who are willing dramatically to modify the old system in a last-ditch attempt to find solutions. Not only must we defeat the pseudo-environmentalists and do-nothing candidates in 1972, we must sustain our efforts until we have removed most of those presently in power from the system and modified it structurally, so that a similar anti-human juggernaut cannot evolve again. The only hope of success lies in organization and persistence.

Organization and persistence could provide the United States with   31
an alternative to the business as usual, Democratic/Republican party brand of politics. People who are sincerely interested in population-resource-environment issues should be offered something new and effective for a change. We think that the emergence of a new major political party may be necessary. Reluctantly, we have come to the conclusion that the two major political parties, left on their own, are unlikely to give us any alternatives. There is simply too much inertia in the ranks of the old-style politicians. Even if we could convince the Democratic or Republican party to adopt strong population-environment planks in their platforms, the candidates would adhere to the old politics and continue, once elected, to permit the government to be run by well-financed business interests. So powerful are these interests — the power lobby, the automobile-highway lobby, the oil lobby, the drug lobby, the food lobby, and so on — that it would be difficult for the new men to counter them, impossible for the old.

An alternative might be provided by a mobilization of grassroots   32
power. It might be possible to unite all the dissatisfied liberal elements of both parties — intellectuals, minority groups, students, and those workers who have come to understand that for them there is no difference between the present Democratic and Republican parties — with any radicals willing to try coalition politics. A coalition might be formed of moderate and liberal Democrats and Republicans, and those to the left and to the right of them who have a stronger interest in survival than in perpetuating over-consumption. Organizations such as *Zero Population Growth* and *Friends of the Earth* might form the nucleus of such a coalition.

Perhaps the most optimistic scenario is one in which the new coali-   33
tion takes over the Democratic Party — making it, in essence, a new party. The Republican Party resulted fundamentally from a single-issue controversy, the debate over the abolition of slavery in the 1850's. The new Democratic Party would concentrate on the single issue of survival. The strength and power of this new party would be to offer alternative candidates, policies, and political styles which neither party

445

in its present form is willing to consider. A coalition victory under the flag of the New Democrats in 1972 could presage the absorption of liberal Republicans into that new party, and a switch of conservative Democrats into the Republican Party. That party could then provide a constructively conservative opposition.

Above all, many more Americans must become deeply involved in politics. In a democracy, the electorate gets only what it deserves and what it is willing to pay for. Expectation sets the limits on realization, and our political system functions no better than we expect it to. As long as much of the American public continues to shun politics as a "dirty business," the American political system will continue to be exactly that. Both the system and the politicians will rarely rise above the mediocre. Unless the American electorate shouts out its disapproval and backs it up with a sustained effort and financial support, the voters will continue to get the same plastic bread and technological circuses which have been their fare for the past two decades. 34

There is, of course, great inertia in the American political system. Student activists, young radicals and others who have the idealism to want to change the system, must show the staying power needed to topple the vested interests of the so-called establishment. The incumbents and the special interest groups, who *do* have the perseverance and the financial backing, have long ago lost their idealism. With a combination of idealism and persistence it may be possible to effect positive changes in the system. 35

Two illustrations of this political reality could be seen in Earth Day and the campus strikes following the American invasion of Cambodia in the spring of 1970. A frenzy of activity and publicity about ecology culminated on April 22nd, Earth Day. After that date, numerous fair-weather "ecologists" got off the bandwagon and presumably went in search of a new fad. But a determined group persisted and helped to defeat a series of environmentally irresponsible candidates in the November 1970 elections. In contrast, the student strikes following the invasion of Cambodia were white hot, and the heat was short-lived. Two weeks after the initial protest, everything was back to "business as usual" on many campuses. The administration was effectively able to defuse the Indochina war issue because not enough people were able to apply continuous political pressure. 36

The environmental battles were often won in close races where conservation votes made the difference; few hawk-dove races were close enough for peace votes to turn the tide. But one should not despair over this result. Intensive political activity by peace groups since 1965 has led to the deposing of one president and an immense change in Ameri- 37 can public opinion at all levels. We must finish the job on the war and move on to attacking the disease of which it is a symbol.

If the present political system is to be revised and a new politics 38 introduced, we must employ political judo. In other words, the momentum and mechanisms within the system must be used against the system. Finesse, rather than force, must be used in order to gain control of the system before it can be changed. This does not mean that power politics and high pressure political tactics will not be employed. On the contrary, nonviolent power must be brought to bear on the politicians and institutions that have used similar force to the public disadvantage in the past.

Organizational Detail

Although there is no single way to organize citizens' action groups 39 and each community has its own political personality, there are several basic guidelines to follow in order to avoid the usual pitfalls into which inexperienced organizers can stray. Start small and build a good, solid, hard-core nucleus of reliable leaders before trying to go community-wide. Most organizations function because of the labors of a very few people. Do not allow a chapter to become cumbersomely large; not beyond 50 or so active members who know one another. When such a size is reached, having sister organizations or chapters working independently, although in communication, is more efficient. Strengthen your communications system by designing a "telephone tree" in which one call generates two more calls, etc. This is important to promote fast action and a short response time, both of which are absolutely critical to succeed at the legislative lobbying game.

The same principle holds true for mailings: make sure you have 40 *complete* information on each member of your group — this includes both home and business phone numbers and addresses. If possible, it is best to standardize this information by putting it on duplicate 3" X 5" cards and *cross-filing* them alphabetically and also by chapter location or function in the organization. Keep an alphabetized master sheet listing all members for quick reference; this should be updated at regular intervals. Too many organizations have collapsed unnecessarily; not from lack of energy, work, or enthusiasm, but rather, because of a poorly organized administrative section. These procedures are really simple to execute and they pay off handsomely in the end, especially under high-pressure crisis situations.

Finances, have also been the downfall of a number of groups and 41 clubs — not merely a lack of funds to support worthwhile programs,

447

but mismanagement of the financial affairs of the organization. Above all else, avoid becoming overextended. Do not commit the organization to long-range projects for which you do not have sufficient funding guaranteed. Being aggressive with your present resources is one thing; being overambitious is quite another. As soon as possible, once the organization is large enough to justify it, locate a volunteer bookkeeper, accountant, and tax attorney for your organization. If you cannot locate a volunteer, it is false economy not to retain the services of professionals, because in the long haul they will save you many more headaches and dollars than you will pay out in fees. Fund raising also benefits from professional advice. Dues, proceeds from sales, fairs, etc., have their place, but concerted and systematic attempts to raise money from donors may make the difference between a viable and a moribund organization.

We would like to reiterate that many problems can be avoided by 42 working through the national organization, which can probably give you guidance. Remember also that great care is usually necessary to avoid internal dissension in volunteer organizations. People are not necessarily compatible merely because they share a common cause. If the world is to be saved, it will be saved by the cooperation of people who agree 50 to 60 percent of the time; 100 percent agreement is rare indeed!

A Last Word

Although we have referred to it several times before, we would like 43 to conclude with a reassertion of our conviction that the population-environment movement is absolutely inseparable from the antiwar movement, the drive for urban rehabilitation, prison reform, and — most importantly — the civil rights movement. The destruction of our environment is tied up to a critical extent with our prevalent philosophy of racism and the exploitation of minority groups, whether they be black, brown, yellow, red, poor, hip, or female. Any attempt to clean the air or water for white, middle-class suburbanites, or to preserve free-running streams or open spaces for the esthetic pleasure of an economic elite which can afford to use them is doomed to failure if the educational and socioeconomic needs of a large, oppressed minority of people in this country are not met at the same time. There is simply no earthly reason for any ghetto dweller to pay taxes or to stand patiently by while the rest of the society seizes the "ccology cop-out" as an excuse for further delay on long overdue social, economic, and educational reforms for the deprived minority.

By the same token, the minorities who are justifiably fighting for their 44
rights must appreciate the necessity of restoring the capacity of our
biosphere to support life on a long-term basis. It is understandable that
when confronted with a choice between laying claim to his own civil
rights as a human being and working wholeheartedly for the ecology
movement, a member of a minority group must choose the former. But
the very quality of humanity which should entitle him to be treated as
a human being also obligates him, if not to support, at least not to
obstruct the honest efforts of others to work on his behalf to guarantee
all of us a place to exercise our equal rights as human beings.

In the long run, it is the sum total of the actions of millions of individu- 45
als that constitutes effective group action, cultural reformation, or revolution. What has become the population-environment movement
began a long time ago with the individual efforts of a few. Even if you
are not committed to the long-term survival of the human race or to
the short-term survival of your neighbor, it is in your own self-interest
to consider your own survival and that of your family. If for no reason
other than that of self-interest, commit yourself to act. The next time
someone asks you, "What can I do?" — tell him to slow down, live
more simply by consuming less, support *Zero Population Growth* and
Friends of the Earth, and get involved in the political process. Then
do it. Otherwise, we shall all eventually find ourselves stranded in space
on a dead Spaceship Earth with no place to go and no way to get there.

Subject

1. This essay was published as an appendix to an entire book describing the problems which need solution; does the appendix make
clear enough what those basic problems are?

2. "There is no a priori reason why the dinosaur should *not* go over
the edge" (paragraph 5). This point does not form a basic premise for
Ehrlich's argument; why is he anxious to make it "crystal clear"?

3. What, according to this essay, is wrong with the radical and the
liberal approaches? What is "wrong" with Charles Reich's theory?

4. How does Ehrlich propose to put consumer power to work?
What is the prime necessity for such a plan to be effective?

5. Ehrlich suggests that military expenditures could be controlled
if people refused to pay part of their income tax; should he have
considered the fact that most people's taxes are deducted from their
paychecks?

6. Does the suggestion for the use of political power seem to be as
workable as that for consumer power?

449

7.   The advice in the section called "Organizational Detail" is not very startling; would it be especially helpful to a group just getting started? Is the simplicity of the advice itself an encouragement to get started?

STRUCTURE

1.   What is added to this essay that is not part of the argument proper? (It might be noted that one omission from a complete argument — the evidence establishing a *need* for something to be done — has been provided by the book which precedes this appendix.)

2.   Does Ehrlich seem to be addressing himself to a general audience or to a special group?

3.   Ehrlich uses an extended dinosaur analogy near the beginning of the essay; why is "dinosaur" a more appropriate choice than, say, "juggernaut" or "mechanical monster"?

4.   Does Ehrlich devote more space to refutation of alternative solutions or to confirmation of his own solution? Should there have been a balance between the two?

5.   What is the chief weakness of the section on political power? How could it have been strengthened?

6.   The appeal of the final paragraph is to self-interest; is this a more effective way to end than by an appeal to humanitarian instincts?

A SCENE,
A STORY,
AND THREE POEMS

Edward Bond

Edward Bond, a British playwright, was born and educated in London. His first play, The Pope's Wedding, *was staged at the Royal Court Theatre in 1962. This was followed by* Saved *in 1965,* Early Morning *in 1968, and* Narrow Road to the Deep North *in 1968. Early Morning won the George Devine drama award. Bond has also written several successful film scripts, including Antonioni's* Blow Up. *The following piece might best be called a requiem. Sharpeville, at Vereeniging in the Union of South Africa, was the scene of a massacre of unarmed black protesters by white troops.*

(Written for the Sharpeville Massacre Tenth Anniversary Commemoration Evening, held by the Anti-Apartheid Movement at the Lyceum Theatre on 22 March, 1970).

Poem: I Cannot Mourn

I cannot mourn men killed at Sharpeville
How can I mourn when I have to say who are they?
Faces I have not seen, unrecognisable in dust anyway
Voices I have not heard, the screams could be anyone's
Hands fighting death, making gestures you see on posters   5
How can I mourn when I can't believe it happened?
How can I believe men shot parents running to hold their children?

How can I believe men shot children?
What men shoot children in the back?

451

But I can understand when I see it like this   10
Sharpeville isn't a village
It isn't even a nation
It's an effect that follows a cause
Be afraid like that
Covet like that   15
Hate like that
Believe in the armed state
That is the font of all wisdom and violence
And the effect follows
Sharpeville is very simple   20
The sentry must challenge the dark and shoot the mountain
The righteous must have their victim
Then the bodies are stacked by my door
I step over them in the street when I go home
I wake and they're piled at my window.   25

Scene: Black Mass

(A church at Vereeniging. An altar and a large cross. The altar is plain   1
and covered by a white cloth. The cross is made of simple wood. A
lifesize Christ is nailed to it. A PRIEST and a PRIME MINISTER. The
PRIME MINISTER kneels for communion)

PRIEST. Ye that do truly and earnestly repent you of your sins and are   2
in love and charity with your neighbours and intend to lead a new life
make your humble confession to almighty god meekly kneeling upon
your knees. (Pause) Meekly kneeling upon your knees ...

P.M. (After a pause) You said something, padre?   3

PRIEST. You have a lot on your mind.   4

P.M. True.   5

PRIEST. Something in particular, prime minister? Perhaps I can help.   6

P.M. You are a help, padre. It's nothing in particular. I wish — I wish I   7
got a little more understanding. Something more in the way of appreciation. Even a bit less abuse. But you know, padre, I tell myself
— I only tell myself in secret, of course — that men of vision are
bound to be misunderstood in their own time and being misunderstood

is part of the privilege of being a man of vision. Well, let's get on. There's a cabinet meeting this afternoon. You were saying?

PRIEST. Meekly kneeling upon your knees.   8

P.M. Ah, yes. Almighty god judge of all men we acknowledge and be-   9
wail our manifold sins and wickednesses which we — and now there's
that crowd of Kaffirs down the road — from time to time most grievously have committed by thought word and deed — just stuck there
— we do earnestly repent and are heartily sorry for these our misdo-
ings the remembrance of them is grievous unto us the burden of them
intolerable have mercy upon us — you'd think they'd have the decency to go, they get pleasure out of causing trouble and giving me a
bad name abroad — padre, yes, have mercy upon us — and what can
I do, they tie my hands and stand in front of the gun and when I squeeze
the trigger it's my fault because they're aggressive enough to get hit,
I must make a note of that for the cabinet meeting (he writes in a little
notebook) — did I say we acknowledge and bewail our manifold? note
how I'm on my knees, I wish they could see that abroad, I'm not
ashamed to pray for guidance, how else could I be sure I was doing the
right thing? — But I mustn't stay here talking, padre, enjoyable
though that is. We must put our hand to the plow, amen.

PRIEST. Lift up your hearts.   10

P.M. We lift them up.   11

   (An INSPECTOR comes in. The PRIEST goes to the altar and prepares   12
   communion)

INSPECTOR. The Kaffirs are still there, sir.   13

P.M. You showed them the planes?   14

INSPECTOR. Did do, sir.   15

P.M. And they still stayed?   16

INSPECTOR. So we brought in reinforcements. The lads didn't like it.   17
They were playing rugger, tennis, cricket, and other mind-cleansing
and body-building games, but they came when they heard the
summons.

P.M. What about the Saracens?   18

INSPECTOR. As useless as the planes.   19

P.M. Oh.   20

INSPECTOR. They're British made, so you wouldn't expect them to 21
work. You might as well send them out on the milk round. Never mind,
we've got our own personal weapons, all made in the home country
— they'll shift them. (He goes to the altar, where the PRIEST is making ritual gestures) Could I disturb you for a moment, padre? (He takes
rifles from under the altar) Could you say a prayer for the boys while
you're at it, padre?

PRIEST. I'm always praying for the boys. 22

INSPECTOR. Thank you padre. We'll do you a good turn some day, man. 23

(The INSPECTOR leaves. The PRIEST turns to the P.M. with the bread 24
and wine)

P.M. Time spent on your knees is never wasted. 25

PRIEST. I wish more people thought like you, prime minister. 26

P.M. So do I. 27

PRIEST. (Offering the bread) Take and eat this in remembrance that 28
Christ died for thee and feed on him —

(Loud rifle fire, off. After twenty seconds the PRIEST speaks again) 29

PRIEST. Do you hear a noise, prime minister? 30

P.M. No. 31

PRIEST. I think perhaps there *is* a sound. Perhaps we should go and see 32
if we can —

P.M. I don't know what you hear, but I can't hear it. *My* mind is entirely 33
concentrated on the appropriate holy thoughts.

PRIEST. Oh so is mine! But I thought I — well, your hearing is better 34
than mine.

P.M. Then let's get on. I can't keep the cabinet waiting. 35

(The rifle fire stops and the INSPECTOR comes in) 36

INSPECTOR. We had to use fire, sir. 37

P.M. Dear me. 38

INSPECTOR. They wouldn't go. And the lads were impatient. They'd 39
been pulled away in the middle of their matches, you see, sir — naturally they were keen to get back and win! There's no fun in shooting
at people nowadays. Too many rules in the game. It doesn't really
qualify as a sport any more — though mind you the lads still try to

play in the spirit of the old amateurs, even if they've turned professional. But it can't hold a candle to wildfowling. You've shot one man and you've shot them all. Still, they put up a show.

P.M. What was the final score?   40

INSPECTOR. 69 — 0. They certainly didn't let the opposition walk over   41
them. The lads really put their backs into the training. There *were* a
few they could have brought off if they'd been on the ball. They set
them up, but they couldn't follow it through. Still, they showed real
style and you can't ask fairer than that. They've gone off to the shower.
Might be as well if you had a word with them, sir. After all, they won.
They're good lads and I don't doubt for one moment they're their own
hardest critics. I watched their faces and you could see how when one
of them missed he knew he'd let the team down. The lady folk have
prepared some beer and sandwiches and a few party dainties — perhaps you'd care to join us, padre?

PRIEST. Later on, I'd like that.   42

P.M. We'll just give them a pat on the head now, while they're hosing   43
down. They like to see the board going round straight after the whistle
— show them you take an interest.

(The P.M., INSPECTOR and PRIEST go. CHRIST comes down from the   44
cross. He raises his hands to speak, but drops them. He puts something
in the communion wine, and goes back onto the cross. The P.M.
and PRIEST return)

PRIEST. Most of them were shot in the back.   45

P.M. (Kneeling) It's the nature of the Kaffir to turn his back when con- 46
fronted with the white man's weapons.

PRIEST. Shall we finish this?   47

P.M. It's a long day but it has its rewards.   48

PRIEST. (Offers bread) Take this and remember that Christ died for   49
thee.

P.M. (Swallows) You know, the lads think it's all over now and they can   50
go home and sleep quietly in their beds like little children, but I'll be
burning the midnight oil — the paperwork a thing like this involves
— the paperwork — it never stops! I only wish you could dispose of
paper as easily as you dispose of people. Paper's more difficult to handle.

PRIEST. (Offers wine) Drink this in remembrance that Christ's blood   51
was shed for thee and be thankful.

P.M. I don't begrudge them their sleep when they've earned it but 52
there are times when I could gladly lay down the burdens of the helm.
(Dies)

(INSPECTOR comes in) 53

INSPECTOR. Did I hear a body falling? Too late! I shall examine the 54
scene of the crime for clues and pounce on the accused with professional speed. Note how, as he faced his maker, he showed the whites
of his eyes.

PRIEST. I wish it could have happened somewhere else. It looks bad 55
here.

INSPECTOR. That's the mark of the black hand — no respect for the 56
proprieties. This is a typical Kaffir foul — behind the umpire's back.
I'm on to something here! A row of little spots. The accused was crying
— unless I'm mistaken and he was peeing himself.

PRIEST. In church? 57

INSPECTOR. Just a little joke, padre. No intention of mocking the cloth. 58
(He follows the trail of spots to the cross) And here we have just what
I was looking for: a little puddle. (To CHRIST) Just a moment, sir. (Takes
out a notebook) Would you mind telling me your name, permanent
address and occupation and explain what you're doing trespassing on
these premises?

PRIEST. I think there's a mistake, Inspector. 59

INSPECTOR. You know this fellow, sir? 60

PRIEST. Yes. 61

INSPECTOR. (Starts to put his notebook away) In that case I take it you're 62
not prepared to vouch for this gentleman's bona fides.

PRIEST. Well . . . not entirely. 63

INSPECTOR. I see. Dearie me then. In that case I must ask the gentle- 64
man to accompany me to the station.

PRIEST. No. I — let me pray for guidance. 65

INSPECTOR. In the circumstances I think prayer comes under the Con- 66
spiracy Act.

PRIEST. That makes it difficult. I'll have to guess the answer. (To CHRIST) 67
I'm afraid I must ask you to leave.

INSPECTOR. I'm sorry, padre. It's gone further than that. 68

456

PRIEST. This is the best way. The whole incident could be blown up out 69
of proportion.

INSPECTOR. You mean the gentleman has friends abroad? 70

PRIEST. Frankly I'm not sure, but it's not worth the risk. 71

INSPECTOR. In that case I'll leave the matter in your hands, as there's 72
no one here to represent Interpol.

PRIEST. (To CHRIST) You've heard, I've been able to spare you some of 73
the public disgrace. But now I must ask you to collect your things and
go immediately. I can't risk your contaminating the young people we
have here. I'm very disappointed in you. Oh, I'm not thinking of myself
and all the wasted effort I've thrown away — but you've let yourself
down. It's too late to say it now, but you weren't without promise —
and you've thrown all that away. You'll regret it in a few years and you'll
look back on this and see we were right. I hope by then you'll have
learned something. You'll never make anything of yourself if you go on
the way you've started. I shall say no more. (CHRIST comes down from
the cross and starts to leave. He stops when the PRIEST talks again) God
knows what your family will think of this. You've got a good family and
they gave you a start in life many others would envy — and you've let
them down, too. I shan't go on. Please leave quietly. It's too late for
explanations and apologies. It's past amends. There is some conduct
that's too underhand to be put right. I've finished now. (CHRIST leans
against the cross in boredom) Why didn't you say if something was
troubling you? You know you could always turn to me. I'm not a hard
man, I'm fairly reasonable and open — I think I can say that. There's
nothing more to be said. The whole thing is best left in silence. In fact
I'm too upset to speak. (CHRIST hangs one arm over the horizontal bar
of the cross) I'd give you another chance if I thought it would help. But
there's no point. I have to remember the others in my charge. It's not
fair on others to allow someone like you to continue to be in a respectable institution like this. Go, and I hope you find somewhere where you
can fit in. Have I made myself clear? (CHRIST goes) It leaves a space. I
shan't get used to a space up there. It seems wrong. The congregation
expect something.

INSPECTOR. I'll help you out, padre. 74

   (The INSPECTOR gestures offstage. A young POLICEMAN comes on. He 75
   is dressed in a fascist-style uniform with an armband)

Here we are, Kedgie. Here's a nice easy job for you. Stand up there on 76
that wooden appliance. Up you get, lad.

PRIEST. Won't he find it tiring? 77

INSPECTOR. No. He's used to controlling traffic. He'll be all right if he 78
puts his mind to it. You can do anything if you put your mind to it.
Comfortable, Kedgie? Keep staring straight ahead, lad. Just think how
they taught you to keep watch on the frontier. (To PRIEST) That makes
the place look tidier.

PRIEST. True, it's an improvement. 79

INSPECTOR. Didn't like the look of the other one. You can pick them out 80
when you've had a few years in my job.

PRIEST. I sometimes had doubts myself. But he had such good refer- 81
ences, so what can you —

INSPECTOR. You're looking fine, Kedgie. You'll be relieved in two hours, 82
lad. Do you know what to do? We'll just have a little rehearsal. We don't
want any slip ups. Church parade is a parade like any other parade. The
same smartness and superior turnout and every movement at the double. (Shouts order) Relief christ, to your post — *march!* (A replica of
Kedgie marches in) Relief christ — *halt!* (The RELIEF CHRIST halts in
front of the cross) Old christ — descend — *cross!* Smartly, smartly,
there! Stop waving your arms about you're not blessing the multitude
now! Watch your step, eyes front, head up, don't look down or you'll fall
through the water! By god, I'll make martyrs of the pair of you! (KEDGIE
has come down from the cross) Relief christ — wait for it, wait for it,
don't anticipate the word of command — mount — *cross!* I don't want
to see you move, I want to see you there! Get up that cross there! Halt!
Put your arms out, put your arms out, lad! Don't stand there with your
arms dangling, you look as though you're going to start playing with
yourself! Wank in your own time, not the army's! — (Turns to PADRE)
There we are, padre, now we're beginning to get somewhere, we're
playing on our home ground.

PRIEST. I feel much safer. There's someone up there watching over me 83
and I can trust and rely on him. (Indicates bread and wine) It's a pity
to waste all this. Would you like to take communion?

INSPECTOR. Oh I — 84

PRIEST. I've changed the wine. 85

INSPECTOR. In that case — it's a very civil thought of yours padre, and 86
I'd be glad to oblige. Call on me any time.

(The INSPECTOR kneels and the PRIEST offers him communion) 87
(Curtain)

Poem: Bird

Fly on, bird   1
Over the winter city on ruins of snow
The beggar with broken wrists
The tanoi that learns speech

Fly on   5
Past men with heads for faces
In cars like snakes fleeing water
One book for rules and another for writing in

Fly on   10
Past time with a hatchet
The member washing blood from under his nails
The youth who says: I go along for the ride
And climbs on the gallows cart

Their glittering corn is deadlier than famine
Their water is dust and chokes cities   15
Sentimentality covers cynicism in their beds

Fly on, blackbird
With claw smashed through beak
Skull cracked
Wings like burned flags   20
Charred cracked firework
Fly on, fly on

Your hands give birth to children
And hold men waiting death
These are small things   25
If the sky is not lived in the earth dies.

Story: Christ Wanders and Waits

Christ was condemned to walk on earth till men were no longer misera-   1
ble. He wandered from place to place. Everywhere he found war,
famine, imprisonment, plague, and people bleeding and crying for
help. There was misery everywhere. Jesus asked every judge and general he met to tell him how to make men happy, but they didn't know

459

how. After many, many hundreds of years he felt he couldn't bear any more of this misery. He'd heard of a wise woman who could do miracles and tell what would happen before it happened. So he went to find her.

He found her living alone, with a few pet animals, in an old house 2 outside a town. The roof was falling in and the path to the door was muddy when it rained. The people in the town wanted to build her a new house near the centre of the town, but she wouldn't move. So they said "Perhaps it's as well. She's clever, but she's mad, too."

Christ said to the old woman "I am condemned to live on earth until 3 men are no longer miserable, but I find misery everywhere. Tell me why men are miserable and how I can make them happy."

The old woman said "You ask very hard questions, Jesus. I'll think 4 about it. Go away and come back tomorrow."

So Christ went away. He decided to stay the night in town with a 5 friend called Simon. When he got to the outskirts of town he saw a procession coming out of town, and one of the women in the procession was Simon's wife. When she saw Jesus she came up to him and said "Simon is dead and we are burying him." Then still crying she caught up with the procession and went with it to the cemetery. Jesus went on into town. He wandered through the streets and then sat on a wall till it was morning. He was too tired to sleep. As soon as it was light he went back to the old woman.

He said "What is the answer?" 6

She said "Jesus, I have never been asked such hard questions. I can't 7 tell you the answers. But I know where you can get them. We will ask someone who's lived all his life and can look back on it and understand everything that's happened to him. Now, I know many skills and I can bring the dead to life." So she took him round to the side of the house where there wasn't much wind and she bent down and picked up a handful of dust and threw it in the air and it drifted into the shape of the dead Simon. Simon recognised Jesus and pressed his hand.

Jesus said to him "Why are men miserable and where can I find a 8 happy man?"

Simon wept and said "I have lived all my life in this town and I hated 9 it. My wife loved me but I made her unhappy. I've always been unhappy and I'm unhappy now I'm dead. There is nothing to tell you. I've learned nothing. What is there to learn? The dead mourn themselves and the living."

The small wind blew and the dust floated away and Simon 10 disappeared.

The old woman said "Shall I bring him back again, Jesus?" 11

Jesus said "No," and went on his way. He wandered on for many more 12 hundreds of years and one day he saw a bird in a tree. The bird had a

worm in its mouth which it was taking to its chicks. Jesus said "I wish
you could speak, bird. Then perhaps you could answer my riddles."

The bird said "I can speak. So tell me your riddles and perhaps I will   13
answer them."

Jesus said "Why are men miserable and how can I make them   14
happy?"

The bird said "Your riddles are very hard but let me think about   15
them. I will tell them to my husband and perhaps he will know the
answers."

But then the worm in the bird's beak spoke. "I can answer your   16
riddles."

The little bird was so startled at hearing the worm speak that it   17
dropped the worm and flew away.

Jesus said to the worm "How can men stop being miserable?"   18

The worm said "Love one another."   19

Jesus said "Where can I find a happy man?"   20

The worm said "The earth is my house yet you walk on it and use it   21
as your own. I don't complain about it, friend, and when you die I
welcome you into my house. We are very close together and I would
like to help you. But how can I tell you where to find a happy man? Still,
I will do what I can. You are very tired. Sit here and I will go round the
world for you, preaching this new philosophy to every man I meet. And
then I will tell him I am christ and ask him if he is happy — and
when I come back I will tell you if I have been able to find such a man."

So the little worm set out to crawl round the earth and Jesus sat down 22
and waited.

Poem: Rest

The body falls   1
An X marking itself
Buries under its own weight
In its own shadow

Under the horizon in its narrowed eyes   5
It rests now

We wander from stretcher to table to fire
Faded like flowers and wire and cards
Using death rattles as slogans
Let it rest   10

The old bitch in her ivory tower
Makes trials of funerals
Calls dead to the stand
And swears virginity in body and mind

Remember it rests   15

I run quickly
Breathing on their breath
Sing in the argument
Dance with the strength of their stillness
They have taken away the rest   20

And I have received the lotus gun.

SUBJECT

1. Is the poem "I Cannot Mourn" intended to be a justification of the Sharpeville massacre? What *is* Bond trying to say?

2. In the "Black Mass," why does the Priest eject Christ from the church? Would you say that the Priest or the Prime Minister is the primary object of Bond's satire? What does each represent?

3. How does the Inspector view the massacre? Is he also an allegorical figure? (Consider particularly his solution to the problem of the empty cross.)

4. In the poem, "Bird," what does the bird represent? What clues does Bond give?

5. Consider the meaning in the final line of "Bird": "If the sky is not lived in the earth dies."

6. The story, "Christ Wanders and Waits," is reminiscent of a Biblical parable; but what is the meaning of the parable? What is the worm that knows more than those who are supposed to be wise?

7. In the final poem, Bond returns to a personal reaction to the massacre; what conclusion, if any, does he come to? If he has "received the lotus gun," what is it and what is he supposed to do with it?

STRUCTURE

1. Do you see any rationale for the order in which these five pieces occur? Why, for instance, is the story separated from the play by the "Bird" poem?

2.   Consider Bond's use of repeated ideas and phrases as a unifying device. Where is this repetition most obvious?

3.   Do you find the irony too heavy handed in the play? Irony loses its punch if it is too obvious; how does Bond try to prevent that from happening? Is he successful?

4.   It might be said that Bond is trying to present an argument to the heart rather than the head, without allowing himself to become overly emotional. Or wouldn't it be more correct to say that the appeal is spiritual rather than temporal?

5.   Regardless of whether or not the reader understands every detail, it should be clear that Bond wants to present an attitude toward the massacre, toward the perpetrators of it, and to suggest what ought to be done about it. Is it possible to summarize his position in expository prose? (We saw in the preceding section, remember, that art cannot always be explained completely.)

8

THE LIBERATION
OF WOMEN

Persuasion

Just as the ancestor of argument was the deliberative oration of the Athenian Senate, so the forefather of persuasion was the forensic oration of Athenian law courts — or judicial assemblies. Its original purpose was to gain acquittal for the defendant. Since the lawyer delivering the oration was less interested in arriving at truth than in getting his client "off the hook," he did not feel obliged to limit his approach to the logical, objective one of the deliberative oration: an acquittal for illogical or emotional reasons was still an acquittal. Although the rather strict formula for the forensic oration is usually disregarded today, our trial lawyers still use many of the same tactics which Aristotle discussed in his *Rhetoric.* Defense attorneys are likely to distract attention from the specific charge by dragging in character witnesses, or by associating the client's cause with the patriotic or religious feelings of the jury by quoting Abe Lincoln and the Bible.

The ideal persuasion, certainly, would not be deliberately illogical, but it would be much less likely than argument to encourage free and impartial discussion of the problem at hand. The strong feelings about his subject which the writer of argument strives to control can actually be put to use in persuasion to sway the reader to the desired position. Normally, too, the writer of persuasion will not be anxious to discuss impartially his opponent's arguments. While he wants the readers to have the impression that his arguments have been presented reasonably and fairly, he is more interested in their having a complete emotional conviction that he is right; hence, the writer does not want to distract them from this goal by allowing any implication of serious weakness in his own position.

The form of a persuasion is basically the same as that of written argument. Normally, it contains the same four parts: analysis of the problem; clear statement of the proposed solution; disproof of the opposition; and positive evidence. In addition persuasion ends with a "peroration," or a final strong emotional appeal. But the difference between persuasion and argument is almost entirely one of attitude: argument seeks to stimulate discussion, persuasion seeks to end it. The writer of persuasion can include anything which does not spoil his case by the obviousness of its intent — appeals to prejudice and sympathies, appeals to such respected authorities as prophets, movie stars, and baseball heroes, arguments against an opponent's character instead of his ideas, and so on. He does not have to take pains to ensure that his evidence is typical, relevant, impartial and sufficient. He can even include brief disgressions on related topics which, while they do not constitute proof, will sway the reader to his side by appealing to religious and political convictions, sense of justice and fair play, and so on. When Mark Antony delivered the famous funeral oration in Shakespeare's *Julius Caesar,* for instance, his aim was to convince the mob that Caesar was innocent of the charge of ambition. But Antony did not confine himself to relevant arguments alone. He aroused the people by displaying Caesar's corpse and pointing out the holes made by the daggers of the various assassins; he read Caesar's will; he made much of Brutus' having slain his best friend. In short, he used any argument which would either make the mob believe that his was the "reasonable" side or incense them against the conspirators.

Because the forensic oration was developed to incite the listeners to *do* something — that is, acquit the defendant — persuasion has traditionally been associated with this original aim. Argument can also be used to stimulate the reader to follow a desired course of action, but usually a reader is more likely to be stirred to action if he is given more motivation than cold logic. Persuasion, then, by combining logic with warmer appeals, is the ideal means of accomplishing such a purpose. (Persuasion can, however, be used simply to sway the reader to believe something without doing anything about it.) If the writer wishes his readers to take some action, he should be specific about the end he has in mind and should outline clearly the steps (process) by which that aim can be accomplished. As in any process, the steps should be in proper order and clearly explained. The P.T.A. speaker who convinces his audience that the town needs better schools may achieve nothing unless he explains a method of getting better schools. Mark Antony incited the mob to anger, but their anger and energy would gradually have dissipated had not Antony suggested specific action to them — to burn Brutus' house and drive the assassins from Rome. Although an audience or reader may be convinced that "something needs to be done," nothing will be done unless he is told how to do it. Even if the writer is not sure that the method he has in mind is the best way of achieving his goal, he should still offer it as a tentative plan: it will show the reader that something *can* be done and it may stimulate him to think of a better plan by giving him something specific to work with.

The greatest danger in writing persuasion is irresponsibility. The student who plans to write persuasion should remember that the aim of writing ought to be honest communication. The freedom to use emotional appeals in persuasion frequently misleads a student into thinking that he is free to use dishonest means to gain honest ends. Good persuasion, like good propaganda, does make use of motivations somewhat less respectable intellectually than those used in logical argument; still, the writer should believe in the rightness of what he wants the reader to do.

Writing persuasion can be an entertaining change of pace from the type of expository prose a student is usually called upon to write. It can also be a useful art: although few students are studying to become politicians or ministers, most of them do have to write home for money occasionally.

HOW MEN WILL
BENEFIT FROM THE
WOMEN'S POWER REVOLUTION

Marya Mannes

Marya Mannes, well known free lance journalist, was born in New York City. She has published two novels, Message from a Stranger *(1948) and* They *(1968); two collections of essays,* More in Anger *(1958) and* But Will It Sell? *(1964); and two volumes of satiric verse,* Subverse *(1959) and* The New York I Know *(1961). She has been feature editor of* Vogue *and* Glamour, *and a columnist for* Reporter, McCall's, *and the* New York Times. *Ms. Mannes has also been a film and TV critic, and has waged a one-woman campaign for improved quality in television programming. Ms. Mannes is also a mother and a wife.*

A great many men must be not only bewildered by, but sick of, the 1
increasing sound and fury of the Women's Liberation movement. They
may also feel threatened.

To these men I would like to extend sympathy and hope. You must 2
know you are not only indispensable but desirable! (Some of my best
friends are men.) And if I thought this revolution (and it is one, in spite
of those too young or too confused to know what the word really means)
concerned the weakening, emasculation, or domination of the male, I
would have no part of it.

For if this movement of women towards social, economic, and politi- 3
cal parity with men is ever to succeed it will do so only if men, too, are
freed of certain burdens and limitations. Those women who consider
men the enemy would fare much better if they enlisted men as allies
— by understanding them. Once men recognize that their new part-
ners in a life that extends beyond the home and into the world are no
less women, they may realize the first fruits of a new masculine freedom.

One, very simply, is relief from the prolonged weight of female de- 4
pendence, emotional and economic. I realize that there is a protective
instinct in you men that needs to be satisfied. To take care of a helpless

or at least passive woman is not only a natural male desire but the source of a satisfying equation: stronger-to-weaker.

It is also one of the easiest ways to bolster an ego not otherwise secure.　5

So you are often the sole support of a woman and family. And you feel,　6 as your wife does, that it is a perfectly fair and equitable return for her to be mother, lover, housekeeper, and cook also. You are supposed not only to keep her forever but love her always.

The irony is that you might love her more if you kept her less. And　7 I do not mean only physically but as a human being. For the first very often militates against the second.

You spend your years at jobs that very often do not satisfy you and　8 living a life that becomes more and more of a pattern. Office hours all week, car or train two or three hours a day, evenings with your wife at your lowest ebb, weekends with your family that end too soon (or not soon enough), TV and small talk to fill the gaps, and endless worry about meeting bills. Your bills, her bills.

"But I love my family!" you may say, or "I love my job." But, surely,　9 sometimes you dream of another life, with another (perhaps less domesticated) woman and time to do all those things you never manage to do?

If you do break away, you are still stuck for life with supporting your　10 wife. Especially if she is of that age when the prospects of marriage in a society of youth are increasingly dim.

Because you have made all the major decisions in her life, she has　11 become almost incapable of making her own. She has lived for twenty years through you and her family and, if you leave her, she has nothing left but alimony and memories. Her capacity to support herself is negligible.

And if you stay, put your children through a costly education that not　12 all of them really want or use and pay for a home which, once flown, they seldom inhabit, what have you got? At the very best a dear companion who cooks and tidies for you and will join you in some retirement community until death.

More often, perhaps, your life has become a habit, with a wife to　13 whom — precisely because she has had no other resources, no other life, no other competences — you have little to say except in the small coinage of daily existence.

She is, if you will, the best possible argument for female — AND　14 male — liberation. She is also one of the women who still resist it most. For it is easier for her to depend on a man than on herself. But

469

even if her marriage fails, the dependent woman will say, "But I have my children!" Has she?

After loving care (cook, servant, chauffeur, tireless user of detergents 15 and waxes) what happens to them? The exclusive company of their peers and almost any messy pad but their tidy homes.

Not all, of course. There is always the daughter brought up to marry 16 in church as early as possible, the son brought up to make it in business. Either way, here is the woman who has lived through everyone but herself and ends up by never knowing what "herself" is.

Now, at last, a rising tide of women are doubting this destiny. And a 17 rising number of men will begin to understand that women's insistence on themselves as identities and not as accessories is a mirror-image of their own needs.

There is no reason any more why a man should be the sole provider 18 all his life. There is no reason why he should not achieve a life-style in which the labors of work and home and raising children are given equal priorities and time.

It is my firm belief, in fact, that a major cause of the alienation of the 19 young from their elders is the absence of their fathers from their lives. Here is the real and dangerous domination of women. In the home — not in the world.

Ironically again, the men take this separation from their families as 20 necessary and preferred because their business lives are more interesting than their wives and homes. They prefer the company of men, with whom they have more in common than with the woman they have chosen to live with (one fifth of the time).

Let me hasten to say that there are a great many men and women 21 who find nothing wrong with it. These are free to pursue accepted patterns and find satisfaction in them, and the wiser female militants should not tamper with the happiness of home-bound females by suggesting that they are unhappy.

A major point of the liberation movement is freedom of choice: free- 22 dom of man and woman as individuals to pursue the life that they most want to live. And if a woman enjoys a purely domestic role, she has every right to it.

But for a great many it is not enough. We do not want to spend our 23 days without men, without the formulation and execution of ideas, without the use of what special talents or skills we have, whether for science or art, for engineering or business, for journalism or technology, for philosophy or broadcasting, for government or law. And whether men like it or not, the universities of this nation are turning out more and more women who are prepared to use their skills and demand that they be used without fear, favor, or discrimination. Many of us — perhaps most of us — want to live with men and bear their children — no more, hopefully, than two. And even, perhaps, none.

Society forgets that not all women are naturally maternal. And all of 24
us must know by now that the large family is no more a blessing than the childless couple is a crime. In fact, the woman who is a copious breeder is doing infinitely more harm than good to this suffocating planet and its crowded broods.

The rest of us really want more men in our lives, not fewer. We want 25
their comradeship at work as well as their company at home. We refuse a life that forces us to live ten hours of every weekday confined to the company of children and women.

We have close women friends, but we choose them more for their 26
intelligence and spirit and talents than for what is repulsively called "girl-talk." We find on the whole that women who work are infinitely more interesting than women who don't.

And I think you men will find that out, too, in time. As a matter of 27
fact, the happiest marriages I know have been between men and women who colaborate in work as well as in the home . . . whether in research, writing, science, or the arts.

At this point, I would like to relieve the male mind of one major 28
apprehension: competition and aggression. You've heard those words time and time again: Why do women want to COMPETE with men? Or, "I don't like COMPETITIVE women — they're AGGRESSIVE," or, "AG-GRESSIVE WOMEN are unfeminine."

Gentlemen, why is it that if you describe a man as competitive and 29
aggressive it's a compliment and in a woman it's a curse? Are ambition and drive and energy exclusive male attributes? And if they are also possessed by many women, why are they feared?

We are not trying to COMPETE with you; we want to collaborate with 30
you. We don't want to be better than you — even if we could be. We don't even want to be LIKE you. We merely want to be equal companions. In honesty, however, I must admit that aggressive militance is no more attractive in a woman than it is in a scruffy youth who yells obscenities while he hurls rocks. You may get attention but you don't get love.

The real aggressors you men should be aware of, in fact, are the 31
killer-sharks in the guise of submissive females. Guerrilla tactics pale before their techniques of ambush and conquests of the male — not necessarily for himself but for his money, power, or his position.

471

Having had work experiences with both sexes in situations of at least   32
some importance, I have found separation of man and woman to blur
and fade entirely. I said separation, not difference. For in the difference
lies our greatest contribution to the work both must do together.

This work is the making of decisions. Decisions that affect every   33
segment of society and its organization, from the Cabinet to the Town
Hall, from state to village, from city to block.

Because of our long experience as nurturers and housekeepers, our   34
constant intimacy with the daily details of life and environment, we can
bring to these decisions elements that humanity sorely needs.

Surely, no intelligent and rational man will deny that his long, abso-   35
lute, and exclusive reign over the destiny of men and nations has
brought neither peace nor order nor joy nor happiness for the vast
majority of people.

In other words, gentlemen, not only do you need help, but we want   36
— and intend — to work for it and give it. We are 51 percent of the
population. Even if only a quarter of us care to, or can, prepare ourselves adequately for participation, we can offer a mighty force for good
that cannot be ignored or rejected.

To accept the offer will mean — unquestionably — many alterations   37
of thinking, of patterns, of accommodation, in men and women. It will
mean a wholly new look at work schedules in terms of time, job altera-
tion, provision for the children of working women and for the dreams
of men who are better fitted to be artists than providers, farmers than
tellers, wanderers than desk-sitters.

Love between a man and a woman should not depend on domination   38
but on fusion. And the fact that above the body what a man loves is a
mind that equals his own should not be a source of conflict but of pride.
Whatever happens, the male ego should remain intact. Not as the con-
queror of woman, so long its most abiding source, but as the sovereign
of himself.

SUBJECT

1.   Does Mannes intend to imply that "male chauvinist pigs" have
insecure egos? (See paragraph 5.)

2.   Do you think her picture of the average bored American male
is a true one or merely a literary cliché?

3.   Would the argument that many women want more men in their
lives likely be taken by men as one argument *against* liberation?

4.   How does Mannes answer the objection that women's libbers are
competitive and aggressive?

5. Mannes suggests (paragraph 31) that the real aggressors are "killer sharks" whose aim is to catch a man; does Mannes consider that most men *like* to be caught? Does "killer sharks" seem an appropriate appellation?

STRUCTURE

1. The essay is ostensibly aimed at male readers; what device does Mannes use to get the men to give her a fair hearing? (If she antagonizes them at the beginning, few men will read the article. Did you notice a growing militance toward the end?)

2. What are the primary appeals used to sway men toward the revolution? How does Mannes make these appeals emotional ones without allowing her own writing to become noticeably emotional?

3. Analyze the careful way in which Mannes refutes what she considers to be the male view of woman's place.

4. What kind of evidence does Mannes present to support her argument for cooperation rather than competition between male and female? (See paragraphs 33 ff.)

5. Discuss Mannes's use of the concession as a persuasive device. Is her statement that happy housewives should not be tampered with by liberationists a "concession"?

6. Is the appeal to male ego in the final paragraph a strong ending for the essay? Does it run any risk of alienating male readers?

I WANT A WIFE

Judy Syfers

The following article appeared in the first issue of Ms., *"the new magazine for women." Ms. bills itself as the voice of the Women's Movement; it is certainly the first quality magazine, published on a regular basis, to avoid the stereotyping and "preparation for housewifery" emphasis of most women's magazines. It is published by Elizabeth Harris and edited by Gloria Steinem. The author of "I Want a Wife," Judy Syfers, is not identified except by name.*

1   I belong to that classification of people known as wives. I am A Wife. And, not altogether incidentally, I am a mother.

2   Not too long ago a male friend of mine appeared on the scene fresh from a recent divorce. He had one child, who is, of course, with his ex-wife. He is obviously looking for another wife. As I thought about him while I was ironing one evening, it suddenly occurred to me that I, too, would like to have a wife. Why do I want a wife?

3   I would like to go back to school so that I can become economically independent, support myself, and, if need be, support those dependent upon me. I want a wife who will work and send me to school. And while I am going to school I want a wife to take care of my children. I want a wife to keep track of the children's doctor and dentist appointments. And to keep track of mine, too. I want a wife to make sure my children eat properly and are kept clean. I want a wife who will wash the children's clothes and keep them mended. I want a wife who is a good nurturant attendant to my children, who arranges for their schooling, makes sure they have an adequate social life with their peers, takes them to the park, the zoo, etc. I want a wife who takes care of the children when they are sick, a wife who arranges to be around when the children need special care, because, of course, I cannot miss classes at school. My wife must arrange to lose time at work and not lose the job. It may mean a small cut in my wife's income from time to time, but I guess I can tolerate that. Needless to say, my wife will arrange and pay for the care of the children while my wife is working.

I want a wife who will take care of *my* physical needs. I want a wife   4
who will keep my house clean. A wife who will pick up after me. I want
a wife who will keep my clothes clean, ironed, mended, replaced when
need be, and who will see to it that my personal things are kept in their
proper place so that I can find what I need the minute I need it. I want
a wife who cooks the meals, a wife who is a *good* cook. I want a wife
who will plan the menus, do the necessary grocery shopping, prepare
the meals, serve them pleasantly, and then do the cleaning up while I
do my studying. I want a wife who will care for me when I am sick and
sympathize with my pain and loss of time from school. I want a wife to
go along when our family takes a vacation so that someone can continue
to care for me and my children when I need a rest and a change of
scene.

I want a wife who will not bother me with rambling complaints about   5
a wife's duties. But I want a wife who will listen to me when I feel the
need to explain a rather difficult point I have come across in my course
of studies. And I want a wife who will type my papers for me when I
have written them.

I want a wife who will take care of the details of my social life. When   6
my wife and I are invited out by my friends, I want a wife who will take
care of the babysitting arrangements. When I meet people at school
that I like and want to entertain, I want a wife who will have the house
clean, will prepare a special meal, serve it to me and my friends, and
not interrupt when I talk about the things that interest me and my
friends. I want a wife who will have arranged that the children are fed
and ready for bed before my guests arrive so that the children do not
bother us. I want a wife who takes care of the needs of my guests so that
they feel comfortable, who makes sure that they have an ashtray, that
they are passed the hor d'oeuvres, that they are offered a second helping of the food, that their wine glasses are replenished when necessary,
that their coffee is served to them as they like it.

And I want a wife who knows that sometimes I need a night out by   7
myself.

I want a wife who is sensitive to my sexual needs, a wife who makes   8
love passionately and eagerly when I feel like it, a wife who makes sure
that I am satisfied. And, of course, I want a wife who will not demand
sexual attention when I am not in the mood for it. I want a wife who
assumes the complete responsibility for birth control, because I do not
want more children. I want a wife who will remain sexually faithful to
me so that I do not have to clutter up my intellectual life with jealousies.
And I want a wife who understands that *my* sexual needs may entail
more than strict adherence to monogamy. I must, after all, be able to
relate to people as fully as possible.

If, by chance, I find another person more suitable as a wife than the   9
wife I already have, I want the liberty to replace my present wife with
another one. Naturally, I will expect a fresh, new life; my wife will take
the children and be solely responsible for them so that I am left free.

When I am through with school and have a job, I want my wife to quit   10
working and remain at home so that my wife can more fully and completely take care of a wife's duties.

My God, who *wouldn't* want a wife?   11

SUBJECT

1.   Note that Syfers never calls the wife she wants "he" or "she." Do
you think she has a man in mind? Does it matter for the establishment
of her point?

2.   Do you think she has been fair in her assignment of tasks to the
wife? Would most husbands expect so much of their wives?

3.   The object of attack is obviously husbands; yet the article appeared in a magazine for women. Who is supposed to be persuaded by
the essay, then, men or women?

4.   What would you say is the persuasive aim of the essay?

5.   If the wife in a typical marriage has this many responsibilities,
doesn't the husband have a commensurate number?

6.   How many of the wife's tasks seem to be the result of marriage
itself. That is, how many are jobs that would not have to be done at all
by bachelors? Does it follow that two people cannot live as efficiently
together as separately?

STRUCTURE

1.   Do you see any progression or order in the list of services Syfers
wants from a wife? What order would be most effective?

2.   Would you say that the persuasive force of this essay derives
primarily from the language or from the subject itself? Should have
made the tone less matter-of-fact?

3.   Is the final sentence necessary? Does it add to or detract from
the force of the persuasion?

4.   The insistence on using "wife" instead of "he" or "she" results
in some rather awkward and unnatural sentences (". . . my wife will
arrange to pay for the care of the children while my wife is working.")
Do you think the advantage gained is worth this awkwardness?

5.   Is Syfers attempting to persuade her audience to a different
attitude or toward some course of action? Upon what kind of emotional
bias is she playing?

PRISONER OF SEX

Norman Mailer

Norman Mailer, poet, novelist, essayist and filmmaker, was born in New Jersey in 1923. Mailer first came to public fame with the publication of his war novel, The Naked and the Dead *(1948). Since then he has published more than a dozen books, including* The White Negro *(1958),* Cannibals and Christians *(1966),* Why Are We in Vietnam *(1967), and* Armies of the Night *(1968), the last of which won a Pulitzer prize. Mailer's latest book,* The Prisoner of Sex *(1971), of which the extract below is the conclusion, is a "woman-lover's" attempt to understand what modern women want. Although Mailer seems particularly unqualified to understand women (he has been divorced four times), he is a fascinating if sometimes irritating writer who merits a hearing. The chief service of this book may be in the response it elicits (see, for instance, the essays following by Pritchett and Oates). Mailer presents his material, not as straight argument or persuasion, but as a kind of personal vogage through the Sargasso Sea of women's liberation. The port at which he finally arrives is described in this concluding passage.*

Still he had not answered the question with which he began. Who finally would do the dishes? And passed in his reading through an Agreement drawn between husband and wife where every piece of housework was divided, and duty-shifts to baby-sit were divided, and weekends where the man worked to compensate the wife for chores of weekday transportation. Shopping was balanced, cooking was split, so was the transportation of children. It was a crystal of a contract bound to serve as model for many another, and began on this high and fundamental premise:

> We reject the notion that the work which brings in more money is more valuable. The ability to earn more money is already a privilege which must not be compounded by enabling the larger earner to buy out his/her duties and put the burden on the one who earns less, or on someone hired from outside.
>
> We believe that each member of the family has an equal right to his/her own time, work, value, choices. As long as all duties are per-

formed, each person may use his/her extra time any way he/she chooses. If he/she wants to use it making money, fine. If he/she wants to spend it with spouse, fine. If not, fine.

As parents we believe we must share all responsibility for taking care of our children and home — not only the work, but the responsibility. At least during the first year of this agreement, sharing responsibility shall mean:

    1. Dividing the jobs (see "Job Breakdown" below); and

    2. Dividing the time (see "Schedule" below) for which each parent is responsible.

There were details which stung: 2

    10. Cleaning: Husband does all the house-cleaning, in exchange for wife's extra childcare (3:00 to 6:30 daily) and sick care.

    11. Laundry: Wife does most home laundry. Husband does all dry cleaning delivery and pick up. Wife strips beds, husband remakes them.*

No, he would not be married to such a woman. If he were obliged to 3 have a roommate, he would pick a man. The question had been answered. He could love a woman and she might even sprain her back before a hundred sinks of dishes in a month, but he would not be happy to help her if his work should suffer, no, not unless her work was as valuable as his own. But he was complacent with the importance of respecting his work — what an agony for a man if work were meaningless: then all such rights were lost before a woman. So it was another corollary of Liberation that as technique reduced labor to activities which were often absurd, like punching the buttons on an automatic machine, so did the housework of women take on magnitude, for their work was directed at least to a basic end. And thinking of that Marriage Agreement which was nearly the equal of a legal code, he was reminded of his old campaign for mayor when Breslin and himself had called for New York City to become the fifty-first state and had preached Power to the Neighborhoods and offered the idea that a modern man would do well to live in a small society of his own choosing, in a legally constituted village within the city, or a corporate zone, in a traditional religious park or a revolutionary commune — the value would be to discover which of one's social ideas were able to work. For nothing was more difficult to learn in the modern world. Of course, it had been a scheme with all the profound naïveté of assuming that people voted as an expression of their desire when he had yet to learn the electorate obtained satisfaction by venting their hate. Still he wondered if it was not likely that the politics of government and property would yet begin to alter into the politics of sex. Perhaps he had been

*Alix Schulman, "Marriage Agreement," *Off Our Backs,* p. 6.

living with the subject too closely, but he saw no major reason why one could not await a world — assuming there would be a world — where people would found their politics on the fundamental demands they would make of sex. So might there yet be towns within the city which were homosexual, and whole blocks legally organized for married couples who thought the orgy was ground for the progressive action of the day. And there would be mournful areas of the city deserted on Sunday, all suitable for the mood of masturbators who liked the open air and the street, perhaps even pseudo-Victorian quarters where brothels could again be found. There could be city turfs steaming with the nuances of bisexuals living on top of bisexuals, and funky tracts for old-fashioned lovers where the man was the rock of the home; there would always be horizons blocked by housing projects vast as the legislation which had gone into the division of household duties between women and men. There would be every kind of world in the city, but their laws would be founded on sex. It was, he supposed, the rationalized end of that violence which had once existed between men and women as the crossed potential of their love, violence which was part perhaps of the force to achieve and the force to scourge, it had been that violence which entered into all the irrationality of love, "the rooting out of the old bodily shame" of which Lawrence had spoke, and the rooting out of the fear in women that they were more violent than their men, and would betray them, or destroy them in the transcendence of sex; yes, the play of violence had been the drama of love between a man and a woman, for too little, and they were friends never to be gripped by any attraction which could send them far; too much, and they were ruined, or love was ruined, or they must degenerate to bully and victim, become no better than a transmission belt to bring in the violence and injustice of the world outside, bring it in to poison the cowardice of their home. But the violence of lovers was on its way to disappear in all the other deaths of the primitive which one could anticipate as the human became the human unit — human violence would go to some place outside (like the smog) where it could return to kill them by slow degree — and equally. But he had made his determination on beginning his piece that he would not write of sex and violence too long, for that would oblige him to end in the unnatural position of explaining what he had attempted in other work. So he would step aside by remarking that a look at sex and violence was the proper ground of a novel and he would rather try it there. And content himself now with one last look at his remark that "the prime responsibility of a woman probably is to be on earth long enough to find the best mate for herself, and conceive children who will improve the species." Was it too late now to suggest that in the search for the best mate was concealed the bravery of a woman, and to find the best mate, whatever ugly or brutal or tyrannical or unbalanced or heart-searing son of misery he might appear, his values nonetheless, mysterious fellow of values, would inevitably present themselves in those twenty-three chromosomes able to cut through fashion, tradition, and class.

There is a famous study of neurotics which shows that patients who   4
received psychoanalysis had an improvement rate of 44 percent; psychotherapy was more effective — a rate of 64 percent; and 72 percent was the unhappiest improvement, for that was the rate of cure of patients who had never been treated at all. The Eysenck study it is called, and later studies confirm its results. It was, the prisoner decided, a way of telling us that the taste in the mouth of explaining too much is the seating of the next disease. One cannot improve the human condition through comfort and security, or through generalized sympathy and support — it is possible the untreated patients got better because the violence of their neurosis was not drained. The cure of the human was in his leap.

But now he could comprehend why woman bridled at the thought   5
she must "find the best mate for herself and . . . improve the species." How full of death was the idea if one looked at any scheme which brought people who were fundamentally unattracted to each other down marriage aisles, their qualifications superb, their qualities neuter. So he was grateful to a writer who wrote a book, *The Lady,* published in 1910, Emily James Putnam, first dean of Barnard. She was a writer with a whip of the loveliest wit. He would give the last quotation to her for she had given the hint of a way.

> Apart from the crude economic question, the things that most women mean when they speak of "happiness," that is, love and children and the little republic of the home, depend upon the favour of men, and the qualities that win this favour are not in general those that are most useful for other purposes. A girl should not be too intelligent or too good or too highly differentiated in any direction. Like a ready-made garment she should be designed to fit the average man. She should have "just about as much religion as my William likes." The age-long operation of this rule, by which the least strongly individualised women are the most likely to have a chance to transmit their qualities, has given it the air of a natural law.*

It was finally obvious. Women must have their rights to a life which   6
would allow them to look for a mate. And there would be no free search until they were liberated. So let woman be what she would, and what she could. Let her cohabit on elephants if she had to, and fuck with

*University of Chicago Press, 1969, p. 70.

Borzoi hounds, let her bed with eight pricks and a whistle, yes, give her freedom and let her burn it, or blow it, or build it to triumph or collapse. Let her conceive her children, and kill them in the womb if she thought they did not have it, let her travel to the moon, write the great American novel, and allow her husband to send her off to work with her lunch pail and a cigar; she could kiss the cooze of forty-one Rockettes in Macy's store window; she could legislate, incarcerate, and wear a uniform; she could die of every male disease, and years of burden was the first, for she might learn that women worked at onerous duties and men worked for egos which were worse than onerous and often insane. So women could have the right to die of men's diseases, yes, and might try to live with men's egos in their own skull case and he would cheer them on their way — would he? Yes, he thought that perhaps they may as well do what they desired if the anger of the centuries was having its say. Finally, he would agree with everything they asked but to quit the womb, for finally a day had to come when women shattered the pearl of their love for pristine and feminine will and found the man, yes that man in the million who could become the point of the seed which would give an egg back to nature, and let the woman return with a babe who came from the root of God's desire to go all the way, wherever was that way. And who was there to know that God was not the greatest lover of them all? The idiocy was to assume the oyster and the clam knew more than the trees and the grass. (Unless dear God was black and half-Jewish and a woman, and small and mean as mother-wit. We will never know until we take the trip. And so saying realized he had been able to end a portentous piece in the soft sweet flesh of parentheses.)

SUBJECT

1. Why does Mailer not want to be married to a woman with whom he has a job-sharing agreement? Is he afraid of work?

2. Do you think Mailer is seriously suggesting political divisions based on sex habits? What is he getting at?

3. On what grounds does Mailer see marriage as a "play of violence"?

4. What does Mailer do with his earlier thesis that a woman's "prime responsibility" is to find the best possible mate and have children by him?

5. Why does Mailer save his last quotation for Emily James Putnam? Does he agree with her?

6. Does the concluding paragraph strike you as sour grapes? Mailer says that "women must have their rights"; does he think the result will

be beneficial? What reservation does he make in the granting of women's rights?

STRUCTURE

1. Comment on the style of Mailer's essay. Would you characterize it as stream-of-consciousness? internal debate? Is the style intended to carry the reader along with Mailer's reasoning, or simply to expose the way his own mind works?

2. Did you find the shifts without warning from almost formal language to slang, even profanity, disturbing? Should Mailer have stayed on one level of diction?

3. Presumably Mailer intends to convince readers rather than simply tell them how *he* feels. What group of readers would be most likely to be persuaded by this essay? Do you think it is directed at men or at women?

4. Is Mailer's supporting evidence selected primarily for its statistical or its emotional qualities? What kind of "evidence" is it?

5. What does Mailer achieve by suddenly bringing "dear God" into the final half-dozen sentences?

6. Does Mailer's style — or organization — cause any difficulty in separating the refutation from the confirmation portion of the essay?

WITH NORMAN MAILER
AT THE SEX CIRCUS

Victor Sawdon Pritchett and
Joyce Carol Oates

Victor Sawdon Pritchett, English novelist and literary critic, was born in 1900. He is literary critic and managing director of The New Statesman, *and has published two dozen novels and books of criticism. He has been visiting professor at a number of universities, including Brandeis, Berkeley, and Cambridge. Currently Mr. Pritchett is at work on a multi-volume autobiography. Joyce Carol Oates was born in New York in 1938 and now teaches at the University of Windsor, Canada. She has published novels, collections of short stories, and volumes of poetry. She received the National Book Award for her novel* Them *(1969). One of her recent short stories, "Bloodstains," is reprinted in this book.*

I. *Into the Cage*

After a bellyful of Kate Millett, Germaine Greer, and Norman Mailer   1
on the subject of the liberation of something called Man and Woman, I am left in a state of total indigestion. To begin with, I am interested only in this man or this woman, not in the generality. In the present state of the world — the eve (I suspect) of an age of tribal invasions on the Genghis Kahn scale — I also think the preoccupation with sex has reached a luxury phase. It is our Ivory Tower which the have-not societies cannot afford. We are evidently uneasy about this, for now, in the second noisy sex circus of this century, our chief sex pundits have taken to the journalistic vices of prophesy and global thinking: when in difficulties about the relations of men and women, enlarge the subject by thinking of it in terms of world revolution. Global thinking is a confession of failure and mediocrity. I don't believe that now that Mrs. X has had forty clitoral orgasms, capitalism will go or the war in Vietnam will stop. She will want only more on the conveyor belt. I don't believe sexual enlightenment would have stopped the massacre in East Pakistan.

I am old enough to look back on the first sex circus of this century with 2
nostalgia. One sees now that it was war that made us think of sex in
terms of weapons. To war, not to argument or enlightenment, we owe
the first large emancipation of women. While men killed, women had
to do the work. It was war that brought in "bad" language and blasphemy and made English Anglo-Saxon again. How delightful it was to
hear a fluting intellectual talk of "copulation" when his father, bemused
by sinful literary periphrasis, was stuck with "sexual congress" or the
creeping blasphemy of "carnal knowledge." To hear the soup spill and
the knives and forks clatter down in a restaurant when some Cambridge girl said "orgasm" in a dashingly cultivated voice designed to
reach the kitchen hands and to show them her superiority, had the thrill
of a motor smash. Women wore the new language as they wore a new
hat. Men felt robbed. Bad language for them was sacred to a soldier's
hatreds; the girls were making it educational. I must say I still resent
this: one hated to see the juicy smut of one's boyhood and the ripe and
genial art of heavy manual workers put to the prim use of intellectual
self-improvement for the middle classes. Still, puritans can be happy
only on principle. As circus turns of the period, we clowns and animals
may have been clumsy, but we were not disinfected.

The second circus which is now culminating in Women's Lib and 3
public do-it-yourself is very different from our innocent affair. Wars
come fast; massacres are everyday; the show begins to have the nasty
smell of the genocide laboratory. It is run by gynecological gunwomen.
The laughs have changed. That old cock of Chatterley's walk, the poor
old penis, is now a relic of the old-style clown; all he has left is his red
nose. The vagina is nothing but an idiotic horse collar — I take the
word from Miss Germaine Greer, who sticks up for it — the clitoris is
Queen. The hysterical spermatozoa swish up the out-of-date vagina,
whiz along the Fallopian tubes; the chromosomes line up like digits on
a computer. It is not quite clear whether we are fooling about in a new
laboratory or watching a Victorian factory grinding along on its last legs.
There is every reason to believe that the womb has had its day: no more
hysteria to drive the male to his pub. The test tube and the bottle are
coming, the breasts will turn into pimples, and Bob, as they say, will be
your Auntie; for Mum herself will be a minor figure, driven to showing
instructional films on how to masturbate in the State infant schools. As
for the language, the hate language of the rocket-makers has taken over
completely. One novelty is that while the mass media show us pictures
of mashed-up bodies of men and women and children most evenings,
the balance is restored by films and picture books of what the animals
looked like, before butchery, while engendering the new season's lamb.
The new circus, as one can see, is even more educational than the one

I have forgotten so much of. The new revolution is ten times more puritanical; it is the puritanism of technology. Where our revolution made us free and clumsy, the new one is political and proposes to turn us into uncomplaining operatives.

At this point Normal Mailer comes in with *The Prisoner of Sex* (Little, Brown, $5.95) and steals the show from the bluestockings. He is what it lacked: a go-getting whistle-stop clown. In an interview, he once let out the joke that he didn't hate women; he just thought they ought to be shut up in cages. Nothing for it then (when one of the women beat him to the front page of *Time* magazine) but to get into the cage with them. A paranoiac with a good boyish punch, a gentle eye, a sentimentalist — four wives, clearly not interested in women but in something they had got — yet with sensible flashes in his rage and savage laughter, determined on the spotlight, he rips around. He is as sweeping and discontinuous as an excited woman, yet he has considerable relics of what Norman Douglas called the "male attributes of humility, reverence and a sense of proportion." He has brought a sparkle to a dismal scene, and if, at the end, one can't make out whether he is swimming or sinking — nor can he — he has one huge advantage over his enemies: he is a brilliant writer with sharp insights, and he has passion, which they have not. His satirical metaphors are very funny. They are also accurate. Miss Kate Millett, author of *Sexual Politics,* is his chief victim: 4

> The style is suggestive of a night-school lawyer who sips Metrecal to keep his figure, and thereby is so full of isolated proteins, factory vitamins, reconstituted cyclamates, and artificial flavors that one has to pore over the passages like a business contract. What explosives are buried in those droning clauses, those chains of familiar aggregates (of words).

Another lady said to him, "We think your views on women are full of shit." He notes, "She had a voice that could have boiled the fat off a taxicab driver's neck."

Still, like all clowns, he is serious. He even has the clown's mock-innocent face. He simply likes to fight women and is apt to find he agrees with them after he has hit them. His heart is really in literature, in the imagination — not reputedly the great female endowment — and so he is more bitter with Miss Millett for chopping off her quotations from Lawrence too soon, so as to force a case, than with her views, which he half shares. His chapter on Lawrence is really excellent. Feminists are enraged by Lawrence's insistence on male dominance, but as Mailer says, the reason was tragic. Weak in health and ruled for so long by his mother: 5

he was bone and blood of the classic family stuff out of which homosexuals are made, he had lifted himself out of his natural destiny which was probably to have the sexual life of a woman ... no wonder he worshiped the phallus, he above all men knew what an achievement was its rise from the root, its assertion to stand proud on a delicate base. His mother had adored him. Since his first sense of himself as a male had been in the tender air of her total concern — now, and always, his strength would depend upon just such outsize admiration. Dominance over women was not tyranny to him, but equality. ...

And, I would say, this is true of the attitude of normal men. The first signal of love for a woman in a man is fear — how to be equal to that dangerous being.

He goes on to Henry Miller and lust and to Genet on buggery with the zeal of a Welsh preacher — in fact, he is really the unfrocked preacher-clown — but he is closest to a seizable point when he at last makes up his mind about Miss Millett: 6

Of course the revolution could also become the first bureaucracy of sex, and the technicians of genetics its intelligentsia. ... The world would seek solutions where technology was faith and you stayed inside the system. ... The passion of the mediocre is to maintain stimulation at its own level. So he had thought it proper to treat Millett with huge attention. If she had not risen any higher on the literary scale than the Upper Mediocre, she was all the more central to the age. She believed in the liberal use of technology for any solution to human pain ... the prose of future prisons was in her tongue ... the power of her argument would be greatest for those who wished to live in the modest middles of the poisoned city. She was a way of life for young singles, a species of city-technique.

The worship of technology is the enemy; the wars of this century have created technological sex. Compute sex as you compute war is the slogan of the last twenty years. So we find Mailer coming round to liberation. "Let her cohabit on elephants if she had to, and fuck with Borzoi hounds, let her bed with eight pricks and a whistle ..." if that is the requirement of free choice; but let the poor old womb alone. And if a couple should blunder upon love — the repressed subject of this century — on the way, let violence ventilate it; though why marital violence should do away with the bully-and-victim syndrome, I can't imagine. Physical violence is the classic method of breaking people.

At one point we find Mailer cheering Germaine Greer for saying in her book, *The Female Eunuch* (McGraw-Hill, $6.95), that clitoral stimulation is "the index of the desexualization of the whole body, the substitution of genitality for sexuality." That, indeed, is the depth to which the sexual revolution has sunk. The notion that one makes love 7 without the whole of the person, moral and physical, is what turns sex into an eccentric exhibition by frustrated acrobats who are surprised to find themselves so regularly falling off the trapeze. And are seen to do so by the public. The second sexual circus is packed with the grimaces of these failures.

Miss Greer's book is an appeal to women to start knowing themselves and thinking about themselves. It contains more interesting facts than Mr. Mailer has patience for, as his ego explodes in midair and he looks back a bit scared by what he has said. Miss Greer writes "like teacher," but she has home-truths. If, for example, it is true to say women have been slaves, then they have the slave mentality. Slaves don't trust each other. But when she says women have become eunuchs, I suggest she tell that to the Wife of Bath and hear what she has to say about "the mastery." *There* was a liberated old girl — as so many old girls are. 8

The one thing that strikes an unliberated male survivor like myself, and that prevents me from burning my underpants in public, having an intimate operation, giving my money away to a few nice chaps, doing my own laundry in office hours, and — most wicked gesture of all — tearing up my will and insurance policies, is the reflection that liberated women are lonely, overworked, and have made it impossible for other women to help them. All they have got is machines that go wrong. When Carlyle heard Margaret Fuller say that she "accepted the Universe," the crusty old man said, "She'd better." It's what, with all the fierce complacency of an anachronism, I'd say about love between men and women (that old stuff!) — they'd better settle for it before the next mushroom goes up. We sleep with people's bodies, but we live with their characters and with their natures: that is where civilization started and not from the waist down with the grunting of four-letter words. 9

V. S. PRITCHETT

II. *Out of the Machine*

... a day had to come when women shattered the pearl of their love for pristine and feminine will and found the man, yes that man in the million who could become the point of the seed which would give an egg back to nature, and let the woman return with a babe who came from the root of God's desire. ...

Norman Mailer, *The Prisoner of Sex*

It is appropriate that Norman Mailer has become the central target of 1
the fiercest and cruelest of Women's Liberation attacks, not because
Mailer is prejudiced against women, or bullying about them, not even
because he claims to know much about them, but because he is so
dangerous a visionary, a poet, a mystic — he is shameless in his passion for women, and one is led to believe anything he says because he
says it so well. He is so puritanical, so easily and deeply shocked, like
any hero, that his arguments, which approach the fluidity and senseless-
ness of music, have the effect of making the dehumanized aspects of
womanhood appear attractive.

Here is Mailer: ". . . why not begin to think of the ovum as a special- 2
ized production, as even an artistic creation?" And: "Yes, through history, there must have been every variation of the power to conceive or
not to conceive — it was finally an expression of the character of the
woman, perhaps the deepest expression of her character — " What,
are artistic creation and the expression of character, for women, not
detachable from their bodies? From the mechanism of their bodies? It
is terrible to be told, in 1971, that we belong to something called the
species, and that we had, throughout centuries, a mystical "power to
conceive or not to conceive." Why didn't we know about this power?

No matter if we protest that sexual identity is the least significant 3
aspect of our lives. No matter if we hope, not absurdly in this era, that
technology might make our lives less physical and more spiritual. None
of this matters for, to Norman Mailer, "the prime responsibility of a
woman is probably to be on earth long enough to find the best mate
possible for herself, and conceive children who will improve the
species."

But we don't know what the *species* is. A post-Darwinist name for 4
"God"? A scientific concept? A mystical concept? A word? An identity?
An essence? Do we locate ourselves in it, or does it push through us,
blindly, with the affection of a stampeding crowd? And how long is
"long enough"? Should we remain on earth for twenty years, or forty,
or dare we hope for an extravagant eighty years, though our last several
decades will be unproductive and therefore unjustified? The machine
of the female body is thought by some to be a sacred vessel, designed
to bring other sacred vessels into the world, for the glory of God; but
it is also thought to be rather foul, as in Lear's words:

> But to the girdle do the gods inherit,
> Beneath is all the fiend's.
> There's hell, there's darkness, there's the sulphurous pit;
> burning, scalding, stench, consumption. . . .

It is also considered a means of improving the species, that is, a machine designed to improve the quality of other machines; and the proper artistic creation of a woman is not a novel, a symphony, not a political theory, certainly, but the cultivation of her womb. The "power to conceive or not to conceive" is, after all, the "deepest expression of [a woman's] character. . . ." Not one kind of expression, not even the most pragmatic expression, but the deepest expression! One sees why the mystic is the most dangerous of human beings.

There is a famous remark of Freud's that ends with the question, "What does a woman want?" A good question. And a woman is inclined to ask, with the same exasperation, "What does a man want?" Indeed, a woman must ask, "What does a *woman* want?" The question is a good one, but it is fraudulent. It suggests that there is a single answer — a single "want" — for a multitude of human personalities that happen to be female. Many women are angry today because they are only women; that is, they possess the bodies of women, the mechanisms for reproducing the species, and they are therefore defined simply as "women." But there is no reality to the class of "women," just as there is no emotional reality to the "species." There are only individuals. The individual may be compartmentalized into any number of compartments, the absurd boxes of the poll-taker (the "Irish Catholic," the "suburbanite, affluent," the "35-year-old divorcée," etc.), but he exists in none of these compartments, and his personality will reject them. The only reality is personality. Not sex. Not sexual identity. No categories can contain or define us, and that is why we draw back from the female chauvinists who claim a biological sisterhood with us, just as we draw back from the male chauvinists who have attempted to define us in the past. 5

"If we are going to be liberated," says Dana Densmore, in a pamphlet called "Sex Roles and Female Oppression," which is quoted in the Mailer article, "we must reject the false image that makes men love us, and this will make men cease to love us." But this viewpoint is not acceptable. It assumes that men demand a false image, that all men demand false images. It does not distinguish between one man and another man. And it assumes that women do not demand, from men, images that are occasionally false. Can an "image" be anything but false? The perfect mate of the toiling, distraught housewife is not a free, marauding male, but a husband stuck to a job that is probably as demeaning as housework, but more grating on the nerves because it is played out in a field of competition. If the woman has become trapped in a biological machine, the man has become trapped in an economic machine that pits him against other men, and for mysterious and shabby 6

489

rewards. Man's fate may be to languish in imaginary roles, wearing the distorted masks of ideal images, but he can at least improve the quality of these roles by using his intelligence and imagination. But only by breaking the machine. Only by abandoning and climbing out of the machine, the traps of "maleness" and "femaleness."

Freud has been attacked from all sides as a representative of typical male prejudice, but his views on the subject are always worthwhile. In that wise, complex essay *Civilization and its Discontents,* he speaks of sex as "a biological fact which, although it is of extraordinary importance in mental life, is hard to grasp psychologically ... though anatomy, it is true, can point out the characteristics of maleness and femaleness, psychology cannot. For psychology the contrast between the sexes fades away into one between activity and passivity, in which we far too readily identify activity with maleness and passivity with femaleness." Obviously, the distinctions are not simple. 7

For if the female finds herself locked in a physical machine marked "passive," the male is as tragically locked in a machine marked "active." As Sylvia Plath says, ironically, "Every woman loves a fascist." What is left, then, but for the man to play the role of a brute? What is masculinity in any popular sense, except the playing of this stupid, dead-end role? In our culture men do not dare cry, they do not dare to be less than "men" — whatever that means. 8

The mechanical fact of possessing a certain body must no longer determine the role of the spirit, the personality. If Women's Liberation accomplishes no more than this it will have accomplished nearly everything. 9

But there are further problems, further areas of masculine uneasiness. Mailer criticizes Kate Millett for believing in "the liberal use of technology for any solution to human pain." Yes, that sounds like a heretical belief so long as human pain is valued as sacred, or important as an expression of personality, or helpful for salvation ... or even conversation. But it isn't. It is nothing, it is a waste, a handicap, a mistake. What good is human pain? We are all going to experience it soon enough, regardless of technology's miracles, so there is no point in our ignoring it or romanticizing it. Human pain — the acceptance of the bodily machine without any rebellion — is a way of making us human, yes, but the rewards are chancy and might be as well accomplished by an act of the imagination. Why shouldn't we ask of technology the release from as much pain as possible? Why not? Why not the disturbing Utopian dream/nightmares of the "extra-uterine conception and incubation" — if they are a means of diminishing pain? Mailer, like all heroic spirits, places a primitive value on suffering. And one feels that he would not shy away from suffering, even the suffering 10 of childbirth, if that were a possibility for him. Yes, to suffer, to feel, to be changed — it is a way of realizing that we live. But it is also a way of becoming dehumanized, mechanized. In fact, a way of dying.

To be mechanically operated, to have one's body moving along in a process that the spirit cannot control, to have the spirit trapped in an unchosen physical predicament — this is a kind of death. It is life for the species, perhaps, but death for the individual. Throughout human history women have been machines for the production of babies. It was not possible for them to live imaginative, intellectual, fully human lives at all, if indeed they survived for very long. They lived long enough to find a mate, to have a number of children, many of whom would not survive . . . but it was the process that mattered, the blind, anonymous reproductive process that gave these women their identities.   11

In a little-known story by Herman Melville, "The Tartarus of Maids," young girls working in a paper factory are seen by a sympathetic narrator: "At rows of blank-looking counters sat rows of blank-looking girls, with blank, white folders in their blank hands, all blankly folding blank paper." They are the pulp that is turned into blank paper out of a certain "white, wet, woolly-looking stuff . . . like the albuminous part of an egg," in a room stifling with a "strange, blood-like, abdominal heat." The process takes only nine minutes, is presided over by a jovial young man named Cupid, and what terrifies is its relentlessness: it is an absolute process, a godly machine that cannot be stopped. "The pulp can't help going," the narrator is told smugly. And he thinks: "What made the thing I saw so specially terrible to me was the metallic necessity, the unbudging fatality which governed it." Melville, who seemed to have no interest at all in the relationship between men and women, and who created no memorable woman character in all his fiction, has given us the best metaphor for the existential predicament of most of the world's women.   12

No wonder that the feminists look to technology for deliverance! As they climb out of their machines they must find other, substitute machines to do the work of women. A body is no more than a machine, if it is not guided by a personality — so why not a surrogate machine, an actual machine, why not the escape from as much impersonal pain as possible?   13

Once we are delivered from the machine of our bodies, perhaps we will become truly spiritual.   14

Perhaps.   15

At the start of *The Prisoner of Sex,* Mailer speaks of having taken care of his large family for several weeks during the summer, cooking, cleaning, turning into a kind of housewife, so exhausted with domestic chores that he had no time to write, to think, to contemplate his ego. *No time*   16

491

to contemplate his ego! After a while, in such a frenzy, one loses his ego altogether . . . one misplaces his personality, and sinks into the routine frenzy of work that adds up to nothing, that comes to no conclusion, no climax. Is this a human life? Can one call an uncontemplated life really a "life" at all? Or is it merely brute existence? One has the time to contemplate his ego — to achieve a personality — only when he or she is liberated from the tyranny of physical burdens, whether they are external in the form of housework to be done eternally, or a commuting distance to be traveled, or whether they are internal, the processes of a body unaltered by technology and human choice. And what grief, what anger and dismay, for the women who — to "liberate" themselves and their men from the possibility of pregnancy — began taking the Pill on absolute faith, only to discover that the Pill carried with it mysterious disappointments and possible catastrophes of its own! — for Technology is probably male, in its most secret essence male.

The problem is: do we control nature, or will we be controlled by nature? A difficult question. A Faustian question. To accept technology and to create surrogate machines that will bear our children — this sounds like madness, perversity. Yet, to deny human choice in the matter of reproduction, as we would never do in the matter of, say, ordinary medicine or dentistry, seems an empty sentimentality. [17]

But after all this, after all these considerations, we are still left with the rage of Women's Liberation. How to explain this anger? And we understand slowly that what is being liberated is really hatred. *Hatred of men.* Women have always been forbidden hatred. Certainly they have been forbidden the articulation of all base, aggressive desires, in a way that men have not. Aggression has been glorified in men, abhorred in women. [18]

Now, the hatred is emerging. And such hatred! Such crude, vicious jokes at the expense of men! Most women, reading the accusations of certain feminists, will be as shocked and demoralized as Normal Mailer himself. Somehow, in spite of all the exploitation, the oppression, somehow . . . there are things about the private lives of men and women that should not be uttered, or at least we think they should not be uttered, they are so awful. Women have been the subjects of crude jokes for centuries, the objects of healthy male scorn, and now, as the revolution is upon us, men will become the objects of this scorn, this exaggerated disgust and comic sadism. [19]

Nothing will stop the hatred, not the passage of legislation, not the friendliest of men eager to come out in support of Women's Liberation. It has just begun. It is going to get worse. [20]

And yet, it will probably be short-lived. Hatred goes nowhere, has no goal, no energy. It has a certain use, but it has no beauty. There will be [21] a place in our society for Mailer's heroic mysticism, at the point in history at which women can afford the same mysticism. Until then, it is better for us to contemplate the blank-faced horror of Melville's pulp factory, rather than the dreamy illogic beauty of Mailer's "ovum-as-artistic-creation."

JOYCE CAROL OATES

SUBJECT

1. In what context does Pritchett make the sweeping statement that "Global thinking is a confession of failure and mediocrity"? Is he right *in context*? Do you agree with the statement as a generalization?

2. Both Pritchett and Oates lament the hatred which is so much a part of the women's liberation movement. Should they consider the fact that all successful revolutions use hatred as a means of unifying the revolutionists? (Castro and Mao Tse Tung, for instance, both used hate-America campaigns so that dissenting factions could join together in a common cause.)

3. Comment on this statement by Pritchett: "The first signal of love for a woman in a man is fear — how to be equal to that dangerous being." Should it be a consolation to a woman to know that the man who loves her does not feel equal to her? How does a man typically go about achieving his equality?

4. What is Pritchett's assessment of Norman Mailer's entrance into the sex circus? Can you tell by the extract from Mailer whether Pritchett's assessment is just?

5. How does Pritchett answer the argument that women do not need men for sex, that clitoral masturbation is a perfectly adequate substitute?

6. Pritchett says that "liberated women are lonely, overworked, and have made it impossible for other women to help them. All they have got is machines that go wrong." Does this seem a fair and objective assessment or the reaction of a male chauvinist? How does such a generalization square with his earlier insistence that he judges people as individuals, not as generalities?

7. What is Oates's chief objection to Mailer's analysis? How does it differ from her main objection to the "female chauvinists" like Dana Densmore?

STRUCTURE

1. Toward what position does Pritchett wish to persuade his readers? On what grounds should the essay be classed as persuasion rather than argument?

2. Point out some non-logical devices Pritchett uses in his essay; are these mainly to ridicule his opponents or to further his own position?

3. Pritchett states his conclusion "with all the fierce complacency of an anachronism"; is he implying that readers shouldn't take him seriously? How can such an admission strengthen his point?

4. Comment on the organization of both these essays. Did you have any trouble seeing their "direction"?

5. Would it be fair to say that Oates's refutation of both Mailer and the female chauvinists is based on reasonable argument, but that the confirmation of her own position falls into the same kind of "mysticism" for which she blames Mailer?

6. Which of these two essays did you find more persuasive? Why?

GOOSE

Ruth Link

In her forthcoming novel, Goose, *Ruth Link has posited a hypothetical society in which sex roles are totally reversed. Turning a set of characters loose in this society, she follows them through situations which are sometimes ludicrous, frequently embarrassing, and always enlightening. The humor, of course, depends on the implied contrast with behavior in "normal" society, but the inversion of roles brings out many inequities and gross absurdities which are not immediately apparent in our own society. The following extract from the book is intended to show men what a traumatic experience for a woman even a simple thing like buying lunch can be.*

Having phoned a few friends and finding nobody free to lunch with him today, Chunk had dropped Tucker at kindergarten, driven to town, parked, walked past a dozen restaurants in a flurry of indecision while trying to appear to passers-by as though he had a definite goal in mind, feeling more forlorn with every step, finally turned into a decent-looking Charcoal Grill and realized he had made a terrible mistake and that there was no way to get out of it. The room was packed with businesswomen. 1

Chunk shrank into himself and pretended he didn't exist for a moment while he tried to regain his bearings. He studied the behavior of a woman who was standing before him surveying the room in search of a table. She strolled in as though she owned the place, sizing people up like items in a shop window, paused and pondered with obvious impatience, cruised on amid the tables, was sighted by a waiter and piloted to a distant booth. 2

Chunk mustered all his courage. Dozens of women were staring at him. He couldn't just stand there. He cursed himself for having worn this yellow shirt and green jacket that suddenly appeared loud and brazen amid all this sober femininity, and knew his wavy hair only made him seem all the more provocative. The longer he hesitated the more they ogled, as though he were on the make. He picked a point at the opposite wall and headed toward it like a ridiculous canoe adrift on 3

Reprinted by permission of the author and Publisher from Sweden Now, March, 1971.

495

a stormy sea. He wanted to feel the back of his jacket to make sure it was down over his behind, but didn't dare, for fear the gesture might be misinterpreted. It was imperative not to let his eyes meet any woman's directly, not to give himself away, to maintain a dignified facial expression that assured all observers that he was a good husband and father, not "available," and merely driven to this daring venture by primitive hunger and thirst. He reached his goal, but there was no table! To stand there so vulnerable, so abandoned, was excruciating torture. Oh, why had he left the safety of "Slimmers" and *Beautiful Road to Happiness?* It was all his wife's fault for getting him into this, he was thinking, when two women rose from a table in the middle of the room, and he groped his way toward it in grateful relief.

Now he felt the eyes of the women at neighboring tables slyly scanning his body. He fingered a dirty fork and glued his eyes to it determinedly. Three women at a neighboring table laughed softly. Chunk trembled. Could he trust his hands to light a cigarette? 4

The waiter walked past, ignoring him. There was something insidious about a man sitting alone. He simply shouldn't. He ventured a glance at the woman in the booth, who was giving her order with easy poise, saying something that made the waiter smile as he arranged the tableware attentively. Chunk snapped his eyes back to the dirty fork. 5

Without thinking, Chunk crossed his legs. He felt the eyes of the woman beside him sexily slide the length of his body, as though the gesture had been an invitation. Enraged and desperate, Chunk looked her squarely and sternly in the face. The woman's mouth curved in a sensual leer. For a mad instant Chunk felt a shiver of pleasure course through his body, and recomposed his face into extreme severity, as he dug out a cigarette. To his horror, the woman held a lighted match in front of him, and Chunk mumbled "Thank you" without looking at her in a voice that emphasized that he was not "that kind" of a man, as goose flesh prickled his arms. 6

By the time the waiter finally cleared away the dirty dishes and grudgingly brought him a menu he was exhausted from tension and the prospect of having to eat was nauseating. He pretended to read the menu with interest. He would have to order something that showed he really was hungry, not too cheap, but average, like the women. But did he dare order the Businesswoman's Lunch? The waiter stood waiting, bored and curt. Chunk could think of nothing to say to make him relent, much less smile. Suddenly he understood he was expected to order something "appropriate." "Give me the Shopper's Special, please, and coffee." "Yeah, mister," the waiter said with contempt, then turned to respond good-naturedly to the women at the adjacent table, who called him by name, asking for their check with bantering familiarity. 7

496

Chunk was relieved when they left and the customers started thinning out. He spotted two men a few tables away, secretaries perhaps, and watched with envy as they sat conversing and eating, apparently undisturbed by their surroundings. Somehow this made him feel more miserable and lonely than ever. He poked over his creamed tuna fish and left the surly waiter too large a tip, as though to apologize for his intrusion.

SUBJECT

1. Why has Chunk tried to call someone who could lunch with him? Why is he embarrassed about going into the restaurant?

2. Would a woman be as self-conscious in this situation as Link makes Chunk out to be? If the point *is* overstated, does that spoil the effectiveness of the story?

3. If, like a woman in our own society, Chunk had been trained from childhood to handle confrontations with the opposite sex, wouldn't he be more relaxed, gracious, perhaps even flattered by the attention he attracts? That is, has Link made only a *partial* reversal of sex roles here?

STRUCTURE

1. Examine the way in which Link informs the reader of Chunk's state of mind; does she do it primarily with interpretive adjectives, or with descriptive phrases which the reader interprets as indicative of a particular state of mind?

2. As this is fiction, it naturally is not cast in the form of a persuasive essay. *Is* it persuasive? Could Link's point have been made just as well in expository prose?

3. Is there any conflict between the story's aim and its chief appeal. That is, toward what readers is the message directed, men or women? Would men or women be most likely to enjoy the story? Could one say, then, that the purpose is more to embarrass than to persuade?

4. Does the situation presented here provide evidence in a case for women's liberation? Can a fictional situation *be* evidence?

A MAYPOP
FROM MERTON

Sylvia Wilkinson

Sylvia Wilkinson (born in 1940) is a native of North Carolina and currently teaches English at the University of North Carolina. She did her graduate study in creative writing on a Wallace Stegner fellowship at Stanford. In addition to her writing, Miss Wilkinson has been a state tennis champion, races sports cars, and has had several painting exhibits. She has published some short stories and three novels, Moss on the North Side *(1966),* Killing Frost *(1967), and* Cale *(1970). Miss Wilkinson was selected in 1965 as one of the Outstanding Young Women in America.*

I won't look up, I just won't. If he starts hollering at me, I'll just act like   1
he's not even there. I know if the school bus doesn't get here soon, he'll make me cry just saying one ugly thing about the way I look. He always says the wrong thing; if it's not that I've got lipstick on my teeth, he'll ask me what that white thing sticking out the bottom of my skirt is and then I go around all day long feeling like I'm just thrown together. With my head down I can't help but cry, the tears just run out even when I don't feel like it and my face will be streaked like I got blood poisoning; it will, I've got that kind of skin. It's delicate and people tell me I should be proud of it but sometimes when I cry when I don't mean to, I mean when I just bend over and tears run out of my eyes, it can just be embarrassing. But he has a way of picking on me and I let it bother me. I don't know why. I just do. I'd give anything in this world if I didn't let somebody like him bother me.

He is a full year older than me and I caught up with him in the   2
seventh grade and he is still there. They let him go on to the ninth grade in Sunday School and I get stuck with him following me around and looking at me like I could ever care two cents for him. Giving me that valentine with his name in numbers thinking I didn't have enough sense to figure it out to be him . . . 13-5-18-20-15-14. I hadn't seen a soul do that since the fifth grade and when I saw it I honestly didn't know it was from Merton because I wouldn't think he would know all the

From *Red Clay Reader* 6 (1969). Reprinted by permission of the publisher.

letters in the alphabet, much less be able to count all the way to 26. I'm not kidding, he really is that dumb. It must have taken him all week to figure that out and I just got mad enough to kick myself after I sat down and worked it all out.

The school bus is stuck somewhere, I bet that's what it is, backed off 3 in a ditch somewhere and I have to sit here in the rain waiting all day for it with that Merton standing across the road just getting soaking wet and waiting for me to look up so he can start talking to me. If I had known, I could have stayed at the house but then I might have missed it and I would have been mud from head to toe before I got there and late to boot. My scarf is so wet that there are just whole drops dripping off the end and after I even ironed the lace separate down the front of my blouse. And there is something over my head in the tree because I hear it rattle in the branches and the water is dumping down like somebody is up there pouring it out of a bucket. I would think it was Merton if I didn't know he was across the road so it must be a squirrel. I hear Merton's silly laugh now, he can see something funny in nothing if you ask me. I just felt every last bit of the curl go out of my hair after I slept all night on those rollers and it's streaking across my face like somebody broke an egg on my head.

"Hey, Rachel! Don't you know enough to come in out of the rain?" 4

I look up at Merton and that darn squirrel starts running up the limb 5 right over my head and washes off every last speck of anything I had put on my face. There just isn't any getting any wetter.

"Merton Hopkins, you see me sitting under a tree and not right out 6 there catching it and I don't fully see how there is any place to go in out of the rain and aren't you someone to tell me about not having enough sense."

I try to see if he is laughing at me and I just know I'm looking like 7 a wet dog. I can see the red lights of the bus blinking down the road and Merton is walking across towards me . . . like he's raking leaves with his feet, that's the way Merton Hopkins walks.

"I heard Mr. Stokes tell you not to plan on coming back to school until 8 you got your hair cut and it sure hasn't been cut," I say.

"You know what I seen?" Merton says and pulls a strand of his black 9 hair down to the end of his nose. "I seen old man Stokes go walking out in the wind the other day and what you know, his hair is longer than mine."

"Oh Merton, you know that's not so. Why he hasn't got enough hair 10 to cover his skin up."

"No, it's the truth. He just grows it all on back so he can comb it up 11 front over his hollow spot."

"It's a bald spot, not a hollow spot and if there's anybody got a hollow spot in the head it's you, Merton Hopkins, and you are fixing to get put out of school for good."   12

"You got black streaks running off your eyes."   13

Oh, he could have gone all day long and not said that. I take a Kleenex out of my pocketbook and wipe under my eyes and it just gets black as tar and it said on the card that it was waterproof. That was why I bought it, so I could go swimming and it would stay on and they would think my lashes were black. Honestly my eyelashes look like they were put on the wrong person, like they should have been on a white rabbit or an albino or something. I just wanted so much for my eyes to show up on stage today. I bet if you were to get at a distance I wouldn't have any face at all, at least that's what Merton said one day when I was walking up to him but he's likely as not got weak eyes and isn't smart enough to know it. I would just love to knock that grinning Merton up beside the head. I would just turn around and go back home this very minute if it wasn't the day my home ec project was due, I would. I wouldn't even go to the tryouts for the ninth grade show and just let Rosey Bell go ahead and get the part of the butterfly. She thinks she's got it anyway.   14

I reach in my pocketbook for my sun glasses but when I feel them, my finger goes right through one of the eye glasses. I don't wear them two times before I bust them. I would have had to say I had pink eye anyway, anybody who'd go stumbling around in the rain in sun glasses. I just know my face is ruint. I take out my compact and start putting powder over the black smudges, now that eyelash stuff decides to be waterproof when it's not where I want it. Every time I try to look up close the glass clouds up so I hold my breath.   15

"You look like a toad frog."   16

My breath all comes out and I shut my compact.   17

"What else nice are you going to say to me today, Merton? Can't you pick something uglier than a toad frog like calling me an old wart toad or something?"   18

"Wart toad made your face turn red." Then he starts into that laughing again. "Toad frogs ain't ugly, they just got pop eyes."   19

See what I mean about him, he never knows when to stop and sometimes I wish I was so big I could just beat him to a speck.   20

The bus stops and all those silly lights come on to stop traffic as if there's going to be any traffic on this road. Maybe if I sit on the outside of the seat Merton will go somewhere else but I ought to know better than that since I've tried it fifty times and all Merton does is crawl over me. Sometimes I'm almost glad when he doesn't go to school, at least   21

I get a little peace and quiet. Maybe they'll just kick him out for good soon. He's just waiting to turn sixteen anyway so he can quit legal.

"I hear you are going to be the butterfly in the play." 22

"Merton, just as loud as you please. Now don't go and talk that all over 23
because sure as everything if you do, Rosey Bell will get it and then I'll
be embarrassed to tears."

"She ain't as pretty as you." 24

"Well, everybody don't think like you do, Merton Hopkins. There's 25
some people who think redheads are prettier than anybody."

"I ain't never seen no redheaded butterfly." 26

"You just tell me when you've seen a blonde-headed butterfly, or any 27
kind of headed butterfly for that matter. Besides her hair isn't natural.
I saw in town what she colored it with and you can see it in the roots
if you look good. I've known Rosey since she was little and her hair was
brown as a mole before she started that coloring in the sixth grade and
her name was Fanny. She changed her name and her hair over the
summer and thought there weren't anyone who was going to notice any
difference and she would go two weeks not talking to anybody who
called her Fanny."

"I think Fanny is the best name for her." 28

"Well I do too." 29

"I bet you don't for the same reason I do." 30

"What do you mean?" 31

"I mean she sure has got a big one if you take the rest of her into 32
account."

"Merton, that was ugly. And she'll be sorry too because my Mama said 33
that the girls who fill out too soon are most inclined to get fat before
their time."

"She goes walking down the hall looking like two little pigs fighting 34
under a blanket."

Merton is laughing at himself now. He says that about everybody, at 35
least everybody with a big tail and he thinks he's the funniest thing
alive.

"I've already planned how I'm going to make my costume," I say, "if 36
I am to get the part that is. I'm going to make it in home ec class and
if I can save enough money I'm going to make it out of real organdy.
I don't want any crepe paper costume like I had to have at Christmas,
not with everybody around pulling on it till it's all stretched out of
shape."

That ought to shut Merton up for a while. He won't say anything to 37
that, not after what he did Christmas when he was supposed to be back
there in charge of pulling the curtain and he stepped on the back of my

holly costume and tore it so bad I had to back clean off the stage. It was a good thing for me I decided to wear bermudas under it just in case or I would have just died. And that Fanny Bell going out there dressed as a Christmas bell, thinking they gave her the part because of her red hair and her last name. Well, though I wouldn't say it to her face, I think they gave it to her because of her shape which is certainly nothing to be proud of. And then she got the boy doing the program to make sure her name was put down as Rosey instead of Fanny like it really is. I honestly wouldn't name a cow Fanny Bell.

"Oh, for goodness sake!"   38

Merton's big foot just landed in my lap.   39

"If you had been born with feet like that, you'd go stepping on the   40
wrong things too!" he says.

"Merton, put your dirty old foot on the floor. You got mud all over   41
my dress."

I shove his foot off my lap and he turns his face out the window. See,   42
that's why he's been so quiet. He was still thinking about stepping on my costume because I told him when he did it, I'd never speak to him again. Now he's pretending his feelings are hurt because he knows that's the only way he can get me to be nice to him. The truth is, that I don't mind Merton so much in the summer when I don't have to be seen with him but when school starts I'd just as soon not know him. There is never any telling what crazy thing he is going to do next. He is really one for picking at you and teasing but if he ever thinks he really did something bad wrong, he'll worry about it forever. I've known that since we were just in the fifth grade together when I was just turned ten and was already getting bumpy faced and worried that I was going to be the ugliest thing alive, because I was the worst cottontop you've ever seen. That was when Merton told me he knew how to make me beautiful.

He told me he was going to give my hair a mud treatment that he   43
had read about on this jar that said "For Beautiful Women Only," and it was guaranteed to make my hair stay curled forever and I could wear the mud for a hat he figured until it came time to take it off. To this day I don't know for sure if he did it for meanness but that Merton had me sitting down there by the pond not moving a muscle while he was piling mud on my head. Then he went running off and told me to wait and I thought he won't never coming back and that it really was just another one of his stunts when he came back with a bunch of blackeyed Susans and stuck them all around in the mud on my head. By this time the mud had started drying and was about to pull my hair out. That was when Merton told me to bend over and look at my pretty hat and I declare I think he did think it was pretty. I saw me for a second in the water

with a big head with things sticking out all over it then splash the whole works went toppling over and liked to have yanked my head bald.

I must have scrubbed my hair twenty times before I didn't feel grit 44 down at the roots and by the time I'd finished, if I ever was to have curly hair, I wouldn't again. Now I know that just sounds like Merton really made a monkey out of me and I've been saying all the time he was the stupid one, but I'm still thinking that Merton might have thought it would make me pretty. The reason I have for that is he never did laugh at me after he had done it, in fact I thought he was going to cry and just start running when he saw the terrible mess he'd made of me. And if it had been on purpose, I'm still figuring he would have made fun of me.

With all his scrambling to get on the bus, Merton will be the last one 45 out when it comes time to get off. You ask him why he has to get by the window and he'll say he wants to see where we're going just like we were going to the ocean or something and he knows good and well we pass the same things every day. I can't even remember when they changed the billboards. Merton will try to read the signs and you can see why he's still in the seventh grade. I have tried to tell him fifty times that it's E-s-s-o not 3-s-s-o, and he still thinks that 7-up spells Zup. He tries to read everything he sees out that window out loud but you just see if you can get him to crack a school book. He just doesn't care I guess. He doesn't ever get excited over anything at school.

Sometimes I wish I could be like that because I can as good as tell you 46 right now that come time for me to try out for the play and my stomach will just feel like it's going to cave right in and I'll fall in behind it. If I didn't go through my part so many times in my head first, I bet I could just walk out and say my part and do my dance and look back at the people out front and quit thinking of them looking at me. That's the trouble. Every time I go to practice in my mind I see myself up there and it's like I'm going out in the audience watching me and it is easy as everything. But when the real time comes to do it, I'm trying to see who's watching me through the lights and I talk too fast so I can get it over with quick. It worries me to death when I got no idea in this world of what I look like and I know all those people out front do know. If only it was just in front of a mirror like at home instead of people, you know what I mean? When you do something wrong, like in this dance I've got to do, you say no and do it over again until it looks right.

I can hear Merton's head thumping against the window and when I 47 look at him, he won't even look at me. Honestly when I hurt Merton's feelings it's like somebody drained the life out of him, just as limp as a dishrag and any normal person would feel his brains shaking out on that window. You could hit Merton in the head with a brick and not raise a swelling, you could. And he's not just hardheaded in the skin; he's hardheaded inside too. He wouldn't do a thing a teacher asked him to do if he thought the world was coming to an end. The last time I asked him what he planned to do with himself, you know what he said? Raise pickles! At first I thought maybe he was dumb enough to think they grew in jars when he said to me, "They'll give me two dollars a bushel for all the cucumbers I can raise long as I don't let them get no longer than three inches before I pull them." But you can't tell Merton anything, he is always trying to raise some fool thing. He's got it in his head that he'll be filling bushels with regular sized cucumbers not three inch ones. Why, it'd take an acre to get one bushel I bet. It's always raising, just try to tell him that there are some things in this world that come about without being planted in dirt.

One time he decided to raise drinking gourds and I don't know a soul who would use a drinking gourd to drink out of if he had one. When I told Merton that everybody I knew used at least a tin dipper if not a glass, he decided to make bird houses out of the gourds but couldn't make the birds decide they wanted to live in one of them. I remember the time he got all these fancy herb seeds out of an order in an oatmeal box. That was the year his cow broke loose and ate them all up then got bloated and he was wondering if it won't a good thing, that maybe all that parsley and sage and stuff would have killed a person. Now his pumpkin crop was really something, you have never seen such pumpkins. I mean they would near about glow in the dark. They looked like the kind you would find in some little kid's book, painted bright orange by somebody who has never seen a pumpkin and makes pigs pink and apples red all over. Well, they were too small for jack-o-lanterns, Merton never paid any attention to what it said on the package — actual size: five inches through and that they were "ornamental." I read the package to him even and said don't you know what ornamental means and he said sure you hang ornaments on the Christmas tree which meant he was about half a hair right and there was no use in the world to try to finish explaining to him so I just let it go. Then he tried to sell them to people for pies and everybody told him they weren't a proper color to be eaten, that they must certainly be poisoned. He slopped the hogs with them until the hogs got sick of pumpkin and rolled them out of the trough and they tell it on Merton that he hauled them all down to the trash pile and busted every last one of them. Well, anyway that's Merton. Just yesterday he was going around singing "I love BERRIES in the springtime." I could make a crow white before I could get that straight in his head.

I really would never have spoken to him again after he tore my holly costume if I couldn't make Merton do things that not a soul on this earth

504

would do. I would be walking along with him in the summer and it would be just as sticky hot as it could be and I'd say, Merton, I want that flower up there on that rock and he would go climbing up twenty feet after it, just howling every time he touched one of the hot rocks. Reason I'm reminded of his howling is I sent him up after this passion flower once. I hadn't seen one of those passion flowers up close since I was a little girl and we were going to the ocean and stopped at one of those roadside places and there was one growing on the girls' privy that I couldn't reach and my daddy wouldn't get it for me which I could understand. Merton said he didn't see the flower up there that day we were walking from the store but I knew it was there because they are hooked onto a long vine and they look like a purple pinwheel because they bloom out flat instead of cupped up and I could see the vine didn't have but one. I was directing Merton to it and he got the idea to snatch down the whole vine but he forgot that was the same vine he was holding to for support with his other hand and when he yanked it loose, he went with it. But you can't hurt Merton; he just let out a yap when he hit and pulled half the hill down on top of himself.

You should have seen my flower once I got it. It was a mess. And just 50 about the stinkingest thing I'd ever smelled. I was cussing at Merton and he said he didn't make it smell, that it won't nothing but a maypop that I almost made him break his neck over and there were thousands of them out in the fields. I did feel a little bad since he had such a time getting it and wished I had said something nice about the flower but it was too late, anyhow I don't think anybody could have said a nice thing about that flower even if they were used to fibbing. Then he tried to show me those thousands out in the fields and I tell you he couldn't find a one after all his big talking and I wanted to know if it really would smell that bad if it wasn't squashed because I wanted to wear it in my hair.

I asked him where in the world he got maypop and he said that was 51 a name for an old tire with cardboard in it that may pop any minute and I said what did it have to do with the flower and he said he didn't know, it was just a maypop. That's the way Merton is. He'll argue until he's blue in the face and not have the slightest notion of what it is he's arguing about.

Merton just groaned and slid down further in the seat. He always does 52 that in the last half mile before school and he'll shut his eyes and be sound asleep before we get there. He's going to really catch it about that hair but I reckon that's why he grew it, so he could get sent home. It's about time for Merton to want to starting planting things. He said yesterday he was going to try grafting this year until he got a tree that would grow apples and pears and plums all at the same time. He did

505

get a pear limb to stick to an apple tree last year but it didn't have any pears . . . just leaves.

It's finally over. After all my worrying, I just went out there and did 53 it but I know I did it a thousand times better at home when the teachers weren't there. And of course there was Merton sitting back there in the auditorium watching me. I don't know why I came back here and sat with him; I just didn't think I could stand to sit down front where all the teachers are.

"You looked good except for that one place you got out of step with 54 the music."

"How do you know whether or not I was in step with the music. You 55 can't even count out the beats."

"I can too. I could play the drums if I had a set." 56

Sometimes I just wish Merton wouldn't say anything at all and would 57 just leave me alone. I worry about things enough without him making it worse. He never knows when he's said enough; now I've got to worry all afternoon that I was out of step. Rosey comes up next. I know she's scared good because I saw her backstage. They had to tell her to get quiet twice because she was talking so loud. I wish Merton would go outside; there are so many times when I just wish he wasn't around or didn't know me or something.

"Hey, Rosey's next." That was Merton and he said it so loud two of 58 the teachers who are down front turned around. Honestly, Merton just doesn't know any better.

"How do you know she's next?" I whisper. 59

"Cause I can see her over there poking her head around the curtain 60 waving at somebody."

The piano starts playing again, The Waltz of the Flowers is the only 61 thing Miss Tripp knows but that doesn't mean she can play it the same way twice. There goes Rosey out; Miss Tripp didn't make a mistake on the introduction for her like she did on mine, how can you be expected to stay in step if the piano player can't even keep the time. Rosey was in my dance class; we both had a year of tap, ballet, and acrobatics but she didn't have such a big tail then. She was just sort of high pockets. I knew she would do the same dance as me since that's the only one we learned all the way through before we quit taking. She never could do a leap without sounding like an elephant when she lands.

"Ka-whomp, ka-whamp, ka-thump, ka-thud!" 62

That was Merton again and one of the teachers turns around but I 63 don't look at Merton this time; I just hit him with my elbow.

"Hey look!" 64

Merton yelled that good and loud. The teachers up front get out of 65
their chairs and go to the edge of the stage. I thought sure they were
coming to throw us out and just ruin my chances for good but . . .
"Merton, where's Rosey?"

"She fell down!" 66

"She didn't fall over the edge, did she? Where is she?" 67

"Behind the curtain. She got her foot caught up in it and crawled over 68
behind it."

I heard one of the teachers call to see if she was all right but she didn't 69
answer. She's crying that's why, I can hear her crying real loud. One of
the teachers has gone up there and I can see her get Rosey to her feet.

"Now she'll limp. I bet she'll limp and try to make them feel sorry for 70
her and think something happened to her besides just being clumsy
footed. Look at her pretending to limp, Merton."

They just told Miss Tripp at the piano something and she folded up 71
her music. I feel my heart go away inside my chest, like a hole just
popped inside me. That means the tryouts are over. Rosey's not going
to go back and do the dance all the way through. She's giving up.

"Rachel Troppin?" 72

"Yes Ma'am, Miss Tripp." I feel myself get up and start down to the 73
front of the auditorium.

"You will be our butterfly then." 74

"Yes, Miss Tripp. Thank you very much." 75

"Rosey is going to be all right. She just turned her ankle but I don't 76
think it would be wise for her to plan on dancing in the play with a weak
ankle."

I see Rosey now sitting on the steps. She is still sniffing but smiling 77
funny like. Her ankle is kind of swollen. The way Miss Tripp smiles at
her, I bet I know what she did. She told Rosey she would have had the
part to get her to stop crying and then told her she had better let me
have it. That's what she did, I bet. "You'll be our butterfly then" she says
to me like I wouldn't have been anyway.

"And Rachel dear, before rehearsals start let me make it clear to you 78
that you shouldn't bring your boyfriend with you unless he sits on the
very back row and stays absolutely quiet."

"Oh, Miss Tripp. Merton's not my boyfriend. He just follows 79
me around because he lives near me. He most certainly is not my
boyfriend."

"Well, I don't care who he is, he was with you and he disturbed our 80
tryouts."

"Yes Ma'am, I'll tell him you don't want him here." 81

The back door just slammed loud; that had to be Merton. Who else 82
hasn't got any more sense than that.

507

"Goodness!" Miss Tripp says.   83

Rosey starts trying to get up and Miss Tripp says, "I guess we had   84
better not try to do any more today in all this confusion. Be here
tomorrow right after school lets out, Rachel."

"Yes Ma'am."   85

I run up the aisle to the door. I want to get outside so bad. If I don't   86
get through the door this second . . . it's still raining. My face must just
be burning hot I'm so embarrassed. And there won't be another bus
home. I'll have to walk now and Merton has gone on without me. The
rain makes my face feel cold but it doesn't feel good even then. I hate
to get wet again. But I don't care about my hair any more, it'll just frizz
all over anyway. I don't care if my face streaks red and black all over.

There's Merton up ahead. He really did start home without me. I   87
can't tell if he's walking slow so I can catch up or not but I will.

"Merton, wait up!"   88

He stops but he doesn't turn around.   89

"Merton, I got the butterfly."   90

He just starts walking again. When I'm beside him he doesn't even   91
turn to say anything to me. Now what have I done to hurt his feelings?

"Miss Tripp must have told Rosey she would have gotten the part if   92
she hadn't fallen down," I say. "You don't believe she would have, do
you Merton?"

"You were glad she fell down."   93

That sounded scary. That didn't sound like Merton.   94

"That's not true. I would rather have gotten the part fair and square." 95

"No, you were glad."   96

Merton is taking bigger steps now. I can't keep up with him and my   97
throat is getting sore from hurrying so hard. I can see the light spots on
his shirt when he swings his arms, he's not rained on there but I feel
rained on all over, so much my clothes are hurting me. He is so far ahead
of me now, he's not walking with me anymore. He's walked off and left
me.

Over the ditch . . . he's taking the short cut over the ditch through 98
the woods path. I don't want to walk by myself; it looks dark already
with the rain.

"Merton, please wait up for me! I don't want to walk all the way by 99
myself."

Merton stops at the edge of the woods.   100

"Well, come on."   101

I'm getting cold. That's not right, it's just not right for him to be like 102
that to me. He's just being plain mean.

"Merton, you know I can't get over that ditch."   103

"I seen you jump that far before." Then he looks hard at me and looks 104
real mean. "I seen you jump farther than that up on that stage."

"But there wasn't a hole there, Merton. Don't make me stand here 105
and freeze. Please come back over and walk the road with me. I'm
scared to try to jump it."

"I want to see you jump over that ditch if you want to walk with me." 106

My eyes are burning now and I couldn't jump, I couldn't jump if the 107
hole wasn't even there.

"You want to see me fall, Merton." 108

I start back up the road. I would give up my butterfly part to be home 109
and dry, I would. I really would if I could be home right this very second
with dry clothes on and dry shoes and socks and be warm in my own
house and not on this road all by myself. And Merton's turned mean to
me. He is just going to go off and leave me and not care a bit if something should happen to me. He won't care a bit.

"He give me three weeks to get it cut." 110

"What! Merton, you scared the stuffings out of me, sneaking up on me 111
like that! I didn't even hear you."

"He give me three weeks because I told him I had to make the money 112
for a haircut or my mama would cut it with a bowl."

"Merton, that's a big fib. I bet you got money enough in your pocket 113
right this very minute for a haircut if you wanted one."

"Yep." 114

"Merton you really *are* going to get thrown out for good." 115

Merton sticks his hands in his back pockets and I see that dry spot 116
under his arm is still there. He didn't listen to one word I said about
getting thrown out.

"Hey Rachel, what you think if I grafted a maypop onto a rosebush? 117
Do you reckon it might smell good?"

SUBJECT

1. Does Rachel dislike Merton? If so, why does she constantly
worry about what he says and does? If not, why does she think such
unflattering and resentful thoughts about him?

2. If Merton is such a clod, why does Rachel allow herself to be
humiliated by him? If she is superior to him, why does she depend on
him?

3. Would you say that Rachel's relationship with Merton is unusual,
or typical in some ways of boy-girl relationships?

4. Is Rachel typically, or unnaturally, concerned with the way she
looks when the rain soaks her at the beginning? To whom do her looks
matter? Why?

5. What do you make of Rachel's thoughts and statements about Rosey Bell? Is Rosey any more "natural" than Rachel?

6. How cogent would this story be as an argument in favor of women's liberation?

STRUCTURE

1. As a ninth grader in the spring, Rachel would probably be fifteen. Does the stream of her consciousness seem appropriate for that age? How much can you tell about her background?

2. Like "Goose," this story cannot be expected to exhibit the form of a persuasive essay; does it present the materials from which a persuasion on women's liberation could be written? What arguments are implicit in the story?

3. The structural formula for this story is "a day in the life of Rachel"; does this arrangement allow Wilkinson to give a clear enough picture of the kinds of worries and humiliations a girl can be faced with? Would a more extraordinary day have been a better choice?

4. The story proceeds by dialog and narrative; but it depends to a considerable extent on descriptive details for its sense of authenticity and its vividness. Were there any particularly vivid details which you can recall without looking back at the story?

5. An irritating problem in writing dialog is having to use "he said" over and over, or else to find substitutes which are even more awkward — "he queried," "he demanded," etc. How does Wilkinson get around this problem?

9

WHERE ARE WE NOW?

Evaluation

The ability to evaluate, to judge, to decide that one way is better than another, is one of the great distinguishing characteristics of the human mind. It is what enables us to make use of our abilities to see likenesses and differences, to form generalizations from particulars, and to accumulate knowledge purposefully instead of indiscriminately as a pack rat saving objects. The discovery of scientific information, for instance, is not nearly so valuable to us as the ability to assess its importance — to see the significance of new facts in relation to known facts.

Evaluation is a practice in which learned minds are constantly indulging and of which everyone is more or less capable. Every time we make a decision we first evaluate the advantages and disadvantages of each possible course of action. We may not do this very carefully or logically, but we do it. Take a familiar example: When a student's alarm clock rings at 7:30 he finds himself faced with a decision. "Should I get up and go to my 8 o'clock class? Should I stay in bed and get some much-needed rest? Should I wander over to the student union for a leisurely and nourishing breakfast of black coffee and cigarette smoke?" The student may be handicapped by an inability to think clearly at this time of day, but he will still evaluate various factors: "I need sleep more than I need food. If I went to class, the professor would put me to sleep. But I sleep better in a prone position than sitting at a desk." A good evaluation, certainly, would be done much more carefully than that, but the basic process would be similar: consider all the pertinent facts and implications and pass judgment in the light of each possibility's relative merits.

Evaluation, whether it be simple or complex, always presupposes the existence of some standard of judgment. Standards may vary greatly with different people and may not be very explicitly formulated, but for any judgment there must be a standard. When a teacher evaluates a student theme, he compares it to certain standards of excellence: "The organization is fair, sentence structure good, clarity excellent, spelling and punctuation atrocious." Then he decides what its overall grade should be. A student does the same sort of thing when he decides "That was a good movie" or "He is a poor teacher." What makes a good movie? — photography, acting, directing, significance of plot, continuity, and so on. The evaluator may not have such explicit standards, however; perhaps he judges from a vague notion, accumulated by watching many movies, that a movie ought to evoke certain emotional responses. But almost no one is totally uncritical — that is, without any standards of judgment.

It will easily be seen from the preceding examples that the amount and diversity of one's experience have much to do with his ability to evaluate. The young child who has seen few movies will be tempted to boo the villain and shout warnings to the good guy; he will admire the good guy and detest the bad guy even if the latter is a much better actor. Similarly, a second grader is not nearly as capable of judging teaching effectiveness as is a college student. And the beginning teacher, lacking the experience which comes from reading thousands of papers of varying quality, may also lack that ability to know automatically what grade a paper should receive; he must make up in eagerness and carefulness what he lacks in experience. Of the two aspects of experience, variety is probably more important for good evaluation than mere quantity of experience, however. A person who has read much poetry but all of it comparatively easy (Service, Whitman, and Sandburg, for example) will still have trouble evaluating the more difficult poetry of Wallace Stevens or Dylan Thomas. His standards of judgment are simply too limited. A story is told of an African tribal chief who was taken to hear his first symphonic concert in an experiment to determine whether or not good music is naturally appealing to someone without prior training. The chief was quite pleased when the orchestra members were tuning their instruments, but the symphony itself left him coldly unappreciative.

In discussing standards of evaluation it is important to keep in mind that standards can be — and usually are — relative instead of absolute. We hold most standards tentatively, with an awareness that there may be specific instances to which a generally valid standard does not apply. Most people who endorse the principle, "Thou shalt not kill," do not hold it absolutely but mean "In *most cases* thou shalt not kill." If one man kills another and we are called upon to evaluate the criminality of his act, we make an exception to the principle if he was fighting in a war, acting in self-defense, or executing a convict. Our courts even distinguish "degrees" of murder: premeditated, un-premeditated, accidental, and justifiable. This same relativity of principles applies in most other areas as well. An English teacher may normally mark off heavily for errors in punctuation or sentence structure, but he is likely to be much more forgiving in these matters if a paper shows considerable insight and imagination. We say that the hero of a tragedy ought to have a recognizable "tragic flaw," but we readily admit that *Hamlet* is great even though its hero has no such flaw.

Evaluation as an essay form can be of three different types. One of these is *primary* evaluation: evaluation of a state of affairs or past action, such as a judgment of the accomplishments of Theodore Roosevelt's administration or of UNESCO's success in fostering mutual understanding among nations. Another type is *secondary,* an evaluation of *someone else's* judgment. This includes book reviews and judgments of paintings, poems, movies — works which express the values of the artist. The process for this kind of evaluation is the same as for primary evaluation except that two sets of standards must be considered: those of the original author or artist and those of the reviewer or critic. Normally, such an evaluation is organized in three parts, answering the following questions: (1) What was the author trying to do? (2) How well did he accomplish his aims? (3) To what extent was the work worth doing? The answers to the first two questions should be in terms of the standards implied by the original author. If an artist was trying to produce an abstract painting it would hardly be fair to condemn his work for being insufficiently representational — that is, not "looking like" the scene which inspired it. The answer to the third question depends on the standards of the reviewer or critic. If he believes that abstract painting is foolish experimentation and that this particular painting cannot be great because it is abstract, such a judgment should come in the third rather than the second part. Thus a critic might conclude that the artist succeeded very well in what he was trying to do but that the attempt was not worth the effort.

The student should remember that any evaluation, no matter how carefully worked out, is still opinion rather than fact. A viewer may be convinced that a certain movie was the "worst" of the year, and perhaps it was that bad if judged by a standard such as acting or plot. But perhaps its producer, his standard of judgment being monetary, might judge it to be "great" if a few suggestive scenes cause it to bring in considerable amounts of money. This is not to say, however, that all evaluations are equally valuable. Enlightened opinion can tell us much; snap judgments tell us little except something about the intellectual nature of the person making the judgment. The student who writes an evaluation should take pains to judge carefully and fairly, to consider as much relevant information as possible, to know and make clear what his standards of judgment are, and to recognize that they may not be the only applicable standards. Pursued properly, evaluation can be a rewarding experience and a valuable contribution to civilization. Done improperly, it can be a mere excuse for perpetrating one's prejudices.

Although *self-evaluation,* the third type, is on a subject obviously familiar to the writer, it is a very difficult kind of writing to handle competently. And it is the one type of writing which is generally more useful to the writer than to his reader. The great Dr. Samuel Johnson always kept a journal, and he urged his friend Boswell to do the same on the grounds that any person, no matter how successful or important he was, could profit by occasionally taking stock of himself. He found that a person, too easily losing sight of his personal values and goals, can drift through life discovering too late that he has not accomplished what he set out to do or anything else worthwhile.

Self-evaluation is especially valuable to a student, for he is in the process of committing himself to a set of standards and aims which will in large measure determine what the rest of his life will be like. The student who comes to school with an exalted and narrow-minded notion of his chosen career, whether it be in medicine, engineering, or creative writing, is likely to be making a tragic mistake if he staggers through a program for which he is not suited and refuses to consider other possible major fields. Again, unless he evaluates himself periodically a student may go through college thinking that a C-average and a house presidency are adequate recommendations for a job, and then suddenly discover too late that he wants to go on to graduate school.

In spite of the obvious benefit from occasional self-evaluation, the student is likely to encounter considerable difficulty in doing it. No one likes to admit that he is making a mistake or that his values are wrong; consequently, it is easier to avoid the possibility of having to make such an admission by dismissing self-evaluation as a "waste of time" or by substituting for honest analysis a few hasty rationalizations. Someone has said, however, that a student's greatest advantage is his right to be wrong: the student who is afraid of making a mistake never learns as much as the one who exposes his ideas to the criticism of his teachers and fellow students. Although a ten-year veteran of a specialized occupation can hardly afford to admit that he has chosen the wrong career, a student can admit it — and change — without too much inconvenience. If he can forget his fear of being wrong and make an honest effort to evaluate himself justly, he can learn a great deal about himself and at the same time gain a clearer view of where he is going and where he wants to go.

A complete self-evaluation contains the answers to two questions: (1) Am I accomplishing my aims and living up to my standards? (2) Are my standards, basic assumptions, and goals the right ones for me? For most students, the first question is probably much easier to answer than the second, for the latter calls into question values which the student has been accumulating for years and about which he may have had no doubts before coming to college. Evaluating these values involves the same kind of difficulty faced by a person who takes a college biology course after having been taught at home or at church that the whole notion of evolution is atheistic nonsense. But because anyone's set of values is likely to include contradictions and unwarranted assumptions, it is particularly worthwhile to examine them before committing one's whole life to them. Most of our "cherished" goals are either handed to us or accumulated unconsciously, so that we have no real reason for being fiercely loyal to them. It would profit any student to take complete stock of himself at least as often as once every school year. The difficulty of the attempt ought to be compensated for by the knowledge that it is the student's own life which is at stake. It is because self-evaluation can be of such vital importance — and because backing off and examining one's self objectively is such a difficult task — that this subject has been reserved for the last part of the text.

DEPRESSING AREAS

Walter Goodman

Walter Goodman was born in New York in 1927, and attended college in England. He has published several books, including The Clowns of Commerce *(1957),* All Honorable Men *(1963), and* The Committee *(1968). Mr. Goodman has written numerous articles on politics and foreign affairs, and currently writes a column, "Fair Game," for* The New Leader. *"Depressing Areas" (1971) is one of his contributions to that column.*

To: The Attorney General 1
From: Head, Internal Security Division

Chief, reports from our faceless undercover agents at home and 2
abroad confirm our worst suspicions — the under-30s are at it again.
Just when the editorial writers were saying that the kids have sown
their oats, that they are going to stop aggravating everybody and go
back to gang rumbles and drunken driving, comes the news that a lot
of soldiers in Vietnam intend to return to their moms, dads and sweet-
hearts as heroin addicts. Sorry, chief — *white* soldiers, too. Having
been given the opportunity to fly clear across the world to serve under
General Abrams and do combat for the national honor, these young
men have chosen to shoot up rather than shoot at. The Vietcong must
be laughing up their pajama sleeves.

Not that one can't make allowances. We're not all fogies up here on 3
Constitution Avenue, no matter what the Trotskyites say. We understand that any young American might feel at loose ends over there in
the battle zone, lacking wholesome entertainment in between Bob
Hope's visits. The least the heads of the Army PXs could have done,
when they weren't busy stealing, was to provide Ping-Pong balls and
Monopoly sets and checked-out girls from high-status gook families for
the GI's leisure time.

As you are aware, it's Pentagon policy for our boys to get to know the 4
way of life of Asiatic peoples, their traditions and customs, no matter

Reprinted from *The New Leader* (June 28, 1971) by permission of the publisher.

how disgusting — it's a real opportunity to broaden one's horizons, become acquainted with unusual lifestyles, as the recruiting posters point out. And (see the memo from Ambassador Bunker) it's not for us sitting in our swivel chairs over here to say a bad word about the Vietnamese citizen who prefers to dream away his days rather than face them fully conscious. And (see the memo from Secretary Rogers) the way business is conducted by government officials in South Vietnam is a matter for decision by democratic process in that little democracy; after all, we don't want to be put in the position of policing the whole world (see what happened to Lyndon Johnson). And we certainly don't want to be accused by the Washington *Post* of trying to tell today's fine young people what they should or should not do with their time off. But heroin? *Ech!*

If that isn't sinister enough, chief, our informants confirm the ac- 5 curacy of that survey the Administration leaked a few weeks ago which showed that a large percentage of VISTA volunteers are being *radicalized* by their experiences in working with America's poor. Stoned on poverty!

As the President has pointed out more than once, everybody in our 6 Administration, from the top right on down the line, is committed heart and soul to all poverty programs; those poor people sure deserve help, and I know that you for one are all for giving them what they deserve. But when you stop and think about it without letting your emotions run away with you, chief (chief, please stop letting your emotions run away with you), what kind of young folks would go into programs like VISTA in the first place? Hustling around out there in Appalachia for peanuts instead of getting a foot in the door in the insurance business back home? The whole thing is just not designed for young folks who cherish our national values. Remember, this was set up by Democrats.

Look at the total picture: Their government sends them forth on the 7 high mission of helping the poor, equipped with plenty of good wishes (if only I had a dollar for every VISTA volunteer I've patted on the back), and just because they find that the poor don't all have indoor privies and local officials are busy uptown, the young folks become *radicalized*. Where's their sense of perspective, for God's sake? J. Edgar is sure that Rennie Davis is at the bottom of the whole mess. (By the way, chief, we hear that the Tobacco Industry Research Council has found a causal connection between Rennie Davis and lung cancer.) But my facelessly informed guess is that the volunteers weren't stable to begin with.

Billy Graham told me on the golf course the other afternoon that the 8 obstinate refusal of a small minority to live the good life bespeaks a want of moral fiber. It's one of those basic virtues that can only be inbuilt by a good home and a good evangelist, Billy said, and made a birdie on the

517

seventh hole (the power of prayer). But no use mincing words. By the time a young fellow is of an age to leave home, he ought to have learned that drugs and poverty are dangerous, and that he should steer clear of them. They are debilitating and demoralizing and distracting; the penalties for pushers cannot be too severe, no matter what the Supreme Court says. Which reminds me, chief — regards from old Harry Carswell. Billy and I met him at the club and had a stimulating chat about moral fiber.

Reentry Pains

Now, these foreign and domestic dilemmas are very much on all our 9
minds in this shop, believe me. We've considered inaugurating a job-training program for addicts, but that seems kind of pointless since there are no jobs available to train them for. It would ease matters if a few thousand of the veterans took a lesson from the North Vietnamese POWS and refused to come home — but excuse me, I'm dreaming.

To get back to nuts and bolts, the first step should be a stiffening of 10
the penalties against marijuana. Between us, that won't have an effect on heroin addiction, but it's guaranteed to smoke out the radicals. Much more important, my staff — in collaboration with Rogers' people and Kissinger's people and J. Edgar's people — has in the works a program to come to grips with everything through a shrewd combination of disengagement and preventive detention. Of course the inspiration, chief, is 100 per cent yours.

Fortunately, we're already well into the Vietnamizing process. As our 11
men return from the bastion of democracy, they will be shipped directly to detoxification centers designed to resemble Uncle Fred's Candy Shoppe Back Home (the Washington, D.C., police force has agreed to handle the logistics). Once there, the veteran will be fed strawberry shakes laced with Southern Comfort until his native tastes reassert themselves and he is ready to find happiness in his own country. (Lawsuits challenging our program of Congenial Rehabilitation will doubtless be instituted by the ACLU in behalf of veterans who are allergic to strawberry flavoring, but our experts assure us there's nothing in the Constitution that guarantees anybody a right to chocolate or vanilla.)

The VISTA volunteers represent a trickier problem. Let me put this 12
on the line, chief — it's unrealistic to expect a strawberry shake to take the taste of Appalachia out of anybody's mouth. The main consideration, here, is that we don't want to appear oppressive — you know how the papers jump on every little thing. J. Edgar's proposal seems to us ingenious but premature; the frontal lobotomy is still a tricky opera-

tion. The Vice President's suggestion that all long-haired youths be shipped to an island off the coast of Italy as part of a Mops for the Wops program would probably upset an ethnic element.

Kicking Poverty

So, to get back to our plan, we want to hand each returned volunteer 13 $10,000 in cash and a Detroit-made automobile to help him resume his acquaintance with the American Way. Get the scenario, chief? We're fighting ideology with ideology. Any radical under 30 who expresses an interest in buying a piece of property will be offered a fat bank loan at advantageous rates, which ought to tie him up pretty effectively well into middle age. Surveys made in Croton-on-Hudson and Martha's Vineyard prove that more Communists have been converted by real estate than by the blacklist. As for the hard-core poverty addict who refuses to take the money, he may have to undergo strawberry shake therapy.

The lesson of this unfortunate experience, chief, is that the poverty 14 program has to be thoroughly reformed. It's just too chancy to continue to expose the middle class to the poor; they catch things from one another. I know it's not prudent politics to point that out in writing, with Jack Anderson checking your garbage can. But we have been sending our troops and our treasure in to help the poor since 1965; surely it's time those people stood on their own ill-shod feet.

Therefore, our intelligence advisory board is suggesting that the 15 President go on TV to announce the following: That the war against poverty is about to be Appalachianized under the dynamic leadership of former Congressman Albert R. Watson of South Carolina, to whom we still owe a job. That all poverty workers will be withdrawn before November 1972. That from then on, helicopters will be flown in over less affluent areas to drop self-help manuals onto those below.

Yes, chief, I know we'll need one-liners to get across our new program 16 to the American people, and the boys in the one-liner shop have come up with a couple of grabbers. The self-help-manual idea can be presented by the President as "Target: The Poor." And the detoxification campaign, naturally, as "Honorable Withdrawal."

SUBJECT

1. Obviously, no one would dare offer seriously the solutions to the two problems discussed here; what kind of thinking do these solutions represent?

2. What, exactly, is the "problem" this fictitious bureaucrat sees in the Vista program? How does he explain the problem's existence?

3. Why is Billy Graham brought into this discussion? Why on the golf course?

4. What differences are there between the bureaucrat's attitudes toward the Vietnamese and toward the poor of America?

5. Does Goodman offer any clues as to how a person can begin thinking along the lines of this bureaucrat? That is, is there something about his very job which encourages such thinking?

STRUCTURE

1. Goodman's article begins as though it was to be an official and formal report, but it soon becomes a chatty newsletter. Should Goodman have made clear from the beginning that the report was to be off-the-cuff? (He could not have gone the other way and made it "official," since this would have necessitated almost unreadable gobbledygook.)

2. Consider Goodman's deliberate use of clichés and prepackaged thoughts to help characterize his bureaucrat. Is this a case when the writer is right to use clichés?

3. This article is curious in that it evaluates an official as *he* evaluates two problems. Goodman's own standards of evaluation must therefore be implied rather than stated; does he make clear what they are?

4. Do you think the satire would have been more effective had Goodman omitted such obvious thrusts as the solutions offered by J. Edgar Hoover and Spiro Agnew?

THE PENTAGON PAPERS
AND HISTORICAL HINDSIGHT

John P. Roche

*John P. Roche (born in 1923) is professor of politics at Brandeis Univer-
sity. He has served as consultant for the State Department and special
consultant to the President (1966–1969), was national chairman of
Americans for Democratic Action and on the executive board of the
Massachusetts Civil Liberties Union. A pacifist and strong supporter of
civil rights, Professor Roche has published many books on American
politics, including* Courts and Rights *(rev. 1965) and* The Quest for
Dream: Civil Liberties in Modern America *(1963). This article appeared in* The New Leader *in July, 1971, between the unauthorized
publication of the Pentagon Papers on Vietnam and the Supreme
Court's decision on their release.*

The real problem created by publication of excerpts from the Pen- 1
tagon's history of our involvement in Vietnam lies not so much in the
act itself as in the effect it will have in the realm of demonology. Nothing has emerged from the series that was not already in the public
domain; the documents themselves were, of course, classified, yet various authors had drawn on their knowledge of classified sources to make
the substantive points. And the Pentagon study has two enormous gaps:
the President and the Secretary of State.

What is important, though, is not what the documents show but what 2
people think they show. Already the foreign press, as well as some of
our more hysterical domestic papers, are trumpeting that the study
"proves" that the United States got involved in the Vietnam war
through a sinister conspiracy, that while Lyndon Johnson was preaching
peace in the 1964 campaign the boys in the back room were drawing
up battle plans. Barry Goldwater has turned out to be helpful on this
matter and is, for the first time in his life, being treated by the doves
as a serious authority on current events.

Now this triumph of "investigative reporting," as the New York 3
Times calls it (a strange description of having a truckload of documents
dumped on your doorstep), does provide a case study of contingency

Reprinted from *The New Leader* (July 12, 1971) by permission of the publisher.

planning, using entirely second- and third-echelon sources. Let us arbitrarily begin with the deposition of Ngo Dinh Diem in 1963. At that
time it was the consensus among policy-makers that Diem and his
brother Nhu were hindering an effective anti-Communist response in
Vietnam. This was also the view of David Halberstam and the New York
Times. But the optimists who looked for a stable successor regime, one
that would inspire South Vietnamese resistance to the ever-increasing
infiltration from the North, were grossly disappointed. Saigon was characterized by revolving-door governments, and the North Vietnamese
regulars and Main Force Vietcong began chewing up ARVN at a terrible
rate.

President Johnson, still fully occupied with the transition from the 4
Kennedy era, acted appropriately: He said to Secretaries Rusk and
McNamara, in effect, "Put your men to work and give me the options.
Once I have seen them, we can talk concretely about how to deal with
the crisis." The men went to work and the results of their efforts have
been chronicled in the *Times* and several other papers. But when the
Times says that a "consensus on bombing" had been reached before the
1964 election, it misstates the case, or perhaps overstates the reality. In
the U.S. government, there is no consensus on anything without the
President. Abraham Lincoln put it tersely when he found himself the
only member of his Cabinet in favor of the Emancipation Proclamation:
"One for, five against — the ayes have it."

What did exist in 1964 was general agreement at the second and third 5
echelons of the relevant agencies that bombing North Vietnam was a
sound policy. There was nothing new about the idea of using air power
to "punish" Hanoi. It had been included as a possible option in General
Maxwell Taylor's report to President Kennedy back in 1961 and it
popped up regularly in subsequent years.

The advocates of air strikes were a strange united front: the Air Force 6
and Navy because they believed it would be effective, and others from
the Armed Services who, while pessimistic about its effectiveness, saw
it as an alternative to a "land war in Asia." It was also argued from
another quarter that bombing the North would stiffen morale in Saigon
and affirm the credibility of American commitments.

But the documents present no evidence that President Johnson had 7
made up his mind one way or the other before November 1964. In fact,
he hadn't. Hung up between two basic responsibilities — one to
peace, and the other to limiting Communist aggression — he did
what he always did under such circumstances: He told Dean Rusk and
Robert McNamara to go on refining their policy options and to set the
wheels in motion, so that whichever approach he finally selected could

be implemented at once. Naturally McNamara increased our airpower assets in the Far East, but we were not committed to bombing. The same thing was done in Korea after the Pueblo crisis, but the planes never took off.

It is seldom hard to construct conspiracy theories of history in retro- 8 spect. Distinguished Southern historians, for example, worked diligently for many years to demonstrate that President Lincoln had deliberately tricked the South into the Civil War, that after the innocent Confederates fired on Fort Sumter, Lincoln rubbed his hands with glee and used the incident to justify mobilizing Union troops. Similarly, Franklin D. Roosevelt was attacked in immense detail by as distinguished an American historian as Charles A. Beard for instigating the Japanese assault on Pearl Harbor. Although these studies had a lunatic logic, they suffer from one overwhelming liability: They are not true.

Lincoln did not want war. Roosevelt did — but with the Nazis, not 9 the Japanese. In fact, if Hitler had not gone completely off his rails and declared war on the United States, we might well have gone roaring off into the Pacific in 1942 and left Europe to its fate. So let us, as we read the memos floating back and forth between assistant secretaries, ask the simple question: Why would Lyndon Johnson have wanted to get mixed up in a war in Indochina? He was well aware of the unpopularity of wars, he recalled vividly the treatment Harry Truman had received over our Korean intervention, and he wanted above all to get down to the serious business of the Great Society.

The Joint Chiefs are paid to plan for wars. They have over at the 10 Pentagon an immense welfare program (Aid to Dependent Colonels, I call it) dedicated to contingency planning. (Back in the 1930s they spent a couple of years deciding how to cope with a combined attack by the British and the Japanese!) You name a country, they have a man on it equipped with detailed maps, target analysis, etc. Obviously a good deal of this is necessary in our uncertain world, but the important thing to note is that most contingencies never occur.

Presidents, on the contrary, are paid to keep us out of wars whenever 11 that is conceivably possible. And while President Johnson, like his predecessors, was committed to containing Communist aggression (whether monolithic or polycentric), the first item on his agenda was how to do so and avoid war. Viewed from this perspective, Step Number One was deterrence, that is, letting the enemy know that if it did certain things, it would get hurt. When deterrence works (as it has, notably with the Soviet Union and Communist China), nobody cheers.

It hardly took a task force to devise the Tonkin Gulf Resolution; it was simply a rewrite of the one passed by Congress in 1958 on the Formosa Straits, which worked.

Unfortunately, Ho Chi Minh was not impressed. Thus the next step 12 was to raise the ante, employing a minimal force level to indicate that we meant business. Enter the air-power spokesmen. Now whatever the assistant secretaries may have written to each other, and despite the optimism of the "air marshals" (as those of us who distrusted the policy called them), bombing North Vietnam was seen as a way of *avoiding* war. Hanoi, it was argued, would appreciate the seriousness of American support for the Republic of Vietnam, calculate that the stakes were too high, and call off its "liberation" movement.

There is no need to detail the rest of the gloomy progression. Johnson 13 ended up with more than 500,000 men in Vietnam and a full-scale land war by opting at each stage for the least repellent alternative. With retrospective omniscience — a wide-spread malady these days — one can argue that he should have gotten off the escalator in 1964 or '65. But history is a very different thing when you are approaching it head-on, rather than with 20-20 hindsight. Without getting into disputes on *how* the war was fought, one could (as I do) suggest that the President's reluctant decisions were a natural and legitimate consequence of the American people's then staunch commitment to freedom for South Vietnam.

That brings us to the issue of disseminating classified information. By 14 a strange coincidence, almost as the *Times* was proofreading the Pentagon papers, the Senate Judiciary Committee was approving the nomination of Otto Otepka to the Subversive Activities Control Board (SACB). A number of Right-wingers looked on this as a vindication of Otepka, who had been fired by those wicked liberals over at the State Department for bootlegging classified information to congressional committees. Recent events, though, may lead the Senate Judiciary Committee and President Nixon, who nominated Otepka, to rethink their stance. If Otepka deserves a slot on the SACB for the trivia he leaked, surely whoever conveyed the Pentagon study to the *Times* merits a spot on the Federal Communications Commission.

And, in fairness, the *Times* and other papers that have been oozing 15 with virtuous editorials about freedom of information and the absurdity of the classification system should immediately support Otepka's appointment. If leaking classified materials is a blow for freedom, one really can't exclude the late Joe McCarthy's "loyal American underground" from the warrior band.

This thought is advanced not in a cynical spirit, but rather to make 16 the point — obscured in the rhetorical mist these past weeks — that, as usual in American politics, one's views on leaking classified material tend to depend, in FDR's phrase, on "whose child has the measles." Let us therefore try to escape from an atmosphere dominated by editors reciting Milton, and government lawyers predicting the end of the bureaucratic world, and take a hard look at some of the real questions before the Supreme Court as this article is being written.

First, has the publication of these documents endangered "national security"? The answer: Of course not. Anyone with a reasonably specialized knowledge of events in 1964 knows, and has known for years, that contingency plans were being considered to deal with the worsening Vietnamese situation. The documents have provided a lot of background; one can argue that their publication was imprudent, but that raises an entirely different issue.   17

Second, has the publication of these documents damaged the operation of the government? This is a tricky one, particularly since one of the worst tendencies in the State and Defense Departments was to over-classify just about everything. During my years at the White House, for example, I was convinced that certain men stamped their missives "Top Secret" simply to attract attention, presumably figuring that nobody would bother to read a merely "Confidential" memo. At the same time, if one expects high government officials to lay their convictions, no matter how unpopular, on the line, there should be some guarantee that confidentiality will be maintained. One of the unfortunate by-products of Joe McCarthy's "loyal American underground" was that dissenters in the State Department responded by keeping unorthodox views to themselves.   18

Part of the historical bias built into the Pentagon papers arose from the fact that such old hands as Dean Rusk and Lyndon Johnson profoundly distrusted the security system. Rusk was known to sit down and type up his "eyes only" memos to the President, and the latter openly held the opinion that to send any sensitive material to the State Department was to guarantee its publication in the next morning's paper. And no one ever sent the minutes of the Tuesday lunches — where crucial decisions were hammered out — anywhere except to the White House files. When President Johnson wanted opinions, he sidestepped the system. In November 1967, for instance, he canvassed a number of advisers on a radical deescalation of the war, and no word of it leaked out.   19

Publication of the documents will undoubtedly encourage bureaucrats to be more noncommittal in their memoranda, and will probably stimulate President Nixon to follow the Johnson-Rusk format. (Nixon's   20

"National Security Council System," which has papers flowing up, down and sideways, is a sitting duck for an ambitious leaker.) But we can survive on that basis. In short, especially given the paranoia that has been generated, I think the full Pentagon history should have been declassified. There is nothing to hide.

SUBJECT

1. Roche clearly does not approve of the way the Vietnam war was handled; on what grounds does he defend the administration from the charge of "sinister conspiracy" to escalate the war?

2. Does Roche's explanation of how the war happened to be escalated despite President Johnson's desire for peace seem to you convincing? Why?

3. What justification does Roche give for the practice of classifying information? Should he give more consideration to the people's "right to know"?

4. What unfortunate result does Roche foresee of the publication of the Pentagon Papers? Is this the same complaint a Pentagon official might voice?

5. What point is Roche trying to make about right-wingers (Otto Otepka and Senator Joseph McCarthy's "underground") who leaked classified information?

STRUCTURE

1. In this essay Roche is evaluating the damage done by public release of secret documents; in a sense, then, it is also an example of cause and effect analysis. Had cause and effect analysis been his sole aim, what would Roche have needed to do differently?

2. Roche makes reference to a number of political figures and events in the past; should he have given them identifying or explanatory footnotes? Is it necessary to know all these references (to Otto Otepka, for instance) in order to understand the essay?

3. Can you find a standard of judgment by which Roche evaluates the publication of secret materials. Is there more than one?

4. What use does Roche make of the examples of Lincoln and Roosevelt in paragraph 8? Do the examples constitute valid evidence that Johnson was not involved in a "sinister conspiracy"?

5. This article contains several satirical thrusts (the jibe about "Aid to Dependent Colonels," for instance). These do not all seem to be slanted in one direction; examine Roche's use of them.

RESPONSES TO
THE GENERATION GAP

Joseph Wood Krutch

*Joseph Wood Krutch, born in Tennessee in 1893, became one of those
rare "complete renaissance men" of our century. A distinguished
professor of English literature, he was also a member of the American
Academy of Arts and Science, the Drama Critics Circle, and the
American Philosophical Society, and was a trustee of the Arizona-
Sonora Desert Museum. Among his more than two dozen books are
works on drama, morality, politics, biography, gardening, desert wildlife, even on the geological history of the Grand Canyon. His best-
known works probably are* Human Nature and the Human Condition
(1959), and The Measure of Man, *which won the National Book Award
in 1954. While in semi-retirement, Dr. Krutch was a contributing
editor of* The American Scholar. *This article appeared in his column,
"If You Don't Mind My Saying So" in 1969.*

I am not sure that the generation gap is any wider today than it has 1
always been. But there is a difference in the responses to it. We elders
used to say, "You will think different when you are older and more
mature." Today it is the young who say to us, "You are too old, too set
in your ways to understand." Neither retort is likely to narrow the gap
and both are to some degree condescending. But to say, "You will
mature," grants the young a possible future; to say, "You are too old,"
is to damn us beyond the possibility of salvation.

In a recent conversation with a sophomore this vast difference was 2
brought home to me. He relented enough to say that if I would listen
to some of his Bob Dylan and Beatles records I might just possibly be
able to understand why the future would recognize them as more
"relevant" than Bach or Beethoven — both of which, so he insisted,
he liked well enough to be sure that it was not incomprehension that
led him to place them in an inferior position. The failure of comprehension was all on my side.

This is the simplest form that can be taken by the current obsession 3
with the "now," but the conviction that there just isn't any usable past
seems to be shared by a good many, including some of those who are
over thirty — the figure commonly assumed by the younger generation to mark the beginning of senility. John Barth (the eccentric novelist
now much esteemed by the *avant-garde* and beginning to reach the
best-seller list where no *avant-garde* writer ought to be) was recently
quoted in the *Chicago Review* as remarking that if Chartres Cathedral
or Beethoven's Sixth were to be created today they would be "simply
embarrassing."

Of course an easy reply would be that this is one sort of embarrass- 4
ment neither Mr. Barth nor, so far as I know, any of our contemporaries
need go in fear of. But I am less interested in being snide than in trying
to understand an attitude now sufficiently widespread to have been
seized upon by a number of advertisers, including those who urge you
to switch from Coca-Cola to a new drink which has "the taste of now,"
just as every rock band now claims to have "the sound of now." When
advertisers begin to catch up with the *avant-garde,* it is in danger of
becoming pop art and so for that matter is any magazine that calls itself
Avant-Garde but takes a full-page ad in the *Saturday Review* headed
"Not for everyone." And then goes on to offer all of us the opportunity
to become members of an elite just by sending in a coupon. "Do you
like face jewels? Mohammed Ali? Edwardian haircuts? Radio? Captain
Lev? Psychedelic art? Mayor Lindsay of New York for President? Grass?
The Pill? Did you like Andy Warhol's films before they became popular? If you can answer yes to most of the above, you are a member of
that small but influential group of pacemakers who set the cultural
trend of the nation."

Grove Press goes one step further in the same direction by offering 5
an Underground Book-of-the-Month Club — which sounds like a contradiction in terms. To become a member you sign a coupon which
begins, "I am an adventurous, literate adult." But since no proof of the
statement is required, I assume nobody ever got rejected on the ground
that he just wasn't adventurous and literate as well as adult. You get as
a bonus two books from a list that includes de Sade and also Forberg's
ancient, learned, pedantic and dull *Manual of Classical Erotology.* One
is no more likely to be rejected by the Underground Book Club than
to be blackballed by the National Geographic Society. Incidentally, I
don't know why a taste for erotica is supposed to be confined to the
mature. I thoroughly appreciated Montaigne's "On Some Verses of
Virgil" when, as a preteen-ager, I discovered it by accident in the local
library. But it was not until I became what *I* call mature that I found
Montaigne's other essays equally interesting.

Those of us who are not only over thirty but over sixty as well still take   6
it for granted that there are some things that are "not for a day but for
all time" and we would put Chartres and Beethoven's Sixth in that class.
To say that neither could be created today is one thing. To say that it
would be "embarrassing" if they could be is quite another. That is
equivalent to saying that they have lost all "relevance" — to use another word that belongs, along with "identity" and "existential," in a list
of those now likely to serve chiefly to conceal thought. But if the whole
business of the artist is to express the spirit of his time and if the spirit
of our time dismisses everything except the "now," then it must be
obvious that those who sought eternal values are merely embarrassing.
Probably that is why perversions of classics like the play *Rosencrantz
and Gildenstern Are Dead* (to say nothing of the British Broadcasting
Company's "Alice in Wonderland" and a more recent "Cinderella")
have been highly praised. They destroy a supposed permanent work of
art and free us from embarrassment by demonstrating the hollowness
of what the past regarded as valid.

I am not sure whether we are supposed to believe that today's "now"   7
will be "simply embarrassing" tomorrow or whether, having got rid of
the past, we have for the first time achieved something that will endure.
Will those now under thirty be ossified as soon as they pass that climac-
teric or is it only the old men of the past and present who are not to
be trusted? An answer to the first part of that question seems to be
implied in the *Saturday Review* where the rock-and-roll critic (yes,
there really is such a thing) writes in the issue for May 31, 1969: "Rock
has muddled around for several months, and while there has been
enough jamming around and back-to-the-roots exploration, there has
been no real breakthrough for quite some time." Obviously the implication is that music is expected to "make a breakthrough" at least every
few months if it is not to become what Mr. Barth calls "embarrassing."

One thing is certain. The justification offered by most previous *avant-*   8
gardes from Dada on is not now so unhesitatingly offered. It used to be
said that destruction would make way for a more glorious future in art
as well as in life. But the tendency nowadays seems to offer nothing but
a future increasingly disorganized. A few months ago a group described
as composed of one hundred "competent intellectuals" assembled in
New York to discuss the question, "The end of the rationalist tradition?"
which most of the intellectuals seemed to regard as hardly worth putting in question form. Said Robert Lowell, "The world is absolutely out
of control now, and it is not going to be saved by reason or unreason."
And if that is merely despairing, Leslie Fiedler had a positive program.
"Reason, although dead, holds us with an embrace that looks like a
lover's embrace but turns out to be *rigor mortis.* Unless we are necro-

529

philes, we'd better let go." For encouragement I might offer him a voice from the embarrassing past. "There is a pleasure sure in being mad which only madmen know." But I shall have to apply to Norman Mailer for an explanation of his statement that "We are heading for a conclusion that consists of Joe Namath grinning hungrily over the line at Earl Morrall."

Sometimes I wonder if I may just possibly be as wrong as it seems   9
obvious to many that I am. Am I as insensitive as my sophomore friend believes when I cannot follow a professional music critic who assures me that the Beatles are the beginning of "a new and golden renaissance of song" and who compares their compositions with "the great eras of song such as that of Monteverdi, Schumann and Poulenc"? Or when Miss Susan Sontag, who is a very "now" critic (or at least was six months ago), tells me that a film that includes "close-ups of limp penises and bouncing breasts . . . shots of masturbation and oral sensuality" is "a beautiful film" and that "an esthetic vision of the world" is perhaps always homosexual"? Or when an art critic assures me that "the fantastic, the strange, the singular or the hitherto unknown perspectives — these are today the only kinds of representation which we accept as the identification mark of a modern artist whose work will genuinely touch us"? Is anarchy in all the arts and on all the campuses really the necessary prelude to a glorious future? Is my belief that what we need is more reason, not less, merely necrophilia?

The only reassurance I have now is that these doubts are very much   10
like those I went through almost forty years ago when nearly every social and literary critic found almost all previous writing as embarrassing as Mr. Barth says he would find a present-day Chartres or Sixth Symphony. "Art is a weapon," so the most radical proclaimed. "Its only meaning is its social criticisms," as the more moderate preferred to put it. Then also there was a theater of the absurd which flourished off Broadway as it now flourishes again and in forms (including audience participation) almost indistinguishable from those now described as unmistakably "now." Only the aged can remember what were then such key ideas as Remy de Gourmont's "dissociation of ideas," Eugene Jolas' "revolution of the word," and the French decadents' confusion of the five senses, one with another. It all gives me very much the sense of a *déjà vu*. Is there really anything new since Dada and shouldn't we find its resuscitation embarrassing? Until recently revived, what was most unmistakably "now" in the 1930s is for the most part as dead as the dodo, while the writers that generation condemned to oblivion are still around — at least to the extent that they have to be destroyed all over again.

Shaw's *Man and Superman* was the first contemporary work that   11
persuaded me to think of myself as a modern. Have I, I now wonder,
become a Roebuck Ramsden? It was he, as I should remind my juniors,
who once boasted to John Tanner, "I was an advanced thinker before
you were born," and got for an answer, "I knew it must have been a
long time ago."

The usual excuse for praising the obscene, the violent and the sadistic   12
in literature seems to be that by listening to those who "tell it like it is"
we come to understand the total corruption of our world and to revolt
against it. But Anthony Burgess in his "London Letter" to the SCHOLAR
(Spring, 1968) seems to champion a pure aestheticism like that of Susan
Sontag. Pornography, he says, is a form of didacticism and the didactic
is the opposite of the artistic no matter what it teaches. "Where *Last
Exit to Brooklyn* [which I have not read] possibly fails as good art is in
its arousal of social conscience. We observe the plight of people living
in a slough of degradation, and we want to do something about it. We
experience pity-and-terror, and we want to discharge that Aristotelian
emotion in an act of charity or compassion. The book is overdidactic,
then, rather than pornographic."

In the London Sunday *Times* (whose *Literary Supplement* used to be   13
an organ of the most respectable academic establishment) Mr. Burgess
has more recently hailed a best-selling American work as "The first
great novel of masturbation" — which, so I suppose, implies that it
did not encourage the activity so called but provided instead a purely
contemplative or aesthetic reaction. Just how a great novel could possibly be written on that subject or how rewarding a field for aesthetic
experience it could possibly provide, I am too "yesterday" rather than
"now" to understand. Moreover, I cling to the conviction that literature
not only tells things like they are but influences to some extent what
that way is. If, as La Rochefoucauld said, few would ever have fallen in
love if it were not for poetry, then art is likely to have a didactic effect
even if it is unintended. I suspect that fewer people would make a
perfect orgasm the Holy Grail they go in search of if it had not so often
appeared as such in contemporary literature.

That a man past his mid-seventies should believe the world is in a bad   14
way and getting worse will surprise no one. Such as he have very
commonly believed just that. But sometimes (if only by accident) they
have been right, and I am inclined to believe that I am one of such.

Is there, I sometimes ask myself, some impulse that unifies all the   15
seemingly diverse tendencies in modern life: the creation of more and

more powerful weapons of destruction; the poisoning of the very air we breathe; the search for the absurd in art and the preference for the antinovel and the antihero; the insistence that man himself is not human but mechanical; and, finally, the rejection of reason itself? All are destructive of something once important and confirm the impression that destruction is, in fact, the essence of the now. Are they all part of a process which one of the most old-fashioned of poets had in mind when he wrote:

> She comes! She comes! the sable Throne behold
> Of *Night* Primaeval, and of *Chaos* old!
> Before her, *Fancy's* gilded clouds decay,
> And all its varying Rain-bows die away.
> *Wit* shoots in vain its momentary fires,
> The meteor drops, and in a flash expires.
>
> • • • • •
> Thus at her felt approach, and secret might,
> *Art* after *Art* goes out, and all is Night.
>
> • • • • •
> *Religion* blushing veils her sacred fires,
> And unawares *Morality* expires.
>
> • • • • •
> Thy hand, great Anarch! Lets the curtain fall;
> And Universal Darkness buries All.

SUBJECT

1. Krutch's response to the generation gap may strike younger readers as the petulant resentment of a bypassed liberal. What is his chief quarrel with what is happening?

2. Does Krutch cite convincing evidence that the "now" culture has rejected reason? Are the authorities he quotes typical of the now generation?

3. What slight "reassurance" does Krutch find from his past experience? (See paragraph 10.) Would *avant-garde* leaders agree that the "now" emphasis is itself a revival?

4. Does Krutch seem to be overly worried about the pornographic side of modern culture? Is it symptomatic, or symbolic, of something to him?

5. In the final paragraph, Krutch equates the irrationality of atomic weapons and air pollution with the rejection of reason in new art and literature. Is he ignoring the cause for the rejection of reason by the "now" generation? Were the bombs made by people who did not believe in reason?

STRUCTURE

1.   What special problem does Krutch have in passing judgment on the "now" culture? What standard of judgment does he use? What standards could he have used?

2.   Krutch apologizes (paragraph 4) for one of his "snide" comments, but he makes a few others later. Do these give the reader a feeling that Krutch is not evaluating justly? Do you suppose they reflect Krutch's frustration at trying to evaluate what he sees as irrational?

3.   What does Krutch do to avoid the charge that he is writing from a prejudiced view rather than in a spirit of open inquiry?

4.   What is the point of ending on a quotation from an "old-fashioned" poet? Does the quoted passage represent a final judgment, or an example of something from the past worth saving?

5.   Criticize the organization of this essay. Does Krutch make clear from the beginning the primary concern? Does he ever drift from the subject? Is there a logical progression in the ordering of materials?

THE LIMITS
OF DUTY

Charles A. Reich

Charles Alan Reich was born in New York in 1928. He earned his B. A. from Oberlin and his law degree from Yale. He has practiced law in New York and Washington, and was, for a time, law clerk to Supreme Court Justice Hugo Black. Reich now teaches at Yale Law School. He is also the author of one of the most controversial books of our time, The Greening of America *(1970), in which Reich argues that America will have to be saved by a new breed of men with "Consciousness III" from the mess made by the organization man ("Consciousness II"). Condemned by critics as a confused pandering to the youth culture, the book is nevertheless widely read and given serious consideration by other writers on American culture.*

In Washington, D.C., during the May anti-war protests, police in automobiles and on scooters aimed their vehicles directly at demonstrators and drove toward them at high speeds in order to herd them off the streets. If one of the protesters had been hit and killed, the police officer driving the vehicle would have been guilty of murder. Not accidental killing or manslaughter but murder. Thus, every one of these officers was potentially guilty of a crime similar to that for which Lieutenant Calley was tried and convicted.   1

The applicable principle is deeply embedded in our common law. A   2
leading early example is Halloway's Case (King's Bench, 1628). Halloway was the woodward of woods belonging to the Earl of Denbigh. He discovered a boy named Payne in a tree, attempting to steal wood. Payne had a rope tied around his middle, probably to aid him in climbing trees. Halloway ordered the boy down from the tree, and when he descended struck him two blows on his back with a cudgel. Then Halloway tied the other end of the rope to the tail of his horse. The frightened horse dragged Payne three furlongs, killing him. The question was whether this was manslaughter or murder, and the court held it to be murder, for Halloway knew, or should have known the reckless and wanton risk he was taking with the boy's life. In such a case, the specific

intention to kill is not required. The deliberate taking of the risk is enough. Halloway was hanged.

Students at Yale, where I teach in the law school, tell me that District 3 of Columbia bus drivers also aimed their buses toward protesters at high speed and drove ahead without slowing down. How strange that those long-suffering civil servants the bus drivers are now guilty of reckless driving and assault, and, but for the agility of their potential victims, would be guilty of murder. Yet this is not an aberration. It is a pattern that is crucial to understanding what has gone wrong with America. Evil now comes about not necessarily when people violate what they understand to be their duty but, more and more often, when they are conscientiously doing what is expected of them. And for this evil the question of individual blame seems almost irrelevant.

Two oil tankers collide on a foggy morning in San Francisco Bay. The 4 bay and ocean are contaminated, beaches are coated, wildlife is exterminated, a fragile beauty is destroyed for millions of people. Yet the tanker captains were doing their duty to move the oil on time, and behind them were company officials concerned with the maintenance of production schedules. No investigation, no technical fixing of blame would be likely to disclose what we have normally imagined to be the root of crime — a guilty mind or a malign heart. And what is true of the San Francisco oil spill is true of the other major evils that we see around us. From wiretapping to the prosecution of the Vietnam war, our crimes have been started and carried out by men zealously attempting to serve as they have been taught to serve.

It is this altered problem of evil that rightly troubles us in the Calley 5 case. I believe that Calley was properly convicted of murdering Vietnamese civilians, even though the same result produced by different means is officially held to be wholly legal. Yet we must all believe that Calley, in his own wrong and frightened way, was seeking to perform his duty — to do what was expected of him. The enterprise upon which he was engaged is not condemned, only the means he chose to carry it out. Hence the profound disquiet among so many Americans, taught to serve employer or country, who cannot understand why the law apparently no longer cares about goals but only about a nicety of method. Plainly, our long-accepted criminal-law concepts do not fit the crimes of today.

The central reality is that evil today is the product of our system of 6 organization and our technology, and that it occurs because personal responsibility and personal awareness have been obliterated by a system deliberately designed to do just that — eliminate or minimize the human element and insure the supremacy of the system. The whole purpose of this system is to reduce the human component; that is why we have organization charts, a hierarchy of supervision, divided responsibilities, specialization. In the main, it is this rational organization of human effort that has brought us to our present stage of civilization, but we should realize that inherent in the very design of the system is the disappearance of individual blame, and hence the obsolescence of our concepts of individual criminal responsibility.

Let us follow the process of creating an evil more closely. A scientist   7
who is doing his specialized duty to further research and knowledge develops the substance known as napalm. Another specialist makes policy in the field of our nation's foreign affairs. A third is concerned with maintaining the strength of our armed forces with the most modern weaponry. A fourth manufactures what the defense authorities require. A fifth drops napalm from an airplane where he is told to do so. The ultimate evil is the result of carefully segmented acts; the structure itself guarantees an evasion by everyone of responsibility for the full moral act. Indeed, the system, especially when it is combined with advanced technology, makes it unlikely that those who participate in the process will have any real awareness of the ultimate consequences. Neither the scientist nor the man in the State Department nor even the pilot actually sees the horrors of burning napalm on human flesh. The basic result of our system of doing things is to destroy awareness, alienate all of us from the consequences of our actions, and prevent the formation of that very responsibility which has been at the center of our idea of criminal justice.

Our traditional criminal law is based on a standard of conduct that   8
assumes each individual to be a morally responsible human being. A man who runs a speedboat carelessly and kills someone is guilty of manslaughter if his actions fall below the standard. A man who allows his passions or desires to direct his actions so that he harms another person is guilty of assault or murder if, according to the standard, he should have controlled himself. The standard represents an ideal. Sometimes it is a cruel and unreasonable ideal, because the individual defendant lacks the capacity for measuring up to it. But the ideal does have a vital function. It establishes a large, even exalted, concept of man.

In the famous case of The Queen v. Dudley and Stephens, decided   9
in 1884, four English seamen were cast away in an open boat on the high seas sixteen hundred miles from the Cape of Good Hope. After eighteen days, they were reduced to the utmost state of desperation, with neither food nor water. Dudley and Stephens then said that if no hope of rescue appeared one of the four should be sacrificed, so that the

others might live. A third man refused to consent to the plan. The fourth, a boy of seventeen or eighteen, was not consulted; he was then in a helpless and weakened state. Dudley and Stephens spoke of their having families, indicating that the boy should be chosen. On the twentieth day, no help appearing, the defendants, after praying for forgiveness, killed the boy, and the three men fed upon his blood and body for four days, after which they were rescued. Dudley and Stephens were brought to England and tried for murder. It was acknowledged that if the boy had not been killed all four would probably have perished before rescue, and the boy would probably have died first. Yet the two men were found guilty.

The opinion of the Queen's Bench was delivered by Lord Coleridge, the Lord Chief Justice of England. Acknowledging that the temptation had been great and the suffering awful, he declared, "We are often compelled to set up standards which we cannot reach ourselves, and to lay down rules which we could not ourselves satisfy." And he went on: 10

> Though law and morality are not the same, and many things may be immoral which are not necessarily illegal, yet the absolute divorce of law from morality would be of fatal consequence . . .

Rather than kill the boy, said Lord Coleridge, the men should have been willing to lose their own lives: 11

> To preserve one's life is generally speaking a duty, but it may be the plainest and the highest duty to sacrifice it. War is full of instances in which it is a man's duty not to live, but to die. The duty, in the case of shipwreck, of a captain to his crew, of the crew to the passengers, of soldiers to women and children, as in the noble case of the *Birkenhead;* these duties impose on men the moral necessity, not of the preservation, but of the sacrifice of their lives for others, from which in no country, least of all, it is to be hoped, in England, will men ever shrink, as indeed, they have not shrunk . . .

Although the circumstances make this case unique, the basic ideal is found throughout the Anglo-American common law. Commonwealth v. Pierce (1884), a classic American case, written by Mr. Justice Holmes, then a member of the Supreme Judicial Court of Massachusetts, dealt with the problem of a physician whose patient died after he had treated her by keeping her wrapped in flannel saturated with kerosene for three days. Admitting that the physician's intentions were good, Holmes said that if the treatment was morally reckless, judged by the standards of a reasonably prudent man, then the defendent must answer for consequences that he neither intended nor forsaw. If the treatment was dangerous according to common experience, "we can-   12

537

not recognize a privilege to do acts manifestly endangering human life, on the ground of good intentions alone." Holmes also wrote:

> The very meaning of the fiction of implied malice in such cases at common law was, that a man might have to answer with his life for consequences which he neither intended nor foresaw . . . his failure or inability to predict them was immaterial if, under the circumstances known to him, the court or jury, as the case might be, thought them obvious.

Recently, I was watching the C.B.S. evening news when a few 13 minutes were devoted to films of one of the favorite antipersonnel weapons used by Americans in Vietnam. It consists of a rocket tightly packed with many ordinary nails. The rocket is fired from a helicopter. The nails scatter widely, propelled with such force that they will go right through the body of anyone in their path. One of the advantages of the weapon, it was explained, is that the gunner doesn't need to see the target at all. The consequences can only be imagined, but what can they be except the reckless maiming of all human beings, old or young, innocent or guilty, who happen to be in the way? Lieutenant Calley is guilty, we are told, but the men who designed these instruments, the men who built them, the men who ordered them to be used, and the men who actually used them were all simply doing their duty. What a diminished view of man this purported version of the law gives us! It tells us that we are all "universal soldiers," in the phrase from one of Donovan Leitch's recordings, morally oblivious of the consequences of our actions. Lord Chief Justice Coleridge completed his argument for full moral responsibility by saying, "It is enough in a Christian country to remind ourselves of the Great Example whom we profess to follow." What has happened when the hard-working, God-fearing people of America are expected to be moral robots, making and firing the nails for mass killings?

Obviously, our thinking has been strained to adapt itself to the reali- 14 ties of technology and organization. That is why all those fixtures of the old criminal law, the guilty mind, the malign heart, actual or presumed malice, the common experience of prudent men, seem so out of place — indeed, ironic — in the Calley case. We all understand that such standards of responsibility are not expected of any of us. Nor would we feel more comfortable about the prosecution of high-ranking generals or political leaders under the Nuremberg theory. They, too, would be found to have been doing their duty.

The Calley case represents a momentary, vestigial reminder of the 15 old law of responsibility. It was unfair to single out one man for such a revival of the old law, to be sure. Still, the reminder sent a shudder of awareness through all of us universal soldiers back home. It was not surprising that President Nixon hastily intervened. What led to his intervention was not just his seeming unconcern for legal processes, or his desire, as the *New Republic* put it, to coddle this particular criminal. The President insists, in every speech he makes, that we should do our small, segmented duties while he — or those in authority — assumes responsibility. The President's intervention was no surprise, because the Calley case confronts us with standards of responsibility that do not fit what the President and others insist are our duties and the limits of our duties. We are all supposed to be motorists on a highway where the maximum speed is sixty and the minimum speed is fifty-nine.

Perhaps the best way to understand those who have resisted the draft 16 — by seeking conscientious-objector status, by going to jail, by fleeing to Canada — is to acknowledge that they are demanding to live and to be judged by the old standards as fully responsible moral beings. They are seeking law, not evading it. Finding no acceptable standard of conduct available in today's organizational society, they have gone to standards that are not their own personal fiat but the old, traditional standards of religion, ethics, and common law. They are saying that they refuse to act in a way that common experience tells them will produce evil — evil that we know about or should know about. Theirs is a revolt for a larger view of man. And for all of us it poses a necessary question: Given that we must all live and work within large organizations, that we must all take only a small part in a large enterprise, how can we restore the awareness, the responsibility, and the law that are the moral essence of free men?

An organization is a hybrid form of machine — one part a tool or 17 system, the other part human. We have made too little use of the human part. We have thought of the humanness as something to be suppressed for efficiency's sake, not something to be valued because it might supply a quality that would otherwise be lacking. All of us who work in organizations should begin to assume a responsibility that is larger than the particular job we do, and this responsibility should ultimately be recognized, protected, and enforced by law. It might take many forms. Perhaps there should be a right — analogous to the long-recognized right to strike for economic objectives — to refuse, on a selective moral basis, to do certain work and perform certain duties. Perhaps this right should be guaranteed to individuals as well as to organized groups. Perhaps the organization should be answerable, on a democratic basis to those who work within it, for its policies and their probable consequences. Surely the present rigid hierarchy of authority must give way to a concept that in an organization all the members have a share of authority.

A corollary to this is that law should be based on the assumption that institutions, far more than individuals, are likely to go astray. Perhaps the primary regulatory work of law should be shifted from that of managing people to that of managing organizations while safeguarding the individuality of the people within them. Because organizations are the most characteristic element of our civilization, the scope of action by the members, employees, or consumers must be widened, and the scope of action by systems and machines must be narrowed and must be supervised by law. In the deepest sense, the purpose of such changes is nothing less than a restoration of one of our richest and most neglected resources — the human potentiality of the great mass of our people. Government by a managerial élite deprives us of the humanity of the many. Policy is made by a few, and the rest are coerced into following by laws that speak in the name of duty. The assumption is made that those who get to the top are naturally qualified to manage and plan for the rest of us, that we must accept what they require of us without allowing our moral knowledge to intervene. Such a neglect of our moral resources is as great a loss as our now well-known neglect of our environmental resources. We need the full participation of each individual. We can no longer afford to be a people who unthinkingly serve.

This brings us back to what happened in Washington. The procedures used against demonstrators who tried to block traffic were flagrantly un-Constitutional. There were arrests without cause — mass round-ups, which often included any young person, however innocent, who happened to be visible to the police. Prisoners were not subject to normal arrest procedure. Many were kept at detention centers without being afforded the basic rights of arrested persons. All this, like the murderous driving, was not the product of officers gone berserk but was part of coldly rational plans sanctioned, and later praised, by high authorities. Indeed, the same high authorities have recommended that similar tactics be used again. Can the policemen and bus drivers in question say they are doing all they can to respect the fundamental law of the land if they simply follow orders? Can the civil servants who drove to work that morning, maybe sympathetic to the peace movement but afraid of a demerit, call themselves law-abiding? I am suggesting that following orders is no longer good enough for any of us — not if we want our Constitution preserved. Each of us has a permanent and personal duty to the supreme law of the land. I do not mean the "law" that the Nixon Administration speaks of — something that I would call "force," or "state power." I think the Nixon Administration is deeply contemptuous of law. We cannot count on Attorney General Mitchell to preserve the law, nor, I fear, can we count on the courts. And, from a certain point of view, that is as it should be. It is our Constitution, not theirs.

SUBJECT

1. On what grounds does Reich claim that the policemen and bus drivers in Washington were potential murderers? Do you suppose one of them would have been found guilty of murder had a peace marcher been killed?

2. Why, according to Reich, is the legal system no longer capable of controlling — or even punishing — evil in America?

3. How does Reich explain the motives of draft resisters? Does he deny that they are breaking the law?

4. "All of us who work in organizations should begin to assume a responsibility that is larger than the particular job we do"; does Reich suggest ways in which this could be done? How can a secretary in the Pentagon assume responsibility for command decisions?

5. Reich thinks laws need to be reworked to apply to corporate responsibility as well as individual responsibility. Do you see ways in which this could be done? (One can't, after all, send a corporation to the electric chair.)

STRUCTURE

1. By what standard does Reich judge the actions of the Washington policemen and bus drivers? Is it the same standard he applies to war criminals and "guilty" corporations?

2. Does Reich make clear his important distinction between obeying the law and following orders?

3. Do the examples Reich gives appear to be typical and relevant? Why does he cite the two instances from British jurisprudence?

4. The concluding paragraph begins, "This brings us back to what happened in Washington"; does it, or is the statement an artificial means of unifying the essay? What is the antecedent of "this" in the quotation? Is it a good idea for Reich to return at the end to the situation he began with?

5. One might expect an essay on law by a law professor to contain a good deal of baffling legal terminology; does Reich successfully avoid this danger?

THE DOOR

E. B. White

*E. B. White (born in 1899) is an essayist and fiction writer. "The Door"
is from* The Second Tree from the Corner *(1939); it was written after
White had read accounts of (1) treatment of certain mental cases by
performing prefrontal lobotomies and (2) of laboratory experiments in
which mice were frustrated into insanity.*

Everything (he kept saying) is something it isn't. And everybody is 1
always somewhere else. Maybe it was the city, being in the city, that
made him feel how queer everything was and that it was something
else. Maybe (he kept thinking) it was the names of the things. The
names were tex and frequently koid. Or they were flex and oid or they
were duroid (sani) or flexsan (duro), but everything was glass (but not
quite glass) and the thing that you touched (the surface, washable,
crease-resistant) was rubber, only it wasn't quite rubber and you didn't
quite touch it but almost. The wall, which was glass but thrutex, turned
out on being approached not to be a wall, it was something else, it was
an opening or doorway — and the doorway (through which he saw
himself approaching) turned out to be something else, it was a wall. And
what he had eaten not having agreed with him.

He was in a washable house, but he wasn't sure. Now about those rats, 2
he kept saying to himself. He meant the rats that the Professor had
driven crazy by forcing them to deal with problems which were beyond
the scope of rats, the insoluble problems. He meant the rats that had
been trained to jump at the square card with the circle in the middle,
and the card (because it was something it wasn"t) would give way and
let the rat into a place where the food was, but then one day it would
be a trick played on the rat, and the card would be changed, and the
rat would jump but the card wouldn't give way, and it was an impossible
situation (for a rat) and the rat would go insane and into its eyes would
come the unspeakably bright imploring look of the frustrated, and after
the convulsions were over and the frantic racing around, then the
passive stage would set in and the willingness to let anything be done
to it, even if it was something else.

"The Door" from *The Second Tree from the Corner* by E. B. White. Copyright 1939,
1967 by E. B. White. Originally appeared in *The New Yorker,* and reprinted by permission of Harper & Row, Publishers, Inc.

542

He didn't know which door (or wall) or opening in the house to jump   3
at, to get through, because one was an opening that wasn't a door (it was
a void, or koid) and the other was a wall that wasn't an opening, it was
a sanitary cupboard of the same color. He caught a glimpse of his eyes
staring into his eyes, in the thrutex, and in them was the expression he
had seen in the picture of the rats — weary after convulsions and the
frantic racing around, when they were willing and did not mind having
anything done to them. More and more (he kept saying) I am confronted by a problem which is incapable of solution (for this time even
if he chose the right door, there would be no food behind it) and that
is what madness is, and things seeming different from what they are.
He heard, in the house where he was, in the city to which he had gone
(as toward a door which might, or might not, give way), a noise — not
a loud noise but more of a low prefabricated humming. It came from
a place in the base of the wall (or stat) where the flue carrying the
filterable air was, and not far from the Minipiano, which was made of
the same material nailbrushes are made of, and which was under the
stairs. "This, too, has been tested," she said, pointing, but not at it, "and
found viable." It wasn't a loud noise, he kept thinking, sorry that he had
seen his eyes, even though it was through his own eyes that he had seen
them.

First will come the convulsions (he said), then the exhaustion, then   4
the willingness to let anything be done. "And you better believe it *will*
be."

All his life he had been confronted by situations which were incapa-   5
ble of being solved, and there was a deliberateness behind all this,
behind this changing of the card (or door), because they would always
wait till you had learned to jump at the certain card (or door) — the
one with the circle — and then they would change it on you. There
have been so many doors changed on me, he said, in the last twenty
years, but it is now becoming clear that it is an impossible situation, and
the question is whether to jump again, even though they ruffle you in
the rump with a blast of air — to make you jump. He wished he
wasn't standing by the Minipiano. First they would teach you the prayers and the Psalms, and that would be the right door (the one with the
circle) and the long sweet words with the holy sound, and that would
be the one to jump at to get where the food was. Then one day you
jumped and it didn't give way, so that all you got was the bump on the
nose, and the first bewilderment, the first young bewilderment.

I don't know whether to tell her about the door they substituted or   6
not, he said, the one with the equation on it and the picture of the
amoeba reproducing itself by division. Or the one with the photostatic
copy of the check for thirty-two dollars and fifty cents. But the jumping

543

was so long ago, although the bump is . . . how those old wounds hurt! Being crazy this way wouldn't be so bad if only, if only. If only when you put your foot forward to take a step, the ground wouldn't come up to meet your foot the way it does. And the same way in the street (only I may never get back to the street unless I jump at the right door), the curb coming up to meet your foot, anticipating ever so delicately the weight of the body, which is somewhere else. "We could take your name," she said, "and send it to you." And it wouldn't be so bad if only you could read a sentence all the way through without jumping (your eye) to something else on the same page; and then (he kept thinking) there was that man out in Jersey, the one who started to chop his trees down, one by one, the man who began talking about how he would take his house to pieces, brick by brick, because he faced a problem incapable of solution, probably, so he began to hack at the trees in the yard, began to pluck with trembling fingers at the bricks in the house. Even if a house is not washable, it is worth taking down. It is not till later that the exhaustion sets in.

But it is inevitable that they will keep changing the doors on you, he said, because that is what they are for; and the thing is to get used to it and not let it unsettle the mind. But that would mean not jumping, and you can't. Nobody can not jump. There will be no not-jumping. Among rats, perhaps, but among people never. Everybody has to keep jumping at a door (the one with the circle on it) because that is the way everybody is, especially some people. You wouldn't want me, standing here, to tell you, would you, about my friend the poet (deceased) who said, "My heart has followed all my days something I cannot name"? (It had the circle on it.) And like many poets, although few so beloved, he is gone. It killed him, the jumping. First, of course, there were the preliminary bouts, the convulsions, and the calm and the willingness. 7

I remember the door with the picture of the girl on it (only it was spring), her arms outstretched in loveliness, her dress (it was the one with the circle on it) uncaught, beginning the slow, clear, blinding cascade — and I guess we would all like to try that door again, for it seemed like the way and for a while it was the way, the door would open and you would go through winged and exalted (like any rat) and the food would be there, the way the Professor had it arranged, everything O.K., and you had chosen the right door for the the world was young. The time they changed that door on me, my nose bled for a hundred hours — how do you like that, Madam? Or would you prefer to show me further through this so strange house, or you could take my name and send it to me, for although my heart has followed all my days something I cannot name, I am tired of the jumping and I do not know which way to go, Madam, and I am not even sure that I am not tired 8 beyond the endurance of man (rat, if you will) and have taken leave of sanity. What are you following these days, old friend, after your recovery from the last bump? What is the name, or is it something you cannot name? The rats have a name for it by this time, perhaps, but I don't know what they call it. I call it plexikoid and it comes in sheets, something like insulating board, unattainable and ugli-proof.

And there was the man out in Jersey, because I keep thinking about his terrible necessity and the passion and trouble he had gone to all those years in the indescribable abundance of a householder's detail, building the estate and the planting of the trees and in spring the lawn-dressing and in fall the bulbs for the spring burgeoning, and the watering of the grass on the long light evenings in summer and the gravel for the driveway (all had to be thought out, planned) and the decorative borders, probably, the perennials and the bug spray, and the building of the house from plans of the architect, first the sills, then the studs, then the full corn in the ear, the floors laid on the floor timbers, smoothed, and then the carpets upon the smooth floors and the curtains and the rods therefor. And then, almost without warning, he would be jumping at the same old door and it wouldn't give: they had changed it on him, making life no longer supportable under the elms in the elm shade, under the maples in the maple shade. 9

"Here you have the maximum of openness in a small room." 10

It was impossible to say (maybe it was the city) what made him feel the way he did, and I am not the only one either, he kept thinking — ask any doctor if I am. The doctors, they know how many there are, they even know where the trouble is only they don't like to tell you about the prefrontal lobe because that means making a hole in your skull and removing the work of centuries. It took so long coming, this lobe, so many, many years. (Is it something you read in the paper, perhaps?) And now, the strain being so great, the door having been changed by the Professor once too often . . . but it only means a whiff of ether, a few deft strokes, and the higher animal becomes a little easier in his mind and more like the lower one. From now on, you see, that's the way it will be, the ones with the small prefrontal lobes will win because the other ones are hurt too much by this incessant bumping. They can stand just so much, eh, Doctor? (And what is that, pray, that you have in your hand?) Still, you never can tell, eh, Madam? 11

He crossed (carefully) the room, the thick carpet under him softly, and went toward the door carefully, which was glass and he could see himself in it, and which, at his approach, opened to allow him to pass through; and beyond he half expected to find one of the old doors that he had known, perhaps the one with the circle, the one with the girl her arms outstretched in loveliness and beauty before him. But he saw 12 instead a moving stairway, and descended in light (he kept thinking) to the street below and to the other people. As he stepped off, the ground came up slightly, to meet his foot.

SUBJECT

1.   What kind of a house is it that the man keeps talking about? To what do the strange names (thrutex, duroid, and so on) refer?

2.   What does the frustrated man out in Jersey have to do with the narrator's problem? Why did he take his house apart brick by brick?

3.   White suggests several times that living in the city may have aggravated the narrator's problem. What is it about the city to which White objects?

4.   The man says that many doors have been changed on him, and he gives four examples. What does each door represent? What is the "food" he is prevented from obtaining? Why does White use symbols instead of stating directly what he means?

5.   Does White mean to imply that someone is deliberately changing the doors in order to frustrate the average man? Who *is* changing the doors? What, according to White, will happen to man when he has become thoroughly frustrated?

6.   What happens to the narrator at the end? What does the doctor have in his hand? If all those unable to adjust to changing conditions underwent a prefrontal lobotomy, frustration would be virtually eliminated; would that solve the problem about which White is writing?

7.   How would White react to the General Electric slogan, "Progress is our most important product"? How would the makers of that slogan probably react to "The Door"?

STRUCTURE

1.   In this story White tried to make the style imitate the actual thinking of a frustrated man. If he has succeeded, he should be able to make the reader see things the way the character sees them. The danger in this method, however, is that the writing may become too incoherent for the reader to understand. The style is admittedly difficult, but you should give the story a second reading before you decide whether or not White succeeds.

2.   Why might White have chosen this particular way of presenting his evaluation? Is it effective? Would it have been just as effective had he stated his points directly in expository prose?

3.   Can you tell what White's standards of judgment are? Are they directly stated, or implied?

THE OTHER SIDE OF THE HEDGE

E. M. Forster

E. M. Forster (1879–1969), a well-known British novelist, wrote comparatively few novels, but several of them have become standard classics. The most famous is A Passage to India. *"The Other Side of the Hedge" appears in* The Collected Tales of E. M. Forster *(1947).*

My pedometer told me that I was twenty-five; and, though it is a shocking thing to stop walking, I was so tired that I sat down on a milestone to rest. People outstripped me, jeering as they did so, but I was too apathetic to feel resentful, and even when Miss Eliza Dimbleby, the great educationist, swept past, exhorting me to persevere, I only smiled and raised my hat. 1

At first I thought I was going to be like my brother, whom I had had to leave by the roadside a year or two round the corner. He had wasted his breath on singing, and his strength on helping others. But I had travelled more wisely, and now it was only the monotony of the highway that oppressed me — dust under foot and brown crackling hedges on either side, ever since I could remember. 2

And I had already dropped several things — indeed, the road behind was strewn with the things we all had dropped; and the white dust was settling down on them, so that already they looked no better than stones. My muscles were so weary that I could not even bear the weight of those things I still carried. I slid off the milestone into the road, and lay there prostrate, with my face to the great parched hedge, praying that I might give up. 3

A little puff of air revived me. It seemed to come from the hedge; and, when I opened my eyes, there was a glint of light through the tangle of boughs and dead leaves. The hedge could not be as thick as usual. In my weak, morbid state, I longed to force my way in, and see what was on the other side. No one was in sight, or I should not have dared to try. For we of the road do not admit in conversation that there is another side at all. 4

I yielded to the temptation, saying to myself that I would come back in a minute. The thorns scratched my face, and I had to use my arms 5

From *The Collected Tales of E. M. Forster.* Published 1947 by Alfred A. Knopf, Inc. Reprinted by permission of Alfred A. Knopf, Inc., and Sidgwick & Jackson Ltd.

547

as a shield, depending on my feet alone to push me forward. Halfway through I would have gone back, for in the passage all the things I was carrying were scraped off me, and my clothes were torn. But I was so wedged that return was impossible, and I had to wriggle blindly forward, expecting every moment that my strength would fail me, and that I should perish in the undergrowth.

Suddenly cold water closed round my head, and I seemed sinking 6 down for ever. I had fallen out of the hedge into a deep pool. I rose to the surface at last, crying for help, and I heard someone on the opposite bank laugh and say: "Another!" And then I was twitched out and laid panting on the dry ground.

Even when the water was out of my eyes, I was still dazed, for I had 7 never been in so large a space, nor seen such grass and sunshine. The blue sky was no longer a strip, and beneath it the earth had risen gradually into hills — clean, bare buttresses, with beech trees in their folds, and meadows and clear pools at their feet. But the hills were not high, and there was in the landscape a sense of human occupation — so that one might have called it a park, or garden, if the words did not imply a certain triviality and constraint.

As soon as I got my breath, I turned to my rescuer and said: 8

"Where does this place lead to?" 9

"Nowhere, thank the Lord!" said he, and laughed. He was a man of 10 fifty or sixty — just the kind of age we mistrust on the road — but there was no anxiety in his manner, and his voice was that of a boy of eighteen.

"But it must lead somewhere!" I cried, too much surprised at his 11 answer to thank him for saving my life.

"He wants to know where it leads!" he shouted to some men on the 12 hillside, and they laughed back, and waved their caps.

I noticed then that the pool into which I had fallen was really a moat 13 which bent round to the left and to the right, and that the hedge followed it continually. The hedge was green on this side — its roots showed through the clear water, and fish swam about in them — and it was wreathed over with dog-roses and Traveller's Joy. But it was a barrier, and in a moment I lost all pleasure in the grass, the sky, the trees, the happy men and women, and realized that the place was but a prison, for all its beauty and extent.

We moved away from the boundary, and then followed a path almost 14 parallel to it, across the meadows. I found it difficult walking, for I was always trying to out-distance my companion, and there was no advantage in doing this if the place led nowhere. I had never kept step with anyone since I left my brother.

I amused him by stopping suddenly and saying disconsolately, "This 15
is perfectly terrible. One cannot advance: one cannot progress. Now we
of the road —"

"Yes, I know." 16

"I was going to say, we advance continually." 17

"I know." 18

"We are always learning, expanding, developing. Why, even in my 19
short life I have seen a great deal of advance — the Transvaal War,
the Fiscal Question, Christian Science, Radium. Here for example —"

I took out my pedometer, but it still marked twenty-five, not a degree 20
more.

"Oh, it's stopped! I meant to show you. It should have registered all 21
the time I was walking with you. But it makes me only twenty-five."

"Many things don't work in here," he said. "One day a man brought 22
in a Lee-Metford, and that wouldn't work."

"The laws of science are universal in their application. It must be the 23
water in the moat that has injured the machinery. In normal conditions
everything works. Science and the spirit of emulation — those are the
forces that have made us what we are."

I had to break off and acknowledge the pleasant greeting of people 24
whom we passed. Some of them were singing, some talking, some
engaged in gardening, hay-making, or other rudimentary industries.
They all seemed happy; and I might have been happy too, if I could
have forgotten that the place led nowhere.

I was startled by a young man who came sprinting across our path, 25
took a little fence in the fine style, and went tearing over a ploughed
field till he plunged into a lake, across which he began to swim. Here
was true energy, and I exclaimed: "A cross-country race! Where are the
others?"

"There are no others," my companion replied; and, later on, when we 26
passed some long grass from which came the voice of a girl singing
exquisitely to herself, he said again: "There are no others." I was bewildered at the waste in production, and murmured to myself, "What does
it all mean?"

He said: "It means nothing but itself" — and he repeated the words 27
slowly, as if I were a child.

"I understand," I said quietly, "but I do not agree. Every achieve- 28
ment is worthless unless it is a link in the chain of development. And
I must not trespass on your kindness any longer. I must get back somehow to the road, and have my pedometer mended."

"First, you must see the gates," he replied, "for we have gates, though 29
we never use them."

I yielded politely, and before long we reached the moat again, at a   30
point where it was spanned by a bridge. Over the bridge was a big gate,
as white as ivory, which was fitted into a gap in the boundary hedge.
The gate opened outwards, and I exclaimed in amazement, for from it
ran a road — just such a road as I had left — dusty under foot, with
brown crackling hedges on either side as far as the eye could reach.

"That's my road!" I cried.   31

He shut the gate and said: "But not your part of the road. It is through   32
this gate that humanity went out countless ages ago, when it was first
seized with the desire to walk."

I denied this, observing that the part of the road I myself had left was   33
not more than two miles off. But with the obstinacy of his years he
repeated: "It is the same road. This is the beginning, and though it
seems to run straight away from us, it doubles so often, that it is never
far from our boundary and sometimes touches it." He stooped down by
the moat, and traced on its moist margin an absurd figure like a maze.
As we walked back through the meadows, I tried to convince him of his
mistake.

"The road sometimes doubles, to be sure, but that is part of our   34
discipline. Who can doubt that its general tendency is onward? To what
goal we know not — it may be to some mountain where we shall
touch the sky, it may be over precipices into the sea. But that it goes
forward — who can doubt that? It is the thought of that that makes us
strive to excel, each in his own way, and gives us an impetus which is
lacking with you. Now that man who passed us — it's true that he ran
well, and jumped well, and swam well; but we have men who can run
better, and men who can jump better, and who can swim better. Specialization has produced results which would surprise you. Similarly,
that girl — "

Here I interrupted myself to exclaim: "Good gracious me! I could   35
have sworn it was Miss Eliza Dimbleby over there, with her feet in the
fountain!"

He believed that it was.   36

"Impossible! I left her on the road, and she is due to lecture this   37
evening at Tunbridge Wells. Why, her train leaves Cannon Street in
— of course my watch has stopped like everything else. She is the last
person to be here."

"People always are astonished at meeting each other. All kinds come   38
through the hedge, and come at all times — when they are drawing
ahead in the race, when they are lagging behind, when they are left for
dead. I often stand near the boundary listening to the sounds of the road
— you know what they are — and wonder if anyone will turn aside. It

is my great happiness to help someone out of the moat, as I helped you. For our country fills up slowly, though it was meant for all mankind."

"Mankind have other aims," I said gently, for I thought him well-   39
meaning; "and I must join them." I bade him good evening, for the sun was declining, and I wished to be on the road by nightfall. To my alarm, he caught hold of me, crying: "You are not to go yet!" I tried to shake him off, for we had no interests in common, and his civility was becoming irksome to me. But for all my struggles the tiresome old man would not let go; and, as wrestling is not my speciality, I was obliged to follow him.

It was true that I could never have found alone the place where I   40
came in, and I hoped that, when I had seen the other sights about which he was worrying, he would take me back to it. But I was determined not to sleep in the country, for I mistrusted it, and the people too, for all their friendliness. Hungry though I was, I would not join them in their evening meals of milk and fruit, and, when they gave me flowers, I flung them away as soon as I could do so unobserved. Already they were lying down for the night like cattle — some out on the bare hillside, others in groups under the beeches. In the light of an orange sunset I hurried on with my unwelcome guide, dead tired, faint for want of food, but murmuring indomitably: "Give me life, with its struggles and victories, with its failures and hatreds, with its deep moral meaning and its unknown goal!"

At last we came to a place where the encircling moat was spanned   41
by another bridge, and where another gate interrupted the line of the boundary hedge. It was different from the first gate; for it was half transparent like horn, and opened inwards. But through it, in the waning light, I saw again just such a road as I had left — monotonous, dusty, with brown crackling hedges on either side, as far as the eye could reach.

I was strangely disquieted at the sight, which seemed to deprive me   42
of all self-control. A man was passing us, returning for the night to the hills, with a scythe over his shoulder and a can of some liquid in his hand. I forgot the destiny of our race. I forgot the road that lay before my eyes, and I sprang at him, wrenched the can out of his hand, and began to drink.

It was nothing stronger than beer, but in my exhausted state it over-   43
came me in a moment. As in a dream, I saw the old man shut the gate, and heard him say: "This is where your road ends, and through this gate humanity — all that is left of it — will come in to us."

Though my senses were sinking into oblivion, they seemed to expand   44
ere they reached it. They perceived the magic song of nightingales, and

the odour of invisible hay, and stars piercing the fading sky. The man whose beer I had stolen lowered me down gently to sleep off its effects, and, as he did so, I saw that he was my brother.

SUBJECT

1. The road, of course, represents life in the modern world. What is Forster's judgment of it? Is he being fair? Most of us, after all, believe in progress of some sort.

2. What kind of life is on the other side of the hedge? Does it seem to you, as to the narrator, a meaningless existence? What about the traditional conception of life in heaven — does it seem meaningless?

3. If the road ultimately leads to this land, wouldn't it be foolish for a person to keep running on the road if he could take a shortcut through the hedge? What does the hedge represent? Why do people on the road refuse to admit that anything exists on the other side?

4. Why won't pedometers, watches, or automobiles work on the other side of the hedge? Would they be of any use if they did function?

5. Does Forster mean to imply that we should quit striving to get ahead and simply give up? If man went out of the ivory gate centuries ago, mustn't he have been dissatisfied with simple happiness without worry? George Bernard Shaw suggest in *Man and Superman* that true happiness lies in facing and trying to solve problems, and that a life without problems would be hell, not heaven. Has Forster left this possibility out of consideration?

STRUCTURE

1. This story is rather clearly allegorical. Is it allegorical in complete detail, or only in broad outlines? What, for instance, do the many things dropped in the road, the ivory gate, and the horn gate, stand for?

2. Why do you suppose Forster wrote his evaluation of modern life in the form of a story? Does the simple form — almost like that of a Biblical parable — emphasize, or weaken, his point?

3. What are Forster's standards of judgment? Does he have a spokesman in the story to make them clear? How else are they conveyed?

4. Note that Forster uses concrete, vivid details throughout, but that he simultaneously maintains a dreamlike atmosphere. How does he accomplish this? Was there anything in the story that should have been more clearly explained? Would he have lost the dreamlike quality if he had explained everything?

THE BURN WARD

Ronald J. Glasser

Dr. Ronald J. Glasser practices medicine in Minneapolis. He was a major in the U.S. Army Medical Corps from 1968–1970. His experience with the Vietnam war is recounted in his book, Three Hundred and Sixty-Five Days *(1971). "The Burn Ward," an excerpt from the book, was first printed separately in* The Washington Monthly *(April, 1971). While the basic story is true, the names of the people and places have been changed, and the time sequence has been rearranged to give the account the form and unity of a short story.*

Edwards picked up the stethoscope from his desk. "Look," he said, "You can say what you want about the Army and its problems, but I learned this much from going home: the Army treats you better dead than alive. I know," he added quickly to keep the captain from talking. "I know, it was my fault. I shouldn't have got involved with taking the body back. But I did." 1

"It's coming," the corpsman said, stepping away from the window. 2

Edwards stuffed the stethoscope into his back pocket. "OK. Tell the ward master. Better fill the whirlpools. I'll be down at the landing pad." He pushed open the double doors to the burn unit. 3

The huge overhead lights were off, leaving only the night lights to flicker feebly across the shiny, tiled floor. He walked quietly down the center aisle of the ward, his footsteps echoing lightly ahead of him. The beds lining the wall were barely visible, the patients no more than lumps against the frames. From the far end of the ward came the faint mechanical hissing of a respirator. He stopped a moment near one of the steel-arched Stryker frames to listen. The machine's slow regular rhythm was almost soothing. How many times he'd heard it before. Someone had once said he'd signed more death certificates than any other doctor in Japan. Probably right, he thought, continuing on his way. At Kishine, the respirator was the sound of death, not life; in all his time there he could not think of one patient who had got off the thing. 4

"Hi, Doc." 5

"Oh, Crowley," Edwards said, coming to a halt near the little cubicle 6
at the back of the ward. "Sorry, I didn't see you in the dark."

The side curtain had been partially pulled. Stretched out on the bed, 7
barely lit by the dials of the respirator, was a shadowy form.

"How's he doing, Sergeant," Edwards asked the ward master who 8
was standing at attention by the machine that was slowly, insistently
hissing air into and out of the charred body.

"Not too good, sir." 9

"What's his temperature?" 10

"105. It was 107 before we put him on the cooling blanket." 11

"Blood cultures growing out anything?" 12

"Yes, sir, the lab called back tonight — Pseudomonas pseudomal- 13
lei. Major Johnson put him on IV [intravenous] chloromycetin and
tetracycline."

Edwards bent over to look more closely at the restrained body 14
spread-eagled across the frame. The air smelled sweet, like a dying
orchard. "When did he come in?" he asked, peering at the grotesquely
crusted body. Even the tips of his toes and fingers were charred and
oozing, nothing had been spared.

"Four days after you left. Seventy percent second degree and 15 15
percent third. At least Major Johnson thought it was second degree, but
it's beginning to look like it's all third."

Edwards examined the crust about the boy's swollen neck and chest. 16
It had a sick metallic green cast to it. "When did he go sour?"

"He was doing fine until this morning. We had to give him Demerol 17
every time he went into the whirlpool, but he's very hard core. Nice
kid. Then yesterday, be became confused and agitated. On the night
shift his temp spiked and he became unconscious. The surgeons trached
him today, and Dr. Johnson put him on the respirator this evening. The
evacs should be in soon, Major."

"Yeah, that's where I'm going. I'll check on him later." 18

"No need, sir, you'll have your hands full. I'll have you called if 19
anything changes."

As he walked away, Edwards could hear Crowley drawing the cur- 20
tains closed behind him. The stairwell was empty and he walked slowly
down to the first floor and out onto the concrete walkway.

It was summer outside and the night was as warm as indoors. He cut 21
across the empty silent field separating the hospital's squat buildings
from the helipad, where the red lights of the landing strip flickered
softly in the misty dark. Far away he heard the muffled dull thudding
of the chopper whopping its way through the heavy air, and suddenly
he felt alone and desperately tired.

"Gentlemen: You have been assembled here at Yokota Air Base to escort these bodies home to the continental United States. Each body in its casket is to have, at all times, a body escort. Those caskets on the plane that do not at the present time have an escort will have them assigned at Oakland. Whatever the case, no casket will be allowed to leave the Oakland area without a proper escort. Escort duty is a privilege as well as an honor. An effort has been made to find an escort whose personal involvement with the deceased or presence with the family of the deceased will be of comfort and aid. Your mission as a body escort is as follows: to make sure that the body is afforded, at all times, the respect due a fallen soldier of the United States Army. Specifically it is as follows: 1) to check the tags on the caskets at every point of departure; 2) to insist if the tags indicate the remains as non-viewable that the relatives not view the body. Remember that non-viewable means exactly that — non-viewable. . . ."

Grimly, with the chopper coming nearer — louder — Edwards 22 walked up a slight rise, past a small, dimly lit sign:

> KISHINE BARRACKS
> 109th UNITED STATES
> ARMY HOSPITAL
> United States Army, Japan
> Burn Unit

"Coastal Airlines loads the bodies on an angle. Be sure that if the body you are escorting is being carried by Coastal Airlines that the caskets are loaded head down — this will keep the embalming fluid in the upper body. If the body is loaded incorrectly, namely, feet down, the embalming fluid will accumulate in the feet, and the body may, under appropriate atmospheric conditions, begin to decompose."

By the time he reached the evac area, the floodlights were on and the 23 chopper had landed. Coming in from the dark around the back of the evac building Edwards was dazzled by the sudden lights. The Huey, low and glistening, its rotors still whirling, sat like a toy exactly in the middle of the arc lights. Its crew chief and co-pilot were already in the open hatchway unstrapping the litters from their carrying hooks. Edwards watched unseen while the corpsmen hurried out to the chopper to off-load the patients. The choppers usually came in about 10 in the morning, but when a bad burn was evac'd to Japan, they were flown in the same night. Burns are a very special kind of wound, and no physician anywhere wants the responsibility of caring for them, not even for a little while. For openers, burns look bad and the patients die.

"Each of the next of kin listed in the deceased 201 file has already been visited by a survivor assistance officer. This was done in person by an

officer in uniform from the nearest army unit. Every effort is made to pick an officer from a similar racial and economic background. These families have already been convinced of the death by either the presentation of personal effects or the relating of an eyewitness report from a member of the deceased's unit. You need not convince the deceased's relatives. The point to remember is that the survivor assistance officer has been there before you and the next of kin have already accepted the death."

He was standing in the reflected glare of the landing lights, with the windy noise of the chopper rushing past him. 24

"Sir. Sir?" one of the corpsmen was shouting above the whining of the motor. "One of 'em's got a head wound, the other is just burned." 25

"Call the neurosurgeon," Edwards shouted back. He gave the empty chopper one more look and then followed the medic into the air evac area. By the time he reached the building, the medics had placed the two litters on the movable stretcher racks and one of them, working on the patient nearest the door, was already setting up an IV. 26

"He's OK, Major," the air evac sergeant said. "The head injury's over there." 27

"One hundred and seventy," the corpsman said as Edwards approached the litter. The wounded soldier, his head wrapped, was lying unconscious on his back, with the blood pressure cuff still wrapped around his arm. "I figured I'd leave the cuff on, sir. He don't look too good." 28

"I'll give you that," Edwards said. He began to unwrap the gauze from around the patient's head. The boy was breathing; other than that he looked dead. Edwards pinched his neck, but there was no response. As he unwound the gauze it became wet and then blood-soaked. Now he was down to the four-by-four surgical pads, and finally to the wound itself. Carefully he lifted up the last pack. Despite himself, he closed his eyes. 29

"He's 47 percent burned," the sergeant said, reading the cover sheet of the soldier's medical record. "Took an AK round a little in front of the right eye. Removed the right eye, traversed the left orbit, removing the left eye and came out near the left temple, apparently blowing out the left side of his head." 30

"Don't worry. I'll be careful, Bob. Honest, I'll be careful. . . ."

"Send him to neurosurgery," Edwards said. "We'll treat his burns up there." 31

"An IV?" 32

"No, just send him up." 33

He walked across to the other wounded trooper. The corpsman had just got the IV started. 34

556

"Sorry it took so long, sir," he said. "Hard to find a vein."   35

The boy was awake, nervously looking at the needle the corpsman   36
had stuck into the back of his hand.

"Hi," Edwards said. "How do you feel?"   37

The soldier looked up at him apprehensively. The skin on his face had   38
been seared red and all his hair and eyebrows and lashes had been burnt
away.

"I know you're nervous," Edwards said soothingly. "Just try to relax.   39
I'm the chief of the burn unit. I'll be your doctor for a while until you
get better." As he pulled back the blanket the soldier grimaced.
"Sorry," he said, lifting the cover more carefully.

The burns, red and raw, ran the whole charred length of the boy's   40
body. Unconsciously Edwards began adding up the percentages of
burned area, tallying them in his mind. He suddenly realized what he
was doing, and for a moment, as he stood there staring at the burns, he
looked stricken. "How did it happen?" he asked gently, carefully dropping back the covers.

"I . . . I was carrying detonators. . . ."   41

*"Dear Bob: We are fighting very hard now. I haven't written Mom and
Dad about it. I don't want to worry them. But we are getting hit and
badly. I'm the only first lieutenant in the company who hasn't been hit
yet. And last week I lost two RTO's. They were standing right next to
me. It gets a bit spooky. I know what you said about my flack vest, but
you haven't been here and you just don't know how hot it can get. On
the move, it's just too damn heavy. You can't carry a 60-pound rucksack in 110 degree heat and an 11-pound flack vest. I make the point
wear his, but then someone else carries his gear. It's like your complaint about patients demanding penicillin — sometimes you just
can't use it. It's the same with a flack vest. Besides, it wouldn't stop a
round and that's what we've been getting lately. But I'll wear it when
I can. By the way, you're beginning to sound like Mom. About what's
been happening lately. I'm not complaining, don't get the wrong idea.
There is, honestly, something very positive about being over here. I
can see it in myself and my men. Not the war itself, God knows that's
hopeless enough, but what happens to you because of it. I'll never be
the same again. I can feel myself growing. Unfortunately you only see
one end of it. That's a bit sad, because there are other endings and even
middles. A lot of guys get out of here OK, and despite what they say,
they're better for it. I can see it in myself. I'm getting older over here
in a way that I could never do at home or maybe anywhere. For the
first time in my life, everything seems to count. All the fuzziness is
gone, all the foolishness. I can't believe the things that used to bother
me, or even that I thought were important. You really see yourself over
here. It works on you, grinds you down, makes you better. Got to go.
Thanks for the R & R. Say Hi to all the guys in the burn unit."*

"What?" Edwards said. 42

"Detonators. I must have taken a round in my rucksack. They just 43
blew up and then I was on fire. Tried to tear my gear off, but my
hands. . . ."

"It's all right," Edwards said. The evac sergeant handed him the 44
patient's medical jacket. Quickly turning the pages, he read: "Eighty
percent second degree and third degree. Debrided under general anes-
thesia at the 60 evac, Chu Ci. Six liters plasmonate . . . catheterized . . .
furacin and sterile dressings . . . Demerol . . 64 mg q three hours." He
looked on the cover sheet. David Jensen, MOS B11; 1/30 E-2, Fourth
Division, 20 years old.

"Twenty years old," he thought, handing back the chart. Grant's age. 45

"David," he said wearily. 46

"Yes, sir." 47

"The first thing we're going to do is put you in a whirlpool bath to 48
soak off your bandages and remove what dead skin we can. It's going
to hurt."

"Yes, sir," David said, his voice wavering. 49

"If it hurts, just let us know. Is that understood?" 50

"Yes, sir." 51

"You don't have to call me sir." 52

"Yes, sir, thank you, sir." 53

"Take him to C-4," Edwards said to the corpsman. "Tell Sergeant 54
Dorsey I'll be right there. And David . . ."

"Yes, sir." 55

"Burns look and feel a lot worse than they are. You're going to get 56
better."

"Yes, sir." 57

"Edwards watched the corpsman wheel the boy out of the evac area, 58
and then left the area himself to go to the neurosurgery ward. It was
a long walk. Like all army hospitals, Kishine is fantastically spread out,
its buildings and wards acres apart so that no one shell or bomb can get
it all. By the time he got to the ward, the neurosurgeon was already in
the treatment room. The patient, partially hidden by the nurse and
doctor, was lying naked on the treatment table. There were blood-
soaked clothes and bandages all over the floor. Cramer turned his head
for a moment, looked at Edwards, and went back to work.

"His frontal lobe is torn up," Cramer said. "I'm going to have to take 59
him up to the operating room and save what I can. What do you think
about his burns?"

Looking over Cramer's shoulder Edwards saw that the surgeon's 60
fingers were deep inside the half shell of the boy's skull. "Don't worry
about the burns," he said, turning to leave.

"Oh, Edwards," Cramer said as he reached the door. "I know how 61 close you two'd become. I'm sorry."

> *"Regardless of the branch of service: The emblem of the Infantry, crossed rifles, will be carried on every coffin. The deceased, where the remains are viewable, will be buried in full military uniform. The emblems on his uniform will be that of the service to which he was attached at the time of his death."*

He walked down the corridor to the elevator. Leaning wearily against 62 the wall, he pressed the button, and without looking stepped in even as the door was opening, almost colliding with one of the patients. "Sorry," he said, moving over to the other side of the elevator. The patient, his bathrobe slung over his good shoulder — the other was wrapped in a plaster cast — smiled politely, and was about to look away when he saw the doctor's name plate on his uniform.

"Excuse me, sir." 63

"Yes?" 64

"Do you have any relatives in Nam?" 65

"Yes," Edwards said, "I do." 66

"First Air Cav?" 67

"Yes." 68

"Is his name Grant?" 69

Edwards nodded as the elevator suddenly slowed to a stop. 70

"Your brother?" The door opened. "I thought so," the trooper said, 71 obviously pleased. "You sort of look like him."

"Come on," Edwards said pleasantly, holding the door. 72

"I saw him about three weeks ago. There isn't a better platoon leader 73 in the whole cav. But I can tell you this, they were handing him some shit to do, when I saw him. His unit was on their way to getting their ass whipped."

> *Are you sure, Grant? Why don't you go into Tokyo? You only have a few days for your R & R. You might as well have a good time."*
> *"But I want to see what you're doing."*
> *"It's not nice."*
> *"And where do you think I've been?"*

He had been surprised at how well Grant had handled himself in the 74 burn unit. He had seen more than one visitor walking through the ward trying desperately to be natural, moving stiffly from bed to bed, smiling and talking as if the boys weren't burnt at all. When Grant visited, there were two ghastly 90 percent burns stretched out, blistered and dying on their Stryker frames, Grant had stopped to talk to them and stayed with each much longer than he had to. He was very much at ease. He didn't ignore their wounds, or pretend not to see that they were so obviously dying. He simply talked to them, interestedly and honestly with a concern so palpable that no one could doubt his sincerity. He was one of them and, for a moment, watching his brother sitting by their frames, Edwards felt suddenly very much outside it all. He was very proud of his younger brother.

"I've seen worse, Bob. Really . . . a lot worse."

"Sir?" 75

"Yes, I know," Edwards said gently. "They did get whipped." 76

When he got back to the burn unit, he found David in the treatment 77 area, already floating full length in one of the whirlpool baths, his head supported on a padded board to keep it above the waterline, the water gently churning about his burnt body. His IV bottle was still working, hanging down from a ceiling hook. A few of the dressings had already soaked off and the medic was picking them out of the water. Taking an admissions chart off the wall rack, Edwards sat down on a chair next to the huge tub.

"OK?" he asked. 78

David, clenching his teeth, nodded. 79

"David," he said, "we're going to debride you a bit — take off the 80 dead skin. We are going to have to do it every day, a little bit at a time. That way it won't be as painful." David was looking anxiously at him. "Once you know what's going on, it won't be so bad. We're going to put you into the whirlpool every day and all the skin that is loose, or loosening, is going to be removed. It has to be done." He hesitated a moment and then went on matter-of-factly. "If we don't take it off, it just stays and decays, forming a place for bacteria to grow and divide, and you'll just get infected. That's what we want to avoid, because if the burns get infected no new skin will form. It's going to hurt, and I'll give you something for the pain when I think you need it."

"Yes, sir." 81

"I've been doing this a long time, David, and I know when it really 82 hurts and when it doesn't. We're going to have to be doing this for some time and we don't want to make an addict out of you, so we're only going to use the pain medicine when we have to. I know you can do it. There have been a lot of troopers, just like you, through here, and I know you're as fine as they are."

David had been staring up at him the whole time. What was left of 83 his lips were clamped tight against the pain of the water churning against his blistered skin. "Yes, sir," he said, his voice trembling.

"OK, John," Edwards said. David looked nervously from him to the 84 corpsman. Pieces of dead skin were already floating free. The corpsman, kneeling down beside the tub, began picking off those pieces that were still attached but had been loosened. "How long have you been in Nam, David?"

"Five ... five months." David said, watching the corpsman pick a 85 chunk of skin off his chest. He had to tug to get it off. David grimaced, barely suppressing a groan.

"How do you like the Vietnamese women?" the medic asked. 86

"Don't know," David said, painfully engrossed in watching the corps- 87 man go after another piece of his skin. "Didn't meet any gooks."

"How come?" the medic asked, scooping a piece of skin out of the 88 water.

"We killed 'em all." 89

Suddenly David let out a scream and the scream, echoing off the 90 spotless tile walls, pierced Edwards to his heart. His eyes clenched tight, the boy was fighting valiantly for control. Blood began oozing from the new patch of raw skin on his chest, and Edwards could see the tears rolling down his burnt cheeks.

> *"Where you from, Doc?" the cab driver asked.*
> *"Japan."*
> *"Oh," the cabbie said, pulling away from the curb, "thought so, saw the Fuji patch on your sleeve. Nice place, huh?"*
> *"No," Edwards said.*
> *"I heard that Japan was paradise."*
> *"I work in a burn unit."*
> *"Oh, get many burns over there?"*
> *"There's a war on. Remember?"*
> *"You mean, you get those guys in Japan?"*
> *"Yeah," Edwards said, "We get those guys ..."*

"Major, Major?" 91

Edwards opened his eyes. It was the ward master. David was still 92 there, sobbing.

"Excuse me, sir. Those flights back from the States are tough. I'm sure 93 you haven't caught up with the time change. Why don't you take a sleeping pill and get some rest."

"Think I'll take your advice," Edwards said, closing his clipboard. He 94 wrote a Demerol order for David and then went to his room. As tired as he was, though, he couldn't sleep. Every time he drifted off, he'd see Grant's tag: "Remains, non-viewable." And all that time in the States, he thought he could handle it. ...

He woke up in the morning exhausted, put on his wrinkled uniform 95 and went to the ward.

561

Johnson was already in the office. "Hi," he said, turning around from   96
his desk. "You know you didn't have to work today — or yesterday,
for that matter."

"I know." Edwards hung up his jacket. "There's really not much else   97
to do."

Both he and Johnson had shared the same office for almost a year now.   98
Johnson had been the plastic surgeon working with the burn unit at
Duke University. He had been drafted and assigned to Kishine.

"You want to go on rounds?" Edwards asked.   99

Johnson pressed the button on the intercom. "Julian, we're gonna   100
start rounds." He pushed himself away from the desk. "Let's go."

"How's the fellow on the respirator?"   101

"He died this morning," Johnson said, picking up his notes. "I told the   102
corpsman to leave you alone."

After rounds, Edwards went down to the bacteriology lab and then   103
to his office. Johnson had gone to X-ray to check on a few films. He sat
down at his desk and looked at the two weeks of correspondence that
had been piled neatly at the corner of his desk. He was reaching
for the first letter when the intercom buzzed. "Major, Jensen's in the
whirlpool."

"OK, be right there, thanks."   104

David was already in the tub, being debrided. Edwards knelt down   105
by the side of the tub and checked the burns. At some places, on the
thighs and chest, he could see down to the muscle fibers criss-crossing
under the burnt fat. "David, I'm going to stop your IV," he said,
straightening up. "You're going to have to start eating. The ward master
told me you didn't touch your breakfast. Hurt?"

Chewing on what remained of his lips, David winced.   106

"Jessie, why don't you give him 25 of Demerol."   107

"Yes, sir," the corpsman said.   108

"Why didn't you eat?"   109

"No one was there to feed me," David said, watching the corpsman   110
open the medicine cabinet and fill the syringe.

"We don't feed you here," Edwards said. "You feed yourself. You've   111
got to start using your hands sometime." He waited while the medic
searched for a place to give the injection. "In his arm," he said.

The corpsman found a small, unburnt area near the elbow and   112
plunged the needle into the skin. David, watching him, visibly relaxed.
He turned his head on the board and looked at Edwards.

"We can help you grow new skin, stop your infections, graft you —   113
if it comes to that. But it will all be for nothing if you leave here with
all your joints tied down by scar tissue. If you don't exercise and keep
the scar tissue and new skin over your joints loose and flexible it will tie

'em down like iron. All that new skin and scar that will be forming has a tendency to contract with time. If you don't keep it loose, you'll leave here as much a cripple as if someone had shot off your arms and legs. Your hands aren't that bad, David. We'll start today with them."

"But I can't hold a fork." 114

"We'll put wooden blocks on them, and as you get used to handling 115 one size, we'll make the blocks smaller. Understood?"

"Yes, sir." 116

"You married, David?" Edwards asked. 117

"No." 118

"Engaged?" 119

"Yes, sir." 120

"Would you like me to write her for you?" 121

David closed his eyes. "No, sir, I don't think so." 122

"All right. I'll check on you later." 123

That evening, despite the fact that Johnson was on call, he went back 124 to the ward. All the patients had been settled in for the night. The ward master was in the treatment room, cutting adhesive tape into 12-inch strips.

"What's new, White?" 125

"Nothing, Doc, really. Same old thing." 126

"How's Jensen doing?" 127

White put his scissors back into his pocket. "He's doing all right. We 128 drew two blood cultures on him this evening and sent a titer off for moniliasis. He had some difficulty using the blocks, but he got a few bites down; seems as if the sulfamyelon is bothering him. Stinging him. You never know who it's going to bother."

Edwards walked out into the unit. David was on a Stryker frame 129 halfway down the ward, lying on his stomach. White sulfamyelon cream was smeared all over his burnt back, buttocks, and legs.

"How's it going?" 130

"Fine, sir." 131

"The ward master told me that you did all right at supper." 132

"Yes, sir." 133

Later that evening, one of David's blood cultures began to grow out 134 Pseudomonas arinosa, a bacillus resistant to most antibiotics. The bacteriology lab called the ward and the ward master called Edwards. He told the ward master to restart David's IV and put him on 200 mg of polymyxin every four hours.

The next morning, after rounds, Johnson got him alone. "About Jen- 135 sen's polymyxin," he said. "Do you think his kidneys are good enough to handle that big dose?"

"What would you suggest?" Edwards said. 136

"You could destroy his kidneys with that much polymyxin." 137
"I could save him, too." 138
"If he's going to die," Johnson said, "He's going to die." 139
"You sure?" 140
"Well, he's 80 percent burned and his blood culture is already grow- 141
ing out Pseudomonas."

When he came back to the ward, he found David lying on his back, 142
and the corpsman was smearing on the last of the sulfamyelon, spreading it over David's charred stomach as if it were butter.

"This stuff stings, honest, Doc," David said. "It just keeps stinging." 143

"I know," Edwards said. "It does that sometimes, but it will get better 144
with time. You sort of build up a tolerance to it. The point is that you
need it now. It keeps your skin from getting infected and gives the new
skin a chance to grow. Believe it or not sulfamyelon is one of the major
breakthroughs in the treatment of burns."

"Can't I have something for the stinging?" 145
"No, David, I'm sorry." 146

That evening, down in the hospital bacteriology lab, his second blood 147
culture started growing out another patch of pure Pseudomonas. When
Edwards came to work up the new admissions, he stopped by to see
David and found him on his stomach again.

"How does the skin grow back?" David asked, speaking to the floor. 148
The day before he had mentioned there were 16 different colors in the
floor tiles. "I mean, where's it gonna come from?"

"From you." 149
"Yeah," David said. "How?" 150

Edwards pulled up a chair. "You have enough, you don't really need 151
very much," he explained. "The skin grows back from the areas around
the hair follicles; the follicles go down pretty deep, down into the area
below the skin. Below the burns the new skin grows out from the lining
of these follicles, like grass out of a valley. These linings are like nature's
reserves. The new skin just keeps growing out from them, creeping
over the burned area, until all these little growing areas come
together."

"Why am I going to have to be grafted then?" David said sullenly. 152

Edwards sensed the despair in his question. "Sometimes," he said, 153
trying to sound reasonable, "if the burns are too deep, deep enough to
destroy the follicles, then there is no skin to grow back, so we have to
graft."

"Where are you going to get the skin for that?" 154

"From your friends, David," Edwards said gently, "from your 155
friends."

The morning culture again grew out Pseudomonas. That afternoon 156
they took David to the operating room and covered his legs and part
of his stomach with cadaver skin. When Edwards visited him again that
evening, he complained that his head hurt and the sulfamyelon was
stinging even more.

"What will you do when you get home?" Edwards asked. 157

David was sullen. "School, I guess." 158

"You've got to be more positive than that," Edwards said coaxingly. 159

"I was positive before I got burned." 160

"I'm telling you, you're going to be OK." 161

"I didn't see it," David said reproachfully. "I was just walking. I wasn't 162
even point. I swear to God, I didn't even hear it. Can you believe that?"
he said loudly. "I couldn't even goddamn hear it."

Within three days, the cadaver grafts failed, refused to take, and 163
Edwards had to order it pulled off, like the rest of the dying skin. David,
lying in the water, saw him as soon as he walked into the treatment
room.

"I'm handling it, dammit," he said belligerently. "Just leave me alone, 164
will you? Just goddamn leave me alone."

That evening David ignored his presence. 165

"I saw you with some letters this afternoon," Edwards said, noting 166
how the whitish scar tissue under David's chin had a pale greenish cast
to it. "Nice handwriting. Your girl?"

"No, my family." 167

"What did they say?" 168

"It's in the drawer." 169

Edwards opened the drawer of the nightstand next to the frame. It 170
was a rather bright letter, careful, measuredly written, filled with support and concern. There was a section about Carol, how much she loved
David and how happy she was that he was finally out of the fighting.

"Did you answer?" Edwards asked. 171

"I didn't know how." 172

"They know you're burned." Edwards refolded the letter. "It seems 173
to me they're holding up quite well. The least you could do is help them
out."

David slowly turned his head. His eyes, hollow holes, stared coldly 174
and defiantly at Edwards. "I've been throwing up all day. I can't keep
anything down."

"Yes," Edwards said calmly, putting the letter back in the drawer. "I 175
know."

"I'm not going to make it, am I? No, no, don't interrupt. I know I'm 176
not. That stuff you keep putting into my IV bottle — the only other

guys who get it are the ones on respirators. I know," he said, almost triumphantly. "I've checked on the way to the whirlpool. I know." It was all there in his eyes — the pain, the suffering, the loss of belief. It caught Edwards off guard.

"I told you about the pain, didn't I?" he said angrily. "Have I bullshit- 177 ted you yet? Look, if you were going to die, I'd let you know. Right? I'd give you the chance to tie things up, understand?" A certain distance entered David's stare, a vague confusion that was more pathetic than his glaring hopelessness.

Edwards got up. "Now, dammit," he said, "I want you to think of an 178 answer to that letter. I'll be back in the morning and I want an answer. Is that clear?"

Depressed and angry, he left the ward. Outside he passed groups of 179 patients from the other wards, some standing around talking, others doing nothing, or being pushed around in wheelchairs by their buddies. Johnson was right, he thought. David would die. He was probably, all things considered, dead the moment the round hit the rucksack.

The phone woke him a little past three the next morning. 180

"Major!" 181

"Yeah." Edwards fumbled across the night table for the lamp switch. 182

"This is Sergeant Cramer. Jensen's temperature just spiked to 105." 183

"OK," Edwards said, switching on the light and sitting up. He cleared 184 his throat. "I'll be right over." Even as he was hanging up, he was reaching under the bed for his shoes.

The ward master met him at the entrance to the unit and followed 185 him hurriedly down the ward.

"He's becoming disoriented." 186

"What about the cultures?" Edwards asked quickly. "Still Pseudomo- 187 nas?"

"No, this morning's grew out Klebsiella." 188

David was lying on the frame. All the covers were off and he was 189 trembling.

"106," the medic said, reading the stool-smeared thermometer. 190

"Better add some kanamycin and Keflin to the chloromycetin. How's 191 the blood pressure?"

"Stable." 192

"How much kanamycin and Keflin?" Cramer asked. 193

"A lot, a lot. Just get it!" 194

Cramer looked at him and quickly left to get the anitbiotics. 195

"David, David," Edwards leaned over the frame. "David!" 196

Slowly he opened his eyes, but there was no light in them, no gleam. 197

"Listen," Edwards said, lowering his voice. "I'm going to have to put 198 you on a cooling blanket. It's not going to be comfortable, but your temperature . . ."

"I can't think of anything," David said, closing his eyes again. 199

"He's been confused for the last hour," the medic said. 200

A moment later, the ward master came back with the antibiotics 201 already drawn up into two syringes. While he shot the drugs directly into the IV bottle, Edwards said, "We'd better put in a central venous pressure. How's his urine output?"

"Down 60 cc in the last two hours." 202

"Does he have any blood crossmatched?" 203

"Four units." 204

"Respirator?" 205

"There's one down in central supply. We can get it any time." 206

"What about his moniliasis titers?" 207

"Still normal." 208

"White count?" 209

"The lab technicians are doing it now." 210

"Let's see his electrolytes." 211

"Doc." 212

Surprised, Edwards turned around. David had stopped shivering. 213

"Doc!" 214

Edwards hurriedly bent over the frame. 215

David stared up at him, his eyes strangely clear and deep. "You didn't 216 have to come, not all the time."

"I wanted to," Edwards said. 217

"They told me about your brother and your taking him home." David 218 was about to go on when, gasping, he suddenly bolted upright and, struggling against the restraints, vomited up a great flood of bright red blood.

Dying in the burn unit is not normally that dramatic. There is usually 219 very little blood; burns die inside out, down at the cellular level, where the billions of struggling cells just simply give up. It is for the most part a kind of gentle going; breathing becomes labored and distant, circulation falls apart, hearts dilate, livers and spleens grow to twice their size, lungs gradually fill with fluid, and there is always a certain period of confusion. But after it, a comfortable time of unconsciousness, where nothing is done and everything — even the last breath — is rather a leisurely giving up.

Suddenly, with the blood still welling out of his lipless mouth, David 220 went rigid and, arching backwards, collapsed against the frame. Edwards grabbed the suction off the wall and, pulling open David's jaw, began sucking out his mouth, trying to clean the blood and vomit out of his airway. The gasping stopped and there was the more comfortable sound of air moving in and out.

"Get the blood," Edwards ordered, reaching for the oxygen mask. He 221 was turning up the oxygen flow, just as Cramer came running back with the blood.

"Call Johnson. Set up a cut-down tray, and get a tracheotomy set." 222

The ward master unhooked the IV from its bottles. "The blood is still 223 ice cold," he said.

"Just hang it," Edwards ordered, holding open David's jaw, trying to 224 get out more of the blood. "Just goddam hang it. And call the general surgeon . . . David! David!" He pressed the oxygen mask over the boy's mouth and he could feel the new skin slipping away under the pressure of the mask's rubber edges. "David! David! Can you hear me? OK, listen, you have an ulcer. We might have to operate tonight. You have a lot of blood and stuff in your lungs. I'm going to have to put you on a respirator. It will help you breathe, so I'll have to make a little hole in your windpipe. It won't hurt." He looked up, checking the blood running down into the IV tubing. "It's just to help you breathe. Honest. Just to breathe."

The corpsman had set up the tracheotomy, and Edwards held the 225 oxygen mask in place while the ward master quickly cleaned David's neck as best he could. The noise coming from inside the lungs was getting louder again. Even with the oxygen David was having to fight to breathe.

"I'm going to make the hole now," Edwards said, removing the mask. 226 Little bits of skin came away with it.

"Doc," David gasped. "Take me home, too . . . Please, Doc, I don't 227 want to go alone. . . ."

SUBJECT

1. Why does Dr. Edwards take a particular interest in David Jensen? (At least two other soldiers die in the course of the story.)

2. Why do you think Edwards consistently lies to Jensen about his chances for survival? Why does Edwards bother with the tracheotomy at the end when Jensen is already as good as dead?

3. It must be a devastating experience to work for a year, not in the worst ward of just any hospital, but in a burn ward for soldiers who have been evacuated from Vietnam — that is, who are expected to die and who consistently fulfill that expectation. What might happen to a doctor whose patients always die? Does Edwards seem to have made an adjustment that makes his position tolerable?

4.   Would you say that the story represents a commentary on burn wards, on the Vietnam war, or on war in general? What indications are there of Glasser's intent?

STRUCTURE

1.   We have said at the beginning of this book that the most powerful examples are those which present the facts vividly and leave the interpretation to the reader. In this story, the only direct commentary occurs in the letter from Grant, Dr. Edwards's brother. Does the story demonstrate, or fail to demonstrate, that evaluation can also be accomplished without "interpretation"?

2.   Note that for the reader's convenience Glasser has clearly marked the flashbacks by putting them in Italic type. Why does Glasser include these flashbacks? They are not directly connected with the story of the burn ward; do they intensify, or distract from, our reaction to the main story?

3.   What effect does Glasser achieve by printing the full Army instructions to people who escort bodies back to the States?

4.   Glasser employs a great deal of medical terminology which would not be familiar to the average reader; does it ever get in the way of the reader's understanding of the story line? Could Glasser have avoided using these terms?

5.   You have doubtless read evaluations of the Vietnam war written in more general expository prose. By choosing the story form and concentrating on a specific experience, Glasser obviously cannot discuss political, legal, and moral considerations. In view of these severe limitations, would you judge Glasser's evaluation to be less effective than others you have read?

6.   Glasser has tried to select specific detail which will not merely turn the reader's stomach, but turn his stomach against war. Do you recall any details which accomplish this particularly well? (What is the point, for instance, of repeating the conversation with the taxi driver?)

BREATH

Samuel Beckett

Samuel Beckett (born in 1906) is an Irish writer who has lived most of his life in France. He is probably best known for his disturbing play, Waiting for Godot *(1948). He has written a number of other plays, including* Endgame *(1956),* Krapp's Last Tape *(1958) and* Happy Days *(1961). Beckett has also published several volumes of poetry, two books of short stories, and six novels, among them* Murphy *(1937),* Malloy *(1946), and* Malone Dies *(1947). A chief concern of Beckett's writing has been the meaninglessness — or at least the impossibility of understanding — the human condition. From the longish* Waiting for Godot *to the recent* Come and Go *(131 words), Beckett has steadily decreased the size of his works, trying to arrive at their essence. Finally, Beckett has created* Breath, *which lasts 35 seconds and contains neither characters nor dialogue.* Breath *was written on commission for Kenneth Tynan's* Oh! Calcutta.

CURTAIN

1. Faint light on stage littered with miscellaneous rubbish. Hold about 5 seconds.

2. Faint brief cry and immediately inspiration and slow increase of light together reaching maximum together in about 10 seconds. Silence and hold about 5 seconds.

3. Expiration and slow decrease of light together reaching minimum together (light as in 1) in about 10 seconds and immediately cry as before. Silence and hold about 5 seconds.

CURTAIN

Rubbish: no verticals, all scattered and lying.

Cry: Instant of recorded vagitus. Important that two cries be identical, switching on and off strictly synchronized light and breath.

Breath: amplified recording.

Maximum light: not bright. If 0 = dark and 10 = light light should move from about 3 to 6 and back.

SUBJECT

1. Beckett refused to allow *Breath* to be used as the opening scene for the London production of *Oh! Calcutta* because Kenneth Tynan had put naked people amongst the rubbish on stage. What difference would the naked bodies make?

2. What kind of commentary can a play having neither dialogue nor characters possibly make about life? (Obviously, meaning cannot be stated; is any implied?)

3. John Calder, who first printed *Breath*, suggests that its theme is that "man's tragedy lies in his sense of time." Do you see how that could be "man's tragedy"? Does the statement help to understand *Breath?*

4. Consider the possibility of similarity between this play and the closing lines of T. S. Eliot's "The Hollow Men": "This is the way the world ends,/ Not with a bang but a whimper."

STRUCTURE

1. Although it is brief and wordless, *Breath* is constructed to have exact symmetry — even the two cries are identical. Is Beckett trying to produce form without content? or meaninglessness in a meaningful structure? Does the structure imply anything about the relationship between art and life?

2. Do you see any reason for the stage direction specifying that the rubbish contain "no verticals"?

3. We have said that an evaluation ought to imply, at least, a standard of judgment; is any such standard implied here? Does your answer give a clue to the play's meaning?

To the student:

We, as publishers, realize that one way to improve education is to improve textbooks. We also realize that you, the student, have a large role in the success or failure of textbooks. Although teachers choose books to be used in the classroom, if the students do not buy and use books, those books are failures.

Usually only the teacher is asked about the quality of a text; his opinion alone is considered as revisions are written or as new books are planned. Now, Little, Brown would like to ask you about this book: how you liked or disliked it; why it was successful or dull; if it taught you anything. Would you fill in this form and return it to us at: Little, Brown and Co., College Division, 34 Beacon St., Boston, Mass. 02106. It is your chance to directly affect the publication of future textbooks.

Book title:_____ School:_____

Course title:_____ Course enrollment:_____

1. Did you like the book?_____

2. CONTENT: Was it too easy?_____ _____

   Did you read all the selections?_____ _____

   Which did you like most?_____

   Which did you like least?_____

3. FORMAT: Did you like the cover?_____

   Did you like the size?_____

   Did you like the margins?_____

   Did you like the illustrations?_____

   Did you like the type size?_____

(over)

4. Were the study questions, review summaries, or other pedagogical apparatus useful?_____

How should they be changed?_____

_____

5. INTRODUCTIONS: Are they useful?_____

How might they be improved?_____

_____

6. Do you feel the professor should continue to assign this book next year?

_____

7. Will you keep this book for your library?_____

8. Please add any comments or suggestions on how we might improve this book, in either content or format.

_____

_____

_____

_____

_____

9. May we quote you, either in promotion for this book, or in future publishing ventures?   _____yes   _____no

_____   _____
date   signature